TABLE OF TECH CASES

D0166193

E-Business Technologies

H. Albert Napier

Phillip J. Judd

Ollie N. Rivers

Andrew Adams

THOMSON ™
COURSE TECHNOLOGY

Australia • Canada • Mexico • Singapore • Spain • United Kingdom • United States

THOMSON

COURSE TECHNOLOGY ™

E-Business Technologies
by H. Albert Napier, Philip J. Judd,
Ollie N. Rivers, and Andrew Adams

Senior Vice President, Publisher:
Kristen Duerr

Managing Editor:
Jennifer Locke

Senior Product Manager:
Margarita Leonard

Developmental Editor:
Ann Shaffer

Production Editor:
Kristen Guevara

Associate Product Manager:
Janet Aras

Marketing Manager:
Jason Sakos

Editorial Assistant:
Christy Urban

Text Designer:
GEX Publishing Services

Cover Designer:
Betsy Young

Title	E-Business/Person	Topic	Chapter and Page
Cascading CRM	Boise Cascade Office Products	Effective implementation of an e-business CRM system	Ch8, P320
Broadcasting Outstanding Content	WGBH Boston	Effective use of Internet technologies in a nonprofit environment and implementing content management technologies	Ch9, P346 and P381
Yet Another Hierarchical Officious Oracle	Yahoo!, David Filo, and Jerry Yang	Development of Internet directory technologies	Ch 9, P365
Stop Me If You've Heard This One	Google, Inc., Sergey Brin, and Larry Page	Development of Internet search engine technologies	Ch9, P367
The Web in Bloom	FTD.com	Successful adaptation of an existing business into an e-business	Ch10, P392 and P416
e-Busted! The Unbelievable Tale of Pixelon, Inc.	Pixelon, Inc. and Michael Fenne	Technology bubble excesses example	Ch10, P393

Brief Contents

Contents

CHAPTER **3**

Internetworking Basics   73

CHAPTER **5**

Wireless Technologies 151

CHAPTER **8**

E-Business Front-End/Back-End Integration   305

CHAPTER **9**

E-Business Web Site Management   345

Preface

E-Business Technologies provides general business students, graduate students, continuing education students, executive education seminar participants, business managers, and entrepreneurs with information about the technologies that make e-business possible. We assume that readers have no previous knowledge of or experience with e-business technologies. This book is designed to help you learn about the key technologies used by e-businesses, from basic networking to Web site content-management technologies.

When we began teaching both an executive education seminar and an MBA-level course in planning and starting an e-business, we found that there were no e-business technology textbooks written specifically with undergraduate or graduate business students, business managers, or e-business entrepreneurs in mind. *E-Business Technologies* is our attempt to fill that void.

Organization and Coverage

E-Business Technologies takes a practical, case-based approach to the discussion of the technologies that allow businesses to exploit the online marketplace. Numerous real-world e-business examples are used in each chapter to illustrate essential concepts.

Important topics covered in this book include:

- The early technological development of the Internet, the factors that led to the commercialization of the Internet, and basic e-business models (Chapter 1)
- Networking basics including types of networks, network topologies, and networking standards (Chapter 2)
- Internetworking basics including hardware such as switches, routers, and firewalls, different ways consumers and businesses connect to the Internet, Internet addressing issues, domain names and the Domain Name System, and organizations that provide oversight for the Internet and World Wide Web (Chapter 3)
- Web site development technologies including markup languages such as HTML, DHTML, and XML, prepackaged Web development applications such as FrontPage and Dreamweaver, a variety of Web browser plug-ins, and multimedia tools such as Flash (Chapter 4)
- Wireless technologies including IrDA and Bluetooth, wireless LAN technologies, cellular and satellite technologies, the Global Position System, and the future of wireless e-business (Chapter 5)
- Network service providers and the Internet backbones, ISPs and Web Hosting companies, content caching and content delivery networks, and application service providers (Chapter 6)
- Physical, internal, external, and transactional risks to e-business Web sites and networks and how to secure against them (Chapter 7)
- ERP, SCM, and CRM systems and the technologies used to integrate e-business front-end (Web site) and back-end (accounting, warehousing, and so forth) operations (Chapter 8)

- Web site management technologies including portals, Web content management systems, directories and search engines, and Web metrics (Chapter 9)
- The causes and effects of the technology bubble of the late 1990s, examples of e-businesses that have successfully or not so successfully married Internet technologies with sound business precepts, emerging technologies that may affect the future of e-business, and future e-business trends (Chapter 10)

Features

E-Business Technologies is unique in its field because it includes the following features:

- **Opening and Closing Case**: A real-world e-business case opens and closes each chapter and provides a unifying theme for the chapter. The case establishes background elements and introduces relevant issues at the beginning of the chapter. The case concludes at the end of the chapter with a discussion of whether those relevant issues were resolved and how they were resolved.
- **Tech Cases**: Other real-world e-business examples are used through the text to illustrate key concepts. A table of these Tech Cases appears in the front of the book.
- **Numerous Illustrations**: The chapter text is well supported with many conceptual figures and screenshots of e-business Web sites.
- **Tips**: Each chapter has multiple margin tips that contain useful additional information about individual topics.
- **Techlist**: Each chapter concludes with a Techlist summary that concisely recaps the most important concepts in the chapter.
- **Key Terms**: Following the Techlist is a list of key terms used in the chapter. These key terms are bolded in the chapter text and defined in the Glossary located at the end of the text.
- **Review Questions and Exercises**: Every chapter concludes with meaningful review materials that include both objective questions and hands-on exercises. The exercises involve experiences that result in a computer output or typed paper. One of the exercises in Chapter 3, for example, asks students to use search tools and Web browser features to research internetworking hardware (switches, routers, and firewalls) and compare and contrast how each device is used in an IP network. Exercises throughout the text ask students to research an issue using the Web, answer questions, and produce a summary of research results and answers to those questions.
- **Case Projects**: Every chapter contains three case projects which allow students to get involved in defining technology solutions to e-business problems. Students are required to apply concepts discussed in the chapter to each scenario and then write a short paper describing the application of those concepts to the case project solution. These three projects can be completed individually or in groups.

- ◆ **Team Projects**: A specially designed team project is included that allows a team of two or three students to work together on the project solution and then make a formal presentation of that solution to others. Team members must work together to complete the project by implementing key concepts from the chapter. This format allows multiple teams to work on the same project and arrive at different solutions. An important aspect of the team project is the requirement to prepare a 5–10 slide presentation illustrating the project solution and then use the presentation materials to formally present the project solution to other students. This allows students to both understand the practical application of key concepts and to experience and practice important presentation skills.
- ◆ **Useful Links**: A list of Web site names and URLs for Web sites providing additional information on the chapter topics is at the end of the chapter.
- ◆ **Links to Web Sites Noted in This Chapter**: An additional list of all the e-business Web sites used to illustrate chapter concepts is also included at the end of the chapter.
- ◆ **For Additional Review**: Every chapter contains a comprehensive list of references to online magazine articles and reports, print magazine articles, newspaper articles, journal papers, and books that students can read to learn more about topics discussed in the chapter. The text's MyCourse Web site will be periodically updated to include references to new reference materials available after the book is published.
- ◆ **Glossary**: A glossary containing the key terms and their definitions appears at the end of the text.

Teaching Tools

- ◆ **Instructor's Manual**: The Instructor's Manual has been carefully prepared and tested to ensure its accuracy and dependability. The Instructor's Manual is available through the Course Technology Faculty Online Companion on the World Wide Web. (Call your customer service representative for the exact URL and to obtain your username and password.)
- ◆ **ExamView**: This textbook is accompanied by ExamView, a powerful testing software package that allows instructors to create and administer printed, LAN-based, and Internet exams. ExamView includes hundreds of questions that correspond to the topics covered in this text, enabling students to generate detailed study guides that include page references for further review. The computer-based and Internet testing components allow students to take exams at their computers and also save the instructor time by grading each exam automatically.
- ◆ **Classroom Presentations**: Microsoft PowerPoint presentations are available for each chapter of this book to assist instructors in classroom lectures. The Classroom Presentations are included on the Instructor's Resources CD-ROM.

Acknowledgments

Creating a quality text is a collaborative effort between author and publisher. We work as a team to provide the highest quality book possible. The authors want to acknowledge the work of the seasoned professionals at Course Technology. We thanks Jennifer Locke, Executive Editor; Margarita Leonard, Senior Product Manager; Kristen Guevara, Production Editor; Jason Sakos, Marketing Manager; Janet Aras, Associate Product Manager; and Christy Urban, Editorial Assistant, for their tireless work and dedication to the project. We also thank Ann Shaffer, our terrific Development Editor, for insightful suggestions and unflagging support.

We want to thank the reviewers for their very helpful comments and suggestions at various stages of the book's development: George Balser, Larry Dugan, Keith Williams, and Yufei Yuan.

H. Albert Napier
Philip J. Judd
Ollie N. Rivers
Andrew Adams

Dedications

To Liz, my wonderful wife

Al Napier

To Michelle, Jacob, and Heather, the world's best antidote for boredom

Phil Judd

To Chris, Jackie, and Taylor, my terrific trio

Ollie N. Rivers

To my wonderful wife Tammy and to Dr. Napier and the Jones School Faculty

Andrew Adams

About the Authors

H. Albert Napier is the Director of the Center on the Management of Information Technology and a Professor of Management in the Jones Graduate School of Management at Rice University, where he teaches graduate and executive development courses related to information technology, e-business, and entrepreneurship. Dr. Napier also makes numerous management development program presentations on e-business and related topics. Additionally, he is associated with Napier & Judd, Inc., a company engaged in computer training and consulting. Dr. Napier is on the board of directors of Hometown Favorites an Internet company that sells hard-to-find specialty foods. Additionally, he consults with clients from a variety of industries including construction, legal and accounting, financial, real estate, energy, agricultural, and manufacturing. Dr. Napier holds a Ph.D. in Business Administration, an M.B.A., and a B.A., all from the University of Texas at Austin. He is the author of more than 20 articles related to management information systems and applications of computer-based decision processes in business and is the co-author of over 60 textbooks on software and entrepreneurship.

Philip J. Judd is a principal of Napier & Judd, Inc. His consulting activities include the analysis and design of automated business systems, planning for large-scale computer operations, the selection and implementation of office automation systems, the development of corporate database systems, and the design and implementation of personal computer network systems including Web site integration. Mr. Judd was previously an instructor in the Management Department at the University of Houston and the Director of the Research and Instructional Computing Service at the university. He received his M.B.A. and B.B.A. degrees from the University of Houston.

Ollie N. Rivers is an associate at Napier & Judd, Inc. where she develops materials for software applications training and e-business courses. She has several years experience in financial and administrative management and holds an M.B.A. and B.S. in Accounting and Management from Houston Baptist University.

Andrew Adams is an Adjunct Professor at the Jones Graduate School of Management at Rice University where he teaches E-Business Technology Strategy. He is also in business development at iMimic Networking in Houston, Texas. He holds an M.B.A. and a B.A. in Economics, both from Rice University, and has several years of industry experience in the technology field.

CHAPTER 1

Introduction to E-Business Technologies

In this chapter, you will learn to:

Describe the early technological development of the Internet

Discuss the origins and evolution of the World Wide Web

Identify the primary events that led to the commercialization of the Internet and the World Wide Web

Define e-business models based on the commercial application of Internet technologies

In the early days of the Internet, only scientists and researchers with UNIX programming skills could readily access Internet resources such as files and programs. In 1992, a team of young programmers at the University of Illinois Champaign-Urbana's National Center for Supercomputing Applications (NCSA) were determined to give users a tool to navigate the Internet and to encourage developers to create Internet content for nonscientific users. To do this, the team, which included Eric Bina, Aleks Totic, Jon Mittelhauser, Chris Wilson, and a young undergraduate computer science student and programmer named Marc Andreessen, began to develop a software application for the Internet called Mosaic. The Mosaic application, which used pictures as well as text to help users find Internet resources, quickly became very popular in the university-based UNIX environment. In 1993, its first year of availability, the number of Mosaic users went from 12 to more than 1 million. Andreessen, who had an eye for business, pondered the potential for profit inherent in Mosaic's soaring popularity. Still, in the early 1990s most people familiar with the Internet thought it was impossible to make money using it. Or was it?

The Early Development of the Internet

Millions of people use the Internet to shop for goods and services, listen to music, view artwork, conduct research, get stock quotes, keep up to date with current events, and communicate with others. At the same time, more and more businesses are using the Internet to conduct their business activities. How did all of this come about, how does it all work, and what new technologies might be around the corner? In this book, you learn how major Internet technologies developed, how they work, how using them has changed the way business is conducted, and how new Internet technologies may affect the future of business.

To the uninitiated, the Internet appears staggeringly complex, with vast resources and millions of users scattered around the globe. But, peel away this outer shell of complexity and an orderly universe emerges — one governed by very clear and specific rules. Early scientists and researchers, working with computers that would now be considered pathetically slow, developed technologies that allowed the Internet to grow beyond their wildest dreams.

In the following sections, you can read about some key developments in the history of the Internet. It's an interesting story, and understanding some of the major milestones can help you appreciate how these ever changing technologies affect today's business world.

Advanced Research Projects Agency (ARPA)

Government has played a crucial role in many scientific advances of the twentieth century, including the development of the Internet. In fact, the groundwork for the Internet was laid in the late 1950s by President Dwight D. Eisenhower. Eisenhower respected the scientific community's value to the country and many well-known scientists of the day served on a variety of panels during his administration. When news of the launch of the Soviet satellite, Sputnik, caused a crisis in 1957, Eisenhower turned to these scientists to foster new research and development programs. Although it would be an oversimplification to say we owe the Internet to Sputnik, the former Soviet Union's first satellite launch galvanized our government's commitment to communications systems and computer systems research.

The intense economic, political, military, and ideological rivalry between the United States and the former Soviet Union, known as the Cold War, was well under way by 1957. The idea that the Soviet Union could be ahead of the United States in anything, especially technology, was intolerable to most American citizens. In order to catch up, the Eisenhower administration created the **Advanced Research Projects Agency (ARPA)** to sponsor research at universities and corporations in areas deemed strategically important, including communications systems and computer technologies.

ARPA, which maintained its offices at the Pentagon, was initially set up to fund military-oriented communications systems and computer research. The abilities of the large mainframe computers that existed in 1957 pale in comparison to the abilities of the average desktop computer found in most businesses and many homes today; however, these mainframes had already proven themselves crucial for complex computational tasks such as cryptography (the enciphering and deciphering of coded messages), weapons control, and other military applications. The military also anticipated that computers would be crucial for spaceflights and in large-scale military command and control operations. It is not surprising, then, that ARPA initially focused on developing a computer information systems edge over the Soviet Union. However, ARPA's computer research and development direction began to change in 1962, when J. C. R. Licklider (Figure 1-1) arrived.

Licklider, an eminent psychologist, was a visionary who believed technological development would "save humanity," and the interaction between humans and computers would lead to better decision making. Before he joined ARPA, Licklider worked at a small consulting and research firm named Bolt Beranek and Newman (BBN). There he published his views on human-computer interaction in an influential paper entitled "Man-Computer Symbiosis." Licklider, commonly called "Lick" by his associates, theorized that people would be more productive if they had access to a good computer system and information databases that they could use directly without having to go through computer operators. The publication of "Man-Computer Symbiosis" outlining these theories redefined Licklider as one of the leading computer scientists of his day.

Because of his theories and his eminence in the computer science community, Licklider was tapped to run two major ARPA projects, a computer research project as well as a new behavioral science project. The first project, called a command and control project, originated from a need to find ways to use computers to help the military make timely decisions and then implement those decisions quickly and effectively. Licklider's theories on man-computer interaction were a natural tie-in to that project and to his work in the behavioral sciences. Licklider's charge at ARPA was to find uses for computers beyond mathematical and scientific calculations. To do this, he identified the country's top computer research centers and scientists and then offered them research contracts. In a short time, scientists from Stanford University, the Massachusetts Institute of Technology (MIT), the University of California, Los Angeles (UCLA), the University of California, Berkeley, and others were working on ARPA research projects.

Figure 1-1
J. C. R. Licklider

By the time Licklider left ARPA in 1964, he had successfully directed ARPA's computer systems research and development emphasis away from military war games and toward time-sharing (where multiple computer users at independent terminals work on one computer at the same time), graphics, and improved programming languages.

ARPANET

ARPA's original Command and Control Research Department was renamed the Information Processing Techniques Office (IPTO), and by 1966 Robert (Bob) Taylor (Figure 1-2), a protégé of Licklider, was the IPTO director. During this time, ARPA began to receive more and more requests for funding to provide IPTO research contractors with computers. Taylor, a psychologist by education whose employment background was more managerial than scientific, believed that providing these researchers with multiple computers was an unnecessary expense. Instead, he set out to find a way for the existing IPTO-funded computers to communicate with each other so that researchers could share computer resources and results. In other words, he wanted to connect the IPTO-funded computers into a network. To accomplish his goals, Taylor provided the funding for building a system of electronic links that would make such a network possible.

Figure 1-2
Robert W.
(Bob) Taylor

Next, Taylor convinced Lawrence (Larry) G. Roberts (Figure 1-3) to join ARPA as chief scientist and manager of the ARPA network project. Roberts had been part of an earlier ARPA-sponsored study that successfully created a link between a computer at MIT's Lincoln Lab in Massachusetts and a computer at the System Development Corporation (SDC) in California using a dedicated phone line.

Roberts, who became the primary architect of the ARPA network, gathered input from his circle of scientific colleagues, including Leonard Kleinrock at UCLA and Douglas Engelbart at Stanford Research Institute (SRI). Roberts reviewed communications systems research by scientists such as Paul Baran (RAND Corporation) and Donald W. Davies (British National Physical Laboratory). Then Roberts created a highly detailed plan for the ARPA network.

Figure 1-3

Lawrence G. (Larry) Roberts

In 1968, the Department of Defense (DOD), operating as the official government sponsor for the ARPA network, sent out 140 Requests for Proposals based on Roberts' plan. (A Request for Proposal, or RFP, is a formal request by a government agency for competitive bids on products and services from a variety of vendors.) These RFPs were sent to companies such as International Business Machines Corporation (IBM), Control Data Corporation (CDC), and Raytheon Company, with the goal of determining which companies might be interested in building the proposed ARPA network. Twelve companies responded with bids. The Raytheon Company was a strong contender, but in the end, the project was awarded to Licklider's former consulting firm, Bolt Beranek and Newman (BBN).

TECH CASE   The Packet-Switching Coincidence

In 1960, the communications division of a think tank called the RAND Corporation was working with limited success on the problem of ensuring that vital communications (for instance, among military personnel) could continue after a nuclear attack. A scientist named Paul Baran suggested the innovative idea that such communications could take place via computer.

To understand the radical nature of Baran's work, you need to be familiar with the concept of a switch. A switch is a central processing location in a communications system. To this day, local telephone systems are organized around centralized switches, which are in turn connected to larger processing stations, which are then connected to create a regional or national telephone system. Baran realized that communication systems with centralized main switches were more vulnerable in a nuclear attack. His first radical idea was to create a computer network without centralized or decentralized switches. Instead, he suggested creating a distributed network of computers connected to each other in a fish net arrangement, with multiple switches available for communications traffic.

His next radical idea was to break up the messages sent across the network into pieces, called message blocks. These message blocks would then take different routes through the distributed computer network to a single destination computer where they would be reassembled. By 1965, Baran had published several volumes of work detailing his theories, but was unable to get enthusiastic support from government agencies or AT&T (who controlled the telecommunications infrastructure at the time) to pursue the project, so he stopped working on it.

Meanwhile a physicist named Donald W. Davies, who worked for the British National Physical Laboratory (NPL) and who had never heard of Baran or his RAND research, was looking for ways to create a public communications network. Davies began proposing a new computer network very similar to Baran's distributed network. In London in the spring of 1966, Davies gave a public lecture describing his idea of sending parts of messages — which he called packets — through a digital computer network. Unlike AT&T, the British telecommunications establishment liked Davies' ideas and encouraged him to seek funding at NPL for an experimental network. In 1967, the NPL Data Network, which used Davies' packet theory to send messages, was developed under his direction.

Continued

Although stemming from two different research objectives — military communications survival vs. a public communications network — Baran's and Davies' (Figure 1-4) revolutionary theories strongly influenced the development of modern packet-switching technologies, which now enable a computer network to send data over multiple paths, bypassing failed connections when necessary. You learn more about packet switching in Chapters 2 and 3.

Figure 1-4
Paul Baran and Donald W. Davies

TIP

As unbelievable as it sounds today, two of the companies that received a DOD RFP, IBM and CDC, declined to bid on the ARPA network project for the same reason: both companies believed that the network could never be built because no computers existed that were small enough to make the network economically viable. When invited to participate in the development of the ARPA network, AT&T argued that the concept of transmitting data in blocks or packets across a computer network just wouldn't work!

Taylor and Roberts decided to have BBN begin building the ARPA network by first connecting the computers of four IPTO contractors: the University of California, Los Angeles (UCLA); Stanford Research Institute (which later became SRI); University of California, Santa Barbara (UCSB); and the University of Utah. These four IPTO contractors were selected because of their close geographic proximity and because of each university's research interests and previous connections to ARPA. In the fall of 1969, the four locations, called **nodes**, were connected and the **ARPANET** was born. Figure 1-5 shows an early sketch of the ARPANET. In 1971, ARPANET had 15 nodes. Then, in 1972, the first international connection brought the University College of London online.

Because of its connection to the Department of Defense, ARPA was renamed DARPA (short for Defense Advanced Research Projects Agency) and the network was renamed the DARPANET in the early 1970s. The number of DARPANET nodes continued to grow as ongoing research developed better ways for these computers to communicate. One essential new development was an agreed upon format for transmitting data between the DARPANET computers, called a **protocol**.

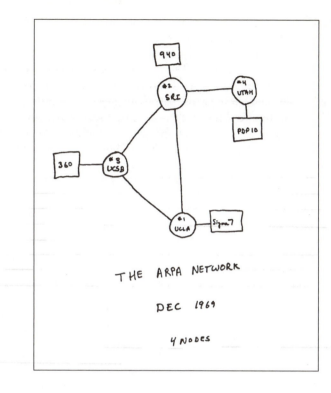

THE ARPA NETWORK

DEC 1969

4 NODES

Figure 1-5
Original drawing of four ARPANET nodes

The new protocol created for DARPANET, named **Transmission Control Protocol** or **TCP**, was developed by Vinton Cerf at SRI and Robert Kahn at DARPA. The TCP protocol made the Internet possible and is the basis for the default data communication networking protocol suite, called TCP/IP, which is currently used on networks throughout the world. Because TCP could connect multiple independent networks, Cerf and Kahn referred to it as an Internetworking protocol, or Internet Protocol for short. These multiple individual networks using TCP were soon commonly called the **Internet**.

TIP

Today, the Defense Advanced Research Projects Agency (DARPA) continues its work for the Department of Defense by managing research and development projects on topics such as communications systems and cyberterrorism.

NSFNET

As the Internet grew, computer scientists developed new ways to send different types of data from computer to computer, including electronic mail (in which a message is transmitted from one computer to another), and bulletin boards (in which electronic messages could be posted and retained at a central location). Also, as the Internet grew, some networks not yet connected to the Internet were absorbed by it (for example, BITNET, which was developed by IBM for Northeastern universities). Meanwhile, other networks were spun off from the Internet to become private networks (for example, MILNET, which became a private military network). The National Science Foundation absorbed some of the costs of supporting the Internet, and created a higher-speed system of interconnections called the **NSFNET** which became the basis for the Internet as we know it today.

This continued growth demonstrated the robustness of the developing Internet technologies. However, managing the diverse interests of the many parties involved in the Internet became more and more difficult. (This was one reason that the military, which could afford a private network, chose to build one.) Commercial activity was still essentially prohibited on the Internet, and it was difficult for most companies to get connected. The majority of Internet users continued to be researchers, students, government employees, and scientists. A few regional networks created to serve universities accepted commercial e-mail interconnections in order to generate revenue; however, the Internet was largely noncommercial. But, that was about to change.

The Origins and Evolution of the World Wide Web

The terms "World Wide Web" and "Internet" are often used interchangeably, but they actually mean different things. The term "Internet" refers to computers and the connections between them. Also, it usually refers to the rules, or protocols, that allow computers to communicate with each other seamlessly. The **World Wide Web (WWW)** is a subset of the Internet — a group of specially formatted documents called **Web pages**. A collection of related Web pages owned and managed by a single individual, organization, or commercial enterprise is called a **Web site**. Web sites reside on Internet-connected computers called servers that deliver or "serve up" Web pages upon request from a **Web browser**, the software application used to locate and display the pages. Figure 1-6 illustrates the WWW.

Figure 1-6
World
Wide Web

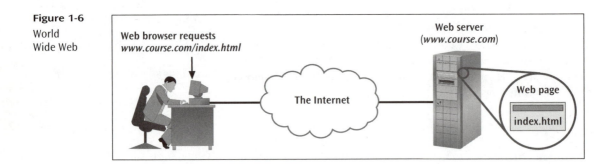

The initial strands of the World Wide Web were woven in 1980 by a young software consultant and programmer named Tim Berners-Lee (Figure 1-7) who was helping to modify the programming for two particle accelerators at CERN, the European Particle Physics Laboratory on the Swiss-French border close to Geneva, Switzerland. Thousands of physicists and engineers from around the world came to CERN to research the basic properties of matter, often bringing with them their own computers, software applications, and operating systems. Berners-Lee decided that for his personal use he needed a way to keep track of the individual researchers, computers, and projects. In his free time, Berners-Lee began playing with a software application to keep track of this information. He called the application Enquire, short for "Enquire Within About Everything." Enquire allowed Berners-Lee to link pages of information stored on a single computer. When Berners-Lee left CERN at the end of his contract, the Enquire software application was lost. But, Berners-Lee's experience with Enquire spurred him on to find a way to link information on computers everywhere.

Figure 1-7
Tim
Berners-Lee

Berners-Lee returned to CERN in 1984 to work with a team that documented the results of individual experiment groups. CERN had grown in the past four years, and its group of scientists and computer systems were more diverse than ever. Berners-Lee quickly realized the need to develop something similar to his original Enquire software application. He used a documentation systems model called **hypertext**, in which text and other objects can be linked to each other, to develop his theories about making information stored on computers anywhere available to everyone. By 1991, Berners-Lee's system of linked documents, which he called the World Wide Web, was a reality.

TECH CASE   From Memex to Xanadu

The concept of linking documents that Tim Berners-Lee pursued at CERN was not a new idea, but an old idea made possible by new technologies. At least three noted visionaries had already conceptualized such a system: Van Bush, Ted Nelson, and Doug Engelbart (Figure 1-8).

Figure 1-8
Bush, Nelson, and Engelbart

Vannevar (Van) Bush (1890-1974) was an engineer, educator, government science administrator, advisor to presidents, and an entrepreneur — in fact, he was one of the original founders of the Raytheon Company. In 1945, Bush published an article in The Atlantic Monthly entitled "As We May Think." In his article, Bush theorized a machine he called Memex that could store linked text and pictures. Bush's Memex machine could also allow users to create a retrievable list of linked documents for easy reference. Unfortunately, the technology to make Bush's theory a reality did not exist in 1945.

In 1965, Theodor Holm (Ted) Nelson, a software designer and theorist, presented a paper entitled "A File Structure for the Complex, the Changing, and the Indeterminate" at the 20th National Conference of the Association for Computing Machinery in New York. In his paper, Nelson outlined a system for "nonsequential writing — text that branches and allows choice to the reader, best read at an interactive screen." In his 1982 book *Literary Machines*, Nelson called this system of nonsequential writing *hypertext*. Nelson went on to design Xanadu, a global hypertext publishing system that allowed a method of accessing text in any document from any other document. Despite millions of dollars and man-hours poured into its research and development, Xanadu was never implemented. In 1994, Nelson moved to Japan where, as a professor at the Shonan Fujisawa Campus of Keio University, he continues his research.

Douglas C. (Doug) Engelbart pursued his research interest in human computer interaction at SRI. In 1963, Engelbart invented a pointing device to control the cursor on a display screen. This device, which was a tremendous breakthrough in computer ergonomics, was called a mouse because of its shape and its connecting wire that resembled a mouse tail. In 1968, at the Fall Joint Conference in San Francisco, Engelbart and his team used a mouse and interactive video conferencing to give what some have dubbed "the mother of all demos" — a groundbreaking demonstration using technology to link users and materials. Engelbart's demonstration included an online session showing the link between two computers and provided a preview of the future of word processing, including document display, editing, formatting, and linking with hypertext. As exciting as the demonstration was for most viewers, Engelbart's award winning work was still way ahead of its time.

In the early 1990s, data traffic on the Internet was growing by 10 percent per month, or more than tripling each year. Initially, the traffic was largely electronic mail and bulletin board related. Activity on the World Wide Web (WWW) also began to grow as CERN made available to the Internet community the specifications for a text-based Web browser called WorldWideWeb. CERN also made available critical software, called a **Web server**, which held Web pages on a server and allowed others to access them. Both the Web browser and the Web server software were developed by Berners-Lee.

As more and more colleges, universities, and other organizations began to participate in the Internet, the demand grew for an easier way to access Internet resources than the existing text-based Web browsers. One of the most important steps in making Internet and WWW resources more accessible to a broad spectrum of users and to encourage developers to create Web site content was the creation of a graphical Web browser. The first graphical Web browser was created at the University of Illinois Champaign-Urbana's National Center for Supercomputing Applications (NCSA) and was called Mosaic. The Mosaic Web browser quickly became very popular for users in the academic community. In quick succession, a commercial Web browser named Navigator (which was based on Mosaic) was released by Netscape Communications. This was followed by Microsoft's Internet Explorer, which is now the dominant Web browser for business users.

Many of the early researchers and scientists who helped develop the Internet and the World Wide Web believed that these technologies should be limited to research and development, academic, and other nonprofit uses. But, as more and more organizations, government agencies, and individuals became aware of the Internet and the WWW, and it became easier to access Internet resources, usage exploded. As soon as businesses and entrepreneurs began to identify opportunities inherent in adapting Internet and World Wide Web technologies to market, sell, and distribute products and services, commercialization was inevitable.

Commercialization of the Internet and the World Wide Web

Rapid adoption of Internet technologies by the world's business community has forever changed the way commercial activities are conducted. Three major events in the early 1990s led directly to this rapid commercialization: (1) the distribution of Berners-Lee's early Web browser and Web server software, (2) the development of easy-to-use graphical Web browsers, and (3) the legalization of commercial activity over the NSFNET.

Commercial activity over the NSFNET was actually illegal until 1992, when Virginia Congressman Rick Boucher introduced an amendment to the National Science Foundation Act of 1950 redefining the "acceptable use" wording of the act to include "additional flexibility for developing in concert with the private sector." This amendment cleared the way for the commercial development of the Internet. On November 23, 1992, President George H. W. Bush signed the amended bill. In 1995, the NSFNET reverted back to a research network and the main portion of Internet traffic was routed through commercial networks.

The widespread electronic linking of individuals and businesses that followed has created a new economic environment. In this environment, time and space are much less limiting, information is more important and accessible, traditional intermediaries are being replaced, and the consumer holds increasingly more power. The terms **electronic commerce** or **e-commerce** are used to describe business activities conducted using Internet technologies. Typical e-commerce transactions include buying and selling products and services, the delivery of information, providing customer service before and after the sale, collaborating with business partners, and enhancing productivity within organizations. Most people today use the term e-commerce interchangeably with **e-business**. In this book the term "e-business" refers to the complete spectrum of Internet business activity.

The Origins of E-Business

The initial development of e-business began in the 1960s and 1970s, when banks began transferring money to each other electronically using Electronic Funds Transfer (EFT), and when large companies began sharing transaction information electronically with their suppliers and customers via Electronic Data Interchange (EDI).

Using EDI, companies exchange information electronically with their suppliers and customers, who are often called "trading partners." The information exchanged includes information traditionally submitted on paper forms such as invoices, purchase orders, quotes, and bills of lading. These transmissions generally occur over private telecommunication networks called value-added networks or VANs. Because of the expense of setting up and maintaining these private networks and the costs associated with creating a standard interface between companies, implementing EDI has usually been beyond the scope of small and medium-sized companies. Now, small and medium-sized companies (and many large companies) are beginning to use the Internet, which is a less expensive network alternative to VANs for the exchange of information, products, services, and payments.

E-Business Models

The commercialization of Internet technologies led to an explosion of different business models as companies and entrepreneurs attempted to exploit perceived marketspace opportunities. As you may know, a company's business model is the way in which it conducts business in order to generate revenue. An e-business model is the way in which an e-business generates revenues. Although there are many different ways to categorize e-business models, they can be broadly categorized as Business-to-Consumer (**B2C**), Business-to-Business (**B2B**), Business-to-Government (**B2G**), Consumer-to-Consumer (**C2C**), and Consumer-to-Business (**C2B**). Within these broad categories, the models are implemented in various ways. Table 1-1 summarizes some of the current e-business models.

E-Business Model	Description	E-Business Example
B2C	Business-to-consumer: sells products or services directly to consumers	Amazon.com (U.S.-based online retailer that sells books, music, toys, and a variety of other consumer goods)
B2B	Business-to-business: sells products or services to other business or brings multiple buyers and sellers together in a central marketplace	Procuron (Canada-based e-business that allows other businesses to buy and sell goods and services)
B2G	Business-to-government: businesses selling to government agencies	B2Gplace (Korean-based global government e-business that facilitates bids and procurement)
C2C	Consumer-to-consumer: consumers sell directly to other consumers	eBay (U.S.-based online auction e-business)
C2B	Consumer-to-business: consumers name own price which businesses accept or decline	Priceline.com (U.S.-based e-business that presents consumer offers for goods and services to participating vendors)

Table 1-1
Summary of E-Business models

Business-to-Consumer (B2C)

Consumers are increasingly going online to shop for and purchase products, arrange financing, arrange shipment of products, take delivery of (in other words, download) digital products like software, and to receive service after the sale. B2C e-business includes retail sales, often called e-retail (or e-tail) and other online purchases such as airline tickets, entertainment venue tickets, hotel rooms, and shares of stock. Many traditional brick-and-mortar retailers such as Barnes & Noble (Figure 1-9) have combined their brick-and-mortar and online businesses and are now known as brick-and-click companies.

Figure 1-9

Barnes&Noble .com and Barnes & Noble storefront

Some B2C e-businesses provide high-value content to consumers for a subscription fee. Examples of e-businesses that follow this subscription model include the Wall Street Journal Online (financial news and articles), Consumer Reports (product reviews and evaluations), and eDiets.com (nutritional and fitness counseling). The Consumer Reports site is shown in Figure 1-10.

Figure 1-10
Consumer
Reports.org

Some businesses supplement a traditional, mail-order business with an online shopping site or have moved completely to Web-based ordering. These businesses are sometimes called catalog merchants. Examples of catalog merchants include Avon.com (cosmetics and fragrances), Chefstore.com (cookware and kitchen accessories), Omaha Steaks (premium steaks, meats, and other gourmet food), and Harry and David (gourmet food gifts). Chefstore.com is shown in Figure 1-11.

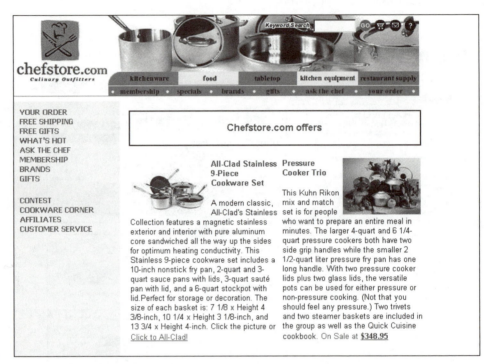

Figure 1-11
Chefstore.com

Figure 1-12
Autobytel
.com

Business-to-Business (B2B)

Although B2C is the most familiar form of e-business, transactions between and within businesses account for a large share of commercial activity. Many of these commercial activities within and between businesses are moving online. Business activities within a company are increasingly transacted online via the company intranet. An **intranet** uses Internet technologies to allow employees to view and use internal Web sites that are not accessible to the outside world.

Business activities between companies can be transacted over an extranet. An **extranet** consists of two or more intranets connected via the Internet. Extranets allow participating companies to view each other's data and to complete business transactions such as purchasing.

Like B2C models, B2B models take a variety of forms. There are basic B2B Internet storefronts, like Office Depot, which allow business customers to purchase products and value-added services. **B2B exchanges** are Web sites that bring multiple buyers and sellers together in a virtual centralized marketspace. In this marketspace, buyers and sellers can buy from and sell to each other at prices determined by the exchange rules. HoustonStreet (an energy exchange site), Covisint (an

TIP

In its 2001 research study *The Evolving eBusiness Web: B2B Market Model Forecast and Analysis, 2001-2005,* IDC (a division of International Data Group, Inc.), says that B2B e-business will reach $4.3 trillion in 2005. This equals a CAGR (compound annual growth rate) of more than 70 percent.

automotive exchange site), and Procuron (an office equipment and electronics exchange site) are all examples of B2B exchanges. The Procuron site is shown in Figure 1-13.

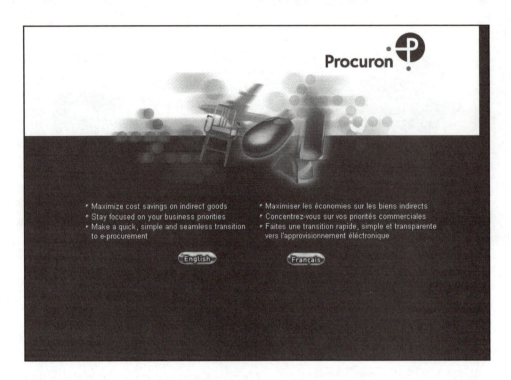

Figure 1-13
Procuron

Another type of B2B exchange is a business trading community, sometimes called a vertical Web community, which acts as a central source of information for a vertical market. A **vertical market** is a specific industry or industry sector in which similar products or services are developed and sold. Examples of broad vertical markets include insurance, construction, real estate, banking, heavy manufacturing, and transportation. An example of a more narrow vertical market is the scrap steel market (which is a sector of the entire steel market). Web sites that serve a vertical market can include buyer's guides, supplier and product directories, industry news and articles, schedules for industry trade shows and events, and classified ads. BuildCentral.com (Figure 1-14) is an example of a vertical market site.

Business-to-Government (B2G)

Another business model, similar to the B2B exchange model, is the business-to-government, or B2G procurement model. B2G e-businesses such as Worldbid.com and B2Gplace (see Figure 1-15) are examples of e-businesses providing a marketspace for businesses to sell their products and services to government agencies.

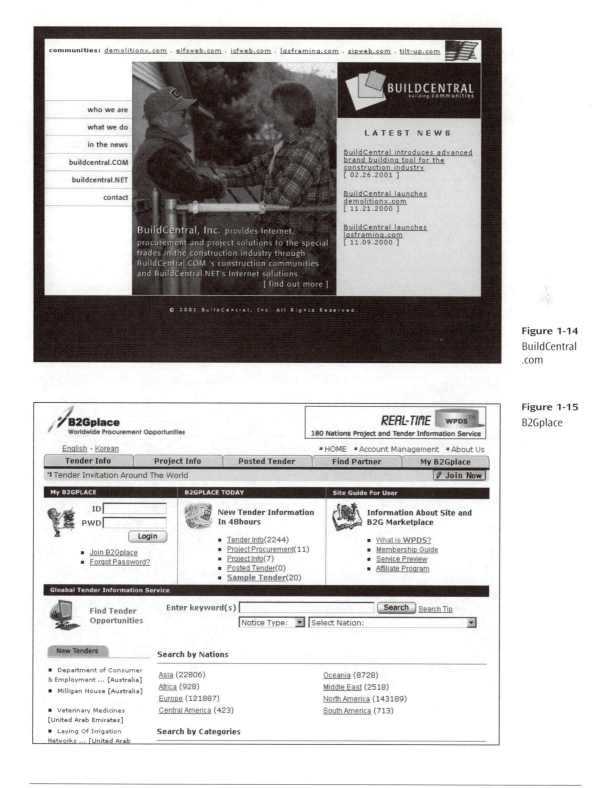

Figure 1-14
BuildCentral
.com

Figure 1-15
B2Gplace

These Boots are Made for Working

Blundstone Pty Ltd (Figure 1-16) is Australia's largest manufacturer of heavy-duty work and safety boots. It has its roots in the skills and experiences brought to Tasmania by British immigrants in the late 1800s. The company prospered throughout the first half of the twentieth century, first as John Blundstone and Son and then as Blundstone Pty Ltd. After World War II, Blundstone became one of Australia's leaders in manufacturing mechanization while pioneering the development of safety and heavy-duty boots for forestry, mining, and other industries.

Blundstone continues its pioneering philosophy by embracing Internet technologies to achieve its goal of being one of the world's most technologically advanced footwear manufacturers. Today, Blundstone uses its Web site to provide its business partners with safe interactive access to the company's internal databases. Using this Web site, Blundstone's business partners can place orders that go directly into the manufacturing system 24 hours a day. This online order processing allows Blundstone to adopt a "just in time" approach to production. Because it can accurately predict what must be manufactured in the near future, Blundstone can purchase raw materials to arrive "just in time" in order to be used in the manufacturing process. This minimizes the expenses related to maintaining raw materials as well as the costs involved in tying up cash in raw materials inventories. Blundstone's business partners also use the Web site to track and pay for orders, manage other account details, and track freight shipments in progress. Blundstone's use of Internet technologies to conduct e-business has helped make it possible to expand its market beyond Australia and surrounding countries to Europe and North America.

Figure 1-16
Blundstone
Pty Ltd

Not only do businesses sell directly to consumers and other businesses online, but consumers are now also interacting with each other to buy, sell, or trade items. This is the basic idea behind the consumer-to-consumer model.

Consumer-to-Consumer (C2C)

In the C2C e-business model, consumers sell directly to other consumers via online classified ads and auctions, or by selling personal services or expertise online. Examples of consumers selling directly to consumers are eBay (auction) and TraderOnline.com (classified ads). The TraderOnline site is shown in Figure 1-17.

Figure 1-17
Trader Online.com

The power shift from sellers to buyers in the new Internet economy has led to another business model, consumer-to-business.

Consumer-to-Business (C2B)

The C2B model, also called a "reverse auction" or "demand collection model," enables buyers to name their own price for a specific good or service. These prices, called demand bids, are often binding. The Web site collects the demand bids and then offers the bids to participating sellers. Auction4Biz.Net (which is used by various industries), and Priceline.com (which deals in travel, telephone, and mortgages) are examples of C2B e-business models. The Auction4Biz.Net site is shown in Figure 1-17.

Figure 1-18
Auction
4Biz.Net

In addition to these broad categories of e-business models, many nonbusiness organizations such as government agencies, not-for-profit institutions, and social or religious organizations are reducing expenses and improving customer service by using e-business models. NPR.org, the National Public Radio Web site, is an example of a not-for-profit institution using an e-business model. As e-business continues to evolve in the marketplace and Internet technologies advance, some e-business models will prove to be unsuccessful and new models will emerge.

E-Business Advantages and Disadvantages

Sellers are finding tremendous advantages in doing business online. They can broaden the scope of sales and operations from local to worldwide, improve internal efficiency and productivity, enhance customer service, and increase communication with both suppliers and customers. At the same time, buyers are enjoying greater access to markets. However, there are some disadvantages to doing business online for both buyers and sellers. Tables 1-2 and 1-3 illustrate some of the e-business advantages and disadvantages for both buyers and sellers.

Advantages for E-Business Sellers	Advantages for E-Business Buyers
Increased sales opportunities	Wider product availability
Decreased transactions costs	Customized and personalized information and buying options
Ability to operate 24 hours a day, 7 days a week from one virtual marketspace	Ability to shop 24 hours a day, 7 days a week
Ability to reach narrow market segments that may be widely distributed geographically	Easy comparison shopping and one-stop shopping for business buyers
Access to global markets	Access to global markets
Increased speed and accuracy of information exchange	Quick delivery of digital products; quicker delivery of information
Multiple buyers and sellers located together in one virtual marketplace	Option to participate in auctions and reverse auctions
Ability to maintain strong customer relationships by direct interaction with individual customers	Ability to create a one-on-one relationship with seller

Table 1-2
E-Business advantages

Disadvantages for E-Business Sellers	Disadvantages for E-Business Buyers
Rapidly changing technology	Concern over transaction security and privacy
Insufficient telecommunications capacity or bandwidth in some areas	Lack of trust for unfamiliar sellers
Difficulty integrating existing systems with e-business software	Inability to touch and feel products before purchase
Problems maintaining system security and reliability	Resistance to unfamiliar buying processes, paperless transactions, and electronic money
Global market issues including language, political environment, and currency conversions	Complicated legal environment
Increased instances of failure to pay for merchandise or fraud	Lack of return policies that are easy to understand

Table 1-3
E-Business disadvantages

In this chapter, you learned about the early development of the Internet and the World Wide Web. You focused on seminal Internet technologies such as networking, data transmission protocols, packet-switching, hypertext, and the graphical Web browser. You also learned how the rapid adoption of these technologies in the business arena forever changed the way business activities are conducted. In subsequent chapters, you learn how these and other Internet technologies work and how they combine with e-business models to maximize e-business opportunities.

In 1993, Marc Andreessen graduated from the University of Illinois and joined Enterprise Integration Technologies, a California company that produced Internet security products. Soon, however, he was contacted by Jim Clark, the founder of Silicon Graphics, who had resigned from the Silicon Graphic's board and was looking for a new venture. The two quickly saw the advantages of combining Andreessen's technical abilities with Clark's business acumen. In 1994, they started their own business, named Mosaic Communications Corporation, with the intention of creating a "Mosaic killer" Web browser application. (In other words, a commercially viable Web browser that would be superior to the Mosaic browser and would replace it.) Then they traveled to the University of Illinois and hired several of the original Mosaic programming team members for the new company.

As you might expect, the University of Illinois was less than thrilled with Andreessen's new venture. When NCSA, which owned the copyright to the Mosaic name and application objected, Andreessen and Clark changed the company name to Netscape Communications and rechristened the revamped Web browser "Mozilla" for "Mosaic Killa'." In October, 1994 Netscape Communications again renamed the Web browser "Netscape Navigator" and released a Beta version on the Internet. The Netscape Navigator software was free for traditional academic and nonprofit users, but businesses were required to buy a license to use it. Netscape made more than $70 million in license revenues in its first year; more than $370 million in its second year; and more than $500 million in its third year.

In fact, until Netscape Communications ran head-on into Microsoft Corporation's Windows operating systems, which integrated the competing Internet Explorer Web browser application, Netscape was one of the fastest-growing companies in history. However, by 1999 Navigator's market share dropped from about 80 percent to about 25 percent and the company's assets were acquired by America Online (AOL) and Sun Microsystems. Andreessen (Figure 1-19) became the Chief Technology Officer for AOL; however, it wasn't "a good fit," and he left to form his own company, an e-business services provider named Loudcloud Inc., in September, 1999.

Figure 1-19
Marc
Andreessen

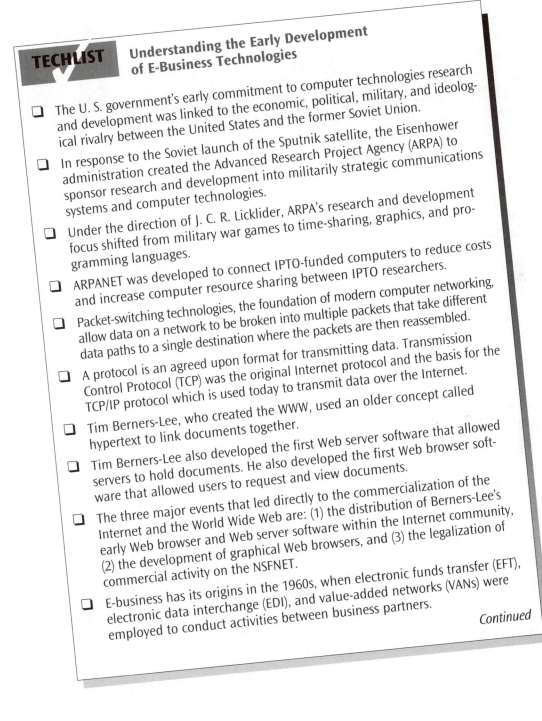

TECHLIST ✓ Understanding the Early Development of E-Business Technologies

❏ The U. S. government's early commitment to computer technologies research and development was linked to the economic, political, military, and ideological rivalry between the United States and the former Soviet Union.

❏ In response to the Soviet launch of the Sputnik satellite, the Eisenhower administration created the Advanced Research Project Agency (ARPA) to sponsor research and development into militarily strategic communications systems and computer technologies.

❏ Under the direction of J. C. R. Licklider, ARPA's research and development focus shifted from military war games to time-sharing, graphics, and programming languages.

❏ ARPANET was developed to connect IPTO-funded computers to reduce costs and increase computer resource sharing between IPTO researchers.

❏ Packet-switching technologies, the foundation of modern computer networking, allow data on a network to be broken into multiple packets that take different data paths to a single destination where the packets are then reassembled.

❏ A protocol is an agreed upon format for transmitting data. Transmission Control Protocol (TCP) was the original Internet protocol and the basis for the TCP/IP protocol which is used today to transmit data over the Internet.

❏ Tim Berners-Lee, who created the WWW, used an older concept called hypertext to link documents together.

❏ Tim Berners-Lee also developed the first Web server software that allowed servers to hold documents. He also developed the first Web browser software that allowed users to request and view documents.

❏ The three major events that led directly to the commercialization of the Internet and the World Wide Web are: (1) the distribution of Berners-Lee's early Web browser and Web server software within the Internet community, (2) the development of graphical Web browsers, and (3) the legalization of commercial activity on the NSFNET.

❏ E-business has its origins in the 1960s, when electronic funds transfer (EFT), electronic data interchange (EDI), and value-added networks (VANs) were employed to conduct activities between business partners.

Continued

- ❑ E-businesses today use Internet technologies to conduct internal business activities on their company intranet or to conduct external business activities with business partners via an extranet.
- ❑ E-business models that exploit Internet technologies to conduct business activities online include business-to-consumer (B2C), business-to-business (B2B), consumer-to-consumer (C2C), consumer-to-business (C2B), and business-to-government (B2G).

Key Terms

Advanced Research Projects
    Agency (ARPA)
ARPANET
e-business
e-business models: B2C, B2B, B2B
    Exchanges, B2G, C2C, C2B
electronic commerce (e-commerce)
extranet

hypertext
Internet
intranet
marketspace
node
NSFNET
protocol
switch

Transmission Control
    Protocol (TCP)
vertical market
Web browser
Web page
Web server
Web site
World Wide Web (Web or WWW)

Review Questions

1. Hypertext is a form of technology that:
    a. Allows text and other objects to be linked.
    b. Enables networked computers to communicate with each other.
    c. Permits businesses to combine brick-and-mortar stores with online stores.
    d. Stores Web pages.

2. The Internet is a:
    a. Network of multiple individual networks.
    b. Data transmission protocol.
    c. Method of linking text between two documents.
    d. Collection of related Web pages.

3. What was the original Internet protocol developed by Vint Cerf and Bob Kahn?
    a. IPX
    b. TCP
    c. ARPA
    d. IPTO

4. An e-business that allows consumers to name their own price for products and services follows which e-business model?
    a. B2B
    b. B2G
    c. C2B
    d. C2C

5. The scientist primarily responsible for the creation of the WWW is:
    a. Bob Taylor.
    b. Larry Roberts.
    c. Tim Berners-Lee.
    d. Vint Cerf.

6. Which of the following is not an e-business advantage?
    a. Increased sales opportunities
    b. Rapidly changing technology
    c. 24/7 operations
    d. Access to global markets

7. The term "hypertext" was coined by Ted Nelson to describe a:

   a. Data transmission protocol.
   b. Method of nonlinear writing.
   c. Computer network.
   d. Graphical user interface for the Internet.

8. The development of Internet technologies is a direct outgrowth of early research and development work sponsored by a government-related agency named:

   a. BITNET.
   b. WWW.
   c. ARPA.
   d. NSFNET.

9. The two scientists who independently formulated theories about transmitting data in blocks or packets between interconnected computers were:

   a. Bob Taylor and Larry Roberts.
   b. Vint Cerf and Bob Kahn.
   c. Tim Berners-Lee and Ted Nelson.
   d. Paul Baran and Donald Davies.

10. A virtual vertical market is a(n):

    a. Online storefront.
    b. Connection of two or more intranets.
    c. Marketspace for a specific industry or industry segment.
    d. Marketspace where consumers buy directly from other consumers.

11. The World Wide Web is the same thing as the Internet. **True or False?**

12. Packet-switching technologies provide an agreed upon format for transmitting data over a network. **True or False?**

13. The Mosaic software application was a graphical Web browser developed and marketed by the Microsoft Corporation. **True or False?**

14. Time, space, and physical location are less limiting factors for e-businesses than for traditional brick-and-mortar businesses. **True or False?**

15. Web server software allows servers to hold Web pages and then provide them to viewers on request. **True or False?**

16. An electronic marketplace is sometimes called a virtualspace. **True or False?**

17. DARPA was created by President Harry S. Truman to preserve the operations research capability developed during WWII. **True or False?**

18. IBM was awarded the contract to build the original ARPANET. **True or False?**

19. Most Internet traffic was routed through commercial networks when the NSFNET reverted to a research network. **True or False?**

20. E-businesses following the C2B e-business model offer products and services directly to consumers who shop online. **True or False?**

Exercises

1. Using Internet search tools or other relevant resources, such as those listed at the end of this chapter, research the origins and history of the Internet and the WWW. Then create a one- or two-page timeline of the major technological developments that made the Internet and WWW possible.

2. Using Internet search tools and other relevant resources, such as those listed at the end of this chapter, research the background and scientific contributions of J. C. R. Licklider. Then write a one- or two-page paper describing his theories and his contributions to the technological development of the Internet.

3. Define the following terms and explain the role each plays in e-business: EFT, EDI, VAN, Internet, intranet, and extranet.

4. Using Internet search tools and other relevant resources, such as those listed at the end of this chapter, research Ted Nelson's Xanadu global hypertext system. Then write a one- or two-page paper briefly describing Nelson's theories and the fate of the Xanadu project.

5. Identify the three major events that led to the commercialization of the Internet and the WWW, and write a one- or two-page paper describing those events and their impact on today's business environment.

CASE PROJECTS

◆ 1 ◆

As part of your job, you maintain a file of Internet and e-business statistical data for your supervisor, the online marketing director for a B2C e-business. He asks you to prepare a report containing current estimates of the number of people who are online in the United States and worldwide, online e-business sales and revenue estimates, and other significant data for the next sales meeting. Using relevant Web sites or other sources (such as those listed at the end of this chapter), gather useful data estimates. Then write a brief report containing the data estimates and their sources for your supervisor.

◆ 2 ◆

You are the executive director of the Internet Technology Historical Society. At the next annual conference, you plan to participate in a round table discussion on the early technological developments that made the Internet possible. You want to focus on the research and contributions made by Doug Engelbart. Using Internet search tools and other relevant resources (such as those listed at the end of this chapter), research Engelbart's technological contributions. Then write a one- or two-page paper describing those contributions.

◆ 3 ◆

You've been asked to present a brief (15 minute) biographical sketch of Tim Berners-Lee and his contributions to the origins, development, and ongoing expansion of the WWW at the next weekly meeting of the Technology Users Group. Using the Internet or other resources (such as those listed at the end of this chapter), research Tim Berners-Lee's work on the WWW. Then using your research, create an outline for your presentation.

TEAM PROJECT

You and three classmates are eager to start your own e-business. Meet with your classmates and use brainstorming and other applicable techniques and resources to expand your e-business idea. Then create a 5–10 slide presentation using Microsoft PowerPoint or other presentation tool describing the e-business and its e-business model. Include in your presentation an analysis of advantages (or disadvantages) you expect to experience when starting your e-business. Present your e-business idea to a group of classmates selected by your instructor.

Useful Links

A Little History of the World Wide Web
www.w3.org/History.html

An Atlas of Cyberspaces — Historical Maps of Computer Networks
www.cybergeography.org/atlas/historical.html

ARPANET Maps
som.csudh.edu/cis/lpress/history/arpamaps/

ArtMuseum.net — Pioneers — Ted Nelson
www.artmuseum.com/w2vr/timeline/Nelson.html

Association for Computing Machinery
www.acm.org/

Bootstrap Institute — Douglas (Doug) Engelbart
www.bootstrap.org

Center for Research in Electronic Commerce
cism.bus.utexas.edu/

Charles Babbage Institute
www.cbi.umn.edu/

CIO.com — Resources for Information Executives
www.cio.com/

Darwin Open Systems: Computing Systems: Myths and Legends
www.darwinsys.com/history/

E-Commerce Learning Center, North Carolina State University
ecommerce.ncsu.edu/

E-Commerce Times — online magazine
www.ecommercetimes.com/

EDI Meets the Internet
www.cis.ohio-state.edu/cgi-bin/rfc/rfc1865.html

Gopher Root at the University of Minnesota
gopher://gopher.tc.umn.edu/

History of the Internet, Packet Switching
www.orangepeel.com/history/packet.htm

Hobbes' Internet Timeline
www.zakon.org/robert/Internet/timeline/

Lynx Viewer
www.delorie.com/web/lynxview.html

Mappa.Mundi
mappa.mundi.net/

Matrix.Net — Internet Research
www.matrix.net/research/index.html

Memex and Beyond
www.cs.brown.edu/memex/

MouseSite — History of Human Computer Interaction
sloan.stanford.edu/MouseSite/

National Science Foundation
www.nsf.gov/

Nerds 2.0.1 Companion Web Site to PBS Series
www.pbs.org/opb/nerds2.0.1/

Netacademy — Electronic Markets Journal
www.electronicmarkets.org/

Netlingo — The Internet Language Dictionary
www.netlingo.com/searchaction.
   cfm?wordsearch =search

PBS, Understanding and Using the Internet
www.pbs.org/uti/utitext.html

Pioneers
www.kerryr.net/pioneers/index.html

RAND, Publications in Paul Baran's *On Distributed Communications* series
www.rand.org/publications/RM/baran.list.html

Short History of HyperText
www.useit.com/alertbox/history.html

Smithsonian Computer History Collection
americanhistory.si.edu/csr/comphist/

Ted Nelson Home Page
www.sfc.keio.ac.jp/~ted/

The Computer History Museum
www.computerhistory.org/index.page

The Internet Archive
www.archive.org/index.html

The Internet Society — All About the Internet
www.isoc.org/internet/history/index.shtml

The Living Internet
www.livingInternet.com/

The Xanadu Model — Deep Hypertext
xanadu.com/xuTheModel/

Tim Berners-Lee Biography
www.w3.org/People/Berners-Lee/Longer.html

Webopedia
www.pcwebopedia.com/

White Papers on Web Technologies
www.itpapers.com/category/intweb.html

World Wide Web — Demographics and Statistics Links
www.devry-phx.edu/webresrc/webmstry/wwwstats.htm

World Wide Web Consortium
www.w3.org/

Links to Web Sites or Companies Noted in This Chapter

Amazon.com, Inc.
www.amazon.com/

AT&T
www.att.com/

Auction4Biz.Net — Internet Cutting Edge
www.auction4biz.net/

Autobytel Inc.
www.autobytel.com/

Avon Products, Inc.
www.avon.com/

B2Gplace
www.b2gplace.com/

Barnes & Noble, Inc.
www.barnesandnoble.com/

BBN Technologies, A Verizon Company
www.gte.com/AboutGTE/gto/bbnt/

Blundstone Pty Ltd
www.blundstone.com/

BuildCentral, Inc.
www.buildcentral.com/

CERN
welcome.cern.ch/welcome/gateway.html

Chefstore.com
www.chefstore.com/

Consumer Reports
www.consumerreports.org/main/home.jsp

Covisint, LLC
www.covisint.com/

Defense Advanced Research Projects Agency (DARPA)
www.darpa.mil/

eBay Inc.
www.ebay.com

eDiets.com, Inc.
www.ediets.com/

Harry and David
www.harryanddavid.com/

HoustonStreet, Inc.
www.houstonstreet.com/

IBM
www.ibm.com/

International Data Group (IDC)
www.idc.com

Jupiter Media Metrix, Inc.
www.jmm.com

Lincoln Laboratory — Massachusetts Institute of Technology
www.ll.mit.edu/

Loudcloud, Inc.
www.loudcloud.com/

Microsoft Corporation
www.microsoft.com/ms.htm

National Center for Supercomputing Applications (NCSA) — University of Illinois
www.ncsa.uiuc.edu/About/NCSA/

National Physical Laboratory (NPL)
www.npl.co.uk/

National Public Radio (NPR)
www.npr.org

Netscape Communications Corporation
browsers.netscape.com/browsers/main.tmpl

Office Depot, Inc.
www.officedepot.com/

Omaha Steaks.com
shop11.omahasteaks.com/servlet/
    OnlineShopping?PCR=1:100

Priceline.com Incorporated
www.priceline.com/

Procuron
www.procuron.com/

PSINet Inc.
www.psi.net/

Raytheon Company
www.raytheon.com/

Silicon Graphics, Inc.
www.sgi.com/

The RAND Corporation
www.rand.org/

Trader Publishing Company
www.traderonline.com/

UUNET, a WorldCom Company
www.uu.net/

Wall Steet Journal Online
online.wsj.com

For Additional Review

Allen, Jamie. 1999. "Netscape Co-founder Relives the Internet Revolution," *CNN Book News*, June 18. cgi.cnn.com/books/news/9906/18/netscape/.

Andreessen, Marc. (aka Mark Andreessen, Marc Andreesen). *Business Leader Profiles for Students*. Gale Research, 2000. Reproduced in Biography Resource Center. Farmington Hills, MI: The Gale Group. 2001. galenet.galegroup.com/servlet/BioRC.

Berners-Lee, Tim. 1999. *Weaving the Web: The Original Design and Ultimate Destiny of the World Wide Web by Its Inventor*. New York: Harper Collins.

Bush, Vannevar. 1945. "As We May Think," *The Atlantic Monthly*, July. www.theatlantic.com/unbound/flashbks/computer/bushf.htm.

Bush, Vannevar. Biographical Essay. *Dictionary of American Biography*, Supplement 9: 1971-1975. Charles Scribner's Sons, 1994. Reproduced in Biography Resource Center. Farmington Hills, MI: The Gale Group. 2001. galenet.galegroup.com/servlet/BioRC.

Cerf, Vinton. 1993. "How the Internet Came to Be," *The Online User's Encyclopedia*, November. www.virtualschool.edu/mon/Internet/CerfHowInternetCame2B.html.

Clark, Jim and Edwards, Owen. 1999. *Netscape Time, The Making of the Billion-Dollar Start-Up That Took on Microsoft*. New York: St. Martins Press, LLC.

Engelbart, Douglas C. and English, William K. 1968. "A Research Center for Augmenting Human Intellect," *AFIPS Conference Proceedings of the 1968 Fall Joint Computer Conference*, December, Vol 33, 395-410. www.histech.rwth-aachen.de/www/quellen/engelbart/ResearchCenter1968.html.

Hafner, Katie and Lyon, Matthew. 1996. *Where Wizards Stay Up Late, The Origins of the Internet*. New York: Simon & Schuster Inc.

Kahn, Robert E. 1994. "The Role of Government in the Evolution of the Internet," *National Academy of Engineering, Revolution in the U. S. Information Infrastructure*. www.nap.edu/readingroom/books/newpath/chap2.html.

Kosiur, David. 1997. *Understanding Electronic Commerce*. Redmond, WA: Microsoft Press.

Landow, George P. 1992. "From Memex to Hypertext: Vannevar Bush and the Mind's Machine, Book Review," *The Journal of Computing in Higher Education*, 121-125. landow.stg.brown.edu/cv/Reviews/Nyce_977.html.

Magid, Lawrence J. 1997. "Inside Netscape: A Conversation with Co-Founder Mark Andreessen," *Computer Currents*, July 21. www.larrysworld.com/articles/Andreessen.htm.

Napier, H. Albert, et al. 2001. *Creating a Winning E-Business*. Boston, MA: Course Technology.

Nelson, Theodor Holm. 1982. *Literary Machines 93.1*. Watertown, MA: Mindful Press/Distributed by Eastgate Systems, Inc. www.eastgate.com/catalog/LiteraryMachines.html.

Nyce, James M. and Kahn, Paul, Ed. 1992. *From Memex to Hypertext: Vannevar Bush and the Mind's Machine*. Boston, MA: Academic Press.

Press Release. 2001. "Autobytel Inc. Meets Heightened Consumer Concern for Price, Safety, and Efficiency; Launches 2002 Buyer's Guide," October 24. Irvine, CA. www.autobytel.com.

Press Release. 2001. "Autobytel Inc. Sites Have More Unique Visitors Than Any Other Car-Buying and Ownership Site on the Web," September 24. Irvine, CA. www.autobytel.com.

Press Release. 2001. "Jupiter to Auto Industry: Internet More Valuable for Deepening Customer Relationships and Consumer Research Than Transactions," December 10, New York. http://www.jmm.com/xp/jmm/press/2001/pr_121001.xml.

Press Release. 2001. "Research Finds Worldwide B2B Purchasing Will Increase 83 percent in 2001," IDC, October 10. www.idc.com/Internet/press/pr/GNET101001pr.stm.

Reid, Robert H. 1997. *Architects of the Web: 1,000 Days That Built the Future of Business*. New York: John Wiley & Sons.

Salus, Peter H. 1995. *Casting the Net: From ARPANet to Internet and Beyond*. Reading, MA: Addison-Wesley Publishing.

Schneider, Gary P. and Perry, James T. 2000. *Electronic Commerce*. Cambridge, MA: Course Technology.

Scully, Arthur B. and Woods, W. William. 1999. *B2B Exchanges, The Killer Application in the Business-to-Business Internet Revolution*. USA: ISI Publications.

Segaller, Stephen. 1999. *Nerds 2.0.1, A Brief History of the Internet*. New York: TV Books, L.L.C.

Shurkin, Joel N. 1996. *Engines of the Mind: The Evolution of the Computer from Mainframes to Microprocessors*. New York: W. W. Norton & Company.

Tasmanian Electronic Commerce Centre. 1999. "Blundstone Pty Ltd." www.tecc.com.au/5Online_Library/2Case_Studies/1Tasmania/sys_Blundstone/.

Waldrop, M. Mitchell. 2001. *The Dream Machine, J. C. R. Licklider and the Revolution That Made Computing Personal*. New York: The Penguin Group.

Wolf, Gary. 1995. "The Curse of Xanadu," *Wired Magazine*, June. www.wired.com/wired/archive/3.06/xanadu.html?person=ted_nelson&topic_set=wiredpeople.

Zachary, Pascal G. 1997. *Endless Frontier: Vannevar Bush, the Engineer of the American Century*. New York: Free Press.

CHAPTER 2

Networking Basics

In this chapter, you will learn to:

Illustrate types of computer networks

Describe LAN transmission media

Discuss LAN physical and logical topologies

Explain the network services provided by LANs

Identify several standards organizations and discuss their role in establishing standards

Describe the Seven-Layer OSI Model

In 1970, the Xerox Corporation created a world-class research facility in Palo Alto, California, called the Xerox Palo Alto Research Center (or PARC). The goal of PARC's scientists was to create "the architecture of information." From this challenge sprang technologies that altered the course of computing history, including personal computers, and laser printing.

In 1973, PARC developed the world's first recognizable personal computer, the Alto. Scientists at PARC wanted to create a network in which each computer could work separately, and yet still communicate and share resources with other computers in the same building — a situation referred to at the time as distributed computing. Robert (Bob) Metcalfe, one of PARC's resident scientists, had earlier networking experience helping to connect MIT computers to the ARPANET. What's more, his original assignment at PARC was setting up a connection between PARC and the ARPANET. Thus, Metcalfe was the natural choice to tackle the problem of creating a smaller, building-wide network.

To solve the problem of how to combine the Alto computers into a network, you might think Metcalfe would have relied on the technology used to connect diverse geographic locations on the ARPANET. Instead, however, Metcalfe made use of research he had done earlier at PARC (on an ARPA-funded experimental network at the University of Hawaii) called the Aloha System, or Alohanet. Alohanet transmitted computer data packets via radio waves instead of the telephone lines used throughout the ARPANET of that time.

On the Alohanet, data packets were sent as needed, regardless of whether other data packets were being transmitted at the same time. If a data packet did not reach its destination because of conflicting traffic, the packet was simply retransmitted after a random interval of time. By contrast, on the ARPANET, conflicting traffic was avoided by waiting for a break in traffic before a packet was transmitted. The primary difficulty with the Alohanet system was its instability and low traffic capacity. Metcalfe's research suggested that a network similar to the Alohanet could be made more stable and could transmit much more data than originally believed. His Alohanet system research also proved vital to solving the problem of connecting the Alto computers.

The Alto local area network had several requirements: it had to be fast, simple to use, reliable, inexpensive, and available anywhere in the building. Metcalfe's solution was to connect the Alto computers with coaxial cable. He theorized that a coaxial cable was simply a "pipe" that carried electronic transmissions in much the same way that a commonplace pipe carried water, only at far greater speeds. Metcalfe believed that using coaxial cable to transmit data "into the ether" (an old term used by physicists for the sky or airwaves) would allow any number of computers and printers to simply connect to the cable to become part of the network. If two or more computers on the network tried to transmit data packets at the same time, they would each back off and try again at random intervals, thereby eliminating the need for a central host computer or network controller. Metcalfe called his system the ETHER network or Ethernet. Over the next few years, Xerox tried unsuccessfully to commercialize Ethernet. Then, in 1979 Metcalfe finally decided to take matters into his own hands!

Types of Computer Networks: LANs, MANs, and WANs

A computer network makes it possible for employees to share expensive resources. For example, rather than purchasing a printer for each employee in the Word Processing Department, a company çould reduce equipment costs by having multiple employees share a single networked printer. Networks also increase productivity by making it easier for employees to share data, communicate with their colleagues, and access the Internet.

A computer **network** consists of two or more computers and other devices such as printers or faxes connected by some form of data transmission media such as cable. A network may be as simple as two computers and a printer connected by cable in a small business office or as complicated as hundreds of computers located around the world connected by a combination of cable, satellites, and infrared devices. Most modern networks rely on a special kind of operating system known as a **network operating system (NOS)**. Popular network operating systems include Microsoft Windows XP, Windows 2000, Linux, and NetWare. All networks (from the most complicated to the simplest) rely on one important device, the **network interface card**, or **NIC**. A NIC is a circuit board, sometimes called an expansion card, which is added to a computer or other device to enable the device to connect to a network. In this chapter, you learn about different types of networks, different types of data transmission media, ways local area networks are connected, and the services local area networks provide.

You start by learning about three broad categories of networks: LANs, MANs, and WANs.

Local Area Network (LAN)

A network that is limited to a relatively small geographical area such as an office or a single building is called a **local area network** or **LAN**. An individual device on a LAN, such as a computer or printer that can process a data transmission, is called a **node**. Each computer on a LAN has its own processing capability, but is able to access files stored on other computers or access other devices (such as printers or fax machines) on the LAN.

For example, assume you need to modify a document created by another employee (and stored on their computer), and then print it on a high-speed printer located in another area of the office. Because your computer, the other employee's computer, and the printer are all connected to the office LAN, you can do this easily. First, you connect to the other employee's computer, and copy the document to your computer. Then you use your computer's processing capability and software to modify the document. Finally, you send the revised document to the high-speed printer — all without leaving your desk!

Local area networks follow two basic designs or architectures: peer-to-peer and client/server.

> **TIP**
>
> As you learned in Chapter 1, packet switching is the practice of breaking data transmission into small packages called packets that can travel independently of each other across a network, much like packages travel independently of each other throughout a postal system.

> **TIP**
>
> A network's architecture refers to its overall structure, the components within that structure, and the relationship between those components.

Peer-to-Peer Network

The simplest design of a local area network is a **peer-to-peer network**. A peer-to-peer network usually consists of six or fewer general-purpose personal computers each of which contains a network interface card or NIC. Often, each of these computers is attached to one or more peripheral devices like a printer. In this type of LAN, computers communicate with each other and share the same files and devices, such as printers, disk drives, CD-ROM drives, and so forth. Every computer on a peer-to-peer network is equal; that is, no one computer is in charge of the other computers. Because peer-to-peer networks are simple and inexpensive to set up, many small and medium-sized businesses start with a peer-to-peer network. Most peer-to-peer networks also include a hub, an inexpensive device that acts as a common connection point on the network.

The first of the following diagrams (Figure 2-1) shows a simple peer-to-peer network without a hub. The second diagram (Figure 2-2) shows a peer-to-peer network with a hub. Note that in Figure 2-2, all the computers on the network connect to the hub. In Figure 2-1, by contrast, all the computers are connected to one main cable, called the **backbone**. Note that the type of hubless network shown in Figure 2-1 can appear to be the simplest option when only two or three devices are involved. But, as the network starts to grow, managing and troubleshooting a hubless peer-to-peer network becomes more difficult. This is partly due to restrictions related to the number of devices that can be attached to the backbone, and the maximum length of the backbone.

The advantages of a peer-to-peer network include the low startup cost and the simplicity of administering the network. Unlike most other types of networks, a peer-to-peer network does not require a special network operating system. Instead, the network users simply modify their desktop operating system options to allow others to read and edit their files.

Figure 2-1
Peer-to-peer network without a hub

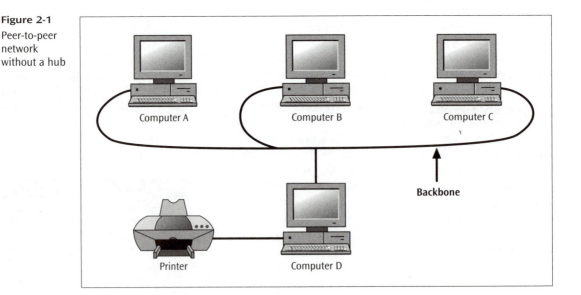

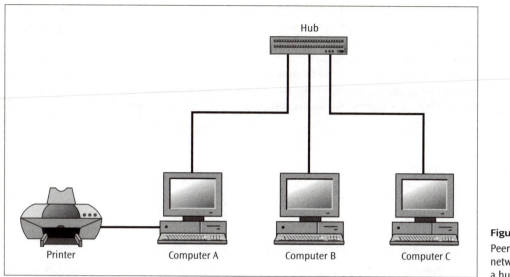

Figure 2-2
Peer-to-peer
network with
a hub

Hub

Printer   Computer A   Computer B   Computer C

While simple and inexpensive, a peer-to-peer network is not practical for more than five or six computers. What's more, because data can be easily accessed by unauthorized users from any computer on the network, a peer-to-peer network may not be very secure. Additionally, a business may quickly outgrow a peer-to-peer network as more employees are added and file sharing and communication needs become more sophisticated.

An alternative to a peer-to-peer network is a client/server network — also called a server-based network.

Client/Server Network

A **client/server network** consists of general-purpose personal computers which are called clients and special high-performance computers called servers. (In many client/server networks, powerful workstation computers are also used as clients.) A server's main task is to enable its clients to share data, data storage space, and other network devices. A server on a client/server network must also run a special network operating system such as Microsoft Windows 2000 Server, UNIX, or Novel NetWare which manages network security, data, and other resources.

The advantages of a client/server network (Figure 2-3) include the ability to manage data storage, network maintenance, and data backups from a centralized location (i.e. from the server). Client/server networks are also more secure than peer-to-peer networks, thanks to the security features included in modern network operating systems. However, setting up and maintaining a client/server network is more difficult than setting up a peer-to-peer network and requires a greater level of technical expertise. In general, client/server networks are also more costly to implement.

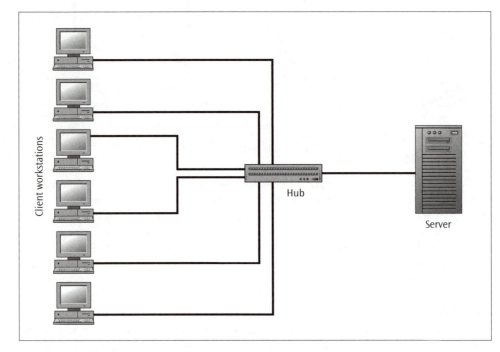

Figure 2-3
Client/server network

Metropolitan Area and Wide Area Networks (MANs and WANs)

A **metropolitan area network** (**MAN**) is a high-speed network connecting two or more LANs (Figure 2-4). A MAN is usually confined to a single metropolitan area, such as a large city and its suburbs.

A **wide area network** (**WAN**) spans a larger geographical area than a MAN and consists of two or more connected LANs. A WAN may connect LANs across the nation or around the world. For example, it's possible to have a WAN consisting of a LAN in the U. S. and a LAN in Australia (Figure 2-5). The Internet is an example of a very complex and extensive worldwide WAN.

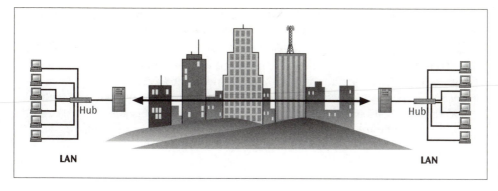

Figure 2-4
Metropolitan area network (MAN)

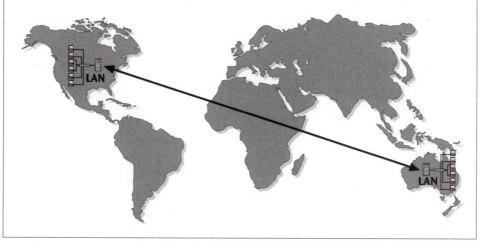

Figure 2-5
Wide area network (WAN)

Issues related to **internetworking**, or the processes and devices needed to allow users to communicate between two or more networks, are discussed in detail in Chapter 3. The remainder of this chapter discusses transmission media, physical connections, and other issues related to LANs.

LAN Transmission Media

When designing a LAN, a network engineer must choose a means for carrying data from one node on the LAN to the next. That is, the engineer must choose a **transmission media**. The only possible transmission media for early networks was coaxial cable. Contemporary networks may include a variety of transmission media, including cable with twisted copper wiring, fiber-optic cabling, infrared transmissions, and radio wave transmissions.

Transmission media are generally divided into two types — cable and wireless. The following list summarizes common types of LAN transmission media:

◆ *Coaxial cable:* The transmission media of choice for early networks. Coaxial cable consists of four parts: a solid metal inner conductor surrounded by insulation, a thin metal outer conductor, and an outer plastic covering (Figure 2-6). The advantages of coaxial cable include the ability to carry heavy network traffic at high speeds and a resistance to interference called "noise." Also, because coaxial cable has been around for so long, you can be certain that most network engineers know how to use it properly. You commonly hear coaxial cable referred to as "coax" (pronounced kō-ax).

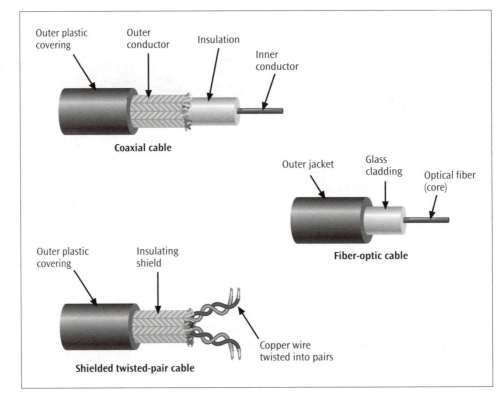

Figure 2-6
Cable LAN
transmission
media

◆ *Twisted-pair cable:* Originally used for telephone transmissions, but now commonly used as a LAN transmission medium. Twisted-pair cabling has gained broad acceptance because it is more flexible, thinner, lighter, and easier to install than either coaxial or fiber-optic cable. A twisted-pair cable consists of insulated copper wires twisted around each other in pairs and then enclosed in a plastic covering. Twisted-pair cables come in many varieties. The two types most commonly used in networking are shielded and unshielded. A shielded twisted-pair (shown in Figure 2-6) has insulating material wrapped around the twisted wires which protects against interference. This improves transmission rates and distances, but can be expensive. An unshielded twisted-pair does not have this insulation, and is less expensive.

◆ *Fiber-optic cable:* Used to carry voice, video, and data signals for very long distances. A fiber-optic cable (Figure 2-6) contains one or more glass fibers at its core, surrounded by a layer of glass cladding and a protective outer jacket. Data is transmitted by pulses of light sent from a laser or light-emitting diode (LED) device and received by a detector that converts the transmission back into the electrical impulses the receiving computer can understand. Because of its capacity and reliability fiber-optic cabling is the transmission medium of choice for high-speed, long-distance transmissions. However, fiber-optic cable is too expensive to be used to transmit data from computer to computer within a small network.

◆ *Infrared (IR) transmission:* A wireless technology that relies on electromagnetic waves with a frequency range above that of microwave but below the visible spectrum. Infrared signals are transmitted through space in the same way a TV remote control device sends signals across a room.

◆ *Radio frequency (RF) transmission:* Another wireless technology that relies on signals sent over specific frequencies, similar to radio broadcasts. RF transmissions (illustrated in Figure 2-7) are regulated by the Federal Communications Commission (FCC) which licenses frequencies by geographic location to ensure that multiple transmitters do not interfere with each others' transmissions. Wireless technologies such as IR and RF transmissions are discussed in more detail in Chapter 5.

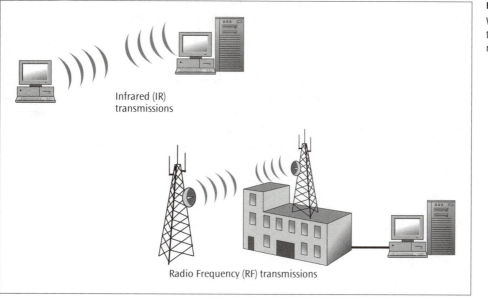

Infrared (IR)
transmissions

Radio Frequency (RF) transmissions

Figure 2-7
Wireless LAN
transmission
media

Two terms engineers use when discussing data transmissions are throughput and bandwidth. Data transmission **throughput** defines how much data can be transmitted during any specified period of time. Throughput is usually measured as the quantity of bits transmitted per second and is expressed as "bps" with a prefix that specifies how many bits. For example, "Kbps" refers to one kilobit or 1,000 bits per second, "Mbps" refers to 1 megabit or 1,000,000 bits per second, and "Gbps" refers to 1 gigabit or 1,000,000,000 bits per second. The throughput for most modern networks is between 10 and 100 Mbps. Data transmission throughput is sometimes called **bandwidth**. However, the term bandwidth is also used to specify the frequency ranges occupied by electronic signals on a specific transmission medium.

Devices such as computers and printers are connected to a network with both physical connections and logical connections.

LAN Physical and Logical Topologies

Broadly speaking, the term **network topology** refers to the way the parts of a network are connected. Technically speaking, there are two types of network topologies: **physical topology** and **logical topology**. The term physical topology refers to a network's physical layout or the pattern in which its devices and cabling are organized. A network's logical topology defines the way in which the data is transmitted between computers on the LAN.

There are three basic LAN physical topologies: the bus, the ring, and the star. Modern LANs generally combine these topologies into a hybrid topology.

LAN Physical Topologies

The **bus topology** (Figure 2-8) is used on peer-to-peer LANs. It consists of a single coaxial cable called a trunk (or backbone, as noted in Figure 2-1) to which all devices are connected. Because the cable is shared, it can carry only one transmission at a time. Before a node sends a transmission it must first announce to the entire network that the transmission is being sent. The destination node then accepts the transmission which is ignored by all other nodes.

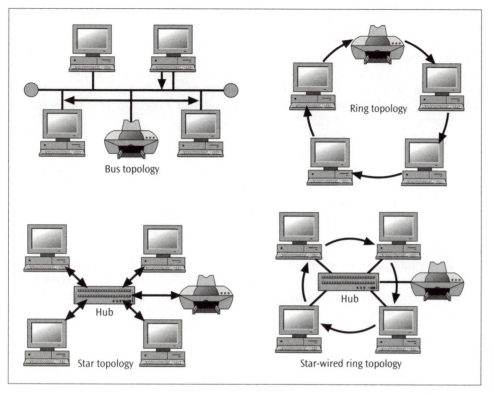

Figure 2-8
Physical topologies

A bus transmission travels from one end of the cable to the other. A device called a terminator is placed at each end of the cable to stop the transmission after it has had a chance to be received by the destination node. If a cable is not properly terminated, the signal moves back and forth continually from one end of the cable to the other, thereby preventing other computers from sending transmissions.

The primary advantage of a bus topology is that it is inexpensive to set up. However, there are several disadvantages including the difficulty of locating the source of a transmission problem, a slowing of transmissions as more nodes are added to the network, and the fact that a single transmission failure can affect the entire network.

TIP

Each data transmission involves at least one sending node and at least one receiving node. Data transmissions that involve one sending and receiving node are called point-to-point transmissions. Transmissions that involve one sending node and multiple receiving nodes are called broadcast transmissions. Networks frequently use simple, fast broadcast transmissions to transmit data. When that happens, it is assumed that all nodes are capable of receiving the data, but only the destination node actually does so.

In the **ring topology** (Figure 2-8) each node is connected to the next node via a single circle of twisted-pair or fiber-optic cable. Data transmissions travel around the circle in a clockwise direction, passing through each node. When a node receives a transmission, it accepts the data addressed to it and then forwards the transmission on to the next node. Ring topologies have two distinct disadvantages. Because a transmission is passed from node to node, the failure of one node can affect the entire network. Additionally, as with the bus topology, adding nodes to a ring topology can slow the transmission process.

In the **star topology** (Figure 2-8) each node is connected to a central hub by a separate twisted-pair or fiber-optic cable. Data is transmitted from one node, through the hub, and out again to the destination node. Although the star topology requires more cabling than the bus or ring topologies, it provides clear advantages. Because each node is connected separately to the hub, a malfunctioning node or cable cannot disable the entire network. The centralized connection point means that star topology networks are easy to modify and move. It's also fairly easy to connect a star topology network with other networks.

At one time, the bus topology was the most common LAN configuration. These days, few LANs use a pure form of the bus, ring, or star topologies. Instead, today's LANs are most often based on a **hybrid topology** that contains elements of two or more topologies. A commonly used hybrid physical topology is the star-wired ring hybrid (Figure 2-8). In this type of hybrid, data travels in a circle, from one node to the next, but each transmission passes through the hub.

LAN Logical Topologies

A logical topology, sometimes called a network transport system, defines the way in which data is transmitted between network nodes. A logical topology specifies several network characteristics such as the rules (called the access method) the nodes must follow in order to access the transmission media, the network's physical topology, its transmission media, and its data throughput rate. Two examples of logical topologies commonly used on LANs are Ethernet and Token Ring.

Ethernet, the most popular and least expensive logical topology, was originally developed by Xerox in the 1970s and later improved by a variety of vendors. The Ethernet access method is called Carrier Sense Multiple Access with Collision Detection (CSMA/CD). CSMA/CD is sometimes referred to as a "traffic cop," because it directs transmission traffic over the network. Using the CSMA/CD access method, a node on an Ethernet network accesses the transmission medium and determines if any other node is sending a transmission. If so, it waits a brief random interval and then checks again. When no transmissions are being sent, the node then broadcasts its transmission to all the other nodes on the network, but only the intended destination responds. If two nodes simultaneously check and then transmit, their two transmissions collide. In this case, both nodes immediately stop transmitting, wait a random interval, recheck, and then rebroadcast. Ethernet networks commonly run on a bus or star physical topology that is connected via coaxial, twisted-pair, or fiber-optic cable. Ethernet networks transmit data at rates ranging from 10 Mbps to 100 Mbps.

The **Token Ring** logical topology was popularized by IBM in the mid-1980s. This type of logical topology combines a star-wired hybrid physical topology with a special kind of access method known as token-passing. In the token-passing access method, a 3-byte packet, called a token, moves clockwise in a circle from node to node. A node that is ready to transmit data takes the token, adds special control information, the data, and the destination node's address, and then passes the token to the next node. All nodes read the token as it passes around the network. Eventually, the destination node picks up the token and sends an acknowledgment of its receipt back to the originating node. When the originating node receives that acknowledgement, it reissues a "free" or unused token and sends it to the next node where it can be used for another transmission. The Token Ring topology provides a high level of dependability because of the absence of transmission collisions; however, it is generally more expensive to install than an Ethernet network. A Token Ring network can use twisted-pair or fiber-optic cabling and can transmit data at 4, 16, or 100 Mbps.

Services provided by networks enable businesses to more efficiently manage assets such as money, equipment, time, and employee productivity.

TIP

Other less commonly used logical topologies are Fiber Distributed Data Interface (FDDI), LocalTalk, Fast Ethernet, Gigabit Ethernet, and Asynchronous Transfer Mode (ATM). FDDI is a standard originally specified by ANSI and ISO in the 1980s in response to Ethernet and Token Ring capacity limitations and can transmit data at 100 Mbps. LocalTalk was designed by Apple Computer, Inc. for its Macintosh computers. Based on the old Ethernet standard, Fast Ethernet supports data transfer rates up to 100 Mbps and Gigabit Ethernet supports data transfer rates up to 1, 000 Mbps. ATM was developed at Bell Labs in 1983 as a higher-bandwidth alternative to FDDI.

LAN Network Services

Probably the most important type of network service, file services, makes it possible to store data in a central location for access by multiple users. Print services provide the ability to print to a variety of printers no matter where the printers are physically located. Meanwhile, mail and communication services enable employees to communicate with each other as well as with customers, vendors, and other interested parties outside the business. Finally, network management services provide the tools necessary to administer and maintain the network itself. You learn more about all of these services in the following sections.

TECH CASE | A Texas LAN

Jesse H. Jones was a remarkable man whose accomplishments are little known outside Texas today. Jones achieved great wealth and success as a Texas businessman by erecting modern buildings that changed the skyline in his adopted hometown of Houston and by dredging the Houston ship channel thus making Houston an international city. Additionally, Jones served a succession of American presidents in various positions in the federal government during the 1930s and 1940s. When Jones died in 1956, he left many wonderful legacies; but perhaps the most wonderful of all is Houston Endowment Inc.

Houston Endowment Inc. (Figure 2-9) was created with a mission to "use the wealth created in the community to enrich the community." By 1956, Houston Endowment had helped 4,000 students get an education via scholarship programs in 57 colleges and universities; by 1979, Houston Endowment was the nation's fifteenth largest foundation; and by the early 1990s, Houston Endowment's management began evaluating how it could manage its assets, improve services to its constituencies, and increase staff productivity by installing a local area network.

Because of the number of workstations involved and the need to have multiuser access to centralized accounting and grant information, Houston Endowment chose to install a client/server LAN using a star physical topology with Ethernet logical topology. Since its original network installation, Houston Endowment's networking needs have grown and changed, and so has its LAN. Recent additions to the network include providing Internet access and the addition of servers that allow users to track telephone activity from their workstations, send and receive faxes directly from their workstations, and access their systems from anywhere in the world. Houston Endowment's LAN enables its staff to more productively manage its assets of more than $1.5 billion and track grants which, in 2001 alone, amounted to almost $70 million.

Figure 2-9
Houston Endowment Inc.

File and Print Services

File services permit the centralized storage of data files. The server that provides file services is called a file server. Data stored on a file server can be accessed by authorized users around the network. A serious business risk faced by an e-business is the potential loss of data resulting from a natural or man-made disaster. One way to protect against damaged or deleted data is to create a backup of the data and store the backup at a different location. Data stored on a file server can be backed up more easily than data stored on several individual desktop computers.

Businesses can also reduce costs and increase productivity by using network **print services** to enable employees to share printers across a network. For example, a business can replace several individual desktop printers with one or two high-quality, high-speed printers that can handle multiple print jobs quickly and efficiently. For example, assume that three employees of NatCo, Inc., Jeff, Tina, and Bob, are working together on an important client contract. Figure 2-10 illustrates the four steps of this process.

◆ *Step 1*: Jeff drafts the client contract using the word-processing software on his computer and stores the contract document on a file server. He calls Tina and asks her to make a few changes to the contract.

◆ *Step 2*: Tina accesses the file server, opens the contract document in her word-processing program, makes her changes, and saves the modified contract on the file server. Then she calls Bob and tells him the contract is ready for review.

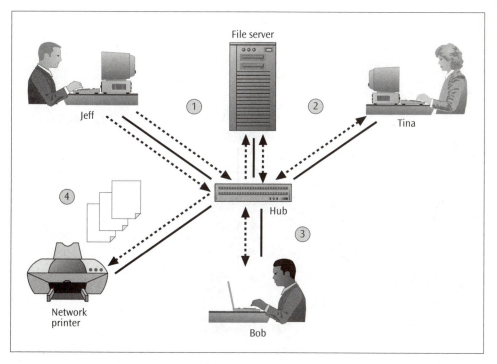

Figure 2-10
File and print services

- ◆ *Step 3:* Bob accesses the file server, opens the modified contract document in his word-processing program, and reviews it. He makes a few changes, saves the document to the file server, and calls Jeff to let him know the modified contract document is reviewed.
- ◆ *Step 4:* Jeff now needs a professional looking hard copy of the contract to send to the client. He accesses the file server and sends a copy of the contract document to a high-speed, high-quality network printer.

You have learned how file and print services allow employees to work more efficiently. Next, you learn how LAN mail and communication services enable employees to communicate more effectively.

Mail and Communication Services

One of the network services most important to business is **mail services**: the sending, receiving, routing, and storage of e-mail. In contemporary businesses, employees use e-mail extensively for internal communications. Many businesses also have employees who travel out of the office, but still require access to the network. Network **communication services** enable traveling employees to connect to the network and access their data files and e-mail messages. Using mail and communication services helps Jeff, Tina, and Bob speed up the process of creating and reviewing that important NatCo, Inc. client contract (Figure 2-11).

Figure 2-11
Mail and communication services

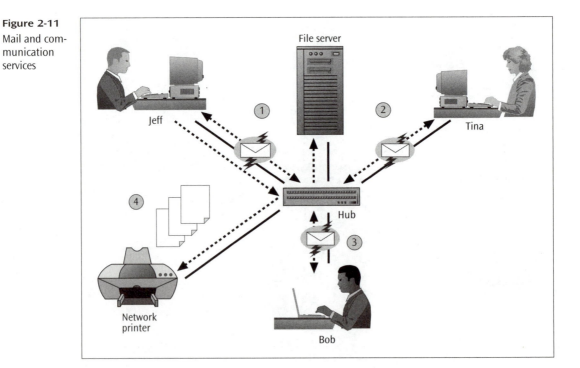

- *Step 1*: Just as before, Jeff drafts the contract and saves a copy of it on the file server. However, this time he routes a copy of the contract document to Tina via intracompany e-mail.
- *Step 2*: Tina receives the routed contract document, opens it in her word- processing program, makes her modifications, and then routes the modified contract document to Bob for review.
- *Step 3*: Bob is traveling on business. When he reaches his hotel, he connects his laptop to the company network via a telephone line, checks his e-mail, and finds the modified contract document routed to him by Tina. Bob reviews the modified contract, makes a few changes, and then routes the reviewed contract back to Jeff via intracompany e-mail.
- *Step 4*: Jeff receives the reviewed contract document from Bob, saves it to the file server, sends the document to a high-speed, high-quality network printer, and then mails the contract to the client for review.

Like mail and communication services, Internet services (described in the next section) enable employees and customers to interact more effectively.

Internet and Management Services

Network Internet services are a critical component of both internal and external business operations today. Network **Internet services** provide external Internet access, internal intranet services, and management of Internet-related technologies such as Web servers, Web browsers, and Internet-based e-mail.

Businesses use company intranets extensively for a variety of internal information-sharing purposes, such as providing computer and systems support or access to employee benefit information. Internet services are, of course, also used to establish and manage external business Web sites to sell products and services, provide customer support, and gather information about potential customers and the marketspace.

Internet-based e-mail allows businesses to maintain contact with customers and suppliers. Using the company intranet and Internet-based e-mail can help Jeff, Tina, and Bob improve service to NatCo, Inc. clients (Figure 2-12).

- *Step 1*: Many of NatCo, Inc.'s client contracts contain standardized wording. In order to make the contract creation process more efficient, Jeff creates a set of standardized contract documents, stores them on a server, and then creates an intranet Web page that lists the available contract documents. The Web page also includes instructions on how to download a copy of a standard contract via a hyperlink on the contracts Web page.
- *Step 2*: Whenever Tina or Bob need to draft a new client contract, they now start their Web browsers and access the NatCo, Inc. company intranet. Then they view the contracts Web page and download a copy of the contract document they need.
- *Step 3*: After downloading the standard contract form, making any client-specific changes, and reviewing the finished contract, Tina or Bob then send a copy of the contract to the client for review via Internet-based e-mail. The client returns the reviewed contract with any noted changes, again via Internet-based e-mail.

File, print, mail, communication, and Internet services enable employees to interact with each other and with customers more effectively. Another important service, network management services, allows administrators to make sure the network is running properly.

Network **management services** enable network administrators to perform many tasks. For example, management services enable administrators to determine how much data transmission and processing is occurring on the network and to ensure that no single network device is overloaded with activity. Additionally, management services enable administrators to detect and solve hardware or software problems on the network. Administrators can also use management services to distribute copies of software applications, such as Microsoft Excel, to users. Thanks to management services, administrators can copy critical data (a process known as backing up data) and store it off-site in case of a fire or other disaster. If the original data is lost or damaged, the administrator can use the back-up copies to restore the data.

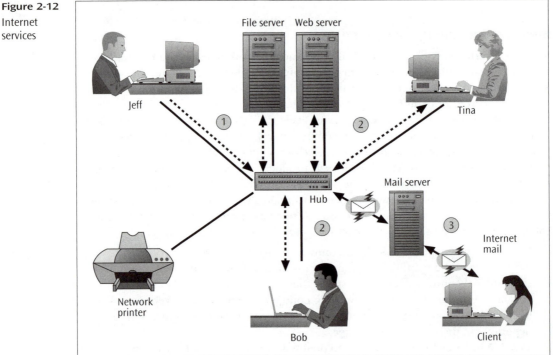

Figure 2-12
Internet services

So far, you have learned about several different types of networks and about the many services a network can provide. As you might imagine, the great variety of technologies in use on modern networks could potentially be the source of a lot of confusion. How do networking professionals know what to expect when installing a new piece of hardware or software on a network? How can they be sure that all the network components will work together as expected? The answer is: standards. All network components are created according to specified rules, called standards, that define how each component works within the network. In the next section, you learn about the organizations that create networking standards.

The Role of Standards Organizations

A standard is a rule, description, or design approved by an established organization or accepted by an industry through common usage. One simple example of a standard relates to units of measurement. In the United States, the mile is the standard unit of measurement for driving distances. If you ask someone in the United States the driving distance between New York and Boston, they'll likely answer with the number of miles between the two cities. However, if you ask the same question of someone in Paris, you'll likely get an answer in kilometers, because kilometers are the standard unit of measurement for driving distances in France.

The fact that France and the United States use different standard units of measurement causes some confusion for travelers, but overall it isn't enough of a problem to bring travel to a halt. On a computer network, however, a lack of generally agreed upon standards can cause major disruptions. After all, modern computer networks often consist of a hodgepodge of equipment acquired from a variety of vendors. To make matters even more complicated, the computers on a network often run a variety of software packages and are used for widely differing purposes. Meanwhile, users may be accessing the network from remote locations anywhere in the world, via numerous types of connections. These many technologies can work together seamlessly only because the world's many hardware and software vendors subscribe to the same basic sets of standards. In this age of globalization, businesses have come to realize that internationally agreed upon standards increase the reliability and effectiveness of the products and services used around the world.

Every industry in the world operates under its own set of standards. For example, manufacturers in the textile industry must create products that adhere to specific flammability standards. In the computer industry, there are standards that specify, for example, how networking cards and other devices are constructed, how computers and other devices connect to a network, and how data is transmitted across networks. For example, the IEEE 802.11b Wireless Fidelity Standard describes how computers and other devices should connect to a LAN using a wireless connection.

Many networking standards cover the formatting and transmission of data. These standards settle questions like: How many wires are in a copper wire cable? What purity should the copper be? What frequencies should be used to transmit data? What size should data packets be? Where should the origin and destination addresses go inside the data packet? If the first half of a data packet arrives but not the other half, what procedure should be followed to request the other half? How should data packets be secured?

Standards are only useful when all (or most) of the people working in a particular industry agree on them. The best way to generate industrywide agreement is to assign the job of creating standards to a third-party organization. Membership in these third-party organizations can include government agencies, scientists and research institutions, consumer groups, engineering professionals, manufacturers, vendors, and other interested parties. You learn about some of the major international standards organizations in the following sections.

The International Organization for Standardization (ISO)

The **International Organization for Standardization (ISO)**, located in Geneva, Switzerland, is a global alliance of national standards bodies drawn from approximately 140 countries (Figure 2-13). Members of ISO include organizations such as the American National Standards Institute (ANSI), the French Association for Standardization Group (AFNOR), the British Standards Institute (BSI), and the China State Bureau of Technical Supervision (CSBTS).

Figure 2-13

International Organization for Standardization (ISO)

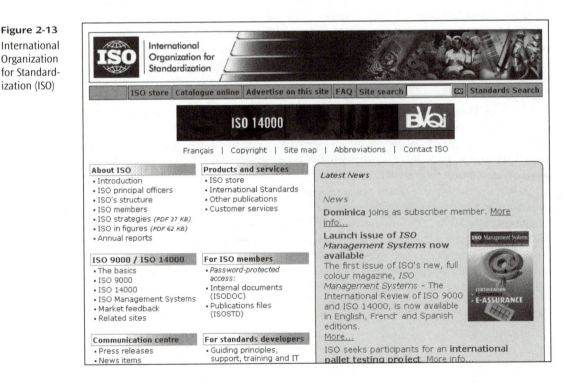

ISO focuses on establishing and publishing standards that help make possible the international trade of goods and services. For example, widely adopted ISO international standards govern areas such as photographic equipment and film speed, quality management and assurance, environmental management, freight container, and paper size standards. Additionally, ISO establishes international standards for the information processing and communication industries in tandem with the International Electrotechnical Commission (IEC).

ISO standards are developed in the following way:

◆ First, the need for a standard is identified by companies within an industry who communicate this need to their national ISO member organization, such as ANSI. The member organization then proposes to ISO that it begin work on the new standard.

◆ Next, a working group of technical experts from a variety of interested countries defines the technical range of the proposed standard. Then the technical details of the proposed standard are examined by manufacturers, vendors, users, and other interested parties until a consensus leads to the formalization of the technical specifications.

◆ Finally, the resulting draft of the new standard is voted on. To be adopted, the standard must be approved by 67 percent of the ISO members that participated in developing the standard and 75 percent of all voting ISO members. Upon approval, the draft is published as an ISO international standard.

One common example of an ISO standard governs the format of credit cards, phone cards, and "smart" cards (a small electronic device approximately the size of a credit card that contains electronic memory) widely used around the world. The ISO/IEC 7810:1995 standard defines the optimal thickness of such cards. By adhering to ISO standards, a company issuing a card in the United States can be certain that customers will be able to use that card in Europe or elsewhere around the globe.

International Electrotechnical Commission (IEC)

The **International Electrotechnical Commission (IEC)**, also headquartered in Geneva, Switzerland, and founded in 1906, has a mission to promote international standards in the fields of electronics, magnetics and electromagnetics, electroacoustics, multimedia, and telecommunications (Figure 2-14). At the IEC, standards are developed through the work of technical committees and their subcommittees and working groups. The IEC technical committee, the **Joint Technical Committee on Information Technology (JTC 1)**, works together with ISO to develop standards for the IT industry, including standards for software engineering, computer graphics, hardware connectivity, and so forth. For example, the ISO/IEC TR 8802-1:2001 standard developed by the JTC 1 provides an overview of LAN networking standards.

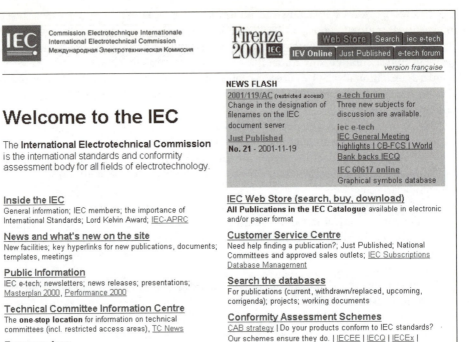

Figure 2-14
International
Electro-
technical
Commission
(IEC)

American National Standards Institute (ANSI)

Headquartered in Washington, D.C., the **American National Standards Institute (ANSI)** is a private, nonprofit organization that acts as the official U. S. representative to international standards organizations such as ISO and IEC (Figure 2-15). Founded in 1918, ANSI's mission is to increase the competitiveness of U.S. businesses in the international business community by encouraging the adoption of U.S. and international standards. ANSI does not develop standards, but rather accredits other qualified organizations to develop voluntary standards which become mandatory only when adopted by the government or when events in the marketplace make adoption of the standard critical. The ANSI membership consists of more than 1,000 U.S. and international business, government, and institutional organizations.

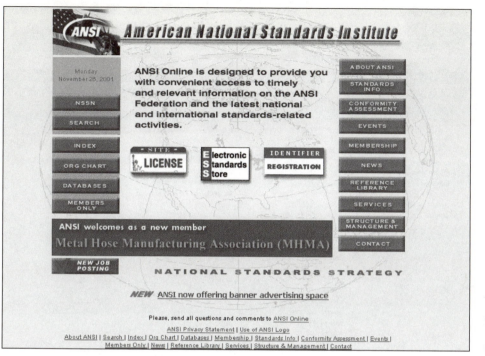

Figure 2-15
American
National
Standards
Institute
(ANSI)

Electronic Industries Alliance (EIA)

Located in Arlington, Virginia, the **Electronic Industries Alliance (EIA)** is a U.S. trade organization with 2,300 plus members affiliated with the electronics industry (Figure 2-16). The EIA is accredited by ANSI and provides a venue for the electronics industry to develop standards for electronic components, consumer electronics, and telecommunications. The EIA acts as an umbrella organization for various other associations with their own standards-setting committees. These other associations include the Consumer Electronics Association (CEA), the Electronic Components, Assemblies, and Materials Association (ECA), the Government Electronics and Information Technology Association (GEIA), the JEDEC Solid State Technology Association (JEDEC), and the Telecommunications Industry Association (TIA).

Institute of Electrical and Electronics Engineers, Inc. (IEEE)

The **Institute of Electrical and Electronics Engineers, Inc. (IEEE)** is a nonprofit association of more than 350,000 technical professionals in 150 countries (Figure 2-17). The IEEE (pronounced "eye-triple-E") has roots in electrotechnology theories and services that go back more than 100 years and is a leading international authority in technical fields including biomedical technology, consumer electronics, computer engineering, electric power, aerospace, and telecommunications. The IEEE publishes over 30 percent of the world's literature on control technologies, electrical engineering, and computer technologies. Additionally, it hosts more than 300 major technology conferences each year and develops electronic and telecommunications standards.

Figure 2-16

Electronics
Industries
Alliance (EIA)

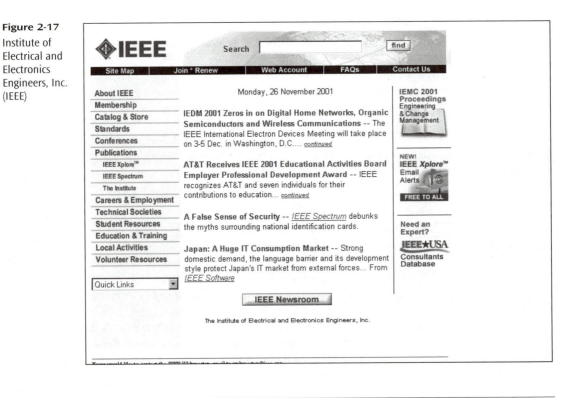

Figure 2-17

Institute of
Electrical and
Electronics
Engineers, Inc.
(IEEE)

International Telecommunication Union (ITU)

The **International Telecommunication Union** (**ITU**) developed out of a need to standardize telegraph networks across international boundaries in the midnineteenth century (Figure 2-18). After WWII, the ITU became a specialized agency of the United Nations. From its headquarters in Geneva, Switzerland, it now provides an international forum where government agencies and members of the telecommunications industry can come together to develop

TIP

The ITU was formerly known as the Consultative Committee on International Telegraph and Telephony (CCITT) and some publications still refer to CCITT standards.

standards for the telecommunications industry. Additionally, the ITU plays an international role in managing the radio-frequency spectrum for wireless communications such as cellular phone and satellite systems. ITU membership consists of 189 countries and more than 650 organizations.

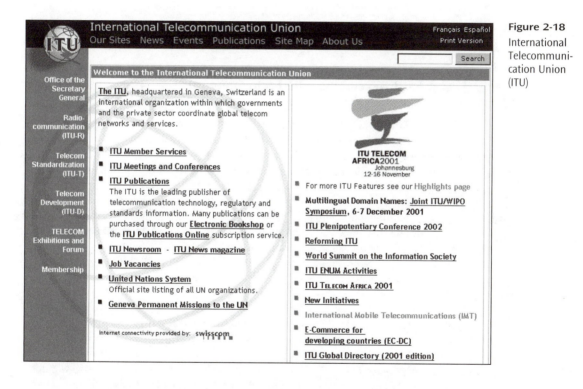

Figure 2-18
International Telecommuni-cation Union (ITU)

European Telecommunications Standards Institute (ETSI)

The **European Telecommunications Standards Institute** (**ETSI**) is one of three recognized European standards organizations that develop standards and documentation for telecommunications, broadcasting, and information technology (Figure 2-19). With 889 members from 54 countries in Europe and elsewhere, the ETSI is a nonprofit organization.

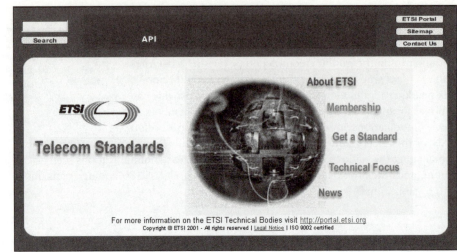

Figure 2-19
European
Telecommuni-
cations
Standards
Institute (ETSI)

TECH CASE Developing a De Facto Standard

A de facto standard is a rule or design that is already widely used in an industry. One example of a de facto standard in the computing industry is the PostScript page description language (PDL) for printers that is widely adopted by the desktop publishing industry.

John Warnock was a graduate student in mathematics at the University of Utah when he set out to help another student solve an extremely difficult programming problem: writing a graphics program that would display the changing view of the New York harbor from the bridge of a moving ship. Warnock's ability to visualize a new, simple, and elegant solution to the student's programming problem drew the attention of the university's administration. They sent Warnock around the country to various universities and seminars to explain his solution. As a result of this experience, Warnock became intrigued and excited about the new possibilities in the developing field of computer science and switched his Ph.D. studies from mathematics to electrical engineering. Ultimately, Warnock became one of the world's experts on computer graphics.

Warnock joined PARC as a principal scientist, and there he collaborated on a language, called JaM. JaM was a special kind of computer language known as a page description language. Its job was to translate objects on a computer screen into entries in a three-dimensional database. JaM evolved into another language, called Interpress, which was used for printing text and pictures on Xerox printers. In 1980, Warnock and his PARC boss, Charles Geschke, tried without success to get Xerox to commercialize Interpress. After Xerox turned them down, the two started their own company, Adobe Systems Incorporated (Figure 2-20), which was named after a stream that ran beside Warnock's backyard.

Continued

Formed in 1982, Adobe Systems developed the PostScript page description language. PostScript was based on the JaM and Interpress language research that Warnock and Geschke had done at PARC. While the PostScript language is primarily used for printing documents on laser printers, it can be adapted to create images on other types of devices. Because PostScript supported the very high-resolution printers used to prepare camera-ready copy, it soon became the de facto standard for desktop publishing. Today, Adobe Systems, creates software for network publishing and is one of the world's largest personal computer software companies with annual revenues in excess of $1.2 billion.

Figure 2-20
Adobe Systems Incorporated

The organizations you've learned about in this section generate standards that relate to a huge variety of technologies and issues. You couldn't possibly expect to be familiar with all of the standards issued by these organizations. But you do need to understand one of these standards very well. This standard, known as the Seven-Layer OSI Model, is used throughout the computer industry to explain how networked computers communicate.

The Seven-Layer OSI Model

ISO began work on a set of universal communication specifications in the early 1980s to assure that computers around the world could communicate openly with each other. To promote widespread understanding of how two nodes communicate on a network, ISO developed a hierarchal model called the **Open Systems Interconnection (OSI) Model**. This generic model, illustrated in Figure 2-21, is often called the Seven-Layer OSI Model because it divides networking design into seven layers: the Physical, Data Link, Network, Transport, Session, Presentation, and Application layers. The OSI Model describes the flow of data from the lowest layer (the physical connections) to the highest layer (interface with user applications) and vice versa. The OSI Model is important because it serves as a kind of map or reference point for technicians thinking about and discussing network communications problems.

Figure 2-21
Seven-Layer
OSI Model

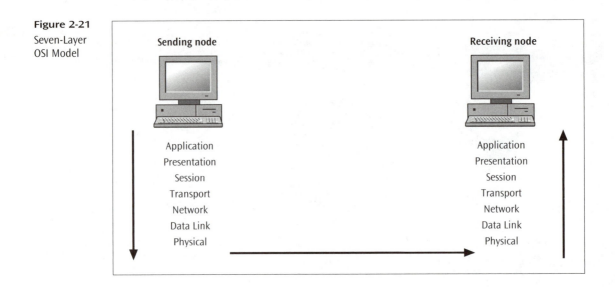

The following list describes each of the OSI layers:

- ◆ *Physical layer*: Defines the physical and electrical characteristics of a system, including cabling, electrical voltage, and data transmission rates. A network interface card or NIC that allows a computer to be connected to a network operates at the Physical layer.
- ◆ *Data Link layer*: Controls communications between the Physical layer below it and the Network layer above it. It is the Data Link layer's job to subdivide data into smaller pieces, known as frames, and then transfer the frames from one computer to another without errors. Each frame consists of the raw data, the sending node's and receiving

node's network addresses, and special information (called error-checking and control information) that ensures the data arrives at the correct destination without errors. After a transmission, the Data Link layer waits for the acknowledgment of a successful transfer. If that acknowledgment is not received, the Data Link layer retransmits the frame. Ethernet technologies function in the Data Link layer.

◆ *Network layer*: Routes data across networks by determining the best path from the sending node to the receiving node based on network congestion and delivery priorities. The Network layer also translates a node's logical address (called IP address) into its physical address (called a MAC address) and can break (or segment) frames into smaller units, if necessary, and then reassemble segmented frames at their destination. You learn about logical IP addresses, physical MAC addresses, and how data is routed from one network to another in Chapter 3.

◆ *Transport layer*: Ensures that frames traveling from the sending node to the receiving node arrive without errors and in the correct sequence. The sending node's Transport layer breaks long frames into smaller units, assigning a sequence number to each unit. The receiving node's Transport layer then uses the sequence numbers to reassemble the units in the correct order. The receiving Transport layer also sends an acknowledgement (ACK) to the sender indicating error-free receipt of the frame.

◆ *Session layer*: Establishes and maintains communications between the sending node and the receiving node. A session is a connection between two nodes that are sending and receiving data. The Session layer sets up a session, decides which nodes can communicate and for how long, and restarts a terminated session, if necessary.

◆ *Presentation layer*: Formats data sent to the receiving node into a format the network can use. The Presentation layer at the receiving node then formats the data into a format an application can use. A bit (short for binary digit) is the smallest unit of data processed by a computer. The sending node's Presentation layer compresses data into the smallest number of bits that need to be transmitted. Encryption translates data into a secret format and decryption translates the data back into its original format. The sending node's Presentation layer can also encrypt data for security purposes and the receiving node's Presentation layer can decrypt it.

◆ *Application layer*: Enables the user's software applications to access network services such as file transfer, file and printer access, and e-mail message management.

It is important to remember that the Seven-Layer OSI Model does not specify hardware or software requirements for each layer, but only provides a conceptual model of how data flows from a sending node to a receiving node on a network.

In this chapter you learned about three types of computer networks: LANs, MANs, and WANs. You also learned about two types of LANs: peer-to-peer and client/server, and the data transmission media and physical and logical topologies associated with them. Additionally, you learned about the importance of industry standards and how the ongoing efforts of several international standards organizations establish the hardware and software standards that

TIP

Keep in mind that no real-world network operates exactly as described by the Seven-Layer OSI Model. However, the model is still a useful tool for understanding data transmissions over computer networks.

permit different makes of computers to communicate with each other over a network. Finally, you learned about one important standard, the Seven-Layer OSI Model, and how it is used to understand the flow of data transmitted from a sending node to a receiving node over a network. In the next chapter, you learn about the technologies involved in transmitting data from one network to another.

... INTO THE ETHER

Frustrated by Xerox's inability to commercialize Ethernet, Metcalfe became an entrepreneur by forming his own company, 3Com Corporation, to sell Ethernet and other networking technologies. A serendipitous combination of events in the early 1980s — the advent of the new, relatively inexpensive (for its day) IBM personal computer and 3Com's development of an expansion card for that computer that allowed an Ethernet connection — encouraged businesses to take a serious look at implementing local area networks. Ultimately, Ethernet became a networking industry standard method of connecting devices on a local area network; 3Com became a huge multibillion dollar success, and Metcalfe became a legend.

Today, Bob Metcalfe (Figure 2-22), who left 3Com in 1990, is a highly respected computer industry "elder statesman" and, as of this writing, is a venture partner in the Boston office of Polaris Venture Partners. He's also the author of Metcalfe's Law, a principle used to explain the dynamic growth of new technologies. Specifically, Metcalfe's law states that the usefulness, or utility, of a network equals the square of the number of users. The analogy most often used to explain Metcalfe's Law is a telephone system. One telephone is essentially useless; however, the more telephones that are added to the system, the more useful the system becomes to its users. The explosive business use of Internet technologies is another dramatic illustration of Metcalfe's Law. Increased use of these technologies to conduct business activities attracts ever more businesses, thereby increasing the value of the electronic marketspace.

Figure 2-22
Robert
Metcalfe

Reviewing Networking Basics

❏ Networks can be categorized geographically as local area networks (LANs), metropolitan area networks (MANs), and wide area networks (WANs). A LAN is a network that covers a small geographical area such as a single office or building. A MAN is a high-speed network connecting two or more LANs usually in a single metropolitan area. A WAN connects two or more LANs across a nation or around the world.

❏ Two common forms for a local area network are peer-to-peer and client/server. A peer-to-peer network consists of six or fewer computers and attached devices connected via cable. A peer-to-peer network is simple and inexpensive to set up. A client/server network uses high-performance computers called servers to allow other network devices to share data, applications, and other devices. A client/server network is more difficult to set up and maintain and more expensive than a peer-to-peer network.

❏ Networks can incorporate a variety of transmission media, including copper wire cable and fiber-optic cable. Wireless technologies such as infrared and radio waves are also options.

❏ In networking, the term "physical topology" refers to the way all the pieces of a network are connected. LAN physical topologies include bus, star, ring, or some combination of the three.

❏ A network's logical topology defines the way data is transmitted between computers. LAN logical topologies include Ethernet and Token Ring.

❏ Networks provide a variety of services that allow businesses to improve communication and save time and money. Network services include file, print, mail, communication, Internet, and management services.

❏ A standard is a rule, description, or design established in two ways: either approved by a standards setting organizations or established as a result of industrywide usage. Without standards in the computing industry, it would be impossible for different vendors' computers to communicate with each other.

❏ National and international standards setting organizations include ISO, IEC, ANSI, EIA, IEEE, ITU, and ETSI.

❏ The Seven-Layer OSI Model describes how data flows from a sending node to a receiving node (and vice versa) over a network.

Key Terms

American National Standards Institute (ANSI)
backbone
bandwidth
bus topology
client/server network
coaxial cable
communication services
Electronic Industries Alliance (EIA)
Ethernet
European Telecommunications Standards Institute (ETSI)
fiber-optic cable
file services
hybrid topology
infrared (IR) transmissions
Institute of Electrical and Electronics Engineers, Inc. (IEEE)

International Electrotechnical Commission (IEC)
International Organization for Standardization (ISO)
International Telecommunication Union (ITU)
Internet services
internetworking
Joint Technical Committee on Information Technology (JTC1)
local area network (LAN)
logical topology
mail services
management services
metropolitan area network (MAN)
network
network interface card (NIC)

network operating system (NOS)
network topology
node
Open Systems Interconnection (OSI) Model
peer-to-peer network
physical topology
print services
radiofrequency (RF) transmission
ring topology
standard
star topology
throughput
Token Ring
transmission media
twisted-pair cable
wide area network (WAN)

Review Questions

1. A de facto standard:
   a. Is approved by an international standards organization.
   b. Plays no part in computer networking.
   c. Is adopted because of common industry-wide usage.
   d. Must be approved by the ANSI.

2. What model is used to describe how data flows from a sending node to a receiving node on a network?
   a. Open Systems Interapplication (OSI) Model
   b. Open Structure Internet (OSI) Model
   c. Open Systems Interconnection (OSI) Model
   d. Open Systems Internetworking (OSI) Model

3. The Transport layer in the OSI Model:
   a. Formats data into an intermediary format.
   b. Translates logical addresses into physical addresses.
   c. Establishes and maintains communications between sender and receiver.
   d. Ensures that frames arrive at their destination without errors and in the correct order.

4. A network that is limited to a small geographical area is called a:
   a. WAN.
   b. LAN.
   c. MAN.
   d. PAN.

5. Which of the following is not true of a peer-to-peer network?
   a. Simple to set up
   b. Requires a special network operating system
   c. Inexpensive
   d. Suitable for six or fewer computers

6. Which of the following transmission media is most commonly used for local area networks?
   a. Coaxial cable
   b. Twisted-pair cable
   c. Infrared transmissions
   d. Fiber-optic cable

7. The bus physical topology connects network nodes:
   a. In a ring.
   b. To a central hub.
   c. Along a single coaxial cable.
   d. In a square.

8. The most popular and least expensive logical topology is:

    a. FDDI.
    b. Ethernet.
    c. Token Ring.
    d. ATM.

9. Which network service allows employees to access their company's network when traveling?

    a. Communication services
    b. File services
    c. Management services
    d. Mail services

10. The leading authority in technical areas of computer engineering and telecommunications is the:

    a. ISO.
    b. IEEE.
    c. CCITT.
    d. ANSI.

11. The advantages of a peer-to-peer network are low startup cost and operational simplicity. **True or False?**

12. Networking transmission media reside at the Physical layer of the OSI Model. **True or False?**

13. Coaxial cable is the medium of choice for high-speed, long-distance data transmissions. **True or False?**

14. The abbreviation "Mbps" refers to the data transmission throughput of 1 megabit per second. **True or False?**

15. The only organization that establishes networking standards is the ITU. **True or False?**

16. The OSI Model specifies required networking hardware and software and all networks must follow the model exactly. **True or False?**

17. Network file services are used to provide access to the Internet or a company intranet. **True or False?**

18. A peer-to-peer network is appropriate when a company has more than 25 workstations and its employees need to access data stored in a central location. **True or False?**

19. The advantages of a client/server network include centralized maintenance, centralized data backup and the security provided by a network operating system. **True or False?**

20. ISO's mission is to develop standards only for the telecommunications industry. **True or False?**

Exercises

1. Using Internet search tools or other relevant resources, such as those listed at the end of this chapter, research several important networking standards. Then write a one-page paper describing at least three standards.

2. Locate a small to medium business in your area that uses a LAN. Interview the business's principals to determine how the LAN is structured and used. Then write a one- or two-page paper describing the business and its LAN. Note: substitute Internet research (or other research) in lieu of an interview, if necessary.

3. Define the acronyms ISO, ANSI, EIA, ITU, and IEEE and explain the role each plays in setting international standards.

4. Using Internet search tools and other relevant resources, such as those listed at the end of this chapter, review the Seven-Layer OSI Model. Then create a one- or two-page paper describing the model, its purpose, and each of its seven layers. Include an illustration of the model.

5. Define the acronyms LAN, MAN, and WAN and create an illustration of each.

CASE PROJECTS

◆ 1 ◆

You are the office manager of a small business that sells products and services directly to consumers. You would like the business's owner to consider setting up a LAN; however, he isn't quite sure how networks work. He asks you to prepare a 15-minute presentation for the next executive committee meeting describing the services a network can provide. Create an outline for your presentation that describes network services including file, print, mail, communication, management, and Internet services. Be sure to explain how these services could improve the business's operations.

◆ 2 ◆

You are the new assistant to your company's network administrator. During a staff meeting, the administrator mentions several logical network topologies with which you are unfamiliar: FDDI, LocalTalk, Fast Ethernet, Gigabit Ethernet, and ATM. You want to know more about these logical topologies before the next meeting. Using the Internet or other resources, research these logical topologies. Then write a one- or two-page paper describing these logical topologies including their uses, advantages, and disadvantages.

◆ 3 ◆

You have been invited to participate in a business conference workshop. The purpose of the workshop is to discuss how networking technologies are affecting businesses today. During the workshop, you want to explore a discussion of Metcalfe's Law. Using Internet search tools or other relevant resources, research the origins and meaning of Metcalfe's Law. Then create a one- or two-page outline you can use to guide the workshop discussion that defines Metcalfe's Law, describes its origins, and illustrates how Metcalfe's Law explains both the value of networks and the value of new technologies.

TEAM PROJECT

Your friend, Elizabeth Wilson, owns a small but growing commercial landscaping business and has asked for your help. She currently has three standalone computers and one printer in her landscaping business office which is located on one floor of a nearby office building. Elizabeth's three office employees need easy access to accounting, payroll, and sales information stored on all three computers. The employees also need to be able to print a variety of documents from any computer. Although the business is growing rapidly, Elizabeth's budget is limited, and she can't afford to invest in any additional computers or printers or hire any additional employees at this time. She is looking for ways to save money and increase her current office employees' productivity. You think a computer network would help meet these two goals.

Working with another classmate, determine the appropriate type of network for Elizabeth's landscaping business. Be sure to specify the appropriate physical and logical topology. Then create a presentation of 5–10 slides using Microsoft PowerPoint or another presentation tool. The presentation should describe why the business needs a network, illustrate your recommended network including its physical and logical topologies, and list the reasons for your recommendation. Present your recommendation to a group of classmates selected by your instructor.

Useful Links

3Com — Small Business Learning Center
learningcenter.3com.com/

Association for Computing Machinery (ACM)
info.acm.org/

Cisco Networking Essentials for Small/Medium Businesses
www.cisco.com/warp/public/779/smbiz/netguide/iii_sbne.html

CNET Glossary
www.cnet.com/Resources/Info/Glossary/

Connectworld — Connectivity Resources
www.connectworld.net/

Context Magazine
www.contextmag.com/

EarthWeb — The IT Portal
www.earthweb.com/

Ethernet Information Page
wwwethermanage.com/ethernet/ethernet.html

GoCertify — OSI Quiz
gocertify.com/quizzes/osi/

IEEE Network — Online Magazine
www.comsoc.org/~nil

IEEE/ACM Transactions on Networking
www.ton.cc.gatech.edu/

IFLANET — Internet and Networking Standards and Organizations
www.ifla.org/II/standard.htm

InformIT
www.informit.com/

Interactive Week — Online Magazine
www.interactiveweek.com/default/0,3660,,00.asp

ITtoolbox — Networking
networking.ittoolbox.com/

ITworld.com — IT resources
www.itworld.com/

James Bond Meets the 7 Layer OSI Model
www.pe.net/~rlewis/Resources/james.html

LabMice.Net — OSI Model Resources
www.labmice.net/networking/OSI.htm

Microsoft Product Support — The OSI Model's Seven Layers Defined and Functions Explained
support.microsoft.com/support/kb/articles/q103/8/84.asp

Network Buyers Guide
www.networkbuyersguide.com/

Network Computing — Online Magazine
www.networkcomputing.co.uk/

Network Professional Association
www.npa.org/

NetworkMagazine.com
www.networkmagazine.com

NetworkWorldFusion — Networking Resources
www.nwfusion.com/index.html

O'Reilly Network — Networking Resources
www.oreillynet.com/

PC Support Advisor — Technical Support and Networking Articles
www.itp-journals.com/

Practically Networked — Networking Resources
www.practicallynetworked.com/index.htm

TechEncyclopedia
www.techweb.com/encyclopedia/

TechFest — Technology Resources
www.techfest.com/index.htm

TechTarget — IT Media
www.techtarget.com/network.html

Telecom Made Simple — Telecommunications Portal
www.telecommadesimple.com/

The Technology Channel
www.the-technology-channel.com/

White Papers on Local Area Networks/Wide Area Networks
www.itpapers.com/category/lanwan.html

White Papers on Network Design
www.itpapers.com/cgi/SubcatIT.pl?scid=291

Links to Web Sites or Companies Noted in This Chapter

3Com
www.3com.com/

Adobe Systems Incorporated
www.adobe.com/main.html

AFNOR — French Association for Standardization Group, French language site
www.afnor.fr/

ANSI — American National Standards Institute
www.ansi.org/

Apple Computer, Inc.
www.apple.com/

Bell Labs
www.bell-labs.com/

BSI — British Standards Institute
www.bsi-global.com/group.xalter

CEA — Consumer Electronics Association
www.ce.org/

ECA — Electronic Components, Assemblies, and Materials Association
www.ec-central.org/

EIA — Electronics Industries Alliance
www.eia.org/

ETSI — European Telecommunications Standards Institute
www.etsi.org/portal.etsi.org/Portal_Common/home.asp

GEIA — Government Electronics and Information Technology Association
www.geia.org/

Houston Endowment Inc.
www.houstonendowment.org

IBM
www.ibm.com

IEC — International Electrotechnical Commission
www.iec.ch/

IEEE — Institute of Electrical and Electronics Engineers, Inc.
www.ieee.org/

ISO — International Organization for Standardization
www.iso.ch/iso/en/ISOOnline.frontpage

ITU — International Telecommunication Union
www.itu.int/home/index.html

JEDEC — JEDEC Solid State Technology Association
www.jedec.org/

JTC1 — Joint Technical Committee on Information Technology
www.jtc1.org/

Microsoft Corporation
www.microsoft.com

Novell, Inc.
www.novell.com/

NSSN — National Standards Systems Network: A National Resource for Global Standards
www.nssn.org/index.html

Palo Alto Research Center Incorporated (Xerox PARC)
www.parc.xerox.com/parc-go.html

Polaris Venture Partners
www.polarisventures.com/index.html

TIA — Telecommunications Industry Association
www.tiaonline.org/

For Additional Review

3Com Corporation. 2001. "Networking Basics." Available online at: learningcenter.3com.com/.

3Com Corporation. 2002. "Who is 3Com." Available online at: www.3com.com/corpinfo/en_US/index.html.

Adobe Systems Incorporated. 2002. "About Adobe, Company Profile, Executive Profiles." Available online at: www.adobe.com/aboutadobe/.

ANSI. 2001. "ANSI - A National Resource," ANSI Publications. Available online at: www.ansi.org/.

ANSI. 2002. "About ANSI." Available online at: www.ansi.org/.

Briscoe, Neil. 2000. "Understanding the OSI 7-Layer Model," *PC Network Advisor*, July, 13. Available online at: www.itp-journals.com/nasample/t04124.pdf.

1Cringely, Robert X. 1996. *Accidental Empires: How the Boys of Silicon Valley Make Their Millions, Battle Foreign Competition, and Still Can't Get a Date*, Revised Edition. New York: HarperBusiness.

Dean, Tamara. 2002. *Network+ Guide to Networks, Second Edition*. Boston, MA: Course Technology.

Derfler, Frank J. 2000. *Practical Networking*. Indianapolis, IN: QUE.

Derfler, Frank J., Jr., 2001. "Buying Guide: Networking," *PC Magazine*, October 5. Available online at: www.pcmag.com/article/ 0,2997,s%253D1610%2526a%253D15864,00.asp.

EIA. 2002. "About the EIA." Available online at: www.eia.org/.

Eley, Stephen F. and Enslow, Philip H., Jr., 2001. "Telecommunications: An Operational Overview," Georgia Institute of Technology. www.gt.ed.net/sf/4375/telecom.html.

Hafner, Katie and Lyon, Matthew. 1996. *Where Wizards Stay Up Late, The Origins of the Internet*. New York: Simon & Schuster Inc.

Hiltzik, Michael A. 1999. *Dealers of Lightning: XEROX PARC and the Dawn of the Computer Age*. New York: HarperBusiness.

Houston Endowment Inc. 2002. "About Houston Endowment Inc." Available online at: www.houstonendowment.org/abouthei/main.htm

IEC. 2002. "Inside the IEC." Available online at: www.iec.ch/.

IEEE. 2002. "About the IEEE." Available online at: www.ieee.org/.

International Organization for Standardization. 2002. "About ISO." Available online at: www.iso.ch/.

ITU. 2002. "ITU Overview - Purpose." Available online at: www.itu.int/.

Kirsner, Scott. 1998. "The Legend of Bob Metcalfe," *Wired Magazine*, November. Available online at: www.wired.com/wired/archive/6.11/ metcalfe_pr.html.

Latimer, Jack. 1997. "Friendship Among Equals: ISO's First Fifty Years," ISO. Available online at: www.iso.ch/iso/en/aboutiso/introduction/ howstarted/fifty/fifty.html.

Limoncelli, Thomas A. and Hogan, Christine. 2001. *The Practice of System and Network Administration*. Reading, MA: Addison-Wesley.

Naugle, Matthew G. 1999. *Network Protocols*. New York: McGraw-Hill Professional.

Newton, Harry and Horak, Ray. 2000. *Newton's Telecom Dictionary, 16th Edition*. San Francisco, CA: Miller Freeman, Inc.

NSSN. 2002. "About NSSN." Available online at: www.nssn.org/.

Palo Alto Research Center Incorporated. 2002. "PARC's History." Available online at: www.parc.xerox.com/parc-go.html.

Press Release. 1998. "Jesse Jones: Brother Can You Spare a Billion?" *KUHT/Houston Public Television*, November 4. Available online at: riceinfo.rice.edu/armadillo/jjones/newsrelease.html.

Press Release. 2000. "Networking At Core of Small Business Internet Use," *Cahners In-Stat Group*, May 10. Available online at: www.instat.com/pr/2000/gn0001rk_pr.htm.

Press Release. 2001. "IDC Forecasts U. S. Market for Metro Ethernet Services Will Surge to $740 Million in 2006," IDC. www.idc.com:8080/communica-tions/press/pr/CM071901pr.stm.

Segaller, Stephen. 1999. *Nerds 2.0.1, A Brief History of the Internet*. New York: TV Books, L.L.C.

Smith, Douglas K. and Alexander, Robert C. 1999. *Fumbling the Future: How Xerox Invented, Then Ignored, the First Personal Computer*. New York: iUniverse.com, Inc.

Steinke, Steve and the editors of Network Magazine. 2000. *Network Tutorial*. San Francisco, CA: CMP Books.

Tanenbaum, Andrew S. 1996. *Computer Networks, 3rd Edition*. Upper Saddle River, NJ: Prentice Hall.

Texas State Historical Association. 2001. "Jesse Holman Jones," *The Handbook of Texas Online*. Available online at: www.tsha.utexas.edu/ handbook/online/articles/view/JJ/fjo53.html.

Thomson, Iain. 2000. "Small Business Networking," *PC Magazine, UK*, October. Available online at: www.zdnet.co.uk/pcmag/labs/2000/10/sbn/00.html.

Waldrop, M. Mitchell. 2001. *The Dream Machine, J. C. R. Licklider and the Revolution That Made Computing Personal*. New York: The Penguin Group.

ZDNET. 2001. "Ethernet Simplified: The Ideal Networking Technology," *ZDNET Business Technology*, July 5. Available online at: www.zdnetindia.com/biztech/resources/ networking/stories/28971.html.

CHAPTER 3

Internetworking Basics

In this chapter, you will learn to:

Identify internetworking hardware, Internet connections, and network addressing issues

Discuss the TCP/IP protocol suite, IP addresses, and logical ports

Explain domain names, the Domain Name System, and Uniform Resource Locators

Identify organizations that provide oversight for the Internet and the World Wide Web

This story of one e-business has all the trappings of a modern-day fable, including hard work and personal sacrifice, romance, and, ultimately, unbelievable success. Sandra (Sandy) Lerner and Leonard (Len) Bosack met in 1977 at Stanford University where she was a graduate student and he was using time-sharing minicomputers in the Computer Science Department. Lerner and Bosack married and continued at Stanford: Lerner as the director of the Stanford University Business School computer facilities and Bosack as director of the Stanford University Computer Science Department.

By 1982, Stanford was home to hundreds of computers (of many makes and models) scattered across the campus. These computers were more or less cut off from each other, because there was no way for them to communicate effectively. In an effort to link this diverse collection of computers, Lerner and Bosack, along with several other Stanford engineers, launched an unofficial experiment involving a computer with special programming called a router. They hoped that this device would allow ordinarily incompatible Stanford computers to connect and communicate. This experimental, router-based network was so successful that it developed into the official Stanford University network.

When word of these new router devices got out, other universities and research centers began clamoring for them. However, when Lerner and Bosack approached the Stanford Office of Technology Licensing (OTL) with a plan to design and build routers for sale to universities, research centers, and businesses under the school's sponsorship, the OTL said "No." Now what were Lerner and Bosack to do?

Internetworking Hardware, Internet Connections, and Network Addressing Issues

In Chapter 2, you learned about networking basics. Among other things, you learned how peer-to-peer and server-based LAN networks are physically arranged and how data moves from computer to computer across a LAN. As you also learned in Chapter 2, a WAN consists of multiple LANs that are connected across long distances. For example, suppose an e-business with offices in New York and Los Angeles has a LAN in each office. Combining the two LANs into a WAN would increase productivity by allowing New York employees to share files and other resources with Los Angeles employees, and vice versa. In this chapter, you learn how data moves from one computer to another across the largest WAN of all, the Internet. Specifically, you investigate the role that hardware, Internet connections, network and internetworking addressing schemes, and Internet protocols play in carrying data across the Internet.

You begin by learning about some essential hardware components. You learn how these devices work on LANs as well as their role in internetworking via the Internet.

Hubs, Switches, Routers, and Firewalls

In its simplest form, a LAN is similar to an old fashioned telephone party line, where you can hear everyone else's conversations simply by picking up the phone and listening. The computer network equivalent of a party line, then, is a situation in which every computer receives every single piece of data transmitted on the LAN. Early LANs were all designed along this party-line model. The problem with the party-line model is that, as more and more computers are added to the LAN, network traffic begins to slow down (because each computer has to "listen" to each transmission) and the network becomes congested.

To reduce network congestion, modern LANs are broken up into pieces, called **segments**. A network segment normally consists of computers that share a common function. For example, on an e-business network all the Accounting Department computers might be on one segment, with the Marketing Department computers on another segment. Special network devices, called switches and routers, control data transmissions within and between such segments. These devices reduce network traffic congestion by assuring that communications between one computer and another computer on the same network segment are transmitted only on that segment. This means that transmissions between one accounting computer and another accounting computer never travel over to the Marketing Department segment. Only when an accounting computer transmits to a marketing computer does the router or switch permit a transmission to travel from the Accounting Department segment to the Marketing Department segment.

Hubs are inexpensive devices used to connect a group of computers (generally fewer than 64) on a LAN. A hub's job is simply to repeat a signal, passing it on to all the other computers or devices on a network segment. Typically, each computer connects to a hub via a cable, with a hub able to accommodate anywhere between four and 64 connections, depending on the hub's make and model. Hubs can connect to other hubs, but every computer connected to any hub or series of hubs can "hear" the other computers on that hub or series — that is, each bit of data a hub receives from one computer is repeated to every other computer. Hubs are useful on small LANs, but can lead to congestion as more computers are added to the network.

As networks grow larger and become congested, network administrators often replace hubs with switches. **Switches** are devices that are similar to hubs in that they are used to transmit a signal from one computer or device to another. However, switches, unlike hubs, are considered intelligent devices and generally cost quite a bit more than hubs. (An **intelligent device** is one that can analyze information passing through it and make decisions about which information to transmit and where to send it.)

A switch has several openings called **ports** to which computers are physically connected via cable. To understand how a switch reduces network congestion, assume that Computer A and Computer B are connected to the same switch and Computer A sends a transmission to Computer B through the switch. Upon receiving the transmission, the switch first determines which computer is connected to which of its ports. The switch then examines the data transmission to determine its destination port. Finally, the switch connects the two ports so that the data is passed only between Computer A and Computer B and is not passed to any other computers connected to the switch.

A typical switch can only handle a few dozen to a few hundred computers at once. As a LAN grows and network traffic becomes more congested, a network administrator might choose to reduce the congestion by replacing some key switches with routers.

Routers are similar to switches in that they are intelligent devices used to manage network traffic. Routers, however, are much more powerful than switches. In fact, they are essentially specialized computers specifically designed to manage data transmissions over large LANs and WANs such as the Internet. Routers do their work by maintaining databases of information about networks and the computers attached to the networks and by closely examining transmitted data packets to direct them to their appropriate destination computers.

Routers are critical to getting data packets transmitted from one network to another via the Internet. Small routers might handle the traffic to computers on a large LAN on multiple floors of the same building. Big routers at the intersection of important Internet data lines are closet-sized, holding gigabytes of memory about the structure of the Internet, and can search through this information quickly enough to correctly forward millions of data packets per second. Such routers are, of course, very expensive. For many years the router market has been dominated by Cisco Systems, Inc. Many large LANs incorporate a mix of hubs, switches, and routers. An appropriate combination of hubs, switches, and routers can help data packets move efficiently and quickly across networks to their destination.

Connecting a LAN to the Internet raises additional concerns. For starters, network administrators must consider the risk of unauthorized network access via the Internet by others outside the network. At the same time, the administrator must be wary of inappropriate Internet access by employees from inside the network. One way to prevent such unauthorized Internet traffic (both into and out of the network) is to install a firewall.

A **firewall** is a security tool, consisting of a specialized hardware device or software or a combination of both. A firewall is placed between a **private network** (such as an e-business LAN) and a **public network** (such as the Internet). The firewall's job is to filter all incoming and outgoing transmissions passing through it and block those transmissions that do not meet specific security criteria. For example, a firewall can stop employees from downloading specific Web pages. It can also filter out unauthorized incoming transmissions from parties outside the network. In Chapter 7, you learn more about firewall techniques and other network security issues.

Figure 3-1 illustrates a two-segment LAN connected with hubs, a switch, and a router behind a firewall. Because Segment 1 computers are connected via a hub, only one computer can talk to the file server or to the router at a time. If the switch in Figure 3-1 were replaced by a hub, only one computer on both segments would be able to talk at a time. The inclusion of the switch, though, means that one Segment 1 computer and one Segment 2 computer can talk to the file server or the router at the same time. The firewall protects the LAN from unauthorized external transmissions and controls employee Internet access.

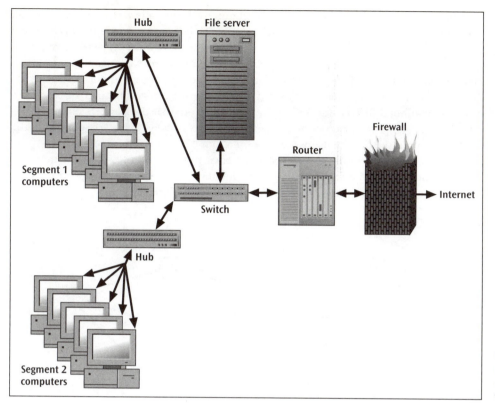

Figure 3-1
Hubs, switch, router, and firewall

As you learned in Chapters 1 and 2, packet switching is the practice of breaking data transmissions into small packages, called packets, which can then travel independently of each other across a network, much like packages travel independently of each other throughout the U.S. Postal System.

When data packets are sent from a computer on one network to a computer on another network via the Internet, an intermediary is needed to receive the packets and route them to the destination network. As you probably have guessed, that intermediary is a router, which acts like a post office by receiving each packet, examining its destination address, and sending it on to the destination computer. Figure 3-2 illustrates data broken into multiple packets (numbered 1-7) and sent from a computer in New York City to a computer in Los Angeles via the Internet. Note that the packets don't all travel the same route. The packet numbers enable the data packets to be reassembled in the correct order at the data transmission's destination.

Now that you are familiar with hubs, switches, routers, and firewalls, you are ready to learn about an important aspect of data communications between networks via the Internet: how consumers and businesses connect to the Internet.

Figure 3-2
Packet switching

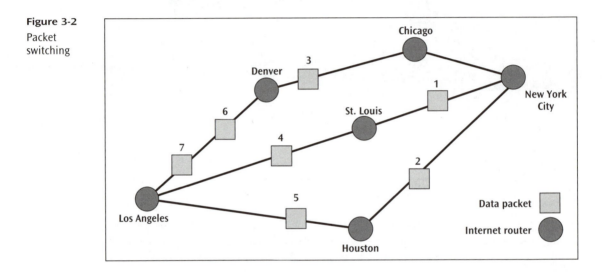

Internet Connections

Internet connections can take place using many different types of telecommunications media, from a **dial-up connection** using a standard phone line and a modem to wireless satellite connections. A modem is a device placed at each end of a phone line to encode (modulate) data into signals that are then decoded (demodulated) at the other end. To access the Internet using a dial-up connection, a user dials a phone number for an Internet service provider (such as America Online) from his or her computer using a modem connected to a standard phone line. Because standard phone lines and modems are readily available and inexpensive, this combination is a popular type of Internet connection for many consumers.

A business, however, may progress through several types of Internet connections as its Internet use evolves. For example, a business may start with a few modems and a shared phone line that enables one employee at a time to access the Internet via a dial-up connection. When it becomes necessary for several employees to access the Internet at the same time, the business might then simply add more standard phone lines. However, once it becomes necessary to transmit large amounts of data over the Internet, dial-up connections often prove inadequate — both because line clarity is not reliable and because the transmission speeds on such connections are too slow. Additionally, paying for multiple standard phone lines may become more expensive than paying for a single, shared connection.

A **shared connection** usually consists of a router on the business's LAN and a telecommunications connection between the router and the Internet. Table 3-1 lists some typical ways businesses connect to the Internet today.

Connection	Description	Speed	Approximate Cost
Dial-up router	Includes a modem that connects to the Internet when it detects an office computer trying to access the Internet	56 Kbps	$40+/month
Leased line/ frame relay	A connection that is always on and much more reliable than a dial-up connection	56 Kbps to 45 Mbps	$400+/month
Integrated Services Digital Network (ISDN)	A dial-up connection about twice as fast as a dial-up router	64 Kbps to 128 Kbps	$120+/month
Digital Subscriber Line (DSL)	A connection that operates over a standard phone line, but on a different set of frequencies than voice conversations; much faster than ISDN and usually less expensive	64 Kbps to 1,500 Kbps	$50+/month
T1 and T3	Communication lines leased from a common carrier such as AT&T suitable for both voice and data	1.544 Mbps and 45 Mbps	$850+/month

Table 3-1

Business Internet connections

In the mid-1980s, few people could have predicted the transforming effect the Internet would have on the way businesses and consumers interact. Nor could many people have predicted the unprecedented consumer demand for Internet access and how this demand would drive the growth of one of the world's largest and most successful e-businesses.

E-business opportunities abound in some of the most unlikely situations. Just ask Steve Case. In 1985, Case was the marketing manager for Control Video Corporation, a failing video game business. At the same time Commodore, manufacturer of one of the first personal computers, was looking for someone to start an online service for its Commodore 64 computer users. Control Video agreed to manage the service and a new company, Quantum Computer Services was formed from the ashes of Control Video. With its limited user base, the new online service, called Q-Link, was only available evenings and weekends. However, within four years Quantum Computer Services was also providing personal computer users with online services through joint ventures with Tandy Corporation and Apple Computer, Inc.

In 1991, Quantum Computer Services became America Online, Inc. (known as AOL) and by December, 1993, AOL had a modest membership base of 500,000. Then the demand for Internet access exploded. AOL's membership base grew from more than 1,000,000 in August 1994 to more than 18,000,000 in 1999 and as of this writing exceeds 33,000,000! Along the way, AOL outpaced its early online service competitors such as Prodigy and CompuServe; survived a number of embarrassing customer support problems; and gobbled up many related technology businesses including Netscape Communications Corporation. In January 2001, AOL took its biggest bite to date by merging with one of the world's largest media and entertainment conglomerates, Time Warner Inc., to form AOL Time Warner Inc.

Steve Case is now the Chairman of AOL Time Warner Inc., and AOL (Figure 3-3), a division of AOL Time Warner Inc., remains one of the world's largest online services. As of January 2002, AOL reported more than two million simultaneous users during peak traffic times, more than 350 million daily e-mail transmissions, and more than 225 million stock quotes accessed each day from its more than 33 million members.

Continued

Figure 3-3
America
Online, Inc.

As you have learned, businesses can connect their LANs to the Internet in a variety of ways. But, no matter how a LAN is connected to the Internet, sending data to another LAN via the Internet requires special addressing schemes. These addressing schemes enable data to be routed precisely and quickly to its destination, similar to the way house numbers and street names are used by the U.S. Postal Service to route mail to its correct destination.

Network and Internetworking Addressing

For data to be transmitted over a network and reach its correct destination, each device on the network must have a unique address. A device's unique physical address is called a **MAC address**. MAC (named for the Media Access Control sublayer of the OSI Data Link layer) addresses are permanently set in a device's network interface card (NIC) by the card's manufacturer. MAC addresses are used in communications between computers on the same network. Computers on different networks communicating over the Internet cannot directly use MAC addresses. Instead, routers and other internetworking devices identify computers via logical (virtual) addresses that identify devices or applications on the Internet. These logical addresses are hierarchical in nature and are easy to break down into components in much the same way you can break down your home address into its various parts: name, street address, city, state, and zip code. These logical addresses are IP addresses, domain names, and logical port addresses.

An **IP address** is a complex numerical address that identifies each device, such as a computer or printer, connected to the Internet. A **domain name** is a simple, easy-to-remember text name that can be translated into an IP address. A **port address** identifies the logical connection between a server and a client application, such as a Web server and Web browser. You learn more about IP addresses, domain names, and port addresses later in this chapter. For now, it's important to remember that sending data over a network requires a set of complex addressing schemes.

To understand how these complex addressing schemes work, you first must learn about Internet protocols, the rules that define how data packets sent via the Internet are formatted and addressed.

The TCP/IP Protocol Suite, IP Addresses, and Logical Ports

As you learned in Chapter 1, the default data communication networking protocol is Transmission Control Protocol/Internet Protocol or TCP/IP. Networks running TCP/IP are often called TCP/IP networks or simply IP networks. **Transmission Control Protocol/Internet Protocol** or **TCP/IP** is actually a group of subprotocols collectively called the **TCP/IP suite** or the **TCP/IP stack**. The TCP/IP protocols operate within specific layers of the OSI Model. Table 3-2 summarizes some TCP/IP suite subprotocols with which you should become familiar.

Table 3-2
Major TCP/IP subprotocols

OSI Model Layer	Protocol	Description
Transport	Transmission Control Protocol (TCP)	Establishes the connection between two computers, transmits data in packets called TCP segments, verifies data integrity, and assures that data is received undamaged
	User Datagram Protocol (UDP)	Sends data in packets called UDP datagrams without error checking or receipt verification; simple and efficient, UDP is often used to broadcast live video or audio over the Internet

Table 3-2
(Continued)

Major TCP/IP
subprotocols

OSI Model Layer	Protocol	Description
Network or Internet	Internet Protocol (IP)	Breaks data into packets called IP datagrams and then routes those packets over an intranet or the Internet, reassembling the packets at their destination
	Address Resolution Protocol (ARP)	Identifies a host computer on a network, and then converts its IP address to its physical MAC address
	Reverse ARP (RARP)	Converts a host computer's physical MAC address into its IP address
	Internet Control Message Protocol (ICMP)	Sends error messages to routers and host computers when problems occur with data transmissions
Application	Hypertext Transfer Protocol (HTTP)	Governs the way Web servers transmit Web pages to a Web browser; HTTP sends a request for a Web page to the server and then returns a copy of the Web page and any related files
	Post Office Protocol 3 (POP3)	Provides centralized storage of e-mail messages on a mail server and forwarding of e-mail messages from a mail server to a user's mailbox upon request from his or her e-mail software
	Simple Mail Transfer Protocol (SMTP)	Sends e-mail messages between mail servers on an IP network
	Internet Mail Access Protocol 4 (IMAP4)	Provides storage and forwarding of e-mail messages like POP3, but also provides remote access to the mail server allowing users to view portions of an e-mail, create mailbox folders, delete e-mail messages, or search for e-mail messages on the server
	File Transfer Protocol (FTP)	Permits the uploading and downloading of files between computers on the Internet using a TCP connection

TCP Segments and IP Datagrams

TCP and IP are two of the most important subprotocols in the TCP/IP suite. The IP protocol is called an "unreliable, connectionless protocol" because it does not first make a connection between the sending and receiving computers; it does not provide error checking to assure the reliability of the data being transmitted; and it does not guarantee data delivery. For example, the IP protocol transmits data without checking to make certain that the destination computer is online and without receiving any confirmation that the data is received. TCP, however, requires that a connection is made between computers before beginning a transmission. Also, TCP contains information that assures the reliability of the data being transmitted.

A **TCP segment** is a data packet created in the Transport layer by the TCP protocol. Figure 3-4 illustrates a TCP segment. The parts of a TCP segment are as follows:

- *Source port*: Specifies the logical port address, for example port 80, at the sending computer
- *Destination port*: Specifies the logical port address at the destination computer
- *Sequence number*: Specifies the position of the data in a flow of data being sent
- *Acknowledgement number (ACK)*: Specifies a confirmation of the receipt of data
- *TCP header length*: Designates the TCP header length
- *Codes*: Specifies any special conditions, such as an "urgent"
- *Sliding-window size*: Specifies the number of blocks of data that can be received by the destination computer
- *Checksum*: Specifies the number of bits in a piece of transmitted data; the checksum is used to verify that all data sent is received
- *Urgent pointer*: Identifies the location of urgent data
- *Options*: Specifies any special options
- *Padding*: Ensures that the TCP header is a multiple of 32 bits
- *Data*: Contains the data sent by the sending computer

Figure 3-4
TCP segment

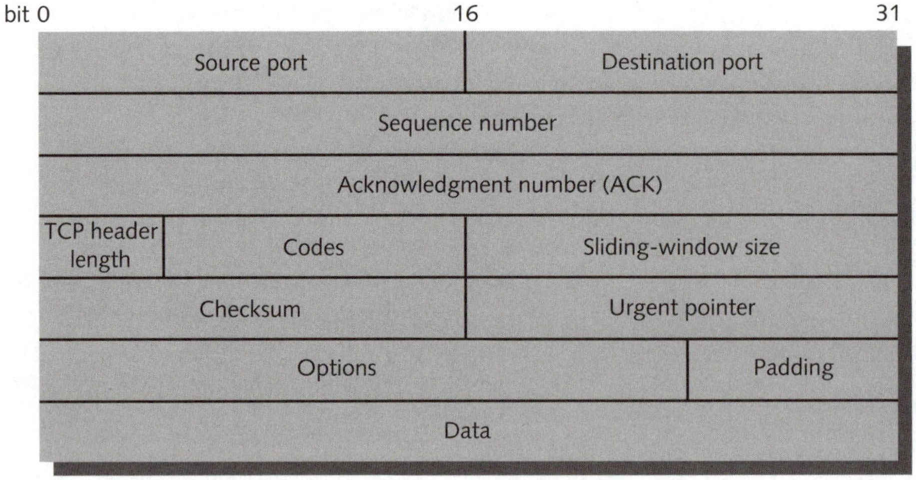

An **IP datagram** is a data packet created in the Network layer by the IP protocol. Figure 3-5 illustrates an IP datagram. The parts of an IP datagram (Figure 3-5) are as follows:

- *Version*: Identifies the version of IP used to format the packet. Today most networks use the IPv4 protocol; however a more advanced version, IPv6, is expected to be widely adopted in the future.
- *Internet header length (IHL)*: Identifies the length of the IP header.
- *Type of service (ToS)*: Specifies the speed, priority, or reliability of the data.
- *Total length*: Specifies the total number of bytes in the IP datagram including both header and data.
- *Identification*: Identifies the specific datagram in a sequence of datagrams; for example, "This is the third datagram in a sequence of sixteen."
- *Flags*: Specifies whether or not the datagram is part of a fragmented sequence of datagrams and if it is the last datagram in the sequence.
- *Fragment offset*: Specifies where the datagram goes in a sequence of fragmented datagrams.
- *Time to live (TTL)*: Specifies how long a datagram can remain en route to its destination computer before it is discarded as undeliverable; in some situations a datagram may have a bad destination address, or the destination computer might be unavailable, thus making the datagram undeliverable.
- *Protocol*: Identifies which protocol receives the datagram, such as TCP or UDP.
- *Header checksum*: Compares the number of bits in the Header checksum with the number of IP header bits received to verify that the IP header has not been corrupted.
- *Source IP address*: Specifies the sending computer's IP address.
- *Destination IP address*: Specifies the destination computer's IP address.
- *Option*: Includes special information, such as routing or timing information, when necessary.
- *Padding*: Includes additional bits, if necessary, to insure that the size of the IP header is in multiples of 32 bits.
- *Data*: Includes the data sent by the sending computer plus the TCP segment which ensures a valid connection, error-checking, and receipt of the data.

By placing a TCP segment inside an IP datagram, TCP and IP work together to ensure that important data transmitted across networks, such as financial data, is received at its destination undamaged.

While the TCP and IP subprotocols are two important components of the TCP/IP suite, the e-mail subprotocols — SMTP, POP3, and IMAP4 — which you learn about in the next section, are also very important.

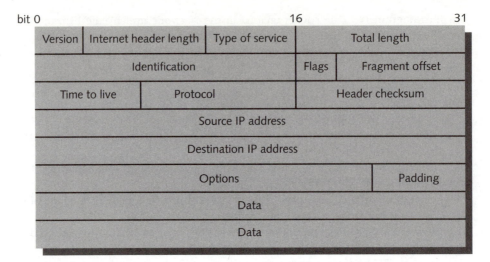

Figure 3-5
IP datagram

SMTP, POP3, and IMAP4 Protocols

Arguably, the single most important networking application is e-mail, which has revolutionized both business and personal communications. The growth in the number of e-mails sent each day is staggering. In fact, some analysts are projecting more than 36 billion daily e-mails will be sent by 2005, and none of these e-mails can be sent without the TCP/IP subprotocols devised specifically for that purpose.

Sending and receiving e-mail requires an e-mail client application and access to a mail server. An e-mail client allows you to compose and send e-mail messages, receive e-mail messages sent by others, and store copies of sent and received messages in folders on your computer. Examples of e-mail clients include: Microsoft Corporation's Outlook and Outlook Express, QUAL-COMM Incorporated's Eudora, Netscape Communication Corporation's Netscape Mail, Pegasus Mail, and the University of Washington's Pine. A mail server is a computer running e-mail server software that permits both the storage of e-mail messages and the forwarding of e-mail messages from one mail server to another. The term "mail server" is usually used to denote both the server hardware and the e-mail server software that runs on it. For example, one of the most popular and reliable mail servers is Sendmail by Sendmail, Inc. Other mail servers such as Microsoft Corporation's Exchange Server are also popular.

TIP

In the early days of e-mail, messages consisted only of text; any other document had to be encoded into text and pasted into the body of the e-mail message. Because this was so irksome, researchers developed the Multipurpose Internet Mail Extensions, or MIME protocol to enable e-mail clients to attach other files such as word-processing documents or spreadsheets to a text message. MIME allows e-mail servers to transmit these "attachments" and also allows e-mail clients to download them.

As noted in Table 3-2, e-mail clients and mail servers rely on the SMTP, POP3, and IMAP4 subprotocols to send and receive e-mail. Figure 3-6 illustrates the process of sending and receiving e-mail messages via SMTP, POP3, and IMAP4. An e-mail client uses SMTP to send an outgoing e-mail message to a mail server. Mail servers, in turn, use SMTP to forward e-mail messages from one mail server to another. An e-mail client uses POP3 or IMAP4 to download incoming messages from a mail server.

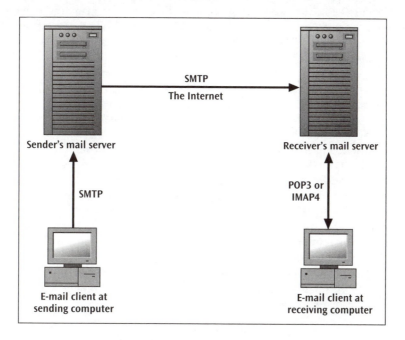

Figure 3-6
Sending and receiving e-mail

You've learned that the TCP/IP protocol suite is essential to the proper transmission of data and e-mail messages between networks across the Internet. Next, you learn how an IP address that identifies a destination computer in a data transmission is assigned.

IP Addresses

Earlier in this chapter you learned that an IP address is a unique number used to identify devices on an IP network. Any device on an IP network, such as a personal computer, that runs an application is called a **host** and requires an IP address. An IP address is a 32-bit number made up of four 8-bit numbers, which are called **octets**. The four octets in an IP address are separated by periods. An example of an IP address might be 194.44.60.43. Groups of IP addresses are assigned to businesses and other organizations by the **Internet Corporation for Assigned Names and Numbers** (**ICANN**), a nonprofit corporation working under the supervision of the U. S. Department of Commerce.

TIP

The largest possible 8-bit number is the binary number 11111111 which equates to the decimal number 255. Each of the four octets in an IP address can be a number between 0-255 allowing for a total of 4.3 billion possible IP addresses.

In October 2001, the world celebrated the thirtieth anniversary of e-mail, the application that forever changed the way individuals and businesses communicate. The father of e-mail is Ray Tomlinson (Figure 3-7), a scientist at BBN (now BBN Technologies), who is credited with sending the first e-mail message. In 1971, Tomlinson was experimenting with an electronic mail program he had written that allowed users sharing the same computer to leave messages for each other in a file called a "mailbox." As part of his experiment, he modified an existing file transfer protocol (a protocol used to upload or download files across a network) to deliver messages to another nearby machine via an ARPANET connection. Just as you have to write an address on an envelope before dropping it in a U.S. mail box, Tomlinson needed some way to address this first e-mail, and eventually settled on the user's login name and the destination machine name separated by the @ sign. You are probably familiar with this format from e-mails you have sent and received. According to Tomlinson, he decided to use the @ sign to identify the destination "mailbox" because the @ sign seemed to make sense to indicate the user was 'at' some other host. Over the years, Tomlinson has often been asked about the contents of that first e-mail message. He says that while he can't remember the exact message, he does remember that it was all uppercase and might have been something like the top row of alphabetic keys on the keyboard — QWERTYUIOP.

Regardless of the first message's content, over the past 30 years e-mail has become a critical component of business communication and an important part of e-business marketing. Permission-based e-mail, where e-mail recipients agree in advance to receive e-mail messages from vendors about their products, is now a critical component of e-business marketing. According to a 2001 research study commissioned by DoubleClick and conducted by NFO WorldGroup, consumers averaged $1,023 in yearly online purchases; 82 percent of online consumers made purchases as a result of permission-based e-mail (also called opt-in e-mail); and 37 percent of online consumers made a purchase instantly by "clicking through" — that is, by clicking a hyperlink in the e-mail message to go directly to the e-business's Web site.

Figure 3-7
Ray
Tomlinson

In the case of a LAN connected to the Internet, the first part of an IP address identifies the network itself, and the remaining part of the IP address identifies the individual host or device on the network. There are several classes of networks — Class A through Class E. Class A networks use the first IP address octet to identify the network and the remaining three octets to identify individual hosts on the network. Class B networks use the first two octets to identify the network and the last two octets to identify individual hosts. Class C networks use the first three octets to identify the network and the remaining octet to identify individual hosts. As you can see from Table 3-3, this numbering scheme gives Class A networks more possible host IP addresses than Class B networks, which in turn have more possible host IP addresses than Class C networks.

Class A IP addresses were largely snapped up by early adopters and are reserved for very large organizations, such as Massachusetts Institute of Technology (MIT, IP address 18.181.0.31), The Boeing Company (IP address 12.13.226.30), and Xerox Palo Alto Research Center (PARC, IP address 13.1.64.14). Class B networks are reserved for large government agencies, organizations, and businesses such as the U. S. House of Representatives (IP address 143.231.86.196), Oracle Corporation (IP address 148.87.9.44) and J. P. Morgan Chase & Co. (IP address 170.148.37.100). A typical small e-business such as Arndt's Fudgery (IP address 209.208.39.210) likely has a Class C network IP address. As you might expect, there are far more Class C networks than Class A networks.

Network Class	Maximum Number of Networks	Maximum Host Addresses per Network	Beginning Octet	Sample IP Addresses for Hosts on the Same Network	Notes
A	126	16,777,214	1-126	90.78.104.33 90.34.112.78 90.107.124.109	All hosts on a Class A network begin with the same first octet
B	16,382	65,534	128-191	160.55.34.107 160.55.78.67 160.55.205.41	All hosts on a Class B network begin with the same first two octets
C	2,097,150	254	192-223	202.78.173.12 202.78.173.13 202.78.173.14	All hosts on a Class C network begin with the same first three octets

Table 3-3
Class A-C networks and IP addresses

When data is transmitted over the Internet, routers use the network portion of an IP address to locate the destination network. When the data reaches the destination network, the host portion of the IP address is used to correlate with an individual host's MAC address to insure that the data is delivered to the correct destination.

When an IP address can be accessed by devices via the Internet, it is called a **public IP address**. (For example, the IP address for Microsoft's public Web site, 207.46.197.113, is a public IP address.) However, network administrators can also assign **private IP addresses** for computers on a private IP network, such as a company intranet, that is isolated behind a firewall. (The IP address for a computer in Microsoft's personnel department might be assigned a private IP address.) Additionally, some IP addresses are reserved for other functions. Table 3-4 lists reserved and currently unassigned IP addresses.

TIP

An e-business wishing to set up its own IP network can register with ICANN for a block of addresses; however, it is usually easier to obtain these addresses from the service providing access to the Internet (an ISP) who has likely already obtained several blocks of numbers from ICANN.

Table 3-4
Reserved and unassigned IP addresses

IP Address	Description
0.0.0.0	Currently unassigned
127.0.0.1	Reserved for communicating with your own machine and is used to troubleshoot TCP/IP-related problems on an individual computer
255.255.255.255	Reserved for broadcasting messages to multiple hosts
10.0.0.0 to 10.255.255.255 172.16.0.0 to 172.31.255.255 192.168.0.0 to 192.168.255.255	Recommended for private networks
Beginning octet 224-239	Reserved for Class D networks which broadcast messages from one host to many hosts (called multicasting), such as occurs in Internet video conferencing
Beginning octet 240-254	Reserved by the Internet Engineering Task Force (IETF) for special experimental networks known as Class E networks

An IP address can be a **static IP address**, in which case it is assigned to a specific host when the computer is originally connected to the network and remains the host's permanent IP address until the network administrator changes it. Static IP addresses are useful in situations when a device's IP address is unlikely to change. Sometimes, however, an IP address is needed infrequently, such as when an employee connects his or her laptop to a network to check e-mail or access the Internet. In this situation, a **dynamic IP address** can be assigned as needed by a server running the **Dynamic Host Configuration Protocol** (**DHCP**). (Such a server is referred to as a **DHCP server**.) When the session is finished and the laptop is disconnected from the network, the dynamically assigned IP address becomes available for use by another host. Dynamic IP addresses also allow for more efficient use of allocated blocks of IP addresses, especially when more hosts are added to a network.

IP addresses are not the only kind of addresses used on the Internet. In addition, client and server applications, such as Web browsers and Web servers, require an address, called a port, in order to make a logical connection between the applications.

Logical Ports

Client and server applications sending or receiving data transmitted via an IP network use a specific port number to make a logical connection. There are 65,536 logical ports, but the vast majority of IP network transmissions are bound for only a few ports, such as:

- *Port 21*: File transfers
- *Port 25*: Outgoing e-mail
- *Port 80*: Web pages
- *Port 110*: Incoming e-mail
- *Port 443*: Encrypted Web pages (such as credit card submission pages)

Figure 3-8 illustrates the logical ports for different types of data being transmitted via an IP network.

Port numbers and IP addresses are generally only used by the software and hardware that make up the Internet. The people who actually use the Internet require yet another type of addressing scheme.

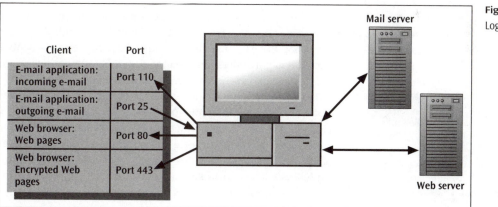

Figure 3-8
Logical ports

Domain Names, the Domain Name System, and Uniform Resource Locators

Machine-readable IP addresses make it possible for one Internet-connected computer to identify another Internet-connected computer. But, complex, numerical IP addresses are difficult for humans to remember. For this reason, a text-based addressing scheme was devised that allows us to use Web addresses like amazon.com and aol.com when requesting a Web page. Text addresses such as these are called domain names. Each domain name address corresponds to a specific IP address. For example, the domain name icann.org corresponds to the IP address 192.0.34.65. Think of a domain name as an alias for a specific IP address; the IP address is the actual address.

Domain names are organized into a hierarchical scheme that first groups Internet-connected computers into domains according to function. (In other words, computers sharing a similar function are grouped into the same domain.) These major domains are called **top-level domains** or **TLDs**. The original TLDs are commercial (.com), education (.edu), government (.gov), military (.mil), other organizations (.org), and network providers (.net). Because of the explosive growth of the Internet, additional top-level domain names have been added or are in the process of being added, such as .biz for business and .aero for the aerospace industry. All the computers in the same domain have the same last three letters as part of its domain name. Thus, all computers in the commercial domain have domain names that end with ".com."

Computers within a single TLD are then divided into subdomains according to each computer's function. For example, within the .com domain, you find subdomains such as microsoft.com (all the computers at the Microsoft Corporation), army.mil (all the computers used by the U.S. Army), and so on. These subdomains are then further divided by function. For example, suppose an e-business that sells office equipment, furniture, and supplies has been assigned the domain name shopoffice.biz. The company's mail server might then be assigned the domain name mail.shopoffice.biz while the company's technical support server might be called support.shopoffice.biz. In e-mail, it's customary to use the @ symbol to refer to a specific user. Thus, you might address an e-mail to Tom Jenkins, an employee of ShopOffice, as follows: TomJenkins@shopoffice.biz.

TIP

Some countries with a serendipitously attractive top-level domain like .md (Moldavia) and .tv (Tuvalu) have tried to encourage companies to register names there, but as of this writing .com remains the standard for e-business.

Also, each country has a two-letter **country code top-level domain** (**ccTLD**): for example, .us for the United States, .ca for Canada, .uk for the United Kingdom (Great Britain), and .au for Australia. Table 3-5 illustrates original, new, and proposed top-level domains, and Table 3-6 provides several real-world domain name examples. As you see in Table 3-6, domain names may or may not include the country code.

Table 3-5
Top-level
domains

Top-Level Domain	Description
.com	Commercial
.edu	Educational
.gov	Government
.org	Other organizations (originally nonprofit organizations)
.mil	Military
.net	Networking companies (originally Internet service providers or hosting companies, but now used by other organizations)
.int	International Treaty Organization
.biz	Businesses
.info	All uses
.name	Individuals
.museum	Museums
.coop	Cooperatives
.aero	Air-transport industry
.pro	Professions

Table 3-6
Domain name
examples

Domain Name	Organization
amazon.com	U.S. online retailer
thehockeyshop.com	Vancouver, Canada online retailer
rice.edu	Rice University, Houston, TX
adelaide.edu.au	Adelaide University, Australia
house.gov	U.S. House of Representatives
gov.on.ca	Ontario, Canada government
tradepartners.gov.uk	Great Britain government
npr.org	U.S. National Public Radio, nonprofit broadcaster
baba.org.uk	British craftsman organization
epilepsyontario.org	Canadian medical special interest
army.mil	U.S. Army
netrazor.net	U.S. Internet Service Provider

Because a computer can't recognize a domain name, it is necessary to translate a domain name into its equivalent IP address before data can be transmitted over an IP network. The Domain Name System makes this translation from domain name to IP address possible.

The Domain Name System (DNS)

ICANN, the nonprofit corporation that assigns IP addresses, also oversees the Domain Name System (DNS). This system consists of servers called **name servers** that contain databases of domain names and their equivalent IP addresses. These name servers are used to translate domain names into IP addresses in a process called "resolving a domain name." At the center of the Domain Name System are 13 root servers located around the world. These **root servers**, which are managed by ICANN, contain databases that keep track of the IP addresses of all the TLD and ccTLD registered entities. This IP address information is regularly downloaded by thousands of Internet-connected computers called **Domain name resolvers** or just **resolvers**. These resolvers, located at Internet service providers or other institutions, respond to requests by clients (that is, by browsers and e-mail clients) to resolve domain names. For example, suppose you enter www.cnn.com in your Web browser. Before the HTTP request can be sent to the Web server, the domain name "www.cnn.com" must be resolved to its IP address. Within seconds a request is sent to a local resolver who first asks the .com registry name server for the IP address of "cnn.com" and then asks a local name server at cnn.com for the IP address for "www.cnn.com." The IP address for www.cnn.com is returned to your computer, the request for the Web page is sent on to the Web server, and the Web page is downloaded. Figure 3-9 illustrates this process.

As you see in the next section, organizations can reserve a specific domain name in the DNS scheme for exclusive use by registering it with an accredited registrar.

Registering a Domain Name

The first registrar for the .com, .org, and .net top-level domains was Network Solutions, Inc., which was overseen by the Internet Assigned Numbers Authority (IANA), a National Science Foundation-funded organization. ICANN, the nonprofit organization regulated by the U. S. Department of Commerce, assumed responsibility for assigning and tracking domain names and IP addresses in late 1998.

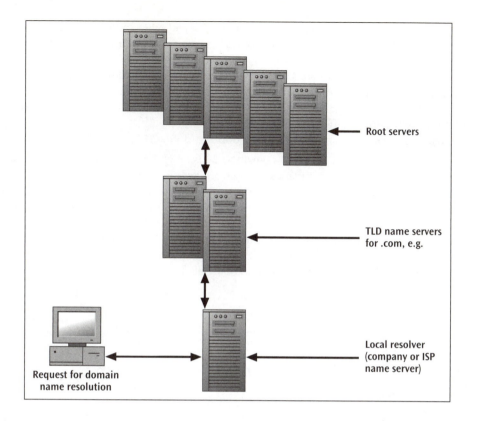

Root servers

TLD name servers
for .com, e.g.

Local resolver
(company or ISP
name server)

Request for domain
name resolution

Figure 3-9
Domain name
resolution

ICANN also manages the domain name registration system (called the **Shared Registration System**, or **SRS**) that allows many private companies such as Register.com (Figure 3-10) to participate in the registration of domain names. These private companies, called accredited registrars, insure that an organization's unique domain name is maintained on the appropriate name servers for a fee ranging from $10 to $35 per year.

The process for registering a business Web site domain name with an accredited registrar is very simple and can be completed quickly online.

◆   *Step 1*: Locate the Web site of an accredited registrar such as Network Solutions, Inc. or Register.com, or use a list of accredited registrars found at the ICANN Web site.
◆   *Step 2*: Search a database of domain names (on the accredited registrar's Web site) to determine whether or not the name you want is available.

> **TIP**
>
> Some alternative root systems compete with the ICANN-controlled DNS system by offering TLDs beyond those approved by ICANN. Also, some e-businesses (such as New.net) provide a registration service for alternative TLDs and offer Web browser enhancements that enable a Web browser to locate alternative TLDs. ICANN opposes these alternative root systems on the basis that their domain names may potentially conflict with ICANN's authoritative DNS system and threaten the "Internet's reliability and stability."

- *Step 3*: Select the domain name including its TLD, and enter the required information which usually consists of the name, address, phone number, and e-mail address of the individual responsible for the domain name.
- *Step 4*: Provide the requested information regarding the IP address of the primary and secondary name servers of the organization hosting your Web site. (See your network administrator or contact your Internet service provider or hosting company for this information, if necessary.)
- *Step 5*: Use a credit card to pay for the domain name.

From a business point of view, a domain name is much more than just the text equivalent of an IP address. Domain names are used to identify an e-business and brand it for marketing purposes. For this reason, selecting an appropriate domain name is a critical step for an e-business. When choosing a domain name, an e-business should try to select a short, easily remembered name to which potential customers can relate, and that ties into the products or services it sells or to its immediately recognizable trademark. Earthlink.net (an Internet service provider), act.com (a contact database software vendor with a product named ACT!), and business.com (online business resources) are all examples of effective domain names.

Figure 3-10
Register.com

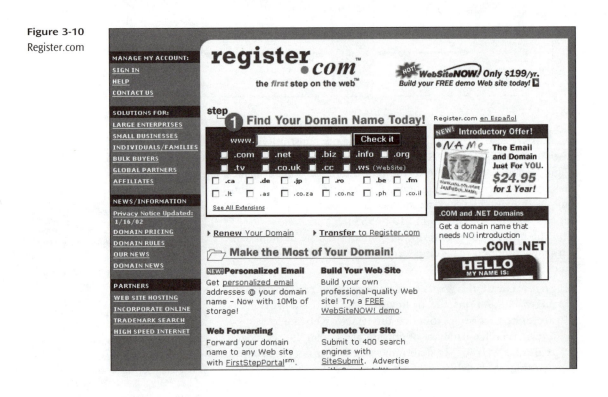

You've just learned that an IP address and its registered alias, its domain name, identify a host machine on an IP network. In the next section, you learn how a short address, called a URL, allows a Web browser to locate specific Web pages.

Using Uniform Resource Locators (URLs)

A **Uniform Resource Locator**, or **URL**, is a short text address entered into a Web browser that identifies the location of a Web page and its related files. A URL includes the TCP/IP subprotocol, host name, domain name, and the path to the Web page file including any subfolders and the filename. For example, assume you want to access a Web page for our previous e-business example that sells office supplies and you want to view the Web page that quotes prices for staplers.

The URL you key in your Web browser might be similar to the one in Figure 3-11, which includes:

◆ The TCP/IP subprotocol for Web pages: HTTP
◆ The host name and domain name: www.shopoffice.biz
◆ The path and filename of the stapler products page: /products/supplies/staplers.html

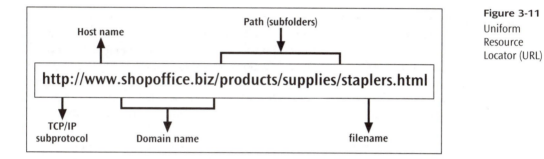

Figure 3-11
Uniform Resource Locator (URL)

It is possible to type the entire URL shown in Figure 3-11 into a Web browser to retrieve the staplers product page. In many if not most cases, however, you simply need to type a host name (usually www for a Web server host) and domain name (shopoffice.biz) to access a Web site's starting or home page. Because the HTTP subprotocol is the default protocol for transmitting Web pages, there is no need to type "HTTP". Web browsers automatically insert this part of the URL for you. Once the Web site's home page is loaded, you can click through a series of hyperlinks (text or picture links to other pages) to find the specific Web page you want. While this may take more time than keying in the complete URL, most users find it more convenient to click hyperlinks than to try type a long URL correctly.

> **TIP**
>
> Tim Berners-Lee originally called the Web page address a Universal Document Identifier. However, through the efforts of the Internet Engineers Task Force (IETF) the Web page address name evolved into "Uniform Resource Locator" (URL). Today, the World Wide Web Consortium (W3C) considers URL to be informal and inappropriate for technical specifications, preferring instead to use the term Uniform Resource Identifier (URI) to define addresses for the broad set of Web resources including Web pages, downloadable files, and so forth.

Returning to our shopoffice.biz example, you might simply type www.shopoffice.biz into your Web browser; wait for the Web site's home page to load; click a Products hyperlink on the home page to download the Products page; click a Supplies hyperlink to download the Supplies page; and click a Staplers hyperlink on the Supplies page to download the Staplers page.

You've learned about how IP addresses are assigned and how domain names are registered. But what organization has the overall responsibility for managing the Internet? As you see in the next section, several organizations provide oversight for the Internet and the World Wide Web.

Organizations that Provide Oversight for the Internet and the World Wide Web

Some people assume that one organization manages or oversees the Internet and the World Wide Web. But, in fact, several different organizations participate in the oversight process.

As you learned earlier in this chapter, the Internet Corporation for Assigned Names and Numbers or ICANN, a nonprofit organization under the direction of the U. S. Department of Commerce, assumed responsibility for assigning and tracking IP addresses and managing domain name registrations in late 1998. ICANN (Figure 3-12) has representatives from business and government on its board, and maintains working relationships with other international bodies.

There have been a number of domain name disputes as a result of **cybersquatting**, the act of registering a domain name that reflects the name of an existing business with the intent to either create a parody Web site or in the hopes of selling the domain name to the existing business. Additionally, some individuals and organizations have purposely registered domain names similar to an existing well-known business name or trademark to attract unsuspecting consumers to their Web sites. Many prominent organizations and individuals including the National Collegiate Athletic Association (NCAA), The Hertz Corporation, Avon Products, Inc., People for the Ethical Treatment of Animals (PETA), and a number of show business and sports celebrities have been involved in domain name disputes. In 1999, the U. S. Congress passed the Anti-Cybersquatting Consumer Protection Act, thus making cybersquatting illegal.

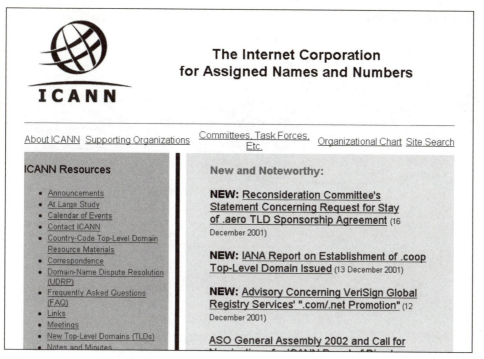

Figure 3-12

The Internet Corporation for Assigned Names and Numbers (ICANN)

Domain name disputes can cross international borders. The **World Intellectual Property Organization**, or **WIPO** (Figure 3-13), associated with the United Nations since 1974, is tasked with globally enforcing copyrights and trademarks. Because of this, WIPO now plays an increasing role in international domain name disputes and their resolution.

The **Internet Society (ISOC)** with offices in Reston, Virginia, and Geneva, Switzerland, reports a membership of more than 150 organizations and more than 6,000 individual members from around the world (Figure 3-14). The ISOC's primary objective is to support the development of Internet standards and protocols through member groups such as the Internet Engineering Task Force (IETF) and the Internet Architecture Board (IAB).

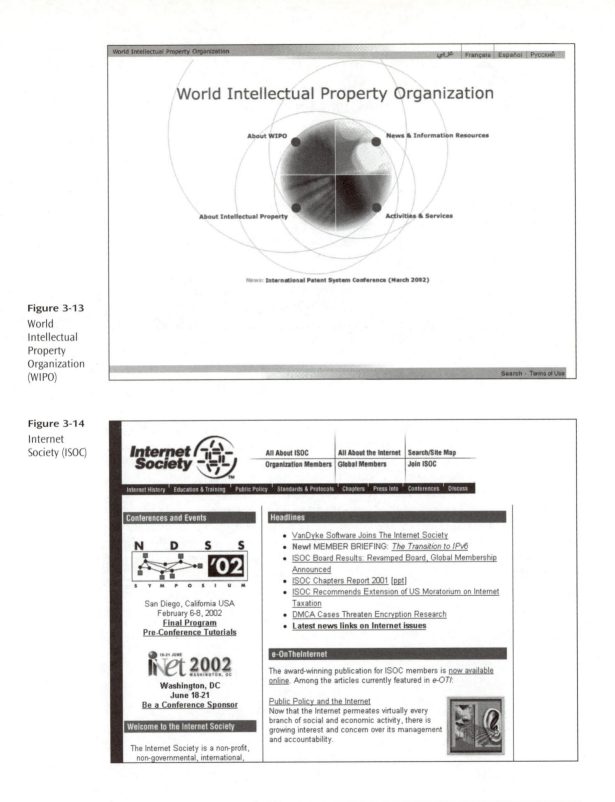

Figure 3-13

World
Intellectual
Property
Organization
(WIPO)

Figure 3-14

Internet
Society (ISOC)

The **World Wide Web Consortium**, or **W3C** (Figure 3-15) was founded by Tim Berners-Lee in 1994 at the Massachusetts Institute of Technology Laboratory of Computer Science (MIT/LCS) as a joint project with CERN, DARPA, and the European Commission. The W3C's mission is to promote standardization and interoperability on the Web to assure that Web languages such as HTML and XML and protocols such as HTTP are compatible with any hardware and software used to access the Web.

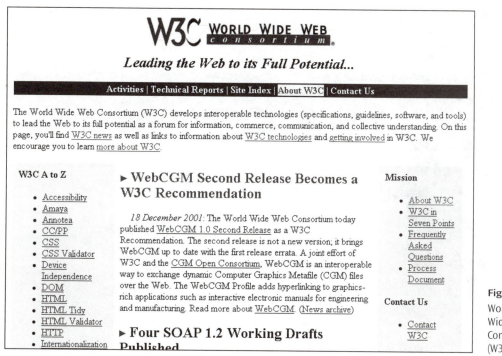

Figure 3-15
World Wide Web Consortium (W3C)

TECH CASE **Farming the Internet**

When John Deere began his blacksmithing career in 1825, he could hardly have imagined the role he and his future company, Deere & Company, would play in using new technologies to change farming practices around the globe. In the nineteenth century, John Deere revolutionized farming and helped enhance the westward expansion of the United States with his introduction of the steel plow. In the twentieth century, Deere & Company incorporated another new technology — the tractor — into its product line, again helping to make farming practices more productive. In the twenty first century, Deere & Company continues to embrace new technologies by "farming the Internet." Today, Deere & Company uses its Internet presence to communicate with customers from around the world. Information gathered from customers is used to provide timely customer support, schedule manufacturing, and develop new products and

Continued

---

services. Additionally, Deere & Company uses Internet technologies to manage its supply chain and perform other activities that reduce costs and improve customer relationships. Deere & Company's Chairman and CEO, Robert W. Lane, stated that one day soon farmers will be able to get help with their John Deere equipment by accessing the Deere & Company (Figure 3-16) Web sites from anywhere, including from a John Deere combine or tractor!

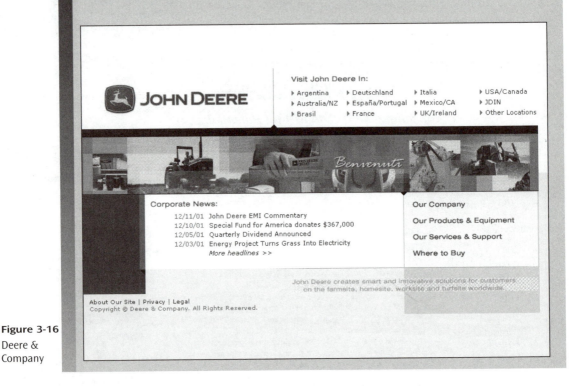

Figure 3-16
Deere & Company

Request For Comment

A **Request for Comment** (**RFC**) is a tool used by Internet scientists to help publicize or improve an idea for a new system or function, such as transferring files between computers. First the scientist creates a model of the proposed function, and then submits an RFC document to the appropriate standards body. The RFC is then assigned a unique number and posted on a public Web site. Interested parties can then submit feedback about potential problems, new features to consider, and so on. In this way, the rules for the new function are refined, tested, refined again, and tested again, until the best parts of the original idea plus the feedback emerge as an Internet standard.

In this chapter, you learned how data is transmitted over an IP network such as the Internet. You also learned how Internet protocols, IP addresses, domain names, and URLs assure those data transmissions reach their destination. Next, you learn about the technologies used to create and maintain Web pages.

Frustrated with Stanford's decision, Lerner and Bosack quit their jobs and, together with engineering friends, spent hundreds of hours a week designing and manufacturing routers in their home. Naming the new business "cisco" (for the last five letters of San Francisco), Lerner and Bosack used their credit cards to finance the e-business's startup costs. By 1986, "cisco" moved into its own offices in Menlo Park, CA, and was making a profit of more than $250,000 a month. By 1987, the now named Cisco Systems needed serious funding in order to keep growing and compete with other networking technology providers. Lerner and Bosack began contacting venture capitalists to raise those funds. After presenting Cisco Systems to 75 venture capitalists with no success, they approached contact number 76, Don Valentine of Sequoia Capital, who agreed to provide $2.5 million for a 32 percent interest in the business.

Valentine brought in a management team and took Cisco Systems (Figure 3-17) public in 1990. Shortly thereafter, Lerner and Bosack left Cisco Systems and sold their Cisco stock for millions of dollars. Lerner went on to cofound the cosmetics company Urban Decay and become involved in the preservation of Chawton House, a family home of the nineteenth century British author Jane Austen. Bosack moved to Redmond, WA, and founded the networking technologies engineering firm XKL. Although no longer married, Lerner and Bosack both support a variety of charitable organizations through their joint foundation, the Leonard X. Bosack and Bette M. Kruger Foundation. And Cisco Systems? As of October, 2001, Cisco Systems, Inc. reported 37,546 employees worldwide and revenues for the year ending July 28, 2001, of $22.2 billion.

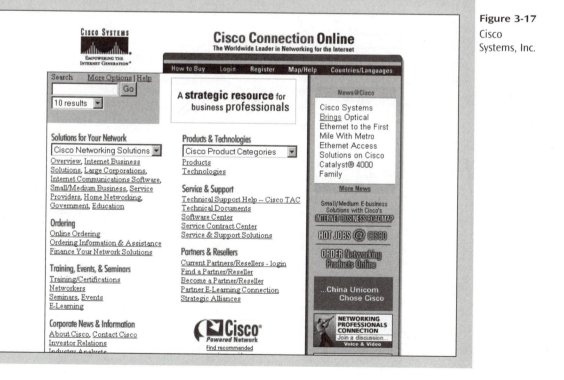

Figure 3-17
Cisco
Systems, Inc.

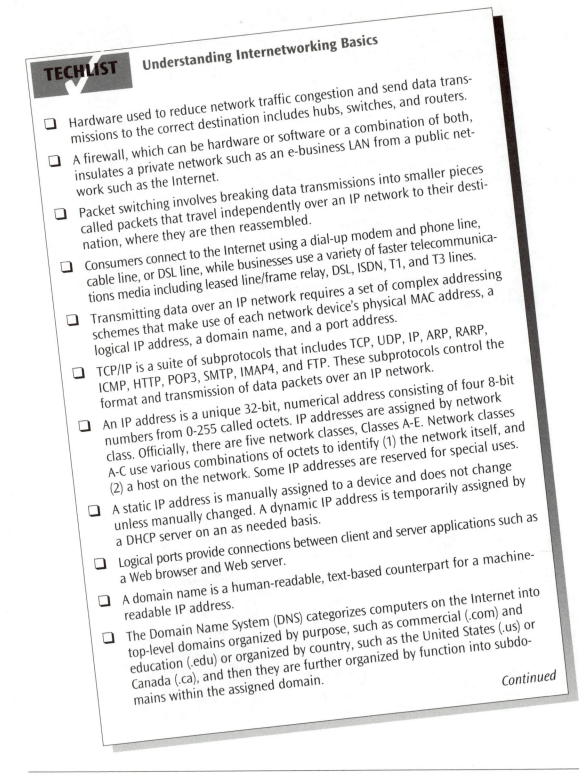

TECHLIST ✓ Understanding Internetworking Basics

❏ Hardware used to reduce network traffic congestion and send data transmissions to the correct destination includes hubs, switches, and routers.

❏ A firewall, which can be hardware or software or a combination of both, insulates a private network such as an e-business LAN from a public network such as the Internet.

❏ Packet switching involves breaking data transmissions into smaller pieces called packets that travel independently over an IP network to their destination, where they are then reassembled.

❏ Consumers connect to the Internet using a dial-up modem and phone line, cable line, or DSL line, while businesses use a variety of faster telecommunications media including leased line/frame relay, DSL, ISDN, T1, and T3 lines.

❏ Transmitting data over an IP network requires a set of complex addressing schemes that make use of each network device's physical MAC address, a logical IP address, a domain name, and a port address.

❏ TCP/IP is a suite of subprotocols that includes TCP, UDP, IP, ARP, RARP, ICMP, HTTP, POP3, SMTP, IMAP4, and FTP. These subprotocols control the format and transmission of data packets over an IP network.

❏ An IP address is a unique 32-bit, numerical address consisting of four 8-bit numbers from 0-255 called octets. IP addresses are assigned by network class. Officially, there are five network classes, Classes A-E. Network classes A-C use various combinations of octets to identify (1) the network itself, and (2) a host on the network. Some IP addresses are reserved for special uses.

❏ A static IP address is manually assigned to a device and does not change unless manually changed. A dynamic IP address is temporarily assigned by a DHCP server on an as needed basis.

❏ Logical ports provide connections between client and server applications such as a Web browser and Web server.

❏ A domain name is a human-readable, text-based counterpart for a machine-readable IP address.

❏ The Domain Name System (DNS) categorizes computers on the Internet into top-level domains organized by purpose, such as commercial (.com) and education (.edu) or organized by country, such as the United States (.us) or Canada (.ca), and then they are further organized by function into subdomains within the assigned domain.

Continued

- ❑ ICANN manages the assigning and tracing of domain names and IP addresses by maintaining the 13 worldwide root name servers. ICANN also manages registration of domain names within the DNS by authorizing accredited domain name registrars.
- ❑ Web browsers use URLs consisting of the TCP/IP protocol, a host name, domain name, path, and filename to locate Web pages.
- ❑ Several organizations provide oversight for the Internet and the World Wide Web including ICANN, the WIPO, the ISOC, and the W3C.

Key Terms

Address Resolution Protocol (ARP)
country code top-level domain
(ccTLD)
cybersquatting
DHCP server
dial-up connection
domain name
domain name resolvers (resolvers)
Dynamic Host Configuration
Protocol (DHCP)
dynamic IP address
File Transfer Protocol (FTP)
firewall
host
hubs
Hypertext Transfer
Protocol (HTTP)
intelligent device
Internet Control Message
Protocol (ICMP)

Internet Corporation for Assigned
Names and Numbers (ICANN)
Internet Protocol (IP)
Internet Society (ISOC)
IP address
IP datagram
MAC address
name servers
octet
port address
ports
Post Office Protocol 3 (POP3)
private IP address
private network
public IP address
public network
Request for Comment (RFC)
Reverse ARP (RARP)
root servers
routers

segments
shared connection
Shared Registration System (SRS)
Simple Mail Transfer
Protocol (SMTP)
static IP address
switches
TCP segment
top-level domains (TLDs)
Transmission Control
Protocol (TCP)
Transmission Control
Protocol/Internet Protocol
(TCP/IP suite or stack)
Uniform Resource Identifier (URI)
Uniform Resource Locater (URL)
User Datagram Protocol (UDP)
World Intellectual Property
Organization (WIPO)
World Wide Web Consortium (W3C)

Review Questions

1. A router is:
   a. An inexpensive device used to connect computers.
   b. Used to resolve an IP address to its domain name.
   c. A device that acts like a "post office" by verifying a packet's delivery address and sending it on to its destination.
   d. An e-mail protocol used to forward messages from a client to a mail server and from mail server to mail server.

2. Unencrypted Web page traffic is sent to which virtual port?
   a. Port 25
   b. Port 80
   c. Port 443
   d. Port 110

3. Which of the following is not a popular e-mail client?
   a. Outlook
   b. Pine
   c. Eudora
   d. Phoenix

4. An 8-bit number that is part of a 32-bit IP address is called a(n):
   a. Octet.
   b. TCP.
   c. PING.
   d. IP.

5. Which of the following protocols provides automatic, temporary assignment of IP addresses as necessary?
   a. SMTP
   b. DHCP
   c. HTTP
   d. POP3

6. The top-level domain originally used to indicate nonprofit enterprises is:
   a. .mil.
   b. .org.
   c. .coop.
   d. .pro.

7. The organization that oversees the Domain Name System is:
   a. WIPO.
   b. W3C.
   c. ICANN.
   d. ISOC.

8. The organization founded by Tim Berners-Lee in conjunction with CERN, DARPA, and the European Commission to promote interoperability on the Web is:
   a. ICANN.
   b. ISOC.
   c. W3C.
   d. WIPO.

9. Which TCP/IP subprotocol provides error-checking and receipt acknowledgement?
   a. ARP
   b. TCP
   c. SMTP
   d. IP

10. Which of the following IP addresses is a possible Class A network host address?
    a. 245.78.193.15
    b. 89.134.43.126
    c. 162.98.60.54
    d. 226.95.172.15

11. When choosing a domain name, an e-business should try to select a short domain name that is easy to remember and which its potential customers can identify. **True or False?**

12. Class C networks can have a maximum of 65,000 host IP addresses. **True or False?**

13. ICANN completely supports the growth of alternative root systems and nonaccredited domain name registrars. **True or False?**

14. Cybersquatting became illegal in the U.S. in 1999. **True or False?**

15. E-mail clients use the SMTP protocol to download e-mail messages from a mail server into a client's inbox. **True or False?**

16. Steve Case is often called the "father of e-mail." **True or False?**

17. The proposed top-level domain for the air transport industry is .air. **True or False?**

18. "Nonprofit.org.uk" is a likely domain name for a not-for-profit organization in Australia. **True or False?**

19. Routers use the network address portion of an IP address to locate a destination network and the host portion of an IP address to locate a specific device on that network by correlating it with a device's MAC address. **True or False?**

20. An IP address can be expressed as a series of four numbers from 0-255 separated by periods. **True or False?**

Exercises

1. Using Internet search tools or other relevant resources, such as those listed at the end of this chapter, locate information about switches, routers, and firewalls. Then write a one- or two-page paper describing each device and comparing and contrasting how each device is used in an IP network.

2. Using Internet search tools or other relevant resources, such as those listed at the end of this chapter, determine the current status of new or proposed top-level domains. Then list and describe each domain's current status.

3. Using Internet search tools or other relevant resources, such as those listed at the end of this chapter, identify instances where an e-business has paid more than $100,000 for the rights to an already registered domain name. Then list at least three e-businesses, the amount paid, and explain why the purchasing e-business was willing to pay such a large amount for rights to the domain name.

4. Using Internet search tools and other relevant resources, such as those listed at the end of this chapter, identify the role the ISOC, ICANN, W3C, and the WIPO play in oversight of the Internet and World Wide Web. Then write a one- or two-page paper describing each organization, its history, and its mission.

5. Using Internet search tools and other relevant resources, such as those listed at the end of this chapter, locate the home page of an e-business and write down its URL. Then using hyperlinks provided on the home page, click through to another page at the Web site and write down its URL. Click through to a third page and write down its URL. Follow this process for at least two more e-businesses. Then create a one- or two-page paper that lists each URL and identifies its component parts: TCP/IP subprotocol, host name, subdomain (if applicable), domain name, path, and filename.

CASE PROJECTS

◆ 1 ◆

You just started a small business which you plan to operate from a home office. You need to set up an Internet connection, and you need to decide what type of Internet connection is best for your business: dial-up modem, cable, DSL, or some other option. Initially, you plan to connect to the Internet several times a day to check e-mail, contact your clients, and purchase your office supplies and products for resale. Research the cost and effectiveness of dial-up, cable, and DSL, and other business Internet connections in your area. (Be sure to check for your options in your geographic region.) Then create a one-page comparison of the connection methods you reviewed, including which method you choose for your business connection and the rationale for your choice.

◆ 2 ◆

You and your friend Bob are considering starting your own e-business. Bob recently read an article about new business-oriented domain names available for registration from e-businesses such as New.net, but that are outside ICANN's managed Domain Name System. Bob suggests that your new e-business register its domain name in this way because of the greater availability of potential names. You are unfamiliar with unaccredited domain name registrars and alternative domain name root systems and need to learn more about them in order discuss the issue with Bob. Using the Internet or other applicable resources, locate articles and Web sites that discuss the issues related to alternative root systems and unaccredited domain name registrars. Create a one-page paper listing the pros and cons of registering with an unaccredited domain name registrar, including why you would or would not use an unaccredited domain name registrar.

◆ 3 ◆

Your supervisor asks you to make a short presentation at the next staff meeting on the IPv6 standard expected to replace the IPv4 standard currently used for IP transmissions. Using the Internet and other applicable sources, locate information about the IPv6 initiative. Then create an outline to guide you through your presentation.

TEAM PROJECT

You and two classmates are planning to start your own e-business. Meet with your classmates and determine the type of e-business model the new e-business will follow and the products or services the e-business will sell. Name the e-business, and choose an appropriate domain name that is easy to remember and representative of the e-business's products or services. Using a domain name registration Web site such as Network Solutions or Register.com, determine whether or not the domain name you want to use is available and how to register it. If the desired name is not available, identify a suitable substitute. Then create a five to 10 slide presentation using Microsoft PowerPoint or other presentation tool that details the new e-business: the e-business model, name, products and services, and proposed domain name. Include details about the registration process. Present the new e-business and its proposed domain name to a group of classmates selected by your instructor.

Useful Links

.EDU Registrar
www.netsol.com/en_US/name-it/edu-us.jhtml;
    jsessionid=J4GZA2PUXERCPWFI3EFCFEY

.GOV Registry
www.nic.gov/

About Domains
www.aboutdomains.com/

BPubs.com — Business Publications Search Engine
www.bpubs.com/Internet_and_E-Commerce/
    Domain_Names/

Electronic Frontier Foundation
www.eff.org/

Google Groups — Newsgroups
www.google.com/grphp?hl=en

ICANN — DNS Security Reading List
www.icann.org/mdr2001/readings.htm

InterNIC
www.internic.org/

ITPRC.com — IT Professionals Resources
www.itprc.com/index.shtml

IP Address to Hostname and Vice Versa — Convert URL to IP Address or IP Address to URL
cello.cs.uiuc.edu/cgi-bin/slamm/ip2name

NTIA — U. S. Department of Commerce National Telecommunications and Information Administration
www.ntia.doc.gov/

Links to Web Sites or Companies Noted in This Chapter

America Online, Inc.
www.corp.aol.com/

AOL Time Warner Inc.
www.aoltimewarner.com/index_flash.adp

Apple Computer, Inc.
www.apple.com

Arndt's Fudgery
www.fudgery.com

AT&T
www.att.com

Avon Products, Inc.
www.avon.com/

BBN Technologies
www.bbn.com/

Business.com
www.business.com/

Chawton House Library
www.chawton.org/index.html

Cisco Systems, Inc.
www.cisco.com

Deere & Company
www.deere.com/nr/deerecom/static/

DoubleClick Inc.
www.doubleclick.com/

Earthlink, Inc.
www.earthlink.net/

IANA — Internet Assigned Numbers Authority
www.iana.org/

ICANN — The Internet Corporation for Assigned Names and Numbers
www.icann.org

Interact Commerce Corporation (ACT!)
www.act.com/

Internet Engineering Task Force (IETF)
www.ietf.org/

Internet Society
www.isoc.org

IPv6 Forum
www.ipv6forum.com/

J. P. Morgan Chase & Co.
www.chase.com

Massachusetts Institute of Technology (MIT)
http://www.mit.edu/

Microsoft Corporation
www.microsoft.com

Momentum Research Group
www.momentumresearchgroup.com/index.html

National Collegiate Athletic Association (NCAA)
www.ncaa.org/

Netscape Communications Corporation
home.netscape.com/ex/shak/index.html

New.net, Inc.
www.new.net

NFO WorldGroup
www.nfow.com/default2.asp

Novell, Inc.
www.novell.com/

Oracle Corporation
www.oracle.com

Palo Alto Research Center Incorporated (Xerox PARC)
www.parc.xerox.com/parc-go.html

Pegasus Mail
www.pmail.com/

People for the Ethical Treatment of Animals (PETA)
www.peta-online.org/

QUALCOMM Incorporated
www.eudora.com/

Register.com
www.register.com

Sendmail, Inc.
www.sendmail.com/

Sequoia Capital
www.sequoiacap.com/

The Boeing Company
www.boeing.com/flash.html

The Hertz Corporation
www.hertz.com

U. S. Department of Commerce
home.doc.gov/

U. S. House of Representatives
www.house.gov/

University of Washington — Pine Information Center
www.washington.edu/pine/

Urban Decay Cosmetics
http://www.urbandecay.com/

W3C — World Wide Web Consortium
www.w3.org/

WIPO — World Intellectual Property Organization
www.wipo.org/index.html.en

XKL
www.xkl.com/index.html

For Additional Review

America Online, Inc. 2002. "Historical Dates for America Online, Inc." Available online at: www.corp.aol.com/.

Andrews, Jean. 2001. *i-Net+ Guide to Internet Technologies*. Boston: Course Technology.

Brain, Marshall. 2001. "How Domain Name Servers Work," *Marshall Brain's HowStuffWorks*. Available online at: www.howstuffworks.com/dns.htm.

Bunnell, David and Brate, Adam. 2000. *Making the Cisco Connection: The Real Story Behind the Real Internet Superpower*. New York: John Wiley & Sons, Inc.

Campbell, Todd. 1998. "The First E-mail Message," *PreText Magazine*, March. Available online at: www.pretext.com/mar98/features/story2.htm.

Carey, Pete. 2001. "A Start-up's True Tale," *Mercury News* as reported by *SiliconValley.com*, December 1.

www.siliconvalley.com/docs/news/depth/cisco120201.htm.

Cavender, Sasha. 1998. "Legends: Ray Tomlinson," *Forbes ASAP at Forbes.com*, October 5. Available online at: www.forbes.com/asap/1998/1005/126.html.

Cisco Systems, Inc. 2001. "Common Port Assignments." Available online at: www.cisco.com/univercd/cc/td/doc/product/access/acs_fix/806/806swcg/tcpports.htm.

Cisco Systems, Inc. 2001. "Fact Sheet," *Cisco Systems, Inc.* Available online at: newsroom.cisco.com/dlls/corpfact.html.

Cringely, Robert X. 1996. *Accidental Empires: How the Boys of Silicon Valley Make Their Millions, Battle Foreign Competition, and Still Can't Get a Date*, Revised Edition. New York: HarperBusiness.

Dean, Tamara. 2002. *Network+ Guide to Networks, Second Edition*. Boston: Course Technology.

Deere & Co. 2001. "General Information: Deere & Company." Available online at: www.johndeere.com/deerecom/_Company+Info/General+Information/default.htm?menu=.

Deere & Co. 2001. "The Story of John Deere." Available online at: www.johndeere.com/deerecom/_Company+Info/History/default.htm?menu=.

Franklin, Curt. 2001. "How Routers Work," *Marshall Brain's HowStuffWorks*. Available online at: www.howstuffworks.com/router.htm.

Fulford, Robert. 2001. "The History of @," *The National Post*, May 22. Available online at: www.geraldinesherman.com/fulford/AtSymbol.html.

Fulford, Robert. 2001. "The Many Names of @," *The National Post*, May 22. Available online at: www.geraldinesherman.com/fulford/AtSymbol2.html.

Glaser, Garrett. 1997. "Cisco Co-Founder Finds New Path," *ZDNet*, November 21. www.zdnet.com/zdnn/content/msnb/1117/242877.html.

IANA.org. 2001. "Port Numbers." Available online at: www.iana.org/assignments/port-numbers.

Internet Society. 2002. "All About the Internet Society." Available online at: www.isoc.org/isoc/.

Internet2. 2001. "About Internet2." Available online at: www.internet2.edu/html/about.html.

InterNIC. 2001. "InterNIC FAQs on New Top-Level Domains." Available online at: www.internic.net/faqs/new-tlds.html.

InterNIC. 2001. "InterNIC FAQs on The Domain Name System: A Non-technical Explanation - Why Universal Resolvability is Important." Available online at: www.internic.net/faqs/authoritative-dns.html.

InterNIC. 2001. "InterNIC FAQs on the Domain Names, Registrars, and Registration." Available online at: www.internic.net/faqs/domain-names.html.

Jesdanun, Anick. 2001. "Weaving More Secure Web: Attacks Prompt Review of Internet's Core Computers," *Associated Press as reported in the Houston Chronicle*, November 12.

Kessler, Gary C. 1999. "An Overview of TCP/IP Protocol and the Internet " April 23. www.hill.com/library/publications/tcpip.shtml.

Knight, Margaret M. 2000. "Pioneers of the Internet: How Rensselaer Alumni Helped Change the Way the World Communicates," *Rensselaer Magazine*, September. Available online at: www.eng.rpi.edu/dept/NewsComm/Magazine/Sep00/Pioneers.html.

Lane, Robert W. 2001. "Farming the Future: Deere's CEO says the Internet Will Change Agriculture as Much as the Tractor Did 80 Years Ago," *Context Magazine, Digital Strategy*, August/September. Available online at: www.contextmag.com/archives/200108/DigitalStrategy.asp.

Leiseboer, John. 1999. "Networking Protocols," *ChipCenter*. Available online at: www.chipcenter.com/eexpert/jleiseboer/jleiseboer029.html.

Lucas, Michael. 2001. "Where Have All the IPs Gone?," The *O'Reilly Network*, March 2. Available online at: www.onlamp.com/lpt/a//onlamp/2001/03/02/ip_gone.html.

Munnariz, Rick. 1999. "A Look at Steve Case CEO and Chairman of America Online," *The Motley Fool, Fool.com*, January 14. Available online at: www.fool.com/specials/1999/sp990114acasestudy.htm.

NetworkIce. 2001. "Port Knowledgebase." Available online at: www.networkice.com/advice/Exploits/Ports/.

NOLO Law for All. 2002. "Cybersquatting: What It Is and What Can Be Done About It," *Nolo.com*. Available online at: http://www.nolo.com/lawcenter/ency/article.cfm?objectID=60EC3491-B4B5-4A98-BB6E6632A2FA0CB2.

Press Release. 2000. "PETA Wins Landmark Cybersquatting Case," *PETA Media Center*, June 19. Available online at: www.peta-online.org/news/600/600dotorg.html.

Press Release. 2001. "36 Billion E-Mails Per Day by 2005," *IDC Research* as reported by *NUA.com*, September 19. Available online at: www.nua.com/surveys/.

Press Release. 2001. "Content and Consent Boost European Email Market," *Forrester Research*, Amsterdam, Netherlands, October 19. Available online at: www.forrester.com/ER/Press/Release/0,1769,641,00.html.

Press Release. 2001. "DoubleClick's Dartmail Study Reveals 88% of Consumers Have Made Purchases as a Result of Permission-Based E-Mail," *DoubleClick*, October 30. New York, N. Y.

Available online at: www.doubleclick.net/us/corporate/presskit/press-releases.asp?asp_object_1=&press%5Frelease%5Fid=2554.

Press Release. 2001. "Internet Business Solutions Expected to Account for 40 Percent of U. S. Productivity Increase Over 10 Years," *Cisco Systems, Inc.*, December 4. Available online at: newsroom.cisco.com/dlls/corp_120401b.html.

Prosise, Jeff. 1996. "A Beginner's Guide to TCP/IP," *PC Magazine Online*, November 19. www.zdnet.com/pcmag/issues/1520/pcmg0030.htm.

Request for Comment #2050. 1996. "Internet Registry IP Allocation Guidelines." ftp://www.arin.net/rfc/rfc2050.txt.

Request for Comment #1939. 1996. "Post Office Protocol - Version 3." Available online at: www.cis.ohio-state.edu/cgi-bin/rfc/rfc1939.html.

Request for Comment #793. 1981. "Transmission Control Protocol, DARPA Internet Program, Protocol Specification." Available online at: www.ibiblio.org/pub/docs/rfc/rfc793.txt.

Robinson, Gail. 1999. "The Best Domain Names in the World...Ever!" *Internet Magazine Online*, November. Available online at: www.findarticles.com/cf_dls/m0CXD/1999_Nov/58326312/p1/article.jhtml.

Robinson, Gail. 2000. "You Paid *How Much* For That Domain Name?" *Web Developer's Journal*, February 3. Available online at: www.Webdevelopersjournal.com/articles/domain_names.html.

Segal, Ben. 1995. "A Short History of Internet Protocols at CERN," *CERN PDP-NS*, April. Available online at: wwwinfo.cern.ch/pdp/ns/ben/TCPHIST.html.

Segaller, Stephen. 1999. *Nerds 2.0.1, A Brief History of the Internet*. New York: TV Books, L.L.C.

Stanford University. 2001. "Bosack/Lerner Endowed Professorship from Cisco Systems, Inc." Available online at: www.stanford.edu/group/cpdcorp/philanthropy/professor.html.

Stanistreet, Michelle. 1999. "The Queen of Urban Chic," *Daily Express Micro Edition*, September 19. www.lineone.net/express/99/09/19/city/m2000queen-d.html#Related_Articles.

Steinke, Steve and the editors of *Network Magazine*. 2000. *Network Tutorial*. San Francisco, CA: CMP Books.

SUNY Institute of Technology. 2001. "What's Inside a Router?" *TEL 316: Data Network Design, SUNY, Utica/Rome*. Available online at: www.tele.sunyit.edu/Router_inside.htm.

Swisher, Kara. 1998. *aol.com: How Steve Case Beat Bill Gates, Nailed the Netheads, and Made Millions in the War for the Web*. New York: Random House, Inc.

The Internet Corporation for Assigned Names and Numbers. 2001. "Background." Available online at: www.icann.org/general/background.htm.

Urban Decay. 2001. "About Urban Decay: Company History." Available online at: www.urbandecay.com/aboutinfo.html.

Waldrop, M. Mitchell. 2001. *The Dream Machine, J. C. R. Licklider and the Revolution That Made Computing Personal*. New York: The Penguin Group.

Warner, Bernhard. 2001. "E-mail is Now 30 Years Young," *Reuters*, October 5. Available online at: http://www.ciol.com/content/news/trends/101100501.asp.

Windbigler, Kristin. 1997. "Exploring the Domain Name Space," *Webmonkey*, January 24. hotwired.lycos.com/Webmonkey/geektalk/97/03/index4a.html.

World Intellectual Property Organization (WIPO). 2001. "About WIPO." Available online at: www.wipo.org/about-wipo/en/.

World Wide Web Consortium (W3C). 2001. "About the World Wide Web Consortium (W3C)." Available online at: www.w3.org/Consortium/.

World Wide Web Consortium (W3C). 2001. "Web Naming and Addressing Overview (URIs, URLs,...)." Available online at: www.w3.org/Addressing/.

CHAPTER 4

Web Site Development Tools

In this chapter, you will learn to:

Consider the importance of planning when developing an effective e-business Web site

Discuss the markup languages used to create Web-based documents

Identify Web development applications

Describe the multimedia tools used to add interest and excitement to a Web page

Discuss ways to add interactivity to Web pages

In the early days of personal computers, buying a personal computer went something like this: Company X builds a computer for $3,000 and distributes it through Distributor Y for $4,500. Distributor Y sells it to Value-Added-Reseller Z for $5,500, and VAR-Z sells it to the end user for $7,500. About this time, a young University of Texas undergraduate named Michael Dell realized the huge difference between the cost of personal computer components and the price of an assembled personal computer purchased from a retail outlet. He decided that if he eliminated the "middle man," he could build and sell less expensive personal computers directly to the end user at a nice profit. He began by building and selling personal computers from his dorm room. Business was brisk, and in 1984 Dell, with $1,000 in his pocket, left the University of Texas to found Dell Computer Corporation based on the proven successful revenue model of selling directly to end users. By 1992, Dell Computer Corporation was included in the Fortune 500 list of the largest companies in the world, and by 1993 Dell was one of the top five computer makers in the world. Still, the company wanted a way to provide an easier purchasing process for customers while providing outstanding customer support. Could the budding World Wide Web be the answer?

Planning an Effective E-Business Web Site

Planning plays a very important role in Web site development. Before creating a Web site for your e-business, you should first carefully consider the Web site's goals, objectives, and overall purpose. Without clear, established, and measurable goals and objectives, your Web site may lack the focus it needs to be effective.

Your Web site's goals and objectives should meet your needs and your customer's needs. Beware: when planning a Web site, e-businesses too often focus on their own internal needs rather than those of customers and potential customers. Never forget that the customer is truly in charge when doing business online, because switching to a competitor's Web site is as easy as the click of a mouse button. Also, potential customers form an impression of your e-business within the first few seconds of their first visit to your Web site. Viewers with a favorable impression of a Web site are much more likely to become customers.

In addition to careful planning, technological advances also play a major role in shaping the online experience of an e-business's customers. New technologies continue to result in faster computers, larger computer screens, better video and sound cards, new Web page development tools, and faster Internet connections. Meanwhile, an e-business that wants to generate more online sales and provide better customer support after the sale must exploit these technological advances in the ongoing development of their Web sites.

In this chapter, you learn about the technologies that e-businesses use to develop interesting, useful, and competitive Web sites. First, you learn about programming technologies, such as HTML, that make it possible for Web pages to be displayed in Web browsers in the first place. Next, you investigate the software used to create Web sites, including FrontPage, Dreamweaver, and GoLive. Then, you learn about multimedia tools, such as Flash and RealOne that you can use to add interest and excitement to Web sites. Finally, you learn about the tools such as forms, ColdFusion, Active Server Pages, and Java applets that you can use to make your Web sites interactive.

Markup Languages

You have learned how networking technologies and the Internet came together to allow computer users with Web browser software to retrieve Web pages from Web servers anywhere in the world. Now you're ready to learn about the technologies involved in actually displaying Web pages in a Web browser. To understand this process, it's helpful to start by thinking about how other applications display documents.

For example, consider a word-processing application such as Microsoft Word. When you open a document in Word, you might see text formatted in various fonts and font sizes, some graphics, and perhaps some tables. What you don't see are the numerous programming codes embedded in the document that tell Word what the document should look like when displayed on the screen or when printed. Although it is possible to display some of these codes in Word, the vast majority are kept hidden to allow you to focus on what really matters — the document itself.

However, a document created in Word may not be fully transportable to another computer that uses different word-processing software. For example, different word-processing software may not recognize some of the Microsoft Word codes; therefore, a Word document might not view or print correctly on that computer. The standard that underlies the technology that allows users to create online documents that are fully transportable between different computer systems is called the Standard Generalized Markup Language (SGML).

Standard Generalized Markup Language (SGML)

The **Standard Generalized Markup Language (SGML)**, an ISO standard published in 1986, specifies a standard format for embedding information called "descriptive markup" within a document. **Descriptive markup** defines the structure of a document, such as, the table of contents section, a chapter heading, a paragraph, and so forth. Because SGML is an international standard, SGML-based documents can be transported easily between different computer systems. SGML applications contain files called **Document Type Definition** files or **DTDs**. A DTD describes the structure of a specific document type, such as a computer systems documentation manual. A DTD identifies the standard document components and specifies how those components are positioned within the document. For example, a DTD for a computer systems documentation manual might specify that the manual be broken into chapters, sections, and individual paragraphs within sections and that each chapter or section must begin with a heading. The actual content of the manual consists of different elements such as titles, headings, paragraphs, lists, and tables. These different elements are identified by codes or **tags** placed within the manual document which mark the beginning and end of each element.

Figure 4-1 illustrates an example of the following SGML tags: <section> and </section>, which identify the beginning and ending of a predefined portion of the document called a section; <subhead> and </subhead>, which define the subheading text content for the section; and <par> and </par>, which define the beginning and end of a paragraph of text content within the section.

```
<section>
<subhead>Subheading Text</subhead>
<par>Paragraph Text</par>
</section>
```

Figure 4-1
SGML example

Programming languages based on the SGML standard are called **markup languages**, and the markup language most commonly used to create Web pages today is the Hypertext Markup Language (HTML).

Hypertext Markup Language (HTML)

One of the most widely used markup languages on the Web today is the **Hypertext Markup Language**, or **HTML**. HTML is so widely used on the Web that the term "HTML document" and "Web page" are more or less interchangeable. You can distinguish an HTML document file from other files by the .html (or .htm) file extensions which are a part of all HTML filenames. For example, a Web page containing frequently asked questions might be named FAQ.html.

When you download a Web page, HTML codes or tags are embedded within the Web page. These tags tell your Web browser how to display the page. For example, one tag might indicate that a photo should be aligned on the left margin, while another might indicate that the document title should be formatted in blue, 14-point font.

When creating a Web page, a Web author has two choices. She can create a simple text document in the Notepad text editor (or some other text editor) that includes all the text that will appear in the Web page, along with the many HTML tags that tell a Web browser how to display the page. Creating a Web page in this way can be tedious work, and requires a fair amount of familiarity with HTML. Figure 4-2 shows an HTML document displayed in the Notepad text editor.

It's also possible to use any one of the numerous software packages such as Microsoft FrontPage or Macromedia Dreamweaver to create Web pages. These applications are often called Web development applications or Web authoring tools. Creating a Web page in one of these Web authoring tools is much like creating a document with a word-processing application. The appropriate HTML tags are automatically inserted in the Web page; however, unlike a word-processing document, the hidden HTML tags can

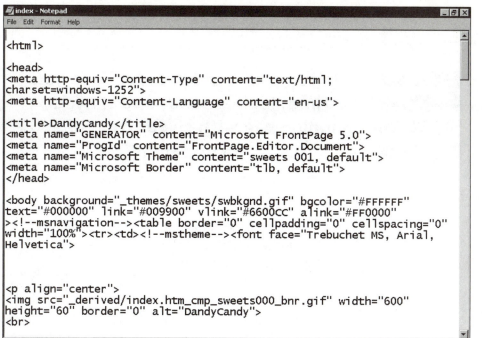

```
index - Notepad
File  Edit  Format  Help

<html>

<head>
<meta http-equiv="Content-Type" content="text/html;
charset=windows-1252">
<meta http-equiv="Content-Language" content="en-us">

<title>DandyCandy</title>
<meta name="GENERATOR" content="Microsoft FrontPage 5.0">
<meta name="ProgId" content="FrontPage.Editor.Document">
<meta name="Microsoft Theme" content="sweets 001, default">
<meta name="Microsoft Border" content="tlb, default">
</head>

<body background="_themes/sweets/swbkgnd.gif" bgcolor="#FFFFFF"
text="#000000" link="#009900" vlink="#6600CC" alink="#FF0000"
><!--msnavigation--><table border="0" cellpadding="0" cellspacing="0"
width="100%"><tr><td><!--mstheme--><font face="Trebuchet MS, Arial,
Helvetica">


<p align="center">
<img src="_derived/index.htm_cmp_sweets000_bnr.gif" width="600"
height="60" border="0" alt="DandyCandy">
<br>
```

Figure 4-2
HTML
document in
Notepad

be viewed if desired. Figure 4-3 shows the HTML document from Figure 4-2 as it appears in a Web development application, and Figure 4-4 shows the same HTML document as it appears in a Web browser.

Figure 4-3
HTML
document
in a Web
development
application

DandyCandy

News
Products
Feedback
Search

Welcome to DandyCandy! Take you time, look around, and fill your shopping bag with sweet treats for t entire family.

Our Mission

Our mission, at DandyCandy, is to provide you with the freshest, best-

Figure 4-4

HTML document in a Web browser

When a Web server receives a request from a Web browser, it fulfills that request by returning a copy of the requested HTML document. It is the Web browser's job to interpret and display the HTML document in a format that's easy to read. This interpretation step is called **parsing**, because it's much like what our brains do when parsing sentences in order to find the subject and verb, analyze any modifiers such as adjectives, and so forth. The Web browser reads the HTML document from top to bottom, picking out elements such as the Web page title or blocks of text and then displaying the elements appropriately in the Web browser window. This process is similar to the way a painter translates what he sees (say, a mountain landscape) into a picture on a canvas. Figure 4-5 illustrates a Web server fulfilling a Web browser request for an HTML document. In keeping with the painter analogy, the Web browser is represented by a hand holding a paintbrush.

Even Web authors who do most of their work with one of the Web development applications need to be familiar with the HTML tags that control how content is positioned and formatted on a Web page. Like many things that first appear complex, HTML is fairly simple once you look under the hood. HTML tags consist of **container tags** that surround and modify a Web page element and **standalone tags** which denote an individual Web page element or contain information about the Web page as a whole. Container tags come in pairs and are used to mark the beginning and ending of Web page elements. Examples include the <html> and </html> tags, which define the beginning and ending of the HTML document itself; the <body> and </body> tags, which define the body section of an HTML document; and the <b> and </b> tags which define boldface formatting for text enclosed within the tags.

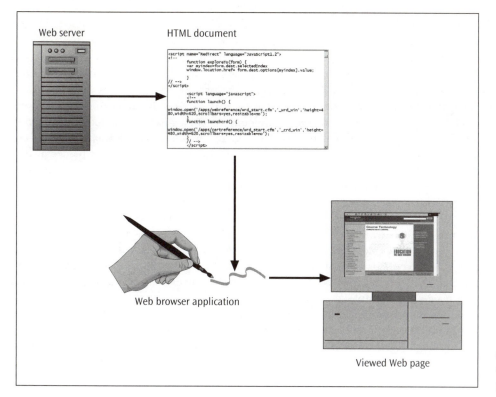

Web server

HTML document

```
<script name="Redirect" language="JavaScript1.2">
<!--
    function exploreTo(form) {
        var myindex=form.dest.selectedIndex
        window.location.href= form.dest.options[myindex].value;
// -->
</script>

    <script language="javascript">
    <!--
    function launch() {
window.open('/apps/webreference/wrd_start.cfm','_wrd_win','height=4
80,width=620,scrollbars=yes,resizable=no');
}
    function launchcrd() {
window.open('/apps/certreference/wrd_start.cfm','_crd_win','height=
480,width=620,scrollbars=yes,resizable=no');
}
    // -->
    </script>
```

Web browser application

Viewed Web page

Figure 4-5
Web browser
process

An example of a standalone tag is the <img> tag that appears once for each picture or other graphical element inserted on a page. This standalone tag tells the browser that it needs to request additional files from the Web server. For example, when a Web browser reads <img src="mr2.jpg"> in an HTML document, the Web browser initiates another request to the same server asking for the mr2.jpg picture file. The Web server returns the picture file and the Web browser positions it on the page. In this way, a Web page is built through multiple requests to the Web server for various page elements.

Another example of a container HTML tag is the anchor tag <a href> that is used to define a hyperlink reference. For example, consider this tag:

<a href="FAQ.html">Click here for answers to some frequently asked questions</a>

This tag tells the browser to take the text "Click here for answers to some frequently asked questions" and format it as a hyperlink (usually using the familiar blue text with an underline). It also tells the browser that when a viewer clicks the hyperlink text, the Web browser should ask the Web server to send the file named FAQ.html. When the Web browser receives this file, it displays it.

> **TIP**
>
> For a look at early Web pages dating back to 1996, check out The Wayback Machine at the Internet Archive Web site.

HTML is just one of several SGML-based markup languages. Another markup language, Dynamic Hypertext Markup Language (DHTML), makes it possible for a browser to display even more sophisticated content.

Dynamic Hypertext Markup Language (DHTML)

Dynamic Hypertext Markup Language, or **DHTML**, is a more sophisticated version of HTML that adapts content "on the fly," making the content react to a viewer's input. DHTML can also change the content to accommodate different screen sizes without sending further requests to the Web server. For example, when a viewer with a large monitor downloads a Web page written in DHTML, the Web browser presents the page in such a way as to take advantage of the monitor. On a smaller or monochrome monitor, the Web browser displays the DHTML page in a much simpler format. In Figure 4-6, the menus on the TrueColor Studios Web page appear in just the right places in two different screen resolutions; the Web browser used the DHTML code to detect the monitor size and adjust menu placement accordingly. In this way, the menu placement remains consistent across multiple browsers and monitor sizes.

DHTML can also be used to change Web page objects based on viewer input. For example, DHTML can be used to link a scale gauge to a map. As a viewer moves his or her mouse pointer along the scale, DHTML can change the level of zoom at which the map is displayed. This level of interactivity makes Web pages more appealing and involving. One of the most common uses of DHTML is in advertising banners that appear on Web pages. For example, the flat banner ad can be replaced with an ad that expands when the mouse pointer is positioned over it. You can also use DHTML to create an ad that briefly covers an entire Web page before shrinking to a smaller banner size.

Although HTML and DHTML tags define how Web page content is displayed in a Web browser, Extensible Markup Language (XML) tags are used to define the content itself.

Extensible Markup Language (XML)

The **Extensible Markup Language**, or **XML**, is similar to HTML in that it uses tags. However, whereas HTML tags are used by the browser to display *content* correctly, the tags in XML are used to provide *information about the content* itself. XML tags are much more powerful than HTML tags and can be customized for any kind of information, as long as both the sender and receiver of the XML document agree on definitions of the tags. The "extensible" portion of the name "Extensible Markup Language" means that new tags can be created at any time, extending the language to fit any kind of information.

To understand why this is useful, you need to understand a little bit about how businesses sometimes exchange information. Some businesses, for example auto parts manufacturers and their customers (auto parts resellers), have to exchange vast amounts of information about parts orders. Because of the quantity of information involved, it's simply not practical for an auto parts reseller to complete paper order forms and mail or fax them to the manufacturers. Nor is it practical for the manufacturers to respond with shipment and back order information via paper documents. Instead, it's faster and more efficient to simply exchange the order/shipping/back order information electronically. But, the information has to be formatted in a way that either recipient can understand.

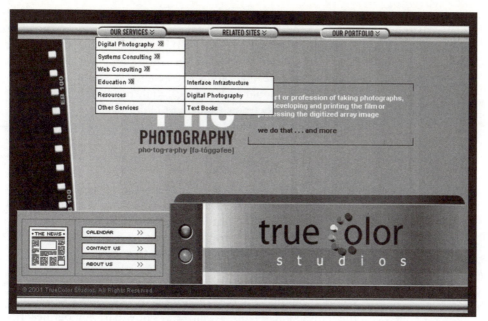

640 x 480 Screen Resolution

1024 x 768 Screen Resolution

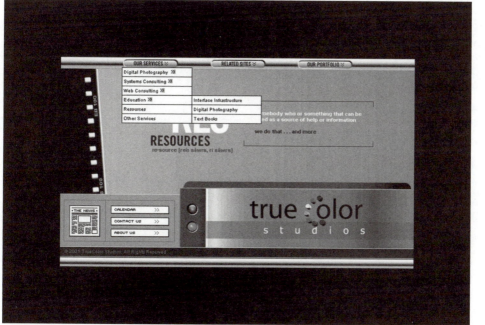

Figure 4-6
Two examples
of menu
positioning
using DHTML

In the past, before XML was available, business partners who regularly traded detailed information would have to create custom software to handle the data exchange. This would entail compiling detailed programming specifications that explained exactly how to exchange the information. In our auto parts manufacturer/reseller example, specifications about the data to be exchanged (such as part number, description, and price) would have to be carefully negotiated between the manufacturer and the reseller or the electronic exchange of information couldn't occur. Those details might include information like: "I will send you data about my parts catalog in 63-character chunks, and the first nine characters will be the part number and the next 21 will be the description and the next five will be the price without a decimal point" and so forth.

Today, XML provides an effective alternative for exchanging this type of business-to-business data online. For example, an auto parts manufacturer might require that all auto parts resellers send their purchase order data to the company in XML format. Auto parts resellers who wish to stock the manufacturer's parts would be forced to comply. In this way, the manufacturer and its resellers can exchange the information necessary to buy and sell thousands of different parts online, without the time and cost of writing special software to handle the transactions. Figure 4-7 illustrates how part number, description, and price information can be transmitted online using an XML document.

XML is also a handy way for the multiple servers running very large Web sites to coordinate with each other. An e-business Web site, for example, might use XML to send credit card information to a server dedicated to handling card authorizations.

Now that you have learned about the major markup languages used to create Web content, you're ready to investigate some prepackaged software applications that automatically generate HTML code.

TIP

In June 2000, Microsoft Corporation introduced .NET, an initiative that supports XML Web services and allows a wide range of applications written in various programming languages to communicate with each other and with systems providing basic services, such as user authentication, over the Internet. Some analysts suggest that the Microsoft's .NET initiative may ultimately change the way Microsoft does business by moving Microsoft away from selling packaged software and toward selling subscription-based software services provided over the Internet.

Figure 4-7
XML example

```
<partnumber>123456789</partnumber>
<partdescription>Medium-sized flange</partdescription>
<partprice>USD$55.00</partprice>
```

Web Development Applications

Web development applications present a **WYSIWYG** (What You See Is What You Get) view of a Web page, allowing the user to enter and format text, insert pictures, and create hyperlinks. This makes creating a Web page similar to creating a document in a word-processing application. These Web development applications automatically generate the appropriate HTML tags as the Web author creates the Web page content. Some of the most popular Web development applications are FrontPage and Visual InterDev by Microsoft; HomeSite by Macromedia Inc., Dreamweaver, and UltraDev; and GoLive by Adobe Systems Incorporated.

Microsoft FrontPage and Visual InterDev

One of the first easy-to-use Web development applications was Microsoft FrontPage. Still popular today because it is so easy to use, **FrontPage** works well with Microsoft's Internet Information Server (IIS) Web server software used to serve up Web pages upon a request from a Web browser. FrontPage includes special utilities (called wizards) that walk you through the process of creating a Web page step by step. It also provides model Web pages (called templates) that a user can customize to create individual Web pages or an entire Web site.

In general, creating a Web page in FrontPage is similar to creating a text document in Microsoft Word or a slide show presentation in Microsoft PowerPoint. However, a Web page created in FrontPage does not always display well in Netscape or other non-Microsoft Web browsers. This is partly because the HTML code generated by FrontPage cannot be read by all non-Microsoft Web browsers. Additionally, FrontPage allows the user to implement features that may not be compatible with non-Microsoft browsers.

Microsoft's Internet Explorer has more than 80 percent of the browser market and Netscape Communications' browser accounts for the lion's share of the rest. However, some e-businesses need to ensure that their Web pages look good on Opera, Netscape for Unix, and WebTV browsers as well. For example, some major companies and governmental organizations are considering or announcing plans to switch from Windows to Linux and thus from Internet Explorer to Netscape; therefore, it's still important to make sure your Web pages work with most Web browsers. FrontPage also doesn't integrate well with some applications and techniques used for complex e-business sites that store information in databases. (You learn more about databases later in this chapter.) For these reasons, FrontPage, although very easy to use, may not be a good choice for a complex e-business Web site. Figure 4-8 illustrates a complete Web site and its home page viewed from within the FrontPage application.

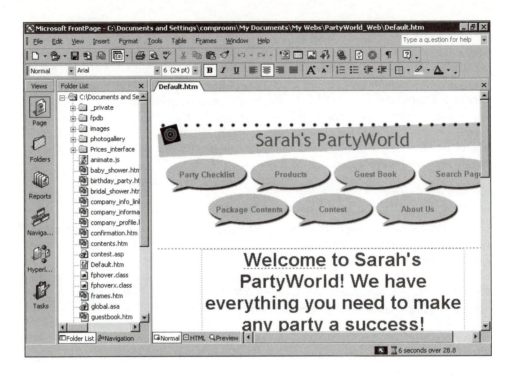

Figure 4-8
FrontPage example

Visual InterDev is Microsoft's high-end Web development application. Going well beyond simple HTML, Visual InterDev can be used to modify large Web sites created with multiple development tools. It also contains features designed to make it easier to manage large Web sites, and to reduce the duplication of work which makes construction of large Web sites so time consuming. But, Visual InterDev is not for the faint of heart — only experienced Web developers can use this product to its maximum potential.

Macromedia HomeSite, Dreamweaver, and UltraDev

Macromedia publishes several Web development applications. **HomeSite**, like FrontPage, is relatively inexpensive and so might initially appear to be intended for beginners. However, HomeSite doesn't contain the breadth of templates and wizards that FrontPage includes, and as a result HomeSite requires a more thorough understanding of HTML than FrontPage.

Dreamweaver by Macromedia is a better choice for newcomers; it contains wizards and online guides to help neophytes build sites. It's also more able to handle complex Web sites and allows developers to integrate more sophisticated features into their Web pages.

UltraDev, Macromedia's most full-featured Web development application, competes with Visual InterDev at the high end of this market. Macromedia's packages generally create HTML code that is displayed properly by major Web browsers, although some manual adjustment of the code is sometimes necessary if compatibility with browsers other than Microsoft Internet Explorer and Netscape Navigator is desired. Figure 4-9 illustrates a Web page in Dreamweaver UltraDev.

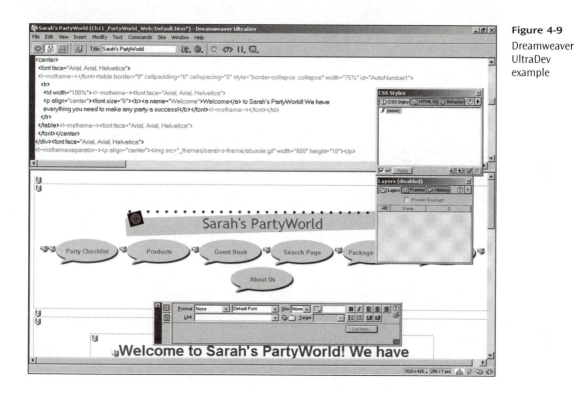

Figure 4-9
Dreamweaver
UltraDev
example

Adobe GoLive

Adobe Systems Incorporated competes in the WYSIWYG arena with the **GoLive** application. GoLive, which includes only a few templates, doesn't have the raft of Web site management features that distinguish Macromedia's applications. GoLive makes up for this, however, with a very easy-to-use interface that can display a Web page as an HTML document (that is, as text with inserted tags) and in a WYSIWYG view simultaneously. This makes GoLive an excellent learning tool for beginners creating their first Web page, because it allows the new Web author to format a Web page using simple menus and toolbar buttons, all the while observing the HTML tags as they are added to the Web page. Figure 4-10 illustrates a Web page in GoLive.

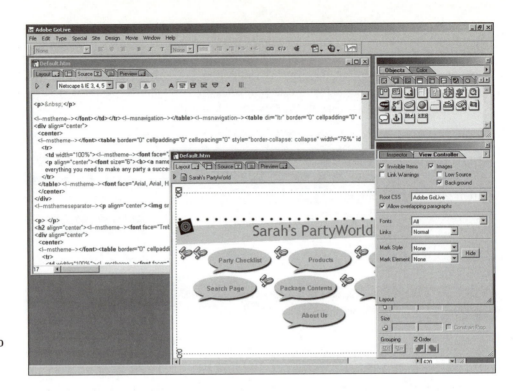

Figure 4-10
GoLive
example

The best way to learn more about Web development applications is to try using them. Macromedia and Adobe provide free trial software at their Web sites, and some versions of Microsoft's Office suite include the FrontPage application. Web authors use pictures, animation, and sound at some Web sites to make them more interesting and attractive. In the next section, you learn about the multimedia tools used to add these effects to Web pages.

Multimedia Tools

As more and more consumers and businesses go online, new types of Web page content are being developed. An e-business may choose to use sophisticated multimedia features such as animated graphics, video clips, and sound to make its Web site more appealing and useful to its customers. Early Web browsers could understand and display HTML, but not video clips or animations of the sort found today on Web sites for such organizations as the National Hockey League or The Coca-Cola Company. First, Web browser capabilities had to be enhanced with additional programs to enable browsers to display multimedia content. Additionally, graphics programs had to be adapted to create more professional looking and appealing graphic content for the Web.

Multimedia tools such as Web browser plug-ins (enhancement software) and state-of-the-art graphics software enable e-businesses to publish exciting, involving, and functional Web sites. You learn about some of these tools in the following sections.

Web Browser Plug-Ins

A **plug-in** is software that adds special features to a Web browser, such as the ability to play sound and video files that are transmitted over the Internet in a continuous stream. Web browser plug-ins include Flash Player by Macromedia which is used to view animated Web page content; RealOne Player by RealNetwork, Inc. which is used to view video clips; and Acrobat Reader by Adobe Systems which is used to view, print, and save documents created in Adobe's Acrobat PDF format.

Macromedia Flash and Flash Player

Flash, created by Macromedia, is an animation technology used to create Web page content which Web browsers can download over a slow dial-up connection. Using this technology, it is possible for Web authors to add animation, stylish menus, sound effects, and other sophisticated elements to a Web page and still have the page download quickly.

To display Flash content, users must install the **Flash Player** plug-in. The first time you download a page with Flash content, you are asked if you want to download the Flash Player. If you click "Yes," the Web browser downloads and installs Flash Player automatically. Without the Flash Player plug-in, Flash content usually displays as a blank white box. Ego Media (Figure 4-11), a consulting firm, uses Flash to display animation at its very complex Web site.

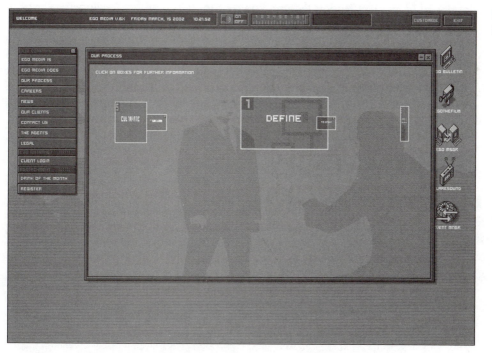

Figure 4-11
Flash example

Streaming Media

Another popular group of plug-ins are those that play streaming sound and video files. (The term **streaming media** is used to refer to sound and video files that are transmitted continuously, similar to a television signal, rather than as separate, individual files.) During the mid-1990s, it was generally thought that the first company to allow users to play video via an Internet connection would reap huge financial gains. In search of these profits, Apple Computer, Inc., Microsoft, and a startup called RealNetworks, Inc. all developed plug-ins that could play downloaded video files as well as streaming video and sound files.

Each company developed its own proprietary video format, and created a plug-in required to display that proprietary video format. The companies made these plug-ins available for free. Apple's plug-in is called **Quicktime**, Microsoft developed the **Windows Media Player**, and RealNetworks released the RealPlayer, recently renamed **RealOne**. While the browser plug-ins are free to consumers, the video encoding software required to compress video and sound, and the server software to transmit it over the Internet are not. In other words, e-businesses that want to provide streaming media to consumers must pay Apple, Microsoft, or RealNetwork for the technology required to do so. This can be expensive, but many e-businesses, including online news providers such as ABCNews, are able to greatly increase their visitor base by providing streaming media.

The key to effective streaming media is the compression technique used to shrink the sound or video clips so that they can be easily transmitted across the Internet without excessively compromising quality. One well-known compression standard was developed by the ISO Motion Picture Experts Group. The group developed a series of standards known as MPEG-1, MPEG-2, and MPEG-3. MPEG-2 is still used in many DVDs and in satellite and digital cable transmissions, since by compressing video data, it's possible for one satellite to broadcast many more channels. MPEG-3 is used the most of the three because it's very good at compressing sound files without a perceptible loss in quality; the transportability of these compressed files led to the explosion in online music swapping. MPEG-4 is a relatively new standard which is gaining popularity under the name DivX. The rapid appearance of these new standards illustrates the usefulness of plug-ins; third-party developers can bring new technologies to viewers without waiting for the major browser manufacturers to develop the technologies.

TECH CASE Streaming to the Top

Growing up in Yonkers, New York, in the 1970s, Rob Glaser was a math whiz who loved baseball. He also benefited from a humanistic program of study during high school while attending the Ethical Culture Fieldston School. At the same time, his politically active parents instilled a strong sense of social responsibility. Glaser continued to pursue academic excellence and social activism at Yale where he graduated with three degrees including undergraduate degrees in economics and computer science and a master's degree in economics.

After graduation from Yale in 1983, Glaser accepted a job with Microsoft Corporation where his superintelligence and aggressive approach quickly made him a star. In his ten years at Microsoft, Glaser worked on a variety of projects, ultimately taking charge of Microsoft's multimedia systems

Continued

group. But, Glaser had a vision of marrying technology with social responsibility. In 1993, he left Microsoft to found his own media technology company called Progressive Networks.

Glaser accurately anticipated a great demand for transmitting audio and video effectively over the Internet, and in 1995 Progressive Networks launched a test program geared toward providing audio on demand via the Internet. The product, called RealAudio, was based on file compression technology that allowed high-quality sound files to be transmitted, stored, and played easily. The Progressive Networks revenue model allowed users to download the software needed to play RealAudio files, called the RealAudio Player, for free. However, e-businesses that wanted to provide RealAudio files would have to buy the server software that allowed RealAudio files to be served up over the Internet. Immediately after RealAudio was launched, the major Web browser makers such as Microsoft and Netscape agreed to distribute the RealAudio Player with their browsers. The RealAudio product was a big hit, and by October 1996 more than 10 million RealAudio Players had been downloaded.

Today, Progressive Networks is called RealNetworks, Inc. (Figure 4-12). The company provides a group of popular media technology products including RealAudio, RealVideo, RealOne (formerly RealPlayer), and RealSystem. In January 2002, RealNetworks reported that RealPlayer was installed on approximately 90 percent of home computers and, furthermore, that RealSystem software was used to provide content on more than 85 percent of streaming media Web pages. Additionally, RealNetworks continues to adhere to Glaser's philosophy of social responsibility by contributing approximately 5 percent of annual net income to charitable organizations as well as participating in other charitable activities.

Figure 4-12
RealNetworks, Inc.

Adobe Acrobat and Acrobat Reader

Another major Adobe contribution to Internet communications is the universal document exchange format called **Portable Document Format** or **PDF**. Sometimes documents created with one application and then opened on another computer system or in a different application do not retain their original formatting or layout. Adobe Acrobat allows users to convert any document, such as a Microsoft Word document, from its original format into the PDF format. This allows the document to be portable, meaning it can be opened on computers with different hardware and software and still look and print the same.

TIP

A full explanation of how markup languages and other Web development tools work is beyond the scope of this book; to learn more, consult one of the many excellent books and references available on these topics. The "Useful Links" and "For Additional Review" sections at the end of this chapter list some additional resources.

To read a document in the PDF format online, you need to use Adobe's **Acrobat Reader** Web browser plug-in. Acrobat Reader is readily available for download from most Web sites that use PDF files. For example, the U. S. government publishes tax forms in the PDF format on the Internal Revenue Service's Web site, so anyone with the Acrobat Reader can view and print them from the Web site.

Adobe Photoshop Graphic Editor

By today's standards, the first Web pages included fairly primitive graphics — grainy photos, simple logos, and square navigation buttons. Today's Web sites often use multiple colors, sophisticated graphic blends, and stylish layouts. Advancements in online graphics are partly responsible for an increase in e-business, because consumers are likely to feel more comfortable buying from a well-designed Web storefront with attractive graphic elements. No graphics software has done more to advance the use of sophisticated Web page graphics than Adobe Photoshop, the "900-pound gorilla" of graphic-editing software.

Using **Photoshop**, a Web author can quickly create a mock-up of a Web page containing sophisticated graphic images. Because large graphic image files require more time to download from a Web server, using image compression to reduce the size of graphic image files without reducing their quality is very important. Photoshop allows a Web author more control over the size of graphic image files by determining how much image compression is used for each file. Photoshop also provides tools for graphical image positioning and alignment on a Web page. Using Photoshop to layout a Web page can result in a more professional looking page with graphic images that are small enough for transmitting efficiently over a dial-up connection, but elegant enough to look good in a Web browser. Figure 4-13 illustrates a graphic image being edited in Photoshop.

Photoshop is expensive (although you can download and try it for free), and can be quite daunting for first-time users. If you want to start with something less complicated, consider using one of Adobe's simpler and less expensive graphics editor applications, such as PhotoDeluxe, Photoshop Limited Edition, and, most recently, Photoshop Elements. These packages are suitable for beginners who are just starting to work with graphics.

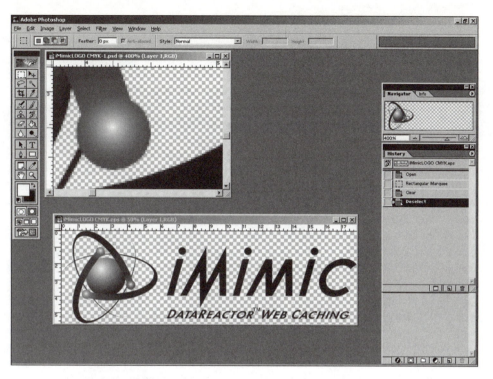

Figure 4-13
Photoshop example

Multimedia tools like Flash, RealOne, and Photoshop can add a lot of excitement to a Web site. But, they do not address the need for customer interactivity at e-business Web sites. In the next section, you learn about some technologies that provide e-business customers with an interactive Web experience.

Interactive Web Sites

E-businesses involve their customers in the online experience by allowing them to search for product or service information, select products, custom-configure those products, purchase the products directly from the Web site, and get online customer support. To achieve this level of interactivity, Web servers must access corporate databases and then create customized Web pages (containing database information requested by the customer) in a matter of moments. In this section, you learn about such tools as Web page forms, Macromedia ColdFusion Studio and ColdFusion Server, Microsoft Active Server Pages and ActiveX technologies, and Java applets that are used to create interactive e-business Web sites.

Forms

The simplest avenue to Web page interactivity is the form. A Web page **form** is similar to a paper form (for example, a job application form), with blank spaces for entering data such as first name, last name, address, and so forth. Forms are often used to collect information from Web page viewers. A form can be very simple, containing only a few text boxes for name and contact information or more complicated, containing check boxes for yes/no answers, option buttons for multiple-choice questions, and drop-down lists for a list of choices such as credit card information.

But, unlike a paper form, data entered into a Web page form is sent to a Web server. The Web server then extracts the newly received data and uses it to complete a task, such as preparing a product order or searching a database for specific product information. Web page forms can be created directly in HTML or by using a Web development application like FrontPage.

Forms are also used to allow a customer to search the databases of an e-business for information. For example, suppose you buy a used car and need to locate an owner's manual for it. You might access the automaker's Web site, and then click an Owners Manual hyperlink to display a search form. In the search form text box, you enter your car's make and model as keywords for the search process. After entering your keyword text, you then click a Submit button to initiate the search. Clicking the Submit button sends the contents of the text box to a Web server. The Web server then compares your entered keywords with an index of the automaker's Web pages to find all the Web pages at the site that contain the keywords. A list of hyperlinks to the Web pages that contain the requested keywords is returned by the server. You then review this list, and click the correct hyperlink to access the appropriate owner's manual.

Table 4-1 illustrates keywords that could be entered in an online search form and the kind of Web-based data that might be accessed based on the keyword search.

Table 4-1
Online search examples

Keywords	Information Accessed
Zip code	Tomorrow's weather
Zip code	Movies playing nearby
Stock symbol	Current price
Date	News on that date
Address	Directions to that address

By involving viewers in an interactive Web site experience, e-business Web sites become "sticky," meaning that viewers spend more time at the site, often making the choice to become paying customers.

Web page forms are one key component in interactivity; however, a Web page form is useless without the interactive capabilities of a Web server. Servers must do more than transmit the same 10 or 20 Web pages; they need to respond to form data and give the customers what they want. In the next section, you learn how a server builds a Web page using both standard content and content that changes depending on the individual viewing the page.

Server-Side Technologies

Server-side technologies such as Macromedia's ColdFusion Server or Microsoft's Active Server Pages operate on the server side of a client/server relationship. (Remember that a Web browser is the client in the client/server relationships we are discussing in this chapter.) How do server-side interactive technologies work? In a nutshell, instead of returning static pages — that is, HTML documents that don't change from one viewer to the next — interactive Web server technologies permit the creation of customized Web pages to suit a viewer's needs. This means that many of the Web pages that you encounter while surfing the Web don't exist on any one Web server as separate, individual HTML documents. Instead, a Web server might start with a basic set of rules that determine what the Web page of an e-business should look like (for example, a logo at the top, standard menu on the left side, and so forth) and then add variable information as necessary. For example, assume you frequently buy books from Amazon.com. When you load the Amazon.com home page in your Web browser, you may see a message at the top of the page welcoming you by name. Additionally, you may see a preselected list of books for sale on the page. The books that appear in the list are selected to appeal to you based on the types of books that you have purchased in the past. A Web server builds the page you see by selecting your name and the book list and plugging this variable information into a Web page template (remember that a template is a model document) along with the standard Amazon.com page content. The resulting complete Web page is then sent to your Web browser. Because the page you receive contains variable content (content that changes frequently), it is called a dynamically generated Web page, or, more simply, a page with **dynamic content**. Before you learn more about dynamic content, however, you need to learn about where Web servers store this variable content.

Database Driven Web Sites

Data is stored on a server in a database. Typically, a database contains one or more groups of similar records, with each record containing specific information about a single item. Groups of related records are stored in a table in a database, and a database can contain many different tables. For example, an online bookstore such as Amazon.com might have a database that contains a table with records for each book available for sale. Each record contains the book's title, author, cost, shipping weight, and perhaps a picture of the book's cover. Another table in the database might contain records with data about each customer's recent book purchases. Web sites that store most of their important information in databases similar to these examples are often called database-backed or **database-driven** Web sites.

Web server applications that interact with databases are incredibly powerful e-business tools. For example, assume you want to purchase a book that contains a group of plays by William Shakespeare (including the play *Romeo and Juliet*) at an online bookstore such as Amazon.com. You can search for books written by Shakespeare using a search form at the bookstore's Web site. First, you type the text "Shakespeare" into the Author text box on the online form, and then you click a button to submit the keyword for the search process. This sends a request for another Web page to the Web server with the data "author=Shakespeare" embedded in the request. In other words, the Web browser tells the Web server "I want you to search your book inventory, and give me a list of all the books for whom Shakespeare is listed as the author."

The Web server interacts with its inventory database and returns a search results Web page containing a list of books in inventory authored by Shakespeare. Each book title in the list is actually a link built by the Web server to another Web page about the specific book. Assume that one of the links is to a book entitled *Romeo and Juliet*. Clicking the Romeo and Juliet link in the search results sends another request to the Web server for the Romeo and Juliet Web page. The Romeo and Juliet Web page is built by the Web server using another Web page template. The Web server accesses a book inventory database to get the book data — the picture, price, title, page count, inventory level, and so forth — and plugs that data into the correct place in the template.

When you purchase the book, the Web server adds a record containing your customer information and information about the book you just purchased to a sales database. The Web server also validates the credit card number in your customer information using the credit card issuer's database. The Web server then modifies the appropriate databases to update the book inventory, schedule the book shipment, and so forth.

Server-side technologies enable Web servers to access databases in order to create Web pages containing dynamic content. But for an e-business, storing content in databases and showing it to the user on demand carries with it an advantage not immediately obvious to those who haven't administered large Web sites. For example, as part of its marketing strategy, an e-business may allow users to access recent news stories and press releases about the e-business from its Web site. These new stories and press releases can be stored in a database that is easily updated and maintained by the e-business's Marketing Department. The Marketing Department employees don't need to know HTML to add the news stories and press releases to the Web site; all they need to do is update the database using a simple form and the Web server, using server-side templates and database access, does the rest.

Now that you've learned where Web servers store the variable data used to create dynamic content, you are ready to learn about two important server-side technologies that create that content: Macromedia ColdFusion and Microsoft Active Server Pages.

Macromedia ColdFusion

One popular tool used today for creating database-driven Web sites is Macromedia's ColdFusion. ColdFusion is actually a set of two products: ColdFusion Studio and ColdFusion Server. **ColdFusion Studio** is used to create Web sites by using templates that the Web server completes on the fly to create the Web pages seen by viewers. **ColdFusion Server** runs on the Web server itself, building and sending Web pages to users as necessary. ColdFusion templates include embedded tags (written in a special markup language called **ColdFusion Markup Language**, or **CFML**). ColdFusion Server interprets these embedded tags *before* sending the page to the viewer. Because Web browsers do not recognize these tags and cannot, on their own, access a database stored on a server, populating a ColdFusion template with variable information from a database and interpreting the CFML tags must take place on the server side.

Figure 4-14 shows tags used in a ColdFusion search form template. The following list explains these template tags:

- The <FORM METHOD> tag identifies the beginning of a Web page form and tells the Web browser to expect some data to be entered.
- The first < INPUT TYPE> tag identifies the data as text and an author's name.
- The second <INPUT TYPE> tag specifies that a search process begins when the user clicks a Submit button.
- The </FORM> tag specifies the end of the form.

In this example, when the user types "Shakespeare" in the search form's text box and clicks the Submit button, the Web browser sends a request to the ColdFusion Web server for a booklist page where Form.author = "Shakespeare."

```
Type the name of the author in this box:

<FORM METHOD="POST"
   ACTION="BOOKLIST.CFM">
<INPUT TYPE="TEXT"NAME="AUTHOR">
<INPUT TYPE="SUBMIT" NAME="SEARCH FOR THIS AUTHOR">
</FORM>
```

Figure 4-14
ColdFusion search form template instructions

The ColdFusion server receives the request for a list of all books by Shakespeare and processes the template instructions that result in the creation of a search results page. Figure 4-15 shows some ColdFusion template instructions. The following list explains these instructions:

- A search for specific records in a database table is called a **query**. Thus, the <CFQUERY> tag initiates the process of finding all of the records in the "books" table of the "booksdatabase" where author = "Shakespeare." The complete query (which consists of the first four lines in Figure 4-15) tells the server to sort the records by title and save the query results temporarily with the query name "getbooksbyauthor." The </CFQUERY> tag ends the query instructions.
- Next, the template specifies that a text message (Thank you for shopping at our bookstore. Below are the books by the author you specified:) be added to the search results page immediately before the search results booklist
- The <CFLOOP QUERY> tag instructs the ColdFusion server to read the "getbooksbyauthor" query and create a Web page that lists the books found in the query (that is, all books by Shakespeare). The list of books includes the book title, publisher's name, book type (hardcover or softcover), and price. The </CFLOOP> tag ends the instructions.
- Finally, the template specifies that another text message (Didn't find the book you're looking for? Click the "Back" button in your browser to search again.) appears below the booklist.

Figure 4-15
ColdFusion query template instructions

After the Web page with the search results is created, it is sent back to the Web browser that originally requested it. Although creating a Web page listing a few books by Shakespeare seems like a complicated process, this ColdFusion template only has to be created once. It can then be used millions of times to allow viewers to search for specific books by any author.

Keep in mind that an e-business using templates created in ColdFusion Studio must also use the Macromedia's ColdFusion Server as its Web server application. Only ColdFusion Server recognizes and acts on the ColdFusion template tags. Other Web servers simply send the tags to the user's Web browser, as if they were part of the HTML code, and the Web browser either ignores them or displays error messages.

Microsoft Active Server Pages

Microsoft is a natural entrant into the server-side data access market, because the company publishes Web server software (IIS) and two very popular database applications (Access, which is part of the Office suite, and SQL Server, a database capable of storing and managing very large amounts of data). Microsoft's offering in this market is called **Active Server Pages (ASP)**. An individual Active Server Page is similar to an HTML document except that it contains small programs called **scripts** and has a file extension of .asp instead of .html.

TIP

ASPs can also be created in two Web development applications by Microsoft, FrontPage and Visual InterDev.

Like ColdFusion templates, ASPs reside on a Web server and contain ASP scripts that perform similar functions to ColdFusion tags. ASP scripts can perform many operations, like modifying the page layout to fit the user's screen before it leaves the Web server, or performing a loan calculation for an online mortgage calculator.

ASP scripts are usually written in VBScript, a programming language that is very much like Microsoft's Visual Basic language. The most important advantage of VBScript is its ability to access databases and create dynamic content as part of the Web page request by a viewer. ASP can be created in any text editor by a programmer familiar with VBScript.

ASP scripts are in some ways more flexible than ColdFusion templates, allowing a Web author more precise control over how Web pages are generated. This flexibility comes at a price, however. ASP scripts can be longer and more complex than the equivalent ColdFusion templates and tags. However, because of ASP's greater ability to interact with other Microsoft software and the established base of Visual Basic programmers, ASP is gaining ground on ColdFusion.

Perl and PHP

A third tool used to get data from a database and display it in HTML format is also gaining market share. In 1994, a Danish programmer named Rasmus Lerdorf, who was adept with UNIX computers, created **Personal Home Page** tools or **PHP**. Like ColdFusion, PHP allows a Web author to create server-side templates and embed non-HTML programming commands into them. Lerdorf chose to make PHP commands very similar to those used in a popular programming language called **Practical Extraction and Reporting Language**, or **Perl**, which is used to extract information from text files. Because Perl was easy for most Web authors to learn, it was a natural choice for extracting information from databases. Lerdorf created PHP to embed Perl scripts in HTML code.

PHP scripts are interpreted and executed by a Web server, in much the same way as ColdFusion templates and tags and ASP scripts. Because Perl was in common use when Lerdorf created PHP, many programmers were able to use PHP as soon as Lerdorf released PHP into the public domain — meaning anyone was allowed to use PHP and modify it.

The original version of PHP wasn't very fast — a given Web server couldn't transmit as many pages or do as many database searches with PHP as with ASP scripts or ColdFusion templates and tags. But, most of the original performance issues were solved by the time PHP 4.0 was released. PHP is often used with a free but powerful database server called mySQL. For those setting up Web servers on a budget, combining the Linux operating system with Perl, PHP, and mySQL make a powerful and entirely free solution for database-driven Web sites.

> **TIP**
>
> In the past few years, a great deal of research has been done on clustering — dividing up tasks across multiple servers — on the Linux operating system. As a result of this research, some very large e-businesses are moving their own Web sites away from one or two huge servers to many small servers running Linux. PHP which runs on Linux is becoming a serious competitor to ColdFusion and ASP.

Now that you've learned about some of the server-side technologies that enable e-businesses to offer their Web site users customized information, let's look at some client-side technologies that make Web sites more useful.

Client-Side Technologies

In the previous section, you learned about the elegant and simple request/receive interaction between Web servers and Web browsers. Each cycle is neat and clean, with no loose ends afterwards. However, there is a downside to the lack of ongoing communications. Some situations call for continuous connection between a Web browser and a Web server. For example, assume that an online trading service similar to Datek Online Financial Services LLC wants to allow its customers to watch the movement of a specific stock. The developers of the online trading service's Web site have a few options.

They can choose to update a page on the Web server every 10 seconds using server-side technologies, and then have customers' Web browsers reload the updated Web page every 10 seconds. (Automatic reloading is accomplished with the meta refresh HTML tag. This tag is a simple way to tell a Web browser to re-request a Web page or go to a new Web page after a specific period of time.) However, in this scenario a customer might miss an update by as much as 9.99 seconds, assuming the update occurs right after the page is reloaded. This might not be a problem for customers who trade infrequently and in small amounts. But if the online trading e-business wants to attract customers who trade frequently in large amounts, it must provide faster updates. Rather than forcing all clients to rerequest Web pages every half second, a method of "pushing" data updates from the server to the viewer as they occur via a continuous connection is a better choice.

As you learned in Chapter 3, virtual ports are used to make sure that incoming data gets to the application that can make use of it. An Applet uses a free virtual port to connect to a stock server or a sports scores server, and then the applet monitors the virtual port for messages from the server.

To make a continuous connection between the Web browser and the Web server, the online trading service's customers can download (via their Web browser) and run an **applet** — a small program that runs on the customer's computer. The applet then maintains a continuous connection to the Web server and receives and displays stock price changes as they occur. Two real-world examples of this continuous connection are Datek's stock ticker and ESPN Internet Ventures' live scoreboard.

Java and the Virtual Sandbox

Two major problems had to be solved to make applets practical: security and interoperability. Because allowing an unfamiliar program like an applet to run on a computer is a bit like handing your car keys to a stranger, customers wanting instant updates needed to feel protected from potential disasters. In theory, a Web browser allows applets to run in an enclosed environment, which protects the rest of the computer from a badly or maliciously written applet. This enclosed environment is sometimes referred to as a **sandbox**, implying that it's a separate space in which an applet can "play." The walls of the sandbox are designed to keep the applets' access to files, CPU time, and other resources tightly controlled. But, the sandbox approach doesn't always work — security holes in sandbox walls can allow malicious applets to access and alter or delete files stored on the computer running the applet. Security holes can be fixed by updating the applet software when the holes are discovered.

TIP

JavaScript is a scripting language that contains some of the features of its big brother, the more complex Java programming language. JavaScript can perform many tasks such as applying special formatting to Web page text when the mouse pointer is positioned over the text. JavaScript can be embedded in HTML and DHTML pages where the scripts are executed in a Web browser. JavaScript can also be embedded in ASP where the scripts are executed by the Web server before the Web page is sent to the Web browser.

The second hurdle for applet developers is the need for applets to run on multiple operating systems, including several versions of Windows, many flavors of UNIX, and multiple generations of Macintosh computers.

Computer scientists at Sun Microsystems, Inc. began working on a way to solve both of these problems at once. First, they proposed a better sandbox, one that not only protected a computer from the applet, but that would appear the same to any applet on any operating system. Thus, the sandbox had to fool the applet into believing it was running on a virtual machine inside the computer. This virtual machine had to behave the same way on all computers, running the same commands, and so forth in all operating systems. With this improved sandbox, a customer could run an applet, confident that the applet would not be able to damage the customer's computer files.

Sun's computer scientists had been working on a new programming language, designed to run on many different types of electronic devices, from remote controls for toasters to computers. Programmable toasters haven't panned out yet, but this new programming language's interoperability turned out to be exactly what was needed for an applet's sandbox. Sun called this language **Java**, and created **Java Virtual Machines**, or **JVMs**, for nearly every major operating system. Now, an applet written in Java and downloaded with a Web page runs in the JVM — the protected virtual sandbox.

TECH CASE Dancing the Marimba

Growing up in Berkeley, California, Kim Polese (pronounced "Polazy") spent many of her free hours in the Lawrence Hall of Science at the University of California at Berkeley playing with computers. While in her teens, Polese's interest in computer technology continued to grow and she began thinking about one day starting her own company. After graduating from the University of California at Berkeley in 1985 with a degree in Biophysics, Polese joined IntelliCorp Inc., a company specializing in developing artificial intelligence technology. Disenchanted with her job, Polese left IntelliCorp in 1989 to join a technical support group at Sun Microsystems, Inc. Eventually growing bored with her technical support duties, Polese jumped at a chance to move into marketing, where she could be more creative and assume more responsibility, ultimately becoming the product manager for Sun's C++ programming language.

Meanwhile, in the early 1990s, a special Sun research team, called the Green Team, was working on a new programming technology called "Oak." The goal of this technology was to allow consumer electronics (such as VCRs and cell phones) to communicate with each other via a handheld device. Like many developing technologies, the original intent for Oak didn't pan out. However, Oak had a powerful advantage: it could be used to write programs for any platform and any application. Because of this interoperability, Oak had the potential to become a powerful tool for Web developers.

Excited about the possibilities for Oak, Polese signed on as its product manager and quickly became involved in everything, including changing its name to "Java," managing Java's product debut in the spring of 1995, and touting Java at trade shows. By the first half of 1996, Java had taken the Web development world by storm as dozens of licensing arrangements were made, including agreements with Microsoft and Netscape. Clearly, Java was destined to become an integral part of Web development.

In early 1996, Polese realized her teenage dream by leaving Sun to join with three other Java team members in forming a new e-business named Marimba, Inc. Marimba, Inc. provides e-businesses with products that help manage their mobile, desktop, and server systems using Web technologies such as Java. As of September 30, 2001, Marimba, Inc. (Figure 4-16) reported more than 200 employees and year-to-date 2001 revenues in excess of $33 million. Polese served as president and CEO of Marimba until July 2000, and as of this writing is Marimba's chairman and chief strategy officer.

Continued

Figure 4-16
Marimba,
Inc.

ActiveX

Microsoft has introduced tools1 similar to Java to enhance the Web experience. Microsoft's competing technology is called **ActiveX**. Active X allows small programs, called **Active X controls**, to be transmitted from the Web server to a Web browser where they are run in "containers," much as Java applets run in virtual machines. The ActiveX technologies allow these controls to be written in several Microsoft languages, including the already popular and widespread Visual Basic. ActiveX can run on several operating systems, but some controls run only in Microsoft's Internet Explorer Web browser.

Like Java, ActiveX is designed to allow programmers to develop programs one time and then run the programs without additional modifications on any operating system or computer platform that supports ActiveX. Like Java, the ActiveX sandbox isn't perfect, and Microsoft does release software updates from time to time that provide security improvements. The capabilities of ActiveX controls fall between Java and JavaScript. ActiveX is useful for Web page animations, but for more complex functions and those that require applets to communicate with servlets (applets that run on a server), Java is the more robust option.

As is frequently the case with Microsoft, however, ActiveX was only the first salvo in Microsoft's response to Java. Microsoft also introduced a new online programming language to compete with Java, called C# ("C sharp") but as of this writing C# has been folded into the larger Microsoft .NET initiative umbrella. C# promises to merge the speed and flexibility of an older but still popular C programming language with the ease of use of Visual Basic.

In this chapter you learned about the tools (such as HTML, XML, FrontPage, Dreamweaver, Photoshop, ColdFusion, Active Server Pages, Java, and Active X controls) that are used by e-businesses to create exciting, effective, interactive Web pages. In the next chapter you will learn about the wireless technologies that may revolutionize e-business.

...A DORM ROOM SUCCESS

Not only could the Web make it easy to provide detailed information about Dell Computer Corporation products, but it also had great potential as a tool for gathering information about customers' preferences. What if customers could design their own computers by choosing the features they wanted, and then buy the custom-designed computers online? What if the company could provide high-quality customer support online? In 1994, Dell Computer Corporation (Figure 4-17) went online with its Web site, and by 1996, customers could buy Dell computers online at the Web site.

Today, the Dell Computer Corporation Web sites make extensive use of high-quality graphics, animations, online forms, and database interactivity to provide customers with exciting and useful online experiences. By using graphic editors, animation creators, and other Web development technologies, Dell Computer Corporation has created some of the world's most effective and busiest e-business Web sites. As of January 2002, Dell Computer Corporation reported more than 600 million page requests quarterly at over 80 international Web sites presented in at least 20 different languages or dialects!

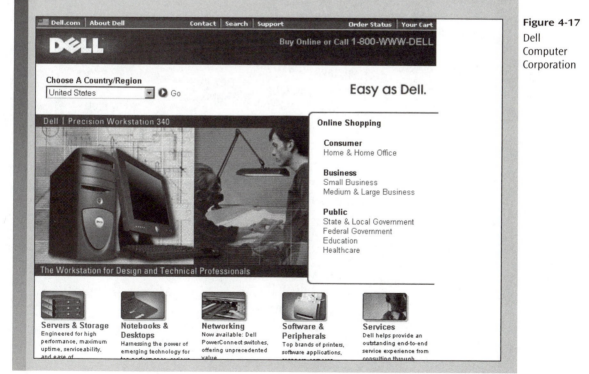

Figure 4-17
Dell Computer Corporation

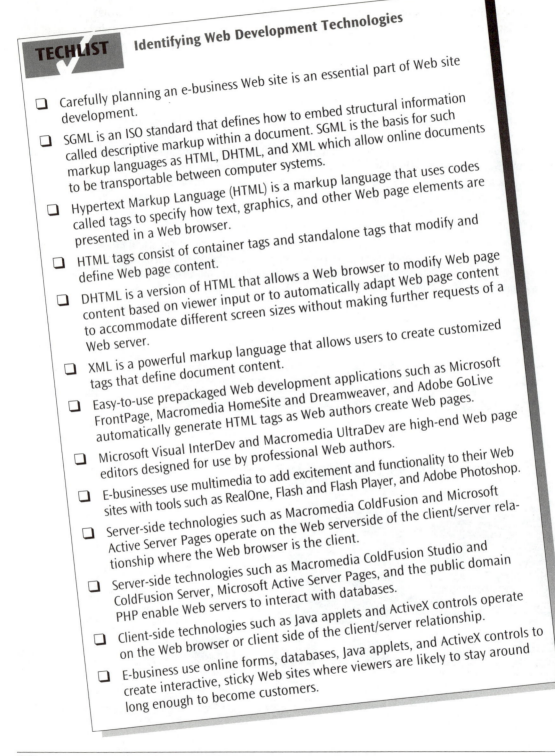

TECHLIST Identifying Web Development Technologies

❏ Carefully planning an e-business Web site is an essential part of Web site development.

❏ SGML is an ISO standard that defines how to embed structural information called descriptive markup within a document. SGML is the basis for such markup languages as HTML, DHTML, and XML which allow online documents to be transportable between computer systems.

❏ Hypertext Markup Language (HTML) is a markup language that uses codes called tags to specify how text, graphics, and other Web page elements are presented in a Web browser.

❏ HTML tags consist of container tags and standalone tags that modify and define Web page content.

❏ DHTML is a version of HTML that allows a Web browser to modify Web page content based on viewer input or to automatically adapt Web page content to accommodate different screen sizes without making further requests of a Web server.

❏ XML is a powerful markup language that allows users to create customized tags that define document content.

❏ Easy-to-use prepackaged Web development applications such as Microsoft FrontPage, Macromedia HomeSite and Dreamweaver, and Adobe GoLive automatically generate HTML tags as Web authors create Web pages.

❏ Microsoft Visual InterDev and Macromedia UltraDev are high-end Web page editors designed for use by professional Web authors.

❏ E-businesses use multimedia to add excitement and functionality to their Web sites with tools such as RealOne, Flash and Flash Player, and Adobe Photoshop.

❏ Server-side technologies such as Macromedia ColdFusion and Microsoft Active Server Pages operate on the Web serverside of the client/server relationship where the Web browser is the client.

❏ Server-side technologies such as Macromedia ColdFusion Studio and ColdFusion Server, Microsoft Active Server Pages, and the public domain PHP enable Web servers to interact with databases.

❏ Client-side technologies such as Java applets and ActiveX controls operate on the Web browser or client side of the client/server relationship.

❏ E-business use online forms, databases, Java applets, and ActiveX controls to create interactive, sticky Web sites where viewers are likely to stay around long enough to become customers.

Key Terms

Acrobat Reader
Active Server Pages (ASP)
ActiveX
ActiveX controls
applet
ColdFusion Markup
    Language (CFML)
ColdFusion Server
ColdFusion Studio
container tags
database-driven
descriptive markup
Document Type Definition (DTD)
Dreamweaver
dynamic content
Dynamic Hypertext Markup
    Language (DHTML)

Extensible Markup Language (XML)
Flash
Flash Player
form
FrontPage
GoLive
HomeSite
Hypertext Markup
    Language (HTML)
Java
Java Virtual Machines (JVMs)
markup languages
parsing
Personal Home Page (PHP)
Photoshop
plug-in
Portable Document Format (PDF)

Practical Extraction and Reporting
    Language (Perl)
query
Quicktime
RealOne
sandbox
scripts
server-side technologies
standalone tags
Standard Generalized Markup
    Language (SGML)
streaming media
tags
UltraDev
Visual InterDev
Windows Media Player
WYSIWYG

Review Questions

1. Perl is a:
   a. Markup language used to instruct a Web browser how to display Web page contents.
   b. Web development software application.
   c. Programming language used to develop Web server database interoperability.
   d. Markup language with customizable tags used to define content.

2. The ISO standard that defines a document's structure by specifying descriptive markup within a document is:
   a. HTML.
   b. SGML.
   c. DHTML.
   d. UML.

3. The markup language that uses customizable tags to define content is:
   a. HTML.
   b. SGML.
   c. UML.
   d. XML.

4. Which of the following is not a popular Web development application?
   a. FrontPage
   b. Dreamweaver
   c. ColdFusion Server
   d. GoLive

5. The popular software application that has done more than any other to advance the use of graphics on Web pages is:
   a. Microsoft.NET.
   b. Photoshop.
   c. DHTML.
   d. ActiveX.

6. Microsoft ActiveX technologies are direct competitors of:
   a. Java technologies.
   b. Flash technologies.
   c. DHTML technologies.
   d. ASP technologies.

7. Java applets run in:
   a. HTML tags.
   b. ASP scripts.
   c. JVMs.
   d. ActiveX controls.

8. Which of the following tools should an e-business wanting to exchange large amounts of information with its business partners specify?
   a. SGML
   b. XML
   c. ASP
   d. ColdFusion Studio

9. A high-end Web development application suitable for use by professional Web developers is:
   a. Visual InterDev.
   b. DHTML.
   c. Active Server Pages.
   d. Java.

10. Which of the following Web development applications provides a concurrent view of the generated HTML code as a user creates Web page content?
    a. ASP
    b. Dreamweaver
    c. HomeSite
    d. GoLive

11. An applet is a small program downloaded by a Web browser that runs on a viewer's computer. **True or False?**

12. Two types of HTML tags are container tags and standalone tags. **True or False?**

13. DHTML is used to add animation to Web pages without running server-side scripts. **True or False?**

14. New Web server technologies allow Web pages to be built on the fly from information stored on the Web server. **True or False?**

15. ColdFusion Studio uses embedded tags written in HTML to interact with databases. **True or False?**

16. RealNetworks, Inc. was originally founded as Progressive Networks by Kim Polese. **True or False?**

17. An important document interchange format for the Internet is Adobe Acrobat. **True or False?**

18. PHP is a Web development software application licensed by Microsoft. **True or False?**

19. The Perl language was originally written to extract information from text files. **True or False?**

20. Microsoft FrontPage is always a good choice for a tool to create a complex e-business Web site. **True or False?**

Exercises

1. Using Internet search tools or other relevant resources, such as those listed at the end of this chapter, research different Web browser plug-ins available for the Web browser you use. Then write a one- or two-page essay listing at least five plug-ins, explaining the purpose of each, and the URL where each plug-in can be downloaded.

2. Using Internet search tools or other relevant resources, such as those listed at the end of this chapter, research the Microsoft Active Server Pages scripting language. Then create a one- or two-page essay describing Active Server Pages (ASP) and its uses.

3. Using Internet search tools or other relevant resources, such as those listed at the end of this chapter, research the Practical Extraction and Report Language (Perl). Then write a one- or two-page essay describing the Perl programming language and its uses.

4. Using The Wayback Machine at the Internet Archive Web site, locate old pages from the Amazon.com Web site. Print at least two pages. Then compare the old pages with current Amazon.com Web pages. Write a one- or two-page essay discussing how the pages have changed. Have evolving Web development technologies made the Amazon.com customer's online experience better? If so, how?

5. Using Internet search tools and other relevant resources, such as those listed at the end of this chapter, research several Web sites or articles that discuss the importance of carefully planning a Web site and the impact of multimedia on Web site attractiveness and usability. Then write a one- or two-page essay discussing the importance of planning in Web development and the advantages and disadvantages of incorporating multimedia in an e-business Web site.

CASE PROJECTS

◆ 1 ◆

You work for an e-business named DraftTime that sells drafting and engineering supplies online and that uses a variety of Microsoft Corporation products throughout the company. Your supervisor recently read an article that briefly introduced the .NET initiative by Microsoft. She is drafting a 5-year plan for DraftTime and wants to know more about Microsoft .NET and how it may affect your company's future operation. She asks you to meet with her next week to discuss Microsoft .NET in more detail. Using the Internet or other resources, create an outline you can use to discuss the Microsoft .NET initiative, including its purpose, current status, and potential impact on the future of DraftTime.

◆ 2 ◆

Note: This case assumes you are using the Internet Explorer Web browser and that the Notepad application is loaded on your computer. If you are using another Web browser or do not have Notepad, your instructor may modify the instructions to display and print the source HTML code.

You donate several hours a month to a local children's charity called LuvOurChildren. You just finished creating a simple Web site for LuvOurChildren using a prepackaged Web development application. Now, you would like to learn more about the HTML code the package generated as you created the Web page content. Using Internet resources, locate several online HTML tutorials. Review the tutorials and work through at least one tutorial of your choice. Then, using the Source command on the Internet Explorer Web browser View menu, display the source code for an existing Web page in Notepad and print it. Next, write a one- or two-page paper listing at least five HTML standalone or container tags in the printed Web page source and explaining the instructions the tags provide for the Web browser.

◆ 3 ◆

At the last meeting of the E-Business Technologies Users Group, Scott Lee asked about the similarities and differences between Microsoft's ActiveX technologies and Sun Microsystems' Java technologies. You volunteer to present a brief overview of the two technologies at the next monthly meeting. Using Internet or other applicable resources, research the origins, similarities, and differences between ActiveX and Java technologies. Include any current news about the relationship of Sun Microsystems and Microsoft in regards to Java and ActiveX. Then prepare an outline of your research to guide your presentation.

Because you and a classmate need extra money, you decide to start a small e-business offering personal concierge services to other students or local professionals too busy to run their own errands. You've worked together and prepared a business plan. The next step is to create an attractive and serviceable Web site to advertise your business and collect information on potential customers. Your classmate wants to create the Web site from scratch using HTML, but you think it might be easier to use a prepackaged Web development application. Meet with your classmate to discuss the issue and make a decision on which approach to take. If you choose to use a prepackaged Web development application, evaluate different products and select the product you plan to use. Then create a 5–10 slide presentation using Microsoft PowerPoint or other presentation tool to explain the details of the name of the e-business and your Web development decision, including the rationale for your decision. Present your e-business and Web development decision to a group of classmates selected by your instructor.

Useful Links

Active-X.com
www.active-x.com/

Arbortext, Inc. — XML White Papers and Online Seminars
www.arbortext.com/html/white_papers_webinars.html

ASP101
www.asp101.com/

ASPFree.com
www.aspfree.com/main.asp

DevelopersNetwork.com — Web Developers Resources
webdevelopment.developersnetwork.com/

DevX — IT Development Resources
www.devx.com/

"How do they do that with HTML?"
www.tashian.com/htmlguide/index.html

HTML Goodies
www.htmlgoodies.com/

HTML White Papers
www.itpapers.com/cgi/SubcatIT.pl?scid=182

Internet.com — BrowserWatch Plug-in Plaza
browserwatch.Internet.com/plug-in.html

Java Boutique
javaboutique.Internet.com/

Java Tutorial
java.sun.com/docs/books/tutorial/

JavaWorld — Online Magazine
www.javaworld.com/

LearnASP
www.learnasp.com/aspng/index.aspx

Microsoft MSDN Library
msdn.microsoft.com/library/default.asp?url=/
    workshop/components/activex/intro.asp

NCSA Beginner's Guide to HTML
archive.ncsa.uiuc.edu//General/Internet/WWW/
    HTMLPrimer.html

Northern Light Special Edition: XML
special.northernlight.com/xml/index.html

Perl Coders
www.perlcoders.com/

Perl.com
www.perl.com/

PowerASP
www.powerasp.com/

Rational Software Corporation — UML Resource Center
www.rational.com/uml/index.jsp

Sun Microsystems — Java Technology Page
java.sun.com/

The ASP Resource Index
www.aspin.com/

The Perl Journal at SysAdmin
www.sysadminmag.com/tpj/

The Unofficial ActiveX Guide
www.longbright.freeserve.co.uk/oldindex.html

The XML Cover Pages — XML/SGML Standards
www.oasis-open.org/cover/sgml-xml.html

Tips, Tricks, How-To, and Beyond — Beginners HTML Guide
tips-tricks.com/begin.asp

Usable Web — Web Site Usability Links
www.usableweb.com/

W3C — Extensible Markup Language (XML)
www.w3.org/XML/

W3C — Overview of SGML Resources
www.w3.org/MarkUp/SGML/

W3Schools.com — Online Web Tutorials (HTML, XML, Browser Scripting, Server Scripting, .NET, Web Building)
www.w3schools.com/default.asp

Web Developer's Journal
www.webdevelopersjournal.com/

XML Magazine
www.xmlmag.com/

XML.com
www.xml.com/

Links to Web Sites or Companies Noted in This Chapter

ABCNEWS.com
www.abcnews.com

Adobe Systems Incorporated
www.adobe.com/

Amazon.com
www.amazon.com

Apple Computer, Inc.
www.apple.com

Datek
www.datek.com/

Dell Computer Corporation
www.dell.com/us/en/gen/default.htm

Ego Media
www.egomedia.com/

ESPN
msn.espn.go.com/main.html

Internet Archive – Wayback Machine
www.archive.org/

Macromedia, Inc.
www.macromedia.com/

Marimba, Inc.
www.marimba.com/

Microsoft Corporation
www.microsoft.com/com/

National Hockey League
www.nhl.com

Netscape Communications
www.netscape.com

RealNetworks, Inc.
www.realnetworks.com/

Sun Microsystems, Inc.
www.sun.com/

The Coca-Cola Company
www.cocacola.com

TrueColor Studios
www.truecolorstudios.com/

For Additional Review

Andrews, Jean. 2001. *i-Net+ Guide to Internet Technologies*. Boston: Course Technology.

Arbortext, Inc. 1995. "A Guide to SGML (Standard Generalized Markup Language) and Its Role in Information Management," *An Arbortext SGML White Paper*. Available online at: www.arbortext.com/data/getting_started_with _SGML/getting_started_with_sgml.html.

ASP101. 2002. "ASP Source Code Examples," *Internet.com*. Available online at: www.asp101.com/samples/viewasp.asp?file= database%2Easp.

Dell Computer Corporation. 2002. "About Dell: The Dell Story." Available online at: www.us.dell.com/ us/en/gen/corporate/michael_003_story.htm.

Dell Computer Corporation. 2002. "Dell at a Glance." Available online at: www.dell.com/us/en/gen/ corporate/factpack_000.htm.

Dell Computer Corporation. 2002. "Dell History." Available online at: www.dell.com/us/en/gen/ corporate/factpack_004.htm.

Dell Computer Corporation. 2002. "Michael S. Dell." Available online at: www.dell.com/us/en/gen/ corporate/biography/biography_generic_michael _dell.htm.

Dell, Michael and Fredman, Catherine. 2000. *Direct from Dell: Strategies that Revolutionized an Industry*. New York: HarperCollins.

Fallside, David C., Editor. 2001. "XML Scheme Part 0: Primer," *World Wide Web Consortium*, May 2. Available online at: www.w3.org/TR/xmlschema-0/.

Ferranti, Marc. 2001. "Glaser Touts RealOne as 'Universal Platform'," *CNN.com SCI/TECH*, December 13. Available online at: www.cnn.com/ 2001/TECH/industry/12/13/realone.glaser.idg/.

Forta, Ben, et al. 2001. *ColdFusion 5 Web Application Construction Kit*. Indianapolis, IN: Que.

Gosselin. 2001. *JavaScript - Introductory, Second Edition*. Boston: Course Technology.

Gray, Douglas F. 2001. "Archiving the Net all the 'Wayback' to 1996," *InfoWorld*, October 25. Available online at: www.idg.net/crd_Web_719143_103.html.

Greene, Jay et al. 2001. "Rob Glaser is Racing Upstream," *BusinessWeek Online*, September 3. Available online at: www.businessweek.com/ magazine/content/01_36/b3747602.htm.

Guthrie and Soe. 2001. *Dreamweaver 4.0*. Boston: Course Technology.

Hattori, James. 2000. "Profile of RealNetworks CEO Rob Glaser," *CNN.com Technology*, August 11. Available online at: www.cnn.com/2000/TECH/computing/ 08/11/glaser/.

Jones, Del. 2001. "Michael Dell to be Named CEO of the Year," *USATODAY.com*, July 18. Available online at: www.usatoday.com/life/cyber/invest/ 2001-07-18-dell-ceo-of-year.htm.

Jones, Jeff. 2002. "XML 101," *SWYNK.com*. Available online at: www.swynk.com/friends/jones/articles/ xml_101.asp.

Kaparthi and Kaparthi. 2001. *ColdFusion*. Boston: Course Technology.

Knowleton and Barksdale. 2001. *Programming BASICS, Using Microsoft Visual Basic, C++, HTML, and Java*. Boston: Course Technology.

Lerdorf, Rasmus. 2002. "Rasmus Lerdorf," *Lerdorf.com*. Available online at: lerdorf.com/bio.php.

Lyons, Daniel. 2000. "Michael Dell's Second Act," *Forbes.com*, April 17. Available online at: www.forbes.com/global/2000/0417/0308102a.html.

Marimba, Inc. 2001. "Corporate Fact Sheet." Available online at: www.marimba.com/aboutus/ corporate_info/corporate_fact_sheet.html.

Marimba, Inc. 2001. "Corporate Profile." Available online at: www.marimba.com/aboutus/ corporate_info/corporate_profile.html.

Marimba, Inc. 2001. "Management Team: Kim Polese." Available online at: www.marimba.com/ aboutus/corporate_info/about-kpolese.shtml.

Microsoft Corporation. 2002. ".NET Defined." Available online at: www.microsoft.com/ net/whatis.asp.

Microsoft Corporation. 2002. "C# Introduction and Overview." Available online at: msdn.microsoft.com/vstudio/nextgen/technology/ csharpintro.asp.

Morneau and Batistick. 2001. *Active Server Pages*. Boston: Course Technology.

Napier, H. Albert and Judd, Philip J. 2002. *Mastering and Using FrontPage 2002*. Boston: Course Technology.

Neilsen, Jakob and Tahir, Marie. 2002. *Homepage Usability: 50 Websites Deconstructed*. Indianapolis, IN: New Riders Publishing.

Perl Mongers. 2001. "The Timeline of Perl and Its Culture," *Perl.org*, May 5. Available online at: history.perl.org/PerlTimeline.pdf.

PHP Manual. 2002. "A Brief History of PHP," *PHP Center*. www.php-center.de/en-html-manual/intro-history.html.

Rational Software Corporation. 1999. *OMG Unified Modeling Language Specification Version 1.3*, June. Available online at: www.rational.com/media/uml/post.pdf.

RealNetworks, Inc. 2002. "Charitable Giving at RealNetworks, Inc." Available online at: www.realnetworks.com/company/giving/index.html.

RealNetworks, Inc. 2002. "Company Profile." Available online at: www.realnetworks.com/company/index.html.

RealNetworks, Inc. 2002. "Management Bios." Available online at: www.realnetworks.com/company/investor/execbios.html.

Reding. 2002. *Adobe Photoshop 6.0 Introductory - Design Professional*. Boston: Course Technology.

Reid, Robert H. 1997. *Architect's of the Web: 1,000 Days That Built the Future of Business*. New York: John Wiley & Sons.

Segaller, Stephen. 1999. *Nerds 2.0.1, A Brief History of the Internet*. New York: TV Books, L.L.C.

Thurrott, Paul. 2000. "Microsoft .NET in Plain English," *Paul Thurrott's SuperSite for Windows: Windows & .Net Magazine*," July 13. Available online at: http://www.winsupersite.com/showcase/dotnet_backgrounder.asp.

Time Digital. 2000. "Michael Dell," *Time Digital Archive: Cyber Elite Top 50*. Available online at: www.time.com/time/digital/cyberelite/10.html.

Volkheimer, Jeff. 2002. "A Quick Introduction to XML Schemas," *DevCentral*. Available online at: devcentral.iftech.com/articles/XML/intro_XML_schemas/default.php.

W3Schools.com. 2001. "Introduction to DHTML." Available online at: www.w3schools.com/dhtml/dhtml_intro.asp.

Zak. 2002. *CGI/Perl*. Boston: Course Technology.

CHAPTER **5**

Wireless Technologies

In this chapter, you will learn to:

Describe the status of wireless e-business today

Discuss the origins of wireless communications and the commercialization of the radio range of the electromagnetic spectrum

Describe two major short-range wireless technologies

Describe a wireless LAN and identify the IEEE 802.11 family of wireless LAN standards

Discuss pager, cellular, satellite, and other wireless networks

Describe the devices, protocols, and languages of the wireless Web

Identify expectations for future wireless e-business

Growing up in New Bedford, Massachusetts, Irwin Jacobs had a gift for science and math. However, he was directed toward hotel management after he graduated from high school because it was expected that he would follow his father into the restaurant business. After less than two years studying hotel management, he returned to his interest in math and science by switching his major to electrical engineering. After graduating from Cornell University, he moved on to the Massachusetts Institute of Technology (MIT) where he earned his M.S. and Ph.D. degrees in Electrical Engineering in only three years. Jacobs then accepted a position at MIT teaching electrical engineering.

In 1966 he packed up his young family and moved across the continent to take a teaching position with the University of California at San Diego. Not long after arriving in San Diego, Jacobs, along with two UCLA associates, Andrew Viterbi and Len Kleinrock, formed a consulting company called Linkabit, which received a contract from DARPA to help European universities, government agencies, and phone companies connect to the ARPANET. Linkabit continued to grow and Jacobs left the University of California to manage the company full time. In 1980 he sold Linkabit to another company but stayed on for another five years; however, in 1985 Jacobs left Linkabit to create another technology startup company, QUALCOMM Incorporated, to develop new commercial wireless technologies.

Traditional commercial wireless technologies relied on a radio signal transmitted on an unchanging frequency. One example of such a signal is an FM radio signal which can easily be found at the same MHz on the radio dial. For some time the military had been using a form of wireless communication called "spread spectrum" in which the wireless signal was deliberately varied from frequency to frequency according to a complex mathematical code known only to the sender and the receiver. This made it difficult for an enemy to jam or intercept the signal. Scientists at QUALCOMM made technological advances that enabled commercialization of a spread spectrum technology called Code Division Multiple Access or CDMA for cellular phones and networks. These advances allowed more signals to share the same bandwidth than were allowed by the other digital wireless technologies used at the time.

By 1989, Jacobs was relentlessly pitching QUALCOMM's CDMA wireless technologies for digital cellular networks, but the reigning telecom companies such as AT&T and Motorola Inc. had already adopted an earlier digital cellular technology called Time Division Multiple Access or TDMA. With an exploding cell phone market, the stakes were high. Could Jacobs successfully challenge the telecom titans?

Wireless E-Business

Wireless communications are increasingly part of everyone's personal and professional lives. You may already have encountered wireless devices of all kinds, including cellular phones, pagers, hand-held computers known as personal digital assistants or PDAs, laptop computers, and hybrid hand-held wireless devices that incorporate phone, pager, and computer features.

Probably the most familiar type of wireless transmission is a radio broadcast. But, the term "wireless technologies" also refers to things such as: a wireless LAN where a laptop computer can transmit a document to a printer three feet away; information transmitted between two PDAs; location positioning from an automobile; and medical images transmitted anywhere in the world via satellite networks. One of the most important wireless devices are digital cellular phones, which are morphing into hybrid devices some call smart phones. These devices are able to browse the Web, connect to corporate databases, hold voice or video calls, and conduct e-business transactions. Figure 5-1 illustrates some popular uses of wireless technologies.

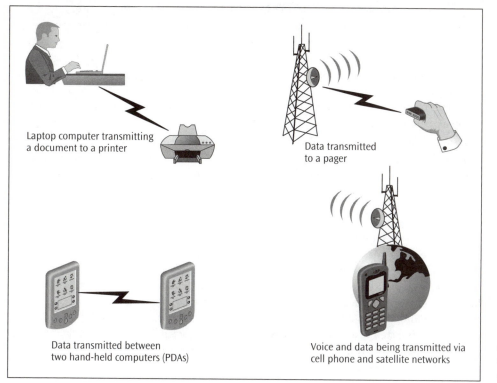

Laptop computer transmitting a document to a printer

Data transmitted to a pager

Data transmitted between two hand-held computers (PDAs)

Voice and data being transmitted via cell phone and satellite networks

Figure 5-1
Wireless transmissions

While estimates of U.S. and global wireless e-business (also called **mobile commerce** or **m-commerce**) markets vary, most analysts predict a huge explosion in the demand for wireless devices, wireless e-business services, and the number of wireless Web users within the next three to five years. For example, one research firm, The Intermarket Group, predicts wireless Web users in the U.S. will grow from two million in 2000 to 89 million by 2005, with the number of worldwide wireless Web users growing from 39 million in 2000 to 729 million by 2005.

Future expectations for the growth of wireless e-business services hinge on the powerful advantages wireless technologies offer, including:

◆ *Immediacy*: Wireless communications are immediate, in the sense that they provide instant gratification, anytime, anywhere. E-businesses can offer immediate services via a wireless device. Need to buy movie tickets while driving to the theater? Use your wireless device to buy them from an online ticketing service.

- *Personalization*: Wireless devices are very personal — even more so than personal computers — because few people share a cell phone or other wireless device. Because wireless devices are highly customizable in terms of style, color, and so forth many users see them as extensions of their personality. In Europe and Asia, for example, wireless devices are more likely to be considered personal accessories than communication tools. E-businesses can exploit this personalization by tailoring information about products and services to specific groups of wireless users. Like to stay informed about current events? News headlines via opt-in text messaging delivered over your wireless device can keep you up to date.
- *Localization*: Wireless users can be localized, meaning a wireless user's specific physical location can be determined through a wireless device. E-businesses can take advantage of localization to guess what a consumer might be interested in based on his or her physical location and then send the consumer advertising and special offers from nearby businesses. Walking past a pizza parlor at the mall? You could receive a coupon for a large pepperoni pizza via your wireless device as you walk past the store.

However, as you learn in this chapter, wireless e-business transactions and other activities (such as purchasing airline tickets, getting stock quotes, playing games, checking bank balances, sending e-mail, downloading video, or buying a soft drink from a vending machine) via a hand-held wireless device are, as of this writing, still more promise than reality. In fact, a 2001 study by the consulting firm Accenture reported that only about six percent of all the U.S. wireless device users who had access to the wireless Web actually accessed the Web with their wireless device.

The reasons for the lag between the expectations for wireless e-business and today's reality are complex. Among other things, this lag is due to the different ways wireless technologies developed globally, challenges to delivering data to wireless devices with greater speed, wireless security issues, challenges to presenting graphical Web-based information on a small device instead of a large computer monitor, and most importantly the lack of a "killer wireless application" — a single wireless application that is so compelling that it alone would drive user adoption (in the same way e-mail drove adoption of business and personal Internet access).

In this chapter, you review the components of the electromagnet spectrum and the origins and evolution of wireless communications. You also learn about modern wireless technologies and standards, the emergence of the wireless Web, and the role wireless technologies are expected to play in the future of e-business.

A Brief History of Wireless Communications

For hundreds of years, humans have tried various ways of communicating with others over long distances, including messenger relays, talking drums, vocalization across mountain passes and valleys, smoke signals from hill top fires, and messages attached to birds trained to fly to specific roosting places. The foundation for wireless technologies used to communicate over long distances was laid in the mid-nineteenth century.

Origins of Wireless Technologies

In 1865, James Clerk Maxwell published his theory of electromagnetic radiation, which described waves of radiating energy (light) passing through the air. In 1873 Heinrich Hertz corroborated Maxwell's theory when he proved that electricity could be transmitted via electromagnetic waves. In 1895, a young inventor named Guglielmo Marconi began experimenting with radio waves to send messages. As the twentieth Century dawned, scientists began to learn more about electromagnetic radiation and the different components of the **electromagnetic spectrum** — the name for all types of electromagnetic radiation.

The Electromagnetic Spectrum

Electromagnetic radiation is represented as a wave that cycles up and down in a pattern of energy peaks and valleys. The number of complete waves or cycles per second is referred to as a wave's **frequency**. Frequency is measured in **Hertz**, with one Hertz equal to one complete wave — one peak and one valley — each second. Two peaks and two valleys equal two Hertz per second, and so on. Various types of electromagnetic radiation have different frequencies.

The useful part of the electromagnetic spectrum starts at a frequency of about 1,000,000 Hertz, or one Megahertz (MHz) for AM radio waves and ranges up to 1×10^{20} (100,000,000,000,000,000,000, or 100 billion billion) Hertz for Gamma rays. Visible radiation, or light, occupies only a tiny fraction of the spectrum at about 1×10^{15} (1,000,000,000,000,000, or one million billion) Hertz.

Wavelength, the distance between peaks, is another defining feature of electromagnetic radiation: the longer the wavelength, the lower the frequency, and the lower the energy radiated. Figure 5-2 and the following list identify the components of the electromagnetic spectrum from the lowest frequency and longest wavelength to the highest frequency and shortest wavelength:

- *Radio*: Radio waves have the lowest frequency and the longest wavelength. Television, FM and AM radio transmissions, use radio waves.
- *Microwave*: Microwaves have the next shortest wavelength. You've probably used them to cook food quickly. Astronomers study microwaves generated throughout the universe.
- *Infrared*: Infrared (IR) waves have a slightly longer wavelength than visible radiation and are used today for wireless communications between computers and other devices and television remote controls.
- *Visible light*: Visible light is that portion of the electromagnetic spectrum that can be seen by the human eye. The range of colors that make up visible light (visible radiation) correspond to a range of frequencies, with red having the lowest frequency and violet having the highest. As frequency increases through the reds, yellows, greens, and blues of visible light, the energy of the radiation increases.
- *Ultraviolet*: Ultraviolet radiation is just beyond the violet end of the visible spectrum. At some point on the visible spectrum, violet light darkens and seems to disappear, but this is only because our eyes can no longer perceive the electromagnetic waves at this frequency.

◆ X-*rays*: X-rays have a very short wavelength and thus high-energy. As you know, X-rays are used by doctors and dentists to create pictures of bones and teeth. Both ultraviolet radiation and X-rays can be damaging in high doses.

◆ *Gamma rays*: Gamma rays have the highest energy, shortest wavelength, and highest frequency radiation and are generated by radioactive materials.

TIP

In the twentieth century, scientists experimented with bouncing electromagnetic waves off solid objects and measuring the time required for a wave to make a round-trip back to the transmitter. These experiments ultimately lead to a technology called radio detection and ranging, more commonly known as radar.

As you have learned, wavelength and frequency are related concepts. To understand this relationship, consider what happens as visible radiation changes from blue to indigo to violet. The change in color corresponds to a change in the light's wavelength: blue light has a longer wave length than violet, so as light changes from blue to violet, the light's wavelength decreases. As the wavelength shortens, more waves can pass a point in space in a second, so we also say that the frequency increases. Thus, a long electromagnetic wave travels at a low frequency, while a short wave travels at a high frequency.

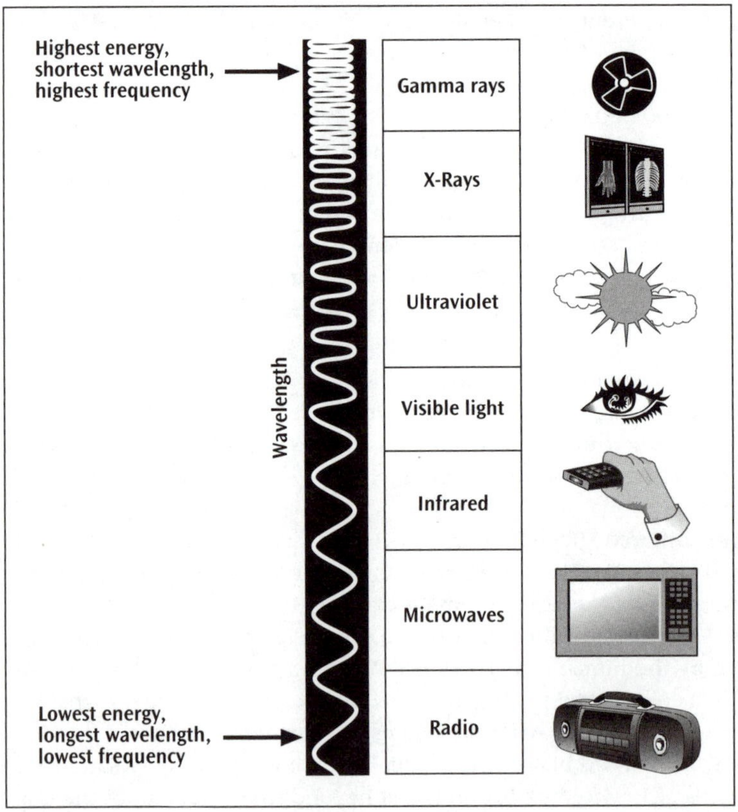

Figure 5-2

The electromagnetic spectrum

Highest energy, shortest wavelength, highest frequency → Gamma rays

X-Rays

Ultraviolet

Visible light

Infrared

Microwaves

Lowest energy, longest wavelength, lowest frequency → Radio

Wavelength

TECH CASE — A Rifle Shot Heard 'Round the World

The wireless age actually began in 1895, when an Italian inventor with little formal training, Guglielmo Marconi (Figure 5-3), demonstrated that it was possible to construct a transmitter and an antenna to emit and detect radio waves and that these waves could travel around obstacles. Most scientists of the day knew about electromagnetic radiation, but believed electromagnetic waves could only travel in a straight line. Marconi's simple experiment placed an assistant approximately three kilometers (1.9 miles) away and behind a hill. Marconi then transmitted the letter "S" (three dots in the Morse code alphabet) via a crude radio transmitter. When the assistant received the letter "S" on his receiver he fired a rifle to let Marconi know that the transmission was a success. Marconi's wireless transmission was man's first use of the electro-magnetic spectrum beyond visible light.

While the Italian government showed no interest in Marconi's discoveries, the British government (with its vast territories spread around the globe) immediately perceived the usefulness of wireless transmissions. In 1897 the British government began providing Marconi the support he needed to continue his experiments and ultimately patent his discoveries. On December 12, 1901, Marconi and his assistant witnessed the world's first wireless transatlantic radio transmission from Cornwall, England to Signal Hill, St. John's, Newfoundland and in 1909 Marconi won the Nobel prize for physics. Thanks to Marconi, the world has now experienced over 100 years of wireless communications!

Figure 5-3
Guglielmo Marconi

Now that you've learned about the early history of wireless communications and reviewed the radiation types included in the electromagnetic spectrum, let's take a look at the commercialization of that portion of the electromagnetic spectrum upon which most wireless communications are based — the radio spectrum.

Commercialization of the Radio Spectrum

Commercial application of the radio spectrum portion of electromagnetic radiation continued to grow and evolve during the twentieth century. The first commercial radio station in the U.S., KDKA, was established in 1920 in Pittsburgh, Pennsylvania. Around that time, a Russian-born inventor named Vladimir Zworykin was working with the Westinghouse Electric Company on technology that could be used to capture, transmit, and view images via wire. Philo Farnsworth, a 30-year old scientist, was the first to actually transmit these signals via radio waves in 1927. Today electromagnetic radiation in the radio spectrum literally permeates modern life. As you read this, transmissions from radio base station towers, man-made satellites, and other sources are passing through you.

Some scientists are increasingly concerned that radio transmissions are not entirely harmless. Some studies tie exposure to high levels of some types of radiation (from extended hours using cell phones, for example) to birth defects and brain cancer. Other scientists dispute these findings. As of this writing, the effects of long-term exposure to radio transmission are still being researched.

Because of the commercial importance of the radio spectrum, governments control and regulate its use. In most countries, the radio spectrum is divided by the government into thousands of groups of frequencies. For example in the United States the **Federal Communications Commission (FCC)** regulates the radio spectrum and in Canada the radio spectrum is regulated by the Department of Communications (DOC). These government agencies grant or sell permits (called licenses) that permit organizations to transmit voice and data on specific radio frequencies. For example, the U.S. commercial radio spectrum is allocated in two parts: the FM band from 88.1 to 107.9 MHz, and the AM band from 540 to 1700 kHz. Within each band, a license to broadcast on a certain frequency is allotted to a specific organization. Some parts of the radio spectrum don't require a license to broadcast on, and other parts aren't used because of interference from other devices that "leak" electromagnetic radiation, such as microwave ovens.

As you might suppose, licenses to transmit over the radio spectrum can be very valuable because there are a finite number of such licenses. In 1994 the FCC began auctioning radio spectrum licenses to raise revenues for the U.S. Treasury. An example that illustrates how valuable these licenses can be is the $3.9 billion bid made by Verizon Communications at the end of 2000 for various radio spectrum frequencies. Verizon, a subsidiary of a major local and long-distance telephone company that was once part of AT&T, wanted the licenses to support an advanced digital wireless network capable of carrying data as well as voice.

TIP

The light you see emanating from a light bulb is made up a wide range of colors, and none of these colors affect the other. For example, blue light doesn't prevent red light from moving across the room. In the same way, traffic on one radio spectrum frequency does not generally interfere with another. In some instances, frequencies that are double or four times one another's wavelength can interfere, but this is a rare case. For this reason radio stations, taxis, military, police, and cell phone networks can all use specific frequencies for transmissions without interference.

Today, inscrutable acronyms like IrDA, IEEE 802.11, TDMA, CDMA, GSM, and so forth pepper reports on wireless technologies by analysts, consultants, and journalists. To make sense of the acronyms that identify wireless standards, it is useful to consider the wireless world in terms of ranges and capabilities. These ranges and capabilities are changing as wireless standards improve, but they are useful nonetheless to broadly categorize wireless technologies.

Short-Range Wireless Technologies

One set of wireless technologies covers what might be called the range of convenience — about 10 feet. Do you lack a cable connection to send a document from your laptop to a printer just a few feet away? Do you need to transmit your business card from your PDA to a business associate's PDA across a conference table? Two wireless technologies were designed to satisfy these needs: IrDA and Bluetooth.

IrDA

Some wireless communications use infrared radiation (IR), the part of the electromagnetic spectrum that lies just below the visible red range. With an infrared-enabled laptop and printer, you can print a document by just pointing your laptop at the printer — no cable connection is necessary.

The **Infrared Data Association** or **IrDA** was created in 1993 to establish standards for the hardware and software used in IR communications; thus infrared technologies are also referred to as IrDA technologies or more simply IrDA. IrDA transmissions between a laptop and a printer require that both devices have a transceiver (a transmitter and receiver combined into one device). Additionally, special IrDA software may be required for these devices.

For IrDA to work there can be no physical obstructions between the transmitter and receiver. In other words, IrDA requires a line-of-sight link. For example, if there is a stapler or some other obstruction between your laptop and your printer, you may not be able to successfully transmit a document to the printer via IrDA. It's possible to have more than one IrDA device in a room; you just have to be sure to point your transmitter to the correct device before sending the transmission. Figure 5-4 illustrates typical IrDA transmissions and Figure 5-5 illustrates the correct positioning of a laptop and a printer for an IrDA transmission. The IrDA transmission takes place within a 30-degree cone of infrared radiation.

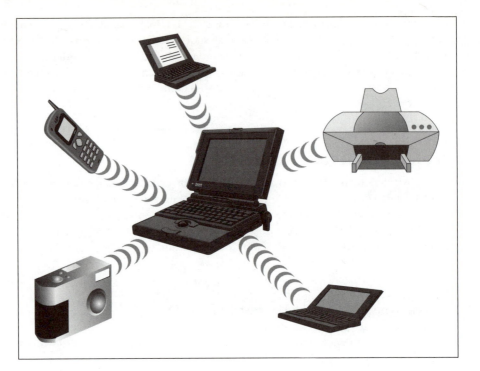

Figure 5-4
Typical IrDA
transmissions

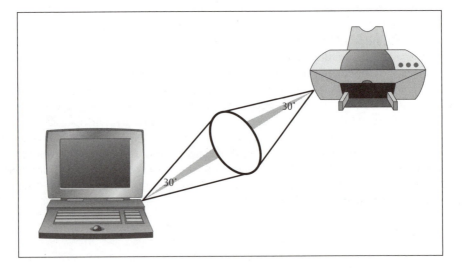

Figure 5-5
IrDA device
positioning

30°

30°

Bluetooth

While IrDA relies on infrared radiation, another type of short-range wireless technology, **Bluetooth**, is a radiofrequency (RF) technology that uses a previously unused range of radio frequencies at 2.45 GHz. Developed in 1994, Bluetooth was originally created to allow mobile phones to communicate with accessories such as headsets. Bluetooth can handle anything IrDA can; however, because radio transmissions can travel through solid objects the line-of-sight problem is not an issue. Bluetooth requires small, low-power transceivers that can be added to a hand-held device such as a cell phone, PDA, or laptop to enable the device for Bluetooth transmissions. Figure 5-6 illustrates Bluetooth hardware.

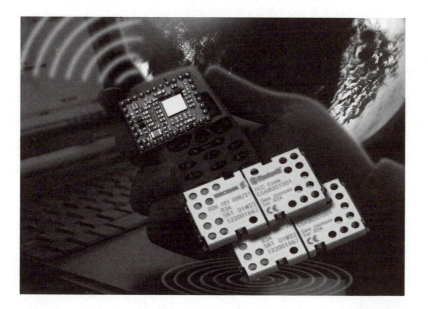

Figure 5-6
Bluetooth hardware

Bluetooth operates on an unregulated section of the radio spectrum. The **unregulated radio spectrum** is a part of the spectrum that can be used without a license. CB radio, walkie-talkie, baby monitor, and ham radio transmissions are examples of unregulated spectrum use. Although using the unregulated spectrum means Bluetooth devices sometimes experience interference from garage door openers, baby monitors, and microwave ovens, Bluetooth devices rapidly change frequencies, using frequency hopping technologies, to handle this interference. (Frequency hopping is discussed in more detail later in the chapter.) Because no line-of-sight link is necessary, Bluetooth can, for example, allow you to transfer addresses to a portable digital address book without removing the device from your briefcase.

> **TIP**
>
> Bluetooth was developed by Telefonaktiebolaget LM Ericsson (a Swedish company that is more commonly called simply Ericsson). It is named for King Harald Blaatand, a tenth century Viking king whose name translates literally into English as "Bluetooth." King Harald unified Scandinavia, so when Ericsson needed a name appropriate for a technology designed to unite many different devices, the name Bluetooth won.

Some inherent problems have slowed Bluetooth's widespread adoption. For starters, adding Bluetooth transceivers to mobile phones and other devices makes them more expensive. Additionally, as of this writing, there hasn't yet been a compelling reason for consumers to demand Bluetooth-enabled devices. Finally, Bluetooth technologies require stronger security and more complex software to allow you to select the device to which you are communicating. This increased complexity makes Bluetooth devices harder to use than comparable IrDA devices, and as a result, Bluetooth hasn't yet taken the market by storm as some predicted. Still, with companies like 3Com Corporation, Ericsson, IBM Corporation, Intel Corporation, Microsoft Corporation, Motorola, Inc., Nokia Corporation, and Toshiba Corporation on the bandwagon, it's a technology that bears watching. A primary source for all things related to Bluetooth is the Bluetooth Special Interest Group Web site (Figure 5-7).

Figure 5-7
Bluetooth SIG

Bluetooth is one of several wireless technologies used to create **Wireless Personal Area Networks** or **WPANs**, which are wireless networks set up to allow nearby mobile and portable devices to communicate without need of cable connections within a range up to 10 meters (approximately 30 feet). WPANs are sometimes called "piconets," for very small networks, or "convenience technologies" because they eliminate the need for bothersome cables. WPANs fall under the auspices of the **IEEE 802.15** Working Group for WPANs, a separate standards body for mobile and portable wireless devices such as cell phones and PDAs.

WPANs are useful when you need to facilitate wireless communication between portable or mobile devices in a small space. When you need to allow wireless devices to communicate with a network that has a physical range greater than a WPAN, you use a wireless LAN. In the next section, you'll learn about the technologies involved in creating a wireless LAN.

Wireless LANs

Operating beyond the range of convenience technologies are **wireless LAN** (also called **WLAN** or **W-LAN**) technologies. These technologies enable workers to roam around an office building, yet stay connected to a LAN at high speed. A wireless LAN most commonly consists of a wired LAN of computers, printers, servers, and other devices, portable devices such as laptops that can connect to the wired LAN when necessary, and access points (also called base stations) that allow the laptops to connect to the wired LAN using radiofrequency (RF) transmissions. A wireless LAN must be located within a limited physical vicinity such as a single office building or building complex.

Examples of Wireless LANs

One common example of a wireless LAN is a school network that includes laptops that must be moved from classroom to classroom. When needed, the laptops are moved to a specific classroom where they connect to the network via an access point. Another example is a hand-held wireless device, such as a PDA, that is used to send data to a wired network. Such a device might be used by:

♦ Warehouse employees transmitting inventory information from the warehouse to the inventory database stored on a file server.
♦ Waiters in a restaurant submitting orders to the kitchen.
♦ Doctors sending patient information, prescription, and nursing orders to a patient database.

Increasingly, airports, hotels, and restaurants offer wireless Internet connectivity for their guests' laptop computers using a wireless LAN. Figure 5-8 illustrates the use of mobile laptops to access a wired LAN.

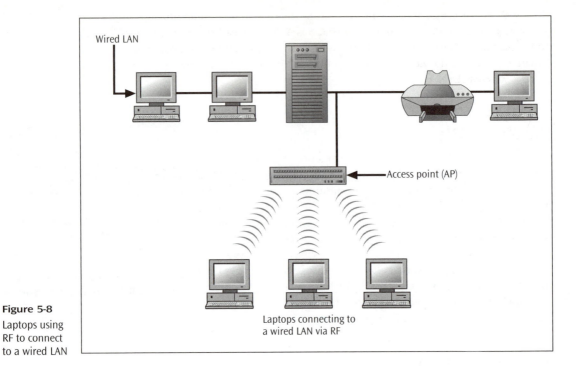

Figure 5-8

Laptops using RF to connect to a wired LAN

Wired LAN

Access point (AP)

Laptops connecting to a wired LAN via RF

The most well-known wireless LAN technologies are based on the IEEE 802.11 wireless networking standards. You learn more about the IEEE 802.11 wireless standards in the next section.

The IEEE 802.11 Family of Wireless Standards

An effort was underway in 1990, long before Bluetooth was under development, to free personal computers from their network cables and create simple wireless Ethernet networks that workers could access from anywhere in an office building or that university employees could access from anywhere on campus. Still, it took the IEEE seven years to approve wireless networking standard 802.11, which supported a data transmission rate of one to two Mbps over the 2.4 GHz unregulated RF range.

The IEEE then immediately started revising the 802.11 standard. The 802.11b standard was the first offshoot to find commercial success. **802.11b** (also known as **Wi-Fi** for **IEEE 802.11 Wireless Fidelity Standard**) supports up to 11 Mbps. Like its predecessor, 80211b operates in the 2.4 GHz RF range up to 300 feet. 802.11b hardware is backward compatible with the original 802.11 standard and is supported by an industry group called the **Wireless Ethernet Compatibility Alliance** or **WECA** that promotes 802.11b as a global standard and certifies 802.11b products. Figure 5-9 shows some examples of 802.11b hardware.

Figure 5-9
IEEE 802.11b
hardware

Although the 802.11b standard can handle 11 Mbps, multiple computers sharing this amount of bandwidth make for crowded airwaves. So **802.11a** was introduced, again under the auspices of the IEEE. At speeds of up to 54 Mbps transmitting in the 5.4 GHz RF range, 802.11a devices can transmit voice, video, and large amounts of data. The main drawback to 802.11a is the lack of backwards compatibility with 802.11b hardware. For multiple reasons, including the fact that they use different radio frequencies, 802.11a devices are currently not backward compatible with 802.11b devices. For example, today a laptop equipped with an 802.11a adapter card cannot connect to a wired LAN via an 802.11b access point. Analysts expect this backward-compatibility issue to be resolved within the next couple of years. Another drawback is range: 802.11a devices have a range of approximately 60 feet which is much less than 802.11b devices. An e-business considering a wireless LAN should carefully evaluate both 802.11b and 802.11a standards before deciding on which wireless LAN standard to implement.

The latest member of the 802.11 family of wireless standards is 802.11g. Like 802.11a, **802.11g** allows a 54 Mbps data rate, but 802.11g is also backward-compatible — allowing older 802.11b devices (such as access points) to operate on the same network as 802.11g devices (such as adapter cards). However, the introduction of 802.11g has become bogged down by disagreements between companies expecting to sell 802.11g equipment and companies that are already committed to the 802.11a standard (which is faster than but not compatible with 802.11b equipment). In November, 2001 the IEEE finally approved a proposal for 802.11g standards and the first 802.11g devices should be available by mid-2002.

Table 5-1 summarizes the short-range wireless standards you've learned about in the previous two sections.

Table 5-1
Wireless standards

Wireless range	Technology	Example
Short-range up to 10 feet	IrDA: IR Transmissions with line-of-sight requirements for sending and receiving devices	Sending a document from a laptop to a printer a few feet away
	Bluetooth: Short-range RF transmissions with no line-of-sight requirements	Sending your business card data from your laptop to another laptop across a conference room table
30 feet	Wireless Personal Area Networks (WPAN) IEEE 802.15	Wireless communications between mobile wireless devices in a small area
Single office building or complex	Wireless LAN (WLAN) IEEE 802.11 standards: 1) IEEE 802.11b – up to 11 Mbps at 2.4 GHz 2) IEEE 802.11a – up to 54 Mbps at 5.4 GHz; not compatible with 802.11b 3) IEEE 802.11g - 54 Mbps; compatible with 802.11b	School laptops moved from classroom to class room where they connect to a LAN. Warehouse employees transmitting inventory information via a hand-held wireless device to a LAN. Doctors sending patient information to a LAN

So far you've learned about wireless transmissions that span a fairly short distance, whether from desk to desk or room to room. In the next section you learn about wireless networks that span much greater distances and the technologies that support them.

Wireless Networks that Span Longer Distances

Networks that provide wireless communications over longer distances than a wireless LAN include pager, cellular phone, mobile data, fixed wireless and fixed wireless broadband, free space optics, and satellite networks. One of the first types of "data networks" as we know them was the pager network.

Pagers and Pager Networks

A **pager** is a small battery-operated device that is used to receive RF transmissions. The first commercial pagers were developed in the 1970s by Motorola and allowed local one-way messaging. These pagers, which had no display capability and no way to store messages, received RF transmissions that simply alerted a user that a message was available. For example, someone wishing to contact another person via a pager would call a phone number and record a message. Operators were used to send an RF signal to the appropriate pager and also playback or relay the actual message when the pager user called a predetermined phone number to access the message.

In the 1980s pagers with display capability were developed which allowed users to view either the phone number of the message sender or a coded message. During the 1980s pagers were primarily used within a limited local range — for example, by doctors and other employees within a hospital.

By the 1990s, pagers could display short text messages. Pagers were also assigned individual phone numbers, thereby making the paging process automatic because operators were no longer needed to send pager signals or read back messages. Someone wishing to contact another person who had a pager could call the pager's phone number and leave a return phone number or a short text message. Also, in the 1990s the broadcast range of paging systems broadened with the advent of pager networks.

Modern paging systems consist of paging terminals, transmitters, and individual pager devices. Paging terminals accept incoming messages and route the messages to a transmitter that has its own local pager area or zone. The transmitter sends the message to the appropriate pager. Multiple local pager zones can be connected (often by satellite) to form a wide area pager network. These networked transmitters can "hand off" a message to another transmitter when the pager is moving between zones. Figure 5-10 illustrates a message being sent from New York to California via a countrywide pager network.

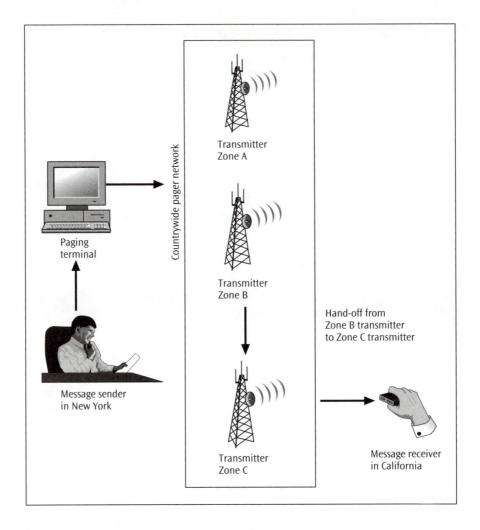

Figure 5-10
Message sent
via a pager
network

You've learned how effective paging systems are for sending a short message or
phone number to someone locally or across the country. Next you learn how cellular
networks are satisfying the ever increasing demand for mobile voice communications.

Cellular Phones and Cellular Networks

A **cellular phone** is actually a rather complex radio that sends and receives RF signals
in the 824-849 MHz range. The "cellular" in "cellular phone" refers to the way an entire
metropolitan area is divided into small transmission areas called **cells**. The facility that

contains the equipment necessary to service the transmissions for one or more cells is called a **base station**. As a cell phone user moves across the boundary of two cells, the base stations agree (by communicating with each other over the wired network to which they are all connected) on how to disconnect the cell phone from one base station at the same instant it's connected to the other. As you might guess, this doesn't work smoothly all of the time, causing occasional connectivity problems for users. Figure 5-11 illustrates a transmission from Caller A's telephone to Caller B's cell phone being handed across cell boundaries from one base station to another as Caller B crosses the boundaries between cells during the transmission.

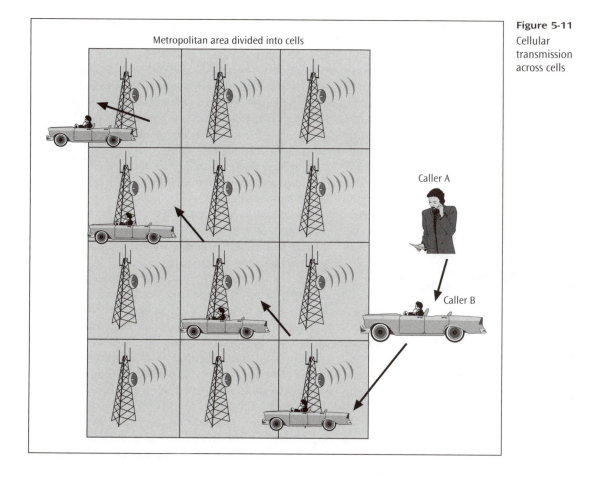

Figure 5-11
Cellular transmission across cells

The original cellular phones were designed for use as car phones and transmitters frequently were located along roadways. **Personal Communication Services** or **PCS** wireless phone systems are similar to the original cellular systems, but require a number of antennas in a calling area or cell. When a PCS user makes a call on his or her phone, the closest antenna picks up the call and sends it to a PCS network base station. PCS networks operate in the 1850-1990 MHz range.

PCS cellular phone technologies are also called "digital cellular" technologies and include the TDMA and CDMA wireless standards developed in the U.S. and the GSM standard adopted in Europe and Asia. Before you learn more about these individual standards, it's important to note that there are several issues affecting the evolution of cellular technologies: the number of phones that can use a certain part of the spectrum; the quality of the phone calls, especially when many phones are sharing a small part of the spectrum; and the amount of data that can be transmitted over a cellular network.

TIP

The terms "cell phone" and "cellular" are commonly used to specify both analog cellular and digital cellular PCS equipment and networks.

It's also important to realize that cellular wireless standards and resulting technologies have evolved differently in the U.S. than in Europe or Asia. For example, the early European adoption of cellular standards that allow cell phones to operate across country borders led to manufacturing economies of scale and much higher market penetration rates for cell phones than in the United States.

Meanwhile, in the United States at least two cellular phone network carriers were named in each metropolitan area, and other carriers entered the market as radio spectrum became available. While this was supposed to benefit the consumer by promoting competition between cellular network vendors, the actual result was an increasingly confusing array of cellular networks, a lack of interoperability between some networks, and an increased cost to the consumer. In theory, a cellular network could handle calls from a cell phone user traveling outside of his or her metropolitan area, but in practice, punitive "roaming" charges were often added by the host network to the user's cell phone. These high roaming charges and a lack of interoperability has hindered the growth of cell phone adoption in the U.S. compared to cell phone adoption in Europe and Asia. European digital cellular networks are more standardized, allowing users to roam across country borders without leaving a compatible network. For this and other reasons, as of this writing, more people use cell phones in Europe and Asia than in the U.S.

TIP

Some analysts suggest that in the U.S. youths and young adults aged 10-24 are the fastest-growing market for wireless data and voice services. For example, Cahners In-Stat Group predicts that the number of wireless subscribers in this age group will exceed 40 million by 2004.

The major cellular standards and services in use today include AMPS, TDMA, CDMA, GSM, GPRS, and i-Mode. Figure 5-12 illustrates the use of these standards and services around the world. You learn more about each of these standards and services in the following sections.

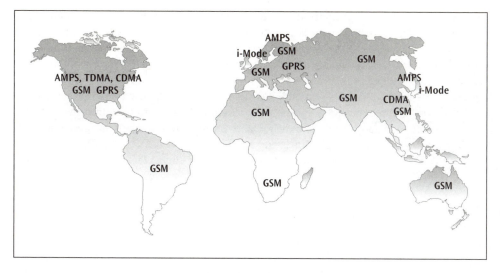

Figure 5-12
Worldwide cellular standards

Advanced Mobile Phone System (AMPS)

Advanced Mobile Phone System (AMPS) is an analog cell phone standard approved by the FCC and commercialized in the United States in 1983. AMPS was also used in analog cellular systems in Japan and Scandinavia as early as 1981. AMPS is based on the **Frequency Division Multiple Access** or **FDMA** analog standard which assigns frequencies to one user at a time. Each AMPS cell phone used two available frequencies — one to transmit and one to receive. Thus, multiple phones could access the same base station by dividing the spectrum of available frequencies among them. But AMPS isn't very efficient — the available spectrum was quickly used up by only a few hundred calls in a given cell — so new digital cellular technologies such as TDMA were developed.

Time Division Multiple Access (TDMA)

In 1994 the Telecommunications Industry Association (TIA) released its **Time Division Multiple Access (TDMA)** interim standard called TDMA IS-136, developed to support increased cellular network capacities, add other services such as fax and text messaging, and generally improve the quality of service. TDMA increases the capacity of a radio frequency (over the AMPS capacity) by dividing each frequency or channel into time slots. The early TDMA technologies allowed up to three users to send timed, synchronized conversation fragments over a shared channel. Today up to six users can share a TDMA channel while it is expected that advanced TDMA technologies will allow up to 40 users to share a channel. TDMA technologies support digital transmissions for voice, fax, data (at rates of 64 Kbps to 120 Mbps), multimedia and videoconferencing, and short text messaging via **Short Message Service** or **SMS**.

TIP

While text messaging via cell phones is not yet widespread in the United States, around the world text messaging (involving SMS and similar technologies such as Unstructured Supplementary Service Data or USSD) is a primary reason for the popularity of cell phones. According to a 2001 study by Accenture, over 50 percent of surveyed cell phone users in Germany, Finland, the UK, and Japan send frequent wireless text messages. Globally more than 15 billion short text messages are sent each month.

SMS is a point-to-point method of transmitting short text messages between wireless devices such as cell phones. These short text messages are sent to a central short message service center (SMSC) which then forwards them to their destination via a wireless network. Originally, SMS was designed to replace paging technology with two-way messaging. Today, notification services — which can, for example, advise you of waiting voice or e-mail messages — are still among the most frequently used SMS services.

However, SMS technologies can be used to send a wide variety of information and entertainment messages such as weather and traffic reports, stock quotes, personal banking information, movie schedules, and so forth.

The TDMA standard was widely adopted in the U.S. and became part of the basis for the GSM digital cellular standard.

Global System for Mobile Communication (GSM)

In the 1980s there were several different analog standards in use by European cellular network providers. In response to the European Commission's directive to develop an international digital cellular standard that could be supported across country borders, the European Conference of Postal and Telecommunications Administrations (CEPT) began working on such a standard in the mid-1980s. By 1987 a framework for the **Global System for Mobile communication (GSM)** was developed, based on a hybrid of FDMA and TDMA technologies. By the early 1990s, GSM was under the purview of the ETSI and was being used commercially across Europe. Like TDMA, GSM allows multiple users to share an RF channel (up to eight users), supports digital data transmissions, and supports text messaging with SMS. GSM operates at 900, 1800, and 1900 MHz.

But, the real advantage of GSM is standardization. Unlike in the United States where the FCC encouraged competition between digital cellular providers (often resulting in adoption of different digital cellular standards by different providers), the European Commission encouraged cooperation between the cellular network providers in its various member countries. This cooperation led directly to adoption of GSM as the European digital cellular standard which in turn enabled manufacturing economies of scale and enhanced consumer demand — a European consumer could now purchase one cell phone from any vendor that would work anywhere GSM was supported. The ultimate result of this standardization is a wide acceptance of GSM not only in Europe, but also globally. For example, the GSM Association reported that as of January, 2002, there were GSM digital cellular networks in 174 countries worldwide with more than 645 million subscribers. Despite the wide adoption of TDMA and GSM digital cellular technologies, some U. S. scientists were working on an even more efficient way to use the radio spectrum. Their efforts resulted in the commercialization of CDMA, a spread spectrum technology used by the U.S. military.

TIP

GSM was adopted as a digital cellular standard in the U.S. in 1995. Unfortunately, although some U.S. cellular networks eventually adopted the GSM standard, they did so using different frequencies than those used in Europe, making the so-called "global" standard not necessarily global in reach.

Code Division Multiple Access (CDMA)

Spread-spectrum technologies involve spreading radio signals over a much larger portion of bandwidth than the original "unspread" signal would use. The advantages of spread-spectrum technologies include a high resistance to detection or interference.

Because of this, spread-spectrum technologies have been used by the U.S. military for some time to prevent an enemy from identifying and "jamming" radio transmissions. There are two primary methods of spreading the spectrum:

◆ *Frequency hopping*: **Frequency hopping spread spectrum (FHSS)** requires that a radio signal "hop" quickly from frequency to frequency based on a complex mathematical formula known only to the sender and receiver.

◆ *Direct sequence*: **Direct sequence spread spectrum (DSSS)** breaks a radio signal into small pieces which, along with a sequencing code called a chipping code, are spread over a large section of bandwidth.

TIP

FHSS and DSSS technologies are also incorporated into the IEEE 802.11 family of standards used for wireless LANs.

TECH CASE **Frequency Hopping in Hollywood**

The origins of frequency hopping can be traced to the early stages of World War II, in a most unlikely place - a Hollywood dinner party. In 1940, the actress Hedy Lamarr and modern music composer George Antheil met at a dinner party. During the evening, Lamarr and Antheil discovered that they shared similar concerns about reports that Allied submarines were having problems with the enemy interfering with the radio signals used to control the torpedoes that targeted enemy submarines.

Lamarr, originally from Austria, had been married to a European arms manufacturer and had paid careful attention to her ex-husband's conversations with others about military weaponry. Antheil was familiar with technologies he used to synchronize several player pianos for one of his compositions. This interesting combination of backgrounds provided the technological framework for what happened next. Lamarr and Antheil met again the following evening, and after hours of discussion, conceived a technique called frequency hopping, in which the radio signals that controlled a torpedo's destination would "jump" through random radio frequencies to avoid enemy detection and interference.

Lamarr and Antheil patented their discovery and gave it to the U.S. Navy. Unfortunately, no use was made of the "frequency hopping" concept during WWII, in part because of the lack of supporting technology to implement it. In 1957, engineers at Sylvania Electric Products, Inc. rediscovered "frequency hopping" and the U.S. Navy finally used the concept in 1962 during the Cuban blockade — three years after the 17 year Lamarr/Antheil patent had expired!

During and after WWII, few knew of the Lamarr/Antheil discovery and neither gained financial rewards from it. In later years, Antheil gave much of the credit to Lamarr, but his experience synchronizing 16 player pianos for his composition titled "Ballet Mechanique" enabled him to envision a practical way to implement frequency hopping. It's no accident that their patent and prototype used 88 frequencies — the number of keys on a standard piano. Today, the Lamarr/Antheil contribution to the early development of digital wireless communications is widely recognized. For example, Lamarr and Antheil (Figure 5-13) were awarded "Pioneer Awards" by the Electronic Frontier Foundation in 1997 in recognition of their astounding work more than 50 years earlier.

Continued

Figure 5-13
Hedy Lamarr
and George
Antheil

Commercial **Code Division Multiple Access (CDMA)** for digital cellular networks is based on DSSS and was developed by QUALCOMM Incorporated. CDMA makes the radio spectrum usage more efficient by breaking up the digitized and compressed voice data into many pieces and, together with a unique code, sending the pieces over many different frequencies — whichever frequencies happen to be available at the moment of transmission. The voice data is then reassembled by the base station using these unique codes. CDMA was adopted by the TIA as an interim standard (IS-95) in 1993 and the first CDMA-based cell phone call was placed from Houston, Texas in October of 1995.

Because CDMA digital cellular technologies significantly increase bandwidth capacity over AMPS and GSM technologies, CDMA has made significant inroads into the digital cellular world. As of this writing, QUALCOMM claims more than 100 million CDMA users; however, GSM has a huge head start on CDMA. Only time will tell which technology will dominate globally.

In the world of cellular technologies, the early AMPS/FDMA analog voice-only cellular technologies are considered the first generation cellular wireless technologies. TDMA, GSM, and CDMA digital voice and data cellular technologies represent the second generation, and for this reason are often called 2G cellular technologies. Next you learn about third generation cellular technologies which allow users to access the Internet.

3G Digital Cellular Networks

The third generation of cellular wireless technologies, called 3G technologies, is still being shaped by technical, financial, and political issues. In fact, 3G has taken so long to appear that in the interim some faster wireless technologies, such as the **General Packet Radio Service (GPRS)** have gained acceptance. GPRS, which is based on GSM, separates voice and data into separate channels and offers IP data transmission from 56 to 144 Kbps. This type of new, interim technology is being touted as 2.5G.

3G technologies are expected to enable users to receive high-speed voice, data, and multimedia transmissions from any location via a cell phone. Projected revenue per customer for 3G services has cellular service providers and equipment vendors very excited, but the costs of building a 3G network are high and a technical misstep could be quite costly. For these reasons, the first commercial 3G system didn't "go live" until October 2001 in Japan.

3G happened first in Japan because of political, technical, and cultural reasons, including the government's eagerness to lift a sagging economy with public investment, a high concentration of potential subscribers in a small geographic area, and a consumer society eager to use the next new device. A Japanese company, NTT DoCoMo (a subsidiary of the government-owned Nippon Telephone and Telegraph, Inc.) launched its **i-Mode** IP-based digital cellular phone service in February 1999 as an easy-to-use method of accessing a limited subset of Internet content created or modified expressly for small displays. i-Mode, initially sporting a maximum speed of 9600 Kbps, enabled users to send and receive e-mail, shop online, access entertainment information, get stock quotes, book airline tickets, play games, download cartoons, and bank electronically all from their i-Mode-enabled cell phone. The i-Mode service is a tremendous success in Japan with more than 28 million subscribers reported by NTT DoCoMo as of this writing.

In October 2001, DoCoMo launched a 3G version of its i-Mode service called **Freedom of Multimedia Access** or **FOMA**. FOMA, based on 3G CDMA technologies, supports delivery of multimedia content and data at 384 Kbps speed. NTT DoCoMo sold 4,000 3G i-Mode-enabled cell phones on day one without even issuing a press release. NTT DoCoMo reported 40,000 3G i-Mode subscribers after only three months, and plans to have at least 1.5 million 3G i-Mode subscribers by the beginning of 2003. 3G i-Mode services are expected to be available in Europe in 2002, and other European telecommunications providers such as Deutsche Telekom also announced 3G services to be launched in 2002. Meanwhile, in the United States AT&T and Verizon launched 3G services in the U.S. in early 2002.

Of the emerging 3G standards, **CDMA2000** appears to have as good a chance as any of finding market acceptance. CDMA2K, as it's sometimes called, has the joint backing of QUALCOMM and Ericsson and calls for three implementation phases at increasing speeds, from 144 Kbps to 2 Mbps, in the next few years. Other CDMA-based 3G standards gaining acceptance are **Wide Band Code Division Multiple Access (W-CDMA)** which provides superior voice quality and high-speed data transmissions up to 2 Mbps and **Time Division Synchronous Code Division Multiple Access (TD-SCDMA)** with enhanced roaming capabilities.

The ITU is supporting 3G technologies via its **International Mobile Telecommunication-2000 (IMT-2000)** initiative, which is essentially a framework for defining 3G standards. The **Universal Mobile Telecommunications System (UMTS)**, developed within the IMT-2000 framework, is a 3G standard based on GMS which enables high-speed mobile IP data transmissions and voice transmissions any-where the standard is adopted.

Table 5-2 summarizes the cellular standards you learned about in this section.

Table 5-2
Cellular standards

Generation	Technology
1G	Frequency Division Multiple Access (FDMA) — analog cellular standard that assigns radio frequencies to one user at a time
	Advanced Mobil Phone Service (AMPS) — analog cellular standard based on FDMA and used in Japan and Scandinavia by 1981; approved for use in the in the United States in 1983
2G	Time Division Multiple Access (TDMA) — digital cellular standard that divides each radio frequency into time slots or channels allowing up to six users to share a channel; supports short text messaging (SMS)
	Global System for Mobile Communications (GSM) — European digital cellular standard based on a hybrid of FDMA and TDMA that allows up to eight users to share a channel; supports SMS
	Code Division Multiple Access (CDMA) — Direct Sequence Spread-Spectrum (DSSS) digital cellular technology that breaks radio signals into pieces and spreads the pieces (along with a sequencing code) across a large section of bandwidth
2.5G	General Packet Radio Service (GPRS) — Interim faster wireless technology based on GSM that separates voice and data into separate channels and provides IP data transmissions from 56 to 144 Kbps
3G	CDMA 2000 — Technology that enables broadband video and multi-media services and that is strongly supported by top vendors
	W-CDMA — Technology that enables superior voice quality and high-speed data transmissions
	TD-SCDMA — Technology that enhances roaming capabilities
	Universal Mobile Telecommunications Service (UMTS) — Technology that enables high-speed IP data transmissions and voice transmissions from anywhere the standard is adopted

Other wireless networks that may play a role in the future of e-business are mobile data, fixed wireless broadband, and free space optic networks.

Mobile Data Networks (MDNs)

Mobile Data Networks or **MDNs** are designed to transmit data from portable termi-nals to LANs and mainframes using hand-held devices similar to PDAs, or by using lap-top computers or other mobile devices. Examples of MDNs are Bell Canada's Bell

Mobility ARDIS network, Motient Corporation's U.S. Wireless Data Network, and RAM Mobile Data in Europe. MDNs provide data services to organizations that have mobile employees such as delivery truck drivers, policemen and firemen, parcel delivery drivers, and taxi drivers. Mobile sales personnel are also increasingly using hand-held wireless devices and MDNs to connect to their companies' networks to submit orders. For example, one large East Coast soft drink distributor was able to increase shelf space at its retail outlets by using hand-held personal computers and an MDN to more efficiently submit orders and other business-critical information to the distributor's network.

MDNs use a variety of RF technologies to transmit data to and from mobile devices. For example, subscribers on the ARDIS network can transmit data from their mobile devices to base stations positioned in specific areas similar to the way base stations are positioned in cellular networks. The base stations then forward the transmissions to a central messaging switch which is cabled to an organization's LAN or mainframe. Figure 5-14 illustrates an MDN.

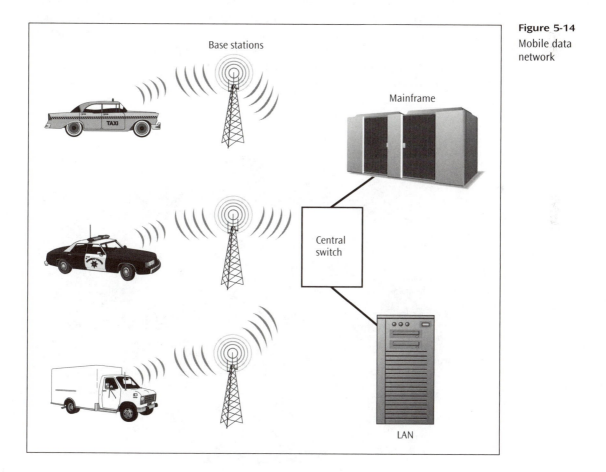

Figure 5-14
Mobile data network

In the previous sections you learned about wireless communications to and from mobile or portable devices via wireless LANs, cellular networks, and mobile data networks. Next you learn about wireless communications from fixed locations.

Fixed Wireless Broadband Systems

Wireless communications to or from a fixed location such as a home or office are called **fixed wireless**. Fixed wireless radio frequencies range from approximately 90 MHz to 40 GHz and are used for both voice and data transmissions. Also, most fixed wireless systems transmit on radio frequencies requiring line-of-sight positioning of antennae over relatively short ranges. As of this writing, some telecommunications providers (including Sprint Corporation) are experimenting with providing high-speed fixed wireless data transmissions called **Fixed Wireless Broadband** or **FWB** at transmissions rate of about 1 Mbps.

FWB is a very effective method for communicating across rural areas with large open spaces and far-flung subscribers. For example, assume an ISP wants to provide high-speed Internet access to a rural community where there is no DSL, cable, or other high-speed wired connections. The ISP could use an FWB system consisting of wireless modems and small antennas at each subscriber's location and large fixed antennas positioned in a geographical range, say a 25 mile-radius, to provide Internet access to all rural subscribers within that radius. Figure 5-15 illustrates a rural FWB system.

Figure 5-15
Fixed wireless broadband

Free Space Optics

Free space optics or **FSO** (sometimes called free space photonics or FSP) is an optical wireless data transmission system based on fiber-optic technology — except that air and not fiber-optic cable is the transmission medium. As you learned in Chapter 2, with fiber-optic cables, lasers send pulses of light along the cable's long glass fibers to detectors at the other end. FSO works in a similar way, except without the cable. That is, instead of sending light along glass fibers, a laser sends light pulses through the air to a detector that can be from just a few feet to approximately three miles away. An FSO system includes laser terminals positioned on a roof or inside a window and central hubs located throughout a metropolitan area which send signals to and receives signals from the laser terminals.

The advantages of FSO wireless transmissions include high transmission speeds (144 Mbps – 10 Gbps) over a currently unregulated portion of the radio spectrum (the terahertz spectrum range or THz), cost, ease of installation, and security. Because there is no need to lay cable, an FSO system can be installed in days or weeks as opposed to months or years, incurring as little as one-tenth the cost of an equivalent fiber-optic system. Also, because the laser beams in an FSO transmission are invisible and very narrow, FSO transmissions are extremely difficult to intercept. One disadvantage of FSO systems is the line-of-sight requirement — there can be no obstructions between the FSO transmission source and its destination. Another disadvantage is FSO's response to poor weather conditions. Rain, snow, and fog can distort an FSO transmission.

TIP

According to a 2001 report by The Strategis Group, a telecommunications market research company, fixed wireless broadband service revenues in the U.S. will grow to more than $6 billion by 2005 with more than five million subscribers. Strategis also predicts European fixed wireless revenues will be more than $8 billion annually by 2006.

Because most office buildings do not have fiber-optic cabling, FSO systems are sometimes used instead to provide the "last mile of connectivity" between fiber-optic cable buried under the street and nearby office buildings. FSO systems can also be used as part of a disaster recovery process when transmissions over fiber-optic cables are interrupted. For example, the fiber-optic cables connecting several Manhattan office buildings housing one of the world's leading financial companies were destroyed during the September 11, 2001, terrorist attack on the World Trade Center. Within two weeks, an FSO system involving three buildings was installed and functioning thus enabling the company to continue its business-critical operations.

Figure 5-16 illustrates FSO transmissions to and from a central hub via laser terminals installed just inside office windows in several metropolitan office buildings.

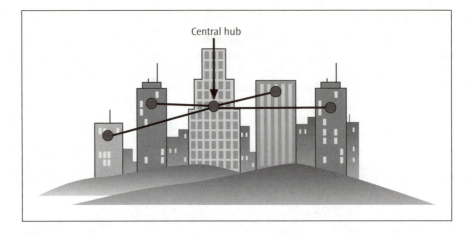

Figure 5-16
FSO
transmissions

Central hub

High-speed wireless data services, voice transmissions, and broadband Internet can be accessed anywhere in the world via communication satellites.

Communication Satellite Networks

A **satellite** is a natural or man-made object that revolves around the Earth (or any planet) in an elliptical or circular path called the satellite's **orbit**. For example, the Earth's moon is a natural satellite. As you learned in Chapter 1, man-made satellites have been orbiting the Earth since 1957 when the Soviet Union rocketed its Sputnik satellite into space.

Today, **satellite networks** consist of strategically positioned Earthbound antennae, ground control facilities, and thousands of weather, scientific, military, and navigational satellites orbiting the Earth. Satellite networks provide current pictures of the Earth's weather, scientific information about natural phenomena such as sun spots, military intelligence, and navigational directions for planes and ships. Additionally, communications satellite networks have hundreds of satellites acting as orbiting radio relay stations. Each of these communication satellites contain thousands of **transponders** (devices that receive and transmit signals) that receive voice, video, or data transmissions from Earth on one frequency and then relay them back to Earth on another frequency.

Satellite networks can be further defined by their type of circular orbit: GEO, LEO, and MEO.

Geostationary Orbit (GEO) Satellite Networks

Geostationary Orbit (GEO) satellites are positioned 22,300 miles from Earth above the equator and support two-way voice, video, and data communications. GEO satellites' speed matches the Earth's rotation, keeping a GEO satellite positioned directly above a specific spot on Earth. A big advantage of a GEO satellite network is the available bandwidth for fixed, high-volume data transmissions. However, because of line-of-sight problems, GEO satellite networks may not be efficient for data transmissions from hand-held mobile devices whose transmissions can be obstructed by trees and tall buildings.

Additionally, because of the distance from the Earth, transmission delays (also called transmission latency) may be experienced with transmissions over a GEO satellite network. One example of a GEO communications satellite network is the 22-satellite network owned by Intelsat, Ltd. which provides digital voice and data communications for telecommunications companies, ISPs, large corporate networks, and broadcasters around the world.

Low-Earth Orbit (LEO) Satellite Networks

Low-Earth Orbit (LEO) satellites are positioned from 400 – 1,600 miles above the Earth. Because of their close proximity to the Earth, LEO satellites orbit the Earth very fast (in 1.5 – 2 hours) to avoid the pull of gravity. Although LEO satellites disappear over the horizon as they orbit the Earth, a LEO satellite network is designed so that more than one satellite in the network is always visible. The major advantage of a LEO satellite network is its proximity to the Earth which helps to reduce transmission latency. Because a LEO satellite network has more than one satellite in view at any time, problems caused by line-of-sight obstructions can be minimized making LEO satellite networks appropriate for mobile wireless communications.

There are two kinds of LEO satellite networks: little LEO and big LEO satellite networks. Little LEO satellite networks use physically small satellites and offer low-bandwidth services such as paging, utility meter reading, cargo tracking, and messaging systems. ORBCOMM LLC and Final Analysis Communications Services, Inc. provide little LEO satellite networks. Big LEO satellite networks carry voice as well as data, often providing these services in geographic areas where users have limited or no access to wired voice communications. Globalstar, a consortium of several international telecommunications companies including QUALCOMM and China Telecommunications Corporation, operates a big LEO satellite network supporting both voice and data communications for remote areas such as offshore drilling rigs.

Medium-Earth Orbit (MEO) Satellite Networks

Medium-Earth Orbit (MEO) satellites are positioned from 1,500 – 6,500 miles above the Earth and offer a compromise between GEO and LEO satellite networks by requiring fewer satellites per coverage area than LEO networks and less transmission latency than GEO networks. As of this writing two MEO satellite networks currently under development are owned by Teledesic LLC and ICO Global Communications, Inc. Both networks are being designed for high-speed IP data transmissions as well as voice and broadband Internet access. The Teledesic and ICO Global MEO networks are being designed to offer data services for large computer networks, telephony, and broadband Internet access to maritime, oil and gas, construction businesses, and to governments. Additionally, both networks will offer Internet access and telephony services to consumers in remote areas not presently served by wired access.

Craig McCaw is one of the least known and most powerful men in the telecommunications industry. Described variously as reclusive, shy, enigmatic, and unassuming, McCaw carefully avoids the public spotlight. McCaw is the son of a pioneering radio and television entrepreneur and a product of Seattle's exclusive Highlands area. He attended the same prep school as Microsoft's Bill Gates and Paul Allen. During his teenage years, McCaw spent his summer vacations working with his father in the family's cable television business learning the business from the ground up. After high school graduation, McCaw enrolled at Stanford University.

Upon the death of his father in 1969, McCaw took control of the family cable television business, actually running it from his fraternity. After graduation McCaw worked hard to make a success of the business and proved to be an astute businessman, always keeping an eye on changing telecommunications technologies. By 1979 McCaw began looking seriously at cellular technologies. He recognized that both cable TV (in which he had already achieved business success) and the new cellular networks were similar in many ways. Both industries operated under FCC regulation, involved transmitters and towers, and made use of radio spectrum assignments. He also noted that none of the major communication companies (such as AT&T) seemed interested in competing in the local cellular market.

In March 1980, McCaw and others created a partnership, Northwest Mobile Telephone. The partnership set about acquiring FCC cellular licenses and by 1982 it had acquired cellular licenses for the Seattle and Portland areas. From that initial partnership grew McCaw Cellular Communications, which by the mid-1990s was the largest provider of wireless communication services in the United States. In 1994 McCaw Communications merged with AT&T in what was, for its time, one of the largest business mergers in U.S. history, worth more than $11 billion. Today McCaw is Chairman and CEO of Eagle River Investments LLC, a telecommunications investment company which has large interests in ICO Global Communications, Inc. (satellite network), XO Communications, Inc. (voice, DSL, VPN services), Nextel Communications (digital cellular services), and Teledesic LLC (Figure 5-17).

Teledesic LLC, a private company whose principal investors include McCaw, Bill Gates, Motorola, and The Boeing Company, was formed in 1990 to build a worldwide, broadband satellite network. The goal of this network is to provide telecommunications services for business computer networks and broadband Internet access for both businesses and consumers. Teledesic received its FCC license in 1997, and as of this writing, telecommunication services to businesses, government agencies, and consumers are targeted to begin in 2005.

Continued

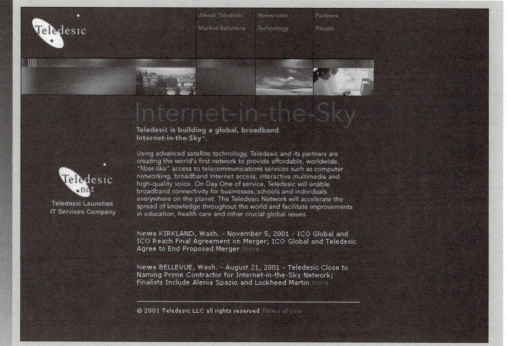

Figure 5-17
Teledesic LLC

The Global Positioning System

The **Global Positioning System (GPS)** is a network of 24 small satellites orbiting approximately 11,000 miles above the Earth in such a way that four to six satellites are always visible on the horizon. Each satellite constantly beams down a signal containing the exact time and its own position in the sky. A special kind of device called a GPS receiver detects these signals and measures how long each signal takes to traverse the distance between the satellite and the receiver. The receiver then uses this information to calculate its own position on Earth to within a few feet. Originally developed for the military, GPS has been a great boon to seaborne navigation and air travel, allowing traffic controllers to precisely position ships and airplanes relative to each other. Commercial GPS receivers can now be found in cars and private pleasure boats while portable GPS receivers are now available for hikers, skiers, balloonists, and others who need to be able to identify their location. Table 5-3 illustrates some additional ways GPS could be used.

> **TIP**
>
> One bit of satellite news: just as satellite TV is taking market share away from broadcast and cable TV, satellite radio is about to take on broadcast radio. In 2001 two companies, XM Satellite Radio and Sirius Satellite Radio, began selling receivers capable of picking up satellite music broadcasts. These broadcasts are beamed from GEO satellites with 18 kilowatts of power, allowing these companies to reach the entire United States.

Table 5-3
GPS services

User	Message
Ship captain	Warning, you are going to hit a reef in 10 minutes.
Road-repair crew	This pothole was repaired by Ed Smith; 5-year warranty.
Parent	Your child is 25 feet away and walking farther away. Turn left to see your child.
Commuter	There's just been an accident ahead; exiting now and taking Monroe Street will save you 45 minutes.
Car owner	Your stolen car has been located in the 9000 block of North Allen Boulevard.

One big promise for the future of wireless e-business involves using GPS to offer Location-based Services. **Location-based Services (LBS)** involve e-business offerings to a customer based on the customer's physical location. For example, with LBS, an electronics retail chain can send an advertising message to a potential customer they know is in one of their stores and standing in front of a big-screen television, or an auto dealer can send an advertising message to a potential buyer sitting in a car on another dealer's lot.

TIP

As of this writing, many analysts predict a rosy future for LBS. The Strategis Group projects annual LBS revenues will exceed $8 billion by 2005 and the Kelsey Group anticipates wireless advertising revenues to exceed $17 billion by 2005.

The level of marketing personalization possible via the combination of wireless devices, the Internet, and GPS is impressive. For example, the Hewlett-Packard Corporation is working on an experimental wireless project in which comments can be linked to locations. Want to know what people think about a given restaurant? In the future you might be able to walk past a restaurant and ask your wireless device to display the comments linked to the space you've just walked through.

For many marketing executives, marketing and advertising strategies that exploit GPS capabilities in cell phones and PDAs or GPS receivers in automobiles may seem to be a logical next step. But, do consumers really want to be constantly assaulted with advertising triggered automatically according to their physical location? Would you really want to be bombarded with advertising for nearby fast food restaurants as you drive down the street?

The possibilities for LBS are endless, but rather disturbing when viewed in light of personal privacy issues. Privacy concerns about the improper use of location information include receiving unwelcome advertising, disclosure of politically damaging or personally embarrassing situations, government observation and cataloging of personal behaviors, and the potential for stalking. As of this writing, wireless location information in the U.S. is protected by the limited disclosure rules of the Wireless Communications and Public Safety Act of 1999 (WCPSA) and the Communications Act of 1996. These acts specify that wireless location information can only be used to provide telecommunications services, specify location to civil authorities in case of emergency, or with "express prior authorization." In other words, consumers must opt-in for LBS and, theoretically unsolicited LBS messages are not allowed.

E-businesses that provide LBS must make clear to consumers how location information will be used, use location information solely for the purpose consumers have requested, and release consumers' information to third-parties only with consumers' permission. However, exactly what form the opt-in authorization will take is still being debated as of this writing. One question is whether consumers should be required to actively choose LBS (in writing or electronically) or whether e-businesses should be allowed to drive or "push" LBS, forcing consumers to accept LBS unless they specifically elect not to use it (that is, unless consumers choose to opt-out). This second option would be similar to the way junk e-mail is distributed to consumers today. To avoid receiving junk e-mail, consumers must opt-out by indicating they do not want to receive any further e-mail advertising from the sending entity. As of this writing LBS is in its infancy and it is too soon to tell which method will prevail.

In the previous sections you learned about the technologies and networks that cover short-range wireless data and voice transmissions over a variety of distances. Next, you learn about the technologies involved in accessing the Web using wireless devices such as cell phones and PDAs.

The Wireless Web

The first major wireless data receiver arrived in living rooms in big wooden cabinets — the radio. Together with the television, the radio initiated a long period of one-way data flow over the airwaves. CB radio operators and ham radio enthusiasts broke this pattern of one-way wireless communication, but what opened the floodgates for broad acceptance of two-way wireless communications was the cell phone. Early analog cell phones which could only transmit voice were heavy, bulky, power hungry, unreliable, and expensive. As you have learned, analog cellular technologies gave way to digital cellular technologies. Digital cellular technologies allowed phones to be smaller, easier to use, to transmit higher-quality voice transmissions, and be less expensive, paving the way for widespread adoption of digital cellular technologies around the world.

The development of digital cellular technologies also meant that data and pictures as well as voice could be transmitted via a hand-held wireless device such as a cell phone. While digital wireless technologies were evolving, the Internet and the Web were becoming both a vital source of information and an important commercial venue. To many it seems only natural that consumers comfortable with their cell phones and PDAs would want the convenience of wireless Web access and that e-businesses would want their Web sites available to mobile customers. Therefore, despite lukewarm interest on the part of most U.S. cell phone and PDA users, many wireless service providers and e-businesses are plunging ahead developing services and content for the wireless Web.

For example, assume you are shopping for a used car and find one you like on a local dealer's lot. Before making your purchasing decision, you need to have more information about the car's history. Thanks to the wireless Web you can now simply take out your Web-enabled cell phone or PDA, access the CARFAX, Inc. Web site, and for a few dollars look up the reported history on the car in question — while you are sitting in the car!

TIP

Some analysts think that using GPS to track people and things that could be lost or stolen such as cars, laptop computers, and small children might turn out to be the much desired "killer app" of the wireless Web.

Of course, the long-term success of the wireless Web hinges on three major issues: 1) making Web-based information designed to be viewed on a large computer monitor fit the small viewing area available with hand-held wireless devices; 2) mitigating slow transmission speeds over wireless networks; and 3) navigation through Web-based information without the use of a mouse. As you'll learn in the next section, a new protocol suite, the Wireless Application Protocol (WAP) and its markup language, the Wireless Markup Language (WML) were developed to make the wireless Web viable on the cell phones and PDAs used today.

Wireless Application Protocol (WAP) and Wireless Markup Language (WML)

The **Wireless Application Protocol (WAP)** is a protocol suite or stack that makes it possible to access Internet resources via a small-display wireless device such as a cell phone or PDA. WAP was developed as a standard for the wireless Web by the WAP Forum, a consortium of wireless vendors including Nokia, Motorola, and Ericsson. The WAP standard defines the wireless application environment and wireless application protocols which work across many different platforms ranging from, for example, an older GSM phone to a new PDA with a color screen. As you would imagine, this ability to bridge different technologies is vital; as with the Internet in general, interoperability is crucial to the success of the wireless Web. The wireless application environment is created with the Wireless Markup Language and the WMLScript programming language. The **Wireless Markup Language (WML)**, also developed by the WAP Forum, is based on XML and is used to design content for small-screen devices such as cell phones and PDAs. A WML document (page) is called a **deck**. Each deck contains one or more **cards**, which contain text, images, markup instructions, and so forth. **WMLScript**, a scripting language similar to JavaScript, is also used to manipulate the content on small screens and perform math functions.

TIP

The Gartner Group estimates that 95 percent of all new digital cellular phones will be WAP-enabled by 2004.

The wireless application protocols in the WAP suite function similarly to the protocols in the TCP/IP suite; however, WAP protocols are not compatible with TCP/IP protocols. This means WAP-enabled devices cannot communicate directly with content servers. Instead, a request for a WML page made from a WAP-enabled cell phone or PDA must first pass through a WAP gateway server. At the gateway, the request is translated into the HTTP protocol and then sent on to the content server. The content server returns the requested page to the WAP gateway server using HTTP. The WAP gateway server then reformats the request back into WAP protocols and sends the page on to the WAP-enabled device.

Table 5-4 specifies the components of the WAP suite and Figure 5-18 illustrates a WAP transmission using a cell phone.

WAP suite	Description
Wireless Application Environment (WAE)	Presentation layer: where the WML and WMLScript tools reside
Wireless Session Protocol (WTP)	Session layer: makes and maintains the connection
Wireless Transaction Protocol (WTP)	Transaction layer: keeps the data moving logically and smoothly; triggers confirmation of received messages
Wireless Transport Layer Security (WTLS)	Security layer: checks for the integrity of the data, handles encryption, authenticates sending terminal and application server
Wireless Datagram Protocol (WDP)	Data Transport layer: provides a common interface between different bearers and the upper protocols; modeled after UDP
Bearer (Network Carrier) Method	SMS, GPRS, GSM, CDMA, and so forth

Table 5-4
WAP suite

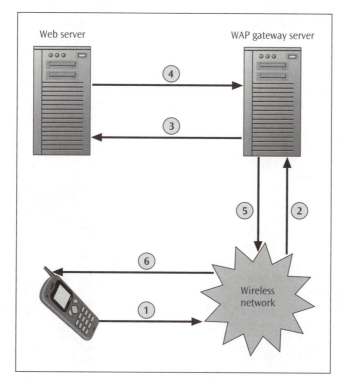

Figure 5-18
WAP
transmission

Despite widespread support, WAP and WML have heavy competition. For example, as of this writing, i-Mode, NTT DoCoMo's 3G IP-based service for cell phones, does not use WAP or WML, but instead supports a mobile version of HTML called i-HTML. Some companies, such as Microsoft Corporation, which currently support WAP and WML as standards for the wireless Web, are pushing toward an evolution of these standards that would make them compatible with current wired Web standards.

Accessing the Wireless Web

As you have learned, it is expected that most users will access the wireless Web by either a Web-enabled cell phone or PDA. In fact, one of the first hand-held wireless devices to make wireless data transmissions possible was Palm, Inc.'s Palm VII PDA which came out of the box with an integrated antenna. A data connection could be arranged for about $70 per month, not unreasonable for the benefits some people found in being connected wherever they went. However, the Palm VII PDA could not be used as a phone. This required consumers to own two wireless devices — both a digital cell phone and a PDA — if they wanted both wireless data access and digital cellular phone access. Soon some companies introduced digital cellular phones with slightly larger and adaptable screens in an attempt to provide both a phone and a PDA. Unfortunately, these screens weren't large enough for practical Web surfing and the lack of a keyboard made their use tedious. Increasingly, the wireless industry is turning to hybrid wireless devices like the Handspring, Inc. Trēo and the Ericsson Communicator that combine the features of a PDA and a cell phone to solve this problem. Figure 5-19 shows two hybrid wireless devices.

Figure 5-19
Hybrid wireless devices

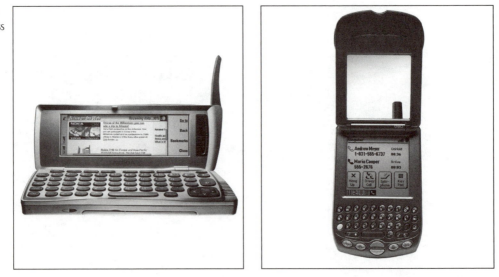

TECH CASE | Beam Us Up, Jeff and Donna

Arguably no one has done more for the popularity of wireless hand-held computers — PDAs — than Jeff Hawkins and Donna Dubinsky. In the early 1990s, Jeff Hawkins, an electrical engineer with at least nine patents for hand-held devices, founded Palm, Inc. Shortly after starting the company, Hawkins was joined by Donna Dubinsky, a Harvard University MBA graduate with several years experience in marketing and logistics support at Apple Computer, Inc. and Claris Corporation.

By 1996 Hawkins had invented the PalmPilot hand-held computer or PDA and Dubinsky, as Palm, Inc. CEO, handled the new product launch. Previous attempts by Apple and others to create a popular hand-held computer were not successful; but consumers fell in love with the PalmPilot PDA and sales took off with more than one million sold in the first 18 months. Along the way, Palm, Inc. captured approximately 80 percent of the PDA market and was acquired by U.S. Robotics which in turn was acquired by 3Com.

Eager to create a new company that could manufacture and market smarter and less expensive PDAs, Hawkins and Dubinsky left 3Com in 1998 to co-found JD Technologies which later became Handspring, Inc. Handspring, Inc.'s original product line included the Visor series of PDAs. As of this writing, Handspring's new Trēo product (which combines digital cellular phone, wireless Internet access, and PDA features in a small package reminiscent of the handheld communications device popularized on the original Star Trek television series), is now available. With this new product, Handspring, Inc. (Figure 5-20) is clearly moving away from the "organizer business" and toward the "communicator business."

Figure 5-20
Handspring, Inc.

In the previous sections you have learned about the evolution of wireless technologies and the advent of the wireless Web. In the next section you learn about the effect of these changes on the future of e-business.

Effects of Wireless Technologies on E-Business

Even during the economic slump of 2001 and early 2002, there was a great deal of activity in the wireless world as wireless service providers spent billions of dollars in the U. S. and Europe leasing radio spectrum, building the infrastructure, and developing the long anticipated 3G wireless technologies that would enable IP data transmissions and high-speed Internet access from hand-held wireless devices — and therefore make wireless e-business a reality. However, as of this writing, U. S. consumers exhibit little interest in "surfing the Web" from their cell phones or PDAs. As you have learned, one reason for this disinterest is the lagging development of 3G technologies in the United States and slow user adoption of hand-held wireless devices compared to Europe and Asia. Ongoing consumer concerns over privacy and security of wireless transactions are another issue. (Wireless security issues are covered in detail in Chapter 7.)

But the primary reason for U.S. consumer disinterest in wireless e-business is the lack of any compelling reason to make purchases using a wireless device. As of this writing, neither the technologies nor the content exist that would ensure a positive purchasing experience via a wireless device. It's just far too early in the evolution of U.S. wireless e-business for this to be practical. However, analysts expect that by 2005 evolving wireless technologies and useful wireless Web content together with increased interest on the part of U.S. consumers will result in billions of dollars in wireless e-business revenues.

TECH CASE **It's All About Useful Content**

When Mari Matsunaga, an experienced magazine editor, joined NTT DoCoMo in 1997 as the new mobile Internet project's editor-in-chief, she had never used the Internet and totally disapproved of "rude" people who made public phone calls from their cell phones. As a self-described "technophobe," Matsunaga seemed a strange choice to be part of a team whose charge was to develop a way for customers to access the Internet via their cell phones. But Matsunaga's gift was her understanding that the wants and needs of the every-day people who used new technologies — not the new technologies themselves — was the critical factor in assuring the success of the mobile Internet project.

Overriding the frequent objections of the project's engineers and consultants, Matsunaga insisted that customers were not interested in the technologies that made Internet access via a cell phone possible; what customers really wanted was useful content and an easy-to-use interface. As the driving force behind the project, Matsunaga focused on the concept that "the newness of an idea matters less than its ease of use" by insisting the new Internet access service, which she named i-Mode, be made to work easily for the general populace and not just business professionals. She also worked tirelessly to line up vendors eager to adapt content for the new i-Mode service.

Continued

Matsunaga's vision for i-Mode was right on target. For a small monthly fee, i-Mode subscribers could download games, do their banking, purchase tickets for entertainment venues, get news headlines, review restaurant guides, play with imaginary animals and friends, and so forth by simply switching on their cell phones and pushing a few buttons. By November 2000 i-Mode had several million subscribers with approximately 50,000 new subscribers signing up for the service every day! As of this writing i-Mode has more than 28 million subscribers and NTT DoCoMo is one of the world's telecommunication heavyweights. When her contract with NTT DoCoMo expired in the spring of 2000, Matsunaga left NTT DoCoMo to form her own startup e-business to provide online services and information useful to Japanese women professionals.

Also in 2000, Matsunaga was named "Asia's Most Powerful Woman in Business" and one of the "Top 25 Women on the Web" by Fortune Magazine. Perhaps one story that's told about Matsunaga best sums up her e-business philosophy and her vital contribution to the success of i-Mode. Upon the announcement that Matsunaga had won an NTT DoCoMo "technical achievement" award, a disgruntled NTT DoCoMo engineer asked one of the managers "So what technology did Ms. Matsunaga develop?" The manager explained that Matsunaga had "developed service technology."

Wireless service providers and equipment vendors are moving ahead by developing, testing, and implementing on a trial or limited basis a variety of wireless e-business propositions such as:

◆ Hotel visitors accessing account information, paying restaurant and hotel charges, and checking in or out by pointing their Bluetooth-enabled PDA to a Bluetooth access point in a hotel's lobby.
◆ Parents tracking their children at a theme park using a GPS-enabled cell phone and tags wrapped around their children's wrists.
◆ Consumers paying for tolls, parking, gasoline, and fast-food meals via a cell phone or PDA.
◆ Stores using point-of-sale wireless devices to ring up consumer purchases while the consumers are standing in line at the register.
◆ Financial services customers checking balances, transferring funds, and purchasing stock via a cell phone or PDA.
◆ Home owners applying for a mortgage, purchasing title insurance, or arranging home warranty services via a cell phone or PDA.
◆ Consumers using their cell phones or PDAs to retrieve personal health information, receive information on drug interactions, and receive medication reminders.

In the not too distant future you may be able to use your digital cellular phone to bid on Star Wars memorabilia in a wireless e-business auction or download the soundtrack from the movie you are watching.

B2C e-businesses and their customers may interact in new ways also, some of them advantageous to one side or the other. How will wireless technologies affect the B2B electronic marketspace? Mahatma Gandhi wrote that "there is more to life than increasing its speed," but it certainly seems that increasing life's speed will be the main focus of much of tomorrow's technology. This will be especially true in the important area of supply chain management, which encompasses all aspects of material purchase and inflow, through production to shipping and customer inventory levels. (You learn more about supply chain management in Chapter 8.) Wireless technologies may become a larger part of the general trend toward vendor/enterprise/customer integration by allowing a B2B e-business's purchasing and production departments to respond immediately to a newly placed large order made by a customer via a wireless device.

The term **knowledge management** is used to refer to the process of organizing, analyzing, and sharing documents, resources, and employee skills. Knowledge management takes place both within an e-business and between an e-business and its business partners. The term **knowledge worker** refers to those employees whose intellectual capacities and experience make them an indispensable asset to the e-business. As you can imagine, managing knowledge can be greatly simplified by wireless technologies, which make it possible for knowledge workers to remain connected to other employees and business partners no matter where the knowledge workers are physically located. Within an e-business, wireless technologies may fuel a growing integration between information generated by its mobile sales staff and its databases. With new wireless technologies, a mobile sales staff may soon be able to access the full range of an e-business's databases.

As wireless data transmission speeds improve, so do the features of hand-held wireless devices. Flat-panel displays, once quite expensive, are becoming cheap enough to build into cell phones, turning them into multifunction wireless devices. Faster chips enable more complex applications. Today's new hybrid wireless devices can function as phones, organizers, portable stereos, hand-held game machines, and so forth.

Another area worth watching in the coming years is the satellite wireless services. The advent of reasonably priced, satellite-based wireless services may bring these services within the reach of small to medium sized e-businesses.

To make wireless e-business ubiquitous, there has to be an e-business "killer app" for wireless devices and, as you have learned, one has yet to appear. Certainly sending and receiving e-mail from a hand-held wireless device is especially useful and accessing the Web via voice commands has great potential. As noted earlier in this chapter, it seems highly likely that GPS services may, in fact, produce that "killer app." For example, mobile videoconferencing which makes use of GPS and other wireless technologies may replace a large segment of business travel. In fact, it's reasonable to assume that some new technologies, such as VoiceXML, may cause a paradigm shift more significant, perhaps, than the introduction of the cell phone. Voice activated Web access vastly extends the potential of wireless e-business from a cell phone or hybrid wireless device. As of this writing, the only thing that's certain about wireless technologies is their potential effect on e-business and their accelerating rate of technological change. The rules and rewards in this new wireless era are being created as we go.

In this chapter you learned about the history of wireless technologies and how they are being used today to communicate over short, medium, and long distances. You've also learned that wireless technologies are evolving rapidly and that the impact of wireless technologies on the future of e-business is still unclear. In Chapter 6, you learn about the technology providers that help e-businesses build their infrastructures.

...SPREADING THE SPECTRUM

Jacobs not only challenged the major telecom companies, he won! QUALCOMM's CDMA technology had one big advantage over other digital or analog technologies — the ability to use DSSS technologies to break phone calls into pieces and distribute them across a frequency. This allowed as many as six times more phone calls over a frequency than TDMA systems and many more than AMPS analog systems. Additionally several new companies were taking advantage of the U.S. auctions of previously unused or repurposed radio spectrum licenses to gain entry into the cell phone business. Many of these new companies adopted QUALCOMM's CDMA technologies making CDMA an excepted digital cellular standard and a big commercial success.

Today, QUALCOMM (Figure 5-21) holds hundreds of CDMA patents. This means that other companies making CDMA-enabled products (such as Nortel, Motorola, Hitachi, Ericsson, and Lucent to name a few) must pay QUALCOMM to use CDMA technologies. In other words, QUALCOMM gets a fee for each CDMA-enabled wireless device sold! As of its fiscal year ending September, 2001, QUALCOMM reported more than 6,000 employees and sales in excess of $2.6 billion.

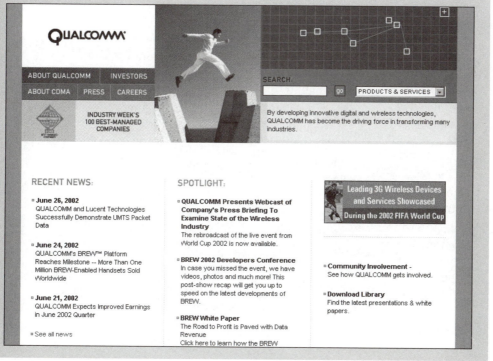

Figure 5-21
QUALCOMM Incorporated

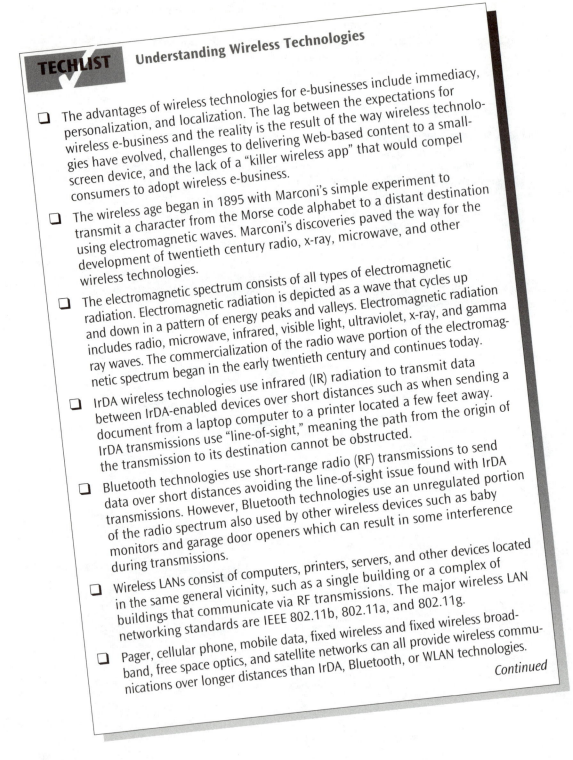

TECHLIST ✓ Understanding Wireless Technologies

❏ The advantages of wireless technologies for e-businesses include immediacy, personalization, and localization. The lag between the expectations for wireless e-business and the reality is the result of the way wireless technologies have evolved, challenges to delivering Web-based content to a small-screen device, and the lack of a "killer wireless app" that would compel consumers to adopt wireless e-business.

❏ The wireless age began in 1895 with Marconi's simple experiment to transmit a character from the Morse code alphabet to a distant destination using electromagnetic waves. Marconi's discoveries paved the way for the development of twentieth century radio, x-ray, microwave, and other wireless technologies.

❏ The electromagnetic spectrum consists of all types of electromagnetic radiation. Electromagnetic radiation is depicted as a wave that cycles up and down in a pattern of energy peaks and valleys. Electromagnetic radiation includes radio, microwave, infrared, visible light, ultraviolet, x-ray, and gamma ray waves. The commercialization of the radio wave portion of the electromagnetic spectrum began in the early twentieth century and continues today.

❏ IrDA wireless technologies use infrared (IR) radiation to transmit data between IrDA-enabled devices over short distances such as when sending a document from a laptop computer to a printer located a few feet away. IrDA transmissions use "line-of-sight," meaning the path from the origin of the transmission to its destination cannot be obstructed.

❏ Bluetooth technologies use short-range radio (RF) transmissions to send data over short distances avoiding the line-of-sight issue found with IrDA transmissions. However, Bluetooth technologies use an unregulated portion of the radio spectrum also used by other wireless devices such as baby monitors and garage door openers which can result in some interference during transmissions.

❏ Wireless LANs consist of computers, printers, servers, and other devices located in the same general vicinity, such as a single building or a complex of buildings that communicate via RF transmissions. The major wireless LAN networking standards are IEEE 802.11b, 802.11a, and 802.11g.

❏ Pager, cellular phone, mobile data, fixed wireless and fixed wireless broadband, free space optics, and satellite networks can all provide wireless communications over longer distances than IrDA, Bluetooth, or WLAN technologies.

Continued

- Advanced Mobile Phone System or AMPS is the analog cellular standard adopted for cellular networks in the early 1980s and was ultimately replaced by the digital cellular standard TDMA.
- Time Division Multiple Access or TDMA is a digital cellular standard developed in the U.S. by the TIA to increase cellular system capabilities and add other services such as text messaging.
- Global System for Mobile communication or GSM is a European digital cellular standard whose wide adoption across country boundaries led to the increased consumer acceptance of digital wireless phones in Europe.
- Commercial Code Division Multiple Access or CDMA is a DSSS technology and digital cellular standard developed in the United States. It was adopted by the TIA and improves spectrum usage by breaking up digital transmissions into many pieces and sending the pieces, together with a chipping code, over many different frequencies.
- CDMA2K, W-CDMA, TD-SCDMA, and UMTS are 3G wireless technologies that improve transmission speeds allowing for faster access to the wireless Web by cell phone and PDA users.
- The first commercial 3G cellular network is NTT DoCoMo's i-Mode service.
- Mobile Data Networks or MDNs use portable terminals and radio base stations to provide wireless communications between mobile employees and a LAN or mainframe.
- Fixed wireless communications emanate from a home or office. Fixed wireless and fixed wireless broadband (FWB) networks can be used effectively in remote areas to provide telephone services, broadband Internet access, and IP data services where a wired communications infrastructure does not exist.
- Free space optics (FSO) use transmitters fixed to the roof of office buildings or positioned inside an office building window to use air instead of fiber-optic cable to transmit data up to three miles. Free space optic networks can be used to provide the "last mile of connectivity" from fiber-optic cable buried under the street to nearby office buildings or can be used as a backup communications media when fiber-optic cables are not functioning.
- Man-made satellites are used to provide weather information, scientific data, military intelligence, commercial wireless communications, and global positioning or location services. Satellite networks are defined by their circular orbit around the Earth: geostationary (GEO), low-Earth (LEO), and medium-Earth (MEO) orbits. MEO satellite networks are currently being developed to provide high-speed IP data services, telephony, and broadband Internet access to businesses, governments, and consumers around the world.

Continued

- The Global Positioning System (GPS) is a network of 24 satellites originally developed by the military that allows location tracking of people and things. Many analysts think that GPS services may turn out to be the "killer app" of the wireless Web.

- Wireless Application Protocol or WAP is the protocol suite that enables small devices such as PDAs and cell phones to access Web-based resources.

- Wireless Markup Language or WML is an XML-based language that, along with WMLScript, is used to create content for the wireless Web.

- In the near future, most users will access the wireless Web via hybrid hand-held wireless devices that combine the features of a PDA and a cell phone.

- As of this writing, wireless e-business is more promise than reality; however, it is expected that more and more e-business transactions will occur over wireless devices as wireless technologies evolve and users feel that there is a compelling reason to purchase items via their cell phones or PDAs.

Key Terms

Advanced Mobile Phone System (AMPS)
base station
Bluetooth
cards
CDMA2000 (CDMA2k)
cells
cellular phone
Code Division Multiple Access (CDMA)
deck
Direct sequence spread spectrum (DSSS)
electromagnetic spectrum
Federal Communications Commission (FCC)
fixed wireless
fixed wireless broadband (FWB)
Freedom of Multimedia Access (FOMA)

free space optics
frequency
Frequency Division Multiple Access (FDMA)
Frequency hopping spread spectrum (FHSS)
General Packet Radio Service (GPRS)
Geostationary Orbit (GEO)
Global Positioning System (GPS)
Global System for Mobile communication (GSM)
Hertz
IEEE 802.11 Wireless Fidelity Standard (Wi-Fi)
IEEE 802.11a
IEEE 802.11b
IEEE 802.11g
IEEE 802.15
i-Mode

Infrared Data Association (IrDA)
International Mobile Telecommunication-2000 (IMT-2000)
knowledge management
knowledge worker
Location-based Services (LBS)
Low-Earth Orbit (LEO)
Medium-Earth Orbit (MEO)
mobile commerce (m-commerce)
Mobile Data Networks (MDNs)
orbit
pager
Personal Communication Services (PCS) (digital cellular)
satellite
satellite networks
Short Message Service (SMS)
spread spectrum technologies

Time Division Multiple Access
(TDMA)
Time Division Synchronous Code
Division Multiple Access
(TD-SCDMA)
transponders

Universal Mobile
Telecommunications
System (UMTS)
unregulated radio spectrum
Wide Band Code Division Multiple
Access (W-CDMA)
Wireless Application
Protocol (WAP)

Wireless Ethernet Compatibility
Alliance (WECA)
Wireless LAN (WLAN or W-LAN)
Wireless Markup Language (WML)
Wireless Personal Area
Networks (WPANS)
WMLScript

Review Questions

1. The age of wireless communications began in:
   a. 1995.
   b. 1985.
   c. 1895
   d. 1940.

2. The short-range wireless transport method using infrared (IR) radiation is:
   a. CDMA.
   b. i-Mode.
   c. IrDA.
   d. Bluetooth.

3. The short-range wireless technology that operates on the unregulated radio wave spectrum is:
   a. CDMA.
   b. GPS.
   c. GPRS.
   d. Bluetooth.

4. Which of the following is a good example of wireless LAN usage?
   a. Sending a business card from one PDA to another
   b. Internet access for school classrooms via laptops that can be moved from room to room as needed
   c. Accessing driving instructions from your automobile
   d. Ordering and paying for a pizza using your cell phone

5. Which of the following is a wireless LAN technology?
   a. AMPS
   b. 802.11a
   c. GSM
   d. IrDA

6. Which digital cell phone technology (developed in Europe) became the pan-European standard?
   a. CDMA
   b. i-Mode
   c. GSM
   d. TDMA

7. Mobile Data Networks were developed to provide:
   a. 3G cell phone technologies.
   b. High-speed data services for pagerlike devices.
   c. Wireless communications for mobile workers who need to send data to a LAN or mainframe.
   d. Broadband Internet access.

8. The protocol suite that makes Internet access possible on small-display wireless devices is:
   a. WAP.
   b. XML.
   c. HTTP.
   d. CDMA.

9. Which of the following cellular technologies use DSSS?
   a. CDMA
   b. TDMA
   c. FDMA
   d. RTMA

10. The FOMA i-Mode digital cellular technology is based on:
    a. 1G technologies.
    b. 2G technologies.
    c. 3G technologies.
    d. 4G technologies.

11. Licenses to transmit wireless communications over the radio spectrum are commercially valuable. **True or False?**

12. Wireless technologies were developed in the same way and at the same pace in the U.S., Europe, and Asia. **True or False?**

13. The Bluetooth wireless technology was developed by the Infrared Data Association as a short-range wireless transmission method using radio waves. **True or False?**

14. Both CDMA and TDMA are 2G digital cellular technologies. **True or False?**

15. Bluetooth is a line-of-sight wireless technology which requires the transmitter and receiver to be positioned so that there is nothing between them. **True or False?**

16. The IEEE 802.11b wireless LAN standard is sometimes called "Wi-Fi." **True or False?**

17. An important feature of TDMA wireless technology is the ability to send text messages. **True or False?**

18. MEO satellite networks are positioned from 400–1,600 miles above the Earth. **True or False?**

19. GPS may provide a big boost to wireless e-business via location-based services. **True or False?**

20. WML is a markup language based on XML and is used to define Web content for small-screen wireless devices. **True or False?**

Exercises

1. Using Internet search tools or other relevant resources, such as those at the end of this chapter, research the short-range wireless technologies IrDA and Bluetooth. Then write a one- or two-page paper comparing and contrasting the two technologies.

2. Using Internet search tools or other relevant resources, such as those at the end of this chapter, research the current status of wireless e-business in the United States, Europe, and Asia. Then write a one- or two-page paper describing the results of your research together with examples of current wireless e-business activities.

3. Define the following terms and explain the role each plays in wireless communications: AMPS, TDMA, SMS, CDMA, GSM, i-Mode, CDMA2K, UMTS, and IMT-2000.

4. Using Internet search tools or other relevant resources, such as those found at the end of this chapter, research the current status of LEO and MEO satellite networks developed to provide broadband Internet access. Then write a one- or two-page paper describing the results of your research.

5. Using Internet search tools or other relevant resources, such as those found at the end of this chapter, locate a Web site that offers a "Wapalizer" feature that demonstrates downloading a Web page to a wireless-Web enabled cellular phone. Experiment with the feature using several Web pages. Then view the same Web pages using your Web browser. Write a one- or two-page paper listing the viewed Web pages and comparing your two viewing experiences for each page.

CASE PROJECTS

♦ 1 ♦

You are the marketing manager for a B2C e-business and have just returned from an industry conference where the buzz was all about the marketing advantages inherent in wireless technologies: immediacy, personalization, and location. You think your company should begin learning how to exploit wireless technologies and you plan to briefly introduce some ideas at your next staff meeting. Using the Internet or other resources, research wireless e-business advantages. Then create a list of the ideas you plan to introduce at the meeting.

♦ 2 ♦

You are the sales manager for a B2B e-business with 30 sales representatives that travel to client sites in the U.S. three or four days per week. Several of the representatives have complained to you about having to carry so much equipment when traveling — a cell phone, a laptop, and a PDA — in order to access their e-mail and the Web, keep appointments organized, and stay in touch with customers and the office. You wonder if one of the new Web-enabled wireless devices that combine phone and PDA features might be used to lighten each traveling representative's equipment load. Using the Internet or other resources, research the features and cost of at least three hybrid wireless devices. Then write a one- or two-page paper comparing the features and cost of the devices. Choose the device most appropriate for your sales team and estimate the total cost of acquiring the devices including any wireless connectivity charges.

♦ 3 ♦

You are to be inducted as the president of the Wireless E-Business Developers Group at its next monthly meeting and want to prepare a few remarks about the evening's discussion topic, "The Wireless Supply Chain." Using the Internet or other resources, research the effect of wireless technologies on supply chain management. Then create an outline detailing your remarks.

TEAM PROJECT

You and your e-business partners are planning to move your staff of 15 employees into offices on the seventh, eighth, and ninth floors of a new office building. You plan to use conference room space located on the fourth floor as needed. You are also preparing plans to set up a LAN in the new facilities. One e-business partner wants to install a wireless LAN so that employees can access the LAN from anywhere in the building. You think a wired LAN is more secure and less expensive, but you aren't sure. Meet with your e-business partners and discuss the advantages and disadvantages of a wired vs. wireless LAN for your e-business and make your decision. Then create a 5–10 slide presentation using Microsoft PowerPoint or other presentation tool describing your e-business and its e-business model and which type of LAN you plan to install. Include in your presentation the rationale behind your decision. Present your LAN decision to a group of classmates selected by your instructor.

Useful Links

100 Years of Radio
www.alpcom.it/hamradio/

3G Newsroom — 3G Portal
www.3gnewsroom.com/index.htm

Anywhereyougo.com — Wireless Resources
www.anywhereyougo.com/

Bluetooth — The Official Bluetooth Web Site
www.bluetooth.com/

Broadband Wireless Magazine
www.broadbandcomputing.com/magazine/index.asp

Business.com — Mobile Commerce (M-Commerce)
www.business.com/directory/Internet_and_online/
    ecommerce/mobile_commerce_m-commerce/

Business2.0 — 3G (Third Generation Wireless Technology Resources)
www.business2.com/webguide/0,1660,18488,FF.html

Cahners Wireless Week
www.wirelessweek.com/

ccWAP.com
www.ccwap.htm

Cool WAP Site of the Day
www.coolwapsiteoftheday.com/index.phtml

CTIA's — World of Wireless Communications
www.wow-com.com/

Ericsson — Wireless Facts
www.ericsson.com/wireless/facts/oh10.shtml

Federal Communications Commission — Electromagnetic Spectrum Auctions
wireless.fcc.gov/auctions/

Federal Communications Commission — Third Generation ("3G") Wireless
www.fcc.gov/3G/

Free Space Optic
www.freespaceoptic.com

Gelon.net — Wapalizer Feature
www.gelon.net/

Geo Informatics Magazine
www.geoinformatics.com/

GPS — Related Links
www.cla.sc.edu/GEOG/rslab/gps.html

GSM World
www.gsmworld.com/index1.html

IEC — Online Education - TDMA
www.iec.org/online/tutorials/tdma/index.html

IEEE 802.15 Working Group for WPANs
http://grouper.ieee.org/groups/802/15/

Imagine the Universe — The Electromagnetic Spectrum
imagine.gsfc.nasa.gov/docs/science/know_l1/
    emspectrum.html

International Engineering Consortium — Web ProForums - WAP Tutorial
www.iec.org/online/tutorials/wap/index.html

International Telecommunications Union
www.itu.int/home/index.html

ITPapers.com — WAP White Papers
www.itpapers.com/cgi/SubcatIT.pl?scid=37

ITtoolbox Wireless
wireless.ittoolbox.com/

Light Reading — The Global Site for Optical Networking
www.lightreading.com/document.asp?doc_id=3124

Marshall Brain's How Stuff Works — Bluetooth
www.howstuffworks.com/bluetooth.htm

M-Commerce Times
www.mcommercetimes.com/

Microwave Journal
www.mwjournal.com/

Mobic — Wireless Resources
www.mobic.com/

Mobile Commerce.org
www.todmaffin.com/futurefile/wireless/shtml

Mobile Internet World — Mobile and Wireless Internet Technologies: Definitions and Links
www.mobileinternetworld.com/technologies/

MobileWAP.com
www.mobilewap.com/mobile/index.html

National Telecommunications and Information Administration (NTIA)
www.ntia.doc.gov/

Nobel Prize Internet Archive — Guglielmo Marconi
nobelprizes.com/nobel/physics/1909a.html

Palowireless.com — Wireless Resources
www.palowireless.com/

PCS Data Knowledge Site
www.gsmdata.com/es53060/default.htm

Spread Spectrum Communications
csd.newcastle.edu.au/users/staff/eemf/ELEC351/
SProjects/Morris/project.htm

SSS Online — Spread-Spectrum Magazine
www.sss-mag.com/

The Diffuse Project — European Commission
www.diffuse.org/

The Tech Museum of Innovation — Satellite Site
www.thetech.org/exhibits_events/online/satellite/

The Wireless LAN.com — Wireless LAN Resources
www.wirelesslan.com/

VoiceXML Forum
www.voicexml.org/

WAP Forum
www.wapforum.org/

WAP.net
www.wap.net/

Wapaw.com — WAP Search Engine and Resources
wapaw.com/index.html

WAPsight.com
www.wap-resources.net/

WebCab.de — WAP Resources Guide
webcab.de/wrg/

Wireless Developer Network
www.wirelessdevnet.com/

Wireless in a Nutshell
www.wap-resources.net/

Wireless Internet Magazine
www.wap-resources.net/
www.wirelessinternetmag.com/

Wireless LAN Association
www.wlana.com/

Wireless Networking Mini-tutorial
www.wkmn.com/newsite/wireless.html

Wireless NewsFactor
wireless.newsfactor.com/

Links to Web Sites or Companies Noted in This Chapter

3Com Corporation
www.3com.com/index2.html

Accenture
www.accenture.com/xd/xd.asp?it=enWeb&xd=
index.xml

AT&T
www.att.com/att/

Bell Mobility
www.data.bellmobility.ca/products/data/default.asp

Bluetooth SIG
www.bluetooth.org/

Cahners In-Stat Group
www.instat.com/

CARFAX, Inc.
www.carfax.com/

CDMA Development Group
www.cdg.org/

CEPT (European Conference of Postal and Telecommunications Administrations)
www.cept.org/

China Telecommunications Corporation
www.chinatelecom.com.cn/en/

Deutsche Telekom
www.telekom.de/dtag/home/portal/

Electronic Frontier Foundation (EFF)
www.eff.org/

European Telecommunications Standards Institute
www.etsi.org/

Federal Communications Commission (FCC)
http://www.fcc.gov/

Forrester Research, Inc.
www.forrester.com/Home/0,3257,1,FF.html

Globalstar
www.globalstar.com/

Handspring, Inc.
www.handspring.com/

Hewlett-Packard Company
www.hewlett-packard.com/

IBM Corporation
www.ibm.com/

ICO Global Communications, Inc.
www.ico.com/

IEEE 802.15 Working Group for WPANS
grouper.ieee.org/groups/802/15/

Infrared Data Association
www.irda.org/

Intel Corporation
www.intel.com/

Intelsat, Ltd.
www.intelsat.com/index.asp

Linksys Corporation
www.linksys.com/

Microsoft Corporation
www.microsoft.com

Motient Corporation
www.motient.com/

Motorola Inc.
www.motorola.com/home/

Nextel Communications
www.nextel.com/

Nokia Corporation
www.nokia.com/main.html

NTT DoCoMo
www.nttdocomo.co.jp/index.shtml

ORBCOMM LLC.
www.orbcomm.com/index.htm

Osram Sylvania
www.sylvania.com/

Palm, Inc.
www.palm.com/

QUALCOMM Incorporated
www.qualcomm.com/

RAM Mobile Data
www.ram.be/

Sirius Satellite Radio
www.siriusradio.com/servlet/snav?/servlet/index.jsp

Sprint Corporation
www.sprint.com/

Telecommunications Industry Association (TIA)
www.tiaonline.org/

Teledesic LLC
www.teledesic.com/

Telefonaktiebolaget LM Ericsson
www.ericsson.com/

The Boeing Company
www.boeing.com/flash.html

The Gartner Group
www4.gartner.com/Init

The Global Positioning System
www.colorado.edu/geography/gcraft/notes/gps/
gps_f.html

The Intermarket Group
www.intermarketgroup.com/

The Strategis Group, Inc.
www.strategisgroup.com/home/index.asp

Toshiba Corporation
www.toshiba.co.jp/index.htm

Verizon Communications
verizon.com/index.html

Westinghouse Electric Company
www.westinghouse.com/

Wireless Ethernet Compatibility Alliance (WECA)
www.wi-fi.com/

World Wide Web Consortium - VoiceXML
www.w3.org/TR/voicexml/

XM Satellite Radio
www.xmradio.com/

XO Communications, Inc.
www.xo.com/

For Additional Review

3Com. 2002. "Pine Crest School," *3Com Case Study*. Available online at: www.3com.com/solutions/en_US/casestudy.jsp?caseid=644.

3Com. 2002. "Wireless LAN Access at the London School of Hygiene and Tropical Medicine," *3Com Case Study*. Available online at: www.3com.co.uk/casestudies/hygiene.html.

About.com. 1999. "Inventors: Selling the Cell Phone - PCS Technology" July 21. Available online at: inventors.about.com/library/weekly/aa072199.htm.

About.com. 2002. "Inventors: History of Pagers." Available online at: inventors.about.com/library/inventors/blpager.htm.

Allen, Doug. 2001. "The Second Coming of Free Space Optics," *Network Magazine*, March 5. Available online at: www.networkmagazine.com/article/NMG20010226S0007.

allNetDevices. 2001. "DoCoMo Starts First 3G Service," *AllNetDevices*, October 1. Available online at: www.allnetdevices.com/wireless/news/2001/10/01/docomo_starts.html.

Andrews, Jean. 2001. *i-Net+ Guide to Internet Technologies*. Boston: Course Technology.

Batista, Elisa. 2001. "Biz Wiz: She Knows What You Want," *Wired News*, May 30. Available online at: www.wired.com/news/print/0,1294,43342,00.html.

Batista, Elisa. 2001. "Wireless Web Isn't Connecting," *Wired News*, September 25. Available online at: www.wired.com/news/business/0,1367,47077,00.html.

Beal, Alex et al. 2001. "The Future of Wireless: Different Than You Think, Bolder Than You Imagine," *Accenture Institute for Strategic Change*, June 4. Available online at: www.accenture.com/isc.

Beaumont, Chris. 2002. "Secret Communications System - The Fascinating Story of Lamarr/Antheil Spread-spectrum Patent." Available online at: www.ncafe.com/chris/pat2/index.html.

Beck, John C. and Wade, Mitchell. 2001. "Wireless: Forget Value, Focus on Relief," *Accenture Institute for Strategic Change mMe Issue Seven*, November 7. Available online at: www.accenture.com/isc.

Beinat, Euro. 2001. "Privacy and Location-based: Stating the Policies Clearly," *Geo Informatics*, September. Available online at: www.geoinformatics.com/issueonline/issues/2001/09_2001/pdf_09_2001/14_17_euro.pdf.

Bell Mobility. 2002. "ARDIS." Available online at: www.data.bellmobility.ca/products/data/default.asp.

Berck, Judy. 1998. "A Brief History of PCS (Digital Cellular) Technology Development in the United States," *PCS Data Knowledge*, April. Available online at: www.gsmdata.com/es53060/history.htm.

Bergeron, Bryan P. 2001. *The Wireless Web: How to Develop and Execute a Winning Wireless Strategy*. New York: McGraw Hill.

Brain, Marshall and Tyson, Jeff. 2002. "How Cell Phones Work," *Marshall Brain's How Stuff Works*. Available online at: biz.howstuffworks.com/cell-phone.htm.

Brown, Gary, 2002. "How Satellites Work," *Marshall Brain's How Stuff Works*. Available online at: www.howstuffworks.com/satellite.htm/.

CDMA Development Group. 2002. "Introduction to CDMA." Available online at: www.cdg.org/tech/a_ross/Intro.asp.

CDMA Development Group. 2002. "Principles of CDMA." Available online at: www.cdg.org/tech/a_ross/Principles.asp.

CDMA Development Group. 2002. "What is CDMA (Code Division Multiple Access)?" Available online at: www.cdg.org/tech/about_cdma.asp.

Charny, Ben. 2001. "The World Waits for 3G Wireless," *CNET News.com*, March 2. Available online at: news.com.com/2009-1033-253483.html?tag=prntfr.

Charny, Ben. 2002. "Verizon Wireless to Debut 3G," *CNET News.com*, January 24. Available online at: news.com.com/2100-1033-822051.html.

Chiampa. 2001. *Guide to Designing and Implementing Wireless LANs*. Boston, MA: Course Technology.

Chidi, George A. 2002. "QUALCOMM Turns Cell Phones into GPS Systems," *PCWorld.com as reported by CNN.com/SCI-TECH*, January 18. Available online at: www.cnn.com/2002/TECH/ptech/01/18/qualcomm.gps.idg/index.html?related.

Chidi, George Jr. 2001. "Satellite Internet: Wireless Medium Looks for a Niche," *NetworkWorldFusion*, June 25. Available online at: www.nwfusion.com/cgi-bin/mailto/x.cgi.

CNET Internet Services. 2002. "Jeff Hawkins and Donna Dubinsky, Founders of Palm Computing," *CNet.com, The Decade in Computing, Part1: Visionaries*. www.cnet.com/Internet/0-3805-7-273986.html.

Cohn, Michael. 2001. "Far-Fetched Wireless: Some Ideas Seem Out of This World, But They Aren't Out of Reach," *Internet World Magazine*, April 1. Available online at: www.internetworld.com/magazine.php?inc=040101/04.01.01m commerce1.html.

Cohn, Michael. 2001. "LANS Sans Wires," *Internet World Magazine*, July 1. Available online at: www.internetworld.com/magazine.php?inc=070101/07.01.01mcomm1.html.

CompassRose International, Inc. 1999. "Introduction to Global Satellite Systems." www.compassroseintl.com/Pubs/Intro_to_sats.html.

ComSilica Inc. 2002. "Technology Introduction: The History of 802.11," *ComSilica Inc.* comsilica.com/technology/.

Corr, O. Casey. 2000. "High Wire(less) Act," *Context Magazine Book Excerpt from Money From Thin Air*, October/November. Available online at: www.contextmag.com/archives/200010/BookExcerpt.asp.

Corr, O. Casey. 2000. *Money From Thin Air: The Story of Craig McCaw, the Visionary Who Invented the Cell Phone Industry, and His Next Billion-Dollar Idea*. New York: Crown Publishing Group.

Cox, John. 2001. "Comdex - Wi-Fi Will Rule, Agere Exec Says," *NetworkWorldFusion*, November 14. Available online at: www.nwfusion.com/news/2001/1114agere.html.

Coyle, Frank P. 2001. *Wireless Web: A Manager's Guide*. Boston: Addison-Wesley.

Crouch, Cameron. 2001. "Will Big Brother Track You by Cell Phone?" *PCWorld.com as reported by CNN.com/SCI-TECH*, April 20. Available online at: www.cnn.com/2001/TECH/ptech/04/20/location.services.idg/index.html??%20related.

Dornan, Andy. 2000. "Emerging Technology: Can Bluetooth Sink Its Teeth into Networking?" *Network Magazine*, November 5. Available online at: www.networkmagazine.com/article/printableArticle?doc_id=NMG20001103S0002.

Dornan, Andy. 2001. "Business Case: Hotel Chain Reserves Room on Space Network," *Network Magazine*, January 5. Available online at: www.networkmagazine.com/article/NMG20010103S0003/3.

Duan, Mary. 2002. "Wireless Web Services: Buzz, Boom, or Bust," *Impulse, A Cooltown Magazine*, January. Available online at: http://cooltown.hp.com/mpulse/0102-wservices.asp?print=yes.

Dynamic Mobile Data. 2002. "Customer Successes: Canada Dry/Pepsi-Cola Franchise Field Sales Solution." www.dmssys.com/successes/default.asp?canadadry.asp.

Eisenhart, Mary. 1998. "How Palm Beat Microsoft," *Salon.com*, September 17. Available online at: www.salon.com/21st/feature/1998/09/17feature.html.

Elstrom, Peter. 2000. "Hunting the Elusive Craig McCaw," *Businessweek Online*, June 19. www.businessweek.com:/2000/00_25/b3686073.htm?scriptFramed.

Encyclopedia.com. 2002. "Development of Radio Technology." Available online at: www.encyclopedia.com/.

Encyclopedia.com. 2002. "Electromagnetic Radiation." Available online at: www.encyclopedia.com/.

Ericsson. 2002. "CDMA2000." Available online at: www.ericsson.com/cdmasystems/3gcdma2000.shtml.

Ewing, James. 2000. "A Brief Overview of the WAP Protocol Suite," *TopXML*. Available online at: www.topxml.com/wap/articles/wapart1.asp.

Ewing, James. 2000. "A Descent Through the WAP Protocol Stack," *TopXML*. Available online at: www.vbxml.com/wap/articles/wapart2/.

Federal Communications Commission. 2001. "Third Generation (3G) Wireless," October 31. Available online at: www.fcc.gov/3G/.

Federal Communications Commission. 2002. "Frequently Asked Questions (FAQs) About the Safety of Radiofrequency (RF) and Microwave Emissions from Transmitters and Facilities Regulated by the FCC." Available online at: www.fcc.gov/oet/rfsafety/rf-faqs.html.

Fusco, Patricia. 2001. "Fixed Wireless Broadbank Competition in Your Backyard," *ISP-Planet*, June 29. Available online at: www.isp-planet.com/fixed_wireless/business/2001/wcai_4.html.

Geier, Jim. 2002. "The BIG Question: 802.11a or 802.11b?" *INT Media Group, Incorporated at Internet.com*, January 24. Available online at: www.80211-planet.com/columns/article/0,4000,1781_961181,00.html.

Geneer. 2000. "The Wireless Future: How to Get Connected and Stay Connected," *Geneer Executive Briefing Series White Paper*. Available online at: www.geneer.com/.

Getgen, Kim. 2002. "Securing the Air - 2001: A Security Odyssey," *IBM DeveloperWorks, Wireless Articles*, January 25. Available online at: www-106.ibm.com/developerworks/library/wi-sec2.html?dwzone=wireless.

Greengard, Samuel. 2001. "Wireless Point of Sale: Retail Giants Are Eyeing Big Benefits from Wireless Checkouts," *Internet World Magazine*, November 1. Available online at: www.internetworld.com/magazine.php?inc=110101/11.01.01mcomm1.html.

Gutzman, Alexis. 2001. "Realistic Expectations for 3G," *M-CommerceTimes*, May 23. Available online at: www.mcommercetimes.com/Technology/128.

Hafner, Katie. 2002. "The Future of Cell Phones is Here, Sort Of," *The New York Times*, February 14. www.nytimes.com/2002/02/14/technology/circuits/14FUTU.html?

Handspring, Inc. 2002. "Executive Team." www.handspring.com/company/excteam.jhtml.

Harley, Stephen. 2002. "Psion: Rising Phoenix or Lost Cause? *osOpinion*, March 20. Available online at: wireless.newsfactor.com/perl/printer/16842.

Hirsh, Lou. 2002. "Satellite Broadband Finding Its Market," *Wireless NewsFactor*, February 8. Available online at: wireless.newsfactor.com/perl/printer/16234.

Hirsh, Lou. 2002. "Why Consumers Are Not Buying M-Commerce," *Wireless NewsFactor*, February 25. Available online at: wireless.newsfactor.com/perl/printer/16484/.

Hoffman, Karen Epper. 2001. "Banking on Wireless," *Internet World Magazine*, February 15. Available online at: www.internetworld.com/magazine.php?inc=021501/02.15.01mcomm1.html.

Hoffman, Karen Epper. 2001. "New Options in Wireless Payments," *Internet World Magazine*, April 1. www.internetworld.com/magazine.php?inc=040101/04.01.01feature3.html.

Hon, A. S. 1993. "An Introduction to Paging - What It Is and How It Works," *Motorola, Inc.* Available online at: www.motorola.com/MIMS/MSPG/Special/explain_paging/ptoc.html.

Hoover's Online. 2002. "Qualcomm Incorporated: Company Capsule." Available online at: www.hoovers.com/co/capsule/6/0,2163,11436,00.html.

Hutchcraft, Chuck. 2001. "Something in the Air: Wireless Technology Applications in Foodservice," *Restaurants and Institutions*, August 15. Available online at: www.findarticles.com.

ICO Global Communications, Inc. 2002. "The Company and Its Aims." Available online at: www.ico.com/about/framemain.htm.

Kageyama, Yuri. 2000. "Easy Enough for 14 Million Subscribers," *Associated Press as reported in The Philadelphia Inquirer*, November 26.

LaForge, Perry M. 2001. "Global View of CDMA History," *CDMA Development Group*, March. Available online at: www.cdg.org/resource_center/GuestCol/laforge_march_01.asp.

Larimer, Tim. 2000. "What Makes DoCoMo Go," *Time Asia*, November 27. Available online at: www.time.com/time/asia/magazine/2000/1127/telecom.docomo.html.

Leinhard, John H. 2002. "Hedy Lamarr, Inventor," *Engines of Our Ingenuity No. 435*. Available online at: www.uh.edu/engines/epi435.htm.

Lewin, James. 2001. "Secrets of the Wireless Web," *The E-Business Enterprise, ITWorld.com*, December 3. Available online at www.itworld.com/nl/ebiz_ent/12032001/pf_index.html.

Leyden, John. 2001. "Business Drives the Wireless Web," *The Register*, November 15. Available online at: www.theregister.co.uk/content/5/22862.html.

Liu, Bob. 2001. "Is 802.11g Doomed?" *Internetnews.com*, November 16. Available online at: www.isp-planet.com/fixed_wireless/news/2001/80211g_011116.html.

Lockheed Martin. 2002. "Satellites," *The Tech Museum*. Available online at: www.thetech.org/exhibits_events/online/satellite/.

Lynch, Patrick et al. 2001. "Location, Location, Location," *Accenture Institute for Strategic Change mMe Issue Two*, June 20. Available online at: www.accenture.com/isc.

Mahoney, Michael. 2001. "Whatever Happened to M-Commerce," *E-Commerce Times*, November 30. Available online at: wireless.newsfactor.com/perl/printer/15042.

McDonough, Dan Jr. 2002. "AT&T 'M-Mode' Takes Page From DoCoMo," *Wireless NewsFactor*, March 22. Available online at: wireless.newsfactor.com/perl/printer/16909.

McLaughlin, Kevin. 2001. "The Next Iridium?" *Business2.0*, March 16. Available online at: www.business2.com/articles/web/0,,15578,FF.html.

Mobile Internet World. 2002. "Mobile & Wireless Internet Technologies: Definitions & Links." Available online at: www.mobileinternetworld.com/technologies/.

Mobilocity, Inc. 2000. "Understanding the Fundamentals of M-Commerce," *Mobilocity.net White Paper*, June. www.pmn.co.uk/corporate/mbusiness/002mcommerce.pdf.

Moore, Matt. 2002. "Treo Melds Phone, Wireless Net, PDA in 'Star Trek' Style," *Associated Press, Houston Chronicle*, January 24.

Mulligan, Paul. 2001. "Business Will Drive the Wireless Web," *eMarketer*, March 20. Available online at: www.emarketer.com/analysis/wireless/20010320_wireless.html.

Murray, James B. Jr. et al. 2001. *Wireless Nation: The Frenzied Launch of the Cellular Revolution in America*. Cambridge, MA: Perseus Books.

Mutsuko, Murakami and Shameen, Assif. 2000. "The DoCoMo Generation," *AsiaWeek.com*, December 1. Available online at: www.asiaweek.com/asiaweek/technology/2000/1201/tt.docomo.html.

National Aeronautics and Space Administration (NASA). 2002. "Electromagnetic Spectrum: Measuring the Electromagnetic Spectrum." Available online at: imagine.gsfc.nasa.gov/cgi-bin/print.pl.

Nee, Eric and Chen, Christine Y. 2000. "QUALCOMM Hits the Big Time," *Fortune Magazine*, May 15. Available online at: www.fortune.com/.

Newell, Frederick and Lemon, Katherine Newell. 2001. *Wireless Rules: New Marketing Strategies for Customer Relationship Management Anytime, Anywhere*. New York, NY: McGraw-Hill.

Newsroom.com. 2002. "Introduction into 3G." Available online at: www.3gnewsroom.com/html/intro_3g/index.shtml.

Notess, Greg R. 2000. "From the Web to WAP," *EContent*, August. Available online at: www.findarticles.com/.

NTT DoCoMo. 2002. "Introducing i-Mode." www.nttdocomo.com/html/i-Mode01_1.html.

NTT DoCoMo. 2002. "Revolutionary 3G Services: FOMA." www.nttdocomo.com/html/i-Mode05_1.html.

Orenstein, David. 2002. "How Badly Do You Want Your E-mail, Anywhere?" *Business 2.0 Wireless Report*, January 9. www.business2.com/articles/Web/print/0,1650,36976,FF.html.

Palowireless. 2002. "What is Bluetooth?" *Palowireless Bluetooth Resource Center*. Available online at: www.palowireless.com/infotooth/whatis.asp.

Pastore, Michael. 2001. "Fixed Wireless Remains Viable Broadband Option," *ISP-Planet*, April 26. Available online at: www.isp-planet.com/fixed_wireless/research/2001/fw_viable.html.

Pastore, Michael. 2001. "Wireless Aims for Widespread Appeal," *CyberAtlas*, February 13. Available online at: cyberatlas.internet.com/markets/wireless/print/0,1323,10094_715841,00.html.

Pastore, Michael. 2001. "Wireless Looks for a Lift to Clear Adoption Hurdles," *CyberAtlas*, March 16. Available online at: cyberatlas.internet.com/markets/wireless/print/0,,10094_715841,00.html.

Press Release. 1995. "National Alliance Places First CDMA Calls on PCS System," *AT&T*, October 31, Dallas, TX. Available online at: www.att.com/press/1095/951031.nsa.html.

Press Release. 1997. "Movie Legend Hedy Lamarr to be Given Special Award at EFF's Sixth Annual Pioneer Awards." San Francisco, CA. Available online at: www.eff.org/Misc/EFF/Pioneer_Awards/6th_pioneer_awards.announce.

Press Release. 2001. "Study Describes Always-on World of uCommerce: The Foundation for Ubiquitous, Unbounded Economic Activity," *Accenture*, October 2, New York. Available online at: www.accenture.com/xd/xd.asp?it=enweb&xd=_dyn/dynamicpressrelease_355.xml.

Press Release. 2001. "Wireless LAN and Bluetooth Will coexist in Europe," *Forrester Research, Inc.*, October 22, Amsterdam, Netherlands. www.forester.com/ER/Press/Release/0,1769,642,00.html.

Press Release. 2002. "GSM Statistics" *GSM World*. Available online at: www.gsmworld.com/news/statistics/index.shtml.

Proxim Inc. 2001. "What is a Wireless LAN?" Available online at: www.proxim.com/learn/library/whitepapers/wp2001-06-what.html.

QUALCOMM Incorporated. 2002. "3G Q & A." Available online at: www.qualcomm.com/main/3G/imj.html.

QUALCOMM Incorporated. 2002. "Executive Profiles: QUALCOMM Incorporated. 2002. "Executive Profiles: Dr. Irwin Mark Jacobs." Available online at: www.qualcomm.com/about/bios/i_jacobs.html.

QUALCOMM Incorporated. 2002. "What Are the Advantages of CDMA?" *QUALCOMM.com* FAQ, White Papers. Available online at: www.cdmatech.com/about_cdma/faq/cdma_adv.html.

Quillian, Jim. 1993. "Stanford Frat Rats," *Red Herring: Over the Wire*, November. Available online at: www.redherring.com/mag/issue06/otwire.html.

Radio Design Group, Inc. 2002. "How It Works: Pagers." Available online at: www.radiodesign.com/pgrwrks.htm.

Rave Technologies. 2002. "Components of WAP Architecture." Available online at: rave-tech.com/WAP/compon.html.

Reinhardt, Andy. 2001. "The Wireless Web Isn't So Wimpy Now," *BusinessWeek Online*, August 13. Available online at: www.businessweek.com/magazine/content/01_33/b3745039.htm.

Rohwer, Jim. 2000. "No. 1 Most Powerful Woman in Asia: Mari Matsunaga," *Fortune*, October 2000. Available online at: www.business2.com/articles/mag/print/0,1643,8612,00.html.

Rysavy, Peter. 2001. "Wireless Broadband and Other Fixed - Wireless Systems," *Network Computing*. Available online at: www.networkcomputing.com/shared/printArticle?article=nc/netdesign/bb1.html&pub=nwc.

Schonfeld, Erick. 2001. "Location, Location, Location: The Wireless Web Needs a Killer App. GPS Could Be Just the Thing," *Business2.0*, February 2. Available online at: www.business2.com/articles/web/print/0,1650,9348,00.html.

Schwartz, Karen D. 2001. "Home Lending Going Wireless," *Enterprise*, July 31. Available online at: www.zdnet.com/ebusiness.

Shapiro, Elizabeth. 2000. "Mari Matsunaga, Reinventing the Wireless Web: The Story of DoCoMo's i-Mode," *Japan Society*, November 14. Available online at: www.japansociety.org/corpnotes/111400.htm.

Stokes, Jeanie. 2001. "Carriers Moving to Free Space Optics?" *Broadband Week*, July 23. Available online at: www.broadbandweek.com/news/010723/print/010723_wireless_free.htm.

Stone, Adam. 2002. "Technology Issues Hindering Mobile Commerce," *M-CommerceTimes*, January 15. Available online at: www.mcommercetimes.com/Technology/206.

Sutherland, Ed. 2001. "The Extraordinary Advantages of a Mundane Technology for M-Commerce," *M-CommerceTimes*, October 4. Available online at: www.mcommercetimes.com/Technology/175.

Suvak, Dave. 2000. "IrDA and Bluetooth: A Complimentary Comparison," *Infrared Data Association*. Available online at: www.irda.org/design/ESIIrDA_Bluetoothpaper.doc.

Swanson, Eric. 1999. "The Telegraph," *Inventors Museum*. Available online at: www.inventorsmuseum.com/telegraph.htm.

Taptich, Brian E. 2002. "The Enigmatic Craig McCaw," *alarm:clock Magazine*. Available online at: www.thealarmclock.com/magazine/magContent/mccaw.htm and www.thealarmclock.com/magazine/magContent/mc2.htm.

Taschereau, John. 2001. "Location Based Services in the Consumer's Hand - Words that Come to Mind are Value, Practicality, Simplicity, Speed, and Choice," *Telecommunications Magazine*, June. Available online at: www.viavis.com/about-us/news/2001-06-01-telecommunications-magazine.htm.

Teledesic LLC. 2002. "About Teledesic: Executive Team." Available online at: www.teledesic.com/about/eTeam.htm.

Teledesic LLC. 2002. "About Teledesic: Fast Facts." Available online at: www.teledesic.com/about/about.htm.

Teledesic LLC. 2002. "Market Solutions." Available online at: www.teledesic.com/ market/m_solu.htm.

Terabeam Corporation. 2002. "Case Studies: Merrill Lynch - Terabeam Provides Rapid Connectivity to Brokerage Firm in Wake of NYC Attacks." www.terabeam.com/equipServ/case/Merrill.shtml.

The Associated Press. 2002. "Locator Madness Pervades Plenty of Devices," *CNN.com/SCI-TECH*, March 28. www.cnn.com/2002/TECH/ptech/03/28/locator.madness.ap/index.html.

The Diffuse Project. 2002. "Mobile Data Communication Standards." Available online at: www.diffuse.org/mobile.html.

The Intermarket Group. 2002. "Wireless Web Population to Soar," NUA Surveys, January 16. Available online at: www.nua.com/surveys/.

The International Engineering Consortium. 2002. "Time Division Multiple Access (TDMA)." *Web ProForum Tutorials*. Available online at: www.iec.org/.

The International Engineering Consortium. 2002. "Wireless Short Message Service (SMS)." *Web ProForum Tutorials*. Available online at: www.iec.org/.

Tobias, Arlyn. 1999. "The Parents of the Pilot Try for an Encore With Handspring - Q & A: A Talk With the Palm Pioneers," *Business2.0*, November. Available online at: www.business2.com/ articles/mag/print/0,1643,5594,FF.html.

Tyson, Jeff. 2002. "How Wireless Internet Works," *Marshall Brain's How Stuff Works*. Available online at: www.howstuffworks.com/ wireless-Internet.htm.

VanderMeer, Jim. 2001. "Will Wireless Location-Based Services Pay Off?" *Business GEOgraphics*, February 1. Available online at: www.geoplace.com/ bg/2001/0201/0201pay.asp.

WAP Forum. 2002. "What is WAP and WAP Forum?" Available online at: www.wapforum.org/what/ index.htm.

Wi-Lan, Inc. 2002. "Hedy Lamarr." Available online at: www.wi-lan.com/inside/main4.html.

Williams, Tish. 2001. "The TSC Streetside Chat: Handspring CEO Donna Dubinsky," *TheStreet.com*, August 4. Available online at: www.thestreet.com/pf/comment/streetsidechat/ 1509882.html.

Williams, Tish. 2002. "On Hold: Telecom's Deferred Comeback," *Thestreet.com*, January 24. Available online at: www.thestreet.com/markets/ tishwilliams/10007382.html.

Wireless Developers Network. 2002. "The Wireless Markup Language (WML) Tutorial." Available online at: www.wirelessdevnet.com/channels/ wap/training/wml.html.

Wireless Review. 2001. "Will Location-Based Services Intersect with Consumer Demand for M-Commerce?" March 1. Available online at: www.viavis.com/about-us/news/ 2001-03-01-wireless-review.htm.

Wrolstad, Jay. 2002. "Next-Gen Wireless I-Mode Service to Hit Europe," *Wireless NewsFactor*, February 25. Available online at: wireless. newsfactor.com/perl/printer/16491/.

XO. 2002. "Our Story: Executive Profile - Craig McCaw." Available online at: www.xo.com/ ourstory/executives/mccaw.html.

CHAPTER **6**

Internet Infrastructure Providers

In this chapter, you will learn to:

Describe network service providers and the Internet backbones

Discuss the role of Internet service providers in providing Internet access to businesses and consumers

Identify Web hosting companies and the services they provide to e-businesses

Discuss content caching and content delivery networks and how they enable large e-businesses to quickly distribute Web content

Describe application service providers and the e-business services they provide

Use the Traceroute utility

In September 1983, several men including Murray Waldron, Bernard J. "Bernie" Ebbers, Bill Fields, and David Singleton, met in a Hattiesburg, Mississippi, coffee shop to talk about starting a telecommunications company that would resell AT&T, wide-area fixed-rate (WATS) long-distance telephone services. Out of this meeting arose a company named Long Distance Discount Services or LDDS. Murray Waldron served as its first president, and Bill Fields took the helm as chairman of the board. Their first customer was the University of Southern Mississippi, which began purchasing long-distance services in January 1984.

By 1985, Bernie Ebbers was the CEO of LDDS. At this time the long-distance telephone marketplace was very complex. The many long-distance companies (referred to as carriers) tended to have small territories. In order for a carrier to send a call to its ultimate destination (which is usually outside the carrier's territory) the carrier had to pay various other companies to transmit the call. Ebbers quickly saw that expansion into other carriers' markets could eliminate these payments. After taking LDDS public in 1989, Ebbers began an acquisition drive rivaling almost any other in U.S. business history. In the early 1990s, LDDS began snapping up other regional and local telephone providers. In 1994, LDDS bought IDB WorldCom, a large, long-distance carrier and LDDS became WorldCom, Inc.

Continuing his aggressive acquisition strategy, Ebbers' WorldCom, Inc. bought MFS Communications Co. in 1996 for $14 billion. At the time, this was the fifth largest merger in U.S. history. Out of the MFS Communications merger came MFS WorldCom, which included UUNET, a large and well-regarded data carrier. Ebbers announced that MFS WorldCom would concentrate exclusively on business customers providing a single source for local and long-distance telephone service as well as Internet and worldwide communication services.

But, Ebbers appetite wasn't satisfied. In early 1998, MFS WorldCom bought MCI Communications, America's second-largest telecommunications company for $35 billion. The merger was hugely disputed by other telecommunications companies as anticompetitive but was finally approved by the FCC in September 1998.

Ebbers finally bit off more than he could chew in 1999. At a time when telecommunications was widely regarded as preparing for a tremendous boom, Ebbers bid more than $120 billion for Sprint Communications Company, which would have created the largest corporate merger in history and would have placed WorldCom, Inc. on an equal footing with rival AT&T. However, the WorldCom/Sprint merger was loudly opposed by other telecommunications companies and consumer watchdog groups. When U.S. antitrust regulators filed suit to block the merger (and European regulators threatened to file suit), WorldCom and Sprint called the merger off.

Even though it failed to swallow Sprint, WorldCom is still an enormous company. With a network spanning the globe and extending into space, in 1999, WorldCom was poised to be the premier provider of what many analysts and telecommunications industry observers expected to be the most precious commodity of the new millennium — bandwidth. But, the marketplace had a few nasty surprises in store for Ebbers and WorldCom.

Network Service Providers and the Internet Backbone

Many telecommunications companies and other technology e-businesses are involved in providing the Internet infrastructure, as well as the services that make the Internet so useful, including data transport, Web site hosting, and e-business application development and management. Before you attempt to purchase Internet connectivity services for an e-business, you need to understand the role these companies play in the world of the Internet. In this chapter, you learn about network service providers (which provide the Internet's primary data transmission lines), Internet service providers (which enable consumers and businesses to connect to the Internet), Web hosting companies (which provide secure facilities for warehousing Web servers), content delivery networks (which enable large e-businesses to get their Web content to end users faster), and application service providers (which enable e-businesses to outsource their custom e-business application development and management). But first, you need to get acquainted with some basic Internet terminology, starting with the term "backbone."

A backbone is a large, data transmission line connected to smaller lines. The **Internet backbone** is that part of the public network made up of high-speed lines spanning long distances to which local or regional networks can connect. As you learned in Chapter 1, the original Internet backbone was the National Science Foundation-supported NSFNET, which used AT&T data transmission lines. However, as the commercial viability of the Internet became important in the mid-1990s, the NSFNET Internet backbone was replaced by interconnected backbones or networks provided by several telecommunications companies including AT&T. Such companies are called **network service providers** or **NSPs**. Soon more NSPs (such as Sprint, WorldCom, and Level (3) Communications) added connections to their own networks via several network access points.

A **network access point** (**NAP**) is an Internet connection point that joins the networks of multiple NSPs. The original four NAPs were located in New Jersey, Washington, D.C., Chicago, and San Jose, California. Today there are many NAPs located across North America and around the world. NAPs enable an Internet user on one telecommunications network to access Internet resources on a different telecommunications network. For example, because the AT&T and WorldCom networks connect at a NAP, a consumer on the AT&T network can access an e-business Web site on the WorldCom network.

> **TIP**
>
> A Metropolitan Area Ethernet Internet Exchange or MAE connection is a short, high-speed Ethernet NAP connection within a metropolitan area. The original San Jose and Washington, D.C. NAPs are both MAEs; called MAE West and MAE East, respectively. There are also five regional MAEs. They are located in New York, Los Angeles, Houston, Dallas, and Chicago. Originally built by Metropolitan Fiber Systems, the MAEs are now owned and operated by WorldCom.

Figures 6-1 through 6-4 illustrate some of today's important North American Internet backbones provided by NSPs.

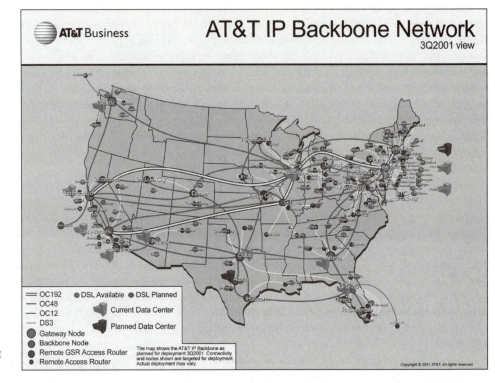

Figure 6-1
AT&T Internet backbone

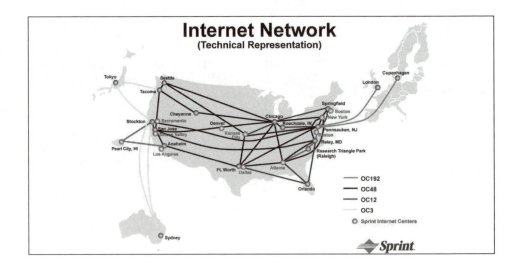

Figure 6-2
Sprint Internet backbone

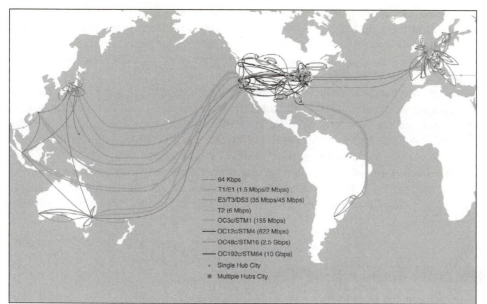

Figure 6-3
WorldCom
Internet
backbone

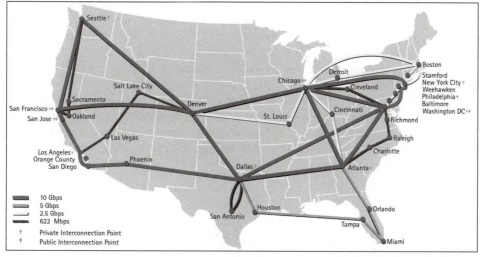

Figure 6-4
Level (3)
Communi-
cations
Internet
backbone

Many telecommunication industry analysts predicted that Internet backbone providers could reap huge revenues by providing additional bandwidth as business and consumer demand for faster and faster Internet access grew. For example, analysts predicted that Internet-based business videoconferencing, Internet-based movies downloaded on demand by consumers, and countless new uses would be found for any additional bandwidth the telecommunications companies could provide. This was the promise that drove a trillion-dollar Internet backbone expansion in the 1990s that, as of this writing, has produced bandwidth capability that far exceeds demand. However, the availability of all of this bandwidth may lead to innovations that would not have been possible had bandwidth remained expensive.

NSPs are responsible for building and maintaining the Internet infrastructure to meet traffic demands. In addition, NSPs wholesale access to their network to smaller e-businesses called Internet service providers, which then resell this Internet access to businesses and consumers.

Internet Service Providers

Internet service providers, or **ISPs** are the data retailers of the online world — they buy Internet access wholesale from NSPs and retail it piecemeal to thousands of customers. Some ISPs focus on providing Internet access to businesses while others are purely consumer oriented, allowing consumers to access the Internet over a dial-up connection for a small monthly fee. ISPs typically offer a variety of services to their customers including Internet access, e-mail accounts, access to newsgroup postings and chat room discussions, and server space for a Web site.

Some NSPs, such as WorldCom, also act as national ISPs, providing Internet access to businesses and consumers across the country. Many ISPs are regional. For example, Southwestern Bell provides Internet access in several Gulf Coast area states. Other ISPs are local, providing Internet access to single cities. A local ISP may purchase Internet access from a regional ISP, which in turn purchases its Internet access from an NSP. Figure 6-5 illustrates some of the ways that businesses and consumers connect to the Internet via local, regional, or national ISPs.

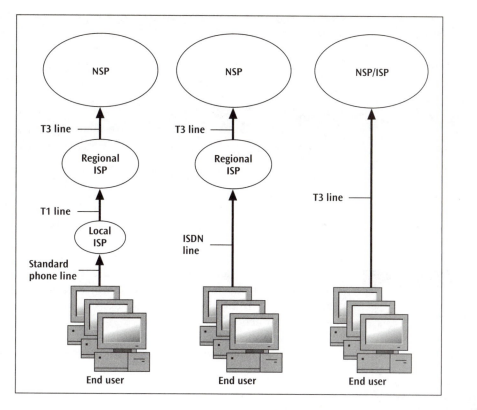

Figure 6-5
Internet access

As you learned in Chapter 3, consumers and most businesses connect to their ISPs using a variety of telecommunications media, ranging from standard telephone lines to dedicated T1 or T3 lines. Additionally, very large businesses (which often need to connect offices around the country or around the world) or ISPs (which need to guarantee very fast, reliable global Internet access for high-speed data transmissions) may use a fiber-optic technology for their data transmissions called **Synchronous Optical Network** or **SONET**, an ANSI standard for connecting fiber-optic networks. Data transfer speeds on a SONET connection are categorized by optical carrier (OC) levels. Each level indicates the supported high-speed data transmission rate. Table 6-1 lists some optical carrier levels and their data transmission rates.

TIP

Telecommunications companies and other e-businesses making huge investments in high-speed Internet access and services may ultimately see their investment pay off within the next several years. In March 2002 the research company Nielsen/NetRatings reported that for the first time, home and business high-speed Internet access hours accounted for slightly more than 50 percent of all Internet access hours in January 2002.

Table 6-1
SONET OC
level speeds

OC Level	Speed
OC-1	51.84 Mbps
OC-3	155.52 Mbps
OC-12	622.08 Mbps
OC-24	1.244 Gbps
OC-48	2.488 Gbps
OC-192	9.952 Gbps
OC-256	13.271 Gbps
OC-768	40 Gbps

TIP

Local ISPs catering to consumers continue to get pushed out of the mix by the Regional Bell Operating Companies (RBOCs) and by cable companies. The RBOCs and the cable companies already own "data pipes" (in the form of telephone lines and cable lines) into nearly every house. Both are marketing new ways to use these pipes. RBOCs have begun selling Digital Subscriber Line (or DSL) service while local cable companies are selling cable modem service.

Because of the high cost involved, SONET technology is not appropriate for small and medium-sized businesses and is most commonly used by major telecommunications companies to link cities and continents.

One interesting result of the way the Internet backbone grew — by connecting many different NSPs and ISPs — is known as the "peering" problem.

Peering

In the voice telecommunications world, local telephone companies that grew into long-distance carriers, such as Sprint and WorldCom, typically pay a local company at the other end of the line to complete a call made from one of their customers. A call placed from a customer of a local phone company to a long-distance carrier customer results in a small payment to the long-distance carrier, for carrying and completing the call. In this way, telecommunication companies that on their own are unable to provide a service can combine with other companies to provide the service and share the resulting revenue.

But, consider how the Internet changes this equation. Suppose an e-business has an arrangement with a national ISP, such as WorldCom, to provide Internet access for a monthly fee. An employee of the e-business connects to the WorldCom network and requests a Web page from a Web server connected to another network. If WorldCom doesn't have a direct connection to the other network, one or more intermediary networks must be used to deliver the Web page request to the Web server and then return a copy of the page to the user.

In this example, the transaction through the WorldCom network is paid for through the e-business's monthly Internet access fee and the Web server operator pays a fee to the network to which it is connected. But, who pays the intermediary networks?

Arriving at a value for the service the intermediary networks provide is difficult for several reasons. Most intermediary networks transport billions of data packets per day along hundreds of thousands of routes to and from thousands of other networks. There's no guarantee that the next intermediary network won't drop the data packet, making it necessary to resend the packet. No accounting or tracking system exists within most IP routers to tabulate per-packet charges; additionally, such recordkeeping would slow router operation considerably.

One solution to this revenue-sharing problem is for larger ISPs to charge connecting ISPs a transit fee or line charge. Another solution is **peering**, an agreement between two or more NSPs or ISPs to exchange Internet traffic destined for each other's network. **Bilateral peering** is an agreement between two entities and **multilateral peering** is an agreement between more than two entities.

TIP

According to an October 2001 report by Cahners In-Stat Group, a marketing research company, the top 10 U.S. ISPs (WorldCom/UUNet, AT&T, PSINet, Cable & Wireless, Sprint, Genuity, Internap, XO Communications, Verio, and Qwest) accounted for more than 65 percent of all Internet access revenues for the prior 12-month period, leading to speculation that it may be more difficult for smaller ISPs to survive without adding additional services such as Web hosting and hardware leasing.

Peering agreements spell out the terms under which networks exchange data and can specify how much traffic can be peered or exchanged, the type of network the peering entities must have, and other requirements. Peering agreements may or may not involve transit fees and line charges. For example, a peering agreement between one NSP and other NSPs or large ISPs might specify that data transfer speeds operate at OC-3 or OC-12 levels. Further, the agreement might require a minimum amount of traffic and specify that no transit or line fees are assessed. However, the same NSP might have different peering agreements with smaller ISPs; for example, such an agreement might require payment of transit fees or line charges.

Public peering is the exchange of Internet traffic at a public switch such as a NAP or MAE. Figure 6-6 illustrates peering between three different NSPs. The lines represent the NSP backbones. The points where they meet (in San Jose and Washington, D.C.) are public peering points, in this case MAE West and MAE East, respectively.

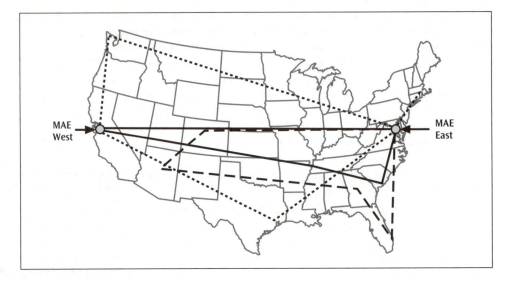

Figure 6-6
NSP peering

NAPs and MAEs can become very congested during the Internet's peak traffic periods. To overcome this congestion some NSPs and ISPs set up **private peering** arrangements — dedicated connections to each others networks — to enable data going between them to bypass the public peering points.

So far you've learned how NSPs and ISPs connect to move data across the Internet. The next section takes a look at how a regional ISP works.

How a Regional ISP Works

As previously discussed, a consumer generally connects to an ISP via a standard telephone line and modem, a DSL line, or a cable connection. A business generally connects to its ISP through its LAN via a router and a dedicated line. A regional ISP's customers typically include both consumers and businesses, as well as smaller ISPs.

Figure 6-7 illustrates how a regional ISP's customers might connect to it and how the regional ISP then connects to an NSP. Consumers and small businesses using a standard dial-up connection are connected to a modem bank. A **modem bank** is a box that accommodates several incoming phone lines and includes an individual modem card for each phone line. A **modem card** is the device that converts the incoming analog signal to a digital signal and then sends the digital signal on to a terminal server via a serial cable. The terminal server combines all the incoming lines into a single line that connects to the ISP's LAN. The group of modems to which the incoming connections to an ISP are randomly allocated is called a **modem pool**.

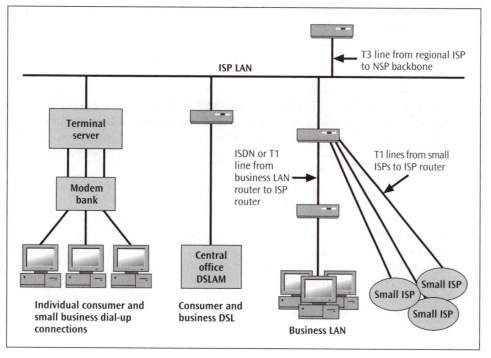

ISP LAN

T3 line from regional ISP to NSP backbone

Terminal server

Modem bank

ISDN or T1 line from business LAN router to ISP router

T1 lines from small ISPs to ISP router

Central office DSLAM

Individual consumer and small business dial-up connections

Consumer and business DSL

Business LAN

Small ISP

Small ISP

Small ISP

Figure 6-7
Regional ISP connections

Dial-up modem connections are increasingly being supplanted by cable modem and DSL connections. Cable modems allow cable system operators to turn their cable networks into LANs, transporting data over cable line on a set of frequencies that doesn't affect the TV-signal carrying ability. Personal computers in homes use DHCP to get an assigned IP address, and the cable company bills the user for an Internet connection as well as cable-TV service. Unlike dial-up modems, in which a customer pays the local phone company for telephone service and an ISP for Internet connectivity, the cable company provides both the data path — the physical cable line — and the Internet connectivity. In some areas, e-businesses also can connect to the Internet via cable. The local cable company connects an e-business to its local network with a standard TV cable (often providing cable-TV in the breakroom), and adds a router to connect and manage the flow of data between the e-business's LAN and the cable network.

A DSL modem connects to a standard telephone line and communicates with a **Digital Subscriber Line Access Multiplexer** or **DSLAM** placed in the telephone company's central office nearest the customer. A typical large city has many telephone central offices, each of which is an aggregation point for telephone lines serving an area 5-10 miles in diameter. In the early days of DSL adoption, it appeared that telephone companies offering DSL services might use those services to drive dial-up ISPs out of business by placing only their own equipment (DSLAMs) in the central offices. Fortunately for business and consumers, the FCC forced telephone companies to allow ISPs to also place DSLAMs in the telephone central offices. This allows businesses and consumers to use the telephone company for voice and an ISP for DSL services. In practice, however, DSL has marginalized smaller ISPs, which can't afford to invest in DSLAM equipment.

DSL and cable-modem service are part of a larger strategy on the part of big telecommunications and media firms to increase the range of services they provide to businesses and consumers. AOL/Time Warner, for example, would like to offer TV, media on demand, Internet connectivity with e-mail and Web hosting services, and local and long-distance phone services over one cable, with one monthly bill. Although integration of these services may bring economies of scale, some analysts are concerned about too much concentration of services resulting in lack of competition as well as too much control over Web, phone, and cable media.

Some businesses and small ISPs connect directly to a regional ISP's LAN via routers that manage data at each end of dedicated data lines — usually T1 lines. Setting up such a connection usually requires only a single point of contact — the regional ISP — which coordinates the installation of the data line in the customer's facility, connecting it to an aggregation point owned by the ISP. The ISP arranges for the line installation and usually provides a router that connects the customer's LAN with the high-speed line. Although this used to be a three-month project, lead time for installations like these in major cities is now measured in weeks. The regional ISP then uses another router and a higher-speed line, like a T3 to connect to an NSP backbone from its LAN.

Whether you are a consumer or a business, choosing the right ISP is an important step.

Choosing the Right ISP

Before you can choose the right ISP for personal or business use you need to understand the services an ISP can provide and the typical fees charged for those services. Additionally, you should be concerned with technical issues such as the type and speed of the Internet connections the ISP provides. Interviewing an ISP's sales representative can help answer many questions you might have about the ISP's services and fees. The Web is also a good source of information on which ISPs are available in which areas and their services and fees. Table 6-2 illustrates some of the issues you should consider when evaluating an ISP for personal or business use.

Table 6-2
Evaluating an
ISP

Category	Issue
Personal and small business dial-up connections	The ISP should provide dial-up numbers in your local area, not just in your area code, so that you don't have to pay long-distance charges.
	Some ISPs may use a combination of older, slow modems and faster modems in its modem pool. If you are considering a standard dial-up connection, the ISP should support a minimum speed of 56K during peak traffic times.
	If possible, determine the ratio of the ISP's customers to the number of modems in its modem pool. If the ratio is too high (two customers to each modem, assuming each customer is online half of a day, for example), it may take longer to connect to the ISP during peak traffic times of the day.
	If you travel on business and plan to access the Internet from a laptop computer, an ISP should provide local dial-up numbers for different area codes so you can avoid paying additional connection charges.
	An ISP should provide alternate local numbers in case there is a problem with the number you usually use to connect.
Personal and business high-speed connections	An ISP should support ISDN, DSL, T1 and other high speed connections. When evaluating a small or regional ISP, determine the type of connections it uses to access an NSP backbone and whether or not the ISP has several connections for backup purposes.
Fees and services	You should determine an ISP's fee structure and then match your Internet access needs with the appropriate fee structure.
	Some ISPs charge a flat monthly fee for unlimited Internet access, several e-mail accounts, and a limited amount of server space for a Web site. Additional charges may be incurred for adding e-mail accounts or increasing the amount of server space.
	Some ISPs provide a flat monthly rate for a maximum number of Internet access hours and additional charges are incurred when the maximum usage is exceeded.
	Some ISPs charge different rates for supporting and maintaining business Web sites.
Technical support	When evaluating an ISP, you should identify its technical support hours and find out whether technical support is available at night or on weekends. You should also try to determine how large its technical support staff is and whether or not support is provided in a variety of ways, including by phone, e-mail, or online via the ISP's Web site.

Table 6-2
(continued)
Evaluating an
ISP

Category	Issue
Reliability	If possible you should determine an ISP's reliability — how often it goes down or has problems with e-mail delivery, and how long it takes to get the service back in operation. This information may be difficult to obtain, although contacting existing customers can be of great help. An alternative may be to use an ISP on a trial basis until you are comfortable with its reliability. You should also determine how long an ISP has been in business and, if possible, contact some of its current clients to see how satisfied they are with the ISP's service.

The Web site services provided by an ISP may be adequate for a small business. However, a medium-sized or large e-business may choose to manage a Web server in-house or outsource its Web site operations to a Web hosting company.

Web Hosting Companies

Large e-businesses may have the staff expertise and budget to allow in-house operations and maintenance of the hardware, software, and high-speed Internet connections necessary for a Web site. But, small to medium-sized e-businesses may find in-house Web site and server management to be cost prohibitive. For these companies, outsourcing Web site operations to a Web hosting company may be the most cost-effective solution.

An e-business can use a **Web hosting company** to warehouse its own Web servers or to share space on the hosting company's servers. For an e-business, the primary advantage for using a hosting company is access to high-speed Internet connections. In addition, hosting companies can also provide secure, air-conditioned storage facilities, Web server administration, e-mail forwarding, data backup, disaster recovery, and Web traffic monitoring. Many national, regional, and local Web hosting companies (including Yahoo! Website Services, Hosting.com, Earthlink, Inc.) offer a variety of services to e-businesses.

For a startup e-business, shared hosting is a good option.

TIP

In a survey conducted in 2001, the market research firm Ovum forecast that the worldwide market for Web hosting services will increase from $10.3 billion in 2001 to $46.9 billion in 2006, with spending on Web hosting in the U.S. and Canada accounting for much of the market growth.

Shared Hosting

Although most, if not all, businesses today need a Web presence, not every e-business needs such a complex Web site as to require its own Web server. Many growing e-businesses start with shared Web hosting by renting space on a Web server for as little as $20-50 per month. For example, Yahoo! Website Services (Figure 6-8) is a popular choice for startup e-businesses, offering starter packages for a setup charge of approximately $15, plus $15 per month for usage. For these fees, an e-business can register a .com domain and upload its Web pages to a Yahoo! Web server to make them available to potential customers shopping online. Yahoo! also handles e-mail services to the company's domain and allows 15 GB of data transfer bandwidth or about 750,000 average-sized Web pages to site visitors per month. Another hosting company, Hosting.com (Figure 6-9), offers several shared hosting packages with a monthly fee ranging from about $20 per month to $200 per month, depending on the amount of disk space reserved, the maximum amount of monthly data transfer bandwidth used, and the number of e-mail accounts.

Paying a small startup fee and a low monthly usage fee may be an economical choice for a startup or small e-business when compared to the several thousand dollars it would cost to own and maintain its own Web server and high-speed Internet connection.

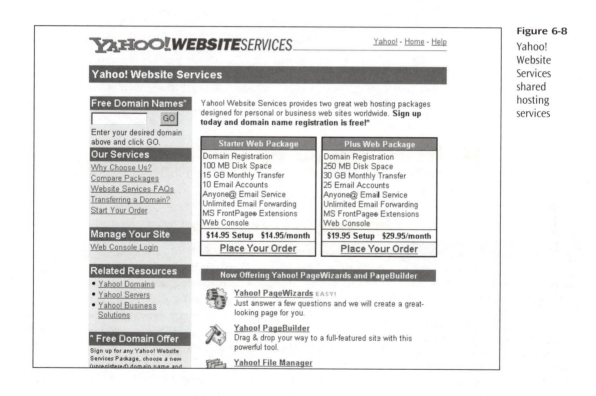

Figure 6-8
Yahoo! Website Services shared hosting services

Figure 6-9

Hosting.com shared hosting services

Inexpensive startup hosting packages may not be cost effective as an e-business grows. Eventually, many e-businesses need to consider paying for their own dedicated Web servers.

Dedicated Hosting Services

As an e-business grows and its Web site traffic increases, it may need to add specialized Web services not available in the inexpensive one-size-fits-all shared hosting services packages. When this happens, an e-business may find it needs a dedicated server just for its Web traffic. Rather than incur the expense of buying its own server, an e-business may choose to take advantage of a Web hosting company's **dedicated hosting services** by renting an entire server from the host for its Web services.

Dedicated hosting services may or may not include Web server administration. For example, Yahoo! Servers provides dedicated hosting services with setup fees ranging from $99–$150 and monthly fees (including a limited amount of data transfer bandwidth) from $150-$400 but Yahoo! Servers dedicated hosting service packages (Figure 6-10) require that an e-business handle its own server administration functions. In another example, Hosting.com (Figure 6-11) offers two levels of dedicated hosting services: self-managed and full-managed. The self-managed option is appropriate for an e-business with an in-house system adminis-tration staff that can handle the day to day chores associated with keeping a Web site up and running. The full-managed option allows Hosting.com's system administrators to handle all of the e-business's server administration functions. Hosting.com's self-managed dedicated hosting service packages have setup fees in the range of $400–$2,200 and monthly fees (exclusive of data transfer bandwidth charges) in the range of $350–$2,200.

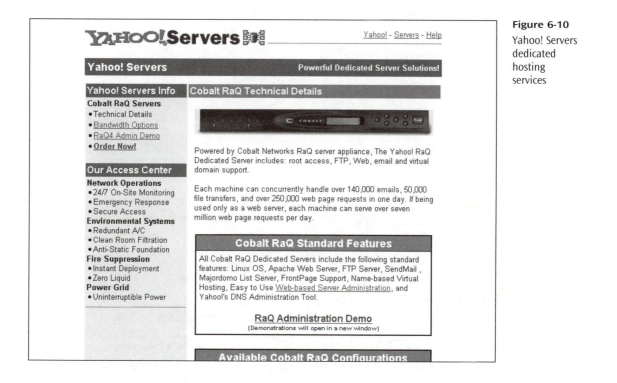

Figure 6-10

Yahoo! Servers dedicated hosting services

Figure 6-11

Hosting.com dedicated hosting services

While some large e-businesses prefer to make use of the hosting company's servers, those with more complex Web sites may choose to run their Web sites on their own private Web servers that are warehoused at a Web hosting company. In other words, these companies choose to make use of co-location services.

Co-Location Services

An e-business's need to integrate its Web site with other services (such as credit card processing) or to run specialized applications often requires that its Web site be housed on its own Web server. This is especially true for database-driven Web sites, where customers look up products and store user information, or where tracking user activity is important. Because complex database interactions require a high level of server-to-user response time, most e-businesses reserve entire servers for database operations. But Web servers require maintenance, storage space, air conditioning, reliable power, physical security, and reliable high-speed Internet connectivity. Many Web hosting companies, such as HostTech Communications (Figure 6-12), also provide facilities, called co-location facilities, where an e-business can house its own servers at a facility dedicated to housing thousands of servers. **Co-location facilities** provide storage space (called "rackspace") in secure, air-conditioned, power-guaranteed buildings with high-speed Internet connections. An e-business can also store related servers (including inventory servers, credit card authorization servers, and so on) at a co-location facility without having to provide a secure in-house facility to accommodate them.

Figure 6-12
HostTech Communications location services

Many NSPs such as WorldCom and Level (3) Communications are also in the co-location business. Because NSPs already manage specialized facilities to house their telecommunications and backbone equipment, adding space for co-located servers is a good business extension for them.

You've learned about the services provided by a Web hosting company; in the next section you learn what issues to consider when deciding which hosting company is right for your e-business.

Choosing the Right Web Hosting Company

What differentiates one Web hosting company service package from another? The most obvious limiters are the amount of server space offered and the total amount of data transfer bandwidth per month a company provides. Most hosting companies offer a certain amount of storage space and a certain amount of total bandwidth per month for a base fee. Should an e-business Web site prove very popular, it might exceed this preallotted bandwidth, resulting in extra charges (similar to using more than your allocated minutes on a cell phone). So it's important to consider not only the base fee, but also any extra charges that might be incurred. Sometimes, as with cell phones, it's better to purchase a package with extra bandwidth than to risk unexpected charges each month.

TIP

A group of servers housed together in one location is sometimes called a server farm or server cluster. When these servers are used for Web sites, the term Web server farm or Web farm is sometimes used. E-businesses such as ISPs or hosting companies that provide Web site hosting on multiple servers are also sometimes called Web farms.

Hosting companies also differentiate their service packages and fees by the other options they provide, such as the number of e-mail accounts. Some hosting companies allow an e-business to set up small databases and use technologies such as ASP, PHP, or ColdFusion to allow customers to interact with their databases. Some hosting companies offer Web site building tools and others offer the means to provide Web site shopping carts and the tools required to set up credit/debit card validation and acceptance services. It's important to consider not only whether a host can handle an e-business's immediate needs economically, but also whether it can offer new services as an e-business grows.

TECH CASE **Searching the Server Farm**

Google, Inc. is an e-business that provides Internet users a way to search the Web for pages containing specific content. Google uses a search engine (you learn about search engine technologies in Chapter 9) to locate Web pages and then adds the pages to its index, or catalog, of available pages. At its Web site, Google presents a search text box in which a user enters a keyword or phrase. Google uses the keyword or phrase to find pages in its index containing the specific keyword or phrase and then returns a list of links to the applicable Web pages. Given the growth in the number of available Web pages, this is becoming a Herculean task. How does Google support this load?

In an increasingly common trend, Google avoids the need to buy the latest helium-cooled supercomputer by using, instead, thousands of rack-mountable servers — essentially hefty personal computers in cases that look like pizza boxes — located at multiple server farms to which are added about 30 new servers *each day*. Google's index of Web pages is broken into hundreds of different pieces and scattered across these racks of servers and server farms. For example, the section of the index relating to Web pages about your congressperson or senator is housed on a different server than the portion of the index relating to Web pages about rebuilding old tractor engines. In order to handle multiple queries and to provide back-up redundancy, each piece of the index database is copied to about 40 servers. A group of sophisticated devices called load balancers identify which server an incoming query should be routed to, and sends it to the least busy server. If a server goes down, queries are allocated to its back-up server. If a cluster of servers goes down, queries are sent to one of the other Google server farms.

Continued

When the flow of requests slows down, another set of servers uses the available bandwidth to find and index new pages. Index updates are parceled out periodically to the servers, which integrate updated information into the existing index. Economy (running the free Linux operating system on cheap PC hardware), efficiency (optimized query routing means each query gets attention quickly), and speed (multiple servers available to share the load on each part of the database results in a fraction of a second response time) keep Google (Figure 6-13) at the front of the pack.

Figure 6-13
Google

Despite the tempting array of services offered by Web hosting companies, many e-businesses, large and small, choose to manage their own Web servers rather than pay a Web hosting company to do so. This is not as difficult as it may sound. An e-business that already has the technical staff to manage other types of servers and a dedicated connection to the Internet of at least 128 Kbps may find it easy to integrate a Web server into its network. Older Web server hardware usually can suffice because even a very slow Web server costing a few hundred dollars can easily handle a half dozen simultaneous page requests. So it's tempting, if a small e-business already has an "always on" connection to the Internet, to use an old computer as a Web host. Rarely, though, does a small e-business have enough data transfer bandwidth to transmit Web content to requesting users as quickly as a reputable Web hosting service can transfer it. If a Web site is popular, users trying to access it may quickly overburden a 128 Kbps line; a 1.5 Mbps T1 line is more appropriate to host Web sites. It's important to note here that without specialized staff, it isn't possible to host complex Web sites in-house; so don't expect to grab an old computer and an $80/month DSL connection to run a high-powered dynamic Web site!

Table 6-3 illustrates issues to consider when evaluating a Web hosting company.

Issue	Description
Data transfer bandwidth	Determine an estimated amount of Web page data transfer from or to your Web site each month. For example, assume your Web site has 25 pages averaging 10 KB each of text with 25 KB of graphics on each page. You project an estimated 100 visitors per day viewing five pages each. Your estimated monthly Web page data transfer bandwidth needs would be:
	(10 KB +25 KB) * (100 visitors * 5 pages) * (30 days) = 525,000 KB or 525 MB of data transfer bandwidth per month, exclusive of the additional bandwidth required to send and receive e-mail and upload or download files to maintain the Web site.
	Look for a hosting company that provides sufficient data transfer bandwidth in its base package fee. Also find out how the hosting company would respond if your account exceeded its base allowed bandwidth: would the hosting company shut down your site? Would extra charges be incurred? Most Web hosting companies include reports on space and bandwidth usage, and most allow package upgrades during the month if demand appears to be headed higher than the bandwidth included in the base package.
Disk space	Determine how much disk space is required to store your Web site files. One easy way to do this is to create a new folder on a computer hard drive and copy all the Web site files you plan to host into the folder; then check the folder size using an operating system tool such as Windows Explorer. Remember to add to your disk space estimate sufficient space for any Web site log files, database files, and other data created and stored with your Web site during Web site operations.
	Look for a hosting company package that provides sufficient disk space. Check with the hosting company to see what procedures are followed if your Web site operations exceed the allowable disk space. Do you have to delete existing files? Would you be prevented from sending/receiving e-mail? What are the additional charges for increasing your disk space?
E-mail	Determine the number of e-mail accounts you require. Decide if you want to have all incoming mail at the host forwarded to an existing e-mail account and whether or not you want an automatic response sent to incoming mail.

Table 6-3
(continued)
Evaluating a
Web hosting
company

Issue	Description
	Look for a hosting package that provides a sufficient number of e-mail accounts in its base fee. Most hosting companies provide e-mail forwarding in which the host forwards all incoming e-mail to an existing e-mail address such as a POP3 account with your ISP. Some hosting companies provide an autoresponder service that sends a predefined message in response to incoming mail.
Interactive Web site needs	If your Web site currently contains interactive content or if you plan to add interactive content, look for a hosting company that supports server-side scripting in Perl, C, C++, and so forth. The company should also support other interactive tools such as Flash, Real Audio, Real Video, and Java elements.
Performance	Look for a hosting company that provides high-quality, high-performance servers and routers and has multiple connections to NSPs via high-speed connections such as OC lines.
Level of Service	Determine whether or not your e-business requires shared hosting, dedicated hosting, or co-location services. If you are looking to co-locate your own Web servers, decide if you want to manage server administration in-house or pay the hosting company to handle all server administration.
Support	Determine the quality of server maintenance, technical support, security, and disaster recovery and backup procedures provided by a hosting company. A hosting company should monitor its servers' performance regularly, provide periodic server software upgrades, and provide systematic backup of data stored on its servers. Its technical support staff should be easy to access 24 hours a day and provide knowledgeable assistance. Adequate security policies and disaster recovery and backup procedures should be established.
Fees	Compare the monthly fees and set up charges for several hosting packages that meet your e-business's needs before you make a decision.

As of this writing, the telecommunications industry is struggling over issues such as overcapacity, enormous debt, and slowing demand for services. Two startling examples of e-businesses losing this struggle are Exodus Communications Inc. and Global Crossing Holdings Ltd.

Exodus Communications Inc. started life in 1994 as an ISP. Soon some of its early customers wanted more than simple Internet connections. Some of Exodus' customers first began asking for space to store their own servers and then began asking for server administration services. Meeting this demand gave birth to the Web hosting e-business model. In 1998, Exodus Communications went public with one of the most successful initial public offerings (IPOs) of the year. By 1999, Exodus had 9.3 percent of the Web hosting market with revenues of about $242 million, had tripled its employees, and increased its customer base from 300 to 1,500. A portion of the Exodus client list read like a "who's who" of e-business: eBay Inc., Yahoo! Geocities, Microsoft Corporation's MSN network, Lycos, Inc., Macromedia, Inc., and Sun Microsystems, Inc. Exodus charged ahead in the new millennium with its plan to increase market share and revenues through building more data centers and acquiring other hosting companies.

Global Crossing Holdings Ltd. is a worldwide telecommunications company involved in building a global fiber-optic network connecting more than 25 countries and approximately 200 primary cities around the world. In 2000, Exodus purchased the GlobalCenter Web hosting division from Global Crossing. As a result of the deal, Global Crossing became the primary network provider for Exodus and Exodus' largest shareholder. By 2001, Exodus had more than 4,000 customers at 44 data centers across the U.S., Europe, and Asia connected via its IP network. What's more, the company was building 10 additional data centers. Meanwhile, Global Crossing finished its global IP fiber-optic network in June 2001, with its final South American connection in Lima, Peru.

But, the slow global economy, telecommunications and hosting overcapacity, and the burst dot.com bubble were already taking their toll. Exodus had lost many e-business startup customers and was having trouble acquiring new customers. Because of its customer acquisition problems, its existing data centers were not operating at capacity even while Exodus was building new ones. Additionally, the company's massive $3.5 billion debt load was quickly draining its cash reserves. By June 2001, Exodus posted a $538 million second quarter loss — ten times greater than the same period in the previous year and its stock price was falling precipitously. At the same time, much of Global Crossing's worldwide communications capacity was going unused.

In August 2001, three of the Exodus board of directors suddenly quit the board for "personal reasons." In early September 2001, its CEO, Ellen Hancock, resigned; and on September 26, 2001, Exodus filed for bankruptcy. Ultimately, Exodus' assets, including 29 data centers in the U.S., Britain, Japan, and Germany were acquired by the British telecommunications company Cable & Wireless plc.

Global Crossing was required to take a huge write-off on the devaluation of its Exodus stock in the third quarter of 2001 and in January 2002, Global Crossing also filed for bankruptcy amid announced investigations by the U.S. Federal Bureau of Investigations (FBI) and the U.S. Security and Exchange Commission (SEC) for accounting improprieties that artificially inflated revenues and stock prices.

So far, you've learned that NSPs and ISPs supply interconnecting networks or backbones for an e-business's data transmissions. You've also learned how ISPs and hosting companies allow e-businesses to make their Web site services available to customers. Another important issue facing e-businesses is the question of how to efficiently make Web site content available to geographically dispersed users without sending and resending data over long distances through many different servers. Content caching and content delivery networks help solve this problem.

Content Caching and Content Delivery Networks

Although The Coca-Cola Company is headquartered in Atlanta, Georgia, few people travel to Atlanta and back just to grab a six-pack of soda. Distributing the Coca-Cola products to consumers involves stocking the sodas at thousands of retail outlets — putting the product close to the consumer regardless of where the product is manufactured or bottled or where the original recipe for the soda resides. For an e-business, however, user requests for Web site services often involve sending data over long distances through many different servers. What if there was a way to avoid these lengthy round trips by a mechanism similar to the stocking of sodas closer to consumers at retail outlets?

Scientists funded by the National Science Foundation began work in the mid-1990s on just this mechanism. Their goal was to establish some method of storing Web pages and other Web content (anything served to users over the Web, including text pages, pictures, sound clips, video files, and so forth) closer to end users. The technology these scientists developed is variously called content caching, proxy caching, or content distribution.

Content Caching

Content caching is done by cache servers connected to networks and positioned between end users and origin servers. A **cache server** intercepts a request for a Web page, then downloads the Web page from the origin server (that is, from the computer where the page was originally posted). The cache server then stores or caches the page, and finally forwards a copy of the page to the requesting user. This activity is essentially transparent to the user who requests the page. The user often doesn't realize the Web page has been provided by a cache server instead of the

TIP

The term "cache" (pronounced "kash"), originally a French word meaning a hidden storage place, is used today to indicate a method of storing data either temporarily in a computer's memory or more permanently on a hard disk.

origin server. The next time the cache server intercepts a request for the same Web page, it doesn't have to download it again; the cache server simply sends another copy of the cached page to the requesting user. Content caching reduces the time it takes for a user to download a Web page and reduces the amount of Web traffic to and from the origin server. Depending on the **latency** — the amount of time it takes for a packet to travel from server to client or vice versa — this time savings can be quite significant.

For example, assume Joan launches her Web browser and downloads the CNN.com home page. A cache server intercepts Joan's request and first downloads the CNN.com home page from the origin server and stores it; then it sends a copy of the page on to Joan. Now another user, David, requests the same CNN.com Web page. David's request is intercepted by the same cache server. Instead of downloading another copy of the page from the origin server, the cache server simply forwards a copy of its cached page to David. Now, assume that David requests a different page from the CNN.com Web site. The cache server first downloads the content of the new page *except* for items such as the CNN logo that are already stored on the cache server. The cache server then sends a copy of the CNN logo and other cached items plus the new page content to David.

When a cache server is full of Web content, it begins deleting Web pages or files requested less frequently to make room for new content. Origin servers tag most content with information about how often it changes and whether or not it can be cached. A stock quote page, for example, might be marked uncacheable or only cacheable for one minute. The CNN.com logo, however, might be cacheable for 24 hours or more. If the cache server receives a request for the CNN.com logo after more than 24 hours, it can query the origin server not for the whole logo, but simply for confirmation that the logo hasn't changed. If the logo has changed, a copy of the new logo is downloaded. If not, the cache server serves up its cached copy of the logo and resets the logo's timer to 24 hours.

Content caching provides two quantifiable benefits. First, the user gets data more quickly because the round-trip time to the cache is typically much shorter than that to the origin server. It usually takes about three seconds for a request to travel from a typical user to an origin server. Cache "hits" — those requests served from the cache — get the requested content back to the user very quickly, often in less than a quarter of a second. Multiplied across thousands of users and thousands of content requests per week, this is a significant benefit. Second, the load on the data lines between the user and the origin server is reduced, usually by about 40 percent. This is because an average group of users tends to have a 40 percent overlap in the Web pages they request.

In another example, an e-business with 200 employees might be straining the capacity of a T1 line enough for the business to consider adding a second line. The e-business can save the $600-900 per month required for a second T1 line by installing a cache server between the end users and the existing T1 line. Assuming that 40 percent of content requests are served from the cache server and do not go out onto the Internet, the load on the T1 would be greatly reduced. Because a cache server capable of handling a 200-person load can be purchased for less than $5,000, the economic motivation for using one at an e-business is powerful indeed.

To illustrate both benefits of installing a cache server, consider figure 6-14, which shows some statistics reported by a cache server for a large organization, in this case a school district.

DataReactor Executive Summary of Running Statistics

CPU workload:	56.44 %
Storage used:	100 %
Total requests served:	114040909 requests
Recent throughput:	1537 req/sec
Peak throughput:	2051 req/sec
Recent response time:	267 msec
-Misses:	1167 msec
-Hits:	3 msec
Recent hit ratio:	88 %
Recent byte hit ratio:	29 %
Recent bandwidth saved:	3979 Kbits/sec
Peak bandwidth saving:	11111 Kbits/sec
Duration:	31.84 hours

Figure 6-14
Cache server statistics

In this example, the cache server is returning requested content already in the cache in three milliseconds, while it's taking 1.167 seconds to fetch noncached content from the Internet. This cache also reports that it's handling 1,537 requests per second, 88 percent of which are **cache hits**, or instances when the cache server can serve the request without forwarding it to an origin server. (A **cache miss** is an instance when the cache cannot serve the request and must forward it to an origin server.) This is a higher hit ratio than most cache servers achieve, but a high percentage of internal users are requesting the same content. (The example comes from a very large school district where hundreds of students and teachers view a specific group of Web sites.) Therefore, 88 percent of requests, or 1,353 per second, are satisfied in 1.164 seconds less than the time it would take to satisfy them otherwise. Each second, the cache saves 1.164 seconds for each of the 1,353 requests that are hits. This equals a total of 26 minutes saved. Of course, this savings is spread across many students and teachers using the cache, but over time these saved milliseconds add up. On a single school day, this school district saves *312 weeks* (26 saved minutes of access time * 3,600 seconds per hour * 8 hours per day = 748,800 minutes saved by the cache each day, divided by 2,400 minutes per week) of time waiting for information to appear on their screens.

Along with the student/teacher viewing time saved, consider the bandwidth savings accrued by not having to forward Web browser requests to origin servers. The peak bandwidth savings

> **TIP**
>
> Another form of Web caching, called browser caching, can be done at an individual computer by setting Web browser options to store Web pages on the computer's hard drive and to test for "freshness" of the page before requesting another copy from the origin server. Clicking the Back button on a Web browser toolbar generally loads a recently viewed page from the user's hard drive cache.

achieved by the cache server during one 32-hour period is 11.111 megabits per second, or the equivalent of more than seven T1 lines. With T1 lines costing about $1,000 each, the cache server in this example obviates the need for $7,000 in telecommunications charges each month. Not bad for a cache server that cost about $20,000! Even with more common cache hit ratios in the 40 percent range, the savings are still quite significant.

There are a few problems with the use of content caching. The issue of most concern to Web advertisers is that they are no longer able to monitor who is requesting which Web pages and viewing which ads, since requests for pages are being intercepted and served without the involvement of the origin server. Because of this, some e-businesses tag all of their Web pages as noncacheable, hoping to force all requests to the origin server. Many cache administrators override such directives, however, leading to a cat-and-mouse game of technical one-upmanship.

For e-businesses, content caching is a double-edged sword. Cache-friendly Web pages — those that allow cache servers to hold a copy — please users because Web content downloads faster, but displeases Web advertisers, because the downloading process is less traceable. Also, sometimes, even though Web pages are updated on the origin server, the cache server might not check for freshness, leading to old content being downloaded by users. However, careful use of the caching information on Web pages by cache servers can remedy this problem.

Although content caching started off as one of the many projects funded by the NSF, commercial cache server e-businesses began to spring up in the mid-1990s. The caching and content distribution marketplace (sometimes called the content acceleration marketplace) is made up of software vendors and server manufacturers. Inktomi Corporation, iMimic Networking (Figure 6-15), and Novell, Inc.'s Volera subsidiary, for example, develop caching and content distribution software which is licensed to server vendors such as Stratacache, Dell Computer Corporation, and Compaq Computer Corporation. Companies such as Cisco Systems, Inc. and CacheFlow Inc. sell preconfigured caching appliances with their own software already installed. E-businesses seeking to speed up delivery of Web pages to internal personnel while saving money on Internet connectivity are the primary customers for these caching appliances, along with telecommunications carriers seeking to reduce the load on their networks.

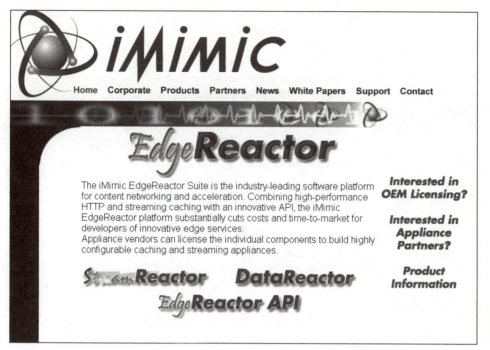

The iMimic EdgeReactor Suite is the industry-leading software platform for content networking and acceleration. Combining high-performance HTTP and streaming caching with an innovative API, the iMimic EdgeReactor platform substantially cuts costs and time-to-market for developers of innovative edge services.
Appliance vendors can license the individual components to build highly configurable caching and streaming appliances.

Interested in OEM Licensing?

Interested in Appliance Partners?

Product Information

StreamReactor   DataReactor   EdgeReactor API

Figure 6-15
iMimic
Networking

One area where caching provides an immediately and obvious benefit is in caching streaming media.

Streaming Media Caching

Streaming media — video and audio content that can be viewed as it is being downloaded, instead of after it is downloaded — is increasingly important to e-businesses. These days, e-businesses are distributing training videos, videoconferences, and other types of managed knowledge internally via intranets and streaming media. Also, online news outlets are turning to streaming media to satisfy impatient consumers who don't want to wait until 11 P.M. for the latest television news. Because data transport across the public Internet operates on a "best efforts" basis, there's no way to guarantee that streamed data will arrive with every frame intact and that data flow will be consistent. This isn't much of a problem with Web pages because a Web browser can simply request the pages again. But dropped frames and interruptions are immediately obvious when watching video clips or listening to music. Also, because streaming content takes up more bandwidth than HTML Web pages, it can quickly overwhelm data lines if the same content is requested by many computers at one time. Figure 6-16 illustrates streaming media without caching where three viewers watching the same stream each need a separate copy sent by the origin server. If each of these three viewers is watching a VHS-quality 500 Kbps stream, and the e-business has a $1,000/month T1 connection to the Internet, these three streams completely fill the 1.5 Mbps T1 line. Any mail delivery or other Web surfing over this line is either blocked or results in poor-quality video.

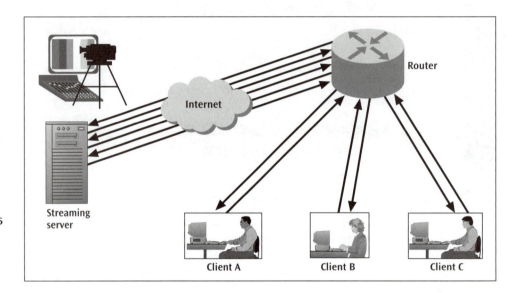

Figure 6-16
Streaming media without caching

These problems with streaming media can be prevented by a special kind of caching known as streaming caching. A user watching a cached clip from a nearby **streaming cache server** (on their intranet or on their ISP's network) is much more likely to have a positive user experience because the delivery channel isn't so constrained and unpredictable. Most corporate networks run at 100 Mbps, which is plenty of speed to carry video from an internal streaming cache server to 200 desktops.

Streaming caching takes two forms: on-demand caching and live splitting caching. **On-demand caching** can be used with a prerecorded video clip of a defined length. A cache server can store the entire clip and restream it to the next requesting user. **Live splitting caching** comes into play with "live" streams — those being delivered over the Internet as they are created, either for the duration of a live concert or continuously, as with a 24-hour news broadcast. In this case, a cache server can intercept a second request for a stream currently passing through the server and split the stream, serving one copy to each requesting computer. When hundreds of people at a given site need to watch a company conference call, line split caching turns out to be a crucial capability for an e-business intranet. A large streaming cache server can split live audio across

8,000 users, or a 400 Kbps training video across 2,000 users. Figure 6-17 illustrates streaming with caching, in which caching solves the overload problem and provides a more consistent and higher quality stream to the users.

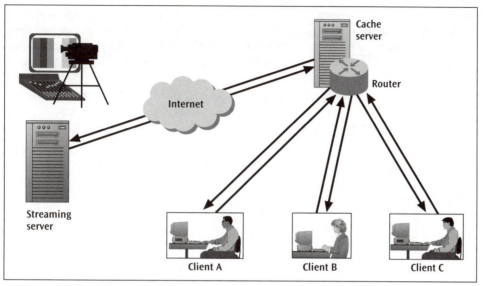

Figure 6-17
Streaming media with caching

Because content caching services are gradually becoming standardized and commoditized, e-businesses specializing in content caching are diversifying into providing many other types of services, such as virus filtering of content and policing requests for appropriateness.

The type of caching you have just learned about in this section is called **passive caching**, because each cache server is choosing what content to retain based on what passes through the cache. Another more proactive caching technique is used by very large Web sites to geographically distribute Web site content.

Content Delivery Networks

Very large Web sites (or those distributing large files such as video clips), often use **active caching**, which involves forwarding (or "pushing") Web content to a geographically distributed group of cache servers ahead of demand (often at night). Networks that push content to cache servers are called **content delivery networks** (sometimes content distribution networks) or **CDNs**. Akamai Technologies, Inc., founded by a group of MIT computer scientists, was one of the first e-businesses to create such a network.

As you learned in the Chapter 4 section on HTML, most Web pages load pictures and video clips from the same server as the text. However, an e-business using Akamai's services serves up the text of a Web page from the origin server and the video and sound from a different server. Before the text is served up from the origin server, the requesting user's IP address is analyzed and the "nearest" Akamai content server is chosen to serve up the larger pieces of content.

Note that "nearest" doesn't necessarily mean geographically close. For example, a user on Southwestern Bell's DSL service in Houston can communicate much more quickly with a server in Dallas that's also on the Southwestern Bell network than with a Houston-based server on a different network because communications from Southwestern Bell's network to a different network must pass through several peering points to reach its destination. So a Southwestern Bell DSL user in Houston requesting a Web page gets the text from the origin server and the large video and other items from an Akamai server connected to the Southwestern Bell network and the user is none the wiser.

Figure 6-18 illustrates a content delivery network. Periodically (once per day, for example), content is pushed from the origin server to the caches on other backbones and onto subnets of those backbones.

Figure 6-18

Content Delivery network

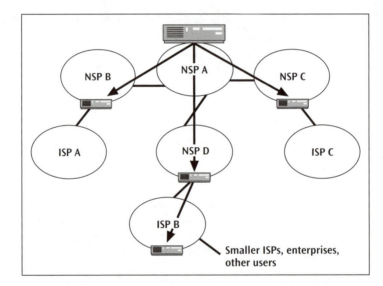

Since all of the cache servers on the Akamai network share information about how many requests they've received for a given piece of content, Webmasters using Akamai have a better idea of how many viewers their Web site is attracting. "Akamized" Web sites can proactively distribute popular content before it is requested, instead of burdening the origin server all at once as it supplies content to passive caches and end users who are not using caching.

When the Internet consisted of mainly simple Web pages, an ISP or hosting service was all that was required to have a Web site. Today, e-businesses need many more services to support a complex Web site and many choose to outsource those services to third parties such as application service providers.

Application Service Providers

Even a simple e-business needs both a shopping cart of some type and credit card clearing services. In addition, an e-business often needs other more sophisticated external or internal Web-based services. For example, an auto dealership might want an online service and reminder tracking system on its Web site as well as an online company directory, calendaring services, sales and inventory tracking, and file sharing across multiple offices. But, it's generally not feasible for a small or medium-sized e-business, such as an auto dealership, to hire an in-house Web site development staff to create and maintain a complex Web site. Thus, many e-businesses turn to third-party technology providers called application service providers to develop and manage their internal or external Web applications.

Application service providers, or **ASPs**, are e-businesses that manage and distribute software services from a central data center across an IP network. In our auto dealership example, an ASP can create a Web-based auto dealer service tracking system, rent the system to several auto dealerships, and run the systems and related Web sites from a central data center or hosting facility.

Applications that are created and managed by an ASP are accessible to the employees of a client e-business via a Web browser. Thus, in our auto dealership example, instead of installing the service tracking system application on every computer at a dealership, the system software and data are kept offsite at the ASP's data center. Dealership employees view the service tracking system and data as a series of Web pages containing the dealership's information.

Once an ASP has created an online system, it's fairly simple (from a database management standpoint) to allow multiple businesses to access the same application with separate data. The ASP model thus promises significant economies of scale for the ASP, which in turn can be passed on to the customer. Also, hiring an ASP involves only a monthly fee, instead of a large software development outlay upfront. One ASP, Intranets.com, enables businesses and other organizations to use an intranet-like application hosted on servers at Intranets.com but accessible over the Web, secured, backed up, and accessible from anywhere in the world, for as little as $3 per employee per month. Such an intranet-like application supplies everything an in-house intranet would: file storage and sharing, contact lists, online meeting and collaboration chat rooms, and so forth. By contrast, the costs of deploying such a system in-house can run into the millions of dollars, especially when the e-business in question has multiple locations or many traveling employees.

As Web pages become more sophisticated in terms of layout, page controls, and supported programming languages such as JavaScript, Java, and C#, the types of applications that can feasibly be fit into a Web browser are growing by leaps and bounds. Another example of an ASP is ANOXWEB (a subsidiary of ANOX Software). ANOXWEB has built a word processor that exists within a Web page and can be used only as needed. Instead of large costs associated with purchasing, installing, maintaining, supporting, and upgrading an e-business's computers with the latest word-processing program, an e-business can rent a word processor on a per user per month basis. Table 6-4 lists a number of major ASPs and their technology specialty.

Table 6-4

Major ASPs

Name	Specialty
Intranets.com, Inc.	Corporate intranet services: calendaring, contact lists, file sharing, online threaded and real-time discussions
Salesforce.com, Inc.	Sales process management tools: bid tracking, customer service management, and reporting
Jamcracker, Inc.	Customized Web-based tools; for example, JamCracker built an online second mortgage application to support DiTech.com's financial business
Digital River, Inc.	A broad variety of custom applications fitting the online needs of individual e-businesses; similar to JamCracker; primarily centered on e-business transactions
ANOXWEB	Application serving: office suites, graphics tools, and so forth

As useful as ASPs appear, there are some cautions to consider before outsourcing applications to ASPs. One is network reliability: if the network link between an e-business and an ASP fails, any ASP applications become inaccessible. In addition, some e-businesses are concerned about crucial business data being maintained by a third party, which might not allow the flexibility that would be possible with in-house management. What's more, while in-house developed applications can be modified to fit business processes as needed, ASPs rarely allow users to change the hosted application, except at regular release intervals.

Some e-businesses have proprietary applications that represent part of the value that they provide to customers. One such example would be geophysical analysis tools that help users to find oil buried in rock formations. Outsourcing one's core competency or intellectual property is rarely a good idea; the ASP could rent the same application to competitors. Finally, if a company already possesses a linked group of applications (for example, manufacturing applications feeding data to an accounting system and a purchasing system) it might be difficult to outsource only one part of the group.

Despite these issues, ASPs will likely capture an increasing percentage of Internet spending. One sign of this trend is the increasing sophistication and specificity seen in the types of applications that are being rented. Online office suites, digital image management systems, and large accounting systems are all available online at reasonable costs. What was once the purview of small ASP startups has become the new arena for the technology industry's super heavyweights. For example, Oracle Corporation has entered the ASP industry in competition with the smaller accounting providers and companies such as Salesforce.com, Inc. Also, Microsoft Corporation's .NET is an initial attempt to address what is seen within Microsoft as the ASP industry's threat to erode Microsoft's core business.

You can actually view the path of information as it flows from its origin to its destination across the Internet by using the Traceroute utility.

Using the Traceroute Utility

You can use your computer to explore the paths through which information flows between it and origin servers such as those at CNN. Most operating systems such as UNIX and Windows include a command-line tool to run a "traceroute" called the Traceroute utility. **Traceroute** sends a packet of information to a destination and reports a list of all of the intermediary routers through which this packet flowed, with the amount of time the packet took to move from router to router.

To practice using Traceroute on a Windows computer:

- *Step 1:* Open a command prompt window.
- *Step 2:* Type **tracert www.mit.edu** and then press **Enter**. You see a list of the hops — the paths from one intermediary router to the next — between your computer and MIT. Each hop represents a router with a host name.

By using the Traceroute utility you can usually watch your data packet move through your ISP's network to an NSP, then to the Internet service provider serving the computer you've identified as your destination (www.mit.edu in the preceding example). You can also use software such as Visualware Inc.'s VisualRoute (Figure 6-19) to run a traceroute. VisualRoute software attempts to correlate the intermediary routers to their physical locations on a map, so you can see where your data physically traveled. You may be surprised to find how circuitous the route is.

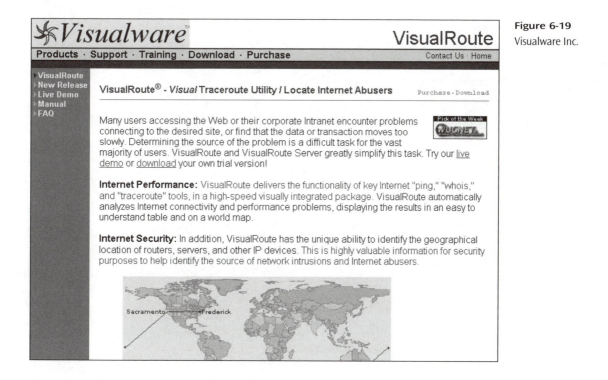

Figure 6-19
Visualware Inc.

In this chapter you have learned how network service providers (NSPs) connect to each other to provide the backbone for the Internet and how Internet users connect to that backbone through Internet service providers (ISPs). You've learned how Web hosting companies provide Web site hosting services to meet almost every e-business hosting need and how caching and content delivery networks (CDNs) enable Web content to reach the end user more quickly. You also learned how e-businesses can save money by outsourcing business application development and management to application service providers (ASPs). Finally, you learned how to trace the flow of a data packet across the Internet using the Traceroute utility. In the next chapter, you learn about network and Web site security issues.

IF YOU BUILD IT, WILL THEY COME?

As it turned out, U.S. capital markets oversubsidized the telecommunications industry. Easy money created a building boom in long-haul networking: railroads, pipeline companies, power companies, and entirely new companies raced to be the first with the fastest global data links. When the bubble finally burst in late 2000, companies such as WorldCom, Inc. awoke to a world where demand filled only three percent of available capacity, leaving many telecommunications companies such as WorldCom, Global Crossing, and Level (3) struggling to generate revenues and bending under mountains of debt incurred to build these networks. As the global economy softened, telecommunications company stock prices began to fall amid rumors of anticipated poor financial results and liquidity problems. An industry that was once the darling of the U.S. capital markets was now a pariah.

Continued

In February 2002, during a conference call with investors and analysts to announce lower than expected earnings, Ebbers was forced to assure investors that WorldCom was in no danger of defaulting on its credit, was not involved in any accounting improprieties, and was not filing for bankruptcy protection as other telecommunication companies such as Global Crossing had recently done. In April 2002, WorldCom (Figure 6-20) was forced to lower its 2002 revenue and earning projections for the second time and Ebbers resigned under pressure from the WorldCom board of directors who were unhappy with WorldCom's falling stock prices and an ever-growing investigation by the SEC. The news just kept getting worse for WorldCom's investors. In late June, 2002 the SEC filed charges against WorldCom when, on June 25, WorldCom's management admitted to massive accounting fraud by reporting operating expenses as capital expenses in its five previous operating quarters. As a result of this accounting fraud, investors, the government, and the public were misled into believing that WorldCom continued to be profitable during the five quarters when, in fact, WorldCom generated losses during this period instead of profits. In an attempt to save the company, in July 2002 WorldCom filed for bankruptcy protection from its creditors — the largest bankruptcy filing in U.S. business history. Despite its bankruptcy, many analysts question WorldCom's long-term viability.

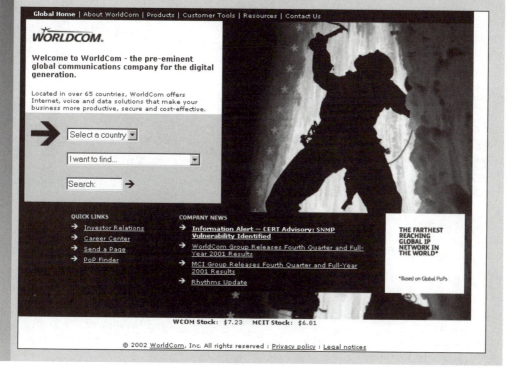

Figure 6-20
WorldCom, Inc.

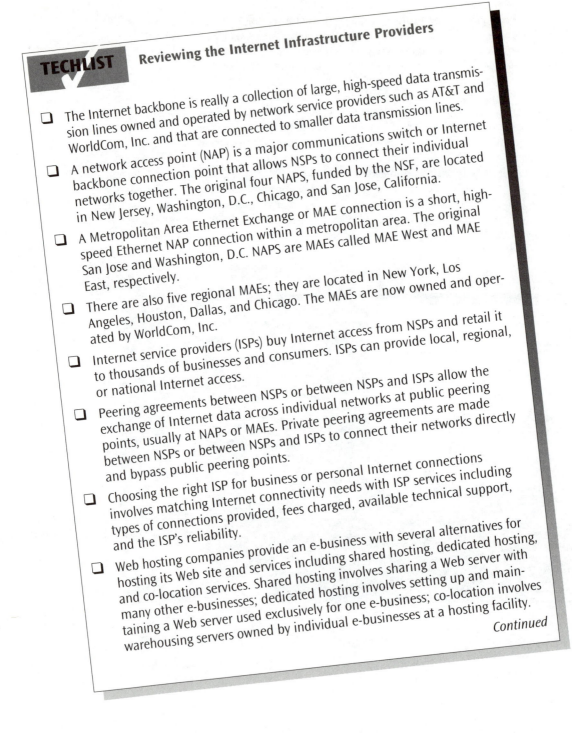

TECHLIST

Reviewing the Internet Infrastructure Providers

❏ The Internet backbone is really a collection of large, high-speed data transmission lines owned and operated by network service providers such as AT&T and WorldCom, Inc. and that are connected to smaller data transmission lines.

❏ A network access point (NAP) is a major communications switch or Internet backbone connection point that allows NSPs to connect their individual networks together. The original four NAPS, funded by the NSF, are located in New Jersey, Washington, D.C., Chicago, and San Jose, California.

❏ A Metropolitan Area Ethernet Exchange or MAE connection is a short, high-speed Ethernet NAP connection within a metropolitan area. The original San Jose and Washington, D.C. NAPS are MAEs called MAE West and MAE East, respectively.

❏ There are also five regional MAEs; they are located in New York, Los Angeles, Houston, Dallas, and Chicago. The MAEs are now owned and operated by WorldCom, Inc.

❏ Internet service providers (ISPs) buy Internet access from NSPs and retail it to thousands of businesses and consumers. ISPs can provide local, regional, or national Internet access.

❏ Peering agreements between NSPs or between NSPs and ISPs allow the exchange of Internet data across individual networks at public peering points, usually at NAPs or MAEs. Private peering agreements are made between NSPs or between NSPs and ISPs to connect their networks directly and bypass public peering points.

❏ Choosing the right ISP for business or personal Internet connections involves matching Internet connectivity needs with ISP services including types of connections provided, fees charged, available technical support, and the ISP's reliability.

❏ Web hosting companies provide an e-business with several alternatives for hosting its Web site and services including shared hosting, dedicated hosting, and co-location services. Shared hosting involves sharing a Web server with many other e-businesses; dedicated hosting involves setting up and maintaining a Web server used exclusively for one e-business; co-location involves warehousing servers owned by individual e-businesses at a hosting facility.

Continued

- ❑ An e-business can reduce costs by outsourcing its Web site operations to a hosting company that provides access to high-speed Internet connections, secure off-site server facilities, trained Web server administrators and technical support staff, regular data backup, disaster recovery plans, and Web traffic monitoring.

- ❑ Large e-businesses move Web content closer to the end users by using cache servers to store frequently requested Web content. Content caching has two primary benefits: it gets Web-based data to the end user more quickly and reduces the amount of traffic to the origin server.

- ❑ Streaming media caching — either on demand or live splitting — allows large e-businesses to more effectively distribute video and audio content to end users.

- ❑ Content delivery networks "push" Web content to cache servers in advance of demand.

- ❑ Application service providers that manage and distribute software services from a central data center or hosting facility provide an e-business with a lower-cost alternative to development and management of custom business applications.

- ❑ You can use the Traceroute utility or software such as VisualRoute to trace the path of a data packet across the Internet.

Key Terms

active caching
application service provider (ASP)
bilateral peering
cache hit
cache miss
cache server
co-location facilities
content caching
content delivery networks (CDNs)
dedicated hosting services
Digital Subscriber Line Access
    Multiplexer (DSLAM)

Internet backbone
Internet service provider (ISP)
latency
live splitting caching
Metropolitan Area Ethernet
    Exchange (MAE)
modem bank
modem card
modem pool
multilateral peering
network access point (NAP)

network service provider (NSP)
on-demand caching
passive caching
peering
private peering
public peering
streaming cache server
Synchronous Optical
    Network (SONET)
Traceroute
Web hosting company

Review Questions

1. Businesses that provide the backbone infrastructure for the Internet are called:
   a. ASPs.
   b. NSPs.
   c. ISPs.
   d. CDNs.

2. Metropolitan Area Ethernet Internet Exchanges or MAEs are owned and operated by:
   a. AT&T.
   b. Sprint Communications.
   c. WorldCom, Inc.
   d. Qwest Communications.

3. The original four NAPs were located in:
   a. San Jose, New Jersey, New York, and Miami.
   b. Washington, D.C., San Jose, Dallas, and Chicago.
   c. Chicago, Washington, D.C., New Jersey, and San Jose.
   d. Houston, Chicago, San Jose, and Dallas.

4. An agreement to exchange Internet data at a NAP or MAE between two NSPs is called a(n):
   a. Data exchange agreement.
   b. Co-location agreement.
   c. Peering agreement.
   d. Dedicated hosting agreement.

5. Which of the following is not an important consideration for an e-business when shopping for an ISP?
   a. Technical support availability
   b. Local dial-up numbers in different area codes for traveling employees
   c. The types of connections the ISP uses to access an NSP backbone
   d. An ISP's geographic location

6. Use of an entire Web server located at a Web hosting facility by a single e-business is called:
   a. Dedicated hosting.
   b. Shared hosting.
   c. Co-location.
   d. Caching.

7. The practice of storing frequently accessed Web content close to the end user is called:
   a. Dedicated hosting.
   b. Content caching.
   c. On-demand caching.
   d. Shared hosting.

8. A server that intercepts Web page requests and fulfills the request from its own stored copy of the Web page is called a:
   a. Transaction server.
   b. Web server.
   c. Origin server.
   d. Cache server.

9. E-businesses that "push" Web content to geographically diverse servers in advance of demand are called:
   a. ASPs.
   b. NSPs.
   c. CDNs.
   d. ISPs.

10. An e-business that wants to outsource the development and maintenance of custom internal or external Web-based applications might hire a(n):
    a. ASP.
    b. NSP.
    c. ISP.
    d. CDN.

11. Internet service providers own and operate the large, high-speed data transmission lines known as the Internet backbone. **True or False?**

12. The five regional MAEs are located in Houston, Dallas, Chicago, New York, and Los Angeles. **True or False?**

13. ASPs are responsible for building and maintaining the Internet infrastructure to meet traffic demands. **True or False?**

14. SONET fiber-optic technology is most commonly used by local ISPs to connect to the Internet backbone. **True or False?**

15. Private peering agreements between NSPs and between NSPs and large ISPs allow them to connect their networks directly and bypass public network access points. **True or False?**

16. Web hosting companies typically offer a variety of services including high-speed Internet access, Web server administration and technical support, e-mail accounts, and secure server storage facilities. **True or False?**

17. The terms "virtual hosting" and "hosting" are generally used synonymously. **True or False?**

18. Co-locating Web servers involves renting space on Web servers owned by a hosting company. **True or False?**

19. The Traceroute utility allows you to trace the path of a data packet across the Internet. **True or False?**

20. A cache server always downloads a fresh copy of Web content from the origin server each time it intercepts a request for the content. **True or False?**

Exercises

1. Using Internet search tools or other relevant resources, such as those at the end of this chapter, identify five ASPs and their specialties. Then write a one- or two-page paper describing the ASPs.

2. Using Internet search tools or other relevant resources, such as those at the end of this chapter, identify five ISPs and the services they provide. Then write a one- or two-page paper describing the ISPs and their services.

3. Define the terms NSP, NAP, MAE, SONET, and OC, and give examples of each.

4. Using Internet search tools or other relevant resources, such as those at the end of this chapter, identify three national or international NSPs and locate and print a copy of each NSP's backbone map.

5. Using Internet search tools or other relevant resources, such as those listed at the end of this chapter, locate three e-businesses involved in content caching or content distribution networks. Then create a one- or two-page paper describing each e-business and its role.

CASE PROJECTS

♦ 1 ♦

You are the owner of a small arts and crafts studio and want to begin providing dial-up Internet access, Internet e-mail, and other Internet-related services for your employees. You are also considering doing business online from your own Web site. Occasionally, you travel out of town looking for new arts and crafts artists whose work you want to display in your studio and you want to be able to access the Internet when traveling.

Your first step in setting up Internet access for your business is to find the right ISP. Using the Internet or other relevant sources, find and review articles and guides explaining how to choose an ISP. Then create your own checklist of important questions to ask an ISP during your search process. Finally, contact at least five ISPs offering services *in your geographical area*. Use your checklist as a guide to determine the services offered by the ISP and its fees. Select one of the ISPs for your business and write a short paragraph explaining your decision.

CASE PROJECTS

◆ 2 ◆

You and Hector, your business partner, operate a medium-sized business that sells rock and roll memorabilia and you are considering doing business online. Because you already have a small business LAN, Hector thinks the business should set up and maintain its own Web server. You are concerned that neither you nor Hector nor any of your current employees has the appropriate expertise and the time to manage an in-house Web server, and you can't afford to hire additional staff at this time. You think the business should outsource its Web site storage and server administration to a Web hosting company.

You and Hector plan to meet tomorrow to make a decision on the best approach to take. Using the Internet or other relevant resources, research the advantages and disadvantages of purchasing and managing a Web server in-house vs. outsourcing the server operations to a hosting company. Then create an outline of your research findings to guide your discussion with Hector.

◆ 3 ◆

You are the manager of a commercial real estate sales and management business with listings and properties in a five-state area. You want to set up Web-based property management and accounting systems for your business but can't afford to hire a Web development staff and Web site and server administration staff. You decide the best approach is to use an ASP. Using the Internet and other resources, identify ASPs that provide real estate systems packages and management of those systems. Then prepare a one- or two-page analysis comparing and contrasting these ASPs.

TEAM PROJECT

You, Maria, and Yong are partners in a C2C auction e-business that specializes in antique glass and figurines. You have been operating your own Web server from your LAN, but the demands on the server and customer complaints about slow access times indicate it's time to consider another option. Maria suggests contracting with a Web hosting company to host your Web site. You know that all your Web site files take approximately 10 MB of hard disk space and that you have 20 Web pages, each averaging 10 KB of text at your site. You estimate each Web page also contains approximately 25 KB of graphics content. You also estimate an average of 200 customers access your Web site each day and each customer views at least 10 pages. Meet with your teammates to determine: (1) your estimated data transfer bandwidth needs, (2) your e-mail account needs including e-mail forwarding and autoresponder needs, and (3) whether or not you can use shared hosting services or require dedicated hosting services. (You may make your own assumptions about facts not presented here.)

Using Internet or other applicable resources, locate at least three Web hosting companies and compare and contrast their hosting packages covering the level of service you require and the fees they charge. Then create a 5–10 slide presentation using Microsoft PowerPoint or other presentation tool describing your e-business, the Web hosting plans you reviewed, and the plan you think is best for your e-business. Include in your presentation the rationale behind your decision. Present your Web hosting decision to a group of classmates selected by your instructor.

Useful Links

American ISP Association
www.americanisps.org/1031/

An Atlas of Cyberspaces — Maps of Internet Service Provider and Internet Backbone Networks
www.geog.ucl.ac.uk/casa/martin/atlas/isp_maps.html

Application Planet — Web-Enabled Applications Resources
www.applicationplanet.com/

ASP Industry Consortium
www.aspindustry.org/

ASPNews.com — ASP Resources and News
www.aspnews.com/

Caching.com — Internet Caching Resource Center
www.caching.com/

ComputerUser.com — Choosing an ISP — Checklist
www.computeruser.com/resources/isp/intquest.html

Computing at Cornell — Choosing an ISP: ISP Checklist
www.cit.cornell.edu/computer/connect/isp/checklist.html

Directorate for Computer & Information Science & Engineering (CISE)
www.cise.nsf.gov/

HostIndex.com — Web Hosting Providers
www.hostindex.com/

HostSearch
www.hostsearch.com/

ISP Planet
www.isp-planet.com/

ISPWorld — Backbone List
www.ispworld.com/isp/bb/Backbone_Profiles.htm

ISPWorld.com — ISP Resources
www.ispworld.com/

MAE Services and Facilities
http://www.mae.net/

Russ Haynal's ISP Page — Links to Internet Backbone Maps
navigators.com/isp.html

SearchEBusiness.com — E-business Resources
searchebusiness.techtarget.com/home/0,,sid19,00.html

Squid Proxy Cache
www.squid-cache.org/

The Internet Weather Report — Animated Maps of Current Internet Lag
www.Internetweather.com/

The List of ISPs — Definitive ISP Guide
thelist.Internet.com/

The Web Host Industry Review — Web Hosting Resources
www.thewhir.com/

Web Caching and Content Delivery Resources
www.web-caching.com/

Web Hosting Magazine
www.whmag.com/content/

Links to Web Sites or Companies Noted in This Chapter

Akamai Technologies, Inc.
www.akamai.com/index_flash.html

ANOX Software - ANOXWEB
www.anoxweb.com/

AT&T
www.att.com/

Cable & Wireless plc
www.cw.com/th_48.asp?ID=global_home

Cable News Network (CNN)
www.cnn.com

CacheFlow Inc.
www.cacheflow.com

Cisco Systems, Inc.
www.cisco.com

Cogent Communications Company (PSINet)
www.cogentco.com/splash.html

Dell Computer Corporation
www.dell.com

Digital River, Inc.
drhome.digitalriver.com/livehtml/newsite/
dr_home_flash_main.html

Earthlink, Inc.
www.earthlink.net/

eBay Inc.
www.ebay.com

Genuity Inc.
www.genuity.com/

Global Crossing Ltd.
www.globalcrossing.com/xml/index.xml

Google, Inc.
www.google.com

Hosting.com
www.hosting.com

HostTech Communications
www.hosttech.com/

iMimic Networks
www.imimic.com

Inktomi Corporation
www.inktomi.com

Internap Network Services Corporation
www.internap.com/index.html

Intranets.com, Inc.
www.intranets.com

Jamcracker, Inc.
www.jamcracker.com/

Level (3) Communications
www.level3.com/us/index.html

Lycos, Inc.
www.lycos.com

Macromedia, Inc.
www.macromedia.com

MCI
www.mci.com/

Microsoft Corporation
www.microsoft.com

MSN
www.msn.com

Network Reliability and Interoperability Council
www.nric.org/

Novell, Inc.
www.novell.com

Oracle Corporation
www.oracle.com

Ovum
www.ovum.com/

Qwest Communications International Inc.
www.qwest.com/

Salesforce.com, Inc.
www.salesforce.com/us/

Southwestern Bell Telephone, L.P.
www.swbell.com/

Sprint Communications
www.sprint.com/

Stratacache
www.stratacache.com/main.htm

Sun Microsystems, Inc.
www.sun.com

The Coca-Cola Company
www.cocacola.com

Vario Inc.
www.verio.com/

Visualware Inc.
www.visualroute.com

WorldCom, Inc.
www.worldcom.com/main.phtml

XO Communications
www.xo.com/

Yahoo! GeoCities
geocities.yahoo.com/

Yahoo! Servers
servers.yahoo.com/

Yahoo! Website Services
website.yahoo.com/

For Additional Review

Andrews, Jean. 2001. *i-Net+ Guide to Internet Technologies*. Boston: Course Technology.

Associated Press. 1996. "WorldCom-MFS Communications Deal Forms Telecom Giant." August 27. New York. Available online at: centralohio.thesource.net/Files3/9608274.html.

Blumenstein, Rebecca and Sandberg, Jared. 2002. "WorldCom's CEO Ebbers Resigns," *MSNBC*, April 30. Available online at: www.msnbc.com/news/745540.asp.

Borland, John and Luening, Erich. 1999. "MCI WorldCom Buys Sprint for $129 Billion," *CNET News.com*, October 5. Available online at: news.com.com/2100-1033-230983.html?tag=prntfr.

Borland, John. 2000. "Sprint, WorldCom Call Off $120 Billion Merger," *CNET News.com*, July 13. Available online at: news.com.com/2100-1033-243110.html?tag=prntfr.

Byron, Christopher. 2002. "Time is Running Out for WorldCom: Sooner or Later the Company Will Almost Certainly Face Liquidation," *MSNBC Opinion*, February 1. http://stacks.msnbc.com/news/697962.asp.

Cable & Wireless plc. 2002. "Cable & Wireless Acquires Exodus Assets," February 1. Available online at: www.exodus.net/feature/customer_letter20020201.html.

Cahners In-Stat Group. 2001. "Business ISPs Will Suffer Consolidation." *NUA Surveys*, October 30. Available online at: www.nua.com/surveys/.

Carolan, Matt. 2001. "Cable & Wireless to Acquire Exodus," *PC Magazine*, November 30. Available online at: www.pcmag.com/print_article/0,3048,a=19256,00.asp.

Caufield, Brian. 2001. "An Exodus from Exodus?" *Business2.0*, November 20. Available online at: www.business2.com/articles/web/print/0,1650,35625,FF.html.

Chidi, George A. Jr. 2002. "Global Crossing Files for Bankruptcy," *ITworld.com, IDG News Service, Boston Bureau*, January 28. Available online at: www.itworld.com/Net/2572/IDG020128globalcrossing/pfindex.html.

ComputerUser.com. 2002. "Choosing an ISP." Available online at: www.computeruser.com/resources/isp/intquest.html?page_type=printer.

Cornell University. 2002. "Choosing an ISP: ISP Checklist." Available online at: www.cit.cornell.edu/computer/connect/isp/checklist.html.

CNN Money. 2002. "WorldCom, Inc.: Telecommunications Firm Misses Quarterly Esitmate, Warns on 2002 Earnings," *CNNMoney*, February 7. Available online at: money.cnn.com/2002/02/07/technology/worldcom/index.htm.

Dean, Tamara. 2002. *Network+ Guide to Networks, Second Edition*. Boston: Course Technology

Eisner, Adam. 2001. "Exodus Communications: The Decline of a Hosting Titan," *The Web Host Industry Review*, September 28. Available online at: thewhir.com/features/exodus928.cfm.

Gilbert, Alorie. 2001. "Exodus To Restructure After Filing For Bankruptcy," *Informationweek.com*, September 26. Available online at: www.informationweek.com/story/IWK20010926S0008.

Global Crossing Ltd. 2002. "The Global Crossing Story." Available online at: www.globalcrossing.com/.

Grise, Corey. 2001. "CEO Hancock out at Exodus," *CNET News.com*, September 4. Available online at: news.com.com/2100-1033-272538.html?tag=prntfr.

HelpWithHosting.com. 2002. "Beginner's Guide to Hosting." Available online at: www.helpwithhosting.com/.

Intel Corporation. 2002. "Technology Strategies." Available online at: www.intel.com/eBusiness/technology/.

Intel Corporation. 2002. "Success Stories: Google." Available online at: www.intel.com/eBusiness/casestudies/snapshots/google.htm.

Internap Network Services Corporation. 2002. "The Internet is a Little Bit Broken." Available online at www.internap.com/about/theproblem.html.

InternetNews.com. 2002. "Web Services: the Next Big Thing?" *ASPNews.com*, February 8. Available online at: www.aspnews.com/trends/article/0,2350,10571_970851,00.html.

Jacobs, April 2001. "Google's Secrets," *NetworkWorldFusion*, September 10. Available online at: www.nwfusion.com/newsletters/accel/2001/00991542.html.

Kende, Michael. 2000. "The Digital Handshake: Connecting Internet Backbones" Office of Plans and Policy, Federal Communications Commission. September. Available online at: www.fcc.gov/Bureaus/OPP/working_papers/oppwp32.pdf.

Landstreet, Linda. 2002. "The Human Factor: Questions to Ask a Potential Web Host" *TopHost.com*. Available online at: www.tophosts.com/articles/?1316.html.

Level(3) Communications. 2002. "(3) Center Colocation (North America)." www.level3.com/us/PDF/colo_USEng_Global_Letter_forscreen.pdf.

Little, Iain and Wright, Julian. 1999. "Peering and Settlement in the Internet: An Economic Analysis." September. Available online at: metric.eco.auckland.ac.nz/~jwright/peering.pdf.

Nottingham, Mark. 1999. "Caching Tutorial for Web Authors and Webmasters," *Web Developer's Virtual Library*, June 21. Available online at: www.wdvl.com/Internet/Cache/index.html.

Network Reliability Council. 2002. "Service Provider Interconnection for Internet Protocol Best Effort Service." Available online at: www.nric.org/fg/fg4/ISP_Interconnection.doc.

Olavsrud, Thor. 2001. "Is the Landscape Changing for Backbone Providers?" *ISP-Planet Market Research*, June 15. Available online at: www.isp-planet.com/research/2001/backbone_study.html.

Pappalardo, Denise. 2001. "When Private Peering Arrangements Go Bad," *Network World*, June 11. Available online at: www.nwfusion.com/archive/2001/121755_06-11-2001.html.

Pastore, Michael. 2001. "Web Hosting Market Just Getting Started," *CyberAtlas*, May 7. Available online at: cyberatlas.Internet.com/big_picture/hardware/article/0,,5921_760171,00.html.

Polito, Julie. 1999. "Stoking the Net's Worth: Industry Veteran Ellen Hancock Talks About How Her Company, Exodus, Keeps its Vast Server Farms Humming," *Salon.com*, October 18. Available online at: www.salon.com/tech/view/1999/10/18/ellen_hancock/index.html.

Reuters Limited. 2002. "Report: Broadband Usage Outpaces Dial-up," *as reported by CNET News.com*, March 5. Available online at: news.com.com/2100-1033-852084.html.

Reuters Limited. 2002. "FBI, SEC Scrutinizing Global Crossing," *as reported by CNET News.com*, February 8. Available online at: news.com.com/2100-1033-832465.html?tag=prntfr.

Romero, Simon. 2001. "Bankruptcy Fears Fuel Drop at Exodus Communications," *New York Times*, September 26. Available online at: www.nytimes.com/2001/09/26/technology/26EXOD.html.

Schmelling, Sara. 2001. "Be Our Guest," *Upside Magazine*, January. Available online at: www.upside.com/texis/mvm/story?id=3a5273f18.

The NetEconomy. 2001. "The Book on Exodus," October 1. www.theneteconomy.com/print_article/0,3668,a=15516,00.asp.

Valdmanis, Thor and Swartz, Jon. 2001. "Cash-Poor Web-hosting Firm Exodus for Sale," *USA Today, Tech Investor*, August 23. Available online at: www.usatoday.com/life/cyber/invest/2001-08-23-exodus-for-sale.htm.

Vaughan-Nichols, Steven J. 2001. "Attention, Backbone Shoppers," *eWeek*, April 16. Available online at: www.eweek.com/print_article/0,3668,a=8983,00.asp.

Wagner, Mitch. 2000. "Google Bets the Farm on Linux," *InternetWeek*, June 1. Available online at: www.Internetweek.com/lead/lead060100.htm.

Wagner, Mitch. 2001. "Google Keeps Pace With Demand: Maintains Speed, Doubles Server Farm Infrastructure to 8,000 Systems," *InternetWeek*, May 7. Available online at: www.Internetweek.com/story/INW20010427S0010.

Wolk, Martin. 2002. "Telecom Sector Takes it on the Chin," *MSNBC*, February 8. www.msnbc.com/news/702780.asp.

Worldcom, Inc. 2002. "Global Overview." Available online at: www1.worldcom.com/global/about/corporate_information/global_overview/.

WorldCom, Inc. 1998. "MCI WorldCom Timeline." Available online at: www.worldcom.com/about_the_company/corporate_timeline/#1983.

E-Business Network and Web Site Security

In this chapter, you will learn to:

Describe general e-business network and Web site security issues

Identify ways to protect the physical security of a network

List internal network security risks and explain how to protect against them

Discuss external network and Web site security risks and explain how to protect against them

Identify the risks associated with an e-business's online transactions

Illustrate a virtual private network

Describe wireless security issues

Discuss the importance of security audits

By midmorning on February 7, 2000, it became clear that something bad was happening on the Web. At 10:30 A.M. Pacific Standard Time users were unable to access several Yahoo! Web sites including its main Web site, Yahoo! Mail, and the GeoCities Web site also owned by Yahoo! The engineers at Yahoo! discovered that the company's routers were so overloaded with false incoming requests for Web pages that the routers were unable to appropriately direct the traffic. It took three hours before they finally restored access to the sites by identifying and removing the unfriendly traffic before it reached the routers.

The next day, February 8, Buy.com, eBay, Amazon.com, CNN.com, and E*TRADE routers were attacked by hundreds of spurious requests. Amazon.com and CNN.com users experienced about two hours of slow service, and the Buy.com site was down for about three hours. On February 9, the E*TRADE and ZDNet Web sites were attacked in the same manner. The E*TRADE attack lasted about one hour before the stock market opened. Approximately 70 percent of ZDNet's Web sites were unavailable to legitimate users for about two hours. Each of these attacks left engineers scrambling to fix the problems, as service at the sites was seriously degraded or halted. The attacks were so severe that then President Clinton called on the FBI to investigate.

The engineers at the affected e-businesses suspected a type of attack called "distributed denial of service" or DDoS. In a DDoS attack, many different computers send an unending stream of data to one destination until the receiving device is overwhelmed and crashes. But no one ever had seen DDoS attacks of such enormity. There were three big questions on everyone's mind: How had such massive attacks been generated? By whom? And why?

General Network and Web Site Security Issues

Security in the broadest sense is about the protection of assets and, for an e-business, those assets include its data and the components of its physical network. The network and Web site asset security risks facing e-businesses can be conceptually divided into four broad areas:

- *Physical risks*: Physical damage to network components and data from natural causes such as fire or flood, or deliberate destruction of equipment and data from employees or outside intruders
- *Internal risks*: Threats originating from within an organization such as lack of awareness of security issues by management and employees, poor data backup procedures, inadequate disaster recovery plans, and unhappy employees
- *External risks*: Threats originating from outside an organization such as unauthorized electronic access to the LAN via the Internet and distribution of destructive programs via Internet e-mail
- *Transactional risks*: Data interception, loss of customer information such as credit card numbers, or inadequate transaction authorization procedures

There is some overlap, of course, and some types of countermeasures can prove useful against multiple risks, but many e-businesses may find to their regret that they are well-prepared against only two or three out of the four main security risks. Therefore, the security issues faced by e-businesses today are exponentially more complex than they ever have been. To make things even more complicated, e-businesses must protect themselves against the unknown. New methods of attacking networks and Web sites and new network security holes are being discovered with disturbing frequency. Nevertheless, by carefully planning its network and Web site security, an e-business can protect against many known and as yet unknown threats.

Even though most losses from security breaches are small compared to the size of the total e-business economy, consumers' perceptions about security affect their willingness to participate in the online marketspace. Just as investors can be frightened away from the capital markets by allegations of widespread faulty accounting practices, customers can choose to avoid online marketspaces that they perceive as insecure, thereby greatly diminishing the usefulness of those marketspaces.

Fortunately, there are countermeasures available to help e-businesses achieve the high levels of security so crucial in the digital economy. In this chapter you learn about the physical, internal, external, and transactional risks faced by e-businesses and the countermeasures they can take to mitigate losses from those risks.

Physical Risks to Network and Web Site Assets

Physical risks to network and Web site security include accidental or deliberate damage to equipment or data as the result of a natural disaster or sabotage. When considering the physical risks to an e-business, it's important to remember that physical risks extend far beyond network equipment. All elements of an e-businesses network infrastructure including network equipment, physical location, redundant access to electrical power, and Internet connectivity need to be secured.

Network Equipment and Physical Location

When managing the physical security of their network assets, e-businesses should start by considering the safety of their network equipment. Some important issues to consider include:

♦   *Network facilities location*: Network equipment (including servers) should be placed in locked rooms to which access is tightly controlled and monitored. The location of the computer facilities should *not* be clearly identified (by signs or on the building directory) in order to make it more difficult for an outside intruder to locate crucial equipment.

♦   *Fire protection*: Water-based sprinkler systems should not be used near network equipment. Instead, special fire-suppression systems should be used to extinguish a fire without irretrievably damaging servers, routers, electrical wiring, and so forth.

- *Network facilities construction*: Network facilities should be built from more substantial materials than the usual office-grade sheetrock; after all, a good steak knife is all that's required to saw a hole in inexpensive sheetrock. Most office buildings use false ceilings to hide electrical and climate control equipment, leaving a 3-foot air space above every office. If the walls of a network facility don't go all the way to the real ceiling, anyone can access the facility simply by pushing two ceiling tiles aside and climbing over the wall.

Electrical Power Backup

Physical data and operational security is essential for reaching "five nines reliability," or 99.999% uptime. At this level of reliability, an e-business's crucial servers can only be unavailable about 5 minutes per year. The most common problems related to uptime are loss of power and loss of Internet connectivity. The best public utility can't always cope with major ice storms, tornados, and other natural events that interrupt power delivery. Because of this, an e-business should consider two levels of backup power: batteries that assume the power load within milliseconds of a failure, and power generators that automatically start when the batteries become exhausted.

Internet Connectivity Redundancy

Concerns about power protection imply a need for Internet connectivity redundancy. An e-business of any size should consider having more than one Internet connection. Major e-businesses, such as ISPs or the data centers of hosting companies, have multiple connections to the Internet, often to different NSPs. Some even have their NSP cable connections exiting their buildings at different points, so an errant backhoe in the parking lot can't cut every line at once. Also, some major e-businesses purchase complete data-center redundancy, which allows them to move their operations to a different data center on very short notice, should a major disaster befall the primary data center.

Outsourcing Physical Risks

Protecting a network and Web site against physical risks can be quite expensive, but for many e-businesses, network or Web site downtime is even more expensive. However, protecting the physical, power, and connectivity requirements of a network are often beyond the reach of many startup e-businesses. The ISPs and Web hosting companies that you learned about in Chapter 6 can help solve this quandary. For a reasonable monthly fee, an e-business can rent servers or co-locate its own servers in facilities that satisfy all physical security requirements. However, it is still an e-business's responsibility to evaluate a Web hosting company's physical security (and, in fact all its security policies) and make certain the security provided is adequate for the e-business's needs.

As improbable as it might sound, internal risks to network and Web site assets (such as malicious damage by an unhappy employee or failure to plan adequately for business continuation in case of a disaster) may be more threatening to an e-business than the physical risks to its network equipment, power supply, or Internet connectivity.

Internal Security Risks

The weakest link in any security system is always the people managing and using it. **Internal risks** are those that come from inside an e-business — either from unhappy employees and contractors or even from management itself as a result of poor security awareness or planning.

Internal security begins with sound security policies. Successful security policies are those that are understood and acknowledged by every employee — from an e-business's top management to its mail room staff. Failure of employees to support certain security policies can be the result of many factors. Employees may not understand a security policy. Sometimes a security policy is so burdensome that employees are not able to follow it or refuse to follow it because it makes it difficult for them to get their work done. Other times, employees may not understand the importance of a security policy. The top management of an e-business must take an active role in not only developing security policies but also in developing a formal, security education plan for employees. Employees must also understand that their role in following security policies is essential to the successful implementation of the policy.

Countermeasures to internal risks include restricting user access to network resources by requiring passwords, biometric identification, or smart card authorization. You learn more about these options in the following sections.

Passwords

The most common means of protecting computers, servers, and other network resources from unauthorized user access is the implementation of passwords. A **password** is a group of characters used to identify a specific computer user and grant that user access to a computer or network. Passwords can be an effective first line of defense for controlling network access, but are only effective when created properly and changed regularly.

Effective passwords are those that have a minimum length of six characters and contain a mix of letters and numbers. Requiring passwords of this type increases the number of potential passwords into the billions and makes it more difficult for an internal user or outside intruder to guess a legitimate password. Additionally, an effective system of passwords should require that a user change his or her password on a regular basis. If a user has access to multiple networks, it is a good idea to require him or her to use a different password on each network. Finally, users should be required to log off the network when not actually using network resources. For example, a workstation on a manufacturing floor that's left logged on at the end of the work day allows access to network resources to anyone who comes by and allows "free passage" around whatever security policies are in force.

Table 7-1 illustrates some do's and don'ts for creating a password. Figure 7-1 illustrates some good and some poor passwords.

Table 7-1
Creating a
password

Do	Don't
Use a minimum of six characters with a combination of numbers and letters	Use a name, date, or number that can be easily guessed by someone who knows you; for example, avoid using your birthday or name
Choose a combination you can easily remember	Pick a common word that is found in a dictionary; some outside intruders are able to penetrate network security by using software that repeatedly tries common words as passwords until one of the words is accepted
Change your password on a regular basis	Pick a new password that is similar to your old password

Figure 7-1
Password
examples

Good Passwords	Poor Passwords
9851JDX	Jones (user maiden name)
N32Y592E	071042 (birthday)
8157ZJ4	test
	user
	apple

Effective password protection is sometimes difficult to implement; many users find it hard to remember where they parked their car, much less a password similar to "h&JK~7" or "T<df8%(." Because of this, some e-businesses are considering biometric identification for network access.

Biometric Identification

Because of unwieldy password protection systems, some e-businesses are considering adding biometric security devices to their systems. The term **biometrics** refers to technology that involves the measurement of biological data. Biometric security devices and software measure and record a computer user's unique human characteristics (such as fingerprints, voiceprint, and eye retina or iris) and then use those characteristics for user identification. For example, a user's retina can be scanned and the results of that scan compared to a database of authenticated users. Once authenticated, the user is granted access to computer or network resources.

As of this writing, biometric security devices are still in the future for most e-businesses; however, interest in replacing or augmenting unwieldy password security with biometric security is growing. For example, biometric security devices demonstrated at the November 2001 COMDEX computer industry trade show included a small video camera with iris recognition software that sits beside a personal computer; a fingerprint scanner embedded in a mouse pointing device; and a tiny fingerprint sensor designed for use with laptops, cell phones, and PDAs.

TIP

One primary concern with biometric technologies is privacy. Many individuals are worried about potential invasion of person privacy if their biometric data is gathered and then shared with other organizations, especially government organizations.

Smart Card Identification

As described in Chapter 2, a **smart card** is a plastic card the size of a credit card that contains an embedded memory chip. Biometric information such as fingerprints can be placed on a smart card for additional confirmation when the user presents the card for identification.

Smart cards can also be used to authenticate a remote user logging into a network. In this situation, the smart card usually contains a display area. When the remote user dials into a network and attempts to log on, he or she is asked to key in a code that is briefly visible in the display area of the card. When the user correctly keys in the code, the smart card then displays a second code the user must enter in order to log on to the network.

One risk associated with such a smart card is the possibility that the card could be lost or stolen. Still, it may not be clear to whoever finds the card which network the card accesses. It is important that a smart card user not make the mistake of writing the network access phone number and his or her username on the back of the card!

Often the most effective way to protect systems is to simultaneously use multiple authentication methods. For example, you might require a user to enter a password and then have a retinal scan. The combination of these two measures would make it highly unlikely that someone other than the authenticated user could access the resource.

TECH CASE **The Justice Files**

One of the most dangerous internal risks faced by an e-business is the risk of damage or theft of assets by greedy, malicious, or disgruntled employees. Here are just three scary examples (from the U.S. Department of Justice files) of internal security breaches.

File 1: In January 2001, a former systems administrator and computer security officer for the U.S. District Court for the District of Alaska was sentenced to three months incarceration followed by three months house arrest, one year of monitored release, 240 hours of public service, and $5,300 in fines. This was his punishment for three attacks on a restricted-use mail server operated by the U.S. District Court for the Eastern District of New York. Displeased by plans to permit additional users on the mail server, the former systems administrator flooded the mail server with e-mails, supposedly to prove its vulnerability to attack. The server was unable to handle the increased activity and had to be taken offline and reconfigured. The source of the attacks was identified by the FBI with the help of the security staff at an Alaskan ISP who traced the IP addresses involved in the attacks back to the former system administrator.

Continued

File 2: In November 2001, an employee of an Ohio executive recruitment firm was sentenced to three years probation and ordered to pay $15,346.71 in restitution for computer fraud against her employer. In the wee hours of the morning one day in April 2000, the employee logged onto her firm's LAN from a laptop at her home. Then using the user ID and password of another employee (without that employee's knowledge or permission) she changed the password of the firm's vacationing chief information officer (CIO.) This prevented the CIO from logging on to the network. The firm had to conduct a complete analysis of its entire network to determine what, if any, additional damage had been done during the unauthorized access and, as a result, incurred expenses of more than $15,000.

File 3: In January 2002, a paralegal was sentenced in a Manhattan federal court to two years and six months in prison for unauthorized computer access, interstate transportation of stolen property, and wire fraud (among other charges) as part of a conspiracy to steal a confidential trial plan valued at several million dollars. The trial plan — for a civil action in a tobacco-related lawsuit — included the firm's trial strategy, portions of depositions, legal summaries, and information about trial exhibits. The paralegal downloaded a copy of the trial plan and, via e-mail, offered the plan for sale to opposing counsel. Opposing counsel turned the matter over to the FBI who planted an undercover agent to negotiate with the paralegal for a $2 million sale of the trial plan.

The ease with which these (now former) employees were able to access their networks and damage or steal assets should give any e-business pause when considering the possibilities of similar security breaches in their own organizations.

Other internal risks to network and Web site assets include failure to adequately back up critical data, failure to properly test existing backup and restore procedures, and the lack of a tested disaster and recovery plan.

Backup and Restore Policies and Procedures

An e-business's **backup and restore policies** describe the company's plan for securing vital data files and software in case of equipment failure or some man-made or natural catastrophe. **Backup and restore procedures** specify when and how critical files and software are copied to backup media. The backup media might consist of magnetic tapes, high-volume removable diskettes, CD-ROMs, or offsite servers.

It's said that there are only two types of businesses — those that have suffered serious computer system failure, and those that will. Computer failure resulting in serious data loss could be the death knell for an e-business. Nevertheless, far too many e-businesses treat data and software backup and restore policies and procedures as an afterthought, often assigning the least senior person to the task. This is a grave error. After all, the simple fact is that computers fail; given the complexity of modern computer systems it's a wonder they don't fail more often.

Backup and restore policies should be clear and the responsibility for assuring that the policies are followed should fall to senior management. Backup procedures should be built into the daily, weekly, and monthly operations of a network. It's important to remember, too, that the backup process is only half of the story — the restore process is the other half. The term **restore** means to return electronic files to their most recently backed-up status. An e-business that doesn't test its restore procedures is asking for trouble. For example, magnetic tapes fail in ways that aren't obvious until it's actually necessary to use them to restore data. Attempting to restore files from damaged magnetic tapes can result in corrupted files. To avoid unpleasant surprises, an e-business should test restore procedures regularly (once a month at least) to verify the integrity of its backup media and files.

Copies of critical data files and software should also be stored off-site to make certain that they are available in case of a disaster involving the business's office and network facilities. Traditional backup media such as magnetic tape, diskettes, or CD-ROMs can be carried off-site and stored in a secure location such as a bank box. It is now also possible to send a backup copy of files off-site to a safe storage facility via the Internet. For example, e-businesses such as Pro Softnet Corporation (with its IBackup products) and Amerivault Corp (Figure 7-2) provide online backup and restore options for files sent to or recovered from their managed off-site servers.

Figure 7-2
Amerivault Corp

Finally, the possibility that a disgruntled IT Department employee, who likely has greater access to network resources than other employees, might attempt to steal or destroy an e-business's data must be considered. Think that is not likely to happen? Just ask Global Crossing Holdings Ltd., the now bankrupt telecommunications giant you learned about in Chapter 6. Beginning in September 2001, an unhappy network technician began stealing other employees' personal information including names, Social Security numbers, and birthdates and then posting the information on a Web site. To make matters worse, Global Crossing didn't begin informing its employees of the security breach until mid-December!

To mitigate potential losses from unhappy IT employees, some e-businesses assign the task of backing up important data outside their IT Departments, so that no single employee can simultaneously destroy current data and all available backups.

No e-business wants to deal with the damage and destruction of a natural or man-made disaster such as a fire, flood, hurricane, riot, terrorist attack, and so forth. But, failing to adequately plan for such a disaster can mean the end of an e-business.

Disaster Recovery Planning

Backup and recovery policies are an important part of **disaster recovery planning** or **DRP**. DRP is sometimes called **business continuity planning** or **BCP** and is concerned with how an e-business deals with a disaster to ensure its continuation as a viable business. The actual contents of a disaster recovery or business continuity plan depend on the type of e-business and other variables. However, one part of any effective DRP or BCP should cover network operations.

The DRP for network operations should explain how an e-business will cope with a catastrophe that results in, among other things, electrical outages, data loss, and security breaches. As with backup and restore procedures, a network DRP is useless without testing. Some e-businesses choose a slow time of the month to unplug their servers or take down other network components to test how well the e-business processes cope with their loss.

Many e-businesses find that their servers and other network components are so absolutely essential to their business viability that they must install redundant servers or other standby network components that automatically take over when the primary components fail or are taken offline. This redundancy is called **failover**. Ideally, a takeover by a redundant secondary network or component occurs so seamlessly that users are not aware of it. It's a good idea to fully test all parts of a DRP or BCP upon its completion and once per year thereafter.

In addition to physical and internal risks, threats to network and Web site assets from outside intruders are greater than ever. In the next section you learn about the external threats from hackers and computer viruses.

TIP

No disaster recovery plan is perfect. When Hurricane Allison inundated Houston, Texas, in June 2001, it turned out that fuel delivery was the weak link in many disaster recovery plans. Because the capacity of the typical generator fuel tank produces less electricity than the 24 to 72 hour's worth of power needed during the electrical outages, some Houston e-businesses, which turned to backup generators for power after the storm, were unable to keep their networks online.

External Security Risks

External risks are those that originate outside a company's protected network, and must first penetrate whatever defenses (often disappointingly minimal) protect the e-business from the outside world. As you have learned, the Internet is a public network consisting of thousands of connected private LANs. Each of these private LANs is therefore exposed to security risks originating from anywhere on the public network. Stringent security measures are necessary to protect against these external risks.

TIP

For a look at business financial loss statistics related to network intrusions and other cybercrimes see the Computer Security Institute's (CSI) sixth annual "Computer Crime and Security Survey" available from the CSI Web site.

External risks have increased exponentially as more users are connected to the Internet. In the following sections you learn about external risks posed by outside intruders and computer viruses.

Hackers

Outside intruders can wreck havoc with a network and its data in many, many ways. These intruders, most commonly called hackers, use many techniques — some simple and some sophisticated — to gain unauthorized access to a network. Originally, "hacker" was a term used to describe gifted software programmers. Now, however, **hacker** is a slang term for someone who deliberately gains unauthorized access to individual computers or computer networks. **Ethical hackers**, sometimes called **white hat hackers**, use their skills to find and make known weaknesses in computer systems without regard for personal gain. Malicious hackers, also called **crackers** or **black hat hackers**, gain access to steal valuable information such as credit card numbers, to attempt to disrupt service, or to cause other damage. Because of the wide popular press coverage of network security breaches, the terms "hacker" and "cracker" are now generally used interchangeably for malicious unauthorized network access. In this book the term hacker refers to anyone who gains or attempts to gain unauthorized access to a network.

TECH CASE **White Hat or Black Hat?**

What do Microsoft Corporation, the *New York Times*, WorldCom, Inc., and Yahoo!, have in common? Adrian Lamo. The networks of all of these organizations (and others not listed here) were hacked by Adrian Lamo, a 21-year old San Francisco resident and self-described "security researcher." Lamo insists his hacking is purely directed toward helping organizations identify security problems and solve them. But, some industry analysts remain skeptical of Lamo's motives.

In August 2001, Lamo hacked into the Yahoo! News databases via three proxy Web servers that connected Yahoo!'s corporate network to the Internet. For three weeks Lamo was able to access Yahoo!'s news production tools and to change the content of news stories. Some of the modified stories remained available to the public for several days until removed from circulation. In September, Lamo notified Yahoo! of the security breaches. Yahoo! quickly took steps to close the loopholes.

Continued

In October 2001, Lamo identified a security problem at a Microsoft Corporation customer service Web site. Although the IP address for the site was unpublished, Lamo simply manipulated the known Microsoft IP addresses until he located the customer service site. Once he was able to access the site, he viewed customer service records including names, addresses, purchasing histories, phone numbers, and e-mail addresses. Microsoft quickly moved to fix the security problem after being notified of the problem by Lamo.

Lamo was just "looking for something to do" in October 2001 when he hacked into WorldCom, Inc.'s administrative network via a proxy server (software that controls user Internet access) that had accidentally been installed on a WorldCom Web server when the server was configured. According to Lamo, access to the administration network "exposed all the information needed to dial into routers belonging to WorldCom's customers" such as America Online or Bank of America. WorldCom used the information provided by Lamo to tighten its security.

Lamo's next publicized hack was in February 2002, when, in less than two minutes, he discovered seven misconfigured proxy servers at the *New York Times*. Once inside the *Times* internal network, Lamo was able to browse the names and Social Security numbers of employees as well as the database that contained information on over 3,000 contributors to the *Times* op-ed page. The op-ed page database included Social Security numbers, phone numbers, editorial comments, and amounts paid to contributors such as actors Robert Redford and Warren Beatty, political commentator William H. Buckley, political activist James Carville, and former president Jimmy Carter. Lamo advised the *Times* of its security holes, and as of this writing, the *Times* is still investigating the problem.

None of Lamo's hacking "victims" have taken legal action against him (as of this writing), and all seem thankful that their security lapses were identified and fixed without a loss of assets. But, many analysts are very concerned about Lamo's actions. Some analysts express dismay at the seemingly "lackadaisical attitude" about security taken by the hacked e-businesses who allowed misconfigured proxy servers to go undetected by their own IT staff. Others are concerned that Lamo is walking a very thin line between white hat and black hat hacking. As one analyst expressed it, "It's the equivalent of someone poking around your house from the outside, finding an open door, and then saying, 'I didn't take anything.'" So, what do you think? Which hat should Lamo wear: white or black?

How does a hacker attack work? The usual objectives of a hacker attack are to expose crucial data, interrupt operations, or use the hacked computer as a base from which to launch attacks on other computers, making the attacks harder to trace. There are many ways to interrupt operations. The most common method is to send confusing data to a server or other computer connected to the outside world. In some cases, the server may not simply throw away the confusing data, but attempt to interpret it, resulting in a crash. For example, for a short while Microsoft's Windows NT operating system could be crashed by a certain type of "bad packet" that a server wasn't able to interpret, causing the server to reboot (or suddenly shut down and then start again).

Rebooting servers isn't the worst problem caused by hackers, however. If a program can be interrupted, confused, or crashed, sometimes the hacker can gain access to a command prompt. A command prompt is a location on the screen where the instructions or commands to execute a program are keyed. The hacker then can execute any command that runs with the same security level as the program that just crashed.

The most common method used by hackers to crash a program is called a **buffer overflow**. To understand how a buffer overflow works, you need to understand the term "buffer," which refers to a temporary space in memory in which data is stored while it is being processed. If a hacker sends more data than can fit in the buffer, the data overflows into other buffers, overwriting their contents. The overflowing data may include destructive instructions to damage files or alter data. Many of the computer viruses you learn about in the next section exploit buffer overflow vulnerabilities in programs.

Most software companies provide regular updates to their programs that fix security problems such as buffer overflow vulnerabilities. Installing these software updates should be a high priority. Unfortunately, many system administrators are so overwhelmed with managing a network and with supporting users that installing software updates is sometimes left at the bottom of the To Do list. For this reason, many e-businesses assign responsibility for network and computer security to a security administrator who can devote his or her full attention to security issues.

Hackers often display a lot of ingenuity. One e-business, Comcast Business Communications, Inc., had to shut down its Web site in February 2002 and review its security after a so-called white hat hacker gained access to its servers and stole a list of potential corporate customers that contained names, contacts, phone numbers, and addresses. The hacker then displayed the list in an online security discussion forum. Why did the hacker pick that particular e-business? Because of a well-publicized acquisition, the hacker knew that the system administrators were swamped with work and that security vulnerabilities would occur.

Hackers can also disrupt operations by sending an unending stream of data or HTTP requests to a network component such as a router or Web server.

Distributed Denial of Service (DDoS) Attacks

A **denial of service** or **DoS** attack is an attack on a network that is designed to disable the network by flooding it with useless or confusing traffic. A **distributed denial of service** or **DDoS** attack uses multiple computers to launch a DoS attack. For example, a Web server undergoing a DDoS attack might receive hundreds of HTTP requests per second. The server then spends so much processing time trying to serve these requests that it cannot handle the load and crashes. The idea is very similar to flooding a company's telephone switchboard with prank calls, making it impossible for regular customers to get through. Prank calls are easily traceable. DDoS attacks can sometimes be traced, but they often originate from computers that have been compromised and are being manipulated remotely to send multiple requests.

Packet Internet Groper or **Ping** is a very simple test used to determine if a network connection is functioning, and can be a very useful troubleshooting tool. Ping enables one computer to send a test message to another computer using ICMP and to then receive a response. Some DDoS attacks are based on sending an unrelenting stream of pings to a host which then becomes overwhelmed and can no longer function properly. Another type of

TIP

A 2001 study by researchers at the University of California, San Diego (UCSD), found that in three 1-week periods, more than 12,000 DoS attacks were launched against commercial Web sites, Internet infrastructure routers, and home PCs. The study found that two to three percent of studied attacks were against name servers used to identify domain names and one to three percent of the attacks were against network routers. Although this is only a small percentage of the total, such attacks against name servers and network routers can potentially affect a larger number of users than attacks on a specific Web site.

DDoS attack involves sending hundreds of huge e-mail messages to a mail server which then crashes when it runs out of storage space for the messages.

While a DDoS attack does not do any technological damage, it can do substantial financial damage to an e-business, because every second an e-business's network or Web site is down may result in lost revenues. The only reward to a hacker for launching a DDoS attack seems to be the opportunity to show off his or her skills. Figure 7-3 illustrates a DDoS attack.

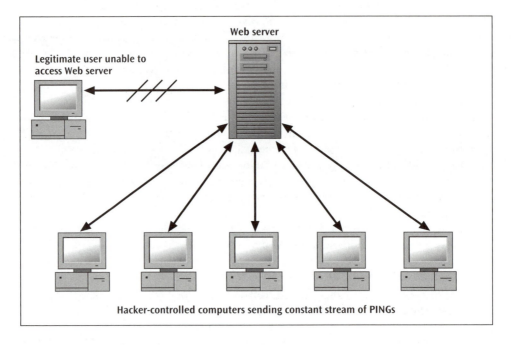

Figure 7-3
DDoS attack

Another threat to Web sites faced by e-businesses is the purposeful altering of Web page contents by a hacker.

Web Site Defacement

Web site defacement or vandalism occurs when a hacker deliberately changes the content of Web pages. Defacement can be the result of a hacker breaking into a network, accessing the Web site files, and modifying the HTML to physically change Web page content. Additionally, a special type of computer virus called an Internet worm (you learn more about worms in the next section) can automatically deface Web pages on vulnerable Web servers (such as a Microsoft IIS Web server which has not been updated with the appropriate software updates). Victims of Web site defacement include the NASDAQ Stock Market, the FBI, the *New York Times*, Goodyear Tire and Rubber Company, NASA, and many, many more.

One recent example of multiple Web site defacements illustrates the security vulnerabilities faced by e-businesses who outsource their Web site hosting to an ISP or hosting company. In July 2001, a group of hackers announced that one of their group had hacked into and defaced 679 Web sites *in less than one minute*! It appears that the Web sites were part of a virtual hosting arrangement and stored on the same Wisconsin-based hosting company server. This made it very easy for the hacker, who exploited a well-known operating system flaw, accessed the hosting company's servers, and then defaced the sites using a simple Perl script that replaced the original home pages with his substitute page. Later review of the hosting company's servers indicated that several network services (including FTP) were left open and available for its customers who remotely managed their Web sites. As one analyst put it "That says to me that convenience, not security, was their [the hosting company's] main concern."

Countermeasures for Hacker Attacks

There are several ways for an e-business to protect its network from external threats. Most involve careful monitoring and attempted blocking of unwanted data flow from the outside world. Most also involve controlling data flow from inside a company to the outside; this is necessary because hackers that manage to infiltrate a company often then attempt to send data to a computer outside the network. As you have learned from some of the previous examples, some common causes of security breaches include simple misconfiguration of servers, leaving discontinued network services turned on, and leaving passwords active that are no longer in use by current employees. An e-business must implement security policies and procedures to prevent these vulnerabilities. Also, an e-business can use firewalls, NAT routers, and proxy servers to control traffic coming into or going out of its network. The most common term for the devices that control data flow and block suspicious activity is "firewall," but many technologies and techniques fall under this title. As you learned in Chapter 3, a firewall is a device that sits between the Internet and an e-business' internal networks, carefully brokering access in both directions while monitoring the flow of information for hints of trouble. Firewalls take many different forms — some are simply monitoring and reporting tools that allow all traffic but watch for suspicious behavior; others block most traffic to a private network or demand authentication to allow certain traffic through. Some firewalls are created by installing special software with operating systems such as Windows 2000 Server or Linux, while others run on proprietary operating systems purposely built for security. Additionally, some firewalls consist solely of hardware that is simply plugged in and configured through a Web browser.

Firewalls are generally designed to resist buffer overflows and other common types of hacker attacks. Because new ways to attack a network are always being developed, a good firewall monitors traffic and notifies a system administrator if certain conditions are met. For example, a sudden burst of traffic from a region of the Internet not previously active could mean an employee who is traveling is accessing the network; however, it might also mean a hacker is accessing an internal computer. Frequent firewall monitoring enables a systems administrator to look more closely at unexpected traffic.

Firewalls are generally classified as one of three types: packet-filtering, circuit-level, and application-level. Which classification applies depends on where in the OSI Model the firewall operates. **Packet-filtering firewalls** operate at the Network layer of the OSI Model. A packet-filtering firewall compares information in the packet header (such as source address, destination address, and port numbers) with predetermined filtering rules. Packets that follow these rules are allowed to pass, while those that don't are blocked. **Circuit-level firewalls** operate at the Session layer of the OSI model by validating TCP and UDP sessions before opening a connection between the source and destination computers. Once the connection is made, all packets that are part of the validated connection are passed through to their destination without further scrutiny. **Application-level firewalls** operate at the Application level of the OSI model and, using a proxy server, pass or block packets depending on the rules specified for the individual network service involved (such as HTTP). Figure 7-4 illustrates an application-level firewall in action.

Figure 7-4
Application-level firewall

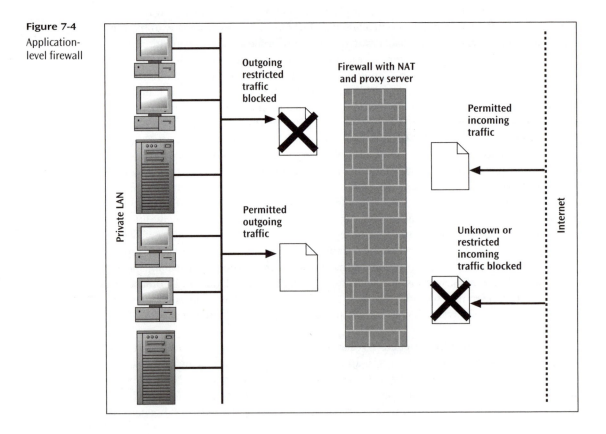

Another firewall technology, **Network Address Translation** or **NAT**, permits internal IP addresses to be converted to different IP addresses for external communications. NAT is used by some firewalls and routers to shield internal IP addresses from identification by anyone outside the internal network.

Another security device that may be used in conjunction with a firewall is a proxy server. A **proxy server**, which may reside on the same server as a firewall or be on a separate server, sits between a user and the Internet and forwards HTTP requests. For example, when a user requests a Web page through a proxy server, the proxy server uses its own IP address to pass the request to the origin server and thereby shields the user's actual IP address. Additionally, a proxy server may also act as a cache server, returning to the user a copy of a cached Web page instead of sending the request on to the origin server. The following steps demonstrate and explain the process of sending an HTTP request to the CNN.com Web site via a proxy server (that does not act as a cache server). This process is also illustrated in Figure 7-5.

1. User launches Web browser and sends request to www.cnn.com URL via a proxy server.
2. Proxy server receives and approves request, remembers which user requested www.cnn.com, and passes the request to the origin server as if the proxy server were the Web browser using its own IP address.
3. The origin server returns the CNN.com Web page, unaware that it's returning the page to a proxy server.
4. The proxy server forwards the requested Web page to the user.

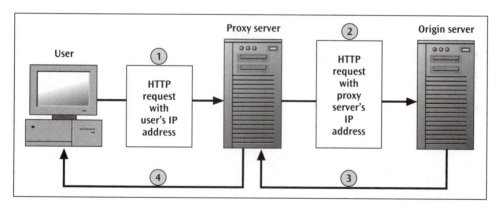

Figure 7-5
Proxy server in action

Both NAT routers and proxy servers may also be used in lieu of a firewall. These devices expose only one IP address to the outside world; all traffic is then channeled through this one IP address. Because hackers can't see the actual internal IP addresses, they can't access them. Vendors sell firewall, proxy server, and caching server hardware and software separately or in packaged combinations. However, the actual setup of any network firewall, NAT router, proxy server or combination depends on an individual e-business's network security needs.

A **filter** is a process or device that screens incoming information and allows only information that meets certain criteria to pass through to the next area. For example, Web traffic on ports 80 and 443 (encrypted traffic) might be allowed through, while e-mail, FTP, telnet, or any other traffic would be blocked. Restricting the types and destinations of incoming traffic is a good idea. For example, even if a server is secured so that only internal computers can talk to it, a hacker can still access that server by first commandeering one of the internal computers and then accessing the server itself. In this scenario, filtering is used to prevent a hacker from accessing the internal computers, thus blocking traffic to the server.

To see how this works, assume you have a network of two hundred computers with IP addresses in the range 204.56.43.1 to 204.56.43.201. Also assume that all internal computers can access a server that is assigned the IP address 204.56.43.210. To prevent a hacker from accessing the server, any unknown incoming traffic not bound for 204.56.43.210 can be filtered out or blocked. Filters can be used effectively to block spurious traffic in a DDoS attack. Figure 7-6 illustrates the filtering process.

Figure 7-6
Filtering in action

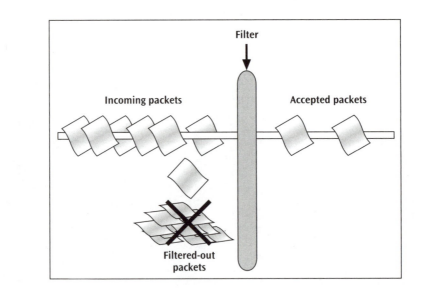

Although filters aren't foolproof (as you have learned by now, no security system is foolproof), when properly monitored they can be an important part of an e-business's security scheme.

An e-business can also purchase network scanning software used to identify technical weaknesses in a network's security. In addition, an e-business can purchase network intrusion detection software and other network security tools. These software packages provide activity logs and other means for determining whether or not a hacker is attempting to breach network security.

Another way hackers can damage or destroy network assets or gain unauthorized access to a network is by creating a computer virus and releasing it to the connected world.

Viruses

Computer viruses are some of the most common external network security threats faced by e-businesses today. A standard computer **virus** is a small, usually destructive, program that inserts itself into other files that then become "infected" in the same way a virus in your body embeds itself in your normal body cells. Viruses can infect executable programs or operating system files and spread when an infected program executes, thereby infecting other programs. Viruses can also be spread via e-mail headers or attachments. Among other things, a virus can prevent a computer system from booting, erase files or entire hard drives, prevent the saving or printing of files, and send repetitive e-mail messages.

A particularly virulent type of computer virus is the worm. A **worm** is a special kind of virus that doesn't alter program files directly. Instead, a worm resides in a computer's memory where it replicates itself. Worms are often not noticed until their uncontrolled replication consumes a computer's resources, slowing the computer or crashing it. Worms are especially effective at infecting systems and crashing servers because of their ability to spread quickly over the Internet.

Another very common type of virus is a macro virus. A **macro** is a short program written in the Visual Basic programming language that is generally used to automate keystrokes when creating a Microsoft Word document or when working in a Microsoft Excel workbook. A **macro virus** is a virus that infects macros. For example, opening a Word document or Excel workbook that contains an infected macro can trigger the macro virus. Macro viruses can be distributed in files such as Word documents or Excel workbooks sent to others as e-mail attachments or transferred via a floppy disk.

A **Trojan horse**, which takes its name from a story in Homer's *Iliad*, is a special type of program that pretends to be something useful or fun but actually does something malicious, such as destroying files or creating a "back door" entry point to give a hacker access to the network. Trojan horse programs are also used by hackers to steal passwords, record a user's keystrokes, locate IP addresses, and plant other destructive programs. A Trojan horse program is often distributed as part of a virus and can be part of an e-mail attachment or a downloaded program. Worm viruses often carry Trojan horse programs as part of their payload. For example, the BadTrans.B worm also carries a Trojan horse named Keylog which is designed to send passwords and operating system information back to a hacker. Table 7-2 lists some examples of destructive standard viruses, worms, macro viruses, and Trojan horse programs.

Table 7-2
Viruses and
Trojan horses

Name	Type	Date Identified	What it Does
W32.Sircam.Worm@mm; also known as (aka): W32/SirCam@mm, Backdoor.SirCam	Worm	7/17/01	Copies itself to shared network drives. Attaches a randomly selected document to itself and then e-mails the document (and worm) to addresses in the user's e-mail address book. On any October 16 it may delete all files and directories on a resident hard drive.
VBS.LoveLetter.CH aka: VBS/Linda.A, VBS.Vbswg2.gen	Worm	3/21/01	Sends itself to addresses in the Microsoft Outlook address book. Spreads to Internet chat rooms using Internet Relay Chat (IRC). Overwrites files on local and network drives.
W32.Alcarys.C aka: W32.Palco.A	Macro	2/28/02	Inserts a macro into the Word Normal.dot master document template, then infects individual Word documents when they are closed. When infected Word documents are closed the message "anti-malicious macros version 1.0 installed" is displayed.
W32.HLLP.Sharpei@mm	Virus, Worm	2/26/02	Sends itself to all addresses in the Microsoft Outlook address book and then deletes the sent messages from the Sent folder to hide its activities. Replicates itself as a file that runs in the Microsoft .NET venue that attempts to infect executable programs and mass mail the virus again.
Backdoor.Surgeon aka: Backdoor.Infector, Win32.Theinf	Trojan horse	2/20/02	Allows a hacker to take control of an infected computer by opening a port (by default, port 35000). Once a hacker has remote control of an infected computer, the intruder can then control the computer's file system, upload and download files, acquire passwords, redirect TCP and IP traffic, log user keystrokes, and so forth.
W32.HLLO.6144	Virus	2/14/02	Overwrites all .com, .exe, and .scr files in all folders with a copy of itself; the overwritten files are not repairable.

Table 7-2
(continued)
Viruses and
Trojan horses

Name	Type	Date Identified	What it Does
W97M.DebilByte.A aka: Macro.Word97.DebilByte	Macro	2/5/02	Infects the Microsoft Word Normal.dot default document template, then infects any Word document that is opened or closed. Disables the Tools, Macro, Macros and Tools, Macro, Visual Basic Editor menu commands.
W32.Badtrans.B@mm	Worm with a Trojan horse	11/24/01	Finds unread mail and responds with an infected attachment. Delivers Trojan horse that logs keystrokes and then sends the log file and intercepted passwords to a variety of predetermined e-mail addresses.
Code Red aka: W32/Dady, I-Worm.Bady, CodeRed, W32/Bady.worm	Worm	7/17/2001	Targets networks running Microsoft IIS 4.0 and 5.0 Web servers running on Windows 2000 or Microsoft Index Server 2.0 and Windows 2000 Indexing Service running on Microsoft NT 4.0 that have not installed appropriate software updates and patches. Received as an HTTP request, lodges in memory, then sends an unending stream of traffic to random IP addresses or sends junk data to a specific IP address. Previously infected systems can be reinfected if the appropriate Web server and Index server software updates are not installed.
W32.Nimda.A@mm aka: W32/Nimda@mm, PE_NIMDA.A, I-Worm.Nimda	Worm	9/18/01	Sends itself in an e-mail message as a Readme.exe attached file to e-mail addresses in .html files or Microsoft Outlook and Outlook Express folders. The attachment may not be visible to the e-mail recipients. Attempts to infect Microsoft IIS Web servers that have not had the appropriate software updates installed. Replaces files with itself and infects executable files. Makes a computer's hard drive (C:\) a shared network drive.

Wireless devices are not immune from viruses. The first **wireless virus** was the "Liberty Crack" Palm Trojan, identified in August 2000. The Palm Trojan virus — which could delete all the applications on a Palm device — was quickly followed by another, more dangerous Palm operating system virus, called "Phage," in September 2000. Phage infected Palm operating system applications and documents and proliferated when a user beamed or shared an infected document with another user. As wireless devices proliferate and become more capable, this is expected to be a growing problem.

There are few known wireless viruses as yet, but antivirus companies like Trend Micro, Inc. have already started releasing products in this field. Network Associates, Inc. through its McAfee Security (Figure 7-7) business unit also provides information about wireless viruses and provides wireless and PDA antivirus products.

Figure 7-7
McAfee wireless security and PDA protection

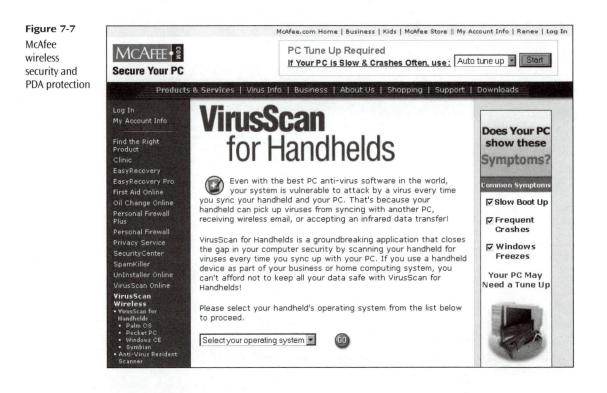

Virus Hoaxes

Some so-called viruses trumpeted in the media or announced via warning e-mails are just hoaxes; however, it can be difficult to tell the difference. The media has created an alarmist atmosphere where false warnings about viruses proliferate as quickly as real viruses and many well-meaning people inadvertently help spread false information about viruses via e-mail. This can create an atmosphere in which a real virus warning might not be taken seriously.

Several antivirus software vendors maintain up-to-date information on viruses, worms, Trojan horses, and hoaxes. You can find this information at the McAfee.com Virus Information Library Web site, the Metropolitan Network BBS Incorporated's AVP Virus Encyclopedia Web site, or the Symantec Corporation's Virus Encyclopedia Web site. Table 7-3 lists some virus hoaxes.

Name	Type	Date Identified	Description
Lump of Coal	E-mail	3/1/99	Warning arrives as e-mail message telling recipient about fictitious virus which travels in an e-mail message dated 12/25 with the subject line "Lump of Coal."
!!?UNAVAILABLE!?	Cell phone	6/21/00	Warning arrives as e-mail message telling recipient that cell phone will be infected with virus if answered when the phone display shows "!!?UNAVAILABLE!?"
48 Hours	E-mail	11/13/01	Warning arrives as an e-mail message telling recipient not to open an e-mail with the subject line "Help" as it contains a virus promulgated by a cyberterrorist.
A Virtual Card for You	E-mail	11/16/00	Warning arrives as an e-mail message telling recipient not to open an e-mail message with the subject line "A Virtual Card for You" because a virus that overwrites the computer hard drive with zeros will be unleashed.
Osama vs. Bush	E-mail	11/8/01	Warning arrives via e-mail message telling recipient not to open e-mail message with subject line "Osama vs. Bush" because the computer's hard drive will be erased.

Table 7-3
Virus hoaxes

If you receive an e-mail warning of a new virus (or hear about one on the evening news), you should first check an online virus encyclopedia to determine if the alleged virus is real or a hoax. Then, if the virus is real, you should make certain your antivirus software is updated to protect against the virus. If you receive an e-mail warning about a virus that turns out to be a hoax, please do not forward that message to anyone else.

Virus Countermeasures

While perfect protection against viruses and Trojan horses is not possible, an e-business can take several important countermeasures to block infections:

- *Antivirus software*: Install and maintain *updated* antivirus software (such as that sold by McAfee and Symantec) that scans disk drives, documents, and incoming e-mail for viruses and then deletes found viruses before they can infect the computer.

- *Employee education*: Educate employees about virus dangers and encourage employees to delete any e-mail and e-mail attachments from unknown senders *without opening the attachments*. Employees should also be discouraged from sending or receiving personal e-mail and attachments from family and friends through the e-business's mail system.

- *Software updates and patches*: Ensure that network operating system and Web server software updates and quick fixes or patches are installed as soon as they become available.

- *Awareness*: Encourage system administrators and other employees to be alert to newly identified viruses and to take the appropriate measures to prevent infection.

- *Application software tools*: Make certain that Microsoft Office Suite applications such as Word and Excel have the appropriate level of macro detection set. An effective countermeasure for macro viruses is to set the macro detection option in Microsoft Office applications to either Medium or High. The Medium option presents a macro warning message when an Office file containing a macro is opened. You can then elect to open the file with the macros enabled (if you are confident of the file's source) or disabled (if you do not want to run the risk of a macro virus infection). The High option allows Office files containing macros to be opened only if they are from previously designated trusted sources. For help in locating these options, use an Office application's online Help feature.

In addition to physical risks such as fire or flood, internal risks from disgruntled employees, and external risks from hackers, viruses, and Trojan horses, an e-business that sells products and services online and accepts customer credit cards in payment is also exposed to transactional risks.

Transactional Risks

Many Internet users believe they face a large risk to their privacy and security when they buy products and services or submit personal information online. Although the perceived risk may be greater than the actual risk, it is still a cause for concern. In order to maintain their customers' trust, e-businesses must adequately address the perceived risks as well as the actual risks associated with transactional security. However, few people realize the complexities involved in addressing transactional security. Transactional security can be divided into four areas:

- *Authentication*: A user must be able to prove his identity to the other party. ("I am Joan Thomas and I live at...")
- *Integrity*: Each party must be comfortable that exchanged information wasn't altered during transmission by a third party or corrupted by misfortune. ("I ordered three items not four...")
- *Nonrepudiation*: Each party must be assured that the counterparty won't be able to deny being the originator or receiver of information. ("I didn't order that item...")
- *Confidentiality*: Parties must be able to exchange information securely without it falling into the hands of a third party. ("My credit card number is...")

Without these four provisions, buying and selling products online would be impossible because of a lack of trust between buyer and seller. Methods for providing authentication, integrity, nonrepudiation, and confidentiality include sending and receiving encrypted messages or data, using digital certificates to authenticate the parties involved in the transaction, and storing retained customer information properly.

Encryption

Cryptography is the art of protecting information by encrypting it. **Encryption** is the translation of data into a secret code called **ciphertext**. Ciphertext that is transmitted to its destination and then **decrypted** (or returned to its unencrypted format) is called **plaintext**. To understand how the encryption and decryption of messages and transactions works, you need to learn a bit more about the encryption/decryption process itself.

Encryption scrambles data in a secret pattern. In order to unscramble that data, you must know the pattern or **key**. The first step in encrypting and exchanging data, then, is to agree on what key to use, and to make sure both parties have access to the key. For example, suppose Charles needs to encrypt and send a confidential database to Maria. First Charles and Maria need to agree on what key to use. If Maria doesn't have a copy of the key, then Charles has to send a copy of the key to Maria. Once both parties have the key, Charles can then encrypt the data and send it to Maria, who then decrypts the data and uses it.

However, exchanging the key via the Internet is not secure. If the key exchange process is compromised, all encrypted transactions based on the key can be compromised as well. One way around this problem is to use two keys: a public key to encrypt information and a private key to decrypt it. An e-business wishing to use encryption with public and private keys contacts a special organization, called a **certificate authority** or **CA**, that, for a fee, creates the keys. Public and private keys are created at the same time and are related in such a way that information encrypted with an e-business's public key can be decrypted with its private key and vice versa. One widely known and respected CA is VeriSign, Inc.

When the public and private keys are created, the public key is posted to a publicly-accessible directory; however, the private key is given only to the e-business requesting the keys. The combination of e-businesses with assigned public and private keys, public key directories, and the certificate authorities that issue and verify security credentials, is called a **public key infrastructure** or **PKI**.

Public Key Infrastructure (PKI)

A PKI is only as trustworthy as the people and technology of which it is composed. When deciding to participate in a PKI, an e-business needs some way to assure that others with whom it exchanges encrypted data are actually who and what they represent themselves to be. Digital certificates provide this assurance. A **digital certificate** is an electronic security credential issued by a CA that certifies an entity's identity. A digital certificate issued to an e-business by a CA such as VeriSign, Inc. can contain the CA's name, the certificate's serial number, expiration date, public key information, and the CA's digital or electronic signature validating that the certificate is legitimate. The digital certificate is made available in a public directory or registry so that e-businesses can look up each other's public keys. Figure 7-8 illustrates a digital certificate.

Figure 7-8
Digital
certificate

The following steps explain how using a PKI solves the transactional security needs of authentication, confidentiality, integrity, and nonrepudiation. (As you read these steps, refer to Figure 7-9.) Assume two e-businesses — MediaTime and ZoneOutlet — are involved in an online order transaction and are participating in a PKI. Both have been issued digital certificates with a public key and both have their own private key. The digital certificate information (including each e-business's public key) is available in a publicly accessible directory.

1. MediaTime, which needs to send purchase order information to ZoneOutlet, finds ZoneOutlet's public key information, encrypts the purchase order data with the public key, and sends the purchase order over the Internet. To provide further

security, the purchase order is signed with MediaTime's digital signature, which is in turn encrypted with MediaTime's own private key.

2. ZoneOutlet receives the purchase order and decrypts it with its own private key. ZoneOutlet locates MediaTime's public key and uses it to decrypt MediaTime's digital signature to verify that the purchase order actually came from MediaTime.

3. ZoneOutlet then creates a purchase order confirmation encrypted with MediaTime's public key, signs the purchase order confirmation with its own private key-encrypted digital signature, and sends the confirmation back to MediaTime.

4. MediaTime receives the encrypted purchase order confirmation and decrypts it using its own private key. MediaTime decrypts ZoneOutlet's digital certificate with ZoneOutlet's public key to verify that the purchase order confirmation came from ZoneOutlet.

Each e-business's digital certificate and digital signature provide authentication that both e-businesses actually are who they say they are. The purchase order transaction and confirmation transaction remain confidential, because only the holders of the private keys can decrypt the transactions. The integrity of the transactions has been preserved because neither transaction can be altered — their contents can only be read and altered by the holders of the private keys. Nonrepudiation is assured because each transaction has been digitally signed by its sender and the digital signature is encrypted with the sender's private key and in turn decrypted with the sender's public key.

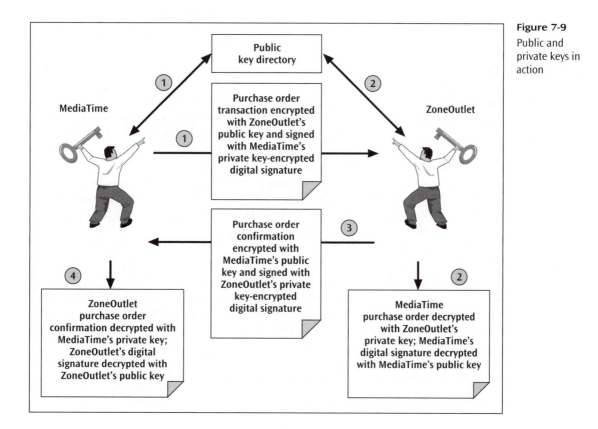

Figure 7-9
Public and private keys in action

The remarkable thing about public key encryption is that, since the mathematical relationship between the two keys is known, it's possible to derive one from the other. How then can such a security system work? Let's start with a small example using prime numbers. A prime number is an integer larger than one that can only be divided by one and itself.

Consider the numbers 3 and 13. It's trivial for a computer to tell us that the product of these two numbers is 39; it only takes a few microseconds. But if we start with the number 39, we need to try several combinations to find 3 and 13 as the lowest prime factors (divisors) of 39. It's fairly easy to tell that 3 and 13 are prime numbers; but what about these two numbers?

2223630206796195325784238989774474055726330242772

1135015321885492199429379788081705800662032233964516617311

They are in fact prime numbers. But even with numbers this large, it takes a computer only a few seconds to multiply them together to get this one enormous number: 25238543549210872218072672045480275651777210748595811525911102542 0004423651526733095299716862664714843487.

But how difficult would it be to start with the enormous number and work backward to determine its two prime factors? This process took a computer with 10,000 processors almost 10 days! This is an example of an asymmetric problem — a problem that's easy to solve in one direction but very difficult to solve in the other direction. Public-key encryption, called **asymmetric encryption**, uses much larger prime numbers (two and a half times longer) than those illustrated here to create public keys which are very difficult to decode or crack.

In practice, using these enormous keys is too slow for lengthy transmissions. To solve this problem public and private keys are used for the initial session greeting and then session keys are used to encrypt and decrypt the data. **Session keys** are shorter keys that are agreed upon in the highly secure initial conversation between the sender and the recipient and used only during the current session and afterward are discarded. In the U.S., session keys usually consist of 16 digits equaling 128 bits. For this reason, session keys are also called **128-bit keys**. 128-bit keys can have $3.4 * 10^{38}$ combinations. This number is adequate today; however, new faster computing technologies may someday make them easier to crack and therefore obsolete.

In the previous section you learned about establishing trust between online buyers and sellers using encryption, digital certificates, and a PKI. Next you learn about the security protocols such as SSL, TLS, and SET that are designed to ensure the security of Internet-transmitted financial transactions such as credit card payments and other secure Internet communications.

Security Protocols

One of the earliest Internet security protocols is **Secure Sockets Layer** or **SSL**, and was originally developed by Netscape Communications. SSL, which uses public and private key encryption and digital certificates, is included in Web browsers and Web server software. To use the SSL protocol, an e-business (or its ISP or Web hosting company) places its Web pages on an SSL secured server. The URL for the SSL-secured Web pages then begins with "https://" instead of just "http://," indicating information is transmitted using the SSL protocol. A Web browser and a Web server can use SSL to connect in an

SSL session and authenticate the server (or in some cases the server and the browser), determine the length of the secure data transmission, and determine the encryption technique to be used. Figure 7-10 illustrates the process of transmitting secure data using SSL.

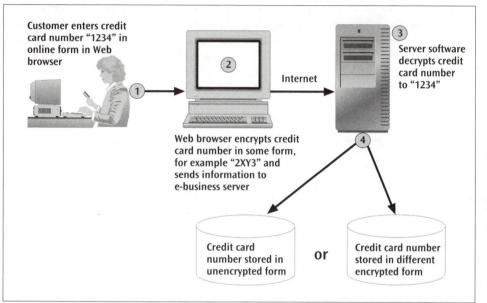

Figure 7-10
Transmitting secure data using SSL

The **Transport Layer Security** or **TLS** protocol suite is used to assure that no third party can access and alter Internet communications. Some experts consider TLS to be the heir to SSL. Based on SSL — but not interoperable with it — TLS consists of two protocols: the TLS Record Protocol and the TLS Handshake Protocol. The TLS Handshake Protocol allows Web browsers and Web servers to authenticate each other and determine the encryption method and keys to be used in the communication. The TLS Record Protocol provides some connection security and encryption using different encryption algorithms than SSL. The TLS Working Group of the IETF continues to work on and promote the TLS protocol suite.

In 1996, Visa and MasterCard, with the backing of Microsoft, IBM, Netscape, and others, announced support for a protocol called **Secure Electronic Transactions** or **SET**. SET is designed to be the standard protocol for presenting credit card transactions on the Internet. SET uses digital certificates, digital signatures, public and private keys, and SSL in its security scheme. Credit card holders, the bank that issued the card, and merchants are all

> **TIP**
>
> One interesting development in encryption is steganography. Steganography is the hiding of confidential data inside a much larger data set so that no one is aware of it. For example, a black-and-white satellite photo can be hidden inside a color photo by subtly changing the colors in ways too faint for human eyes to see. Unless you knew to look for the hidden photo you would be unaware of it. Using steganography to hide messages inside pictures is reportedly one method used by international terrorists to communicate with each other via the Internet.

required to have digital certificates for authentication. Credit card holders maintain an electronic or digital "wallet" that contains their digital certificate and credit card information. Merchants, and the card-issuing bank, use public and private encryption keys to exchange payment information.

No matter which encryption or transport method an e-business uses to protect its financial transactions, customer data such as names, address, and credit card numbers must be carefully protected. Theft of personal information (sometimes called identify theft) has reached epidemic proportions in the U.S. One frequent target of hackers is the information that identifies an e-business's customers including their credit card numbers. If an e-business stores this information online where it is vulnerable to a hacker attack, it should be stored in an encrypted format. An even better idea is to store this information offline, where it cannot be accessed by a hacker.

TECH CASE **Guess Who Has Your Credit Card Number?**

In February 2002, a 19-year old "independent software developer" in California discovered that by manipulating URLs the Guess? Inc. Web site was vulnerable to hackers who could easily access a customer information database — which also contained credit card numbers. The software developer attempted to warn Guess? of the problem; but, despite several attempted e-mails and a voice mail message, he couldn't get anyone at Guess? to respond. After waiting a week, he contacted a well-known security issues Web site, SecurityFocus Online, told the staff about the problem, and demonstrated how he was able to hack into the Guess? Inc. site. SecurityFocus Online then contacted Guess? — got someone's attention — and the vulnerability was quickly closed.

In addition to a security weakness, the network managers at Guess? failed to make it easy for anyone to let them know that a security weakness existed. According to some analysts, the inability to find the right person at an e-business to advise of a security vulnerability is far from uncommon. Some analysts suggest that a standard method of identifying and disclosing security holes that software vendors, users, and white hat hackers could follow would help solve this problem, but no standard notification method exists as of this writing.

In this section you learned how the SSL, TSL, and SET protocols enable secure online credit and debit card transactions. Next you learn about using a WAN (generally the Internet) to create a secure connection for two parts of a private LAN or between a remote user and a private LAN in order to transmit data securely.

Virtual Private Networks (VPNs)

One way an e-business can reduce costs involved in transmitting data between offices over long distances is to take advantage of the existing telecommunications infrastructure of the largest WAN of all, the Internet. A **virtual private network** or **VPN** is a private network that uses a large public network to transmit its data. For many VPNs, that public network is the Internet. VPNs use firewalls, public and private key encryption, and digital certificates as part of their security scheme.

Tunneling is a process by which one protocol is encapsulated within another protocol. VPNs that use the Internet encapsulate encrypted data, sending and receiving IP addresses, and a special tunneling protocol within a regular IP packet. The encapsulated information is routed to its destination network using the IP protocol. Once the encapsulated packet reaches the VPN destination, VPN software (usually installed as part of a firewall) removes the IP protocol information. Then the tunneling protocol transmits the packet to its final destination computer. A number of tunneling protocols are used by VPNs, including the Point-to-Point Tunneling Protocol or PPTP, the Generic Routing Encapsulation Protocol or GRE, the Layer 2 Tunneling Protocol or L2TP, and the Internet Protocol Security Protocol or IPSec. The manner in which VPN data is encrypted and encapsulated depends on the tunneling protocol used. Figure 7-11 illustrates a remote user transmitting data to a private network over a VPN.

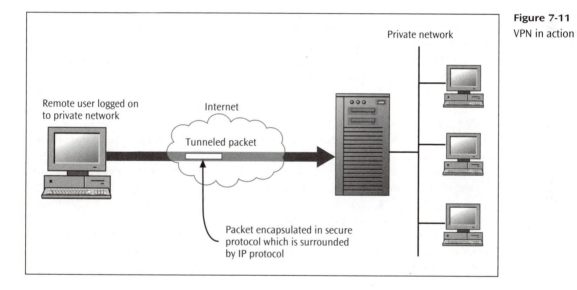

Figure 7-11
VPN in action

No discussion of security issues today would be complete without introducing some important security concerns related to wireless data transmissions.

Wireless Security Issues

In Chapter 5 you learned about FDMA, TDMA, and CDMA wireless technologies used by cellular networks. The early FDMA technologies required that a device stay on one frequency for the duration of a call. Listening in on such a call was fairly simple; you just needed a listening device able to intercept the transmission located near the phone or the tower serving it. Intercepting TDMA calls wasn't much more difficult; all that was needed was equipment that could listen for one third of each second (or one eighth, depending on the TDMA standard), and then decompress the audio signal into a full second of speech. Any electrical engineer could build such a device with off-the-shelf components. CDMA, which incorporates FHSS or DSSS, poses more of a challenge. However, an eavesdropper with enough resources can simply monitor all frequencies in use, reassemble every conversation, and throw away those not important. As cellular equipment gets cheaper, this scenario becomes more and more plausible. Clearly, something more sophisticated — such as data encryption — is in order.

WAP and WTLS

In Chapter 5, you also learned about WAP, the protocol stack or suite that makes it possible to access the Internet via cell phones or PDAs. WAP's internal encryption standard, **Wireless Transport Layer Security** (**WTLS**), uses encryption and digital certificates to establish a secure transmission session between a WAP server and a cell phone.

For example, assume you want to purchase something online via your cell phone. First you access a secure WAP site with your cell phone's minibrowser, which requests a secure connection with the WAP server. The WAP server sends its digital certificate (containing its public key) back to your cell phone's minibrowser which verifies the validity of the digital certificate by determining that it has been digitally signed by a CA. Once the validation process is complete, your cell phone's minibrowser generates an encrypted session key and sends it to the WAP server which decrypts the session key. Now, your cell phone's minibrowser and the WAP server can use the session key to send and receive encrypted secure communications.

As of this writing, the WLAN security issues are of great concern. These include the ease with which hackers can locate WLAN access points and encryption weaknesses in the IEEE 802.11b security protocol.

WLANs and Security

With the greater availability of IEEE 802.11 standard equipment and the explosive use of wireless devices, many organizations and businesses are installing WLANs. While problems with WLAN security are generally well known to IT security specialists, many business executives and managers may be surprised to learn how easy it is for a hacker to locate information about their WLAN access points. Once an access point is identified, a hacker can then exploit a WLAN's security vulnerabilities.

The term **war driving** is used by hackers and security analysts to describe driving around in a car (or parking a car across from a store or office building) and using an

802.11b-enabled laptop, an inexpensive antennae, and WLAN access point detection software such as NetStumbler to locate WLAN access points. For example, one analyst in a Southeastern seaboard city drove around the city with this type of simple setup to see if he could locate any WLAN access points. To the analyst's amazement, he was able to locate and map access points on more than 200 WLANs!

Additionally, the analyst discovered that many of the access point devices were named in such as way as to make it easy for a hacker to trace the access point back to the business or organization that owned the WLAN or, even worse, still had the manufacturer's default name (and likely the default password) assigned giving a hacker a head start on infiltrating the WLAN. The analyst's last surprise came when he contacted several of the WLAN owners to tell them he had easily located an access point to their WLAN and identified problems with the access point device's setup. The responses he received varied from "I just took it out of the box and plugged it in," to "We hired a professional to install it and never discussed security," and "It's just for a specific group, and we don't care if someone outside the organization can access it." Another illustration that people are always the weakest link in any security system!

The IEEE 802.11b Wi-Fi standard uses the **Wireless Equivalent Privacy (WEP)** security protocol to provide encryption and authentication of wireless transmissions to and from a WLAN. However, the analyst in the above example was able to determine that only 33 of the WLANs he identified (16 percent) were WEP enabled! Combining easy-to-locate access points and unencrypted wireless transmissions of sensitive data is a recipe for certain disaster. For example, Best Buy originally set up a small number of wireless cash registers that could be moved from department to department in its stores, thereby expanding checkout service in those departments with numerous waiting customers. In May 2002, Best Buy suspended the use of wireless cash registers after an unknown party reported to a security-focused e-mail mailing list that he had been able to locate a Best Buy WLAN access point and intercept unencrypted credit card numbers being transmitted to one of Best Buy's wireless cash registers. As of this writing, Best Buy is reportedly reviewing its WLAN security measures.

Security is still a concern for those businesses with WLANs that *are* WEP enabled because university researchers have recently identified serious short comings in WEP encryption standards. The IEEE 802.11b consortiums are working on improving WEP encryption standards; however, in the meantime, many organizations are simply not using WLANs at this time because of the potential ease with which a hacker can locate an access point and intercept sensitive data or infiltrate their network.

In addition to WLAN security, IrDA and Bluetooth technologies also raise serious security issues.

IrDA and Bluetooth Security

Because of the short distances and line-of-sight requirements for IrDA devices, it would be difficult to interpose a "sniffer" (a device that monitors network traffic) unobtrusively between two IrDA-enabled laptops. However, many analysts are concerned about another problem: namely, that laptop users are not aware of security issues related to using laptops with IrDA ports in public places such as airports. Analysts are concerned that many of these laptops still have the default IrDA port settings which automatically allow networking with other devices without authentication or passwords. This makes the laptops vulnerable to nearby hackers. Analysts suggest one way to protect an IrDA-enabled laptop from hackers when it is being used in a public place is to unplug the laptop's NIC and cover the IrDA port when they are not being used.

Bluetooth devices use several methods to establish a secure transmission including a link key (a 128-bit random number) to authenticate a connection between two Bluetooth-enabled devices; a private encryption key (8 to 128 bits in length and derived from the link key) to encrypt data, and a user-selected PIN code that identifies the Bluetooth device. Additionally, each Bluetooth device has a unique address. Security concerns arise in two areas: privacy and PIN storage. A Bluetooth device's unique address is transmitted with each message; therefore, it is possible to track the device and its activities (and, therefore, its human user). The use of PIN numbers can be an irritant to users who may choose to store the PIN number in the device. If the Bluetooth device is lost or stolen, whoever finds it may then be able to locate the stored PIN number and use it to authenticate a Bluetooth connection. The latter is more of a social problem than a technical one, since anyone practicing good computer hygiene should be careful not to store important PIN numbers or passwords anywhere on a device itself.

An e-business shouldn't wait for a white hat hacker to advise it of security vulnerabilities or for a disgruntled employee to take advantage of a security weakness. Security audits that include penetration testing can help an e-business prevent security breaches before they happen.

Security Audits

A **security audit** is a comprehensive review and assessment of an e-business's security vulnerabilities. A complete security audit should involve reviewing security policies, taking a look at employee training on security policies and procedures, and reviewing the physical security of the e-business's offices and network facilities. A security audit should also involve examining the technical security of a network via **penetration testing** or actual attempted hacking attacks by security audit personnel. Many e-businesses specializing in security services and many accounting firms offer security auditing services. Often an e-business wishing to purchase insurance coverage to protect against loss of assets because of damage or theft by employees, physical intruders, or hackers must undergo a security audit.

A thorough security audit should contain at least three components:

◆ *Organizational audit*: Identifies weaknesses in an existing formal security plan or the lack of a formal security plan; reviews effectiveness of a formal security awareness program for all employees; reviews security training procedures for all new employees including acceptable use standards for corporate computer assets; reviews employee hiring and firing policies including background checks and procedures for monitoring computer access by terminated employees.

- *Technical audit*: Identifies internal weaknesses in network security caused by poorly configured servers, firewalls, and routers; reviews the effectiveness of the password system used to control access to the network; identifies ports left open for discontinued network services; uses internal and external scans (penetration tests) of the network's security to identify any weaknesses that could be exploited by hackers.
- *Physical audit*: Identifies how easy or difficult it is to gain unauthorized access to computer facilities, offices, and unattended computers; notes effectiveness of doors, locks, and other barriers to entry of the general office and network facilities; identifies whether or not employees challenge the presence of unknown outsiders in offices or computer facilities; reviews the location of the computer facilities and notes whether those facilities are readily identifiable to outsiders; reviews the effectiveness of cameras, motion detectors, and human security inside the general office facilities and the network facilities.

> **TIP**
>
> Some security audits may include using social engineering techniques — human-to-human interactions — to trick employees into divulging important security information such as passwords, the physical location of the computer facilities, or other information that might compromise security. However, because these social engineering exercises *are almost always successful* (remember, humans are always the weakest link in any security system), many security auditors don't even bother trying them!

TECH CASE Banking on a Security Audit

When a New England bank launched its online banking Web sites, it realized that it needed to take a close look at the security risks related to its Web sites and LAN. The management of the bank understood the importance of treating security risks just like any other business risks; therefore, it formed a technology risk committee that included the executive vice president, the vice president of IT, and the chief financial officer among others. The first order of business for the technology risk committee was to determine where the bank's LAN and Web site security was vulnerable.

To determine its LAN and Web site vulnerabilities, the bank hired a security firm to perform a security audit which included penetration testing. To prepare for the security audit, the security firm conducted a preliminary interview with the bank's internal auditor and the IT vice president to determine the audit's objectives — which were to test the security of its two Web sites (one that handled its customers' online banking and the other that handled static information pages) and to test its LAN security (especially its mail server security). Because the security firm wanted to use only publicly available information — the same information available to potential hackers — it did not ask the bank for any details about the Web sites or the two companies that hosted them.

The security firm began the audit by using the bank's Web sites to locate every IP address related to the hosted sites. Next, it set up its testing team, which would attempt to breach the Web sites' security in the early morning hours over the next several days. Within 30 minutes of the first attempted intrusion at the bank's online transaction Web site, the hosting company notified the bank by phone message and by e-mail that the bank's site had been scanned by an unknown third party. Within 12 hours of the scan, the hosting company had traced the scan back to the security consultant's IP address, got the security firm's phone number, and called the firm to find out what was going on. The bank was thrilled with the hosting company's quick identification of the scan and its thorough response to it. The security audit report on the LAN and e-mail server security was also positive.

Continued

Unfortunately, the second hosting company, which hosted the bank's static information pages, did not respond to the scan and, in fact, was not aware of it until notified by the bank. While there was no access to sensitive customer information at this Web site, the site was vulnerable to Web site defacement, which could embarrass the bank and adversely affect its reputation. The hosting company agreed to upgrade its security and the bank elected to continue the relationship. For the bank, the cost of the security audit was money well spent.

Hiring a security firm to perform a security audit is an important step. When evaluating a security firm that performs a penetration test of the network as part of the security audit, there are several factors to consider:

◆ *Proof of insurance*: Ask for proof of insurance to protect you against the security firm's accidental damage to your system or system downtime because of the tests.
◆ *Nondisclosure agreements*: Have everyone on the security firm's team sign a nondisclosure agreement and consider requiring a third-party background check on each member of the security firm's team. Is the firm using white hat hackers? Are you comfortable with that?
◆ *Scanning tools*: Find out what security scanning tools the security firm is going to use. Are they using prepackaged tools your own staff could use (much less expensively) or are they using custom tools?
◆ *Scope of engagement*: Determine a clear scope for the audit and a workable time frame that is agreed to by all parties.
◆ *Documentation*: Make sure the final report from the firm includes an accounting of all attacks attempted and whether or not they were successful, a return of all the paper or electronic information gathered by the firm, and recommendations on how to fix any problems discovered during the tests.

An e-business cannot expect to achieve perfect security for its network and Web site. Instead, e-businesses should strive for security that is good enough to protect the e-business's assets, revenue stream, customer privacy, and its own reputation. In other words, e-businesses should strive for adequate security, not perfect security. However, security measures that are adequate for one company might be impossibly inadequate for another company. The definition of "adequate" depends on an individual e-business's situation. For example, a Web site providing information on vegetarian recipes may not require the same level of security that a bank might require. An e-business must determine its security needs based on the risks involved, the value of the assets at risk, and the cost of implementing a security system.

In this chapter you have learned about the physical, internal, external, and transactional risks for which an e-business must be prepared and some countermeasures an e-business can take to lessen those risks. In the next chapter you learn about the technologies that allow e-businesses to integrate their Web site operations with their administrative operations.

...MAFIABOY MADNESS

Before February 7, 2000, most people outside of IT personnel and network security specialists had never heard of distributed denial of service attacks. That changed dramatically when several of the biggest names in e-business were brought to their knees by DDoS attacks. Financial losses for these DDoS attacks are estimated to be more than $1.2 billion.

Who was behind the attacks? Within three days of the attacks U.S. and Canadian officials were able to trace the CNN.com attack to a Canadian teenager, known in chat rooms as "Mafiaboy." He was identified via his computer's IP address that was found on a computer log at the University of California at Santa Barbara (UCSB). Additionally, Mafiaboy had been bragging about his attacks in online hacker chat rooms.

How did he do it? After several months of investigation it was determined that Mafiaboy had accessed several computers on U.S. university networks including UCSB, Harvard, and Duke University. Mafiaboy planted instructions on the computers telling them to send unending streams of traffic to various Web sites. In August 2000, Mafiaboy was charged with 10 counts of attacking Yahoo!, Amazon.com, eBay, and other Web sites, plus an additional 54 counts of unauthorized access to university networks. Mafiaboy pleaded guilty to the DDoS attacks and incidents of unauthorized network access and, in September 2001, he was sentenced to two successive four-month sentences and one year's probation. Additionally, he was prohibited from owning any software used to break into computer systems, from visiting Web sites that promote such software, and from benefiting financially from his crimes.

Why did he do it? Apparently the attacks were launched simply for bragging rights!

TECHLIST ✓ Understanding Network and Web Site Security

❑ Security concerns the protection of assets. An e-business's network and Web site assets include both equipment and data.

❑ Network and Web site security must protect against physical, internal, external, and transactional risks.

❑ Physical risks include accidental or deliberate damage to equipment and data as a result of a natural disaster or sabotage. Countermeasures for physical risks include adequate barriers to office and network facility entrances, controlled and monitored access of network facilities, adequate fire-suppression systems, and adequate network facilities construction including floor to ceiling walls, backup electrical power supply, and backup Internet connections.

Continued

- Internal security risks are those that originate from inside an e-business and include threats to assets from unhappy employees and failure by management to institute security policies, procedures, and education. Internal security risks also include failure to prepare timely backups of data and to test restore procedures. Finally, internal security risks also include failure to properly plan for disasters. Countermeasures to internal security risks include a password system for network access and biometric and smart card identification systems.

- Password systems are only effective if they are well constructed and monitored. Passwords should be at least six characters long and consist of both letters and numbers. Poorly constructed passwords include names, dates, and common words that might be easily identified by another employee or an outside intruder.

- Backup of data and testing of data restoration should be done on a regularly scheduled basis. At least one set of backup data should be retained off-site.

- Every e-business should have a disaster recovery or business continuity plan to assure that, in case of a catastrophe, the business can remain viable. A disaster recovery or business continuity plan should be tested periodically once it has been developed.

- External security risks include network intrusion by hackers. Hacker attacks can include denial of service attacks and Web site defacement. Countermeasures for hacker attacks include firewalls, NAT and proxy servers, filters, and network intrusion detection software.

- External security risks include computer virus infections. A standard computer virus is a small destructive program that infects other programs and can damage files, programs, and data. A worm is a virulent type of virus that resides in computer memory and replicates itself. A macro virus infects Microsoft Office documents. Some so-called viruses are just hoaxes, but an e-business must be able to tell the difference and protect against real viruses. Countermeasures for viruses include antivirus software, employee education, operating system software updates, general virus awareness, and proper use of macro detection tools for various applications.

- A Trojan horse is a program, sometimes part of a virus's payload, that looks like something fun or interesting but that is actually a program that, once planted on a computer, allows a hacker to access that computer remotely and gather confidential information.

Continued

- ❑ E-business transactional risks include failure to authenticate parties to a transaction, interception and alteration of data during data transmission, refusal to acknowledge a transaction, and breach of confidentiality of transaction contents including customer information.

- ❑ Encryption is the translation of data into secret code called ciphertext; decryption is the process of returning ciphertext to plaintext.

- ❑ The four necessities of transactional security are: authentication, integrity, nonrepudiation, and confidentiality. E-businesses that use a public key infrastructure to encrypt and decrypt transactions fulfill these four transactional needs.

- ❑ Security protocols also used to protect data from interception and alteration during transmission are SSL, TLS, and SET.

- ❑ A virtual private network is a secure connection over a public network, usually the Internet, between two parts of a private LAN or between a remote user and a private LAN. Data transmitted over a virtual private network is first encrypted (along with sending and receiving IP addresses and a special tunneling protocol) and then encapsulated in a regular IP packet. The IP packet information is stripped away at the VPN's destination, at which point the tunneling protocol forwards the data to its final destination.

- ❑ WTLS is the security protocol component of the WAP wireless protocol suite. WTLS uses encryption and digital certificates to enable secure data transmissions over a cell phone or PDA. The ease of locating a WLAN access point coupled with poor internal management of WLAN security, and a weak security protocol (WEP) make WLAN security so problematic that many businesses are avoiding implementing WLANs. IrDA and Bluetooth security issues involve user failure to properly shield IrDA ports from hackers or to protect Bluetooth PIN numbers when a device is lost or stolen.

- ❑ A security audit can provide an e-business with information about the effectiveness of its security policies, procedures, and employee security training and awareness. Additionally, a security audit should identify technical network weaknesses such as poorly configured servers. Finally, a security audit should point out physical security weaknesses such as inadequate control and monitoring of access to office and network facilities.

Key Terms

128-bit key
application-level firewalls
asymmetric encryption
backup and restore policies
backup and restore procedures
biometrics
black hat hacker
buffer overflow
business continuity plan (BCP)
certificate authority (CA)
ciphertext
circuit-level firewalls
crackers
cryptography
decrypted
denial of service attacks (DoS)
digital certificate
disaster recovery plan (DRP)
distributed denial of service
    attacks (DDoS)

encryption
ethical hacker
external risks
failover
filter
hacker
internal risks
key
macro
macro virus
Network Address Translation (NAT)
Packet Internet Groper (Ping)
packet-filtering firewalls
password
penetration testing
physical risks
plaintext
proxy server
public key infrastructure (PKI)

restore
Secure Electronic Transactions (SET)
Secure Sockets Layer (SSL)
security audit
session keys
smart card
Transport Layer Security (TLS)
Trojan horse
tunneling
virtual private network (VPN)
virus
war driving
Web site defacement
white hat hacker
Wireless Equivalent Privacy (WEP)
Wireless Transport Layer
    Security (WTLS)
wireless virus
worm

Review Questions

1. Which of the following is a worm that attacks Microsoft's IIS Web server?

  a. Code Red
  b. 48 Hours
  c. VPN
  d. DDoS

2. Which of the following is not a physical risk to a network?

  a. Unlocked network facilities
  b. False ceilings
  c. Door sign identifying the network facilities
  d. Only one Internet connection

3. Which of the following is a well-constructed password?

  a. Smith
  b. XC13
  c. 091157
  d. AZ17XD

4. Another name for a DRP is:

  a. VPN.
  b. DoS.
  c. BCP.
  d. TLS.

5. Web page defacement:

  a. Enhances the appearance of a Web page.
  b. Secures the Web page from intruders.
  c. Embarrasses Web site owners.
  d. Prevents against credit card theft.

6. A program that appears to do something useful or entertaining but actually does something malicious is called a:

  a. Macro.
  b. Virtual private network.
  c. Virus.
  d. Trojan horse.

7. Which of the following is not an effective virus countermeasure?

   a. Antivirus software
   b. Employee education
   c. Operating system software updates
   d. Organizational audit

8. Which of the following is not a security protocol?

   a. VPN
   b. SSL
   c. TLS
   d. SET

9. Which of the following is likely to be the greatest threat to an e-business's network and Web site security?

   a. Viruses
   b. Hackers
   c. Security audits
   d. An e-business's employees and management

10. An organizational security audit is likely to uncover:

    a. Poorly configured servers.
    b. Inadequate door locks.
    c. Poorly constructed passwords.
    d. Inadequate security training for employees.

11. White hat hackers use their skill to gain access to networks to steal or damage assets. **True or False?**

12. Intrusion detection software enables an e-business to send secure data over the Internet. **True or False?**

13. A buffer overflow occurs when more data is sent to file on a hard disk than the file can hold. **True or False?**

14. Network and Web site security is always the top priority for e-business management and employees. **True or False?**

15. Biometric security devices and software can enhance or replace an ineffective and unwieldy password system. **True or False?**

16. External security risks are those that originate inside an e-business. **True or False?**

17. A DDoS attack might consist of hundreds of pings sent to a host from other computers. **True or False?**

18. Circuit-level firewalls operate at the Application level of the OSI Model. **True or False?**

19. Filters can be used effectively to block spurious traffic in a DDoS attack. **True or False?**

20. A virtual private network uses a public network such as the Internet to transmit secure data by encapsulating that data inside a regular IP packet. **True or False?**

Exercises

1. Using Internet search tools or other relevant resources, such as those at the end of this chapter, research famous (or infamous) network or Web site hacking events over the past two years. Then create a timeline of these events including a description of each event.

2. Using Internet search tools or other relevant resources, such as those at the end of this chapter, research articles on the differences between white hat and black hat hackers. Then write a one-page paper describing the differences including recent, real-world examples of both.

3. Using the several security-focused Web sites, such as SecurityFocus.com or others listed at the end of this chapter, review current news about security issues, including wireless security issues. Then write a one- or two-page paper describing three to five current network and wireless security issues of particular concern to e-businesses.

4. Using the Virus Information Library at McAfee.com, the Antiviral Toolkit Pro Virus Encyclopedia, Symantec's Virus Encyclopedia, or other relevant resources, such as those at the end of this chapter, note 10 recently identified computer viruses, worms, and Trojan horses. Then write a one-page paper listing the items including name, date identified, type, and destructive capability.

5. Using Internet search tools or other relevant resources, such as those at the end of this chapter, locate five e-businesses that provide security audit services. Then write a one-page paper comparing and contrasting the e-businesses and their audit services.

CASE PROJECTS

♦ 1 ♦

You are the assistant to the president of a startup e-business that sells extreme sports equipment online. James Wong, the president, wants to create a business culture that supports system security and asks you to draft an announcement to all employees about the importance of network security. Using any relevant resources, draft a one-page announcement explaining the importance of network security and especially the correct use of passwords and other security measures.

♦ 2 ♦

You are the assistant to Juanita Luna, the president of a large e-business that provides Web hosting services from several data centers around the country. Luna is considering installing biometric security devices at each of the data centers to control access. She asks you to research the current status of biometric security devices that would be suitable, including information about specific devices and software and their vendors. Using the Internet or other relevant resources, research information about the current status of biometric security, the types of devices and software available, and the vendors that sell the devices. Then create an outline that you can use to discuss your findings in the next meeting with Luna.

♦ 3 ♦

You and your e-business partner, LaTisha Washington, have decided to hire a security firm to conduct a security audit to identify any network or Web site security weaknesses your e-business may have. You are meeting with a representative of the firm tomorrow and want to be prepared for the meeting. Create an outline of the topics you need to discuss during the meeting before you consider hiring the firm.

TEAM PROJECT

You and two classmates have just been hired as an auditing team by an e-business that provides security auditing services. Next week your team is going on its first assignment: auditing a medium-sized e-business that publishes an online magazine. The client is trying to purchase cybercrime insurance and a security audit is required by the insurance company. The client has 20 employees, a private LAN with a Web server, and a mail server, and all employees have Internet access. (You can make up any other facts not presented here.) Meet with your team to plan the audit assignment.

After your meeting, use Microsoft PowerPoint or other presentation software to create a 5–10 slide presentation that presents an overview of your security audit plan. Then present your security audit plan to a group of classmates selected by your instructor.

Useful Links

Center for Secure Computer Systems — George Mason University — Security links
www.isse.gmu.edu/~csis/links.html

CERT® Coordination Center — Carnegie Mellon Software Engineering Institute
www.cert.org/

CNN.com — News Special: Insurgency on the Internet
cnn.com/TECH/specials/hackers/

Computer Security Resource Center (CSRC) — U.S. Department of Commerce
csrc.ncsl.nist.gov/

Disaster Recovery Journal
www.drj.com/

DShield.org — Distributed Intrusion Detection Information
www.dshield.org/

Electronic Frontier Foundation
www.eff.org/

eSecurityPlanet.com
www.esecurityplanet.com/

Hackers Hall of Fame at Discovery.com
tlc.discovery.com/convergence/hackers/hackers.html

IDG.net — Biometrics Special
www.idg.net/biometrics

Information Systems Audit and Control Association & Foundation
www.isaca.org/

InfoSysSec — Security Portal
www.prognosisx.com/infosyssec/

InfoWar — Security Portal
www.infowar.com/

IT Papers.com — Biometric White Papers
www.itpapers.com/cgi/SubcatIT.pl?scid=442

IT Papers.com — Disaster Recovery White Papers
www.itpapers.com/cgi/SubcatIT.pl?scid=76

McAfee Wireless Security Center
www.mcafee.com/wireless/handscan/?

Microsoft Security
www.microsoft.com/security/

National Infrastructure Protection Center (NIPC)
www.nipc.gov/

National Security Institute — Security Resources
www.nsi.org/compsec.html

Prime Numbers and Factoring Links
www.ontko.com/~rayo/primes/

SANS Institute Online
www.sans.org/

Security Administrator — Windows IT Security
www.ntsecurity.net/

Security World Wide Web Sites
www.alw.nih.gov/Security/security-www.html

SecurityGeeks
securitygeeks.shmoo.com/

SecuritySearch.net — Security Resources
www.securitysearch.net/

TekCentral — Disaster Recovery and Business Continuity Resources
www.tekcentral.com/teknetwork/Disaster_Recovery/

The Biometric Consortium
www.biometrics.org/

The Biometric Digest
webusers.anet-stl.com/~wrogers/biometrics/

The Jargon File — The New Hacker's Dictionary
www.tuxedo.org/~esr/jargon/html/index.html

The PC Guide — Backups and Disaster Recovery
www.pcguide.com/care/bu/index.htm

The PKI Page — PKI Links and Resources
www.pki-page.org/

The WWW Security FAQ
www.w3c.org/Security/Faq/

U.S. Department of Justice — Cybercrime Site
www.cybercrime.gov/

Virtual Private Network Consortium (VPNC)
www.vpnc.org/

Virus Protection and Software Primer — Clemson University
virtual.clemson.edu/client/repprob/vprimer.htm

Links to Web Sites or Companies Noted in This Chapter

Amazon.com
www.amazon.com

Amerivault Corp.
www.amerivault.com/

AVP Virus Encyclopedia
www.avp.ch/avpve

Best Buy
www.bestbuy.com/

Biometric Consortium
www.biometrics.org/

Buy.com
www.us.buy.com/

CNN Interactive
www.cnn.com/index.html

Comcast Business Communications, Inc.
www.comcastbusiness.com/

Computer Security Institute (CSI)
www.gocsi.com/

eBay
www.ebay.com

E*TRADE
www.etrade.com

Federal Bureau of Investigation
www.fbi.gov

Global Crossing Holdings Ltd.
www.globalcrossing.com/

Goodyear Tire and Rubber Company
www.goodyear.com/

Guess? Inc.
www.guess.com

Key3 Media — COMDEX
www.key3media.com/comdex/

McAfee Virus Information Library
vil.mcafee.com/default.asp?

McAfee Wireless Security Center
www.mcafee.com/wireless/handscan/?

Metropolitan Network BBS Inc. — AVP Virus Encyclopedia
www.avp.ch/avpve/findex.stm

Microsoft Corporation
www.microsoft.com

National Aeronautics and Space Administration (NASA)
www.nasa.gov

NetStumbler.com
www.netstumbler.com

Pro Softnet Corporation
www.pro-softnet.com/

SecurityFocus.com
www.securityfocus.com/

Symantec Corporation — Virus Encyclopedia
securityresponse.symantec.com/avcenter/vinfodb.html/

The NASDAQ Stock Market, Inc.
www.nasdaq.com/

The *New York Times*
www.nytimes.com

Trend Micro, Inc.
www.antivirus.com/free_tools/wireless/

U.S. Department of Justice
www.usdoj.gov/

VeriSign, Inc.
www.verisign.com/

WorldCom, Inc.
www.worldcom.com

Yahoo!
www.yahoo.com/

ZDNet
www.zdnet.com

For Additional Review

Anand, Nikhil. 2001. "An Overview of Bluetooth Security," SANS Institute, February 22. Available online at: rr.sans.org/wireless/bluetooth.php.

Andrews, Jean. 2001. *i-Net+ Guide to Internet Technologies*. Boston: Course Technology.

ArrowPoint Communications: White Papers. 2000. "Web Site Security and Denial of Service Protection." www.arrowpoint.com/solutions/white_papers/Web _Site_Security.html.

Blakey, Elizabeth. 2000. "Commit a Cybercrime? You're Hired!" *E-Commerce Times*, July 17. Available online at: www.ecommercetimes.com/ perl/printer/3789/.

Cisco Systems. 2000. "Intrusion Detection Planning Guide." Available online at: www.cisco.com/ univercd/cc/td/doc/product/iaabu/idpg/.

CNN In-Depth Specials. 1999. "Two Views of Hacking." Available online at: cnn.com/TECH/specials/ hackers/quandas/.

CNN.com. 2000. "Cyber-attacks Batter Web Heavyweights," February 9. Available online at: www.cnn.com/2000/TECH/computing/02/09/ cyber.attacks.01/index.html.

CNN.com. 2000. "E*TRADE, ZDNet Latest Targets in Wave of Cyber-attacks," February 9. Available online at: www.cnn.com/2000/TECH/computing/ 02/09/cyber.attacks.02/.

Coles, Robert. 2000. "Safety Net," 150(895), *The Banker*, September 7.

Computer Security Institute. 2000. "2000 Computer Crime and Security Survey," May 22. Available online at: www.gocsi.com/.

Costello, Sam. 2001. "Study: Nearly 4,000 DoS Attacks Occur Per Week," *IDG News Service* as reported by CNN.com, May 24. Available online at: www.cnn .com/2001/TECH/internet/05/24/dos.study.idg/.

Cowell, Ruth. 2001. "War Dialing and War Driving," *SANS Institute*, June 11. Available online at: rr.sans.org/wireless/war.php.

Daudelin, Art. 2000. "E-security Advances for Everyday Banking," 13(2), *Bank Technology News*, February 1.

de Borchgrave, Arnaud et al. 2000. "Cyber Threats and Information Security: Meeting the 21st Century Challenge," *Center for Strategic and International Studies*, December. Available online at: www.csis.org/ homeland/reports/cyberthreatsandinfosec.pdf.

Dean, Tamara. 2002. *Network+ Guide to Networks, Second Edition*. Boston: Course Technology.

Delio, Michelle. 2001. "The Greatest Hacks of All Time," *WiredNews*, February 6. www.wired.com/news/ print/0,11294,41630,00.html.

Dube, Jonathan and Ross, Brian. 2000. "Mafiaboy Arrested," *ABCNews.com*, April 19. Available online at: abcnews.go.com/sections/tech/ DailyNews/webattacks000419.html.

Duffy, Daintry. 2000. "Test Your Defenses," *Darwin Magazine*, December. Available online at: www.darwinmag.com/read/120100/defenses.html.

Edwards, Joseph. 2000. "Something Old, Something New: DNS Hijacking," *Windows IT Security*, February 16. Available online at: www.ntsecurity.net/ Articles/Print.cfrm?ArticleID=8170.

eMarketer, Inc. 2000. "While the Boss is Away, the Mice Surf," as reported by *Websense Inc.*, May 23. Available online at: www.netpart.com/company/ news/features/00/052300.cfm.

Felton, Edward W. et al. 1997. "Web Spoofing: An Internet Con Game," Department of Computer Science, Princeton University. Available online at: www.cs.princeton.edu/sip/pub/spoofing.pdf.

Fennelly, Carole. 2000. "Hacker's Toolchest: Techniques and Tools for Penetration Testing," *SunWorld*, May. Available online at: www.sunworld. com/sunworldonline/swol-05-2000/swol-05- security_p.html.

Festa, Paul. 2001. "Microsoft Closes Window to Customer Data," *CNET News.com*, October 10. Available online at: news.com.com/ 2102-1023-274207.html.

Festa, Paul. 2001. "Yahoo News Hacked, Story Changed," *CNET News.com*, September 20. Available online at: news.com.com/ 2102-1023-273284.html.

Forbes.com. 2001. "Wireless Security: Guess Who's Listening," May 22. Available online at: www.forbes .com/2001/05/22/0522wireless_print.html.

Fratto, Mike. 2001. "Tutorial: Wireless Security," *Network Computing*, January 22. Available online at: www.nwc.com/shared/printArticle?article=nc/1202/ 1202fld1.html&pbj-nwc.

Gast, Matthew. 2002. "Wireless LAN Security: A Short History," *O'Reilly Network*, April 19. Available online at: www.oreillynet.com/pub/a/wireless/2002/04/19/security.html.

Getgen, Kim. 2001. "Securing the Air — 2001: A Security Odyssey," IBM, January. Available online at: www.105.ibm.com/developerworks/papers.nsf/dw/wireless-papers bynewest?OpenDocument&Count=500.

Gibson, Steve. 2001. "The Strange Tale of the Denial of Service Attacks Against GRC.com," *Gibson Research Corporation*, June 2. Available online at: grc.com/dos/grcdos.htm.

Greenemeier, Larry. 2000. "IBM Offers Web-Site Checkup — Three Levels of Global Services' Web Security Scan Augment Firewalls and Encryption," *Information Week*, June 5, 139.

Harris, Donna. 2000. "Security Expert Offers Tips to Stop Web Site Defacement," 74(5865), *Automotive News*, March 13.

Harvey, Thomas W. 2000. "Asleep at the Packet Switch," *CFO, The Magazine for Senior Financial Executives*, 16(11), Fall.

Henry-Stocker, Sandra. 2001. "Deconstructing DoS Attacks," *CNN.com SCI-TECH*, March 7. Available online at: www.cnn.com/2001/TECH/internet/03/07/dos.attacks.idg/.

Hopper, D. Ian. 2000. "Denial of Service Hackers Take on New Targets," *CNN.com*, February 9. Available online at: www.cnn.com/2000/TECH/computing/02/09/denial.of.service/.

Howell, Ric. 2002. "WAP Security," *Concise Group Ltd*. Available online at: www.vbxml.com/wap/articles/wap_security/default.asp.

Hurwitz Group, Inc. 2000. "Web Application Security: Protecting e-Business from Attack," Sanctum, Inc. Available online at: www.sanctuminc.com/security/more/index.html.

Huston, Brent. 2001. "Types of Penetration Testing," *ITWorld.com*, October 24. Available online at: www.itworld.com/nl/security_strat/10242001/pf_index.html.

Inam, A. 2000. "Companies Now Confront Cyber Risk," *Global Finance*, 14(6), June 1.

Jesdanun, Anick. 2002. "Snoops Cause Wireless Networking Worries," *Associated Press* as reported in the *Houston Chronicle*, May 3.

Krebs, Brian. 2002. "Sites Revealed Passwords for Thousands of Ameritech Users," *Newsbytes*, February 22. Available online at: www.newsbytes.com/cgi-bin/udt/im.display.printable?client.id=newsbytes&story.id=174719.

Kuhn, Larry and Hargreave, Andrew. 2001. "Preparing for Security in the Wireless World," *Geneer Corporation*. Available online at: www.geneer.com/publications/index.asp.

Lamm, Gregory et al. 2001. "Bluetooth Wireless Networks Security Features," *IEEE Workshop on Information Assurance and Security at the United States Military Academy*. Available online at: www.itoc.usma.edu/Workshop/2001/Authors/Submitted_Abstracts/paperW2A2(26).pdf.

Lamos, Robert. 2001. "Hacker Had WorldCom in His Hands," *CNET News.com*, December 6. Available online at: news.com.com/2102-1001-276711.html.

Lamos, Robert. 2001. "Hacker Helps Excite@Home Toughen Defenses," CNET *News.com*, May 29. Available online at: news.com.com/2102-1001-261728.html.

Lamos, Robert and Kane, Margaret. 2002. "Hacker Penetrates *N.Y. Times'* Network," *CNET News.com*, February 27. Available online at: news.com.com/2102-1023-846215.html.

Larsen, Eric and Stephens, Brian. 2000. *Web Servers, Security, & Maintenance*. Upper Saddle Rivers, NJ: Prentice-Hall, Inc.

Lawton, George. 2001. "Lock Up Your Wireless LAN," *Enterprise*, August 23. Available online at: techupdate.zdnet.com/techupdate/stories/main/0,14179,2806945-2,00.html.

Lemos, Robert. 2001. "Year of the Worm," *CNET News.com*, March 15. Available online at: news.com.com/2102-1001-254061.html.

Lipschultz, David. 2001. "Security Haunts the Wireless Web," *InternetWeek*, July 10. Available online at: www.internetweek.com/indepth01/indepth071001.htm.

MacPhee, Allan. 2001. "Understanding Digital Certificates and Wireless Transport Layer Security (WTLS)," *Entrust, Inc.*, Available online at: www.entrust.com/resources/pdf/understanding_wtls.pdf.

Mandeville, David. 1999. "Hackers, Crackers, and Trojan Horses: A Primer," *CNN.com*, March 29. Available online at: cnn.org/TECH/specials/hackers/.

Masland, Molly. 2000. "The Dark Side of Online Shopping: Trail of Fraud Leads From Amazon.com to Thailand," *MSNBC*, June 24. Available online at: www.msnbc.com/news/283239.asp.

McDaid, Cathal. 2001. "Bluetooth Security," *Palowireless Bluetooth Resource Center*, February-March. Available online at: www.palowireless.com/bluearticles/cc1_security1.asp.

McDonough, Dan Jr. 2001. "PDA App Attacks 'Wireless Security Gap'," *Wireless NewsFactor*, July 31. Available online at: wireless.newsfactor.com/perl/printer/12392.

McMillan, Dan and Goldfield, Robert. 2000. "Internet Security Firms Profit From Hack Attack," 16(52), *Business Journal-Portland*, February 18.

McMurray, Mike. 2001. "Wireless Security," *SANS Institute*, January 22. Available online at: rr.sans.org/wireless/wireless_sec.php.

McWilliams, Brian. 2001. "Mass Site Defacement Relied on Cheap Trick," *Newsbytes*, July 13. Available online at: www.newsbytes.com/news/01/167942.html.

Mikal, Philip. 2002. "WTLS: The Good and Bad of WAP Security," *Advisor Wireless Technology*. Available online at: http://www.advisor.com/Articles.nsf/aid/MIKAP001.

Miller, Sandra Kay. 2001. "War Driving," *Information Security Magazine*, November. Available online at: www.infosecuritymag.com/articles/november01/technology_wardriving.shtml.

Moran, John M. and Halloran, Liz. 2000. "Hackers Jam More Internet Doors — Concern Rises Over Web Site Security, Privacy," Issue PSA-2532, *The Hartford Courant: Statewide*, Main (A) Section.

MSNBC News. 2000. "Vast Online Credit Card Theft Revealed: And Related Stories," March 17. Available online at: www.msnbc.com/news/382561.asp#BODY.

Napier, H. Albert et all. 2000. Creating a Winning E-Business. Cambridge, MA: Course Technology.

NetAction.org. 2001. "NetAction's Guide to Using Encryption Software." Available online at: www.netaction.org/encrypt/.

Newmediary, Inc. 2001. "Tech Guide: Security for Today's Enterprise," *Techguide.com*. Available online at: www.itpapers.com/techguide/security.pdf.

Niccolai, James. 2001. "COMDEX - Biometrics Puts a Face (or Finger) on Security," *ITWorld.com*, November 16. Available online at: www.itworld.com/Sec/2054/IDG011116biometrics/pfindex.html.

Null, Christopher. 2000. "How to Hire a Hacker," *Ziff Davis Smart Business for the New Economy*, July 1.

Olson, Scott. 2000. "Protection From Hackers Available for E-tailers," 20(50), *Indianapolis Business Journal*, February 21.

Pappalardo, Denise 2000. "Avoiding Future Denial-of-Service Attacks," *NetworkWorld* as reported by *CNN.com*, February 23. Available online at: www.cnn.com/2000/TECH/computing/02/23/isp.block.idg/index.html.

Pastore, Michael. 2001. "Internal Threats Justify Increase in Security Spending," *CyberAtlas*, June 19. Available online at: cyberatlas.internet.com/big_picture/applications/print/0,,1301_787251,00.html.

Plummer, Don. 2002. "Wireless Systems are Simple to Hack," *The Atlanta Journal-Constitution*, March 2. Available online at: www.accessatlanta.com/ajc/news/0302/31wireless.html.

Poulsen, Kevin. 2001. "War Driving by the Bay," *Security Focus Online*, April 12. Available online at: online.securityfocus.com/news/192.

Poulsen, Kevin. 2002. "Guess? Leaks Credit Cards of the Fashion Conscious," *SecurityFocus.com* as reported by *The Register*, March 6. Available online at: www.theregister.co.uk/content/6/24315.html.

Poulsen, Kevin. 2001. "Proxy Exposes Excite@Home Data," *SecurityFocus*, May 29. Available online at: online.securityfocus.com/news/209.

Poulsen, Kevin. 2001. "Yahoo! News Hacked," *SecurityFocus*, September 18. Available online at: online.securityfocus.com/news/254.

Poulsen, Kevin. 2002. "*New York Times* Internal Network Hacked," *SecurityFocus*, February 26. Available online at: online.securityfocus.com/news/340.

Press Release. 2000. "Alaska Man Indicted for Alleged Attack on United States Court Computer System," *U. S. Department of Justice*, April 19. Available online at: www.cybercrime.gov/dennis.htm.

Press Release. 2001. "Chardon, Ohio, Woman Sentenced for Computer Fraud via Unauthorized Access of Employer's Computer System," *U.S. Department of Justice*, December 13. Available online at: www.cybercrime.gov/brownSent.htm.

Press Release. 2001. "Former Federal Court Systems Administrator Sentenced for Hacking Into Government Computer System," *U.S. Department of Justice*, January 22. Available online at: www.cybercrime.gov/dennisplea.htm.

Press Release. 2002. "Manhattan Man Sentenced for Theft of Litigation Trial Plan," *U.S. Department of Justice*, January 30. Available online at: www.cybercrime.gov/farrajSentence.htm.

Radding, Alan. 2001. "Crossing the Wireless Security Gap," *Computerworld*, January 1. Available online at: www.computerworld.com/cwi/Printer_Friendly_Version/0,1212,NAV47_STO55583-,00.html.

Rapoza, Jim. 2000. "Locking Up Content — Lockstep Security Application Stops Web Attacks," *eWeek*, July 3, 57.

Raymond, Eric S. 2000. *The New Hacker's Dictionary — 3rd Edition*. Cambridge, MA: The MIT Press.

Reuters. 2002. "Disgruntled Employee Sentenced for Sabotage," *ZDNet News*, February 27. Available online at: news.zdnet.co.uk/story/0,,t281-s2105124,00.html.

Rothberg, Alan. 2002. "Tales of a White Hat War Driver," *O'Reilly Network*, March 29. Available online at: www.oreillynet.com/pub/a/wireless/2002/03/29/wardriver.html.

Saarinen, Markku-Juhani. 2002. "Attacks Against the WAP WTLS Protocol," *University of Jyväskylä*. Available online at: www.cc.jyu.fi/~mjos/wtls.pdf.

Sametband, Ricardo. 2002. "Crooks Cause Chilean Car Chaos," *WiredNews*, April 26.

San Francisco Chronicle. 2002. "Hacker Saw Plenty in Files of *N.Y. Times*," *Houston Chronicle Technology Section*, February 28, 2002.

SANS Institute Resources. 2001. "Security on Internet Satellite — Any Different than Wired or Wireless?" May 28. Available online at: rr.sans.org/wireless/satellite.php.

SANS Institute Resources. 2002. "The Twenty Most Critical Internet Security Vulnerabilities (Updated)," January 30. Available online at: www.sans.org/top20.htm.

Santalesa, Rich. 2001. "The War Over 802.11x Security, " *ZDNet.com*, July 9. Available online at: zdnet.com.com/2001-11-0.html.

Savino, Lenny. 2000. "Teen Hacker Charged in Canada May Face Matching Charges in U.S.," *Knight-Ridder/Tribune News Service*, August 4.

Schneier, Bruce. 2000. *Secrets and Lies: Digital Security in a Networked World*. New York, NY: John Wiley & Sons.

Schultz, Eugene. 1999. A Strategic View of Penetration Testing," *Information Security*, September. Available online at: www.infosecuritymag.com/sept99/pen_test.htm.

Schwankert, Steven. 2002. "Wireless Viruses: 2002's Looming Threat?" *IT World.com*, February 21. Available online at: www.itworld.com/AppDev/1312/IDG020221wireless/.

Schwartz, Karen D. 2001. "Driving Secure E-Commerce Forward," *ZDNet Enterprise*, August 9. Available online at: techupdate.zdnet.com/techupdate/stories/main/0,14179,2802510,00.html.

Shimmin, Bradley F. 2000. "Deconstructing Denial of Service Attacks," *ZDNet Help*, February 8. Available online at: www.zdnet.com/zdhelp/stories/main/0%2C5594%2C2434548%2C00.html.

Singletary, Tim. 2000. "The Internet Worm," *Zen and the Art of the Internet*. Available online at: sunland.gsfc.nasa.gov/info/guide/The_Internet_Worm.html.

Smith, Gary. 2001. "A Brief Taxonomy of Firewalls — Great Walls of Fire," *SANS Institute*, May 18. Available online at: rr.sans.org/firewall/taxonomy.php.

Stone, Adam. 2001. "Wireless Security: An Oxymoron?" *MCommerce Times*, May 15. Available online at: www.mcommercetimes.com/Solutions/125.

Stone, Martin. 2000. "Data Spill Blamed for De Beers Web Site Security Leak," *Newsbytes*, April 5.

Sullivan, Bob. 2002. "Best Buy Closes Wireless Registers," *MSNBC Technology*, May 1. Available online at: www.msnbc.com/news/746380.asp?cp1=1.

Sullivan, Bob. 2002. "*N.Y. Times* Source Database Hacked," *MSNBC Technology*, February 27. Available online at: www.msnbc.com/news/716753.asp.

Sundaram, Aurobindo. 2000. "An Introduction to Intrusion Detection," *Association for Computing Machinery*. Available online at: www.acm.org/crossroads/xrds2-4/intrus.html.

Sussis, Don. 2001. "Biometrics in the Digital Realm," *E-Commerce Guide*, November 27. Available online at: ecommerce.internet.com/news/insights/econsultant/article/0,,10418_929651,00.html.

Sutherland, Ed. 2001. "The Chaotic State of Wireless Security," *MCommerce Times*, September 26. Available online at: www.mcommercetimes.com/Technology/173.

Taylor, Laura. 2002. "How to Choose the Right Enterprise Firewall," *eSecurityPlanet.com*, February 13. Available online at: www.esecurityplanet.com/views/article/0,,10752_974501,00.html.

The Applied Technologies Group, Inc. 2001. "Securing E-Business," *Techguide.com*. Available online at: www.itpapers.com/techguide/secebus.pdf.

The Industry Standard. 2001. "Mafiaboy Sentenced to 8 Months in Detention," *IDG*, September 13. Available online at: www.thestandard.com/article0%2C1902%2C28975%2C00.html.

Thomas, Pierre and Hopper, D. Ian. 2000. "Canadian Juvenile Charged in Connection with February 'denial-of-service' Attacks," *CNN.com*, April 18. Available online at: www.cnn.com/2000/TECH/computing/04/18/hacker.arrest.01/.

Trantor Standard Systems, Inc. 2002. "Public Key Encryption Explained," *DataHush*. Available online at: www.datahush.com/public.htm.

Tucker, Darla Martin. 2000. "California-Based Internet Service Companies Fall Victim to Hacker Attacks," *Knight-Ridder/Tribune Business News*, August 28.

Ulfelder, Steve. 2000. "Hackers for Hire," *Earthweb IT Management*, July 1. Available online at: itmanagement.earthweb.com/secu/print/0,,11953_601251,00.html.

Vaas, Lisa. 2000. "Security Checkup — One Bank's Experience at Having Its E-Biz Links Poked, Prodded, Scanned," *eWeek*, August 14.

Vainio, Juha T. 2000. "Bluetooth Security," *Department of Computer Science and Engineering, Helsinki University of Technology*, May 25. Available online at: www.niksula.cs.hut.fi/~jiitv/bluesec.html.

Vamosi, Robert. 2002. "How Can We Prepare for the Next Big Virus?" *ZDNet, Anchor Desk*, February 27. Available online at: zdnet.com.com/2100-1107-846099.html.

Vamosi, Robert. 2002. "Watch Out! 2002 Could be the Year of the Trojan Horse," *ZDNet News, Anchor Desk*, February 6. Available online at: zdnet.com.com/2100-1107-830278.html.

Varcoe, Bill. 2000. "Three Ways Your Site is Vulnerable to Attack." *workz.com*. Available online at: www.workz.com/content/1187.asp.

Vijayan, Jaikumar. 2002. "Employee Data Exposed on Web," *Computerworld*, February 11. Available online at: www.computerworld.com/.

Violino, Bob and Larsen, Amy K. 1999. "Security: An E-Biz Asset," *Information Week*, February 15, 44.

WAP Forum. 2002. "Wireless Application Protocol WAP 2.0 Technical White Paper," January. Available online at: www.wapforum.org/what/WAPWhite_Paper1.pdf.

Websense International Ltd. 2001. "Web@Work Survey 2001." Available online at: www.websense.com/company/news/research/webatwork-employee2001-europe.pdf.

Weil, Nancy and Crouch, Cameron. 2001. "Wireless Security Flawed, Researchers Report," *PCWorld*, February 5. Available online at: www.pcworld.com/resource/printable/article/0,aid,40442,00.asp.

Weiss, Todd R. 2001. "Hacker Explains Recent Exploits Inside WorldCom Network," *Computerworld*, December 7. Available online at: www.computerworld.com/.

Weiss, Todd R. 2002. "Comcast Business Communications Site Shut After Hacker Exposes Data," *Computerworld*, February 8. Available online at: www.computerworld.com/.

Wexler, Joanie. 2002. "The Wireless LAN Security Quagmire," *NetworkWorldFusion*, April 10.

Williams, Martyn. 2000. "Immense Network Assault Takes Down Yahoo," *ComputerWorld* as reported by *CNN.com*, February 8. Available online at: www.cnn.com/2000/TECH/computing/02/08/yahoo.assault.idg/index.html.

Wolverton, Troy. 1999. "Butterball's Data Security For the Birds," *CNET News.com*, May 4. Available online at: news.cnet.com/news/0-1005-200-342072.html.

CHAPTER **8**

E-Business Front-End/Back-End Integration

In this chapter, you will learn to:

Define e-business front-end and back-end operations

Describe enterprise resource planning (ERP) systems

Discuss Supply Chain Management (SCM) systems

Define Customer Relationship Management (CRM) systems

Describe the technologies used to integrate ERP, SCM, and CRM systems

GOING ONCE, GOING TWICE, GONE —
TO THE CONTEST WINNER...

During the late spring and summer of 1999, eBay, Inc., the top C2C online auction site, suffered a series of embarrassing and costly system failures or "outages" that prevented users from bidding on items or tracking the results of a previous bid. On May 3 and May 20, 1999, eBay experienced outages for five and seven hours, respectively. Then on June 10 and June 11, 1999, eBay experienced an outage again — this time lasting 22 hours! But, it didn't stop there. In early August 1999, there was a 10-hour eBay outage. These outages resulted in millions of dollars in lost revenue from auction fees and — because investors became very concerned about eBay's ability to maintain stable operations — millions more in lost market capitalization as a result of declines in stock prices.

The reported reasons for the system outages included problems with Sun Microsystems, Inc.'s Solaris operating system software, Sun's server hardware, and Oracle Corporation's database software. But, the real culprit was the unqualified massive success of eBay! Founded as a hobby by a man who knew little about auctions but believed they created a "perfect marketplace" where fair prices would prevail, eBay had grown since 1995 into a tremendously popular and active site. The strain of handling thousands of Web accesses per minute was beginning to show. Also, because of the massive number of auction transactions, eBay had been devoting more resources to creating and managing its Web applications and fewer resources to the management and maintenance of its database applications. The operating system software, server hardware, and database software used to drive eBay's back-end operations, such as its customer databases, just couldn't keep up with the volume of transactions generated by the real-time bidding applications in its front-end Web operations.

By early August 1999, it was clear that eBay had to act quickly to mitigate the outages and to convince both customers and investors that the eBay auction operations were stable. On August 9, 1999, eBay announced it had hired Maynard Webb, a former Senior Vice President and CIO at Gateway, Inc. with a strong reputation as an expert in building e-business IT infrastructures, to be the president of eBay Technologies. Webb's charge was to oversee the efforts needed to improve eBay's technology infrastructure including developing better integration between eBay's front-end and back-end systems. Upon his arrival, Webb found well-designed, front-end systems, but identified problems in the interaction between eBay's transaction and database servers. Webb began reducing the number of outages by making more Sun servers available and by dividing the back-end workload between different Oracle databases. Although Webb continued to fine-tune the existing operations, sporadic outages continued during 2000; but, by December 2001, eBay was able to report a 99.9 percent uptime performance.

After shoring up eBay's back-end database systems with a "warm backup"— a backup system of servers that could step in and handle database transactions from the front-end when the original database servers experienced problems — Webb began looking for a longer-term solution. What eBay needed was a standard method of passing data from the front-end systems to the back-end systems that could expand with eBay's needs. In the late summer of 2001, eBay announced it was going to replace its outmoded auction-management software. At this point, the big three — Microsoft Corporation, Sun Microsystems, and IBM — came courting. Each company wanted to supply eBay's new auction-management software. Microsoft's proposal was based on its .NET technologies while Sun's and IBM's proposals were based on Sun's Java 2 Enterprise Edition (J2EE) technologies.

Continued

In order to evaluate each company's software proposal, eBay devised a contest in which the winner would win a very big prize worth millions in revenues and bragging rights — the chance to solve eBay's auction operations problems. Each competing company was given some sample programming code from eBay's existing auction software and asked to develop a trial application that would process sample auction transactions. eBay then evaluated each company's trial application against its current software to see how well the trial software performed under a variety of conditions. Additionally, eBay evaluated the software proposals in light of its stated e-business objectives to: "achieve annual sales of $3 billion by 2005; handle $50 billion in merchandise auctions annually by 2005; expand the annual gross profit margin beyond the current 82 percent; and enhance customers' online experience by making the buying and selling process easier." Now the big question was…which of the big three would win the prize?

E-Business Front-End and Back-End Operations

An e-business's **front-end operations** consist of the hardware and software with which its customers directly interact and over which its customers exert some control. For example, an e-business's front-end operations include the Web site processes that its customers use to view information, purchase products and services, and access online customer support. An e-business's **back-end operations** are not directly accessed by its customers and include the hardware and software that handle accounting and budgeting, manufacturing, marketing, inventory management, distribution, and order tracking.

An e-business's front-end operations require much of the same data already stored in its back-end operations, including customer data, product availability, and pricing. Additionally, new data being gathered by the front-end operations (such as order information) must be made available to the back-end operations (such as accounting, billing, payment processing, product delivery, and inventory management). Integrating front-end and back-end operations not only provides an e-business with more useful information about its overall business efforts, it also reduces costs by allowing data to be shared across front-end and back-end applications. Figure 8-1 illustrates the integration of an e-business's front-end and back-end operations.

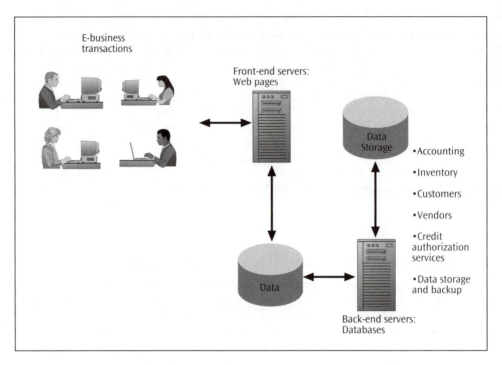

Figure 8-1
Integration of
front-end and
back-end
operations

In fact, the economic benefits to an e-business of seamlessly integrating its customers' and vendors' data into its ordering, purchasing, manufacturing, billing, and delivery systems is so important that an entire sector of B2B e-business is devoted to developing and selling front-end and back-end integration technologies. In this chapter you learn about this B2B e-business sector and the technologies e-businesses use to integrate their front-end and back-end operations.

Enterprise Resource Planning (ERP) Systems

Traditionally, a business's planning, manufacturing, warehousing, accounting, finance, sales, marketing, and human resources departments would each have their own individually tailored computer applications. The advantage of this traditional approach is the high-level of customization possible in each department's applications. But, the major drawback to this approach is the inability to capture data once and then share the data across applications. For example, under the traditional approach the data from a customer order might have to be entered multiple times: once for the Sales Department, again for the warehouse, and again for the Accounting Department. As you can imagine, this duplication of labor is expensive and time consuming. The traditional approach also had a negative effect on customer service. A customer calling the Finance Department to arrange new credit terms would likely be told to "call back and speak to someone in the warehouse" to determine if a recent order had been shipped.

These days, most businesses have abandoned the traditional approach in favor of enterprise resource planning, which allows different functional areas of a business to share information. The term **enterprise** is used to define organizations of all sizes, but especially large organizations, that use computer networks to interact with employees, vendors, and customers. **Enterprise resource planning (ERP)** is a term used to refer to a system that links individual applications (for example, accounting and manufacturing applications) into a single application that integrates the data and business processes of the entire e-business. Figure 8-2 illustrates an ERP system.

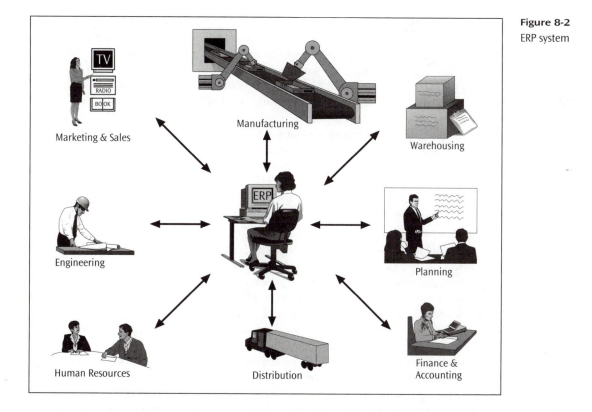

Marketing & Sales
Manufacturing
Warehousing
Engineering
ERP
Planning
Human Resources
Distribution
Finance & Accounting

Figure 8-2
ERP system

As you learn in the next section, traditional ERP systems had their origins in the 1960s in manufacturing systems.

Origins of ERP Systems

Early ERP systems incorporated raw-materials planning, purchasing, shop-floor management, and distribution systems required by

TIP

The term "ERP systems" is used to mean both the overall process of integrating data between business processes and the software used in the integration process.

manufacturing systems. ERP systems grew out of a function called **materials resource planning (MRP)** which was used to allocate resources for a manufacturing operation. For example, a manufacturing company's front office staff could enter orders into an MRP system which would queue up the orders and schedule the ordered items for production on a specific machine on the factory floor. When raw materials were needed, the MRP system could automatically allocate them from stock, and then order more raw materials when stock levels got too low. The MRP system could also track the manufactured items through shipping and billing. MRP systems software ultimately became very complex allowing for efficiencies of scale not previously possible — for example, allowing one purchasing manager to handle more and larger operations. Production job scheduling was automated, eliminating resource-allocation inefficiencies such as idle factory equipment.

Even more sophisticated ERP systems began to replace MRP systems in the 1980s and by the early 1990s, other enterprise activities such as engineering, project management, accounting, finance, and human resources were being incorporated into ERP systems. ERP systems software was more flexible than MRP systems software and could be configured to help manage not just manufacturing operations but also service organizations, food processors, and so forth. ERP systems software also helped managers control processes and organizations spanning multiple locations. Properly implemented ERP systems allow managers to quickly spot trends, good and bad, in sales patterns, manufacturing costs, if applicable, and a business's financial position on almost a real-time basis. Today, an ERP system can encompass, but is not limited to, the following functions:

◆ *Sales and order entry*: Information about customers and what they purchase can drive other business processes. For example, customer sales orders generate the transaction data that defines sales volume, total accounts receivable, total accounts payable, and other critical business operational data benchmarks. ERP systems can integrate this sales and order information with other business processes such as manufacturing and accounting to provide up-to-date information.

◆ *Raw materials, inventory, purchasing, production scheduling, and shipping*: The ability to fulfill promised orders is important in any business. The tracking of raw materials, inventory levels, purchasing requirements, production processes, and shipping can ensure that customer orders are fulfilled in a timely manner. ERP systems are used to track the components of production and help guarantee availability of products, maintain accurate inventory levels, and ensure prompt delivery of orders.

◆ *Accounting*: Part of running a successful business is accurate accounting and record keeping. Accounting functions track sales, customer balances (accounts receivable), amounts owed to vendors (accounts payable), the amount of cash available, the control and disposition of physical assets, the calculation of profits, and so forth. An ERP system can integrate accounting functions with other business processes to, for example, facilitate customer collections and the timely payment of vendors' invoices to better manage accounts receivable, accounts payable, and cash flow.

◆ *Human resources*: The most important asset any business has is its employees. Human resources functions, often simply called HR, include managing the hiring and firing processes, controlling payroll costs, managing employee benefits programs, and managing training programs. ERP systems can integrate HR functions with other business processes to, for example, manage workforces including job scheduling, match skills with job requirements, better manage payroll and benefits costs, and track employee training.

◆ *Resource and production planning*: One of the biggest constraints many businesses face is a limit on their resources. For example, a manufacturing business may only be able to make a given number of products on a specific assembly line each day. A business offering product delivery, installation, and service may have a limited number of delivery trucks and technicians available each day. By using an ERP system, businesses can more effectively manage the allocation of these and other types of resources.

ERP systems are based on databases that store all of the data needed by the different ERP systems software modules. These databases must be capable of handling large numbers of records and many requests for data at the same time. In addition, the databases must protect the data from being changed or accidentally erased while another application is using the data.

Complete ERP systems are generally found in very large enterprises such as Fortune 2000 companies. For small and midsized e-businesses, it may not be necessary or cost effective to fully integrate all aspects of the business. For these businesses, an ERP solution might consist of two or three critical applications that are integrated via the Web. For example, many e-businesses don't do any manufacturing, so extensive manufacturing-support functions of an ERP system would not be needed. If an e-business is primarily providing services instead of products, then the accounting and human resources portions of an ERP system may be all that's required.

Today, many vendors, suppliers, customers, and outside sales representatives use the Internet or a company intranet to access an e-business's ERP system.

E-Business ERP Systems

An e-business must keep track of and process a tremendous amount of information. For example, most e-businesses need to be able to update product and pricing information on its Web site very quickly. A B2C e-business may also need to allow a customer to verify that the product he or she placed in a shopping cart is actually in inventory. Completed orders then must be routed quickly to the warehouse for order fulfillment and delivery.

By the time the Internet became a commercial medium in the 1990s, many large businesses had already implemented ERP systems. These businesses realized that much of the information they needed to run an e-business — stock levels at various warehouses, cost of parts, projected shipping dates — could already be found in their ERP system databases. So, a major part of the online efforts of many e-businesses involved adding Web access to an existing ERP system.

It turns out that many e-businesses want the same things from their business infrastructure. Nearly every major e-business needs inventory tracking, credit card authorization services, shipment tracking, online customer service, and other services. Thus, rather than custom build these applications, many companies prefer to use prepackaged ERP system software, which is often more efficient and less expensive to implement. For example, once a software vendor has solved the problem of how orders feed directly from an e-business to its suppliers, the software vendor can then market this capability to any e-business with similar operations. By using a common framework that applies to many businesses, ERP vendors develop and sell software that can achieve much more in less time than software created expressly for a specific e-business.

Vendors such as J. D. Edwards, PeopleSoft, Inc., Oracle, and SAP AG (Figure 8-3) provide ERP systems, or components of ERP systems. As a result of the e-business explosion, these major ERP vendors set about rewriting their applications to make them accessible via a Web browser, instead of via dumb (text-only) terminals or proprietary applications. Figure 8-4 illustrates a SAP Web interface to an ERP system.

Figure 8-3

SAP AG

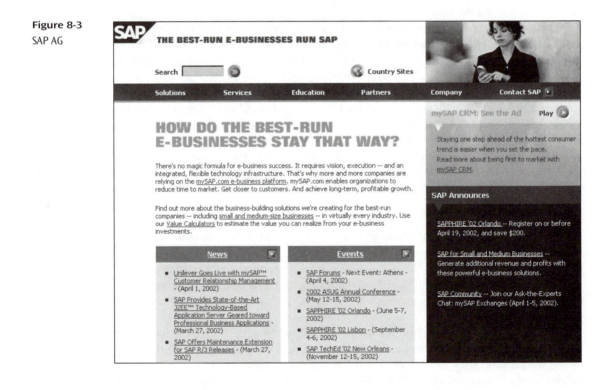

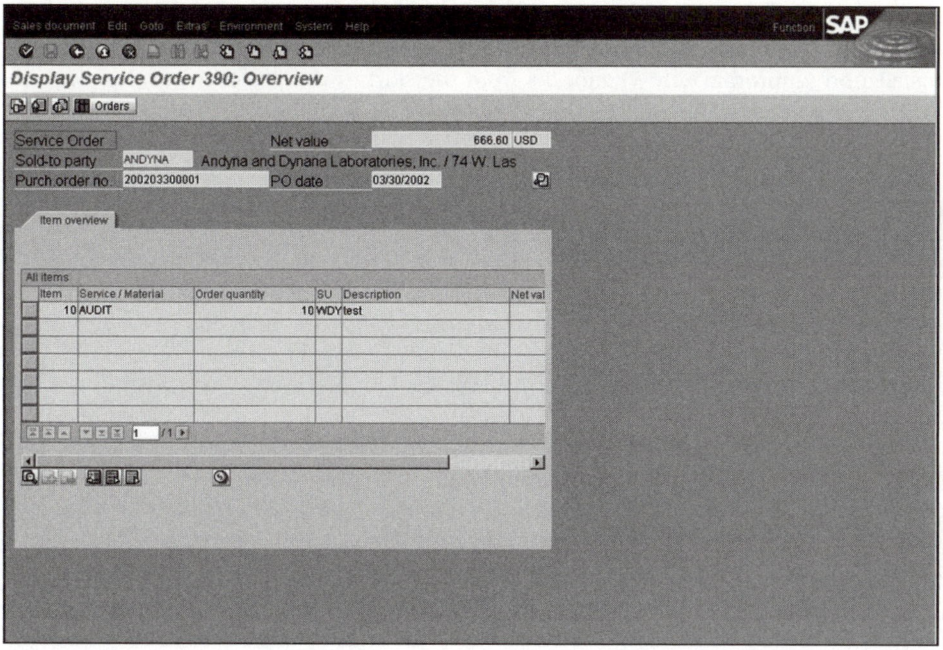

Figure 8-4
SAP Web ERP interface

Implementing an ERP system can be expensive and challenging, as explained in the next section.

Cost of Implementing ERP Systems

Most businesses need extensive help from consultants to configure their ERP system software around their existing business practices, or to suggest changes in business practices in order to better fit the ERP system requirements. This process of mutual adaptation is called **systems integration**. The consultants who supervise the integration process are often referred to as **systems integrators**. Systems integrators generally provide part or all of the personnel doing the system integration, and handle the training of in-house employees.

The total cost of ownership (TCO) of an e-business's ERP systems including fees to systems integrators, can run from thousands to millions of dollars. The actual cost of an ERP system, however, is often dwarfed by the time and effort a business must spend to fully integrate its business processes with the ERP system. The return, however, can be equally significant. For example, in a year 2000 study, the META Group, a research and consulting firm, surveyed 63 small, medium, and large companies that had implemented ERP systems. The study found that the total cost of ownership of the ERP systems, which included up to three years of implementation and management, ranged from about half a

TIP

Employee training costs for a new ERP system is a major line item in an ERP systems implementation budget, since ERP systems software typically is used by nearly every employee. Without training in the proper use of such software, incorrect data may be entered for customer orders, raw-materials purchases, manufacturing processes, and so forth resulting in poorly implemented ERP systems.

million to \$300 million, with an average TCO of approximately \$15 million. The study also found that businesses didn't begin seeing benefits for at least eight months after installation (approximately 31 months from the start of the project) and that the new ERP systems generated a median annual savings of \$1.6 million.

TECH CASE **The Blame Game: When Good ERP Goes Bad**

Attempting to integrate an ERP system into every e-business process is a complex undertaking, and there is no shortage of things that can go wrong. An improperly implemented ERP system can lead to disruptions of normal business processes, lost data, and huge amounts of wasted time and dollars. Too aggressive a schedule, a lack of employee commitment or training, inept consultants, and software unsuited for the nature of the e-business in question are the most common causes of implementation problems. In the 1990s several major businesses experienced infamously disastrous results from ERP system installations gone horribly wrong. Let's take a look at some of the players in the ERP "blame game":

Player #1: W. L. Gore & Associates, Inc. — In the mid-1990s Delaware-based W. L. Gore & Associates, Inc., the manufacturer of GoreTex waterproof fabrics, embarked on installing a new ERP human resources system to be used by payroll, personnel, and other departments to track its more than 6,000 employees in over 40 locations around the world. When the HR system went "live" in 1997 it failed miserably, resulting in miscalculated paychecks, benefits, and taxes. The system also failed to provide a way for Gore to track employee vacation or sick time. In 1999, Gore filed a lawsuit against the HR software manufacturer PeopleSoft and Deloitte & Touche — the consultants hired as the systems integrator — alleging that the HR system failed to work properly. Gore's suit alleged that the Deloitte & Touche consultants were inexperienced and poorly trained and were not the "experts" they claimed to be. Gore alleged that installation costs (exclusive of software costs) had more than doubled from Deloitte & Touche's original estimate to \$2.5 million and that Gore had incurred several million dollars in additional costs trying to salvage the system.

Player #2: FoxMeyer Corporation — In 1993, FoxMeyer Corporation, a \$5 billion drug distributor in Carrollton, Texas, embarked on a \$65 million ERP system designed to radically improve its distribution operations. However, after more than a year, the system was only installed in six of 23 warehouses and could only process 10,000 invoice lines per night — far short of the more than 400,000 invoice lines per night processed by the old system the ERP system was meant to replace. FoxMeyer alleged the system also miscounted inventory, created customer billing errors, and was prone to frequent crashes. By 1996, FoxMeyer was in bankruptcy and in 1998 FoxMeyer's bankruptcy trustee filled a \$500 million law suit against the ERP systems maker SAP AG and it's U.S. subsidiary and another \$500 million law suit against Andersen Consulting (the systems integration consultant on the project). The suits alleged that SAP AG misrepresented the capabilities of their R/3 software, which was designed for manufacturing operations and not distribution operations. The suit also alleged that Andersen's integration team consisted of inexperienced recent college graduates and that the combination of inappropriate software and an inexperienced integration team created a failed ERP system and, furthermore, that the failed system directly contributed to FoxMeyer's descent into bankruptcy.

Player #3: Department 56 — In 1996, Department 56, a Minnesota-based seller of collectible items, hired Arthur Andersen to upgrade its J. D. Edwards ERP systems to not only accommodate

Continued

Y2K requirements but also to add warehouse and distribution modules. In early 1998, preliminary tests of the new system were performed and implementation problems were discovered including, according to Department 56, communication problems between the system integration consultants and the in-house members of the integration team. In the meantime, Department 56 changed some of its business practices by, among other things, adding new products and altering its commission scheme; this made the conversion to the new ERP system even more problematic. Finally, in January 1999, the new ERP system went "live" and chaos ensued. Orders were not processed accurately, inventory couldn't be tracked properly, and hundreds of customers were billed inaccurately. When Department 56 refused to pay Andersen several thousand dollars in billings, Andersen sued. Department 56 countersued for $6 billion alleging it was damaged as a result of Andersen's poor performance. Department 56 also alleged that Andersen's original quote of $3 million ballooned to more than $12 million in actual costs. In March 2002, Andersen paid Department 56 $11 million to settle the countersuit.

Outsourcing ERP Systems

As you have learned, one response to the challenge of managing a complex ERP system is to outsource it. Most companies that install an ERP system hire systems integrators to handle the job on a time-and-materials basis (hourly), which if not managed closely can result in huge cost overruns. An alternative is a flat fee contract which can be used to hold development and installation costs within budget. For example, while employed as the CIO at Bay Networks, Maynard Webb contracted with Andersen Consulting (now Accenture) to install an ERP system for a flat fee (equivalent to 70 person-years of time, believe it or not). The contract also included incentives for an early and satisfactory finish, and penalties for tardiness or postinstallation problems. In the end, Andersen beat the targets and reaped the reward. Considering the multitude of horror stories surrounding ERP implementations gone bad, Webb was likely happy to pay those incentives.

Some businesses go farther than this, choosing to outsource not only the installation but also the ERP system software. Companies such as Oracle and Salesforce.com, Inc. currently provide ERP systems software and other applications over the Web, making it unnecessary to install hardware or software at the user's site. Instead of selling their applications for a huge up-front fee, these software vendors rent their applications, thereby reaping a steady income. The businesses who rent the applications avoid a heavy initial cost, and pay extra for increased functionality only as their business requirements warrant it. Therefore, application rental can be a plus for both the software vendor and the user. It seems likely that this type of software rental will become more popular in the future.

As businesses finished installing ERP systems to manage internal processes, they began to consider the benefits of integrating their ERP system directly with their vendors.

Supply Chain Management (SCM) Systems

Supply chain management, or **SCM**, is the management of the materials, money, information, and other resources that go into a business' products for resale. SCM systems use technology to more effectively manage supply chains. A typical SCM system might address the following issues:

◆ *Planning*: Employing strategies that assure the resources (time, materials, money, and so forth) required to meet customers' demands for products and services are available

◆ *Vendor selection*: Identifying the right vendors to supply resources, including pricing and delivery options

◆ *Manufacturing*: Producing, testing, and packaging the finished product

◆ *Logistics*: Warehousing the finished products and selecting carriers for delivering the finished product

The two basic types of SCM system software are **supply chain planning software (SCP)** and **supply chain execution software (SCE)**. SCP software uses mathematical models to predict inventory levels based on the efficient flow of resources into the supply chain. SCE software is used to automate different steps in the supply chain such as automatically sending purchase orders to vendors when inventories reach specified levels. Figure 8-5 illustrates an e-business supply chain.

Figure 8-5
The supply chain

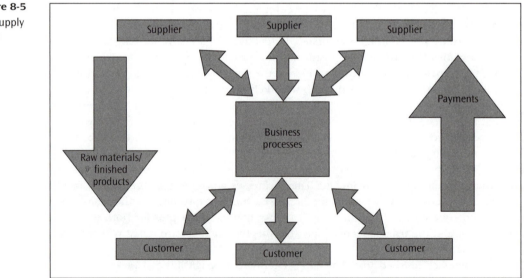

An SCM system is an important part of an e-business's overall ERP system. Manufacturing companies have relied on SCM systems for years as a vital management tool. Some businesses install SCM systems because they simply want an easier way to transmit orders for raw materials to their suppliers. Other businesses have gone farther, allowing vendors direct access to their SCM systems in order to gather information that would allow the vendors to anticipate the business's needs.

A famous example of the latter relationship is the cooperative arrangement between The Proctor & Gamble Company and Wal-Mart Stores. Proctor & Gamble has direct access to inventory information at Wal-Mart's distribution centers. When inventory of specific Proctor & Gamble products runs low, the SCM system automatically alerts Proctor & Gamble to send more products. With this type of information, Proctor & Gamble can anticipate when to produce and ship products to the Wal-Mart distribution centers. Of course, invoicing by Proctor & Gamble and payment by Wal-Mart are also automated. The savings Proctor & Gamble realizes by more efficient manufacturing, reduced inventory, and lower order processing costs result in lower costs to Wal-Mart and lower retail prices to Wal-Mart's customers.

With the advent of the Internet, however, e-businesses began to demand different things from their SCM systems. Most importantly, SCM systems vendors (largely the same vendors that provide ERP systems software) had to modify their products to include a Web-based interface.

The advent of the Internet also sparked an explosion of B2B e-businesses that provide SCM services. One such e-business is Suppleyes, Inc. To understand the success of Suppleyes, Inc., you need a little background. More than two million cataract surgeries are performed in the U.S. each year and the facilities that perform these surgeries require a steady supply of intraocular lenses and related items used in these surgeries. Based in Akron, Ohio, Suppleyes, Inc. is devoted to meeting that need. Using the online marketspace at Suppleye.com, a surgery center manager can order lenses and other supplies from a variety of vendors in just a few minutes. Other services offered at Suppleye.com (Figure 8-6) include bar code scanning for building online orders, an online "stockroom" for each individual customer in which inventory information is maintained, the ability to place orders with multiple vendors simultaneously, and online tracking of orders.

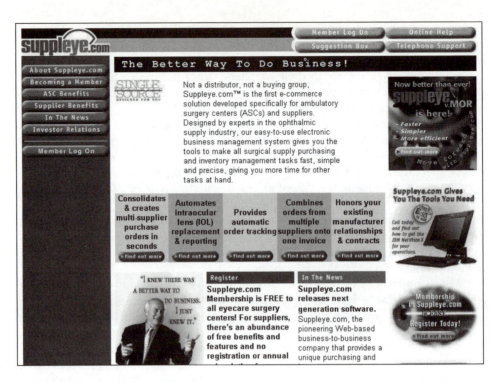

Figure 8-6
Suppleye.com

The ultimate goal of a business ERP system is complete optimization of internal business processes. Once businesses began to see that dream become a reality, they began to look for other uses for their ERP systems. Many businesses, and especially e-businesses, soon realized that the same technology could be used to offer customers a better purchasing experience while at the same time gathering vital data during every customer interaction.

Customer Relationship Management (CRM) Systems

For all e-businesses, getting and keeping customers is a top priority. **Customer relationship management (CRM)** systems, sometimes called **e-CRM** systems, use technology to help an e-business manage its customer base. CRM allows an e-business to match customer needs with product plans and offerings, remind customers of service requirements, and determine what products a customer has purchased. CRM applications connect databases with different data sources (such as sales figures, call center activities, Web transactions, and mobile transactions) in order to gather relevant information about customer interactions.

CRM systems are sometimes broken down into two components: **operational CRM**, which includes direct customer interactions, and **analytical CRM**, which takes the data captured by operational CRM processes and uses it to identify trends. ERP systems software vendors such as SAP and Oracle also provide CRM systems software. Other CRM system software vendors include E.piphany, Inc. and, as of this writing the top CRM vendor, Siebel Systems, Inc. (Figure 8-7).

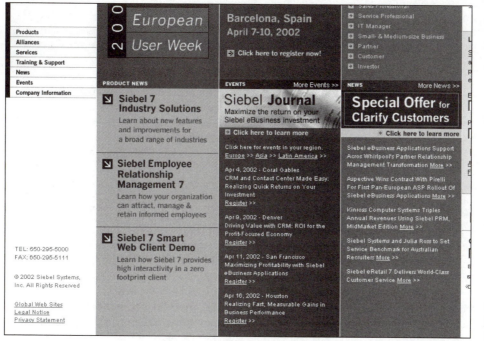

Figure 8-7
Siebel Systems, Inc.

However, as of this writing, some businesses have expressed dissatisfaction with the gap between the potential of CRM systems and the results of CRM systems implementation. For example, a 2001 Merrill Lynch & Co., Inc. survey of CIOs at large businesses indicate at least 45 percent of the respondents were not satisfied with their CRM installations. While the CRM market is expected to grow to almost $46 billion by 2003, many CRM systems fail to deliver either the expected cost savings or increased sales. Some analysts suggest this can happen because many businesses that implement CRM systems focus on the new "cool" technologies rather than viewing CRM as part of an overall business strategy. While technologies that can be used to track customers' purchasing preferences are exciting, some businesses that implement CRM technologies may not have a clear strategy on how to turn that purchasing preference information into increased profits. For example, the Gartner Group predicts that about 75 percent of CRM projects that fail through 2004 will do so as the result of *poor business decisions*, not because of problems with the CRM technologies.

TIP

As a result of the terrorist attack on the World Trade Center in New York on September 11, 2001, some CRM systems software vendors such as Siebel Systems are using their customer-tracking experience to develop CRM-style systems that can be used by government agencies to track potential terrorists.

TECH CASE Cascading CRM

When Christopher Milliken, the CEO of Boise Cascade Office Products Corporation, surveyed the B2B office supplies industry in 1999, he decided that the only way to survive the increased competition and its attendant cut-throat pricing strategies was to offer business customers something different. That difference, Milliken believed, was improved customer service, which he hoped would give the business customer a better reason to purchase their paper, pens, and binder clips from Boise. In order to achieve this goal, Milliken decided to spend more than $20 million on a CRM project, called One Boise, which would enable Boise to provide the most personalized services in the industry.

While the notion of customer service was not a new one to Boise, Milliken's plan was a radical approach requiring that customer needs and a single, unified customer database actually drive Boise's business. Milliken was adamant that "collecting and then acting on user information" would enable Boise to add extra value to its customers' office supplies transactions. Milliken and his management team decided that if Boise was going to have one unified customer database, then the logical business model was to have one unified group working with all customers instead of the existing three business units. So, the first thing Boise did was change its business practices by consolidating its three business units into one entity in the winter of 1999. After this consolidation, Boise was then ready to consider the CRM technologies it would implement.

Milliken and his management team realized that integrating Boise's legacy systems with new CRM technologies that would gather information from any customer transaction — from a call center, a field sales rep, or the Web — would be an incredibly complex undertaking. First, Boise created an executive steering committee in order to involve all company leaders in the One Boise project and get their support. Then in March 2000, Boise hired a consulting firm, KPMG Consulting, Inc., to select the CRM technologies and to assist Boise's IT staff in implementing the technologies. Following a steady but also speedy development schedule, by the summer of 2001 most of the CRM technologies were operational. For example, customers who logged on to the Boise Web site were greeted by name by a Boise sales agent.

One important facet of the success of the ongoing One Boise CRM project was the company's ability to successfully manage change. As a result of the consolidation, company managers were required to review job titles, descriptions, and employee reporting relationships to eliminate redundant positions. Boise also embarked on a major internal marketing campaign to assure that all employees were aware of Boise's new customer-centric orientation. At the same time, Boise provided extensive training sessions in the new CRM technologies.

While the One Boise CRM project was not without its long hours and implementation problems, Milliken and Boise's management are pleased with the first phase of implementation that came in within one percent of its budget and within six weeks of its targeted deadline. Boise's customers are also responding well to the new changes. One big advantage of the One Boise initiative has been the consolidation of customer profitability information. Armed with this new information, Boise has been able to negotiate better pricing with some major customers and eliminate unprofitable customers by modifying discounts, pricing, and other account terms until the unprofitable customers become profitable or switch to another supplier.

According to Milliken "sales are up from Boise's most valuable customers" and continued investment in CRM is "going to be the key to the success of the company." Boise's successful CRM implementation has not gone unnoticed by the e-business world. In September 2001, Boise (Figure 8-8) won the Gartner, Inc. CRM Excellence Award for its outstandingly effective CRM implementation.

Continued

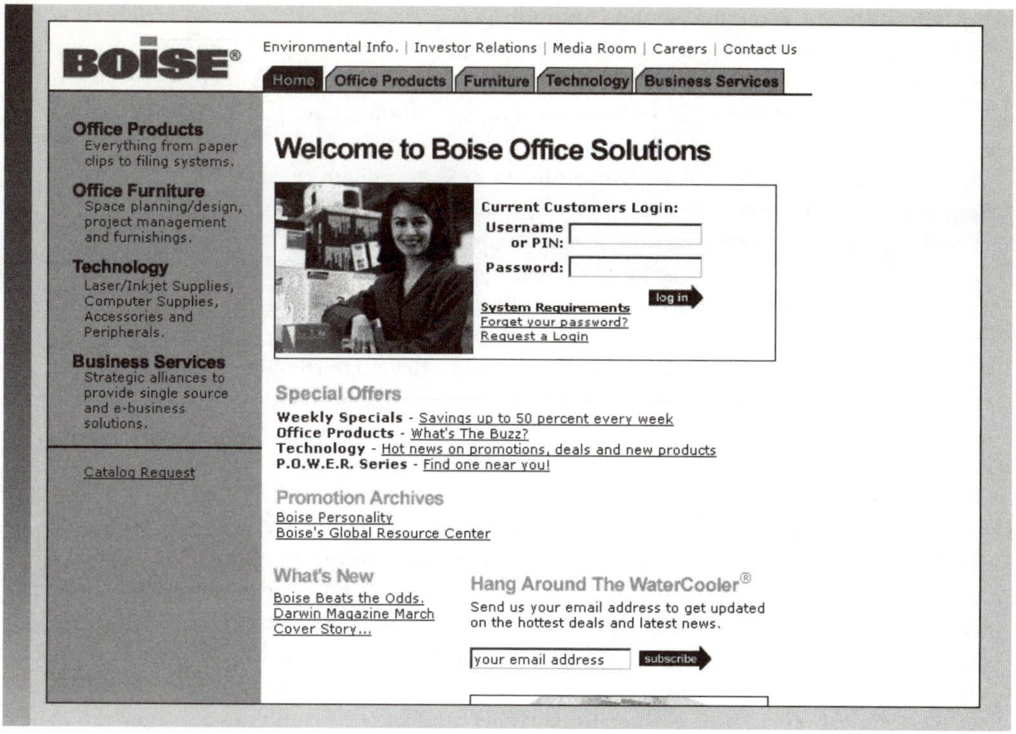

Figure 8-8
Boise
Cascade

A major benefit of CRM technologies is the ability to tailor, or personalize, a customer's online purchasing experience.

Personalization and CRM

Personalization ensures that each customer's Web experience is tailored to their specific needs. Some personalization software simply concentrates on recommending products to returning online customers based on their past purchasing history. But, effective personalization software goes further, by offering products or services tailored to the individual customer — whether or not the products or services have been previously purchased.

These personalization software products draw information from e-business databases in order to customize Web-site content for each individual customer. When a customer logs on to an e-business Web site that uses personalization software, information about recent orders, customer sales profitability, the customer's physical location, and a host of other relevant data (number and ages of children, make and model of automobile, owner or renter of primary residence, and so forth) is used to determine what content and advertising messages the customer sees.

Obviously, the more information about its customers an e-business stores in its databases, the more powerful personalization technologies can be. For example, an automobile maker might use personalization software to select the advertising banners displayed at its Web site so that a 60-year-old viewer living in a retirement-heavy zip code in Arizona and who owns a four-year-old luxury car might see an advertising banner for a new luxury car, while a 25-year-old single viewer living in Seattle might be shown an advertising banner for a sports utility vehicle.

Major CRM software vendors that also provide personalization software include BroadVision, Inc., BEA Systems, Inc., Art Technology Group, Inc. (ATG), and IBM. Rather than using off-the-shelf personalization software from one of these vendors, many e-businesses create their own in-house personalization software or combine customized off-the-shelf personalization software with software developed in-house to better meet the e-business's information needs. Three examples of e-businesses that successfully exploit personalization technologies to enhance their customers' online buying experiences and drive sales are the B2C e-businesses Reflect.com LLC and eDiets.com, Inc. and the B2B e-business Physician Sales and Service, Inc.

Reflect.com LLC (Figure 8-9) is a San Francisco-based e-business (backed by Procter & Gamble) that caters to women who prefer to purchase skin care and makeup products customized just for them. At the Reflect.com Web site, customers can order cosmetics, shampoos, conditioners, and other personal care items that best suit their individual skin and hair needs. New Reflect.com customers complete a questionnaire that provides the data used to create the customized skin care products and cosmetics. In order to maximize the personalization of all customer interactions, Reflect.com combines personalization technologies developed in-house with IBM's WebSphere platform and a master database of customer information that is accessed as needed by its transaction, manufacturing, and fulfillment systems.

Its use of personalization technologies allows Reflect.com to cross-market its products. For example, when a customer orders a bottle of shampoo, a message pops up recommending a customized conditioner. The customer's action — declining the conditioner or adding it to her shopping cart — is recorded in the database. If a customer declines to purchase the conditioner, she will not continue to receive marketing messages about it. Meanwhile, Reflect.com can use the information it knows about women who do purchase the conditioner to further target its marketing efforts.

Figure 8-9
Reflect.com

Originally founded in 1996 as DietCity.com, eDiets.com, Inc. is a highly successful subscription-based e-business that offers customized weight loss and fitness plans. With more than 30,000 new subscribers each month, as of this writing eDiets.com has 300,000 registered subscribers and more than 9.5 million opt-in newsletter subscribers. eDiets.com uses personalization technologies developed in house.

A new subscriber to eDiets.com completes a questionnaire about his or her food preferences, level of physical activity, and medical history. The data from that questionnaire is stored in the eDiets.com subscriber database. Then eDiets.com uses the subscriber database together with meal plan and fitness plan databases to create customized meal and fitness plans. Subscribers log on to the eDiets.com Web site each week to record their weight and print out their meal and exercise plans and, if desired, a shopping list tailored from the meal plan. eDiets.com also offers emotional support via a number of online support groups for subscribers with similar interests or concerns. Additionally, eDiets.com (Figure 8-10) uses its personalization technologies to encourage subscribers who haven't logged on in a while to do so by sending them e-mail messages.

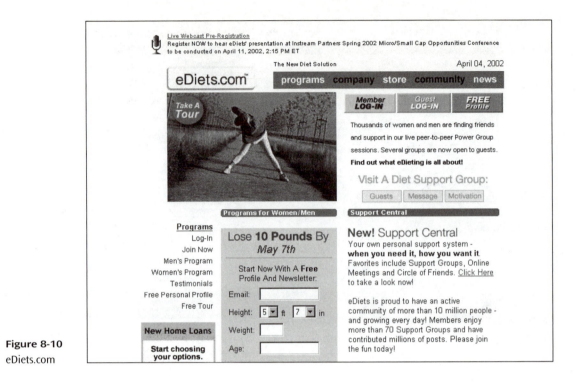

Figure 8-10
eDiets.com

When Patrick Kelly and three associates founded Physician Sales and Service, Inc. (PSS) in 1983, their mission was to "fulfill the inventory needs of office-based physicians." Today PSS, headquartered in Jacksonville, Florida, is part of PSS/World Medical, Inc., a $1.8 billion distributor of medical supplies. PSS is a leading provider of medical supplies with 51 service centers distributing medical supplies to approximately 92,000 physician offices in all 50 states. PSS installed the first Web-enabled, order-processing system in the medical supply industry, changing the way physicians' offices order supplies and access information about those supplies. As of this writing, PSS controls about 15 percent of the physician medical supply market.

PSS uses personalization technologies developed by BEA Systems, Inc. and a master customer database to create customized online catalogs for each of its customers based on the customer's type of medical practice and prior purchases. To further customize the online catalogs, it adds the customer's name and logo to them. When a new customer creates an account with PSS, he or she can choose to view only the products that are relevant to their medical practice. As the customer makes purchases, those purchases are added to a list of previously purchased items the customer can access to make it easier to order replacement items. PSS (Figure 8-11) also uses this list to show a customer what other customers in the same type of medical practice are purchasing. Using personalization to drive sales has resulted in a 20 percent higher average order size for PSS online customers vs. those who order via phone or through a sales rep.

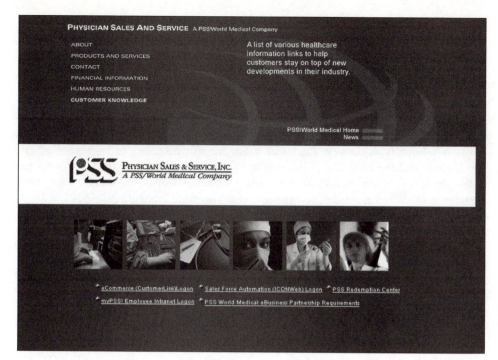

Figure 8-11
Physician
Sales and
Service, Inc.

An important facet of CRM systems is the ability to manipulate stored customer and transaction data to find patterns of behavior. Because even a small e-business Web site generates more customer data than any human can easily handle or summarize manually, data-mining techniques are used to meet this challenge.

Data Mining/Web Mining

A tremendous amount of valuable information lies hidden away in the large customer and sales databases of most e-businesses. Because of the large volume of data, this data is not easily examined in its raw form. Numerous techniques have been devised to make sense of these huge databases. **Data mining** is the process of using mathematical techniques to look for hidden patterns in groups of data, thereby discovering previously unknown relationships among the many pieces of information stored in a database. For example, data mining can help e-businesses identify customers with common interests. A **data warehouse** is a database (often a mirror of a company's production database that isn't pared down to recent data or optimized for buy/sell transactions) that contains huge amounts of data, such as customer and sales data. Data-mining techniques can be used to extract new patterns of data from a data warehouse that can then be used by management to aid in decision making.

> **TIP**
>
> Blockbuster Inc. uses data mining of its data warehouse (which contains information on more than 36 million households and over 2 million daily transactions) to help its rental customers pick out movies and to encourage customers to rent more movies. Acquiring new customers is very expensive; increasing the revenue per customer can boost the bottom line more quickly.

Web mining uses data-mining techniques to discover previously unknown patterns or trends in data gathered via the Web. Web-mining sources include customer and sales data from online transactions and the data captured in Web server logs such as the number of visitors to a Web site, the number of times a specific Web page is viewed, the IP addresses of visitors to the Web site, the URL of the page visitors were viewing when they "clicked through" to the Web site, and so forth. Using data- and Web-mining techniques, marketers can identify many interesting statistics and correlations that can help an e-business better attract and sell to its customers.

Data mining is not a new field, but it has been revolutionized by the needs of e-businesses and the capabilities of modern computers. E-business are faced with an avalanche of data about their customers, their customers' buying habits, and their own operations. Once upon a time, companies were insulated from their customers by a multilayered wholesaler/retailer network, and accumulating data about customers was an expensive and time-consuming proposition involving surveys, focus groups, and other such tools. Now, every customer who visits a Web site provides clues regarding what parts of the site are useful or attractive, what products are enticing alone or in combination with other products, and what products are purchased as gifts or for personal use. Many companies, such as the American Express Company and Wal-Mart, have been using data mining since before the Web existed. However, the Web presents an ideal opportunity to use data mining because every action performed by a customer at a Web site generates an electronic record.

In fact, one potential problem with collecting customer data from a Web site is collecting too much data. For example, if every customer visit to a Web site provided 100 valuable **data points** (useful pieces of information), and 20 customers visited per minute, 259 million data points per quarter would be generated (or more than one billion per year). Making use of, or even making sense of, such an immense quantity of data is a daunting prospect. Because the rewards of paying attention to such data can be very great, e-business are turning to data-mining/Web-mining software to sift through their data.

Data-mining/Web-mining software is specialized software that enables e-businesses to apply sophisticated statistical tools to their databases in order to identify patterns in data that would otherwise have remained hidden. For example, an e-business might use a last-minute, pop-up advertisement window to entice shoppers to add one more item to their cart before they finalize their purchases. Data-mining/Web-mining software can help identify an e-business's impulse buyers — that is, buyers who like to make purchasing decisions at the moment of checkout. Better still, an e-business could use information discovered via data or Web mining to increase sales by basing that last-ditch sales pitch on items that compliment what the customer already has in his or her shopping cart. For example, if a customer fills his or her cart with business books, the purchase of a briefcase or a PDA might be encouraged.

E-businesses can use data-mining software to determine how one event leads to another, later event. For example, an e-business can use data mining to show how a customer's purchase of a product leads to the customer's later purchase of another product.

Companies can find hidden synergies between product lines or consumption patterns that allow fine-tuning of advertising strategy. Data mining/Web-mining software can also be used to identify associations between events. For example, data-mining might be used to determine what percentage of new car buyers shopped online for their new car.

By discovering these hidden patterns, e-businesses can attempt to forecast future results. This is one area where knowledge really is power. Because of its impressive capabilities, data-mining/Web-mining technologies have moved out of the back room to become an essential tool for e-business marketers. Vendors that provide data-mining/Web-mining software include SPSS Inc. (Figure 8-12), SAS Institute, Inc., and NetIQ Corporation (WebTrends).

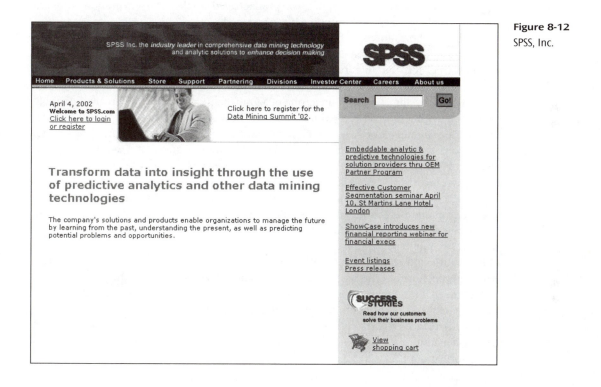

Figure 8-12
SPSS, Inc.

In the previous sections you've learned how e-businesses integrate their back-end and front-end operations with ERP systems, how they can streamline their supply chain with SCM systems, and how they can increase sales by giving customers just exactly what they need via CRM systems. Next, you learn about the technologies that help tie an e-business's ERP, SCM, and CRM systems together.

Integrating E-Business ERP, SCM, and CRM Systems

How do all of the applications involved in ERP, SCM, and CRM systems link to each other? Prior to the1990s, even reasonably large businesses had one application (usually an ERP or a simpler MRP program) running on a mainframe with one database, displaying output on many connected terminals. In today's e-business world, an enterprise is faced with multiple applications serving different constituencies on different devices, from PDAs to voice-command phone links to networked personal computers. Finding a way to make multiple applications interact with each other is not an easy task, but it is a ubiquitous e-business problem. Solving this problem can be expensive. Most e-businesses have been forced to choose between extremely expensive, custom-designed application integration software, and less expensive prepackaged application integration software designed to meet the most common e-business needs.

Consider the following analogy. Two home builders each set out to build a house that follows the same design and floor plan. One builder starts with a forest and a mine, and mills trees into suitable lumber and refines ore into metal to make nails. Each bit of lumber is then individually incorporated into the house, with beams nailed together by hand. The result is a very nice, one-of-a-kind handcrafted house, at an incredibly high price, with a long delivery horizon. This is how in-house, custom application integration tools are developed — very expensively and over a long time frame. When building custom application integration software, e-businesses often start with one of the two best-known application integration technologies, Sun Microsystems, Inc.'s **Java 2 Enterprise Edition (J2EE)** and Microsoft Corporation's **.NET**.

Businesses that balk at the expense of developing custom application integration software can choose a more generic solution. To return to the house analogy, this would be like the second builder who orders precut lumber, prefabricated roof trusses, buys nails by the pound, has premixed concrete poured, adds preassembled window frames, and prefabricated siding. While both home builders start off with the same priorities (for example, four bedrooms, 3.5 bathrooms, and a two-car garage), the second home builder meets these priorities sooner and at a lower cost by using precut, preassembled, and prepackaged components. When looking for the advantages of lower cost and faster implementation, e-businesses needing to integrate applications often turn to prepackaged application integration software called middleware. In the next two sections you learn more about J2EE, .NET, and middleware.

J2EE and .NET

Both Sun's Java 2 Enterprise Edition (J2EE), and the Microsoft .NET technologies are "low-level" technologies, meaning they are very flexible and can be adapted to handle nearly any programming situation. The term "interface" refers to the way a computer is asked by a human or another computer for data, such as how a weather-service computer is asked by humans or another computer for the current temperature in a given location. For example, a vacationer, a farmer, and a commodities-trading computer may all need to know how hot it will be in Kansas tomorrow and can use some type of computer interface to access that information.

The term "implementation" refers to the internal structure of a computer, for example, the language in which its programs are written, how data is stored, and so forth. Both J2EE and .NET allow for the separation of interface and implementation. Why is this separation important? Using our weather-service computer analogy, the request for tomorrow's Kansas temperature may come from the vacationer and the farmer via a Web browser while the request from the commodities trading computer may come in the form of an XML document. Because of this, the weather-service computer must be able to accomodate different "interfaces" for handling these queries.

By separating the interface from implementation, applications for either side — interface or implementation — can be revised or rewritten without the need to rewrite both sides of the transaction. For example, the weather-prediction software used by the weather-service computer could be modified or completely rewritten without users noticing, as long as the interfaces remained the same. It's a powerful concept which .NET and J2EE have embraced.

Both technologies provide programmers with prewritten interfaces (mostly using XML) that, out of the box, enable communication with similar interfaces in other applications. For example, many .NET applications can interact with J2EE applications and vice versa by using these XML interfaces. This allows programmers to be more concerned with complex functionality rather than making the "nuts and bolts" of communicating between two different applications go together easily.

However, there are also some substantial differences between J2EE and .NET. Some .NET applications can only operate on computers running the Microsoft Windows operating systems. By contrast, programs that use the J2EE framework can run on any operating system including Windows, UNIX, and Linux. While .NET technologies are Windows-centric; they use a "common language runtime" (CLR) which means .NET applications can be written in one of many languages such as C# and Visual Basic. Although it is an oversimplification, it is helpful to think of J2EE technologies as being "platform independent and language specific" while .NET technologies are "platform specific and language independent." Another important difference between J2EE and .NET technologies is that J2EE technologies provide a framework for Web services provided by third parties, while Microsoft plans to be a primary provider of .NET services.

Finally, an important part of the .NET technologies is the Microsoft Passport authentication service (electronic wallet) which allows consumers to enter all their personal information such as their name, address, and credit card numbers in one centralized database creating a single source of authentication information for all Web-based transactions from any Web-enabled device. E-businesses using the .NET technologies can use the centralized Passport authentication database to authenticate customer transactions instead of developing and maintaining their own authentication databases and systems.

Expressing great concern over the possibility that a single vendor such as Microsoft could control customer information from centralized databases, Sun and other companies such as Nokia, NTT DoCoMo, and General Motors came together in the Fall of 2001 to form the **Liberty Alliance Project**, a group dedicated to developing standards for a decentralized open-platform authentication service as an alternative to the Microsoft Passport proprietary authentication service. While, as of this writing, these standards are only in the formative stage, they are expected to allow participating e-businesses to store customer information on their own servers while allowing consumers to authorize an exchange of appropriate information, such as name and credit card number, between e-businesses as the consumers browse the Web.

The overall effect of the J2EE and .NET rivalry on e-business is yet to be determined. However, in the future, it is highly likely that e-businesses will use some combination of J2EE and .NET technologies in their front-end and back-end operations. J2EE and .NET are useful as general-purpose integration technologies. However, some e-businesses need to integrate their front-end and back-end applications without going to the time and expense of creating their own integration applications. These e-businesses can elect to use one of several "higher-level" integration tools called middleware.

Middleware

Applications written by different programmers on different systems at different times often send and receive data in very different ways — different languages, protocols, formats, and so forth. **Middleware** is software that helps two applications communicate by translating messages and transmitting them in a way that each application understands. **Enterprise Application Integration** tools or **EAI** is middleware designed specifically for integrating legacy system applications with ERP, SCM, and CRM systems applications.

Middleware applications typically work by creating a centralized "message space," or data bus, through which data can travel from one application to another. For example, suppose an e-business has back-end J. D. Edwards ERP applications and front-end BroadVision CRM applications that need to communicate. The e-business can use middleware such as IBM's WebSphere, which understands the specific data and format requirements of both vendors' applications. When a customer attempts to purchase a product at the e-business's Web site, a BroadVision application sends a stock-level query via WebSphere to a J. D. Edwards ERP application to determine the product's availability in inventory. WebSphere accepts the front-end, stock-level query and places it in a message queue — a waiting list of data items flowing between applications through the middleware — destined for the J. D. Edwards application. The WebSphere adapter manages the message queue, feeding the queries and receiving the result data as quickly as the application components can handle the workload. The resulting response from the J. D. Edwards application is then placed by WebSphere in a message queue for the Broad-Vision application, which picks it up and finishes building a Web page containing information about the availability of the item in question.

Another example of middleware was created by TIBCO Software, Inc. TIBCO's middleware helps bridge the gap between the NASDAQ and its traders — certainly one of the more daunting middleware implementations to date. The NASDAQ market, unlike the New York Stock Exchange, has no central trading floor; buy and sell orders are matched by computer and execution notices are sent to participating traders. Communications between the order-matching systems, accounting systems, market information compilation systems, more than 350,000 information terminals, and the NASDAQ Web site form the lifeblood of the NASDAQ market. NASDAQ uses TIBCO middleware to allow systems to subscribe to various data feeds which are published into the TIBCO middleware and distributed to all subscribers. Thus, distribution of information such as current stock prices is much more efficient than in a system where the NASDAQ computers have to manage a sprawling network of disparate recipient terminals, each of which may expect data in a slightly different format. For example, upgrades to one component of NASDAQ's infrastructure don't require wholesale changes to other components, because each is separated by the TIBCO middleware.

What language do these middleware tools use to handle communications between disparate applications? More and more often, it's XML. XML is compact, modular, and has become a standard format for transmitting data. As you learned in Chapter 4, XML tags are extensible and can be modified to suit the needs of many different kinds of business applications. Since XML is fairly new, many older applications don't work with XML. But both J2EE and .NET support the use of XML by implementing parsers, or programs that translate application output (if it's not in XML already) into XML and the XML into the format expected by the receiving application. A parser knows precisely the format the receiving application expects. So even if a business is still using older ERP system software which does not recognize XML input or output, it's still possible to implement a robust middleware strategy centered around XML for inter-application communications.

Managing an e-business in this quickly changing technological climate isn't easy. Many e-business CIOs find that just as the e-business finishes one major technology implementation, technological improvements necessitate starting the cycle again. E-businesses of reasonable size must be prepared for significant costs to implement and manage their ERP, SCM, and CRM systems. One way to mitigate these expenses and get the best return on investment is to develop systems with reusable components and standard communications interfaces. This allows new components to be added or existing components to be modified, without requiring systemwide changes.

In this chapter you learned about the differences between front-end and back-end operations and the importance of integrating these operations. You also learned how ERP, SCM, and CRM systems are used by e-businesses to control costs, manage their supply chains, and increase sales. Finally, you learned about some of the technologies that allow ERP, SCM, and CRM systems to work together to achieve e-business goals. In the next chapter, you learn about Web site content management, portal, and search engine technologies used by e-businesses.

After the contest participants submitted their trial applications to eBay (Figure 8-13), eBay evaluated the results. And the winner was: IBM's WebSphere platform, built around Sun's J2EE technologies. eBay decided to replace its outdated, in-house auction management software with WebSphere application server software and the WebSphere Commerce software suite (which provides shopping carts and other e-business features). As part of the change, eBay is moving from a two-tier server arrangement, in which front-end software and servers send Web pages to customers and then integrate data generated by customers with its overworked back-end servers and databases, with a three-tiered server arrangement. In this three-tiered arrangement, front-end servers continue to provide Web pages to eBay users and gather data; a second tier of servers process auction data, and the third-tier of servers handle the back-end databases. IBM, which plans to spend at least 16 months installing WebSphere and related products, expects eBay's WebSphere solution to support billions of daily transactions and any number of additional service applications.

According to Chuck Geiger, an eBay technologist, one important reason the WebSphere platform was selected was "to increase our developer productivity over what we have today…WebSphere allows us to buy systems-level software; and therefore allows us to get our talented development staff to move on to creating business-differentiating functionality." In other words, eBay's technology selection allows eBay's IT development staff to spend time increasing the distance between eBay and their nearest competitors, rather than reinventing the wheel. By letting the WebSphere products handle the data flow, eBay's IT development staff can concentrate on the bigger picture — managing trouble-free systems, developing innovative services, and driving bigger profits.

Figure 8-13
eBay Inc.

Understanding E-Business Front-End/Back-End Integration

❑ An e-business's front-end operations consist of the hardware and software with which its customers interact, such as its Web site.

❑ An e-business's back-end operations include those systems not directly accessed by its customers, such as its accounting and budgeting, manufacturing, marketing, and inventory management systems.

❑ Because an e-business's front-end and back-end operations share data, it is important to reduce costs and duplication of data entry by integrating the applications that are part of both operations.

❑ Enterprise resource planning (ERP) systems, which originated in manufacturing materials resource planning (MRP) systems, allow different functional areas of an e-business such as an Accounting Department and a warehouse to share the same data by linking functional area software into a single application.

❑ Supply chain management (SCM) systems link together the planning, vendor selection, manufacturing, and logistics functions of an e-business to enable the e-business to more efficiently manage its supply chain resources such as materials, money, and information.

❑ Customer relationship management (CRM) systems allow an e-business to monitor and control its interactions with its customers and then use data from those interactions to drive sales and customer service. One of the major benefits of CRM is the ability to personalize a customer's online purchasing experience.

❑ Data mining and Web mining use mathematical techniques to identify previously unknown trends in an e-business's data including that data generated by Web server logs.

❑ Sun's Java 2 Enterprise Edition and the Microsoft .NET technologies are competing technologies used to integrate e-business applications.

❑ Middleware is software that resides between two applications and helps link them together. Enterprise Application Integration (EAI) software is middleware used to integrate an e-business's legacy systems with its ERP, SCM, and CRM systems.

Key Terms

.NET
analytical CRM
back-end operations
customer relationship management (CRM or e-CRM)
data mining
data points
data warehouse
enterprise

Enterprise Application Integration (EAI)
enterprise resource planning (ERP)
front-end operations
Java 2 Enterprise Edition (J2EE)
Liberty Alliance Project
materials resource planning (MRP)
middleware
operational CRM

personalization
supply chain execution software (SCE)
supply chain management (SCM)
supply chain planning software (SCP)
systems integration
systems integrators
Web mining

Review Questions

1. Which of the following functions is not part of an e-business's back-end operations?

   a. Accounting
   b. Budgeting
   c. Online ordering
   d. Inventory control

2. Enterprise resource planning systems grew out of:

   a. ERP.
   b. MRP.
   c. CRM.
   d. SCM.

3. Which of the following subsystems cannot be part of an ERP system?

   a. Human resources
   b. Resource and production planning
   c. Sales and order entry
   d. All can be part of an ERP system.

4. The system that allows an e-business to monitor and control its customer interactions and then use data gathered from these interactions to personalize each customer's online purchasing experience is:

   a. CRM.
   b. SCM.
   c. ERP.
   d. J2EE.

5. The SCM software that uses mathematical models to predict inventory levels is:

   a. SCE.
   b. SCM.
   c. SCP.
   d. SAP.

6. The part of a CRM system that is concerned with analyzing data from customer interactions is:

   a. Operational CRM.
   b. Behavioral CRM.
   c. Analytical CRM.
   d. Investigative CRM.

7. Tailoring a customer's online personal experience using information about the customer's preferences and purchasing habits is called:

   a. Data mining.
   b. Personalization.
   c. Supply chain management.
   d. Implementation.

8. A data warehouse is a:

   a. Large building where products to be sold are stored.
   b. System for integrating front-end and back-end operations.
   c. A group of mathematical techniques used to analyze data.
   d. Database that contains huge amounts of customer and related sales data.

9. The TCO of installing an ERP system can include the costs for:

   a. Software.
   b. Consultants.
   c. In-house time and effort.
   d. All of the above are part of the TCO of an ERP system.

10. According to analysts, if a CRM system is going to fail, it's probably because of:

    a. Problems with CRM technologies.
    b. Lack of consultant expertise.
    c. Poor business decisions.
    d. Too many CRM vendors.

11. Back-end operations are those operations with which customers directly interact. **True or False?**

12. The economic benefits of front-end and back-end operations are so important that an entire sector of B2B e-business has evolved to develop and sell integration technologies. **True or False?**

13. An enterprise is an organization of any size that uses computer technology to interact with customers, vendors, and employees. **True or False?**

14. MRP software is used to personalize an e-business customer's online purchasing experience. **True or False?**

15. Implementing an ERP system is usually an inexpensive and problem-free process. **True or False?**

16. Contracting with a consultant on a time-and-materials basis to implement an ERP or CRM system is the best way to insure that the ERP or CRM project stays within its budget and on schedule. **True or False?**

17. SCE software automates the different steps in an SCM system. **True or False?**

18. An effective SCM system can help an e-business acquire and retain customers. **True or False?**

19. Web mining uses data-mining techniques to analyze data acquired via the Web. **True or False?**

20. J2EE technologies were developed by Microsoft. **True or False?**

Exercises

1. Using Internet search tools or other relevant resources, such as those at the end of this chapter, research the J2EE and .NET technologies and then write a one- or two-page paper comparing and contrasting the two technologies.

2. Using Internet search tools or other relevant resources, such as those at the end of this chapter, locate five middleware vendors. Then create a one-page paper that lists the vendors and describes their middleware offerings.

3. Using Internet search tools or other relevant resources, such as those at the end of this chapter, find two examples of e-businesses using data mining/ or Web mining to analyze their business data. Then write a one- or two-page paper describing the e-businesses and how they used data mining/ or Web mining.

4. Define the following terms: ERP, SCM, CRM, personalization, data mining, and Web mining, and give examples of each.

5. Using Internet search tools or other relevant resources, such as those at the end of this chapter, identify two e-businesses *not discussed in this chapter* that use personalization technologies to drive sales and improve customer interactions. Then write a one- or two-page paper describing the e-businesses and how they are using personalization.

CASE PROJECTS

◆ 1 ◆

You are the owner of EduTown.biz, an e-business that sells toddler, pre-K, and kindergarten educational materials online directly to parents and educators. You want to build your customer base and increase sales by tailoring your product offerings to each of your customers' special interests. Using the Internet or other relevant resources, research CRM and personalization topics. Then create a list of ways you could accomplish your goals using CRM and personalization.

◆ 2 ◆

You are the assistant to the IT manager for a medium-sized, B2B e-business, EquipCare.biz, that provides a marketspace for other businesses to buy and sell used office furniture and equipment. The manager is preparing a proposal for the installation of a CRM system and asks you to create a list of CRM vendors she can take to a meeting next Monday. Using the Internet or other relevant resources, research at least five CRM vendors. Then create a one- or two-page paper listing each vendor and describing their CRM products and services. Based on your research, recommend one of the vendors for the proposed CRM project. Be sure to list the reasons for your recommendation.

◆ 3 ◆

You are the logistics manager for Tile Designs, Inc., an e-business that manufactures custom-designed ceramic kitchen and bathroom tiles for the luxury home market. The e-business has grown dramatically along with the house building boom of the past two years and you think installing an SCM system to manage and control the Tile Designs supply chain would save several million dollars a year in idle inventory and material costs. You will mention your idea tomorrow when lunching with the president. Using the Internet or other relevant resources, research SCM topics. Then create a list of "talking points" about SCM systems you can use in your discussion with the president.

TEAM PROJECT

You and two partners are operating a successful B2C e-business; however, it is becoming clearer that the e-business's accounting, sales, inventory control, and other back-end functions need to be integrated more closely with the front-end, Web-site order processing in order to reduce duplication of data entry efforts and provide better customer service. One of your partners suggests that the e-business implement an ERP system; however, you have heard many "horror stories" about scope creep, cost overruns, and unfulfilled expectations of ERP system implementations.

Using the Internet or other relevant resources, research successful and not-so-successful ERP implementations. Then meet with your partners and work together to define a set of expectations, a TCO range, and an implementation time frame. Then draft an outline of the steps you think will be necessary to assure the success of an ERP implementation for your e-business —

an implementation that comes in on time, within budget, and meets your operational expectations. After your meeting, use Microsoft PowerPoint or other presentation software to create a 5–10 slide presentation that identifies your B2C e-business, states your ERP expectations, TCO range and time frame, and the steps your team thinks are necessary to have a successful ERP implementation. Then present your ERP system implementation plan to a group of classmates selected by your instructor.

Useful Links

Baseline Magazine
www.baselinemag.com/

BusinessTechnology.com — IT Financial Management Issues
www.businesstechnology.com/

CIO Magazine — ERP Center
www.cio.com/research/erp/index.html

CommunityB2B
www.communityb2b.com/

CRM Magazine
www.crmmagazine.com/

CRMCommunity — CRM Resources
www.crmcommunity.com/default.htm

CRMDaily.com — CRM News and Resources
www.crmdaily.com/

CRM-Forum.com — CRM Resources
www.crm-forum.com/

CRMguru.com
www.crmguru.com/

CRMXchange
www.crmxchange.com/

Data Mining and CRM Technologies
www3.primushost.com/~kht/index.htm

Data Warehousing Online
www.datawarehousingonline.com/

Distributed Systems Online — Distributed Database and Content Management Resources
dsonline.computer.org/index.htm

DM Review — Business Magazine
www.dmreview.com/default.cfm

EAI Journal
www.eaijournal.com/

ebizQ — E-business Integration
www.ebizq.net/

EContent Magazine
www.econtentmag.com/

ERP Fan Club
www.erpfans.com/

ERPCentral.com — ERP News and Resources
www.emergenet.com/

ERPWorld.org — Enterprise Computing Information
www.erpworld.org/

Evolt.org — Web Developer Resources
www.evolt.org/index.html

IntelligentCRM — CRM Resources
www.intelligentcrm.com/

IntelligentEnterprise — Enterprise Resources
www.intelligententerprise.com/

IntelligentERP — ERP Resources
www.intelligenterp.com/

Intranet Journal
www.intranetjournal.com/km/

ITToolbox — Data Mining and CRM Resources
businessintelligence.ittoolbox.com/

ITToolbox — ERP Resources
www.erpassist.com/

ITToolbox — SCM Resources
supplychain.ittoolbox.com/

KDNuggets — Data Mining Resources
www.kdnuggets.com/

KMWorld — Knowledge Management Resources
www.kmworld.com/

KnowledgeStorm, Inc.
www.knowledgestorm.com/MainServlet?ksAction=
    home;jsessionid=fa80f9b4eccc4fa288a5f9cf22bce
    88cKoQAC_wdB

Middleware Resource Center
www.middleware.org/

Object Management Group, Inc.
www.omg.org/ and www.corba.org/

SearchCRM.com — CRM Resources
searchcrm.techtarget.com/home/0,,sid11,00.html

SearchDatabase.com — Database Resources
searchdatabase.techtarget.com/bestWebLinks/
    0,,sid13_tax281649,00.html

SearchEBusiness.com — E-Business Resource
searchebusiness.techtarget.com/bestWebLinks/
    0,,sid19_tax282990,00.html

SearchWebServices.com — Web Services Resources
searchWebservices.techtarget.com/

Supply Chain Management Review
www.manufacturing.net/scm/

TechRepublic — CRM Briefing Center
www.techrepublic.com/briefingcenter.jhtml?id=b015

TechRepublic — ERP Resources
www.techrepublic.com/briefingcenter.jhtml?id=b004

The Data Mine — Data Mining Resources
www.the-data-mine.com/

**The Stanford Global Supply Chain Management
Forum**
www.stanford.edu/group/scforum/

The Supply Chain Council Inc.
www.supply-chain.org/

WebSphere Advisor — IBM WebSphere Resources
www.advisor.com/www/WebSphereAdvisor

Links to Web Sites or Companies Noted in This Chapter

Accenture (formerly Andersen Consulting)
www.accenture.com/xd/xd.asp?it=enWeb&xd=
    index.xml

Amazon.com
www.amazon.com

American Express Company
www.americanexpress.com/homepage/
    mt_personal.shtml

Art Technology Group, Inc. (ATG)
www.atg.com/en/index.jhtml

Arthur Andersen
www.arthurandersen.com/

BEA Systems, Inc.
www.beasys.com/index.shtml

Blockbuster Inc.
www.blockbuster.com/

Boise Cascade Office Products Corporation
www.boiseoffice.com/

BroadVision, Inc.
www.broadvision.com/

Deloitte & Touche
www.deloitte.com/vs/0%2c1151%2csid=2000%2c00.html

Department 56
www.department56.com/

E.piphany, Inc.
www.epiphany.com/index.html

eBay Inc.
www.ebay.com

eDiets.com, Inc.
www.ediets.com

Electronic Frontier Foundation
www.eff.org/

Electronic Privacy Information Center
www.epic.org/

Gartner Inc. (Gartner Group)
www4.gartner.com/UnrecognizedUserHomePage.jsp

Gateway, Inc.
www.gateway.com

General Motors
www.ge.com

IBM
www.ibm.com

J. D. Edwards
www.jdedwards.com/

KPMG Consulting, Inc.
www.kpmgconsulting.com/

Liberty Alliance Project
www.projectliberty.org/

Merrill Lynch & Co, Inc.
www.ml.com/

META Group
www.metagroup.com/cgi-bin/inetcgi/index.html

Microsoft Corporation
www.microsoft.com

NetIQ Corporation (WebTrends)
www.webtrends.com/default.htm

Nokia Corporation
www.nokia.com

NTT DoCoMo
www.nttdocomo.com

Oracle Corporation
www.oracle.com

PeopleSoft, Inc.
www.peoplesoft.com/corp/en/public_index.asp

Physician Sales & Service, Inc. (PSS)
www.pssd.com/

PSS/World Medical, Inc.
www.pssworldmedical.com/

Reflect.com LLC
www.reflect.com/

Salesforce.com, Inc.
www.salesforce.com

SAP AG
www.sap.com

SAS Institute, Inc.
www.sas.com

Siebel Systems, Inc.
www.siebel.com/

SPSS Inc.
www.spss.com/

Sun Microsystems, Inc.
www.sun.com

Suppleyes, Inc.
www.suppleye.com

The NASDAQ Stock Market, Inc.
www.nasdaq.com/

The Proctor & Gamble Company
www.pg.com/main.jhtml

TIBCO Software, Inc.
www.tibco.com/

W. L. Gore & Associates, Inc.
www.gore.com/

Wal-Mart Stores, Inc.
www.walmart.com/

For Additional Review

Accrue Software, Inc. 2000. "Web Mining White Paper: Driving Business Decisions in Web Time." March 23. www.accrue.com/pdf/webminingwhitepaper_1099.pdf.

Andrews, Jean. 2001. *i-Net+ Guide to Internet Technologies*. Boston: Course Technology.

Aponovich, David. 2001. "Case Study: Data Software Has Eyewear Seller Seeing Clearly," *IT Management*, September 14. Available online at: itmanagement.earthweb.com/datbus/article/0,,11969_884631,00.html.

Aponovich, David. 2001. "Case Study: Insurance Firm Reaps Extranet Benefits," *IT Management*, July 16. Available online at: itmanagement.earthWeb.com/datbus/print/0,,11969_802081,00.html.

Ard, Scott and Clark, Tim. 1999. "eBay Blacks Out Yet Again," *CNET News.com*, June 13. Available online at: news.com.com/2100-1017-226987.html.

Baldwin, Howard. 2002. "Prescription for Healthier CRM," *Enterprise Magazine*, March 18. Available online at: techupdate.zdnet.com/techupdate/stories/main/0,14179,2854592,00.html.

Bass, Alison. 2002. "Too Much of a Good Thing: Why IT Executives Are Not Rushing to Buy CRM From the People Who Brought Us ERP," *CIO Magazine*, March 19. Available online at: comment.cio.com/crm/031902.html.

Blakey, Elizabeth. 2001. "Any Outrage Over E-Commerce Outages?" *E-Commerce Times*, January 8. Available online at: www.ecommercetimes.com/perl/printer/6513/.

Bray, Mike. 2000. "Software Technology Review: Middleware," *Carnegie Mellon University, Software Engineering Institute*, September. Available online at: www.sei.cmu.edu/str/descriptions/middleware.html.

Brickley, Peg. 1999. "High-Tech Firm Sues PeopleSoft, Deloitte," *Philadelphia Business Journal*, November 5. Available online at: philadelphia.bizjournals.com/philadelphia/stories/1999/11/08/story5.html.

Carnegie Mellon Software Engineering Institute. 2002. "Middleware." Available online at: www.sei.cmu.edu/str/descriptions/middleware_body.html.

Chung, Sungmi and Sherman, Mike. 2002. "Emerging Marketing," *Inc.com*, March 13. Available online at: www2.inc.com/search/24004.html.

Clark, Tim. 1999. "eBay Online again After 14-hour Outage," *CNET News.com*, August 6. Available online at: aolaustralia.com.com/2102-1017-229518.html.

Clark, Tim. 1999. "eBay Recovers After Outage," *CNET News.com*, May 21. Available online at: news.com.com/2102-1017-226166.html.

Clark, Tim. 1999. "Outages Plague eBay Again," *CNET News.com*, June 29. Available online at: news.com.com/2102-1017-227811.html.

CNET News.com. 2002. "Is CRM All It's Cracked Up to Be?" April 3. Available online at: news.cnet.com/investor/news/newsitem/0-9900-1028-9602165-0.html.

Cohen, Adam. 2002. *The Perfect Store: Inside eBay*. New York: Little, Brown and Company.

ComputerWire. 2002. "Sun Launches Java Alternative to Mobile .NET," *The Register*, March 26. Available online at: www.theregister.co.uk/content/4/24580.html.

ComputerWire. 2002. "Sun Opens Java to Open Source Community," *The Register*, March 26. Available online at: www.theregister.co.uk/content/4/24579.html.

Computerworld. 2000. " Halloween Less Spooky for Hershey's This Year," *ITWorld.com*, November 6. Available online at: www.itworld.com/App/679/CWST053358/.

Coursey, David. 2001. "Sun's Stand: How the Liberty Alliance Could Save E-Commerce," *ZDNet*, September 28. Available online at: www.zdnet.com/anchordesk/stories/story/0%2C10738%2C815289%2C00.html.

Darwin Magazine. 2002. "Executive Guide: Customer Relationship Management." Available online at: guide.darwinmag.com/technology/enterprise/crm/index.html.

Darwin Magazine. 2002. "Executive Guide: Enterprise Resource Planning." Available online at: guide.darwinmag.com/technology/enterprise/erp/index.html.

Deck, Stewart. 2001. "CRM Made Simple: Three Companies Zero in on Exactly What they Need From CRM — and then Make It Happen," *CIO Magazine*, September 15. Available online at: www.cio.com/archive/091501/simple.html.

Dignan, Larry. 2002. "CRM: Dream or Nightmare?" *ZDNET News*, April 3. Available online at: zdnet.com.com/2100-1106-874430.html.

Doherty, Patricia. 2000. "Web Mining — The E-Tailer's Holy Grail," *DM Review*, January. Available online at: www.dmreview.com/portal.cfm?NavID=91&EdID=1891&PortalID=9&Topic=1.

Donahue, Sean. 1999. "Mr. Fix-It," *Salon.com*, September 20. Available online at: www.salon.com/tech/view/1999/09/20/maynard_Webb/.

Donovan, Michael. 2000. "ERP: Successful Implementation the First Time," *The CEO Refresher*. Available online at: web.idirect.com/~vfr/!erp1.

Dornfest, Rael. 2001. "Identity," *The O'Reilly Network*, July 18. Available online at: www.oreillynet.com/cs/weblog/view/wlg/481.

Dragoon, Alice. 2002. "This Changes Everything: The CEO at Boise Cascade Office Products Saw Boosting Customer Service as His Only Chance to Win-So He Did," *Darwin Magazine*, March. Available online at: www.darwinmag.com/read/030102/changes.html.

Earls, Alan. 2001. "Integrating ERP and CRM," *ebizQ*, February 12. Available online at: eai.ebizq.net/erp/earls_1.html.

Edelstein, Herbert A. 2001. "Pan For Gold in the Clickstream," *Informationweek.com*, March 12. Available online at: www.informationweek.com/828/prmining.htm.

Evers, Doris and Vance, Ashlee. 2001. "Sun, Others to Issue Competitor to Microsoft Passport," *InfoWorld*, September 26. Available online at: www.idg.net/ic_700281_1794_9-10000.html.

Farley, Jim. 2001. "Picking a Winner: .NET vs. J2EE," *Software Development Magazine*, March. Available online at: www.sdmagazine.com/print/documentID=11085.

Ferguson, Renee. 2002. "Managing the Supply chain Via the Web," *eWeek*, March 26. Available online at: www.eweek.com/article/0,3658,s=1884&a=24579,00.asp.

Fisher, Dennis. 2001. "Liberty Alliance Support Grows," *eWeek*, December 19. Available online at: www.pcmag.com/article/0%2C2997%2Cs=1582&a=20302%2C00.asp?kc=PCNKT0107KTX1K0000360.

Gage, Deborah. 2001. "Without a .NET," *Baseline Magazine*, October. Available online at: www.baselinemag.com/print_article/0,3668,a=17021,00.asp.

Gardner, Dana. 1999. "Consultant, ERP Firm Face Lawsuit Over HR App," *InfoWorld*, November 1. Available online at: www.infoworld.com/articles/hn/xml/99/11/01/991101hnncconsultanbt.xml.

Girard, Kim. 2002. "Blame Game: Why Andersen Cracked in IT Suit," *Baseline Magazine*, March 6. Available online at: www.baselinemag.com/article/0%2C3658%2Cs=2101&a=23650%2C00.asp?kc=BANKT0110KTX1K0000464.

Girard, Kim and Farmer, Melanie Austria. 1999. "Business Software Firms Sued Over Implementation," *CNET News.com*, November 3. Available online at: news.com.com/2100-1001-232404.html?tag=prntfr.

Grant, Elaine X. 2002. "What Does Microsoft's .NET Mean for E-commerce?" *E-Commerce Times*, April 5. Available online at: www.ecommercetimes.com/perl/printer/16966/.

Greening, Dan R. 2000. "Data Mining on the Web: There's Gold in that Mountain of Data," *New Architect*, January. Available online at: www.webtechniques.com/archives/2000/01/greening/.

Grushkin, Barry. 2001. "Meaningful Encounters of the Second Kind: Although Technology Still Can't Mimic Complex Human Relationships, Understanding the Way Your Customers Think May Be the Next Step in Personalization," *Intelligent Enterprise*, September 18. Available online at: www.intelligententerprise.com/010918/414decision1_1.shtml?ebusiness.

Hakala, David. 2001. "Sky-High Expectations: ERP and CRM Integration," *eWeek*, July 23. Available online at: www.eweek.com/article/0%2C3658%2Cs=723&a=10109%2C00.asp?kc=EWNKT0110KTX1K0000440.

Harreld, Heather. 2000. "Avoiding ERP Disaster," *Federal Computer Week*, May 29. Available online at: www.fcw.com/fcw/articles/2000/0529/tec-erp-05-29-00.asp.

Henig, Peter D. 1999. "When Outages Hit, Should Investors Run?" *Red Herring*, August 13. Available online at: www.redherring.com/insider/1999/0813/inv-outages.html.

Hertzberg, Robert. 2001. "Bada-Boom," *Baseline Magazine*, December 10. Available online at: www.baselinemag.com/article/0%2C3658%2Cs=25064&a=19488%2C00.asp?kc=BANKT0110KTX1K0000464.

Hesterbrink, Christoph. 1999. "Integrating E-business and ERP," *PricewaterhouseCoopers*, October. Available online at: www.intel.com/eBusiness/business/plan/5/hi15020.htm.

Hunter, Philip. 2001. "Holding It All Together," *Computer Weekly*, August 24. Available online at: www.findarticles.com/.

IBM. 2000. "Suppleye.com," *Supply Chain Management (SCM) Case Studies*. Available online at: www-5.ibm.com/e-business/uk/components/scm/case_studies/scm_cs_suppleye.html.

Jaroneczyk, Jennifer. 2002. "CRM Stumbles on the Catwalk," *InternetWorld*, April 1. Available online at: www.internetworld.com/magazine.php?inc=040102/04.01.02fastforward6.html.

Katz, David M. 2001. "Beware of 'Scope Creep' on ERP Projects," *CFO.com*, March 27. Available online at: www.cfo.com/Article?article=2432.

Katz, David. M. 2001. "Of Men and Mice: An ERP Case Study," *CFO.com*, March 21. Available online at: www.cfo.com/Article?article=2348.

Katz, David M. 2001. "What If Your ERP Can't Deliver," *CFO.com*, April 19. Available online at: www.cfo.com/article/1,5309,2791,00.html.

Koch, Christopher. 2002. "The ABCs of ERP," *CIO Magazine*, February 7. Available online at: www.cio.com/research/erp/edit/erpbasics.html.

Koch, Christopher. 2002. "The ABCs of Supply Chain Management," *CIO Magazine*, January 22. Available online at: www.cio.com/research/scm/edit/012202_scm.html.

Krasner, Herb. 2000. "Ensuring E-Business Success by Learning from ERP Failures," *ITProfessional Magazine as reported by IEEE Computer Society*, January/February. Available online at: www.computer.org/itpro/cover_stories/jan_feb/erp_1.htm.

Layman, Andrew and Montgomery, John. 2002. "XML, Web Services, and the .NET Framework," *TopXML*. Available online at: www.vbxml.com/xml/articles/dotnetintro/default.asp.

Levinson, Meridith. 2002. "Getting to Know You: A Guide to Personalization 101, Brought to You by Three Companies That Are Doing It Right," *CIO Magazine*, February 15. Available online at: www.cio.com/archive/021502/know.html.

Mahoney, Michael. 2001. "The Future of E-Commerce: Caught in a .NET?" *E-Commerce Times*, December 26. Available online at: www.ecommercetimes.com/perl/printer/153631.

Markoff, John. 2002. "Microsoft Has Shelved Its Internet 'Persona' Service," *The New York Times*, April 10. Available online at: www.nytimes.com/2002/04/11/technology/ebusiness/11NET.html.

Maselli, Jennifer. 2002. "Front-to-Back: Integration Plays a Role in BroadVision's Plans," *InformationWeek*, February 21. Available online at: www.informationweek.com/story/IWK20020221S0032.

McCartney, Laton. 2000. "Law and Disorder," *Smart Player*, October 23. Available online at: techupdate.zdnet.com/techupdate/stories/main/0,14179,2643712-2,00.html.

McDonald, Tim. 2002. "The Problem with .NET," *NewsFactor.com*, March 20. story.news.yahoo.com/news?tmpl=story&u=/nf/20020320/tc_nf/16843&c.

McGeever, Christine. 1999. "GoreTex Maker Files Suit Over Software Installation," *Computerworld*, October 29. Available online at: www.computerworld.com/cwi/Printer_Friendly_Version/0,1212,NAV47_STO29312-,00.html.

McNaughton, Kora. 1999. "eBay Suffers Prolonged Outage," *CNET News.com*, May 3. Available online at: news.com.com/2102-1017-225285.html.

Mearian, Lucas. 2000. "Petsmart CEO: SAP Project 'Far More' Difficult than Expected, " *Computerworld*, November 17. Available online at: www.computerworld.com/cwi/Printer_Friendly_Version/0,1212,NAV47_STO54169-,00.html.

Mello, Adrian. 2002. "Six Mistakes That Will Sink Your CRM," *Enterprise Magazine*, March 18. Available online at: techupdate.zdnet.com/techupdate/stories/main/0,14179,2854618,00.html.

Mena, Jesus. 2000. "Bringing Them Back: Customer Retention is the Name of the Game, and Web Mining Your Customer Interactions Can Help You Win It," *Intelligent Enterprise*, July 17. Available online at: www.intelligententerprise.com/000717/feat2.shtml.

Metz, Cade. 2001. "Microsoft and the Liberty Alliance," *PC Magazine*, December 13. Available online at: www.pcmag.com/article/0%2C2997%2Cs=1490&a=19953%2C00.asp?kc=PCNKT0107KTX1K0000360.

Morphy, Erika. 2001. "Integrating CRM: The Myth of Seamlessness," *CRM Daily.com*, October 4. Available online at: www.crmdaily.com/perl/printer/13947/.

Nash, Kim S. 2000. "Companies Don't Learn From Previous IT Snafus," *Computerworld*, October 30. Available online at: www.computerworld.com/cwi/Printer_Friendly_Version/0,1212,NAV47_STO53014-,00.html.

Nash, Kim S. 2000. "Users Say Consultants Play Role in IT Disasters,: *Computerworld*, November 6. Available online at: www.computerworld.com/cwi/Printer_Friendly_Version/0,1212,NAV47_STO53331-,00.html.

Nelson, Scott and Eisenfeld, Beth. 2002. "Salvaging a Failed CRM Initiative," *Enterprise Magazine*, February 22. techupdate.zdnet.com/techupdate/stories/main/0,14179,2849379,00.html.

Nerney, Chris. 1999. "eBay Move to Solve Outage Woes Paying Off So Far," *The Internet Stock Report*, August 16. www.Internetstockreport.com/tracker/article/0,,4661_183121,00.html.

Norris, Grant et al. 2000. *E-Business and ERP: Transforming the Enterprise*. New York: John Wiley & Sons.

Office of New York State Attorney General Eliot Spitzer. 1999. "Points of Reference: E-Commerce Failures."Available online at: www.oag.state.ny.us/investors/1999_online_brokers/points_reference.html.

Osterland, Andrew. 2000. "Blaming ERP," *CFO.com*, January 1. Available online at: www.cfo.com/printarticle/0,5317,1684|,00.html.

Pal, Ashim. 2002. "CRM: Best Practices from the Field," *Enterprise Magazine*, March 7. Available online at: techupdate.zdnet.com/techupdate/stories/main/0,14179,2852076,00.html.

Palfini, Jeff. 2001. "The Sultans of CRM," *The Industry Standard*, August 6. Available online at: www.thestandard.com/article/0,1902,28227,00.html?body_page=1.

Patton, Susannah. 2001. "Talking to Richard Dalzell: Amazon.com's CIO Talks About Investing in Technology at the Company Known for Having the Best CRM on the Web," *CIO Magazine*, June 12. Available online at: www.cio.com/research/crm/edit/061201_amazon.html.

Patton, Susannah. 2001. "The Truth About CRM," *CIO Magazine*, May 1. Available online at: www.cio.com/archive/050101/truth.html.

Pender, Lee. 2001. "The 5 Keys to Supply Chain Success," *CIO Magazine*, July 15. Available online at: www.cio.com/archive/071501/keys.html.

Physician Sales and Service. 2002. "About." Available online at: www.pssd.com/about/about.htm.

Plexico, Kevin. 2000. "Taking the Risk Out of ERP," *Federal Computer Week*, April 3. Available online at: www.fcw.com/fcw/articles/2000/0403/tec-plexico-04-03-00.asp.

Porter, Michael E. 1985. *Competitive Advantage: Creating and Sustaining Superior Performance*. New York: The Free Press.

Press Release. 1998. "SAP Sued for Firm's Collapse," *Wired News*, August 27. Available online at: www.wired.com/news/print/0,1294,14684,00.html.

Press Release. 2001. "IBM and eBay Forge Broad E-Business Alliance," *IBM*, September 6. www-3.ibm.com/software/info1/Websphere/news/ibmnews/pr010907.jsp?S_TACT=102BBW01&S_CMP=campaign.

Press Release. 2001. "Sun Microsystems Calls for Industry Support Around Liberty Alliance Project," *Sun Microsystems, Inc.*, September 26. Available online at: www.sun.com/smi/Press/sunflash/2001-09/sunflash.20010926.1.html.

Radosevich, Lynda. 1998. "Bankrupt Drug Company Sues SAP," *InfoWorld*, August 27. Available online at: ww1.infoworld.com/cgi-bin/displayStory.pl?980827.wcsapsuit.htm.

Ricciuti, Mike. 2002. "Testimony Highlights .NET Disarray," *CNET News.com*, May 10. Available online at: news.com.com/2102-1001-909216.html.

Saliba, Clare. 2000. "eBay Apologizes for Service Outages," *E-Commerce Times*, October 24. Available online at: www.ecommercetimes.com/perl/printer/4622/.

Schonfeld, Erick. 2002. "This Is Your Father's IBM, Only Smarter: How a Former Has-Been Kicked Its Old Habits, Got Open-Source Religion, and Regained Its Status as One of the Biggest, Baddest Tech Companies on Earth," *Business2.0*, May. Available online at: www.business2.com/articles/mag/print/0,1643,39361,FF.html.

Seybold, Patricia B. 1998. *Customers.com: How to Create a Profitable Business Strategy for the Internet and Beyond*. New York: Random House.

Slater, Derek. 2000. "Middleware Demystified," *CIO Magazine*, May 15. Available online at: www.cio.com/archive/051500/middle_content.html?.

Sliwa, Carol. 2002. "Java Creator Gosling Says .NET Falls Short of Expectations," *Computerworld*, March 29. Available online at: www.computerworld.com/storyba/0,4125,NAV47_STO69691,00.html.

SmartPros. 2001. "Andersen Worldwide Slapped With $6 Billion Lawsuit". March 3. Available online at: accounting.smartpros.com/x29650.xml.

Smith, Tom. 2002. "Staples Offers Customers Free E-Procurement Integration," *InternetWeek*, March 19. Available online at: www.Internetwk.com/story/INW20020319S0008.

Songini, Marc L. 2001. "Users See Greater Benefits in Tight Supply Chain Links," *Computerworld*, July 2. Available online at: www.computerworld.com/industrytopics/manufacturing/story/0;10801,61773,00.html.

Stedman, Craig. 1999. "Failed ERP Gamble Haunts Hershey," *Computerworld*, November 1. Available online at: www.computerworld.com/1999/story/0,11280,37464,00.html.

Sterner, Stafford G. 2000. "E-Commerce — Beyond the Web Site Case Study from the Materials Handling Industry," Logistics/Supply Chain at About.com, November 20. Available online at: logistics.about.com/library/weekly/uc112000a.htm.

Strauss, Gary. 1999. "When Computers Fail," USA Today, December 7. Available online at: www.usatoday.com/life/cyber/tech/ctg838.htm.

Sun Microsystems, Inc. 2000. "ERP Platform-Related Analysis Total Cost of Ownership: A Platform-Related Cost Analysis of ERP Applications." February 11. Available online at: www.sun.com/servers/workgroup/tco/metastudy.html.

Suppleye.com. 2002. "About Suppleye.com." Available online at: suppleye.com.

Sykes, Rebecca and Busse, Torsten. 1998. "SAP Denies R/3 Caused Firm's Collapse," *NetworkWorldFusion*, August 28. Available online at: www.nwfusion.com/news/0828sap.html.

Symons, Allene. 1998. " FoxMeyer Litigation Continues With Suites Against SAP, Deloitte & Touche," *Drug Store News*, September 21. Available online at: www.findarticles.com/.

Talarian Corporation. 2000. "Everything You Need to Know About Middleware," *ebizQ*, October. Available online at: www.messageq.com/communications_middleware/talarian_1a.html.

Thomas, Nigel. 2002. "In Pursuit of the Extended Enterprise: Integrating CRM, ERP, and E-Commerce," *ebizQ*. Available online at: b2b.ebizq.net/e_commerce/thomas_1.html.

Toft, Dorte. 1999. "eBay Shares Drop 18 Percent After Outage," IDG News Service, *Boston Bureau*, June 14. Available online at: www.idg.net/english/crd_ebay_76336.html.

Weiss, Todd R. 2001. "EBay Plans to Build Trading System Around WebSphere," *ComputerWorld*, September 10. Available online at: www.computer-world.com/cwi/story/0%2C1199%2CNAV47_STO63692%2C00.html.

Wheatley, Malcolm. 2000. "ERP Training Stinks," *CIO Magazine*, June 1. Available online at: www.cio.com/archive/060100_erp_content.html?.

Wice, Nathaniel. 1999. "Can a Man Named Webb Keep eBay From Crashing?" *ON Magazine*, August 10. Available online at: www.onmagazine.com/on-mag/reviews/article/0,9985,29297,000.html.

Wolverton, Troy. 1999. "eBay Outages Enrage Users," *CNET News.com*, June 11. Available online at: news.com.com/2102-1017-227015.html.

E-Business Web Site Management

In this chapter, you will learn to:

Discuss issues related to managing an e-business Web site

Discuss portals and the role they play in e-business

Define Web content management and describe the components of a Web content management system

Describe directories and search engines and define the role they play in building a Web site's audience

Identify ways to measure a Web site's performance

When television viewers consider the programs available on their local public television stations, many inevitably look for such high-quality programming as NOVA, Frontline, and Masterpiece Theater. These and many other excellent programs are produced for public television by WGBH Boston, arguably the leading public broadcasting organization in the U.S. The award winning (Emmys, Peabodys, Oscars, and more) WGBH Boston, was a pioneer in public radio and television. Its heritage actually goes all the way back to 1836, when John Lowell Jr. left a bequest intended to create "free public lectures for the benefit of the citizens of Boston." By 1946 the Lowell Institute had formed an alliance with six Boston colleges in order to broadcast its public lectures on commercial radio stations. Then, in 1951, the WGBH Educational Foundation launched its first radio broadcast of a live musical concert — and WGBH was on its way.

By 2000, WGBH had evolved into a huge organization with three public radio services, three television channels, and three production facilities, which together provided a variety of products including IMAX films, CD-ROMs, and television and radio programming for public broadcasting stations across the U.S. Like most large organizations, WGBH also had its own Web site. That Web site started out as a simple collection of static pages. But, by 2000 the Web site no longer met the needs of WGBH. One of the problems with the site was that updating and maintaining information at the site took too much time and effort. WGBH needed some way to automate the process. The management at WGBH also wanted to provide more exciting, timely, and useful Web site content in order to attract new Web site viewers. Much of the funding for public broadcasting comes from donations in the form of audience memberships. Attracting new Web site viewers would give WGBH the opportunity to encourage these viewers to join WGBH's audience membership program. What could the management at WGBH do to solve these problems?

Managing an E-business Web Site

As an e-business grows, its Web site **content** — the text, images, sound, video, hyperlinks, and so forth included in its Web site — often becomes more and more complex, drawing on material generated from many different internal and external sources. Unless carefully managed, an e-business's growing Web site can quickly degenerate into a disorganized hodgepodge of confusing information. Managing an e-business Web site can include:

- Presenting timely and useful content to viewers
- Controlling who creates and approves content, and controlling how and when that content is presented
- Increasing a Web site's audience
- Measuring a Web site's performance against expectations

In this chapter, you learn about portals and how an e-business can use different types of portals to make appropriate Web content available to its employees, vendors, customers, and the general public. Then you learn how an e-business can use a Web content management system to control the development of Web site content and to schedule when that content appears. Next, you learn about search engine technologies and how an e-business can exploit these technologies to help drive viewers to its Web site. Finally, you learn how an e-business can use technology to evaluate its Web site's effectiveness.

Portals

A **portal** is a Web site that serves not as a viewer's final destination, but as a starting point for finding useful information. The goal of a portal is to be the "first place a viewer looks" when locating Web-based information or services. Analysts often categorize portals either by audience type or by content. The following sections divide portals into types based on audience: general consumer portals, personal portals, vertical portals, industry portals, and corporate portals.

General Consumer Portals

General consumer portals, sometimes called **publishing portals**, provide a wide range of information suitable for a generalized audience with varied interests. The Yahoo! and AltaVista Web sites are examples of general consumer portals. In addition to providing a way to search for Web sites, the Yahoo! and AltaVista sites draw viewers interested in news headlines, shopping, personal, travel, auction, and other services. They do this by providing links to content directed at those varied interests. For example, a viewer can start his or her Web browsing day at the AltaVista (Figure 9-1) Web site by checking the latest news headlines and then return to the Web site as needed throughout the day as browsing interests change.

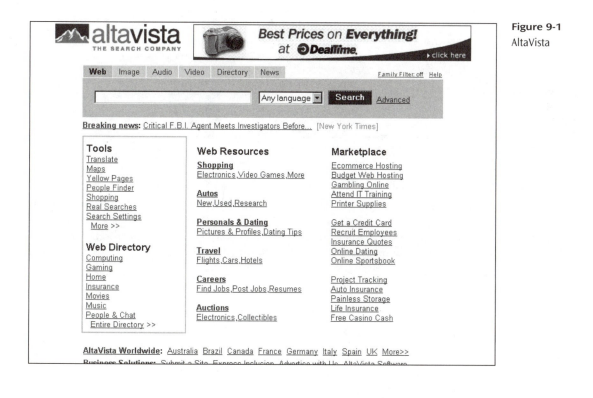

Figure 9-1
AltaVista

Personal Portals

Personal portals, sometimes called **horizontal portals**, are a type of consumer portal that allows viewers to customize content in order to satisfy their own particular interests. The objective of a personal portal is to use customized content — weather, sports scores, news headlines, and so forth — as a draw to encourage a viewer to make the personal portal his or her default starting point when accessing the Web. My Excite (Figure 9-2) and My Yahoo! (Figure 9-3) are two examples of personal portals.

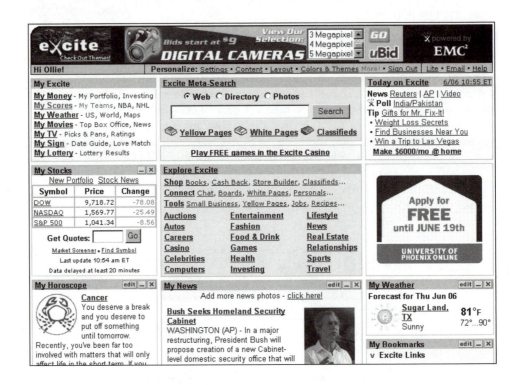

Figure 9-2
My Excite

Vertical and Industry Portals

Vertical portals attract a narrow group of viewers with common interests. An example of a vertical portal is the BMW of North America, LLC Web site (Figure 9-4) where BMW owners (or potential owners) can learn about BMW cars, read current news and reviews about BMW products, and chat with other BMW owners.

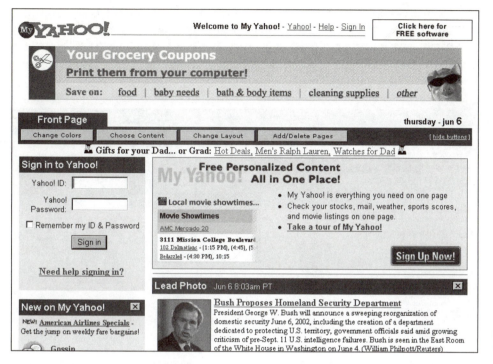

Figure 9-3
My Yahoo!

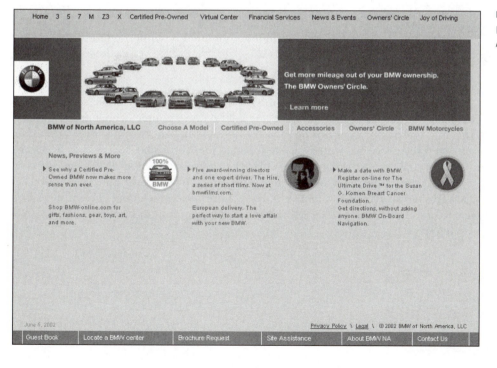

Figure 9-4
BMW of North America, LLC

Another example of a vertical portal is the government portal for New York City, NYC.gov (Figure 9-5), which provides information about city services, links to the Web sites of city agencies, personalized weather data, New York City news and special features, and special information from the mayor's office — all targeted at citizens of New York.

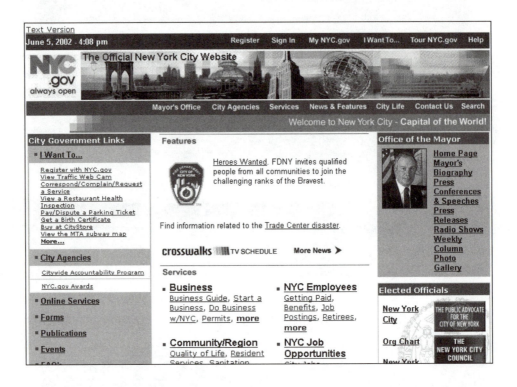

Figure 9-5
NYC.gov

A subtype of the vertical portal is the **industry portal**, which attracts viewers who are looking for information about a specific industry. An example of an industry portal is TruckNet, a portal for the trucking industry. Users of the TruckNet (Figure 9-6) Web site can match their services with available trucking jobs (or loads), chat with other users, read news about the trucking industry, place and answer classified ads, and so forth.

Another example of an industry portal is USAutoNews.com (Figure 9-7). Viewers at this Web site can access automotive industry information including current news articles, automotive industry stock quotes, and employment opportunities in the automotive industry.

Figure 9-6
TruckNet

Figure 9-7
USAutoNews.com

Often, an e-business Web site combines industry information along with information specific to that e-business. This combination approach is designed to increase the e-business's total viewing audience and enhance the e-business's profile within its particular industry. Some analysts also consider these Web sites to be industry portals. Providing industry-specific content at a Web site can be a very effective way of marketing an e-business within its own industry. To see how hosting an industry portal might be an effective way to market an e-business within its own industry, let's compare the Web sites for two competing energy industry firms: the Halliburton Company and Schlumberger Ltd.

The Halliburton Web site (Figure 9-8) is a destination Web site where viewers can find information about Halliburton and its services. However, the Schlumberger Web site (Figure 9-9) contains much more than just information about Schlumberger. Schlumberger's Web site content includes news articles about the oil and gas industry, other energy-related industries, and other technology industries in which Schlumberger is involved. Additionally, the content includes energy industry stock market information, a tool for viewing stock quotes, and a feature that tracks the number of drilling rigs in various locations around the world, a key energy industry market indicator. Energy industry viewers — vendors, customers, and employees of energy-related companies — can use the Schlumberger Web site as a starting point each day to keep up to date with current industry news and events. Meanwhile energy industry-oriented viewers can't help learning about Schlumberger and its products and services — clearly Schlumberger's plan!

Figure 9-8
Halliburton
Company

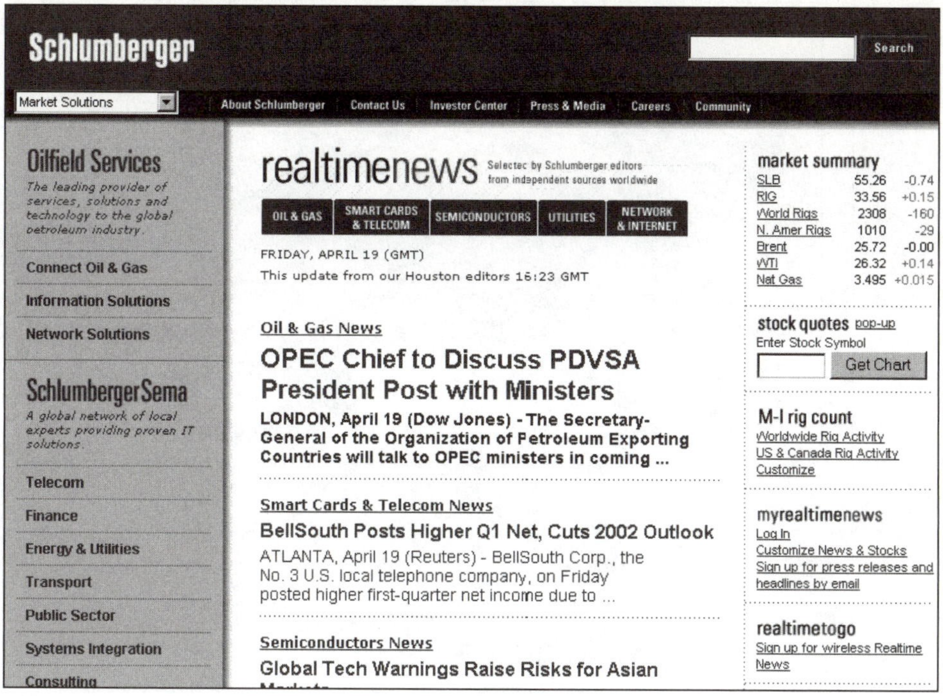

Figure 9-9
Schlumberger Ltd.

Corporate Portals

Corporate portals, also called **enterprise information portals (EIP)**, are internal Web sites used by employees, vendors, customers, and other business partners to access proprietary business information and conduct business transactions. In Chapter 8, you learned about ERP, SCM, and CRM systems. A corporate portal is a single browser-based interface used by employees, vendors, customers, and other business partners to access all the underlying applications and databases that are part of an e-business's ERP, SCM, and CRM systems as well as other internal systems and applications. In other words, a corporate portal makes it possible to access all these resources via the same browser interface, in lieu of requiring separate interfaces for each. Figure 9-10 illustrates a corporate portal.

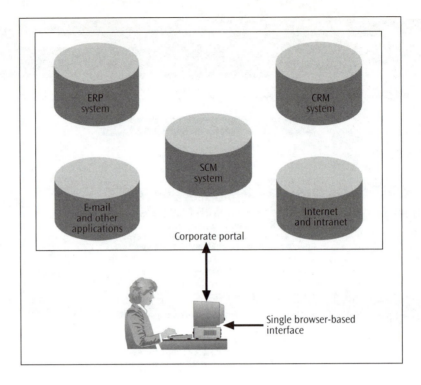

Figure 9-10
Corporate
portal

The content of a corporate portal is defined by the user's needs, and varies from one user to another. The content presented to an employee might provide access to information about benefits or other human resources-oriented information as well as access to specific applications and databases related to the employee's job. For example, an employee in the accounts receivable area of an Accounting Department could track customer invoices and payments as well as update his or her own health insurance information via the corporate portal. Meanwhile, corporate portal content for customers and vendors might provide access to product, service, order, shipment, invoice, and payment information tailored specifically to their needs.

Portal software offered by such vendors as Plumtree Software, Inc. (Figure 9-11), SAP AG, PeopleSoft, Inc., and Epicentric, Inc. provides the integration technologies necessary to build a portal by pulling together the varying data, applications, and services that users access. Additionally, portal software provides the personalization technologies needed to assure that users — employees, vendors, customers, business partners, and others — have access to the appropriate portal content.

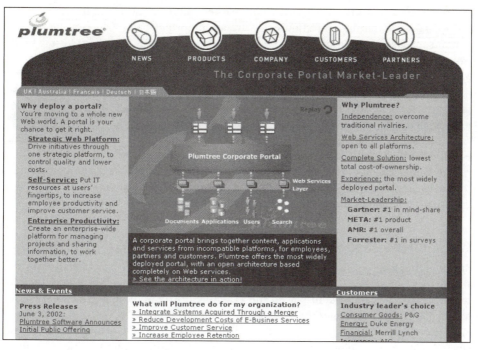

Figure 9-11
Plumtree
Software, Inc.

In this section, you learned about different types of portals and how they are used by e-businesses. Next, you learn how e-businesses can better manage the dynamic Web content at portals and other complex Web sites.

Web Content Management

Content management involves organizing and classifying information from many different sources. These information sources can include printed documents, e-mails, and electronic files containing text, pictures, audio, video, and so forth. After the information is organized and classified it is then stored in a common location, from which it can easily be retrieved, reused when necessary, and published in a variety of different formats for multiple users. When users access content via a Web browser, content management is often referred to as **Web content management** and this terminology is used for the remainder of this chapter.

> **TIP**
>
> As you learn about Web content management, you may realize that a new set of terminologies or industry jargon has evolved to explain Web content management issues. It may be difficult to separate the jargon from the issues at times; but just remember, Web content management is all about getting the right information to the right user in the most effective way.

Technologies such as those that you learned about in earlier chapters — SGML, XML, databases, and data warehouses — are an important part of an e-business's Web content management. Other Web content management technologies are also available from vendors such as Documentum, Inc., Interwoven, Inc., Vignette Corporation, and Microsoft Corporation. However, Web content management is about much more than just technology; effective Web content management involves the careful analysis of user information needs, identification of information resources, and a comprehensive planning process designed to coordinate these resources and needs.

Web content management is an important factor in the overall management of an e-business's Web site. Well-executed Web content management ensures that a site's content is accurate, timely, comprehensive, well organized, easy to locate, and personalized to meet each user's needs. Take a look at an example that illustrates how the lack of effective Web content management can create problems for an e-business.

Web Content Management Example

Suppose that Joan purchases a new mountain bike online for her son's birthday present. It's the day before her son's birthday party and Joan is beginning to assemble the bike when she realizes she has misplaced the assembly instructions. Joan isn't worried; she simply logs on to her computer, launches her Web browser, and accesses the e-business Web site where she purchased the bike. However, Joan begins to worry after spending several minutes searching the Web site and following confusing and misdirected links. Finally, Joan locates the assembly instructions and downloads and prints them — only to realize that the instructions are mislabeled. The instructions labeled for this year's bike model are actually for last year's model.

Frustrated (and running out of time) Joan calls the toll free, customer service number listed at the Web site and receives a recorded message explaining that the phone number has changed. When she finally gets through to a customer service representative she is told that the representative does not have access to the database containing the new assembly instructions, but someone will get back with her in two days. By now Joan is furious and the e-business has likely lost a valuable customer.

How could Web content management have avoided this situation? By managing its Web content effectively, the e-business could have ensured the assembly instructions for its bikes were easy to find at its Web site; the assembly instructions posted at the site were accurately labeled for each specific bike model; the customer service phone number listed at the site was up to date; and the customer service representative had access to the database containing the new assembly instructions.

Web Content Management System

A **Web content management system** includes the people, policies, procedures, processes, and technologies used to manage an e-business's Web content. How can an e-business determine if it needs to implement a system to manage its Web content?

Generally, when an e-business meets one or more of the following criteria, implementing a content management system should be considered:

- A large e-business has multiple Web sites covering different business lines; for example, General Electric maintains separate Web sites for its appliances and financial services business lines.
- Web page content comes from multiple sources such as advertising agencies, freelance writers, and multiple authors within the e-business.
- Multiple approvals are required before Web page content is published; for example, the legal, marketing, product development, shipping, fulfillment, and manufacturing managers may all need to approve an e-business's online product catalog.
- The Web site contains content that needs to be continuously updated or frequently revised, such as adding new products or changing prices, maintaining current news headlines, stock quotes, and so forth.
- The Web site content needs to be personalized for each viewer; examples of personalized content include made-to-order cosmetic products or sports scores for specific teams.
- Legal liability issues affect the published content; for example, when issues related to marketing to a restricted audience or publishing scientific or legal content creates a requirement that the content may need to be reconstructed at any point in time.

As explained in the next three sections, employee knowledge and expertise, digital document inventories, and special Web content lie at the heart of an e-business's Web content management system.

Knowledge Base

An e-business's **knowledge base** consists of everything the e-business "knows" — information found in paper and electronic documents as well as its employees' knowledge about the business, their work experiences, and their technical expertise. Managing its knowledge base is an integral part of an e-business's Web content management system and is called knowledge management (KM). In Chapter 5 you learned that KM encompasses organizing, analyzing, and sharing documents, resources, and employee skills.

> **TIP**
>
> A comprehensive discussion of Web content management including knowledge management, document management, and all the processes and systems that support them is beyond the scope of this book. For more information on these topics, see references located in the "For Further Review" section at the end of this chapter.

Translating its employees' knowledge and expertise into information available to the users who need it is a tremendous challenge for any e-business. For example, assume that an e-business's sales manager has been "on board" since the inception of the e-business several years earlier. An important part of the e-business's knowledge base is the years of operational experience and the vast amount of information about vendors and customers the sales manager has accumulated during his tenure. Undoubtedly, the e-business would suffer some business loss if the sales manager suddenly left or retired and his knowledge and expertise were no longer available.

To avoid this type of business loss, more and more e-businesses are implementing a knowledge management system. A **knowledge management system** includes the employees (called knowledge workers), the processes, the procedures, the policies, and the technologies that enable employees to transform their knowledge and expertise into electronic documents.

In order to avoid an overload of data in a KM system, employee knowledge must first be analyzed so that business-critical knowledge is separated from that which is noncritical; only the critical knowledge should be translated into electronic documents. The KM system then specifies a standard method by which employees create these electronic documents. For example, a KM system might require that all documents be created using XML. The electronic documents are then stored in a database that can be accessed by different applications and operating systems. AskMe Corporation (Figure 9-12), IBM, and OpenAir, Inc. are among the many vendors that offer knowledge management technologies.

Figure 9-12
AskMe
Corporation

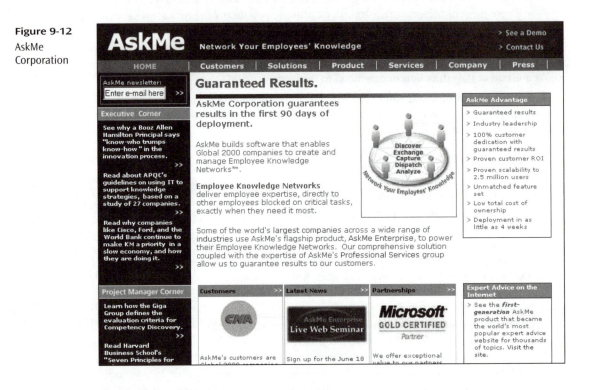

Document Inventory

Web content management systems have their roots in the systems used to categorize, track, and file paper documents. Such systems, which now bear the fancy title "manual document management systems" consisted simply of rows of filing cabinets. Each cabinet contained manila folders labeled with color-coded labels identifying the folder's contents. These days, most modern document management systems consist of databases containing electronic documents.

In Chapter 4, you learned how databases can be used to keep track of discrete bits of information, such as part numbers or product prices. However, modern databases can also easily store complete documents or files. In fact, the ability of modern databases to maintain relationships between electronic documents makes them ideal for storing an e-business's electronic document inventory.

Special Web Content Elements

A Web content management system includes special Web content elements that are also stored in databases:

- *Templates*: The Web page models you learned about in Chapter 4
- *Style sheets*: Worksheets that control the appearance of Web pages including colors, text fonts, and so forth
- *Graphics files*: Images that might be generic to all Web pages such as an e-business's logo as well as specific images that appear on Web pages such as pictures of people, products, or maps
- *Imported data*: Data provided by third-party sources, such as news or weather information

Figure 9-13 illustrates a Web content management system.

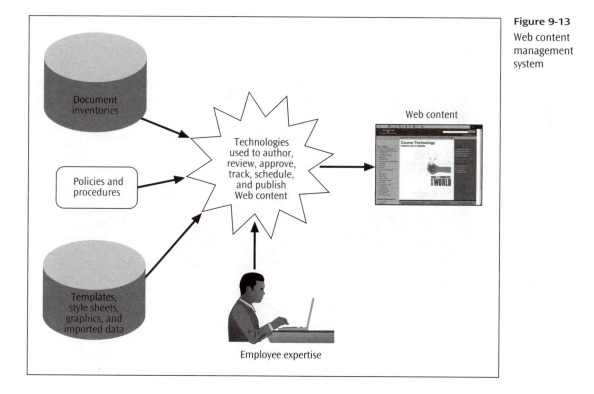

Figure 9-13
Web content management system

You have learned that electronic documents and other Web content elements are stored in databases. In a Web content management system, those databases are called content repositories.

Content Repository

A **content repository** is a database in which electronic documents and other Web content are stored. A content repository may also contain pointers to files stored on a file server. There are several advantages to using a content repository:

♦ Web content, stored in a common location, can easily be accessed and, when necessary, reused in a variety of ways.

♦ A standardized "look and feel" is easily maintained for Web pages when the content, templates, and style sheets are stored in a content repository.

♦ Content can be created, modified, and updated from any location, but approval of the content and its scheduled publication to a Web site can be controlled. For example, news reports can be entered into a content repository from reporters anywhere in the world, but the flow of those news reports to a Web site can be tightly scheduled and controlled.

Figure 9-14 illustrates a content repository.

Figure 9-14
Content repository

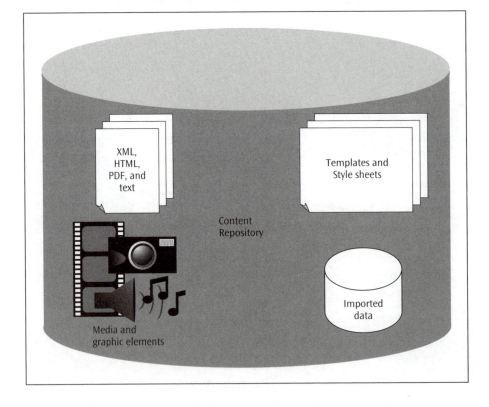

To understand how a Web content management system could generate a Web page from elements stored in content repositories, let's take a look at the British Broadcasting Corporation (BBCi) home page (Figure 9-15). A Web page such as this could be constructed by drawing individual content elements such as text or graphics or groups of related content elements (called **content modules**) from content repositories and then inserting these elements into a Web page template to present personalized content while achieving a standardized look and feel.

TIP

Branding is the consistent presentation of a unique set of factors that differentiates an e-business from its competitors. Web content management systems allow an e-business to control when and how branding components (such as company logo graphics) appear at its Web site.

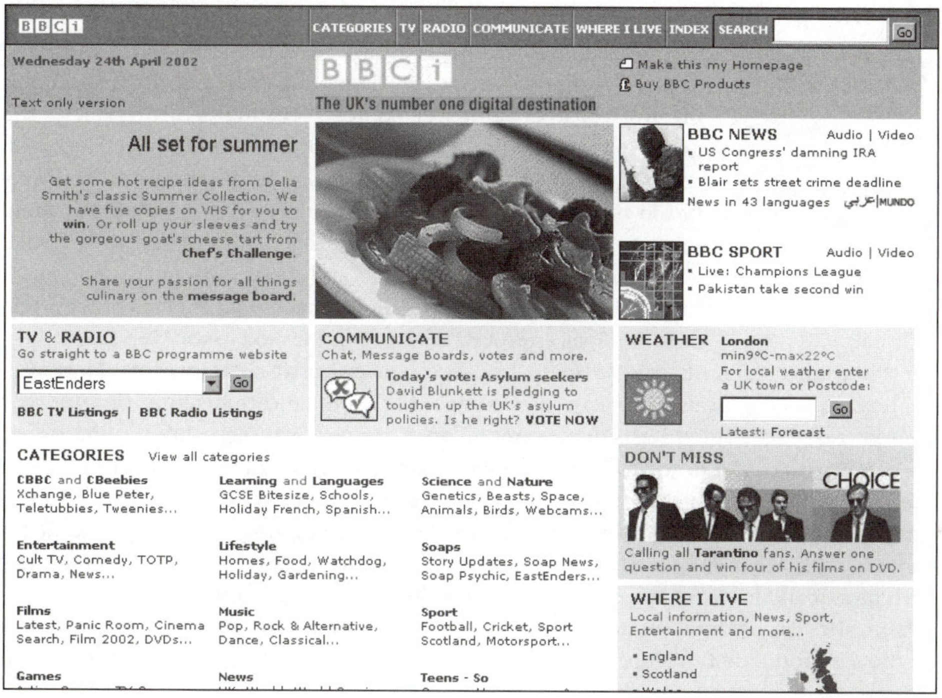

Figure 9-15
BBCi

BBCi's logo and marketing slogan — "The UK's number one digital destination" — are significantly displayed on the page and are both items that can be stored separately in a content repository and then added to a Web page as specified by the Web page template. On the remainder of the page, the content is highly modular, consisting of content modules that can easily be replaced by more current or personalized content. For example, the "All Set for Summer" content module could easily be replaced by a content module containing a sports program schedule or other personalized content.

TIP

Another type of Web content stored in content repositories is banner ads. These ads can be stored in databases that track how often the ads are displayed and also coordinates the ads with personalization information from a CRM system in order to target the ads to viewers with specific interests.

Certain areas of the Web page are populated (filled with content drawn from a content repository) according to the time of day a viewer downloads the page. Likewise, each time a viewer downloads the page, a Web content management system could query a CRM system's personalization information to determine where the viewer lives so that locality-specific weather information stored in a content repository can be displayed. The BBCi Web page Categories section helps to direct viewers to specific categories of content. This categorized content is also stored in a content repository so that it can be easily accessed, updated, and published.

In-house content authors work together with editors and approvers to create most of the content stored in content repositories.

Content Collaboration and Distribution

Content collaboration is a term used to describe the workflow process — the authoring, reviewing, approving, storing, and tracking involved in creating Web content. Creating standard policies and procedures for author, editor, and approver workflow collaboration can help an e-business to better manage its Web content. For example, in the collaboration process multiple versions of Web content might be created. A Web content management system can save each version of the new Web content and then track each version as it moves through the Web content management process ensuring that only the final, approved version is published to the Web site.

Publishing content to a Web site is also called **content distribution**. Most Web content management systems can also control the automatic publishing of approved content on a scheduled basis; for example, an e-business can schedule an important press release about a new product or about a management change to appear at its Web site at just the right time. High-end Web content management systems can also automatically adapt content for different devices; for example, adapting the same content for viewers with a handheld wireless device and for viewers using a personal computer with broadband Internet access. Automatically distributing updated and new content to a Web site can reduce an e-business's Web site administration costs and improve employee productivity. Figure 9-16 illustrates the content collaboration and distribution process.

Content Not Developed In-House

Some Web content is not developed by in-house authors, but is instead purchased from vendors. For example, one type of content especially popular at portals is current news. E-businesses such as YellowBrix's iSyndicate (Figure 9-17) and Interest! Alert Inc. sell or syndicate news and other types of content to other e-businesses. Including current news works well as an addition to a portal for several reasons. Current news gives a portal a fresh feel, and attracts viewers looking for the most recent news updates. As you learned in the earlier Schlumberger Ltd. example, filtered news — news articles chosen as specific to an industry or other readership — is attractive to many viewers who do not have time to filter news for themselves.

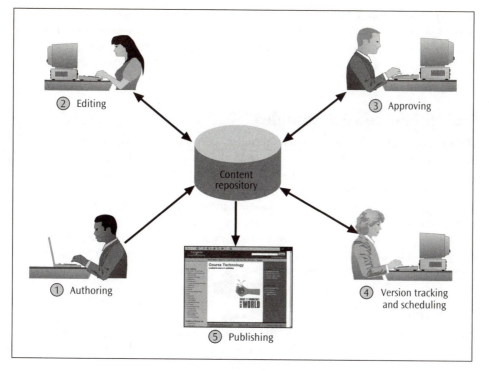

Figure 9-16

Content collaboration and distribution

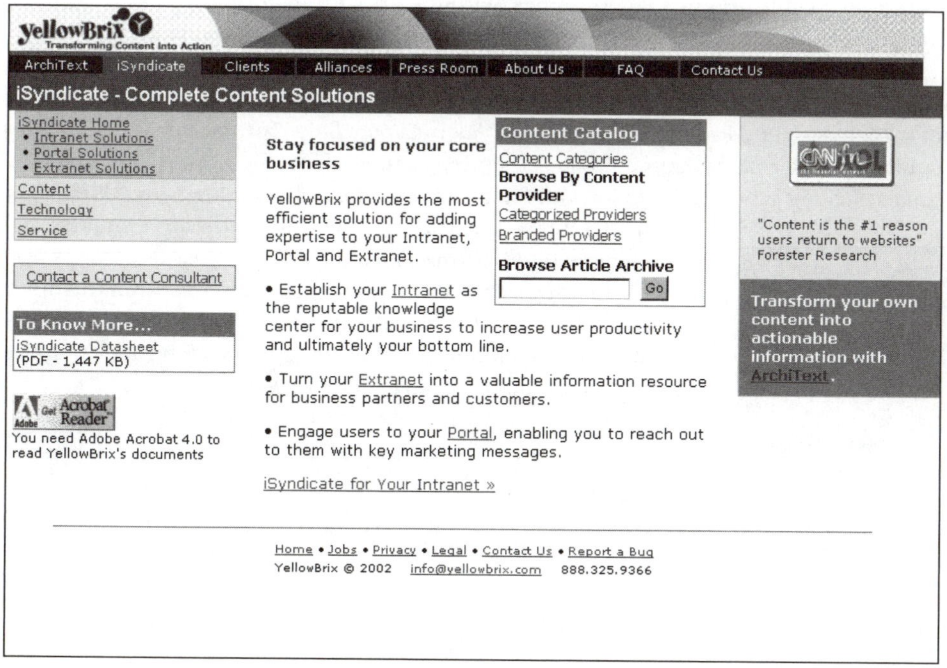

① Authoring

② Editing

③ Approving

④ Version tracking and scheduling

⑤ Publishing

Content repository

Figure 9-17

iSyndicate

So far you've learned how e-businesses can use portals and Web content management systems to ensure that appropriate and timely Web content is presented to specific viewers. In the next section, you learn how e-businesses can use search engine technologies, HTML meta tags, and other techniques to help drive viewers to their Web sites.

Search Engine Technologies

The Internet and the World Wide Web have brought with them a crush of information. Directories and search engines are the search tools that help Web viewers sort through this crush to find specific information. You have undoubtedly already used directories and search engines when looking for information on the Web. Consumers often use search engines and directories when looking for e-businesses that offer specific products and services; therefore, anyone responsible for an e-business Web site must have a basic understanding of directories and search engines in order to maximize his or her e-business's placement in search results lists. In the next two sections you learn more about how directories and search engines work.

Directories

A **directory** is a Web site that maintains an index of other Web sites and categorizes these other Web sites by subject. For example, a directory might first categorize all the entertainment-related Web sites in its index into a broad general category such as Entertainment. Additionally, each entertainment Web site might belong to a subcategory such as Movies or Television or Video Games. Within each subcategory, a Web site might be further categorized by type of movie, or television show, or game, and so forth.

A directory's Web pages contain links to each of its Web site categories and subcategories. For example, when a viewer clicks the Entertainment category link, he or she may then see the Movies, Television, and Video Games links. To find links to Web sites containing information about Movies, the viewer then clicks the Movies link and continues clicking subcategory links until finally finding links to individual movie Web sites.

In Chapter 4 you learned how internal search engines can help viewers find information at a Web site. Most directories also provide an internal search engine that is used to search the directory's own index. Yahoo! is arguably the most famous and widely used directory search tool. Other directory search tool examples include Galaxy and LookSmart (Figure 9-18).

> **TIP**
>
> A directory might also provide review comments and ratings for the Web sites in its index.

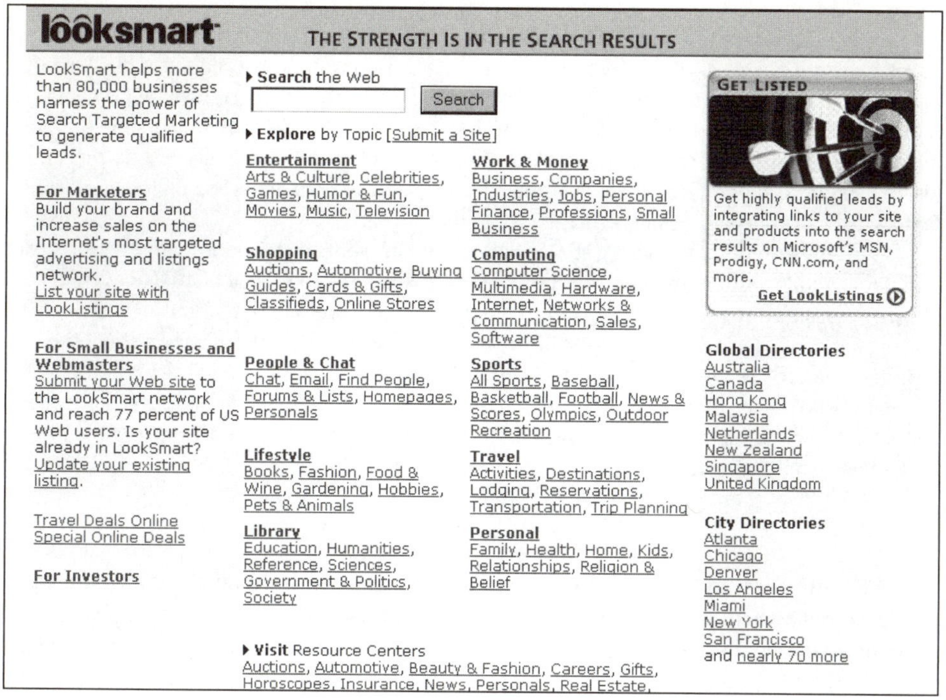

Figure 9-18
LookSmart

TECH CASE   Yet Another Hierarchical Officious Oracle

Jerry Yang, a native of Taiwan raised in San Jose, California, took his undergraduate and graduate degrees at Stanford University. David Filo, a Louisiana native, graduated from Tulane University and Stanford University. In early 1994, Yang and Filo were both still at Stanford working on their doctorates in electrical engineering and were both getting a little bored with their doctoral programs.

These were the early days of the Internet and both Filo and Yang found themselves spending increasingly more time looking for new and interesting information on the Internet using the Mosaic browser. (You learned about the Mosaic browser in Chapter 1.) The Mosaic browser had a feature called a "hotlist" which was a list of links to previously viewed items. Each time Filo and Yang found something interesting that they wanted to view again, they added the link to the Mosaic "hotlist." It wasn't long before their "hotlists" — which could only be read sequentially — had so many links that they were no longer useful.

To solve this problem, Filo and Yang wrote Perl scripts that allowed them to reorganize their "hotlists" into a hierarchical list categorized by subject. This hierarchical method of categorizing the list made working with it much easier. At first the categorized list was only available to Filo and Yang on their Stanford computers. Then they made the list, which they renamed Jerry's Guide to the World Wide Web, available to other Internet users. At first not many users were aware of Jerry's Guide; however, word of mouth about Jerry's Guide began to grow as more and more Internet users became aware of it.

Continued

By June 1994, when Filo and Yang began allowing others to submit links, Jerry's Guide was developing into something much more significant than a list of Yang's and Filo's personal Web site favorites. By the fall of 1994, Jerry's Guide had been renamed Yahoo! (an acronym for "yet another hierarchical officious oracle") and the Yahoo! Web site was getting more than one million user hits a day. Realizing the significance of their Web site list, Filo and Yang became business partners in March 1995 by incorporating Yahoo! By April, 1995 they had secured almost $2 million in startup financing for their new e-business and the rest, as they say, is history!

As of this writing, the Yahoo! Web site has evolved into one of the world's largest and most popular general consumer portals. Additionally, Yahoo! Inc. sells a variety of e-business services to other e-businesses, including customized enterprise portal software and e-business storefront hosting and management services. One of the most successful early e-businesses, Yahoo! Inc. reported sales of $717.4 million and net income of $92.8 million for the fiscal year ending December 2001. And cofounders Filo and Yang? As of this writing both Filo and Yang, known as Yahoo! Inc.'s "chief Yahoos," remain involved: Filo as chief technologist and Yang as a member of the board of directors.

Web sites are added to a directory's index when an individual or an e-business requests that a particular Web site be added. By contrast, a search engine is a search tool that automatically updates its index.

Search Engines

A **search engine** is a Web site that maintains a searchable index of keywords found in Web pages. Search engine indexes are updated automatically by software called spiders (or robots). Spiders follow links between Web pages throughout the entire Web, adding any previously unindexed Web pages to the search engine's index. An individual or e-business can also submit its Web site information to many search engines. This ensures that a Web site is added to a search engine's index more quickly than if the Web site's administrator simply waited for the search engine's spider to locate and index the site. Some of the most popular search engines include AltaVista, HotBot, Northern Light, and Google. Most online consumers are familiar with popular search engines such as Google and AltaVista. For example, a consumer trying to purchase and send flowers online might visit the Google or AltaVista Web site and type in a search keyword such as "florists." The AltaVista or Google search engine would then return a list of links to Web pages containing the "florists" keyword.

TIP

As you might imagine, searching a huge index for Web pages requires a great deal of computing power. Think back to the Google Tech Case presented in Chapter 6 and reflect on the thousands of computers Google uses to store its index and allow searches across it.

Because of the ever increasing number of Web pages on any given subject, the people who manage search engines must struggle with the question of how to prioritize the list of Web pages (often called a list of hits) returned by each search process. For example, as of this writing, searching the Web for "florists" via the AltaVista search engine returns a list of more than 241,000 Web pages that might be relevant. Obviously a search results list of this size is impossible to review completely;

therefore, the Web pages listed in the search results list must be placed in some order of priority for the list to be useful.

Early search engine technology prioritized the items in a search results list according to the number of times each search keyword appeared on a Web page. In this scenario, the more times the search keyword is found on a Web page, the higher that Web page appears in the search results list. However, Web authors quickly learned to exploit this method by "spamming" search engines — repeating search keywords such as "florists" hundreds of times in hidden text within a Web page in order to move the page closer to the top of a search results list. This "spamming" created search results lists with Web pages containing the most repeated keywords at or near the top of the list instead of the most useful and relevant Web pages.

Today, search engines use a combination of factors to rank Web pages in a search results list. For example, Google uses a proprietary ranking system called PageRank, which considers how many other Web pages are linked to each Web page in the search results list. Each linked Web page is considered a "vote," and more votes means a Web page is likely to be a more useful page. But each vote isn't equal — a linked Web page that itself is linked to many other Web pages has a more important vote. Therefore, to appear near the top in a Google search results list, a Web page must not only have many Web pages linking to it, but these linking Web pages must themselves have many Web pages linking to them. Google's proprietary PageRank technology returns a search list of Web pages that most viewers find extremely useful, thus separating Google from the rest of the search engine pack.

TIP

One site that is especially useful for anyone creating or managing a Web site, or for someone who wants a better understanding of how search engines and directories work, is Search Engine Watch.

TECH CASE **Stop Me If You've Heard This One**

Did you hear the one about the two graduate students at Stanford University who developed one of the most widely used Internet search tools....and then became fabulously rich and.....but wait! This story isn't about Jerry Yang and David Filo of Yahoo! fame as you might expect. No, this story is about two *other* Stanford graduate students, Sergey Brin and Larry Page, and *their* award-winning and wildly popular (and profitable) search tool — Google.

Originally from Moscow, Sergey Brin attended the University of Maryland at College Park where he received a B. S. in Mathematics and Computer Science. Brin left Maryland for Stanford University where he completed his Master of Science degree and began working on his Ph.D. While Brin was toiling at the University of Maryland, Larry Page was earning his undergraduate degree in engineering from the University of Michigan. Page also went on to Stanford for his master's degree in computer science where he met Brin in 1995. By 1996, Brin and Page, who shared an interest in the Web and in data mining, were collaborating on a research project. At that time, they developed a new proprietary search engine technology that could analyze the "back links" — links from other pages — to a Web page. As it turns out, these "back links" are a very good predictor of the relevance of a Web page to a particular set of keywords. The more "back links" a Web page has, the more relevant the Web page is to the search keywords — and the more useful the Web page is likely to be to the user. Brin and Page called their new search engine technology BackRub and soon word of mouth began to spread around the Stanford campus about the usefulness of the BackRub search engine.

Continued

By September 1998, Brin and Page, with the encouragement of Yahoo! cofounder David Filo and seed money from Andy Bechtolsheim, one of the founders of Sun Microsystems, Inc., started Google, Inc. The Google Web site (a play on the term 'googol' which is the number 1 followed by 100 zeros) featured Brin and Page's proprietary search engine technology called PageRank. Google's PageRank technology was so effective in creating search lists with relevant Web pages that by December 1998, Google had made it to the list of the top 100 Web sites and search engines. By February 1999, Google was responding to more than 500,000 search queries each day.

Within the next three years, the Google Web site became the 15th most-visited Web site in the U.S. As of this writing, Google is the top search engine on the Web with more than 120 million search queries each day in 26 languages. Google, Inc. boasts a staff of more than 250 employees, at least 50 of which are Ph.D.s focusing on improving search engine technologies.

Because of the huge number of possibly relevant Web pages in most search results lists, most viewers only pay attention to the first 10-15 Web pages in a search results list, assuming that these are likely to be the most relevant pages. This means e-businesses need some way to ensure that their Web pages are listed at or near the top of any search list. In response to this need, some e-businesses such as Overture Services, Inc. (Figure 9-19) offer search engines that combine traditionally prioritized search results with those generated by "pay for placement" services.

An e-business can pay Overture to place its Web page at or near the top of an Overture search results list. Generally, the more an e-business pays, the higher its Web page will appear in the search results list. A **click through** occurs when a viewer clicks a link at one Web page to download another Web page. With a pay-for-placement service, the e-business pays a certain amount each time a viewer clicks through from the search results list to the e-business's Web site.

For example, Figure 9-19 illustrates the results of a search at the Overture Web site using the keyword "florists." In the resulting search list, Usaflower.com is shown first because it bid $3.13 for a click through. In other words, Usaflower.com pays Overture $3.13 each time a viewer clicks through from the Overture site to the Usaflower.com site. The second highest bidder, Coast to Coast Flowers, is only willing to pay $3.12 per click through.

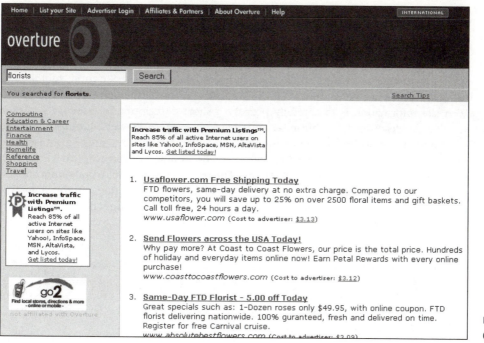

Figure 9-19

Overture

Online florists that choose not to "pay for placement" at Overture may find their Web page links positioned far down the search results list — well below the point a typical viewer stops reading. For example, as of this writing, Florists.com which did not bid on placement, is in the 99th position in the search results list. FindWhat.com, Google AdWords, and Espotting are other examples of search engines offering pay-for-placement services.

In this section, you learned about directories and search engines, how they create their indexes, and how some search engines prioritize search results lists. Next, you learn how an e-business can exploit search engine technologies to help build an audience for its Web site.

Using Search Tools to Build a Web Site Audience

An e-business can exploit directory and search engine technologies to help drive customers to its Web site. As you have learned, e-businesses can submit their Web site information to directories. Additionally, most search engines combine a submission system with an automated system to build their indexes. E-businesses make these submissions using forms accessed at the search tool's Web site. Generally, the first step in submitting Web site information is to carefully prepare a short description of effectively chosen words that describe the e-business and that can capture viewers' interest. Next, an e-business usually submits a set of approximately 25 primary keywords or phrases that potential viewers might enter when using a search engine or directory to locate Web sites similar to the e-business's Web site. These keywords should not duplicate the description, but complement it. Figure 9-20 illustrates the description and the keywords that might be submitted to various search tools by a B2C e-business that sells specialty foods that are hard to find.

Figure 9-20

Sample description and keywords

Description:
Famous restaurant specialties and regional delicacies. Local food and hard to find food. Food you never forget!

Keywords:
specialty food, regional food, comfort food, local flavors, great food, hometown favorite, home style cooking, food from home, Texas, Louisiana, BBQ, regional gourmet, online food store

Instead of submitting its own Web site information to a list of search engines and directories, an e-business can instead hire a submission service to submit this information. Search engine submission services such as Add URL, SubmissionPro, or EZ-Submit.Net (Figure 9-21) provide a single place for an e-business to complete and submit the necessary forms to all of the major search engines as well as some lesser known search engines and directories.

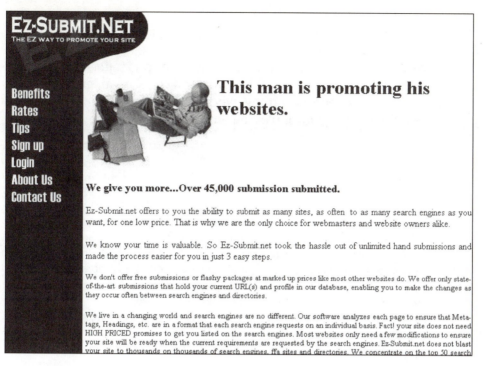

Search engines use multiple methods to get their indexing information from a Web page, including the Web page's HTML meta tags, the Web page's text content, and the Web page's descriptive titles. In Chapter 4 you learned about HTML code or tags. **Meta tags** are small segments of HTML code that are read by search engines. Meta tags are found between the <head> and </head> HTML tags on a Web page and use the following format:

<META NAME="description" CONTENT="*Description goes here.*">

<META NAME="keywords" CONTENT="Keywords go here, separated by commas.">

Figure 9-22 illustrates an example of meta tag keywords that might be used by a B2B e-business selling products and services to the energy industry.

In addition to using meta tags, it is equally important that each Web page at a Web site have a descriptive title. This descriptive title appears on the title bar of a browser when the Web page is being viewed. Not only do some search engines use this descriptive title for indexing purposes, some search engines display this title in their list of returned search results to more clearly identify the Web page.

> **TIP**
>
> You can view a Web page's HTML tags (including its meta tags) in a Web browser. For example, if you open a Web page in Internet Explorer and click the Source command on the View menu, the source HTML code opens in the Notepad application window.

Figure 9-22
Meta tag
example

```
<meta name="keywords" content="energy, resource,
trading, exchange, crude, oil, crude oil, refined, products,
refined products, gas, electricity, power, buyer, seller, bid,
offer, hit, lift, market, liquid, buy/sell, swap, spread, global,
commodities, energy trading, wholesale, online trading,
real time, energy resources, e-commerce">
```

It is a good idea for an e-business to periodically review search engine results using the e-business's keyword or meta tag list to make certain its Web pages are being properly listed by search engines. Also, monitoring search engine results can provide other useful information regarding the existence of a new competitor or a sudden improvement in a competitor's Web page rankings. When a competitor's Web pages appear higher in a search results list, it is then a good idea to review the competitor's Web site, including its meta tags, to see if any useful conclusions can be made about why the competitor's pages rank higher for any specific set of keywords.

In this section, you learned how an e-business can use search engine technologies to help get its Web site noticed. In the next section you learn about setting measurable goals for Web site performance and some of the technologies used to measure actual results against those goals.

Measuring Web Site Performance

Comparing actual financial results to a company's business plan is essential when attempting to measure the performance of any business. When measuring an e-business's performance, though, it's perhaps equally important to measure the effectiveness of the e-business's Web site. However, for many e-businesses, measuring Web site effectiveness or performance is more difficult than measuring traditional financial results. For example, the benefits that adhere to an e-business from investments in Web content management and other Internet technologies are sometimes nebulous. Nevertheless, measuring a Web site's performance is very important. Success or failure for many e-businesses is determined by the e-business's ability to learn from experience and make necessary changes. Therefore, the most important reason for an e-business to measure its Web site performance is to learn how to improve it. An e-business can use benchmarks and Web metrics to evaluate Web site performance.

Benchmarks

A **benchmark** is a performance-based objective. Part of measuring a Web site's performance includes setting benchmarks and then measuring the Web site's actual performance against those benchmarks. This process enables an e-business to make better business decisions for its current operations and for its long-term business strategies. Typical benchmarks for a Web site's performance might include the number of visitors to the Web site or the number of user actions taken at the Web site, such as placing orders or submitting registrations. The process for setting and evaluating benchmarks includes:

- Determining individual Web site operating goals
- Setting benchmarks
- Comparing actual results against these benchmarks
- Drawing reasonable conclusions about these comparisons

For example, a typical Web site has multiple operating goals. Assume one Web site goal is to increase sales; the e-business should then set benchmarks for increases in sales attributable to online ordering. Assume that another Web site goal is to reduce operating expenses; the e-business should then set benchmarks that reflect changes in operating expenses over time, both in total expense dollars and as a percentage of sales. Benchmarks such as these examples may be developed from the actual performance of similar e-businesses, from industry averages, or from historical performance.

Once a set of benchmarks is determined, the e-business must then compare its Web site's actual results to the benchmarks to determine if the Web site performed as well as, better than, or worse than the benchmarks. Whether or not the Web site meets its benchmarks, it's most important that the e-business's management reaches meaningful conclusions about why the benchmarks were met, exceeded, or not met at all.

During the goal-setting process, it is possible for an e-business to establish Web site goals that are unobtainable or that are too easily achieved. Therefore, it may even be necessary to reevaluate the original Web site goals and benchmarks to determine if they were reasonable. By going through this goal setting, benchmarking, and comparing process, an e-business can better evaluate the performance of its Web site. Armed with better information, an e-business can then do a better job of setting future Web site goals and establishing benchmarks upon which to measure those goals.

A number of measurements are used to evaluate Web site performance. These measurements are called Web metrics.

Web Metrics

Because any e-business requires a large investment in resources (people, money, time, technology, and so forth), some return on those invested resources is naturally expected. Traditional calculations that determine a return on investment (called **ROI**) are applied to an e-business's financial data and measure an e-business's profitability. However, an e-business must also be concerned with its Web site ROI, which is much more difficult to calculate and which may not immediately translate into profits. For example, Web site investments that increase customer satisfaction may not be immediately measurable in profits; however, in the long run, increased customer satisfaction should lead to increased revenues and increased profits.

No single performance measure can define Web site ROI. In the early days of e-business, the most important measure of Web site ROI was a hit. A hit is a recorded event in a Web site's server log for each element of a Web page downloaded to a viewer's browser. A hit actually bears no relationship to the number of pages viewed or visits to a site. For example, when a viewer downloads a Web page containing three graphics, the Web server records four hits: one for the Web page and one for each of the three graphics.

Today, several **Web metrics** (such as pages viewed, the number of Web site visitors, the ratio of actual orders to Web site visitors, and so forth) are used instead of hits to measure Web site ROI. In general, Web metrics are divided into simple metrics (also called basic metrics), and more complicated metrics (called advanced metrics). A Web site's server log files are often the source of basic Web metrics, such as the date and time certain Web pages were accessed at the Web site. Advanced metrics require the combination of several basic measurements. An example of such an advanced metric is the number of unique visitors. (You learn about unique visitors later in this chapter.) While the needs of an individual e-business determine the level of Web metrics it wants to use, all e-businesses should, at a minimum, exploit log file analyses to evaluate Web site ROI.

Log File Analysis

Web servers record everything they do or respond to (that is, all events) in the form of special files called log files. For example, every time a browser asks a Web server for a Web page or an image, or submits a form, the event is recorded in the Web server log file. In addition to the event, other information such as date, time, the IP address of the computer making the request, and browser type may also be recorded. These log file entries offer an e-business a bounty of useful information. Figure 9-23 illustrates a section of a sample log file for a cache server. The log file shows requests for pages, pictures, and supplementary files over an eight-second period.

Figure 9-23
Cache server log file example

IP Address	Date and Time	Request
168.159.1.88 - -	[20/Feb/2003:17:30:54 -0500]	"GET / HTTP/1.0" 304 0
168.159.1.88 - -	[20/Feb/2003:17:30:54 -0500]	"GET /robots.txt HTTP/1.0" 404 148
168.159.1.88 - -	[20/Feb/2003:17:30:54 -0500]	"GET /favicon.ico HTTP/1.0" 304 0
168.159.1.88 - -	[20/Feb/2003:17:30:54 -0500]	"GET /default.css HTTP/1.0" 304 0
168.159.1.88 - -	[20/Feb/2003:17:30:55 -0500]	"GET /images/TopLogo-1.gif HTTP/1.0" 304 0
168.159.1.88 - -	[20/Feb/2003:17:30:55 -0500]	"GET /index9d28.html HTTP/1.0" 304 0
168.159.1.88 - -	[20/Feb/2003:17:30:55 -0500]	"GET /indexadda.html HTTP/1.0" 304 0
168.159.1.88 - -	[20/Feb/2003:17:30:55 -0500]	"GET /images/TopLogo-19.gif HTTP/1.0" 200 9248
168.159.1.88 - -	[20/Feb/2003:17:30:55 -0500]	"GET /indexe63d.html HTTP/1.0" 304 0
168.159.1.88 - -	[20/Feb/2003:17:30:56 -0500]	"GET /images/TopLogo-12.gif HTTP/1.0" 304 0
168.159.1.88 - -	[20/Feb/2003:17:30:56 -0500]	"GET /indexad2d.html HTTP/1.0" 304 0
168.159.1.88 - -	[20/Feb/2003:17:30:56 -0500]	"GET /images/TopLogo-14.gif HTTP/1.0" 200 9272
168.159.1.88 - -	[20/Feb/2003:17:30:57 -0500]	"GET /index5f70.html HTTP/1.0" 304 0
168.159.1.88 - -	[20/Feb/2003:17:30:57 -0500]	"GET /images/TopLogo-10.gif HTTP/1.0" 304 0
168.159.1.88 - -	[20/Feb/2003:17:30:57 -0500]	"GET /index3a07.html HTTP/1.0" 304 0
168.159.1.88 - -	[20/Feb/2003:17:30:57 -0500]	"GET /index7e96.html HTTP/1.0" 304 0
168.159.1.88 - -	[20/Feb/2003:17:30:57 -0500]	"GET /index0ef8.html HTTP/1.0" 304 0
168.159.1.88 - -	[20/Feb/2003:17:30:58 -0500]	"GET /images/Heartbeat-Blue.jpg HTTP/1.0" 304 0
168.159.1.88 - -	[20/Feb/2003:17:30:58 -0500]	"GET /images/bar_support.gif HTTP/1.0" 304 0
168.159.1.88 - -	[20/Feb/2003:17:30:58 -0500]	"GET /images/LeftBar.jpg HTTP/1.0" 304 0
168.159.1.88 - -	[20/Feb/2003:17:30:58 -0500]	"GET /indexb0d1.html HTTP/1.0" 304 0
168.159.1.88 - -	[20/Feb/2003:17:31:01 -0500]	"GET /images/Line.jpg HTTP/1.0" 304 0
168.159.1.88 - -	[20/Feb/2003:17:31:02 -0500]	"GET /index38b8.html HTTP/1.0" 304 0
168.159.1.88 - -	[20/Feb/2003:17:31:02 -0500]	"GET /index701e.html HTTP/1.0" 304 0
168.159.1.88 - -	[20/Feb/2003:17:31:02 -0500]	"GET /images/VertLine.jpg HTTP/1.0" 304 0

Each line in the log file in Figure 9-23 represents a request for one picture or HTML page. Reading left to right, the first column contains the IP address of the requesting computer. You can see that all requests made during this particular eight seconds were made by the same computer. The second column contains the date and time the request was made. IP addresses can be tracked over time to show how long a specific user viewed specific Web pages and the path the user took through the Web site. The "-500" at the end of the date/time field is the difference from Greenwich Mean Time. It's useful for site administrators to know this if they need to correlate traffic on multiple servers around the world.

The column on the far right contains the request itself. After the "GET" instruction, the specific page or picture being requested is listed; notice that both image files and HTML files are being requested. As you learned in Chapter 3, Web browsers request the HTML file first, then parses it to determine which image files need to be retrieved from the Web server to complete the page.

After the filename, you see "HTTP/1.0," signifying that the request was made using the HTTP1.0 protocol. Finally, each request is followed by a result code indicating how the server responded to the request. "304," the most common request in this log file example, means "Not Modified." As you learned in Chapter 6, a cache server checks with an origin server to verify whether or not the Web page item it has cached is current. The 304 code means the page is current and does not need to be modified. There are a number of common result log file codes with which you may want to be familiar. Table 9-1, presented here for general information, lists the other common result codes found in server logs:

Code	Description	Explanation
200	OK	Normal result; information transmitted to the browser
206	Partial content	Partial result transmitted to browser (some browsers request only partial content if the browser already has part of the file being requested, in case of a partially completed file download, for example)
301	Moved permanently	Browser is told to look elsewhere for this file
302	Found	Browsers sometimes ask "Is the file there" instead of "Send me the file"
304	Not modified	Browser asks if stored copy is still current, or has the content been modified since the stored copy was made
400	Bad request	Request syntax unacceptable — return address might be bad, or request doesn't conform to HTTP syntax
401/403	Unauthorized/ Forbidden	User doesn't have permission to access the requested resource
404	Not found	Requested information doesn't exist on server
500	Internal server error	Covers a wide array of problems — server busy, server can't access storage, and so forth

Table 9-1
Server log result codes

In order to do a more sophisticated and advanced analysis of Web site performance, an e-business can use special log analysis software.

Log Analysis Software

A number of vendors offer software products designed to combine information from server log files with customer databases and other sources to provide information on Web site performance. For example, e-businesses such as WebTrends (part of NetIQ) and DeepMetrix Corporation sell log analysis software that pulls the data from the server log files and customer databases and reports it in a format that is easy to understand. Other e-businesses such as WebSideStory, Inc. provide log analysis on an outsourced basis.

Log analysis software enables an e-business to analyze server logs to calculate other measurements of Web site ROI. The following list describes examples of useful Web site ROI information an e-business can develop from its server logs by using log analysis software:

- *Visitors*: Indicates the actual number of viewers to the Web site. A count of actual visitors is more meaningful than the number of hits.
- *Page views*: Indicates the number of times a specified Web page has been viewed. Page views can be reviewed to determine exactly what content people are (or are not) viewing at a Web site.
- *Page views per visitor*: Measures how many pages viewers look at each time they visit a Web site. Page views per visitor is calculated by dividing the number of page views by the number of visitors. A large number means that the Web site content is "sticky"; in other words, visitors are looking at more pages and spending more time at the Web site.
- *IP addresses*: Determine a viewer's origin by identifying which countries and networks its Web site visitors are coming from.
- *Referring URLs*: Indicates how visitors get to a Web site - whether they type the URL directly into a Web browser or whether they click a link at another Web site to get to the e-business's Web site. If the referring URL is a search engine, the keywords that the visitor used to find the Web site can often be determined.
- *Browser type*: Indicates the type of Internet browser a visitor is using. An e-business can check this information to make certain that its Web site can be viewed properly by the browser that is most common among its visitors. Nonstandard browsers (such as WebTV) could present viewing problems for the viewers who use them because these browsers may not support all of the components that are supported by the two major browsers, Microsoft Internet Explorer and Netscape Navigator.

- ◆ *Conversion rate*: Indicates which viewers are taking some action at a Web site. For example, by dividing the number of orders by the number of visitors, a conversion rate related to sales can be determined. This sales conversion rate is an important measure of how well an e-business's Web site content converts shoppers into buyers.
- ◆ *Errors*: Indicates errors recorded by a log server. An example of an error a visitor might encounter is the "404 - File Not Found" error. An e-business can analyze these and other error messages to discover broken links or other problems at its Web site.

Figure 9-24 illustrates a server log analysis created by WebTrends software charting the number of visitors per day (the columns on the far right represent future days, for which there is not yet any data). Figure 9-25 shows an analysis of which individual pages were requested over time. Using this type of analysis, an e-business can learn about viewer preferences and can tailor the Web site's content to match those preferences.

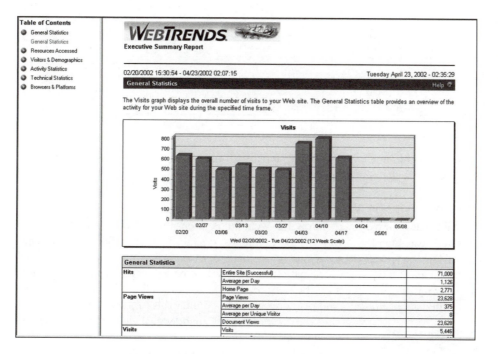

Figure 9-24
Server log analysis — number of visitors

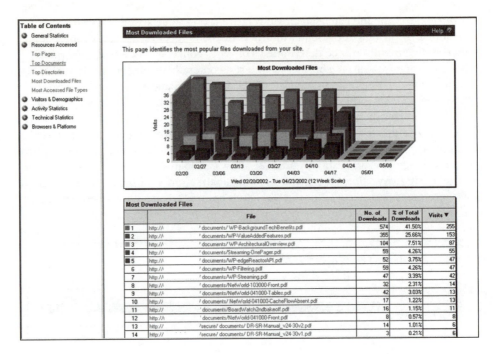

Most Downloaded Files   Help

This page identifies the most popular files downloaded from your site.

Most Downloaded Files

		File	No. of Downloads	% of Total Downloads	Visits ▼
■	1	http://^ ' documents/ WP-BackgroundTechBenefits.pdf	574	41.50%	255
■	2	http://^ ' documents/WP-ValueAddedFeatures.pdf	355	25.66%	153
■	3	http://^ ' documents/ WP-ArchitecturalOverview.pdf	104	7.51%	87
■	4	http://^ ' documents/Streaming-OnePager.pdf	59	4.26%	55
■	5	http://^ ' documents/WP-edgeReactorAPI.pdf	52	3.75%	47
	6	http://^ ' documents/WP-Filtering.pdf	59	4.26%	47
	7	http://^ ' documents/WP-Streaming.pdf	47	3.39%	42
	8	http://^ ' documents/NetWorld-103000-Front.pdf	32	2.31%	14
	9	http://^ ' documents-041000-Tables.pdf	42	3.03%	13
	10	http:// ' documents/ NetWorld-041000-CacheFlowAbsent.pdf	17	1.22%	13
	11	http:// ' documents/BoardWatch2ndbakeoff.pdf	16	1.15%	11
	12	http:// ' documents/NetWorld-041000-Front.pdf	8	0.57%	8
	13	http:// /secure/ documents/ DR-SR-Manual_v24-30v2.pdf	14	1.01%	6
	14	http:// /secure/ documents/ DR-SR-Manual_v24-30v1.pdf	3	0.21%	6

Figure 9-25

Server log analysis — requested pages

It is possible not only to identify what Web page a viewer is accessing, but also to determine how the viewer moved through a Web site.

Tracking Web Site Viewers

The path that a viewer takes through a Web site is often referred to as a **click trail**. An e-business can identify a viewer's click trail by organizing information on the pages accessed from a specific IP address in sequential order. One problem with analyzing a click trail is that an IP address may originate from a firewall or proxy server that corresponds to the many individual viewers on the network behind the firewall or server. (In Chapter 7 you learned about firewalls and proxy servers.) To counter this problem, many e-business Web sites use cookies to track an individual viewer as he or she travels through their Web sites.

A **cookie** is a message passed to a Web browser by a Web server and then stored on the viewer's hard drive as a text file. The cookie's text is available to the originating Web server each time the Web browser requests a Web page from it. Even if multiple viewers access the same site through the same proxy server, each viewer has a unique cookie on his or her hard drive, which enables the Web server to identify each viewer as unique. Using cookies helps an e-business determine the correct number of unique viewers.

TIP

In addition to tracking viewers, cookies are used by e-businesses in a number of ways. For example, an e-business might use a cookie to enable a viewer to more easily log on to a password-protected Web site or to provide customized Web site content for the viewer. However, using cookies remains controversial in light of increasing concerns about viewer privacy.

Viewer tracking software can determine if a visitor is returning or is visiting the site for the first time. This software can track visitors as they click through a Web site. This software can also identify how the visitor got to the site, whether by clicking a banner ad, following a link from another site, responding to a special offer in an e-mail, or keying in a unique URL. The software then

TIP

As you learned in Chapter 4, a sticky Web site is one where viewers spend more of their viewing time.

identifies a visitor when he or she returns to visit the Web site. In addition to tracking a visitor through an individual session, it is also important to track the frequency with which the visitor returns to the site. This frequency is also a measure of a Web site's "stickiness."

It is also important to identify the last page a viewer looks at before exiting the site. This information may tell an e-business whether or not visitors are finding the information they expect to find at the Web site or whether they are getting frustrated and leaving the site before finding useful information. For example, if a large number of visitors exit a Web site after looking at a particular page, an e-business may need to determine if visitors found all of the information they needed on that page or if there is a problem with the page that discourages visitors and prompts them to go elsewhere.

Another important piece of visitor data an e-business should examine is the search keywords viewers use to search within the Web site. In Chapter 4, you learned that many e-businesses provide search forms at their Web sites allowing visitors to perform a keyword search for products and information. Analyzing visitors' keywords provides valuable information about visitors' interests at the Web site. For example, perhaps many visitors are looking for information or products that are not available at the site; however, if enough visitors are searching for the same information or products, an e-business may want to add those products or that information to its Web site.

Another way to measure Web site performance is with Web site visitor traffic reports.

Web Site Traffic Tracking and Auditing Services

Some vendors offer services that track the visitors at an e-business's Web site and prepare reports analyzing that visitor traffic. Many e-businesses have the capability of generating their own visitor traffic reports; however, it may be necessary at times to have an independent third-party audit and validate these visitor traffic reports. For example, if an e-business sells advertising, its advertisers often want an audit of visitor traffic data by an independent third party in order to verify that the expected number of viewers are seeing their ads. Another example is when an e-business's investors want to see an audit of the e-business's Web site traffic. Whether the e-business is privately funded or is a public company, investors still want to know that the e-business is reporting accurate visitor data. E-businesses such as WebAudits LLC (Figure 9-26) and ABC Interactive independently audit visitor traffic reports by analyzing an e-business's Web server log files to determine the number of unique visitors.

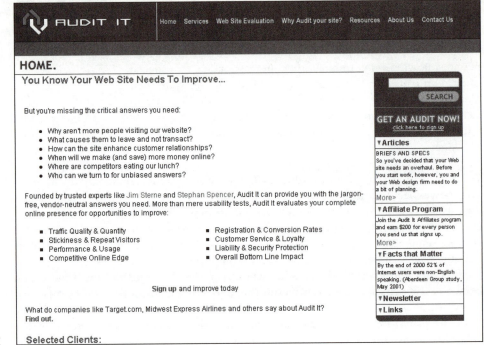

Figure 9-26
WebAudits LLC

While objective measures of Web site performance are essential, it is also important to remember that no single measurement or metric can satisfy every e-business. Also, Web metrics continue to evolve from the original idea of Web site hits to various methods of calculating Web site ROI. One challenge for an e-business is to sort through the mountains of data and then decide what Web site metrics are appropriate for its particular situation. Another challenge, of course, is for an e-business to use those Web site metrics to evaluate its Web site's performance and then to implement appropriate changes.

In this chapter you learned about different types of portals, methods for managing Web site content, and ways to use search engine technologies to help build a Web site's audience. You also learned about the importance of measuring Web site performance against objective goals and about some of the Web metrics used in those measurements. In the next chapter you learn how certain e-businesses have been successful in combining Internet technologies and business precepts and about some e-businesses that have not been successful in doing so. Additionally, you learn about new and emerging technologies and their potential affect on the future of e-business.

In the fall of 2000, WGBH contracted with a consulting firm to plan and install a Web content management system that would help WGBH staffers and other content authors to more efficiently add and update content at the Web site. The Web content management system WGBH installed provides content authors with easy-to-use customized forms for entering new content or revising existing content. Templates control the appearance of the Web site while pulling data and pictures from a common content repository. For example, a WGBH content author can use a form or wizard in conjunction with a template to pull data, images, online discussions, and poll results stored in the common content repository into an article to be published as Web site content. As the drafted article passes from the author through the editing process, workflow features in the Web site content management system allow tracking of each version of the article. When the final draft of the article is approved, the article is then automatically published to the Web site according to a predetermined release date.

The new Web content management system also provides for personalization by allowing audience members to create a personal profile indicating particular topics and programs of interest. When an audience member logs on, a list of relevant programming notes, articles, and other information based on the member's profile is presented. Finally, the Web content management system allows radio and television schedule administrators to establish scheduling rules such as "every Thursday from 9:00-10:00 P.M." Radio and television programming schedules are then automatically filled in based on these rules.

The implementation of a Web content management system that provides easy-to-use input forms, a common content repository, templates that provide a consistent appearance, and workflow processes to track items in the content repository enable WGBH (Figure 9-27) to present far more timely and original content with far less effort than would be expended without such a system.

Figure 9-27
WGBH
Boston

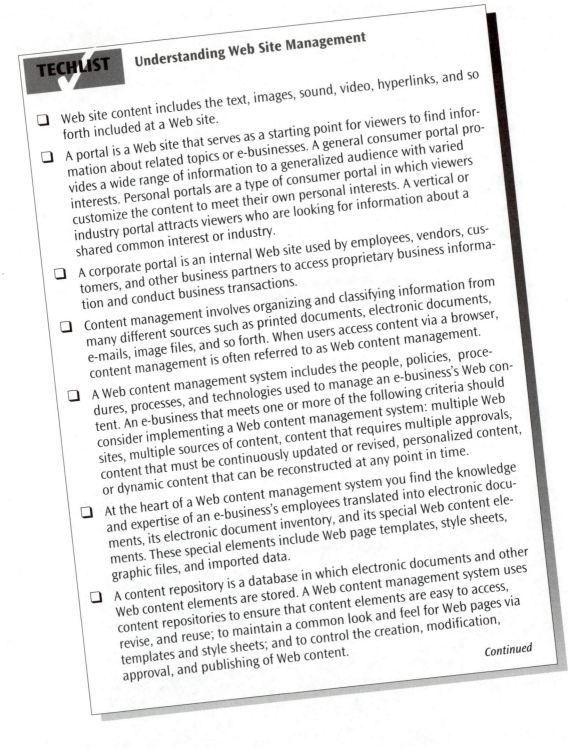

TECHLIST — Understanding Web Site Management

❏ Web site content includes the text, images, sound, video, hyperlinks, and so forth included at a Web site.

❏ A portal is a Web site that serves as a starting point for viewers to find information about related topics or e-businesses. A general consumer portal provides a wide range of information to a generalized audience with varied interests. Personal portals are a type of consumer portal in which viewers customize the content to meet their own personal interests. A vertical or industry portal attracts viewers who are looking for information about a shared common interest or industry.

❏ A corporate portal is an internal Web site used by employees, vendors, customers, and other business partners to access proprietary business information and conduct business transactions.

❏ Content management involves organizing and classifying information from many different sources such as printed documents, electronic documents, e-mails, image files, and so forth. When users access content via a browser, content management is often referred to as Web content management.

❏ A Web content management system includes the people, policies, procedures, processes, and technologies used to manage an e-business's Web content. An e-business that meets one or more of the following criteria should consider implementing a Web content management system: multiple Web sites, multiple sources of content, content that requires multiple approvals, content that must be continuously updated or revised, personalized content, or dynamic content that can be reconstructed at any point in time.

❏ At the heart of a Web content management system you find the knowledge and expertise of an e-business's employees translated into electronic documents, its electronic document inventory, and its special Web content elements. These special elements include Web page templates, style sheets, graphic files, and imported data.

❏ A content repository is a database in which electronic documents and other Web content elements are stored. A Web content management system uses content repositories to ensure that content elements are easy to access, revise, and reuse; to maintain a common look and feel for Web pages via templates and style sheets; and to control the creation, modification, approval, and publishing of Web content.

Continued

❑ A directory is a Web site that offers a search tool based on an index of Web sites created from manually submitted information. A search engine is a Web page search tool that is updated automatically by software called spiders (or robots). Today, most popular search engines use a combination of manual submissions and spiders to update their indexes. Many popular search tools such as Yahoo! and AltaVista have also evolved into general consumer portals.

❑ A major problem with search results lists relates to how the items in the lists are ordered. Early search engines ordered their search results based on the number of times the search keyword appeared in a Web page. Some search engines provide a pay-for-placement service which allows e-businesses to pay to have their Web pages listed at or near the top of a search results list. Most search engines use a combination of methods to order a search results list in a most relevant to least relevant order.

❑ An e-business can request that its name, business description, URL, and other information be added to a search tool's index. Other techniques for maximizing Web site placement in a search engine's search results list include using HTML meta tags to add keywords to a Web page.

❑ An e-business should identify appropriate measurements for its Web site return on investment (ROI). One way to begin is by setting Web site performance benchmarks and then comparing actual results to those benchmarks. Web server log files combined with log file analysis software and Web site traffic auditing can help an e-business identify specific measures of Web site performance, such as the number of unique visitors, which Web pages are being viewed and for how long, and a viewer's click trail.

Key Terms

benchmark
click through
click trail
content
content collaboration
content distribution
content management
content modules
content repository
cookie

corporate portal
directory
enterprise information portal (EIP)
general consumer portal
horizontal portal
industry portal
knowledge base
knowledge management system
meta tags

personal portal
portal
publishing portal
ROI
search engine
vertical portal
Web content management
Web content management system
Web metrics

Review Questions

1. Which of the following items is not an important consideration for managing an e-business Web site?
   a. Presenting timely and useful content
   b. Controlling the "who, what, when, and where" of Web content publishing
   c. Measuring a Web site's performance against expectations
   d. All are important considerations.

2. A portal is a(n):
   a. Method of measuring Web site ROI.
   b. Set of unique factors that differentiates an e-business.
   c. Guide to positioning Web page content.
   d. Web site that serves as a starting point rather than a final destination.

3. General consumer portals are also called:
   a. Vertical portals.
   b. Horizontal portals.
   c. Publishing portals.
   d. Corporate portals.

4. A benchmark is a(n):
   a. Web traffic auditing tool.
   b. Performance-based objective.
   c. Element of a Web content management system.
   d. A new search tool.

5. Which of the following is not a component of content collaboration?
   a. Indexing
   b. Authoring
   c. Editing
   d. Approving

6. A content repository is a(n):
   a. Method of publishing Web content.
   b. List of Web pages known to a directory or search engine.
   c. Central source for Web content.
   d. Method of calculating unique Web site visitors.

7. Which of the following items is not found in a content repository?
   a. Web page templates and style sheets
   b. Text, PDF, HTML, XML, and other types of electronic documents
   c. Paper documents generated from an ERP system
   d. Data provided by third-party sources such as news or weather data

8. Which of the following Web sites is an industry portal?
   a. TruckNet
   b. CNN
   c. Halliburton
   d. Yahoo!

9. Web site ROI measurements are also called:
   a. Traffic auditing.
   b. Web metrics.
   c. Log analysis.
   d. Branding.

10. HTML tags used by search engines to index a Web page are called:
    a. XML tags.
    b. Body tags.
    c. Image tags.
    d. Meta tags.

11. Corporate portals provide a single browser-based interface to an e-business's back-end applications and databases. **True or False?**

12. A KM system is used by an e-business to translate its employees' knowledge, experience, and expertise into electronic documents. **True or False?**

13. Some search engines also use a Web page's descriptive title when indexing the page. **True or False?**

14. Web sites with a few static Web pages are perfect candidates for a Web content management system. **True or False?**

15. A content module is a group of related content elements stored in a content repository. **True or False?**

16. Publishing Web content to a Web page is also called content collaboration. **True or False?**

17. Search engines use programs called spiders to link from Web page to Web page while building and updating their index. **True or False?**

18. News, weather, and other content items popular at portal sites can be purchased from vendors instead of being created by in-house authors. **True or False?**

19. Popular search engines include Yahoo!, Galaxy, and LookSmart. **True or False?**

20. The content presented at a corporate portal is personalized to meet the needs of employees, vendors, customers, and other users. **True or False?**

Exercises

1. Using Internet search tools or other relevant resources, such as those at the end of this chapter, research topics on measuring a Web site's performance. Then write a one- or two-page paper describing ways an e-business can evaluate the performance of its Web site.

2. Using Internet search tools or other relevant resources, such as those at the end of this chapter, locate five portals. Then create a one- or two-page paper describing each portal and identifying its portal type based on its audience.

3. Define and illustrate by example the following terms: directory, search engine, and Web metrics.

4. Using Internet search tools and other relevant resources, such as those at the end of this chapter, research log analysis software or service vendors. Then create a list containing at least five vendors including name, URL, and a brief description of their products and services.

5. Using Internet search tools and other relevant resources, such as those at the end of this chapter, locate and review several articles on Web content management systems. Then write a one- or two-page paper describing Web content management and its importance in managing an e-business's Web site.

CASE PROJECTS

◆ 1 ◆

You and your friend Larry are operating an e-business named HotShots that sells photography equipment and supplies online to professional photographers. You need to increase your Web site's audience, so you decide to submit information about your site to a number of Web directories and search engines. Create a brief description and the keywords that best identify your e-business. Then research the submission requirements for two directories and two search engines. Create a one- or two-page paper that describes the directories and search engines and their submission requirements.

◆ 2 ◆

You have been asked to discuss the term "cookie" during a short (15 minute) presentation at the next meeting of the E-Business Managers Group. Using the Internet and other relevant resources, research the term "cookie." Then create an outline for your presentation that defines cookie, explains how cookies are used by e-businesses, describes the security implications for cookies, and discusses the controversy surrounding cookies and viewer privacy.

◆ 3 ◆

You own an e-business named AsiaArts that sells jewelry and crafts imported from the Far East. You realize that you need to drive more traffic to your B2C e-business in order to increase sales, so you are considering participating in a pay-for-placement service. First, identify five keywords for which you want pay for placement, and then using the Overture search tool (or other search tool that offers a pay-for-placement service) determine how much you would have to bid per click through in order to have your Web site placed at the top of the list. Note that each keyword you select may require a different bid value. Then create a list of your keywords and bid values.

TEAM PROJECT

You are the assistant to the president of a growing B2B e-business. The president is concerned about an increasing number of employee complaints surrounding the amount of time it takes to create and publish content to your Web site and the escalating number of customer complaints about errors and inconsistencies at your Web site. He asks you to create a committee to investigate the problems and find some solutions. Select two classmates to be on your committee. Working together as a committee, create a business profile for your company (you may assume any facts not presented here). Then evaluate how a Web content management system could solve your workflow and content problems.

Working with your committee, use Microsoft PowerPoint or other presentation software to prepare a 5–10 slide presentation that defines your e-business, lists the current workflow and content problems, and explains how implementing a Web content management system could solve those problems.

Useful Links

bPubs.com — Knowledge Management
www.bpubs.com/Management_Science/
    Knowledge_Management/

ClickZ Today
www.clickz.com/

Content Management Systems
www.Webgenz.com/cms-resources.html

CookieCentral.com
www.cookiecentral.com/

Cookies FAQ
www.azc.com/htmls/faqs/cookies.html

EContent Magazine
www.ecmag.net/

e-Doc Magazine — Enterprise Content Management Resources
www.edocmagazine.com/

ITPapers.com — Portal White Papers
www.itpapers.com/cgi/SubcatIT.pl?scid=189

KM World — Best Practices in Enterprise Portals
www.kmworld.com/publications/whitepapers/
    portals/default.htm

Line 56 Magazine
www.line56.com/

MagPortal.com — Magazine Article Search
www.magportal.com/

Portals Community
www.portalscommunity.com/default.htm.

Search Engine Guide
www.searchengineguide.com/

Search Engine Showdown
notess.com/search/

Search Engine Watch
www.searchenginewatch.com/

SearchEngines.com
www.searchengines.com/

The Conference Board — E-Commerce
www.conference-board.org/expertise/ecom.cfm

The Spider's Apprentice
www.monash.com/spidap3.html

Traffick — The Guide to Portals and Search Engines
www.traffick.com/default.asp

Links to Web Sites or Companies Noted in This Chapter

ABC Interactive
www.abcinteractiveaudits.com/index.html

Add URL
www.1-add-url.com/

AltaVista
www.altavista.com

AskMe Corporation
www.askmecorp.com/default.asp

BMW of North America, LLC
www.bmwusa.com/

British Broadcasting Corporation
www.bbc.co.uk/

City of New York
www.nyc.gov

Coast to Coast Flowers
www.coasttocoastflowers.com/

Deepmetrix Corporation
www.deepmetrix.com/index.asp

Documentum, Inc.
www.documentum.com/

Epicentric, Inc.
www.epicentric.com/

Espotting
www.espotting.com

EZ-Submit.net
www.ez-submit.net/

FindWhat.com
www.findwhat.com

flowerwhisper.com
www.flowerwhisper.com

Galaxy
www.galaxy.com/

Google, Inc.
www.google.com

Halliburton Company
www.halliburton.com/index.jsp

HotBot
www.hotbot.com

IBM
www.ibm.com

InterestAlert Inc.
www.interestalert.com

Interwoven, Inc.
www.interwoven.com/

iSyndicate
www.yellowbrix.com/pages/www/index.nsp?
    id=isyndicate

LookSmart
www.looksmart.com/

Microsoft Corporation
www.microsoft.com

My Excite
www.excite.com/

My Yahoo!
my.yahoo.com/

NetIQ
www.Webtrends.com/

Northern Light
www.northernlight.com

NYC.gov
home.nyc.gov/portal/index.jsp?pageID=nyc_home

OpenAir, Inc.
www.openair.com/home/

Overture Services, Inc.
www.overture.com/

PeopleSoft, Inc.
www.peoplesoft.com

Plumtree Software, Inc.
www.plumtree.com/

SAP AG
www.sap.com

Schlumberger Ltd.
www.schlumberger.com/

Search Engine Watch
www.searchenginewatch.com/

SubmissionPro
www.submission-pro.com/

TruckNet
www.trucknet.com

USAutoNews.com
www.usautonews.com

Vignette Corporation
www.vignette.com

WebAudits LLC
www.auditit.com/?source=goto

WebSideStory, Inc.
www.Websidestory.com/

WGBH Boston
www.wgbh.org

Yahoo!
www.yahoo.com

For Additional Review

Alexander, Steve. 2000. "e-Metrics," *Computerworld*, December 11. Available online at: www. computerworld.com/managementtopics/ ebusiness/story/0,10801,54915,00.html.

ArsDigita. 2001. "WGBH.org Case Study." www. arsdigita.com/customers/casetudies/wgbh.html.

Baker Robbins & Company. 2001. "Bringing a Portal to Life: A Twelve Step Program for Law Firm Success," *Managing Partner Magazine*, June. Available online at: www.brco.com/downloads/articles/ a_AN_Portal.pdf.

Bitta, Michael Della. 2001. "Cookie Rejections Way Down, Says Survey," *PC Magazine*, April 18. techupdate.zdnet.com/techupdate/stories/ main/0,14179,2709269,00.html.

Bount, Sumner. 2002. "The Problem With Portals," *eBizQ*. Available online at: b2b.ebizq.net/ e_commerce/blount_1.html.

Bruemmer, Paul J. 2002. "Defining Search Technology," *ClickZ Today*, January 30. Available online at: www.clickz.com/search/opt/article.php/964231.

Builder.com. 2002. "Looking at Web Portals." Available online at: builder.cnet.com/webbuilding/pages/Business/Portal/ss01.html.

Burgert, Philip. 2001. "Business Intelligence: Content Growth Challenges B2B Operations," *E-Commerce World Magazine*, March 1. Available online at: www.ecomworld.com/magazine/issues/article.cfm?ContentID=643.

Buxbaum, Peter A. 2001. "It's Difficult to Get a Clear View of Portal Concept," *SearchEBusiness*, November 5. Available online at: www.searchebusiness.com/originalContent/0,289142,sid19_gci779661,00.html.

CIO Magazine. 2001. "A Business Person's Guide to Enterprise Portal Terms and Business Impacts." Available online at: www.cio.com/sponsors/portalswhitepaper.pdf.

Collins, Heidi. 2001. *Corporate Portals: Revolutionizing Information Access to Increase Productivity and Drive the Bottom Line*. New York: AMACOM.

Copeland, Lee. 2001. "Users Extend Use of Web Portals to Supply Chain for Materials Procurement," *Computerworld*, June 11. Available online at: www.computerworld.com/softwaretopics/erp/story/0,10801,61276,00.html.

Cutler, Matt. 2001. "Understanding Online Behavior," *NewMedia*, July 17. Available online at: www.newmedia.com/nm-ie.asp?articleID=2841.

Cutler, Matt and Sterne, Jim. 2000. "E-Metrics: Business Metrics for the New Economy," *NetGenesis*. www.netgen.com/downloads/pdf/emetrics/e-metrics_business_metrics_for_the_new_economy.pdf.

Dreier, Troy. 2002. "Real World Intranets, Parts 1-7," *Intranet Journal*, May, 2001-March, 2002. Available online at: www.intranetjournal.com/.

Elgin, Ben et al. 2001. "Why They're Agog Over Google," *BusinessWeek*, September 24. Available online at: www.businessweek.com/magazine/content/01_39/b3750036.htm.

Erickson, Jim. 2001. "The Portal Comes of Age," *Line56*, November 29. Available online at: www.line56.com/articles/default.asp?ArticleID=3175.

Finkelstein, Clive. 2001. "The Enterprise: Enterprise Portal Success," *DM Review*, March. Available online at: www.dmreview.com/master.cfm?NavID=198&EdID=3083.

Forbes.com. 2000. "Google Searches for Business," May 2. Available online at: www.forbes.com/2000/05/02/feat.html.

Gaspar, Suzanne. 2001. "Content Management Tools Automate Web Page Production," *Network World*, February 19. Available online at: www.itworld.com/App/1041/NWW0219feat2/.

Google, Inc. 2002. "All About Google." Available online at: www.google.com.

Google, Inc. 2002. "Google Technology." Available online at: www.google.com/technology/.

Hackos, Joann T. 2002. *Content Management for Dynamic Web Delivery*. New York: John T. Wiley & Sons.

Hansell, Saul. 2002. "Google's Toughest search is for a Business Model," *The New York Times*, April 8. Available online at: www.nytimes.com/2002/04/08/technology/ebusiness/08GOOG.html?todaysheadlines.

Harbrecht, Douglas Ed. 2001. "Google's Larry Page: Good Ideas Still Get Funded," *BusinessWeek*, March 13. Available online at: www.businessweek.com/bwdaily/dnflash/mar2001/nf20010313_831.htm.

Holt, Mark and Sacoolas, Marc. 1995. "Chief Yahoos: David Filo and Jerry Yang," *Sun Microsystems*, May. Available online at: www.sun.com/950523/yahoostory.html.

Kontzer, Tony. 2001. "Curing the Content Migraine: Managing Content is Becoming a Gigantic Pain, But It Doesn't Have To Be That Way," *InformationWeek*, May 28. Available online at: www.informationweek.com/839/online_cm.htm.

Kontzer, Tony. 2002. "Vignette CEO Sees Growing Momentum for Content Management," *InformationWeek*, March 6. Available online at: www.informationweek.com/story/IWK20020306S0013.

Lee, Kevin. 2001. "What Search Engine Strategy?" *ChannelSeven/Ad-Insight*, June 8. Available online at: www.channelseven.com/adinsight/commentary/2001comm/comm20010608.shtml.

Lloyd-Martin, Heather. 2002. "Four Common SEO Writing Mistakes to Avoid," *RankWrite Roundtable*, January 24. Available online at: www.searchengineguide.com/rankwrite/2002/0124_rw1.html.

Marsan, Carolyn Duffy. 2000. "Web Site Performance Measurement Yields Results," *NetworkWorldFusion*, October 9. Available online at: www.nwfusion.com/archive/2000/108923_10-09-2000.html.

McCluskey-Moore, Nancy. 2002. "Untangling Web Content Management: Intranet, Extranet, and Otherwise," *Intranet Journal*. Available online at: www.intranetjournal.com/articles/200004/im_04_18_00a.html.

Meckler, Alan. 2001. "The Value of Unique Visitors," *ChannelSeven Ad/Insight*, June 1. Available online at: www.channelseven.com/adinsight/commentary/2001comm/comm20010601.shtml.

Moore, Andy. 2001. "Content, the Once and Future King," *KMWorld*, May. Available online at: www.kmworld.com/publications/whitepapers/ECM/moore.htm.

PriceWaterhouseCoopers and SAP AG. 2001. *The E-Business Workplace: Discovering the Power of Enterprise Portals*. New York: John Wiley and Sons, Inc.

Reddy, Ram. 2001. "One Quick Hit at a Time: Using Portal Technology Can Help You Extract Value From Your Supply Chain One Step at a Time," *Intelligent Enterprise*, November 12. Available online at: www.intelligententerprise.com/011112/417infosc1_1.shtml?ebusiness.

Robertson, James. 2002. "How to Evaluate a Content Management System," *Step Two Designs Pty Ltd*, January. Available online at: steptwo.com.au/papers/kmc_evaluate/.

Rutherford, Emelie. 2000. "Is This Any Way to Build an Intranet," *CIO Magazine*, April 1. Available online at: www.cio.com/archive/040100_intranet.html.

Ryan, Janet. 2001. "Drafting an E-Metrics List," *ClickZ Today*, March 26. Available online at: www.clickz.com/res/analyze_data/article.php/839321.

Schiffman, Betsy. 2001. "Eric Schmidt is Gaga Over Google," *Forbes.com*, August 6. Available online at: www.forbes.com/2001/08/06/0806google.html.

Shook, David. 2002. "Overture's Big Score," *BusinessWeek*, February 21. Available online at: www.businessweek.com/bwdaily/dnflash/feb2002/nf20020221_4802.htm.

Sullivan, Ben. 2001. "Content Management for the Masses," *Online Journalism Review*, June 28. Available online at: www.ojr.org/ojr/technology/1015018005.php.

Sullivan, Dan. 2001. "Five Principles of Intelligent Content Management," *Intelligent Enterprise*, August 31. Available online at: www.iemagazine.com/010831/413feat1_1.shtml.

Thumlert, Kurt. 2002. "Eye in the Sky E-Metrics: Creative Surveillance for Streamlined e-Business," *eCom Resource Center*. Available online at: www.ecomresourcecenter.com/ecom_connection/eye.html.

Time.com. 1998. "Jerry Yang of Yahoo!" Available online at: www.time.com/time/community/transcripts/chattr072398.html.

Weisman, Robyn. 2001. "In or Out: Navigating the Web Portal Maze," *ECommerceTimes*, February 12. Available online at: www.ecommercetimes.com/perl/story/7409.html.

Wesker, Mark. 2001. "Using a Portal to Solve Business Problems," *KMWorld*, July/August. Available online at: www.kmworld.com/publications/whitepapers/portals/wesker.pdf.

WGBH.org. 2002. "About WGBH." Available online at: main.wgbh.org/wgbh/about/gettoknow.html.

Whalen, Jill. 2002. "Is Search Engine Optimization a Dying Art," *RankWrite Roundtable*, February 15. Available online at: www.searchengineguide.com/rankwrite/2002/0215_rw1.html.

Winkler, Ramona. 2002. "Portals — The All-In-One Web Supersites: Features, Functions, Definitions, Taxonomy," *SAP Design Guild*. www.sapdesignguild.org/community/innovation_articles/edition3/portal_definition.asp.

Yahoo! Media Relations. 2002. "The History of Yahoo! — How It All Started…" Available online at: docs.yahoo.com/info/misc/history.html.

Yockelson, David. 2001. "ROI Can Be Found in Enterprise Portals," *InternetWeek*, October 2. Available online at: www.Internetweek.com/enterprise/enterprise100201.htm.

Zimmer, Mike. 2001. "Enterprise Content Management is a Key Success Factor for an e-Business Infrastructure," *KMWorld*, May. Available online at: http://www.kmworld.com/publications/whitepapers/ECM/zimmer.htm.

CHAPTER **10**

E-Business Past and E-Business Future

In this chapter, you will learn to:

Discuss the development of the technology bubble of the late 1990s

Describe the technology and other factors affecting the success or failure of several e-business models

List several emerging technologies

Identify future e-business trends

The Technology Bubble

In the previous nine chapters, you learned about the technologies that gave birth to the Internet, the World Wide Web, modern networking, and Internetworking technologies. You also learned about the current status and future promise of wireless technologies, Internet infrastructure providers, the technologies that enable e-businesses to support and manage attractive, interactive, and complex Web sites, and the technologies used to integrate these Web sites with e-business back-office operations. Along the way, you also learned about many of the individual e-businesses that provide these technologies and about other e-businesses that use them.

In this chapter, you learn about several early e-businesses that either succeeded or failed at exploiting these new technologies in the marketplace. You also learn about emerging technologies and how these new technologies may create innovative e-business opportunities. Finally, you learn about the trends that are most likely to influence the future of e-business.

Before you learn about individual e-business successes and failures, it is helpful to consider the speculative environment related to e-business startups in the late 1990s. **Speculative bubbles**, situations where overly exuberant optimism (and often pure greed) on the part of investors drives a market far beyond its sustainable performance, are nothing new. Consider the sixteenth century's frantic Tulipmania speculation in Dutch tulip bulbs; or the infamous South Sea Bubble of the 1720s when British investors clamored for shares of a speculative trading company doing business in Latin America; or the U.S. stock market crash of 1929, and so forth. Many future historians will undoubtedly add the dot.com bubble of the late 1990s to this list. The dot.com bubble, also called the Internet or **technology bubble**, refers to

TIP

For a very funny look at some of the worst excesses of the technology bubble and other unbelievable business "moments," check out "Boo! And the 100 Other Dumbest Moments in E-Business History" (dated May 2001) and "The 101 Dumbest Moments in Business" (dated April 2002) at the Business2.0 Web site.

investors' unbridled infatuation with the commercial possibilities of new Internet technologies and the resulting meteoric rise (and astounding fall) of many e-businesses in the so called "new economy" of the late 1990s and early 2000.

But what caused the technology bubble? There's plenty of blame to go around — predatory investment banks, gullible investors, greedy venture capitalists, and entrepreneurs looking to get rich quick. The problem was exacerbated by a collective wish on the part of investors, entrepreneurs, and others that every new e-business would be viable, that the value of e-business-related stocks would keep going up, and that consumers would quickly adopt Internet technologies and flock to the online marketplace. As with previous speculative bubbles, any initial investor nervousness was countered by a generalized overconfidence — this time in the ability of Internet technologies to drive the marketplace.

However, this marketplace overconfidence began eroding as many new e-businesses failed to attract the customer base needed to produce sufficient revenues to cover costs — much less generate profits. Many businesses, such as those in the telecommunications industry you learned about in Chapter 6, invested heavily in Internet technologies in anticipation of a huge demand for Internet-related equipment and services. When the demand didn't materialize, these businesses found themselves burdened with overly large sales staffs, more servers and IT equipment than necessary, and so forth. Therefore, many industries, especially telecommunications, consulting, and equipment manufacturing, faced a huge drop in demand as new sales slowed to a crawl.

The eroding investor confidence made it increasingly more difficult for new or existing e-businesses to find the additional investment dollars needed to keep operating and more failed — leading to a downward spiral of eroding confidence and failed e-businesses. In fact, Webmergers.com reported that for the period beginning January 2000 and ending February 2002, more than 800 e-businesses from B2C retailers to B2B marketspaces to technology and infrastructure providers either closed or filed for bankruptcy.

TIP

For an interesting look back at various speculative bubbles and social manias, check out the now classic book *Extraordinary Popular Delusions & the Madness of Crowds* by Charles MacKay and Andrew Tobias.

TECH CASE   E-Busted! The Unbelievable Tale of Pixelon, Inc.

Few tales better sum up the rampant obsession with the commercialization of Internet technologies than that of Pixelon, Inc. and its founder Michael Fenne. In early October 1999, Pixelon, Inc. announced several exciting new technological innovations: a new encoding technology that would allow the broadcasting of high-quality streaming media over the Internet at a much faster rate than the competing Microsoft and RealNetworks technologies; a new streaming media distribution network using OC48 Sonat technology; satellite redistribution of broadcasts to reach millions of viewers; enormous server capacity distributed across the country in a number of server farms; personalization technologies that would permit custom advertising to be embedded in streaming media directed to a specific viewer; new encryption technologies that would protect artistic property from being stolen or duplicated during a broadcast; and a new interactive "Pixelon Player" that viewers could use to view the streaming media and to interact by providing feedback, responding to polls, and so forth.

Continued

Fenne founded Pixelon, Inc. in 1998 in San Juan Capistrano, California. A physically imposing man with a magnetic and charming personality, Fenne had little trouble lining up investors for Pixelon. Astoundingly, several angel investors (individual investors who invest in startup companies) and a venture capital firm were so eager to reap the anticipated rewards of an investment in exciting new Internet technologies that they quickly handed over more than $30 million — without bothering to extensively check out Pixelon's technology claims or to check out Michael Fenne. But more about that later.

Pixelon decided that the best way to launch the new e-business was with a live, streaming media show from Las Vegas that would showcase Pixelon's new, proprietary technologies. Dubbed "iBash 99," the event was held on October 29, 1999, at the MGM Grand and included significant musical acts such as the Dixie Chicks, Kiss, Brian Seltzer, Faith Hill, Tony Bennett, and The Who in a special reunion performance. To pull off the event, Pixelon reportedly spent from $12–$16 million, or about half its startup funds. Immediately following "iBash 99" things started unraveling for Pixelon and Fenne.

First, many viewers complained that Pixelon's much touted technological innovations didn't work as promised during the streaming media broadcast of "iBash 99." Only a very few viewers with extremely high-speed connections were able to see the performances. Next, upon hearing about the huge price tag for the event, the increasingly unhappy venture capitalists flew to San Juan Capistrano, gathered up the members of the board of directors, and ousted Michael Fenne from his own company.

Then, in early April 2000, while trying to transform Pixelon from a streaming media broadcaster into a technology reseller, Pixelon's investors and board of directors received the biggest shock of all: the Virginia State Police called Fenne and demanded that he turn himself in. Fenne complied. It seems that Fenne, whose real name is David Stanley, had been convicted in 1989 of bilking more than $1 million from elderly investors in Virginia and Tennessee. Stanley, who received a 36-year sentence (28 years of which were suspended) was released on probation in the mid-1990s so he could work to reimburse his victims. Stanley broke the terms of his probation in 1996 and fled Virginia. He remained on Virginia's list of most wanted criminals until he was discovered in San Juan Capistrano under the name of Michael Fenne. Pixelon's shocked management hired a top accounting firm to audit Pixelon's books; to their relief, the audit failed to indicate any embezzlement of funds.

But, the news just kept getting worse for Pixelon's management and investors. In May 2000, a Pixelon executive and a few employees began admitting that Pixelon's much ballyhooed new technological innovations were anything but innovative and that Pixelon had been misleading investors by claiming proprietary technologies. In fact, Pixelon had used open source MPEG 1 technologies in its streaming media demonstrations to investors, its MPEG encoding technologies had been previously developed by firms such as FutureTel and LocoLabs, and its media player technologies were so similar to those developed by Microsoft for the Windows Media Player as to be valueless. Additionally, some employees admitted that the personalization features of Pixelon's supposedly proprietary technologies couldn't possibly work. Within two weeks, Pixelon had laid off 55 employees, leaving only a few unpaid executives. Its creditors were trying to force the e-business into bankruptcy and other potential investors were running for their financial lives!

Continued

The old adage "If it looks too good to be true…" certainly applies to the unhappy tale of Pixelon, Inc. Today, it's hard to believe that investors failed to thoroughly investigate the new technologies or failed to perform a simple background check that would have told them that "Michael Fenne" didn't exist. But in the heat of the white-hot technology bubble, the desire to grab onto a sizzling deal and make the next Internet fortune clearly overrode what now, of course, seems to be only sound, logical business sense.

In spite of the burst technology bubble, many new e-businesses continue to be successful in developing market share and are actually profitable. Next, you consider several successful and not so successful e-businesses and the factors, including technological factors, which are integral to that success or failure.

E-Business Models: What Went Right and What Went Wrong

Investment strategy errors were not the only reasons the technology bubble burst — far from it. While some e-businesses successfully married Internet technologies to their e-business models, some did not. Additionally, some early e-businesses followed poorly conceptualized e-business models that failed to generate sufficient revenue. A variety of other mistakes and miscalculations also contributed to the downfall of some early e-businesses. Let's take a look at some of the factors, including technological factors, which played a role in early e-business successes and failures.

Successful E-Business Models

E-businesses like eBay, NetBank, and the Hotel Reservations Network have succeeded by focusing on the main strength of Internet technologies — moving information quickly from one place to another. E-businesses such as these stay away from physical product inventories and their resulting high costs of product purchasing or manufacturing, warehousing, and shipping, and either function as intermediaries or offer electronic products and services.

eBay

As you learned in Chapters 1 and 8, eBay uses Internet technologies to bring buyers and sellers together in an online auction marketspace. Founded in 1995, eBay generates revenues from auction listings and selling fees and was profitable almost from the start. As of this writing, eBay continues to report astounding growth in both sales and profits; for example, for the fiscal year ending December 2001, eBay reported sales of $748.8 million and net income of $90.4 million.

NetBank

Opened for business in 1996, NetBank (Figure 10-1), with headquarters in a suburb of Atlanta, Georgia, is the largest online FDIC-insured Federal savings bank and one of the only online banks still operating as of this writing. NetBank offers traditional financial services such as checking accounts, money market accounts, bank loans, and so forth. How has NetBank thrived when its online banking contemporaries such as Bank One's Wingspanbank.com and CompuBank failed to even survive? NetBank, with more than $2.9 billion in assets and over 245,000 accounts across 50 states and 20 foreign countries, survived the old-fashioned way — by being profitable!

Unlike other early online banks, which put a higher priority on account acquisition and increasing market share than on profitability, NetBank focused on profits from the beginning. In fact, when asked about NetBank's success, its vice chairman and CEO responded, "I tell people I'm old-fashioned enough to believe that running a business is about making a profit." In order to remain profitable, NetBank is pursuing a strategy of slowing its account acquisition growth rate from 150 percent per year to 40 to 50 percent per year and has acquired two mortgage lending firms, putting it among the country's top 20 mortgage lenders.

NetBank uses Internet technologies to insure efficient operations, provide customer service, and reduce customer acquisition and marketing costs. For example, NetBank provides a secure transaction environment (and satisfies customer concerns about security) by employing passwords, firewalls, and encryption technologies. In the early years, NetBank offered higher than market interest rates on checking, saving, and money market accounts in order to acquire new customers. Today, NetBank reduces customer acquisition costs by using opt-in e-mail (you learned about opt-in e-mail in Chapter 3) to offer new products and services to existing customers or to extend existing products and services to new customers. NetBank also uses Web site technologies to create special Web "landing pages" that describe these products and services each time an opt-in mailing goes out. The e-mail recipients can click through to the related "landing page" at NetBank's Web site directly from the e-mail.

Other Internet technologies employed by NetBank include: cookies, which are used to track click throughs, which are in turn a measure of the success of opt-in e-mailing; e-mail mailing lists, which are used to send periodic financial services newsletters; and HTML and other Web page creation tools, which help keep the NetBank Web site easy to use and navigate. To help hold down costs (and increase profits) NetBank also uses a variety of tools to carefully measure the ROI of its Web site and other technology projects.

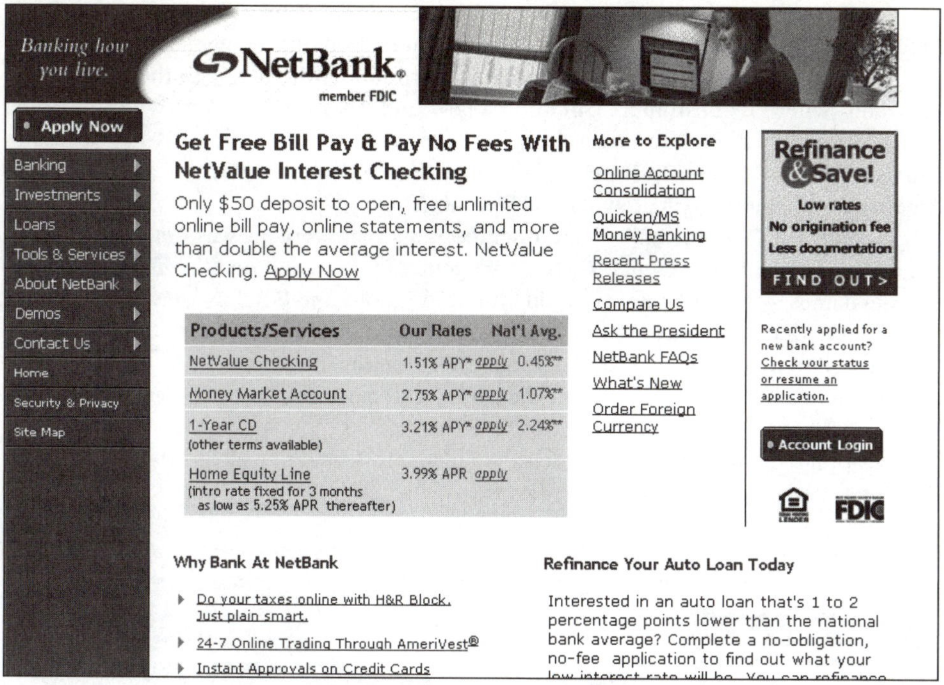

Figure 10-1
NetBank

Hotel Reservations Network

Most hotels do not fill all their rooms every night, a fact that one e-business was able to capitalize on. Hotel Reservations Network (HRN), founded in 1991 in Dallas, Texas, purchases huge blocks of hotel rooms at a big discount from hotel chains and independent hotel operators that can't fill their rooms. HRN (Figure 10-2) then marks up the room rates and resells the rooms to consumers who are still getting a bargain of up to 70 percent off what they would pay if they booked their rooms directly with the hotels.

Originally, HRN sold hotel rooms via toll-free call centers. In 1995, HRN moved part of its operations to the Web by running multiple Web sites such as 180096hotel.com, allluxuryhotels.com, and hoteldiscount.com. Additionally, HRN entered into affiliate relationships with other travel-oriented Web sites (such as Travelocity) which either directed potential customers to the HRN Web sites for a small commission or actually booked rooms for customers through HRN while booking the customers' airline reservations. Fees paid by the affiliates that used the HRN room search and booking technologies to book rooms for customers at their own Web sites generated additional revenues. By 1998, HRN was consistently profitable with a reported average annual revenue growth of approximately 80 percent, and in 1999, HRN was purchased by USA Interactive (formerly USA Networks). In 2000, HRN went public, and although it maintained its call centers for customer support, by this time most of its revenues were generated online either at its own Web sites or at its affiliates' Web sites. Continuing to be profitable, HRN reported $536.5 million in sales and $12.9 million in net income for the fiscal year ending December 2001.

In addition to using its Web sites to sell hotel rooms, HRN also uses Internet technologies to gather information about its customers' booking habits such as in which geographical areas its customers are looking for rooms. HRN then uses the information regarding where its customers can and cannot find discounted rooms when deciding which geographical area to target for expansion. As of this writing, HRN has access to rooms at more than 4,500 hotels in Western Europe, Asia, the Caribbean, and North America and has approximately 24,000 Web affiliates.

Despite HRN's successful online operations, its management was not satisfied with the e-business's online presence. HRN's management was concerned that the e-business's domain names — 180096hotel.com, allluxuryhotels.com, and hoteldiscount.com — were too difficult for customers to remember. HRN's management also was concerned that having three different Web sites fragmented HRN's online presence. Thus, in 2002, HRN changed its name to Hotels.com and began an extensive media campaign to build the Hotels.com brand with the goal of becoming the world's biggest provider of hotel rooms and vacation lodgings. Ultimately, Hotels.com plans to close down all its other Web sites as the Hotels.com brand becomes better known.

Figure 10-2
Hotels.com

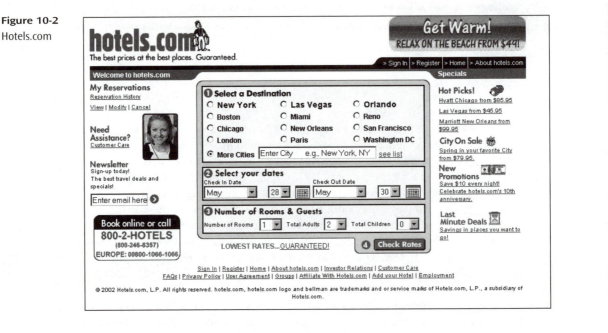

Other Successful E-Businesses

A "pure play" e-business retailer is one that sells its products and services online only and does not have sales from brick-and-mortar stores or printed catalogs. The most famous pure play e-business retailer is, of course, Amazon.com. While Amazon.com continues to increase its market share with aggressive marketing and acquisition strategies, as of this writing it has yet to report an annual profit. For example, for the fiscal year ending December 2001, Amazon.com reported a net loss of $567.3 million on sales of $3.12 billion; however, Amazon.com did report its first ever profitable quarter in the fourth quarter of 2001. It again reported a profitable quarter in the first quarter of 2002 and projects annual profitability for 2002.

Some retailers that traditionally sold their products via stores or printed catalogs (such as Barnes & Noble, Godiva Chocolatier, Crate and Barrel, and Hickory Farms) already had distribution and order fulfillment operations and were able to integrate their Web operations with these existing operations. Many other e-businesses (such as Ask the Builder) started small — often without any startup investment by venture capitalists or angel investors — managed their revenue growth and costs effectively, and remain viable by selling a variety of products and services to niche markets.

Additionally, many traditional companies, such as Bristol-Myers Squibb Company, Whirlpool Corporation, and others discussed previously in this text, use Internet technologies to streamline their supply chains and boost customer support, which contributes to their overall profitability. Also, some B2B marketspaces such as MetalSite (raw goods and refined metals) and ChemConnect (chemicals and plastics) have been able to develop their marketspaces through strong relationships with sellers and buyers and high sales volumes.

But, despite these success stories and many others not noted here, many, many horror stories of disastrous e-business failures exist. In the next section, we take a look at a couple of e-businesses that failed to merge new Internet technologies and sound business precepts into successful e-businesses.

TIP

Here's a quote to consider from John G. Sifonis, a director of Cisco Systems, Inc.'s Internet Business Solutions Group: "The 'e' in e-business is silent. The great lesson of the dot.com meltdown is that business is business. The difficult part of the equation is making a solid business between the many possible infrastructure investments a company has in its portfolio."

Unsuccessful E-Business Models

Many early e-business entrepreneurs and investors miscalculated the speed with which consumers would adopt the new Internet technologies. These companies created online marketspaces from which both individual and business consumers stayed away in droves. For example, some early B2B marketspaces such as Chemdex (chemicals) and PointSpeed (discounted office supplies and products for small businesses) failed because they could never build the supplier/buyer base needed to operate successfully.

Some early e-business models were based on the idea that new online marketspaces would quickly and completely replace traditional offline marketplaces — and, of course, that did not happen. Others, such as the pure play e-business retailers eToys, Pets.com, and GroceryWorks.com tried to adapt the traditional brick-and-mortar retailing model to the Web and found that product, marketing, advertising, warehousing, and order fulfillment costs far outstripped revenues. Other early e-business entrepreneurs and investors focused their e-business models on rapid

TIP

For a cinema verité-style look at "the good, the bad, and the ugly" of an e-business startup, check out *Startup.com*, a documentary film about the rise and fall of govWorks, Inc., an e-business that attempted to create e-business solutions (such as portals) for local governments. The film, which was released in 2001, is produced by D. A. Pennebaker, directed by Chris Hedgus and Jehane Noujaim, and is available on DVD with a 103-minute runtime.

growth and increased market share, failing to consider that in the final analysis an e-business must still follow the basic rule of any for-profit business — the need to generate revenues in excess of expenses in order to create profits. Lacking sufficient revenues, these e-businesses failed when the technology bubble burst and funding dried up.

Many early e-businesses were based on an e-business model that involved generating revenues by selling advertising. The basic idea behind this e-business model was to create a compelling Web site, often by offering free products or services, which would become popular with a large number of viewers. These viewers would, in turn, view the advertising messages presented at the site. Initially it was expected that advertisers would be happy to pay for exposure to a large number of "eyeballs." Unfortunately, in many cases advertisers were not convinced that Web advertising was effective and the necessary advertising revenues never materialized. Two of these failed e-businesses, AllAdvantage.com and ThirdVoice, also completely misjudged the effect of Internet technologies on the marketplace.

AllAdvantage.com

AllAdvantage.com, which launched its Web site in March 1999, is an example of an e-business with an e-business model that included generating revenues by selling advertising space. Additionally, AllAdvantage.com's e-business model completely failed to adequately plan for one very powerful aspect of doing business online — the network effect. In Chapter 2, you learned about Metcalfe's Law, also called the network effect, which essentially states that the value of a network increases as more and more entities are added to the network. AllAdvantage.com attempted to exploit the network effect by recruiting Web viewers to become "members" of a marketing program in which each member profited by encouraging others to become members. (This type of marketing program is often called a multilevel marketing program or scheme and is similar to offline businesses that pay their sales representatives bonuses or commissions when they recruit others to be sales representatives.)

AllAdvantage.com's e-business model involved paying its members a few cents per hour to browse the Web. The e-business model also included a referral program that paid a member an additional bonus amount per hour while any new members he or she referred to AllAdvantage.com browsed the Web. Further, an original member earned a second bonus amount per hour when a new member he or she referred to AllAdvantage.com then referred someone else. Revenue generation in the AllAdvantage e-business model involved selling advertising space on a "viewing bar" or Web browser plug-in that members downloaded and left open on their screens as they browsed the Web.

How well did the AllAdvantage.com e-business model work? Let's see. In the first week of operation, an unexpected 100,000 new members enrolled at the AllAdvantage.com Web site. Although AllAdvantage.com expected to sign only 20,000 members within its first three months of operations, it found itself with 1 million members — and its membership continued to grow. By late spring of 2000, AllAdvantage.com had 6.7 million registered members and about 2.5 million active members, with membership continuing to grow at 15,000–16,000 new members a month. The network effect was working spectacularly!

Unfortunately, the revenue generation portion of the AllAdvantage.com e-business model was not working as expected. AllAdvantage.com tried to sell advertisers on the idea of targeting advertising to its captive viewing audience, but advertisers were very slow to accept the concept. In the first quarter of 2000, AllAdvantage.com's advertising revenues amounted to only $9 million while payments to members in the same first quarter topped out at approximately $40 million. Altogether, AllAdvantage.com lost more than $102 million in its first year of operation!

In the fall of 2000, AllAdvantage.com attempted to survive by reducing the amount it paid members for browsing. This resulted in a very unhappy and vocal membership base who blasted AllAdvantage.com in Internet chat rooms and in e-mail to other members. In November and December of 2000, AllAdvantage.com severely reduced its staff and attempted to retool its e-business model to become a technology provider. But by the spring of 2001, the B2B auction house DoveBid was advertising a complete "liquidation" of AllAdvantage.com's servers, switches, routers, firewalls, laptops, desktops, desk phones, and more.

ThirdVoice

Another e-business with an e-business model that involved generating advertising revenues but that also failed to accommodate the effect of Internet technologies on the marketplace was ThirdVoice. ThirdVoice offered Web viewers a highly innovative but very controversial way to use Internet technologies to share information — by creating electronic comments or "sticky notes" related to a specific Web page.

In May 1999, ThirdVoice began offering a free Web browser plug-in that allowed viewers to create electronic "sticky notes" that could be read by any viewer using the ThirdVoice plug-in. Web pages were not physically altered because the electronic "sticky notes" were not actually attached to a Web page. Instead, the electronic "sticky notes" were stored on ThirdVoice's own servers. When a viewer using the ThirdVoice plug-in downloaded a Web page, the plug-in automatically sent the page's URL to the ThirdVoice servers which returned any "sticky notes" stored about the Web page. Revenue generation in the ThirdVoice e-business model involved selling advertising space in a small "window" in a viewer's Web browser.

As you might expect, the response to ThirdVoice's innovative use of Internet technologies ranged from a celebration of free speech to accusations that ThirdVoice was spreading "electronic graffiti." Outraged e-businesses (appropriately concerned with managing their online presence) were not amused by negative comments posted in "sticky notes" by disgruntled customers or hecklers. "Say No to ThirdVoice" lobbying groups and anti-ThirdVoice Web sites quickly sprang up.

In April 2000, ThirdVoice published a new version of its plug-in that turned selected words on a Web page into hyperlinks to related Web pages and discussion groups. But by then the novelty of creating electronic "sticky notes" was wearing thin and expected advertising revenues were not being generated. In April 2001, ThirdVoice posted a message at its Web site telling users that it was no longer supporting the plug-in and provided instructions on how to uninstall it.

In the last sections, you have reviewed some of the causes and effects of the technology bubble and have taken a look at some e-business models that have successfully or not so successfully combined Internet technologies and sound business practices. Next, you learn about some exciting emerging technologies that will likely affect the future of e-business.

Emerging Technologies

As of this writing, many exciting technological changes and innovations are taking place. More than a few of these changes and innovations will likely have a significant impact on the future of e-business. In this section, you learn about technological innovations such as Web services, peer-to-peer computing, collaborative commerce initiatives, intelligent agents, and the Semantic Web. You also learn about other emerging technologies that may influence the development of future e-business models, including: the executable and extended Internet, the Electronic Product Code, Internet2, nanoscale computing, quantum computing, and bioinformatics.

Web Services

In Chapter 8, you learned about some of the technologies used to facilitate the exchange of data between different e-business applications. Such an exchange of data is sometimes called application integration. As of this writing, the latest buzz phrase related to e-business application integration is "Web services." The phrase **Web services** refers to the technologies involved in exchanging data between different applications and systems over an IP network such as the Internet. Web services technologies include XML (discussed in Chapters 4 and 8), UDDI, WSDL, and SOAP. These technologies were or are being developed jointly by Microsoft Corporation, IBM, Ariba Inc., and other Web technology providers.

UDDI or **Universal Description, Discovery, and Integration** is an XML-based directory (similar to the Yellow Pages business telephone directory) in which e-businesses list themselves and provide a description of the Web-based services they offer to other e-businesses. The Web-based services descriptions included in a UDDI directory are created using **WSDL (Web Services Description Language)** which is an XML-based markup language. An e-business wishing to access specific Web-based services can use a UDDI directory to identify which e-businesses offer the desired Web services.

SOAP or **Simple Object Access Protocol** is the protocol used to exchange XML files between applications on different operating systems using HTTP and an IP network. SOAP is used to actually transmit data between e-businesses in the form of XML files.

Another XML-based technology for Web services is ebXML. **ebXML**, sponsored by the United Nations Center for Trade Facilitation and Electronic Business (UN/CEFACT) and the Organization for the Advancement of Structured Information Standards (OASIS), is a globally supported set of standard XML specifications that support B2B transactions over the Internet. ebXML specifications are used to identify an e-business and the Web-based services it offers. Analysts expect that ebXML will be used in conjunction with UDDI and SOAP technologies in future e-business data exchanges.

Throughout most of this text, you've learned how computers exchange data in client-server networks, in which a client application such as a Web browser requests data stored on a server. However, not all valuable data is stored on servers; most users also store useful and important data on their individual personal computers. This sometimes makes sharing the data with others problematic. But, what if users could access data stored on individual personal computers no matter where the computers were located? This is the promise of peer-to-peer, or distributed computing.

Peer-to-Peer Computing

You learned about the basic components of peer-to-peer LANs in Chapter 2. However, when discussing distributed computing, **peer-to-peer computing (P2P)** refers to the uploading or downloading of files (stored on individual computer hard drives) between computers on the same LAN or between computers on different LANs over an IP network such as the Internet. P2P has been around for many years as an idea, but it was brought to the forefront in the late 1990s by two events: the SETI@home project and an e-business named Napster.

SETI@home Project

One dramatic use of P2P is aggregating the unused computing power of individual personal computers into a computer power grid to create a virtual supercomputer. Some analysts suggest that today's Internet-connected personal computers with their vastly improved resources represent more than 10 billion Mhz of processing power and 10 thousand terabytes of storage — with more than half of that capability going unused! An interesting example of tapping into that unused computing power is the SETI@home project.

When researchers at the University of California at Berkeley faced a lack of funds to pay for computer analysis of radio telescope data gathered for the SETI (Search for Extraterrestrial Intelligence) SERENDIP project, they found a unique solution: harnessing the unused power of thousands of personal computers around the world. The SETI@home project allows people interested in participating in the radio telescope data analysis to download a screensaver program from the SETI@home Web site. When their computer is turned on but not being used, the screensaver program downloads chunks of radio telescope data and examines it for patterns. The results of the analysis are then uploaded to the SETI@home project servers and combined with the patterns analysis performed by thousands of other personal computers participating in the project. The SETI@home (Figure 10-3) project has likely surpassed the wildest dreams of its creators as more than 3.7 million people have downloaded the software, contributing almost one million years of computing time to the project.

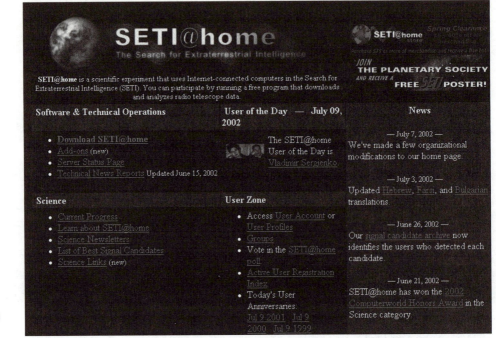

Figure 10-3
SETI@home

Napster

Peer-to-peer's next big event was Napster, an e-business that allowed users to share music and other files (stored on their individual personal computers) with other users via the Internet. Technically speaking, Napster didn't employ a pure P2P network. That's because, in a pure P2P network, every file search traverses the entire P2P network, returning a list of all computers on the P2P network that contain a copy of the searched for file. By contrast, Napster relied on a master server that maintained a searchable list of all available files and the files' locations. (A pure P2P network would not include a master server.) To find a music file, Napster users first searched for files on the master server list and then directly contacted the individual computer where the files were stored to download the files.

File swapping — especially music files — exploded in popularity and soon millions of people were using Napster to share music files. Of course, the recording industry was not pleased and several suits were filed against Napster for copyright violations. The courts agreed with the recording industry that Napster's music file sharing operations violated copyright laws. In the summer of 2001, the courts ordered Napster to shut down its Web site until it could demonstrate a reliable way to prevent the swapping of copyrighted files. By June 2001, the embattled Napster, without revenues or sources of additional funding, filed for bankruptcy protection and its assets were acquired by Bertelsmann AG, the German media conglomerate.

Other P2P Technologies: Gnutella, KaZaA, and JXTA

The courts' actions against Napster did not stop file sharing or progress in the development of P2P technologies, of course. One example of a pure P2P technology is Gnutella. The Gnutella open-source P2P technology (developed originally by the late Gene Kan and others) allows file sharing directly between individual computers across an IP network. However, Gnutella exposed a fundamental inefficiency in many P2P networks: it didn't scale well. In other words, as more people became part of the Gnutella P2P network, file searches became slower and slower, because each file search had to traverse the entire P2P network.

The solution to this P2P scalability problem was the introduction of **supernodes**, computers with fast connections that act as hubs for several computers. The supernodes can also be supplemented by super-supernodes, computers that act as hubs and indexes for multiple supernodes. Thanks to the supernode solution, P2P file searches now only have to traverse a limited number of super- and super-supernodes. One e-business that uses this technique to allow file searching and sharing between its customers is KaZaA, which has a P2P network developed by Sharman Networks.

The Gnutella network is declining in size now that a better solution (supernodes) is being provided by competitors such as KaZaA. By some measures, the Gnutella network is, as of this writing, only about one-quarter the size it reached in mid-2001 at the height of its popularity.

Other technology providers such as Sun Microsystems, Inc. are also involved in developing P2P technologies that can be used for more than just music file sharing. For example, Sun's JXTA project involves developing P2P technologies that would allow any devices connected to a network (such as servers, personal computers, wireless cell phones, or PDAs) to communicate with each other in a P2P environment.

Commercial Use of P2P

And how are e-businesses using P2P today? As of this writing, P2P technologies are being used to share drug data between more than 10,000 employees and researchers at a major drug manufacturer. One technology provider uses P2P technologies to distribute computer-based training materials to employees more efficiently. And a major aircraft manufacturer uses P2P technologies (instead of a wind tunnel) to create a computing power grid that simulates wind flow over a structure.

P2P technologies may become an integral part of future knowledge management systems. Additionally, P2P technologies may be used to extend the benefits of the ERP and SCM systems you learned about in Chapter 8 by enabling e-businesses to interact as peers and share information about product supply and demand. The new buzz phrase for this type of interaction is "collaborative commerce."

Collaborative Commerce

Collaborative commerce or **c-commerce** is a new term that refers to the interrelationships between multiple e-businesses that use Internet technologies to work together to form "trading communities" in which information about the development of products and services can be exchanged between trading partners. Additionally, trading community participants can buy and sell each other's products and services. Analysts envision that the next wave of ERP and SCM systems will allow e-businesses and their trading partners to collaborate in a way that substantially reduces costs. This collaboration may make it possible to instantly share product information, business forecasts, customer information, promotional opportunities, and a host of other business information. This sharing of information would all take place via the Internet.

Analysts also expect that, in the future, many of our personal and business interactions with computers may involve intelligent agents and the Semantic Web.

Intelligent Agents and the Semantic Web

An **intelligent agent**, often just called an agent, is a computer program that can act independently by using simple logic to carry out scheduled tasks. In the future, intelligent agents may provide much of the computing needed to manage the increasingly complex transactions involved in the daily life of an individual or an e-business. For example, intelligent agents may be used to help e-businesses provide better customer support while reducing costs. A customer needing to know the difference between stone-washed and acid-washed jeans may be able to get that information quickly at an e-business's Web site via an intelligent agent instead of having to contact someone in the e-business's Customer Support Department. Also, the more powerful computers expected to be available in the future may use intelligent agents that respond to voice commands to manage tasks such as file searching.

The term **Semantic Web** refers to a plan (generated by Tim Berners-Lee and others at the W3C) describing a possible future for the World Wide Web — a future in which intelligent agents radically improve your ability to find and manipulate data. According to Berners-Lee and the W3C, the next step in the evolution of the World Wide Web is to make computers require less human intervention in order to find and manipulate data. This new capability would rely on an XML-based technology called **Resource Description Framework**, or **RDF**.

Consider the following futuristic example. Suppose an attorney is interested in researching lawsuits involving taxi passengers. Old research methods required hours of manually searching through books. By contrast, current Internet search technologies make it possible to enter the words "taxi" and "passenger" into a search engine and retrieve a list of lawsuits that may or may not be relevant. This is certainly an improvement over the older method, but it's not perfect. The list generated by a search engine may also contain references to lawsuits about water taxis and passenger pigeons! In the future however, RDF technologies might be used to embed information about the plaintiff, the defendant, the nature of the complaint, the award, and so forth in stored lawsuit data. Then our attorney might be able to use the Semantic Web, an intelligent agent, and a voice command to quickly search for and list the most appropriate lawsuits.

As of this writing Berners-Lee's concept of a Semantic Web is still just an interesting idea. But some analysts have another view of the Internet's future, which they call the executable and extended Internet.

X Internet

The term **X Internet**, which stands for both "executable Internet" and "extended Internet", was coined in 2001 by analysts at Forrester Research, Inc., who were attempting to see into the future of the Web and e-business. These analysts expect the Web to evolve into an environment where consumers and e-businesses use disposable (use once and throw away) executable programs that could be downloaded to computers or handheld devices. These disposable programs could be used to get real-time information or to provide a variety of interactive online experiences. Analysts dubbed this new online environment the **executable Internet**. AOL Instant Messenger and Napster's P2P file swapping are examples of early executable Internet applications. Sun Microsystems' JXTA P2P open-source project and Microsoft's .NET technologies are precursors of future executable Internet technologies.

Predicting more than 14 billion Internet-enabled devices by 2010, these same analysts also foresee an **extended Internet** where nearly every electrical device is Internet-enabled and work with applications and intelligent agents that sense and control the world around us. Part of that control may be exerted by tagging items with an Electronic Product Code.

Electronic Product Code (ePC)

The Universal Product Code (UPC) is the barcode that appears on packaging for consumer products such as cereal, soup, and paper items. Store clerks simply pass products marked with a UPC over a scanning device to record a purchase. The UPC revolutionized product distribution and supply chain management by vastly reducing errors and speeding up the process of inventory and product-movement tracking. The **Electronic Product Code (ePC)** standard takes these principles to a new level by providing a unique identification code for *each individual product* that emerges from a manufacturing process. For example, using ePC, a supply chain management system could track every bag of chips, every razor blade, or every can of soda from manufacturing through distribution and sale! ePC technologies are being developed by researchers at the Auto-ID Center (Figure 10-4) at MIT with the sponsorship of major businesses such as Wal-Mart Stores, Procter & Gamble, Sun Microsystems, Inc., The Coca-Cola Company, and so forth.

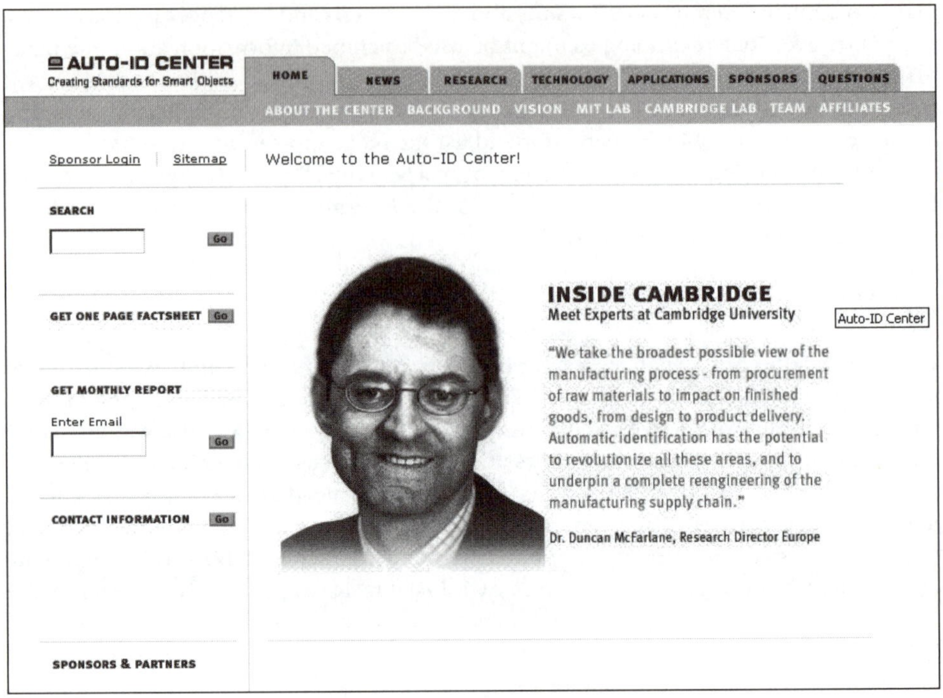

Figure 10-4
Auto-ID
Center

These new ePC technologies use a 96-bit numbering code consisting of a header, a manufacturer ID, product ID, and an individual serial number. This 96-bit code is attached to an item via a very small electronic "smart tag" which uses **Radio Frequency Identification (RFID)** technologies to absorb energy from an incoming radio signal. (The small electronic security tags that bookstores place in books is another example of RFID technologies.) The smart tag then uses the absorbed energy to send a response whenever the tagged item is near a special reading device. For example, in the future you may be able to fill your shopping cart with ePC tagged items and simply *walk by* an ePC reader device to automatically have your credit card billed for your purchases. At the same time, suppliers would be automatically advised to restock the store shelves.

One major concern about ePC technologies is, of course, privacy. While ePC technologies are designed to improve supply chain management and product distribution, other uses will surely be found for these technologies. Do you really want someone else scrutinizing the contents of your shopping cart? Or someone tracking your whereabouts by an ePC tag in your clothing? Or others watching what you read, view, or purchase by tagging items such as books, videos, medications, or certain controversial items such as firearms and ammunition? As you can imagine, privacy watchdog groups are keeping an eye on the development of ePC technologies.

Two components of ePC technologies are the Object Naming Service and the Physical Markup Language. The **Object Naming Service (ONS)**, partly based on the DNS but expected to be much larger, acts as a "post office" by using ePC tag addresses to locate data on each tagged item. The **Physical Markup Language (PML)**, an XML-based markup language, is a generalized language that can be used to describe physical objects. Such a language is necessary because, unlike humans, computers do not have a method of describing physical objects to each other. A better way of understanding the physical world using technologies such as PML may allow computers to be more effective in manufacturing where they are used to design complex objects. Additionally, PML may be useful in everyday life when computerized appliances and other devices such as ePC smart cards need to know more about the environment in which they operate to be effective.

As Internet usage grew rapidly during the 1990s, some scientists became worried that the volume of personal and business traffic on the Internet would outpace the ability of the Internet to handle that traffic. These scientists feared that this scenario would restrict scientific and academic Internet usage. Their solution to the problem? A second Internet.

Internet2

In October 1996, 34 scientists and researchers came together in Chicago to find a way to solve what they perceived to be the troublesome problem of increasing traffic on the Internet brought about by its commercialization. Their proposed solution was a separate high-speed network for the scientific and academic world that would allow scientists, researchers, and educators to work together in real time. Within six years that network, called **Internet2**, was a reality. Internet2 (Figure 10-5) connects colleges and universities, government agencies, and other scientific and educational facilities in North America, South America, Europe, and Asia via two high-speed fiber-optic backbones.

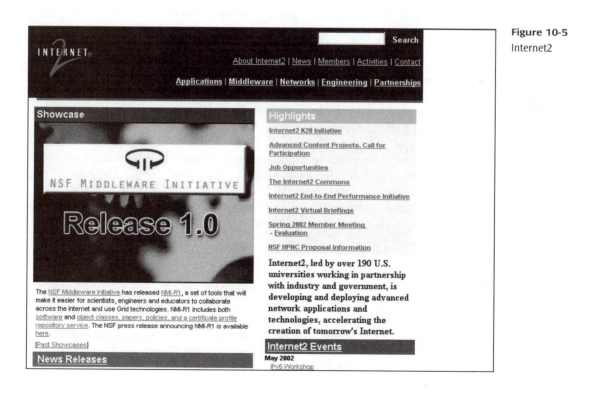

Figure 10-5
Internet2

Commercial network providers are studying the development of Internet2 to determine what Internet2 technologies should be introduced into the e-business marketplace. But, as you learned in Chapter 6, the anticipated bandwidth crunch that stimulated development of Internet2 has not occurred. As of this writing, the amount of available bandwidth exceeds the demand. Also, many consumers do not yet have high-speed Internet connections in their homes; therefore, high demand for bandwidth-intensive applications such as video-on-demand is not developing as many analysts predicted. As of this writing, there appears to be no strong demand for the commercial application of Internet2 technologies.

One area so new and exciting that it's difficult to speculate on where it might lead is nanoscale and quantum computing.

Nanoscale and Quantum Computing

Nanoscale computing is computing with devices or components smaller than a nanometer (one billionth of a meter). Beyond nanoscale computing is **quantum computing**, in which individual atoms are used to store data. Both nanoscale and quantum computing offer potential advances in memory capacity, processing speed, and storage capacity that may make today's most advanced microprocessors and storage devices seem as antiquated as yesterday's transistor radios or floppy diskettes.

Moore's Law, promulgated by Gordon Moore, one of the founders of Intel Corporation, essentially states that microprocessors double in power every 18 months as transistors get smaller and smaller, allowing more computing power to be added to each microprocessor. In other words, computers continue to get smaller, faster, more powerful, and less expensive. In the future, nanoscale and quantum processing and storage capabilities may make using voice commands to direct the actions of intelligent agents a more realistic option.

As of this writing, no e-business applications for nanoscale and quantum computing exist. However, it is not unreasonable to assume that advances in computing capabilities such as these will have a positive effect on e-business. For example, advances in computing technologies may allow SCM systems to more accurately track raw materials and manufacturing output, or allow CRM systems to more efficiently personalize customer transactions. Nanoscale and quantum computing technologies may also make possible new e-business models that rely on more powerful and less expensive computing capabilities. E-business activities that rely on portable computing, where power and storage are at a premium, may be the first commercial activities to benefit from nanoscale and quantum computing.

Another technology area which is progressing rapidly and which may have implications for e-business opportunities is biotechnology.

Biotechnology and Bioinformatics

Clearly, some astonishing biotechnology developments are on the way. For example, in 2002 scientists announced that light-powered chips had been inserted into the retinas of blind people, allowing them to see again. Also, in 2002, research results detailed how a brain implant was used to control a rat's behavior and how another brain implant enabled a monkey to control an onscreen cursor with its thoughts. These and other advances in biotechnology promise great improvements in the lives of people with disabilities.

But how may biotechnological advances affect e-business? As you have learned from the many Tech Cases and other examples throughout this text, e-business opportunities are found in virtually every technology and business sector — and the biotechnology sector is no exception. One example in the biotechnology sector is biotechnology portals such as BioExchange (Figure 10-6). Biotechnology portals enable scientists and researchers to exchange information about the biotechnology sector. They also provide venues for biotechnology-related e-businesses to interact.

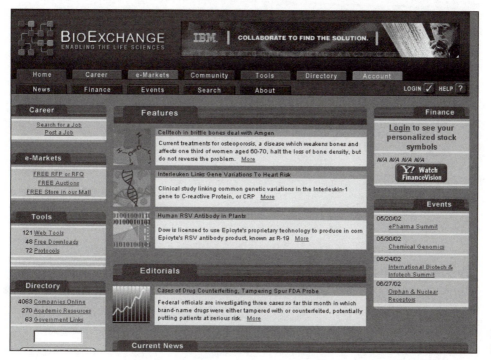

Figure 10-6
BioExchange

Advances in biotechnology could also create opportunities for new e-businesses related to biological or pharmaceutical research. Such e-businesses might involve **bioinformatics**, which is the use of computers and databases to augment biological research. The most famous application of bioinformatics is the Human Genome Project, an ongoing, collaborative attempt to identify the 80,000 genes in human DNA. This greater understanding of human DNA has led to a variety of interesting businesses, perhaps the most unusual of which are e-businesses that offer DNA testing for everything from establishing paternity to identifying a genealogical link to our earliest female ancestors. Examples of such e-businesses include DNA Diagnostics Center and Oxford Ancestors (Figure 10-7). Some new e-businesses actually participate in or support pharmaceutical research. For example, Clinical Trials Online (Figure 10-8) conducts clinical trials over the Internet, while Veritas Medicine provides up-to-date information on available clinical trials and their status.

Oxford Ancestors
Putting the genes in genealogy

Home | About the Daughters of Eve | MatriLine™ | MyMap™ | Y-Line™ |
Vikings | Order Form | FAQs | Real Life Stories | Feedback

The Seven Daughters of Eve

Discover your ancestral mother

50% OFF BESTSELLERS

Buy the book from
Amazon.co.uk

US visitors can buy
the book here!

Over the past decade research in Oxford and other universities throughout the world, has shown that our mitochondrial DNA (or mtDNA for short), which is inherited exclusively through the maternal line, uncovers a genetic legacy which has been invisible until now.

This female genealogy has created an evolutionary framework going back 150,000 years, and reveals that almost everyone in Europe, or whose maternal roots are in Europe, is descended from one of only seven women. Each of them founded a maternal clan whose descendants make up well over 95% of modern Europeans.

These seven women, the 'Seven Daughters of Eve', have been given the names Ursula (Latin for "she-bear"), Xenia (Greek for "hospitable"), Helena (Greek for "light"), Velda (Scandinavian for "ruler"), Tara (Gaelic for "rock"), Katrine (Greek for "pure") and Jasmine (Persian for "flower").

You can now find your own place within this genealogy - by far the world's largest

Figure 10-7
Oxford
Ancestors

Figure 10-8
Clinical Trials
Online

home

internet clinical trial systems

overview   our methods   current trials   who we are?   contact us

about icts

We specialize in the conduct of clinical trials (studies) of therapeutic products - *entirely over the Internet.*

Our *clinical trials online* system replicates traditional <u>trial methods</u> yet allows people from all over the Country to participate from the convenience of their own homes.

Our approach is most applicable evaluation of safe products, such as nutritional remedies and medical devices, in the treatment of disorders that can be evaluated by means of online questionnaires.

See our <u>current Trials.</u>

why do clinical trials online?

What are clinical trials?
Clinical trials are research studies that are designed to test the effectiveness of medicines and remedies in treating medical disorders. They help us find out which treatments work, and which do not.
What's the problem with traditional clinical trials?
Traditional clinical trials require participants to journey repeatedly to a hospital or clinic for medical assessments, and often cost *millions* of dollars. The difficulties in in recruiting enough participants often result in studies which are too small to be meaningful. This, together with the prohibitive costs, limits the number of remedies which can be tested in

Finally, as you learned in Chapter 7, biotechnology is already being used to make e-business networks more secure. As the risks to e-business network assets and data escalate, the use of biometric identification techniques becomes increasingly important.

Which e-business models have the best chance of exploiting these many emerging technologies in the future? As you have learned, it will likely be the e-business models that find an innovative use for the technologies, manage growth carefully, generate a revenue stream, and control expenses — in other words, the creative and profitable ones! Next, you learn about some of the e-business trends that may prove to be the most important in the next few years.

Focusing on the Future

Many analysts expect that e-business will continue to be influenced by trends such as a continued growth in B2C and B2B transactions, an explosive growth in wireless e-business transactions, the ever increasing need for network and Web site security, the continued shift in marketplace power between buyer and seller, and the globalization of e-business.

B2C and B2B Transactions

Most analysts expect that B2C online transactions will continue to grow steadily as more and more consumers become comfortable purchasing items online. For example, a 2002 study by the research company Ovum projects that global B2C revenues will exceed $360 billion by 2007. B2B online transactions will also continue to grow as businesses work together to use the Internet and the Web in new and creative ways. In fact, a 2002 study by the research company Gartner argues that global B2B sales will grow from $1,930 billion in 2002 to $8,530 billion in 2005.

Wireless E-Business Transactions

As of this writing, wireless e-business — conducting e-business transactions via hand-held wireless devices such as personal digital assistants (PDAs) and cell phones — is still in its infancy. (You learned about wireless e-business in Chapter 5.) Nevertheless, some analysts expect that within the next few years, evolving wireless technologies, more useful wireless Web content, and increased interest on the part of consumers may result in billons of dollars in wireless e-business revenues. For example, the same 2002 study by the research company Ovum (mentioned earlier in regard to B2B and B2C business) projects that global wireless B2C transactions will grow to more than $30 billion by 2007.

TIP

Many analysts think that the artificial "e-business" distinction of the past few years will fade and at some point in the future "e-business" will become ubiquitous. Analysts will then cease to discuss e-business activities as though they were totally different and distinct from traditional business activities.

Security, Security, Security

In Chapter 7, you learned about the importance of protecting customer data and securing Web site, network, and information assets against physical, internal, external, and transactional risks. As businesses become increasingly more dependent on their networks and the Internet to conduct their activities, the demand for improved network and Web site security will continue to grow. The networked world is, unfortunately, becoming more hazardous; with the growing threat of independent and state-sponsored cyberterrorism, ever more stringent network security will become a fact of life for every e-business.

Customers, Customers, Customers

As you learned in Chapter 1, one of the important aspects of e-business is the power shift from seller to buyer. Commercialization of the Internet has led to an empowerment of both business and individual consumers who now have access to better information and more product choices. The process of buying a new car is one example that illustrates the power shift from seller to buyer. A buyer shopping for a new car is no longer at the mercy of a dealer's sales staff when trying to negotiate price. He or she can approach the negotiation armed with pricing information and quotes from a number of dealerships simply by using the services available at e-businesses such as Autobytel.com.

Also, as you learned in Chapter 8, customer relationship management systems and the use of personalization will become more important as both businesses and individual consumers are confronted with an ever growing slate of e-businesses from which to choose. Who will thrive in such a marketplace? The e-businesses that use personalization technologies to establish and maintain strong relationships with their customers.

Globalization of E-Business

As you learned in Chapter 1, the Internet, which allows millions of consumers and businesses around the world to stay "connected," creates a marketplace where business opportunities are no longer constrained by geographical boundaries. The potential customer base for a smart e-business looking to globalize its market share continues to grow as more and more consumers around the world gain Internet access. Let's take a look at two different estimates of the number of potential customers available to global e-businesses as of this writing.

According to Nua Internet Surveys, an Internet consultant firm, the number of people with Internet access worldwide has increased from 171 million in March 1999 to 544.2 million in February 2002, an increase of more than 200 percent! Figure 10-9 illustrates the number of people around the world with Internet access, and is based on data compiled by Nua Internet Surveys in February, 2002.

	1st Qtr
☐ Africa	4.15
☐ Asia/Pacific	157.49
☐ Europe	171.35
☐ Middle East	4.65
☐ Canada & USA	181.23
☐ Latin America	25.33

Source: Nua Internet Surveys. 2002. "How Many Online?" Available online at: www.nua.ie/surveys/how_many_online/index.html.

Figure 10-9
Number online

The numbers in a March 2002 study by Global Reach, a marketing consulting firm, are slightly higher, estimating that 567 million people worldwide are now online. The Global Reach study provides another interesting estimate: unlike a few years ago, as of this writing only 40 percent of those online today speak English as their native language. Figure 10-10 illustrates the Global Reach study's estimated percentage of people online by native language.

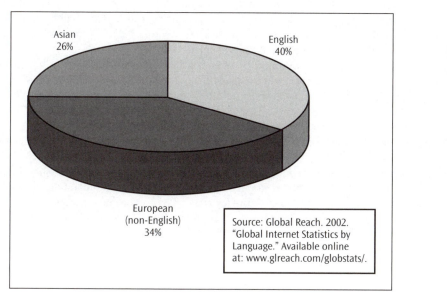

Figure 10-10
Online population by language

Asian 26%
English 40%
European (non-English) 34%

Source: Global Reach. 2002. "Global Internet Statistics by Language." Available online at: www.glreach.com/globstats/.

The significance of these online population estimates on the future of U.S. e-business should not be overlooked. More and more potential consumers around the world are getting connected and fewer and fewer of them speak English as their native language. E-businesses in the U.S. that do not realize the importance of the globalization of the Internet and its effect on the e-business marketspace will likely miss out on huge opportunities to reach new customers.

In this chapter, you have learned that, while some e-businesses have faltered because of an inability to exploit new technologies or accurately read the marketplace, many more are succeeding, proving that e-businesses that are based on sound e-business models and that follow good business practices are here to stay. Meanwhile, the anticipated ability of current and future e-businesses to successfully exploit emerging technologies and e-business trends offers the world a bright e-business future.

...THE WEB IN BLOOM

As of this writing, FTD.com, the "3-year old company with the 93-year old history" is an unqualified e-business success story. In September 2001, FTD.com reported its fifth consecutive quarter of profitability with $4.3 million in net income on sales of $21.9 million! But, how did FTD.com make profits in spite of the economic slowdown of 2001-2002 while other e-businesses failed? Several factors, including technological ones, came together to help FTD.com's e-business model succeed. Perhaps most importantly, FTD had the advantage of a ready and willing consumer base for online flower and gift sales. Consumers were already comfortable with ordering flowers via the telephone and therefore were very receptive to ordering flowers and gifts online.

Other success factors are specific to FTD.com and the way its management implements its e-business model. First of all, FTD.com makes effective use of Internet technologies and its proprietary FTD fulfillment network (called the Mercury Network) to funnel orders placed at the FTD.com Web site to the FTD-affiliated florists who actually fulfill the orders. FTD-affiliated florists can choose to connect to the Mercury Network with software that provides a Web interface and allows them to receive orders and perform certain back-end functions such as accounting and inventory control. Smaller FTD-affiliates can choose to use a less sophisticated connection with a Web interface that simply lets them receive and manage orders.

Because FTD.com simply takes floral and gift orders and relays the orders to a member florist for fulfillment, FTD.com incurs no inventory or fulfillment costs. Additionally, years of goodwill and positive consumer experiences are connected to the FTD brand. Because FTD.com doesn't need to build its brand, it is able to hold down marketing costs and exploit FTD's offline network of florists to maintain a high level of customer awareness.

FTD.com's management has also made several important strategic decisions: to ignore the "grow at all costs" philosophy that hurt some early e-businesses by keeping the pace of growth manageable; to market FTD.com with e-mail campaigns and Web portal partnerships rather than expensive television and billboard ad campaigns; and, perhaps most importantly, to operate FTD.com (Figure 10-11) in such a way as to focus on both revenue growth and profitability by carefully managing its marketing effort and controlling costs.

Continued

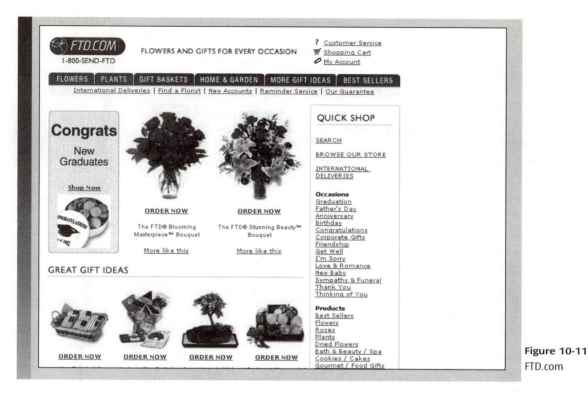

Figure 10-11
FTD.com

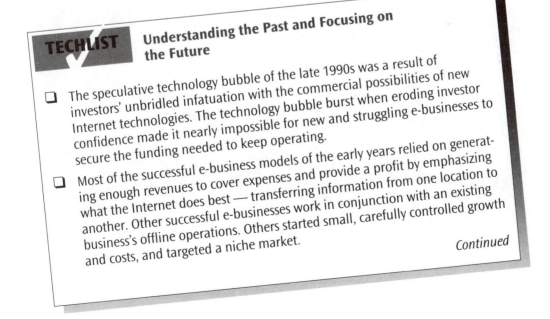

TECHLIST ✔ Understanding the Past and Focusing on the Future

☐ The speculative technology bubble of the late 1990s was a result of investors' unbridled infatuation with the commercial possibilities of new Internet technologies. The technology bubble burst when eroding investor confidence made it nearly impossible for new and struggling e-businesses to secure the funding needed to keep operating.

☐ Most of the successful e-business models of the early years relied on generating enough revenues to cover expenses and provide a profit by emphasizing what the Internet does best — transferring information from one location to another. Other successful e-businesses work in conjunction with an existing business's offline operations. Others started small, carefully controlled growth and costs, and targeted a niche market.

Continued

- E-businesses that failed in the early years generally misjudged how quickly consumers would adopt Internet technologies, relied on traditional business models that didn't translate well into online businesses, and misjudged the power of Internet technologies.

- "Web services" refers to the new technologies involved in exchanging data between e-businesses, including SOAP, UDDI, WSDL, and ebXML.

- "Peer-to-peer (P2P) computing" refers to the uploading and downloading of files that are stored on individual personal computer hard drives via an IP network such as the Internet.

- "Collaborative commerce" is a term many analysts use to refer to the interrelationships of multiple e-businesses that work together as trading partners using Internet technologies.

- An intelligent agent is a program that can act independently to carry out scheduled tasks. The Semantic Web is a conceptual plan for the future of the Web. According to this plan, intelligent agents would work to improve our ability to find and manipulate Web-based information.

- Futurists see the executable Internet as an environment where executable programs that are used once and then thrown away are downloaded to computers or hand-held devices. Such programs would provide real-time information or provide an interactive online experience. Futurists also project the development of an extended Internet, which would involve making nearly every electrical device Internet enabled.

- The Electronic Product Code (ePC) provides a unique identification for each item produced in a manufacturing process. The Physical Markup Language (PML) and the Object Naming Service (ONS) are two components of ePC technologies.

- The Internet2 is a high-speed network created especially for scientists, researchers, and educators.

- Nanoscale computing and quantum computing may provide e-businesses with cheap and powerful computing power, and advances in biotechnology research may provide future opportunities for new e-business models.

- In the future, B2B, B2C, and wireless e-business transactions are expected to grow, network security will become paramount, and the globalization of the Internet will enable e-businesses to reach an ever increasing number of potential customers.

Key Terms

bioinformatics
collaborative commerce
   (c-commerce)
ebXML
Electronic Product Code (ePC)
executable Internet
extended Internet
intelligent agent
Internet2
nanoscale computing
Object Naming Service (ONS)

peer-to-peer computing (P2P)
Physical Markup Language (PML)
quantum computing
Radio Frequency
   Identification (RFID)
Resource Description
   Framework (RDF)
Semantic Web
Simple Object Access
   Protocol (SOAP)

speculative bubbles
supernodes
technology bubble
transparent commerce
Universal Description, Discovery,
   and Integration (UDDI)
Web services
Web Services Description
   Language (WSDL)
X Internet

Review Questions

1. Which of the following items is likely not a cause of the technology bubble?

   a. Predatory investment banks
   b. Investor overconfidence
   c. Greedy venture capitalists
   d. E-business models with a focus on generating revenues from day one

2. Which of the following e-businesses focused on growth and building market share rather than early profits?

   a. eBay
   b. Amazon.com
   c. Hotels.com
   d. NetBank

3. Which of the following failed e-business models followed the "advertising revenues" model?

   a. eToys
   b. Pets.com
   c. AllAdvantage.com
   d. GroceryWorks.com

4. Which of the following is not a Web services technology?

   a. UDDI
   b. X Internet
   c. WSDL
   d. SOAP

5. Which of the following is not a peer-to-peer technology?

   a. KaZaA
   b. Gnutella
   c. ONS
   d. JXTA

6. An intelligent agent is a(n):

   a. Program that can act independently of its user.
   b. Data transmission protocol.
   c. New concept describing the future of the Web.
   d. XML-based language designed to describe physical objects.

7. Which of the following technologies holds promise for increased computer processing speeds?

   a. Quantum computing
   b. UDDI
   c. Nanoscale computing
   d. Bioinformatics

8. Which characteristics define the e-business models that have the best chance of successfully exploiting emerging technologies?

   a. Creative
   b. Well-managed
   c. Profitable
   d. All of the above

9. What is a major concern about the implementation of Electronic Product Code technologies?

   a. Creation of a speculative bubble
   b. Ease of use
   c. Privacy
   d. Cost

10. Which failed e-business neglected to consider the social ramifications of its innovative use of Internet technologies:

    a. eToys
    b. ThirdVoice
    c. AllAdvantage.com
    d. PointSpeed

11. Many successful e-business models act as intermediaries or offer electronic products and services rather than physical products. **True or False?**

12. The most famous "pure play" e-business selling physical products is eBay. **True or False?**

13. Many early e-business entrepreneurs and investors miscalculated the speed with which consumers would adopt Internet technologies. **True or False?**

14. Some early e-business entrepreneurs and investors were correct in their assumption that new online marketspaces would completely replace offline marketplaces. **True or False?**

15. One important lesson from the burst technology bubble is that it is more important for a new e-business to grow market share than to generate profits. **True or False?**

16. Transparent commerce is a term used to refer to online transactions of the future, which may take place without the explicit participation of a human. **True or False?**

17. AOL Instant Messenger is an early example of the executable Internet. **True or False?**

18. ePC "smart tags" use RFID technologies to receive and send radio signals. **True or False?**

19. Commercial network providers are rushing to implement Internet2 technologies for commercial customers. **True or False?**

20. Collaborative computing initiatives may assure the continued growth of B2C e-business. **True or False?**

Exercises

1. Using Internet search tools or other relevant resources, such as those at the end of this chapter, identify two successful and two unsuccessful e-businesses *not previously discussed in this text*. Then create a one- or two-page paper describing the origins of the e-businesses and the factors (including technological factors) that led to their success or failure.

2. Using Internet search tools or other relevant resources, such as those at the end of this chapter, research the dot.com or technology bubble of the late 1990s. Then write a one- or two-page paper describing the factors leading to the creation of the bubble and explaining why it burst.

3. Define the following terms and explain the role each may play in the future of e-business: collaborative commerce, the Semantic Web, intelligent agent, Internet2, and X Internet.

4. Using Internet search tools or other relevant resources, such as those found at the end of this chapter, research the origins, history, and background of eBay and Amazon.com, two successful pure play e-businesses. Then write a one- or two-page paper comparing and contrasting the two e-businesses, focusing on their successful use of Internet technologies.

5. Using Internet search tools or other relevant resources, such as those at the end of this chapter, research the globalization of the Internet and then write a one- or two-page paper describing the effect of globalization on the U.S. and worldwide e-business marketspace.

CASE PROJECTS

◆ 1 ◆

At the next E-business Managers Roundtable meeting, you will moderate a panel discussion entitled "Dot.Coms and Dot.Bombs: What Have We Learned?" Using Internet search tools and other relevant resources, research the dot.com or technology bubble and today's e-business environment. Then create an outline of the talking points you can use to guide the moderated discussion. Be sure to include specific e-business examples to make your talking points more effective.

◆ 2 ◆

You are a member of the Young Professionals Book and Movie Club. At the next meeting, you and several other members plan to review a book or movie about a real-world, e-business startup. Using Internet search tools or other relevant resources, such as those listed at the end of this chapter, locate an appropriate book or movie that you would like to review. Read the book or watch the movie and then create a two- or three-page review to share with the club members. Be certain to pay special attention to the way in which the e-business startup used technology as well as the other factors related to its success or failure.

◆ 3 ◆

You are the executive assistant to Bonita Daversa, the president of TopMetal, an e-business that operates a B2B marketplace for the scrap metal industry. Ms. Daversa has been invited to give a 15-minute presentation on "E-Business and Emerging Technologies" during the industry's annual trade show and conference. She asks you to prepare an outline that describes five emerging technologies and their anticipated effect on e-business. Using Internet search tools or other resources, research emerging technologies and the future of e-business. Then prepare the outline.

TEAM PROJECT

You and two classmates are finally going to take the plunge and start your own e-business, and you are working together to develop a business plan. As part of the plan, you need to prepare a summary of the technologies that will become an integral part of your e-business. First, meet with your classmates to select a name, domain name, and e-business model, and to create a descriptive business purpose for your e-business. Then determine the networking, Internet-working, Web development, Internet access, wireless, security, back-office integration, content management, and other technologies that you will use to make your e-business a success. Finally, using Microsoft PowerPoint or other presentation software, prepare a 5–10 slide presentation that defines your e-business and explains your technology selections. Present your e-business and technology selections to a group of classmates chosen by your instructor.

Useful Links

AgileBrain.com — E-business Ideas and Resources
www.agilebrain.com/

AIM — RFID Resources
www.aimglobal.org/technologies/rfid/

Auto-ID Center
www.autoidcenter.org/main.asp

BioInformatics.org
bioinformatics.org/

Center for Nanoscale Science and Technology
cnst.rice.edu/

Compinfo — The Computer Information Center
www.compinfo-center.com/tpagnt-t.htm

Computational Publications — Nanotechnology and Computers
www.comppub.com/links.phtml?cat=Computing

eAI Journal — E-business and Application Integration
www.eaijournal.com/

ebXML
www.ebxml.org/

Forbes.com — Future Tech
www.forbes.com/futuretech/

Forbes.com — Personal Tech
www.forbes.com/personaltech/

Foresight Institute
www.foresight.org/homepage.html

Gnutella.com
www.gnutella.com

IBM — The Intelligent Agents Project at T. J. Watson Research Center
www.research.ibm.com/iagents/

National Nanotechnology Initiative
www.nano.gov/

Peer to Peer Central
www.peertopeercentral.com/

SemanticWeb.org
www.semanticweb.org/

Soap.Weblogs.com
soap.weblogs.com/

The Institute of Nanotechnology
www.nano.org.uk/

Universal Description, Discovery, and Integration (UDDI)
www.uddi.org/

W3C — The Semantic Web
www.w3.org/2001/sw/

WebServices.org
www.webservices.org/

Links to Web Sites or Companies Noted in This Chapter

Amazon.com
www.amazon.com

Ariba Inc.
www.ariba.com/

AsktheBuilder.com
www.askthebuilder.com

Barnes & Noble
www.bn.com

BioExchange
www.bioexchange.com/

Bristol-Myers Squibb Company
www.bms.com/

Business2.0
www.business20.com/

ChemConnect
www.chemconnect.com/

Cisco Systems, Inc.
www.cisco.com

Clinical Trials Online
www.clinicaltrialsonline.com/

Crate and Barrel
www.crateandbarrel.com/

DNA Diagnostics Center
www.dnacenter.com/

DoveBid
www.dovebid.com/

eBay
www.ebay.com

Forrester Research, Inc.
www.forrester.com/home/0,6092,1-0,FF.html·

FTD.com
www.ftd.com

Global Reach
www.glreach.com/globstats/

Godiva Chocolatier
www.godiva.com/

Hickory Farms
www.hickoryfarms.com/welcome.asp

Hotels.com
www.hotels.com

IBM Corporation
www.ibm.com

Intel Corporation
www.intel.com/

Internet2
www.internet2.org/

KaZaA
www.kazaa.com/en/index.php

MetalSite
www.metalsite.com/

Microsoft Corporation
www.microsoft.com

Napster
www.napster.com/

NetBank
www.netbank.com

Nua Surveys
www.nua.ie/surveys/

Ovum
www.ovum.com

Oxford Ancestors
www.oxfordancestors.com/daughters.html

Proctor & Gamble
www.pg.com/?rc=-5

SETI@home
setiathome.ssl.berkeley.edu/

Sharman Networks — KaZaA
www.kazaa.com/en/index.htm

Sun Microsystems, Inc.
www.sun.com

The Coca-Cola Company
www.cocacola.com/

Travelocity
www.travelocity.com

USA Interactive
www.usanetworks.com/

Veritas Medicine
www.veritasmedicine.com/

Wal-Mart Stores
www.walmart.com/

Webmergers.com
www.webmergers.com/

Whirlpool Corporation
www.whirlpool.com

For Additional Review

Adams, John. 2002. "NetBank's Attention to Retention," *FutureBanker*. Available online at: www.futurebanker.com/fb/currentissue/fb-db.html.

AllAdvantage.com. 2000. "The Company," www.alladvantage.com.

Arango, Tim. 2002. "FTD.com Buyout Wilts in the Sun," *The Street.com*, March 4. Available online at: www.thestreet.com/_intuit/stocks/timarango/10011455.html.

Ashbrook, Tom. 2000. *The LEAP: A Memoir of Love and Madness in the Internet Gold Rush*. New York: Houghton Mifflin Company.

Barkow, Tim. 2001. "The New E-commerce," *WebReview*, January 26. Available online at: www.webreview.com/soapbox/2001/01_26_01.shtml.

Barnes-Vieyra, Pamela and Claycomb, Cindy. 2001. "Business-to-Business E-Commerce: Models and Managerial Decisions," *Business Horizons*, May, 44:3.

Bellini, Heather et al. 2001. "The Birth of Collaborative Commerce," *SalomonSmithBarney*, June 20. Available online at: www.karat.com/images/pdfs/SSB_Birth_Collaborative_Commerce_final.pdf.

Berman, Dennis K. 2000. "What's the Trick: Some Dot-Coms are Actually Making Money. And Others Predict Profits This Year," *Business Week*, July 17. Available online at: www.hotels.com.

Berners-Lee, Tim et al. 2001. "The Semantic Web," *Scientific American*, May 1. Available online at: www.sciam.com/2001/0501issue/0501berners-lee.html.

Bhattacharjee, Debashish et al. 2002. "Expert Panel: The Future of Enterprise Applications," *Intelligent Enterprise*, March 28. Available online at: www.intelligententerprise.com/020328/506feat2_1.shtml?ebusiness.

Bicknell, Craig. 2000. "From iBash to iBusted," *Wired News*, April 14. Available online at: www.wired.com/news/print/0,1294,35691,00.html.

Black, Jane. 2001. "Where the Web is Really Revolutionizing Business," *BusinessWeek Online*, August 27. Available online at: www.businessweek.com/magazine/content/01_35/b3746669.htm.

Borck, James R. 2001. "Web Services Bring E-businesses Together," *InfoWorld*, September 14. Available online at: www.infoworld.com/articles/tc/xml/01/09/17/010917tcpit.xml.

Breidenbach, Susan. 2001. "Peer-to-Peer Potential," *NetworkWorldFusion*, July 30. Available online at: www.nwfusion.com/research/2001/0730feat.html.

Brock, David L. 2001. "The Physical Markup Language," *Auto-ID Center*, February. Available online at: www.autoidcenter.org/research/MIT-AUTOID-WH-003.pdf.

Burriesci, Jeanette. 2002. "Companies to Watch 2002: Collaborative Commerce," *Intelligent Enterprise*, January 1. Available online at: www.intelligententerprise.com/020101/501feat2_4.shtml.

Carvell, Tim et al. 2002. "The 101 Dumbest Moments in Business," *Business2.0*, April. Available online at: www.business2.com/articles/mag/0,1640,38604,00.html.

Cassidy, John. 2002. *Dot.con: The Greatest Story Ever Sold*. New York: HarperCollins.

Cavuto, Neil. 2002. "Robert Diener, President of Hotel Reservations Network," *Fox News*, March 26. Available online at: www.foxnews.com/story/0,2933,48809,00.html.

Cerami, Ethan. 2002. "Top Ten FAQs for Web Services," *O'Reilly Network*, February 12. Available online at: www.oreillynet.com/pub/a/Webservices/2002/02/12/Webservicefaqs.html.

Chabria, Anita. 2001. "For FTD.com, a Name Goes a Long Way," *The Industry Standard*, February 8. Available online at: www.google.com.

Charny, Ben. 2002. "Sprint to Test Net Access Through Walls," *ZDNet News*, May 7. Available online at: zdnet.com.com/2100-1105-901738.html.

Classen, Michael. 2002. "What Web Services Are NOT," *Webreference*. www.webreference.com/xml/column/50.

Cover, Robin. 2001. "Physical Markup Language (PML)," *XML Cover Pages*, December 20. Available online at: xml.coverpages.org/pml-ons.html.

Cover, Robin. 2002. "Electronic Business SML Initiative (ebXML)," *The XML Cover Pages*, March 20. Available online at: xml.coverpages.org/ebXML.html.

Dignan, Larry. 2001. "An E-Government Pill for the Tech Sector," *CNET News.com*, December 17. Available online at: news.com.com/2100-1017-277085.html.

Dominguez, Alex. 2002. "Monkey Moves Cursor by Thinking," *Salon.com*, March 13. Available online at: www.salon.com.

Dumbill, Ed. 2000. "The Semantic Web: A Primer," *XML.com*, November 1. Available online at: www.xml.com/pub/a/2000/11/01/semanticweb/.

E-CommerceGuide.com. 2002. "E-Commerce: What Works & What Doesn't," February 8. Available online at: ecommerce.Internet.com/news/insights/trends/article/0,3371,10417_971301,00.html.

eCompany. 2001. "Boo! And the 100 Other Dumbest Moments in E-business History," *Business 2.0*, May. Available online at: www.business2.com/articles/mag/0,1640,12416,00.html.

Edmonds, Christopher. 2002. "Bottom of the Barrel: Bank on NetBank for Profits," *TheStreet.com*, February 6. Available online at: www.thestreet.com/_yahoo/comment/chrisedmonds/10008294.html.

Enos, Lori. 2001. "Report: English-Only a Mistake for U. S. Sites," *E-Commerce Times*, May 17. Available online at: www.ecommercetimes.com/perl/story/9812.html.

eRetail News. 2002. "The Electronic Product Code." Available online at: www.eretailnews.com/Features/0105epc1.htm.

Featherly, Kevin. 2001. "Forget the Web, Make Way for 'X Internet'," *Newsbytes*, May 7. www.newsbytes.com/news/01/165405.html.

Fingar, Peter et al. 2001. *The Death of 'e' and the Birth of the Real New Economy: Business Models, Technologies, and Strategies for the 21st Century*. Tampa: FL: Meghan-Kiffer Press.

Fortune Small Business. 2001. "Don't Give Up on the Web: Smart, Patient, Creative Companies Can Still Win Online." February 1, 11:1.

FTD.com. 2002. "About Us." Available online at: www.ftd.com.

Fukuyama, Francis. 2002. *Our Posthuman Future: Consequences of the Biotechnology Revolution*. New York: Farrar Straus & Giroux.

Gimein, Mark. 2000. "Meet the Dumbest Dot-Com in the World," *Fortune*, July 10, 142:2.

Glasner, Joanna. 2000. "Perilous Fall of Pixelon," *Wired News*, May 16. Available online at: www.wired.com/news/exec/0,1370,36243,00.html.

Global Reach. 2002. "Global Internet Statistics by Language." Available online at: www.glreach.com/globstats/.

Goodin, Dan. 2000. "Pixelon Decimates Its Ranks," *The Industry Standard*, May 11. Available online at: www.thestandard.com/article/display/0,1151,15054,00.html.

Goodin, Dan. 2000. "Pixelon Misled Investors, Exec Admits," *The Industry Standard*, May 14. Available online at: www.thestandard.com/article/display/0,1902,15115,00.html.

Goodin, Dan. 2000. "The Imposter," *The Industry Standard*, July 3. Available online at: www.thestandard.com/article/0,1902,16309,00.html?body_page=1.

Gralpois, Bruno. 2001. "Speaking the Language of E-Internationalization," *ClickZ.com*, March 20. Available online at: www.clickz.com/em_mkt/int_em_mkt/article.php/838881.

Griffin, Jane. 2002. "Information Strategy: Collaborative Commerce and the eXtended Intelligent Enterprise," *DMReview.com*, March. Available online at: www.dmreview.com/master.cfm?NavID=193&EdID=4815.

Grimmelmann, James. 2001. "Peer-to-Peer Terrorism," *Salon.com*, September 26. Available online at: www.salon.com/tech/feature/2001/09/26/osama_bin_napster/.

Gulati, Ranjay and Nemmers, Michael L. 2001. "Future Directions in E-Business," *Kellogg Graduate School of Management, Northwestern University*. Available online at: www.ranjaygulati.com/art/present/present-futuredirs.pdf.

Hamm, Steve. 2001. "The Tech Challenge: Businesses are Fed Up With Paying for Underperforming Technology. They Are Looking for Products That Will Save Money and Spur Growth," *BusinessWeek Online*, August 27.

Harrison, Ann. 2001. "Bill Joy Spins the Future of P2P," *NetworkWorldFusion*, July 2. Available online at: www.nwfusion.com/newsletters/fileshare/2001/00898095.html.

Helft, Miguel. 2001. "The E-Commerce Survivors," *The Industry Standard*, July 16. Available online at: www.thestandard.com/article/0,1902,27593,00.html.

Hess, Diane. 2002. "Travel Shares Find Room for Upside," *TheStreet.com*, January 28. Available online at: www.hotels.com.

Hesseldahl, Arik. 2001. "Death of the Pager?" *Forbes.com*, December 13. Available online at: www.forbes.com/2001/12/13/1213tentech.html%20.

Hesseldahl, Arik. 2002. "Motorola Gets a Hip Transplant," *Forbes.com*, April 5. Available online at: www.forbes.com/technology/personaltechnology/2002/04/05/0405tentech.html.

Hesseldahl, Arik. 2002. "Wiring Teens: The Next Wireless Fad," *Forbes.com*, April 3. Available online at: www.forbes.com/technology/personaltechnology/2002/04/03/0403wildseed.html.

Hibbard, Justin. 2000. "And of Course, the Anti-Entrepreneur," *Red Herring*, September. Available online at: www.redherring.com/mag/issue82/mag-anti-82.html.

Hibbard, Justin. 2000. "Can Peer-to-Peer Grow Up?" *Red Herring*, December. Available online at: www.redherring.com/mag/issue86/mag-grow-86.html.

Hibbard, Justin. 2000. "Fraudcasting: The Blunderful and Horrible Life of Pixelon," *Red Herring*, September. Available online at: www.redherring.com/mag/issue82/mag-fraudcasting-82.html.

Hotels.com. 2002. "About Us." Available online at: www.hotels.com.

Hotz, Robert Lee. 2002. "Brain Probes Give Rats Their Marching Orders," *Los Angeles Times*, May 2. www.latimes.com/news/yahoo/la-000031153may02.story?coll=la%2Dnewsaol%2Dheadlines.

Internet2. 2002. "About Internet2." Available online at: www.internet2.edu/html/about.html.

InternetNews.com. 1999. "Pixelon Intros TV-Quality Broadcast Network Technology," October 18. Available online at: www.Internetnews.com/bus-news/article/0,,3_220791,00.html.

Jacobus, Patricia. 2000. "Pixelon Issues Sweeping Layoffs After Founder's Arrest," *CNET News.com*, May 12. Available online at: news.com.com/2100-1023-240493.html?legacy=cnet&tag=st.cn.sr.ne.2.

Jimenez, Helen A. 2002. "B2C E-commerce Gaining Foothold," *BusinessWorld*, April 3. Available online at: globalarchive.ft.com/globalarchive/article.html?id=020403001923&query=ovum.

Joy, Bill. 2000. "Why the Future Doesn't Need Us?" *Wired Magazine*, April. Available online at: www.wired.com/wired/archive/8.04/joy_pr.html.

Kador, John. 2002. "Profiting From e-Business Innovation," *eAI Journal*, February. Available online at: eaijournal.com/PDF/InnovationKador.pdf.

Kawamoto, Wayne. 2001. "NetBank," *App-Planet Apps in Review*, February 1. Available online at: www.google.com.

Kayl, Kammie. 2001. "ebXML: The Key Components," *Sun Microsystems, Inc.*, September. Available online at: java.sun.com/features/2001/09/ebxmlkey.html.

Kayl, Kammie. 2001. "Electronic Business XML: Revolutionizing the Engines of Business," *Sun Microsystems, Inc.*, September. Available online at: java.sun.com/features/2001/09/ebxmlrev.html.

Kemp, Ted. 2001. "Online Retailers Smell the Roses," *Internetweek*, September 17. www.internetweek.com/customers091701.htm.

Kirby, Carrie. 2001. "Pay-to-Surf Not Paying Off for Web Sites," *San Francisco Chronicle*, July 12. Available online at: www.sfgate.com/cgi-bin/article.cgi?file=/chronicle/archive/2000/07/12/BU90515.DTL.

Kirsner, Scott. 2001. "Future Tense: X Internet," *Fast Company*, October. www.fastcompany.com/online/51/future_xInternet.html.

Koenig, David. 2000. "Dallas Company Dominates Field of Booking Hotel Rooms on the Internet," *Associated Press Newswires*, July 23. Available online at: www.hotels.com.

Kopytoff, Verne. 2001. "Online and Profitable: Amid the Dot-Com Carnage, Some Firms Found Success on the Web," *San Francisco Chronicle*, July 9. Available online at: www.sfgate.com/cgi-bin/article.cgi?file=/chronicle/archive/2001/07/09/BU205110.DTL.

Kuo, David and Kuo, J. David. 2001. *dot.bomb: My Days and Nights at an Internet Goliath*. New York: Little, Brown & Company.

Lemley, Brad. 2002. "Internet2: A Supercharged New Network with True Tele-presence Puts the Needs of Science First," *Discover Magazine*, May. Available online at: www.discover.com/may_02/gthere.html?article=featinternet2.html.

Levitt, Jason. 2000. "Peer-to-Peer Anarchy: The Next Big Thing?" *Informationweek*, May 15. www.informationweek.com/author/Internet35.htm.

Limewire.com. 2001. "2001 Rolling Host Count: Gnutella Network Hosts." Available online at: www.limewire.com/historical_size2001.html.

Little, Darnell. 2001. "Why FTD is Flowering on the Web," *BusinessWeek Online*, October 31. Available online at: www.businessweek.com/technology/content/oct2001/tc20011031_4135.htm.

Macaluso, Nora. 2001. "U. S. E-Commerce Losing Global Edge," *E-Commerce Times*, January 11. Available online at: www.ecommercetimes.com/perl/story/6637.html.

Mahoney, Michael. 2001. "The Future of E-Commerce: Caught in a .NET?" *E-Commerce Times*, December 26. Available online at: www.ecommercetimes.com/perl/story/15363.html.

Mann, Charles C. 2000. "Peer-to-Peer: An E-mail Exchange With Gnutella Developer Gene Kan," *The Atlantic Monthly Online*, September. Available online at: www.theatlantic.com/issues/2000/09/mann-kan.htm.

Marketingsherpa.com. 2001. "Case Study: NetBank Achieves 12 Profitable Quarters by Obsessively Tracking Marketing Metrics," July 27. www.financialmarketingbiz.com/sample.crfm?contentID=1771.

Maturion, Damon. 2000. "Is the AllAdvantage Viewbar a Scam?" *New Business News*, April 24. Available online at: www.newbusinessnews.com/story/04240001.html.

McDonald, Tim. 2002. "Sneak Peek: The Computer Screen of the Future," *NewsFactor Network*, April 4. Available online at: www.newsfactor.com/perl/story/17066.html.

McDonough, Dan Jr. 2002. "How Mobile Chips Could Change Computing," *Wireless NewsFactor*, April 4. Available online at: www.wirelessnewsfactor.com/perl/story/17108.html.

McDougall, Paul. 2000. "The Power of Peer-to-Peer," *InformationWeek*, August 28. Available online at: www.informationweek.com/801/peer.htm.

McHugh, Josh. 1999. "Wisecrack-Ware," *Forbes*, July 26. www.forbes.com/1999/0726/0214026a_print.html.

Mello, Adrian. 2001. "Global E-Business: Walking the Talk," *ZDNet Tech Update*, November 14. Available online at: techupdate.zdnet.com/techupdate/stories/main/0,14179,2824486,00.html.

Micek, John L. 2001. "FTD.com Profitability Blooms Anew," *ECommerce Times*, January 23. Available online at: www.ecommercetimes.com/perl/story/6931.html.

Microsoft Corporation. 2002. "Web Services: Interoperability Across Platforms, Applications, and Programming Languages," February 6. Available online at: www.microsoft.com/net/ws-i.asp.

Miller, Tim. 2002. "Top Ten Lessons From the Internet Shakeout," *Webmergers.com*. Available online at: www.webmergers.com/editorial/article.php?id=48.

Morrone, Megan. 2001. "After Napster: What's Next for P2P?" *TechTVNews*, March 12. Available online at: www.techtv.com/news/specialreport/story/0,24195,3316556,00.html.

Murphy, Chris. 2000. "A Financial Advantage?" *InformationWeek*, June 12. Available online at: www.northernlight.com.

Negroponte, Nicholas. 1995. *Being Digital*. New York: Random House (Knopff).

NetBank. 2002. "The NetBank Story." Available online at: www.netbank.com/about.

Netmarkets Europe. 2001. "E-collaboration: A Hand-in-Hand Route to Success," *The Insider's Guide to B2B*, March. Available online at: www.netmarketseurope.com/summite/ecollaboration.pdf.

Nicholls, Sean. 2002. "Electronic Tags May Rule the World," *The Age.com*, February 27. Available online at: www.theage.com.au/articles/2002/02/26/1014471638902.html.

Nua Internet Surveys. 2002. "How Many Online?" Available online at: www.nua.ie/surveys/how_many_online/index.html.

Oakes, Chris. 1999. "The Web's New Graffiti?" *Wired News*, June 9. Available online at: www.wired.com/news/technology/0,1282,20101,00.html.

Oakes, Chris. 1999. "Third Voice Rips Holes in Web," *Wired News*, July 9. Available online at: www.wired.com/news/technology/0,1282,20636,00.html.

Oestricher, Dwight. 2001. "Lodging Industry Woes a Boom for Hotel Reservations Network," *Dow Jones Newswires*. Available online at: www.hotels.com.

Olavsrud, Thor et al. 2002. "Web Services Moving Beyond the Hype," *InternetNews.com*, March 13. Available online at: www.Internetnews.com/ent-news/article/0,,7_990981,00.html.

Olsen, Stefanie. 2000. "Pay-to-Surf Site Hopes to Ride a Different Wave," *CNET News.com*, August 22. Available online at: news.com.com/2100-1017-244753.html.

Orr, Andrea. 2002. "NetTrends: Amazon Brings Back Old Rules in New Economy," *Reuters*, May 1. news.moneycentral.msn.com/ticker/article.asp?Symbol=US:AMZN&Feed=RTR&Date=20020501&ID=1605593.

Overby, Stephanie. 2001. "Survivor III: We Return to Six Businesses We Profiled Last Year to See Who is Still Standing and Who has Been Kicked Off E-Com Island," *CIO Magazine*, May 1. Available online at: www.cio.com/archive/050101/survivor_content.html.

Palan, Petr. 2001. "The Future of E-Business is in Online Marketplaces," *Emerce Industry Day*, July 11. Available online at: www.europemedia.net/showfeature.asp?ArticleID=6546#.

Pastore, Michael. 2001. "The End of the Web as We Know It," *CyberAtlas*, May 17. Available online at: cyberatlas.Internet.com/big_picture/applications/article/0,,1301_767831,00.html.

Patsuris, Penelope. 1999. "Talking Back on the Web," *Forbes*, May 21. Available online at: www.forbes.com/1999/05/21/feat.html.

Paul, Noel C. 2002. "Hotels Follow Airlines into Online Bookings," *The Christian Science Monitor*, May 6. Available online at: www.csmonitor.com/2002/0506/p17s01-wmcn.htm.

PC Magazine. 2001. "E-business: What Went Right…What Went Wrong…," July 1. Available online at: www.pcmag.com/article/0,2997,s=400&a=5001,00.asp.

Plansky, John and O'Grady, Tom. 2001. "E-Markets Business Model V2," *Line 56*, August 9. Available online at: hamlet.line56.com/articles/default.asp?NewsID=2832.

Press Release. 2001. "The Death of the Web is Inevitable, " *Forrester Research*, Inc., May 17. Available online at: www.forrester.com/ER/Press/Release/0,1769,567,00.html.

Radjou, Navi et al. 2001. "The X Internet Invigorates B2B Apps," *Forrester Research, Inc.*, October. Available online at: www.objectfx.com/literature/XInternet.pdf.

Raik-Allen, George. 1999. "New Startup Gives Browsers Their Voice," *RedHerring*, May 18. Available online at: www.redherring.com/insider/1999/0518/vc-thirdvoice.html.

Reddy, Ram. 2002. "The Evolution of Supply Chain Technologies," *Intelligent Enterprise*, January 14. Available online at: www.intelligententerprise.com/020114/502infosc1_1.shtml.

Reddy, Ram. 2002. "The Evolution of Supply Chain Technologies — Part 2," *Intelligent Enterprise*, February 21. Available online at: www.intelligent enterprise.com/020221/504infosc1_1.shtml?ebusiness.

Regan, Keith. 2002. "Five E-Commerce Trends to Watch," *E-Commerce Times*, April 3. Available online at: www.ecommercetimes.com/perl/story/16967.html.

Roberti, Mark. 2001. "Peer-to-Peer Isn't Dead," *The Industry Standard*, April 23. Available online at: www.findarticles.com/cf_dls/m0HWW/16_4/73746906/p1/article.jhtml.

Roberts-Witt, Sarah L. 2001. "Peer Pressure," *PC Magazine*, June 19. techupdate.zdnet.com/techupdate/stories/main/0,14179,2775032,00.html.

Rountree, David. 2001. "NetBank Celebrates Its Fifth Anniversary," *Bank Technology News*, November. Available online at: www.banktechnews.com/btn/articles/btnnov01-04.shtml.

Sandsmark, Fred. 2000. " Reload: Now It's ThirdVoice, Take Two," *RedHerring*, July. Available online at: www.redherring.com/mag/issue80/mag-reload-80.html.

Saunders, Christopher. 2001. "All Over at AllAdvantage," *Internetnews.com Advertising Report*, February 1. Available online at: www.Internetnews.com/IAR/article/0,,12_577561,00.html.

Saunders, Christopher. 2001. "Lacking Business Model, Phones, AllAdvantage Still in Business," *Internetnews.com Advertising Report*, February 6. Available online at: www.Internetnews.com/IAR/article/0,,12_581071,00.html.

Sausner, Rebecca. 2001. "Meet the Future: the 'X Internet'," *NewsFactor Network*, May 25. Available online at: www.wirelessnewsfactor.com/perl/story/10012.html.

Schonfeld, Erick. 2001. "IBM Gets Small: Big Blue Researchers are Trying to Move Quantum Computing from Theory to Reality," *Business 2.0*, December 5. Available online at: www.business2.com/articles/web/print/0,1650,35998,FF.html.

Shankland, Stephen. 2001. "Tech Giants Update E-commerce Standard," *CNET News.com*, June 18. Available online at: news.com.com/2100-1001-268529.html?legacy=cnet.

Shankland, Stephen. 2002. "Digital Dog Tags: Would You Wear One?" *CNET News.com*, February 8. Available online at: news.com.com/2100-1001-833379.html?legacy=cnet&tag=lh.

Shirky, Clay. 2000. "What is P2P…and What Isn't," *O'Reilly Network*, November 24. Available online at: www.openp2p.com/pub/a/p2p/2000/11/24/shirky1-whatisp2p.html.

Shook, David. 2001. "The Davids of E-Commerce," *BusinessWeek Online*, April 23. Available online at: www.businessweek.com/bwdaily/dnflash/apr2001/nf20010423_511.htm.

Siddalingaiah, Madhu. 2001. "Overview of ebXML," *Dot-Com Builder*, August 17. Available online at: dcb.sun.com/practices/webservices/overviews/overview_ebxml.jsp.

Singer, Michael. 2001. "AllAdvantage at a Disadvantage," *siliconvalley.Internet.com*, February 1. Available online at: siloconvalley.Internet.com/news/print/0,,3531_577581,00.html.

Smith, Geoffrey. 2002. "An Online Bank That Could — and Is," *BusinessWeek Online*, March 19. Available online at: www.businessweek.com/technology/content/mar2002/tc20020319_2987.htm.

Snel, Ross. 2002. "HRN Seeks Brand Awareness," *The Wall Street Journal*, April 24. Available online at: www.hotels.com.

Steenhuysen, Julie. 2002. "Bionic Retina Gives 6 Patients Partial Sight," *Yahoo! News*, May 8. Available online at: story.news.yahoo.com/news?tmpl=story&u=/nm/20020508/sc_nm/health_optobionics_dc_1.

Stone, Martin. 2000. "AllAdvantage.com Alienates Ad-Watchers," *Newsbytes*, June 5. Available online at: www.northernlight.com.

The Associated Press. 2000. "Man Who Started Pixelon.com Was a Fugitive," *Las Vegas Review-Journal*, April 15. Available online at: www.lvrj.com/lvrj_home/2000/Apr-15-Sat-2000/news/13382037.html.

The Associated Press. 2000. "Pixelon Founder Turns Self In," *ABCNews.com*, April 14. Available online at: abcnews.go.com/sections/us/DailyNews/pixelon041400.html.

The Industry Standard. 2001. "Life and Death: Private Dot-Coms," July 2. Available online at: www.thestandard.com/article/0,1902,27626,00.html.

The Wall Street Journal. 2002. "E-Commerce," *The Wall Street Journal Reports*, April 15.

Third Voice, Inc. 2000. "Company History," www.thirdvoice.com.

Time, Inc. 2001. "They Love the Slump: These Online Businesses are Profiting Not in Spite of the Tech Slowdown but Because of It," June 11, 157:23.

Trottman, Melanie. 2001. "The Web @ Work / Hotel Reservations Network Inc.," *The Wall Street Journal*, September 17. Available online at: www.hotels.com.

Tsuruoka, Doug. 2001. "Travel Site Enjoys Solid Profits in the First Quarter, Web Company Reported Earnings of 20 Cents per Share," *Investor's Business Daily*, June 20. Available online at: www.hotels.com.

Tsuruoka, Doug. 2002. "Hotel Reservations Network Rebrands Itself With New Web Address," *Investor's Business Daily*, April 18. Available online at: www.hotels.com.

Tweney, Dylan. 2001. "The Defogger: Think Globally, Act Locally," *Business 2.0*, October. Available online at: www.business2.com/articles/mag/0,1640,17423,00.html.

UDDI.org. 2001. "UDDI Executive White Paper," November 14. Available online at: www.uddi.org/pubs/UDDI_Executive_White_Paper.pdf.

Vigoroso, Mark W. 2002. "The World Map of E-Commerce," *E-Commerce Times*, April 2. Available online at: www.ecommercetimes.com/perl/story/16942.html.

Vizard, Michael. 2001. "J. D. Edwards' CEO Ed McVaney Banks on Collaborative Commerce to Drive Business," *InfoWorld*, April 23. Available online at: www.infoworld.com/articles/hn/xml/01/04/23/010423hnmcvaney.xml.

Vizard, Michael. 2002. "Gazing at the Future," *InfoWorld*, January 25. Available online at: www.infoworld.com/articles/fe/xml/02/01/28/020128fecto.xml.

von Lohmann, Fred. 2001. "Peer-to-Peer File Sharing and Copyright Law After Napster," *Electronic Frontier Foundation*, February 27. Available online at: www.eff.org/IP/P2P/Napster/20010227_p2p_copyright_white_paper.html.

Vranica, Suzanne. 2002. "Dot-Com Ads Reappear on TV, Signaling Advertising Rebound," *The Wall Street Journal*, April 10.

Webmergers.com. 2002. "Internet Shutdowns and Bankruptcies Pass 800 Mark in February". Available online at: www.webmergers.com/editorial/article.php?id=54.

Wingfield, Nick. 2002. "Bertelsmann Acquiring Napster Assets," *MSNBC*, May 17. Available online at: www.msnbc.com/news/753696.asp.

Wolk, Martin. 2002. "The New Economy Re-examined." MSNBC.com, March 12. Available online at: www.msnbc.com/news/720239.asp.

Workopolis.com. 2001. "The Rise and Fall of e-Hopes," October 22. Available online at: globeandmail.workopolis.com/servlet/News/fasttrack/20011022/SBEHOP.

Young, Steve and Jorgensen, Jim. 1999. "CEO AllAdvantage.com," *CNNfn Digital Jam*, July 1. Available online at: www.northernlight.com.

Glossary

.NET Flexible, low-level Internet technologies developed by Microsoft Corporation that allow programs written in many different languages to run primarily on networks using Windows operating systems.

128-bit key Session keys consisting of 16 digits equaling 128 bits.

Acrobat Reader A plug-in developed by Adobe Systems Incorporated to read PDF files.

active caching Forwarding or pushing Web content to a geographically distributed group of cache servers ahead of demand.

Active Server Pages (ASP) A server-side technology developed by Microsoft Corporation that uses scripts to help construct Web pages or perform calculations.

ActiveX A programming technology created by Microsoft Corporation similar to Java that runs small programs called ActiveX controls in containers (similar to a virtual sandbox) on a user's computer.

ActiveX controls Small programs downloaded by a Web browser that run in containers on a user's computer similar to the way Java applets run in virtual sandboxes.

Address Resolution Protocol (ARP) A protocol that identifies a host computer on a network and converts its IP address to its physical MAC address.

Advanced Mobile Phone System (AMPS) An early analog cellular phone standard approved by the FCC and commercialized in the U.S. in 1983.

Advanced Research Projects Agency (ARPA) A government agency created during the Eisenhower administration to sponsor research at universities and corporations in strategically important areas such as communications systems and computer technologies.

American National Standards Institute (ANSI) A private, nonprofit organization that acts as the official U.S. representative to ISO and the IEC.

analytical CRM That portion of a CRM system that takes the data captured by operational CRM processes and uses it to identify trends.

applet A small program downloaded via a Web browser that runs on a user's computer.

application service provider (ASP) E-businesses that manage and distribute software services from a central data center across an IP network.

application-level firewalls Firewalls that operate at the Application layer of the OSI Model and use a proxy server to pass or block packets depending on the rules specified by the individual network service involved.

ARPANET The network of university computers sponsored by ARPA.

asymmetric encryption The encryption method that uses very large prime numbers to create public and private keys.

B2B An e-business model in which revenues are generated by selling products and services only to other businesses not directly to consumers.

B2B Exchange An online marketspace where e-businesses buy and sell products and services from and to other e-businesses.

B2C An e-business model in which revenues are generated by selling products and services directly to consumers.

B2G An e-business model in which revenues are generated by selling products and services to government agencies.

backbone The main cable connecting computers and other devices on a peer-to-peer network without a hub.

back-end operations Those processes and systems not directly accessed by customers such as accounting, manufacturing, and marketing systems.

backup and restore policies Policies that describe a company's plan for securing vital data files and software in case of equipment failure or disaster.

backup and restore procedures Procedures that specify when and how critical files and software are copied to backup media.

bandwidth The frequency ranges occupied by electronic signals on a specific transmission medium. *See also* throughput.

base station The facility that contains the equipment necessary to service the transmissions for one or more cellular network cells (metropolitan coverage areas).

benchmark A performance-based objective.

bilateral peering A peering agreement between two entities.

bioinformatics The use of computers and databases to augment biological research.

biometrics The technologies involved in the measurement of biological data.

black hat hacker Malicious hackers who gain unauthorized access to a computer or network to steal valuable information, disrupt service, or cause other damage.

Bluetooth A radio frequency (RF) technology that uses a previously unused range of radio frequencies at 2.45 GHz.

buffer overflow A disruption to a running program that occurs when a hacker sends more data than can fit into a temporary space in computer memory called a buffer.

bus topology A peer-to-peer LAN topology consisting of a single coaxial cable called a trunk or backbone to which all devices are connected.

business continuity plan (BCP) A company's plan for dealing with a disaster to ensure its continuation as a viable business. *See also* disaster recovery plan (DRP).

C2B An e-business model in which revenues are generated by consumers offering a set price for products or services offered online and the offer is then accepted or declined by the e-business providing the products or services.

C2C An e-business model in which revenues are generated by consumers selling products and services directly to other consumers online.

cache hits Instances where a cache server can fulfill a Web browser request for Web content without forwarding the request on to the origin server.

cache miss   An instance where a cache server must forward a Web browser request for Web content to the origin server.

cache server   An intermediary server used to store Web content that sits between the origin server and the user and intercepts Web browser requests filling the requests with its copy of the Web content.

cards   Elements of a WML deck that can contain text, images, WML instructions, and so forth.

CDMA2000 (CDMA2k)   A 3G digital cellular standard based on CDMA.

cells   The transmission area division of a metropolitan area used by cellular phone networks.

cellular phone   A complex radio that sends and receives RF signals in the 824-849 MHz range.

certificate authority (CA)   A business that, for a fee, creates public and private keys used to encrypt and decrypt data and the digital certificates used to validate an organization's identity.

ciphertext   Text that has been encrypted.

circuit-level firewalls   Firewalls that operate at the Session layer of the OSI Model by validating TCP and UDP sessions before opening a connection between the source and destination computers.

click through   The action by a viewer who clicks a hyperlink on one Web page to download another Web page.

click trail   The path a viewer takes through a Web site.

client/server network   A LAN that consists of general-purpose computers (clients) and special high-performance computers (servers) that enable clients to share data, data storage space, and other network devices.

coaxial cable   The transmission media of choice for early networks consisting of four parts: a solid metal inner conductor, insulation, a thin metal outer conductor, and an outer plastic covering.

Code Division Multiple Access (CDMA)   A digital cellular standard that breaks up digitized and compressed voice data into many pieces and sends the pieces together with a unique code over many different frequencies.

ColdFusion Markup Language (CFML)   The Macromedia, Inc. markup language used to embed tags in ColdFusion templates. *See also* ColdFusion Studio and Cold-Fusion Server.

ColdFusion Server   A server-side technology developed by Macromedia, Inc. that builds and sends Web pages to users as needed.

ColdFusion Studio   A Web page development tool published by Macromedia, Inc. that allows Web servers to use templates to build Web pages as they are requested.

collaborative commerce (c-commerce)   The interrelationships of multiple e-businesses who use Internet technologies to work together to form trading communities which are online communities where participants buy and sell each other's products and services and exchange data.

co-location facilities   Air-conditioned, secure facilities with high-speed Internet access in which e-businesses can rent space to house their own servers.

communication services   The network services that allow traveling employees to connect to the network and access their data files and e-mail messages.

container tags   Paired HTML tags that surround and modify a Web page element.

content   The text, images, sound, video, hyperlinks, and so forth included at a Web site.

content caching   A method of storing Web content on an intermediary server called a cache server that resides between the origin server and the viewer.

content collaboration   The process of authoring, reviewing, approving, storing, and tracking Web content.

content delivery networks (CDNs)   Networks that push Web content to cache servers ahead of demand.

content distribution   The process of publishing approved content to a Web site on an automatic or scheduled basis.

content management   The process of organizing and classifying Web content derived from many sources such as printed documents, electronic documents, and e-mails.

content modules   Groups of related Web content elements such as text and related graphics.

content repository   A database in which electronic documents and other Web content are stored.

cookie   A message passed to a Web browser from a Web server and then stored on the viewer's hard drive as a text file.

corporate portal   An internal Web site used by employees, vendors, customers, and other business partners to access proprietary business information and conduct business activities.

country code Top-Level Domain (ccTLD)   A two-letter country code that is part of a domain name.

crackers   Malicious hackers who gain unauthorized access to a computer or network to steal valuable information, disrupt service, or cause other damage.

cryptography   The art of protecting information by encoding or encrypting it.

customer relationship management (CRM or e-CRM)   A system that enables an e-business to manage its customer base, to match customer needs with product plans and offerings, to determine what products customers might want, and to provide customers with a personalized online experience.

cybersquatting   The act of registering a domain name that reflects the name of an existing business with the intention to either create a parody Web site or in the hopes of selling the domain name to the existing business.

data mining   The process of using mathematical techniques to look for previously unknown patterns in groups of data.

data points   Useful pieces of information gathered at a Web site.

data warehouse   A database that contains huge amounts of data gathered from a number of sources such as customer interactions and sales data.

database-driven   Web sites that store most of their important information in databases.

deck   A WML-based document.

decrypted   The process of returning encrypted data to its original form.

dedicated hosting services   Services provided by a Web hosting company that allows an e-business to rent or lease an entire server rather than renting or leasing space on a shared server.

denial of service attack (DoS)   An attack on a network designed to disable it by flooding it with useless or confusing information.

descriptive markup   Information embedded in a document that identifies the document's structure.

DHCP server   A server running the Dynamic Host Configuration Protocol (DHCP) that assigns temporary or dynamic IP addresses as needed.

dial-up connection   An Internet connection that uses a standard phone line and modem.

digital certificate   An electronic security credential issued by a certificate authority that certifies an entity's identity.

Digital Subscriber Line Access Multiplexer (DSLAM)   A device located in a telephone company central switching office that provides consumers and businesses high-speed, always-on DSL (Digital Subscriber Line) Internet access via telephone lines.

Direct sequence spread spectrum (DSSS)   Spread-spectrum technologies that break a radio signal into small pieces which, along with a sequencing code, are spread over a large section of bandwidth.

directory   A Web site that maintains an index of other Web sites and categorizes these other Web sites by subject.

disaster recovery plan (DRP)   A company's plan for dealing with a disaster to ensure its continuation as a viable business. *See also* business continuity plan (BCP).

distributed denial of service attack (DDoS)   A denial of service attack that uses multiple computers to send useless or confusing information in order to disable a network.

Document Type Definition (DTD)   A file that describes the structure of a specific type of document (such as an employee manual) by defining the document's components and the position of those components within the document.

domain name   A simple and easy-to-remember text name that can be translated into an IP address.

domain name resolvers   Thousands of Internet-connected computers used to resolve a domain name to its IP address.

Dreamweaver   A Web development package published by Macromedia, Inc. that can handle complex Web sites and that allows users to integrate more sophisticated features into their Web pages.

dynamic content   Web page content that is variable and changes frequently.

Dynamic Host Configuration Protocol (DHCP)   The protocol used to assign temporary or dynamic IP addresses by a server.

Dynamic Hypertext Markup Language (DHTML)   A sophisticated version of HTML that adapts Web page content by making the content react to a viewer's input.

dynamic IP address   An IP address that is assigned as needed by a DHCP server.

e-business   A term used to describe a broad spectrum of business activities using Internet technologies. *See also* e-commerce.

e-business model   The method in which an e-business generates revenues: for example, by selling directly to consumers, to other businesses, or to government agencies or e-business Web sites that bring multiple buyers and sellers together in a virtual centralized marketspace. Possible e-business models include: B2C, B2B, B2B Exchanges, B2G, C2C, and C2B.

ebXML   An XML-based set of B2B transactions standards sponsored by an agency of the United Nations.

e-commerce   A term used to describe business activities conducted using Internet technologies. Short for "electronic commerce."

electromagnetic spectrum   The name for all types of electromagnetic radiation.

Electronic Industries Alliance (EIA) A U.S. trade organization affiliated with the electronics industry and accredited by ANSI.

Electronic Product Code (ePC) A standard that provides for a unique identification code for each individual product that emerges from a manufacturing process.

encryption The translation of data into a secret code called ciphertext.

enterprise Organizations of all sizes (but especially large organizations) that use computer networks to interact with employees, vendors, and customers.

Enterprise Application Integration (EAI) Middleware designed especially to integrate legacy system applications with ERP, SCM, and CRM systems.

enterprise information portal (EIP) An internal Web site used by employees, vendors, customers, and other business partners to access proprietary business information and conduct business activities.

enterprise resource planning (ERP) A system that links individual applications such as accounting and manufacturing applications into a single application. This application integrates the data and business processes of the entire e-business.

Ethernet The most popular and least expensive logical topology that uses the CSMA access method and which was originally developed by Robert Metcalfe at Xerox PARC and later improved by a variety of vendors.

ethical hacker Hackers who supposedly use their skills to find and make known weaknesses in computer systems without regard for personal gain.

European Telecommunications Standards Institute (ETSI) One of three recognized European standards organizations that develop standards and documentation for telecommunications, broadcasting, and information technology.

executable Internet A term coined by futurists who predict that the Web will evolve into an environment where consumers and e-businesses download and use disposable executable programs.

extended Internet A term coined by futurists who predict that the Web will evolve into an environment where nearly every electrical device is Internet-enabled.

Extensible Markup Language (XML) A markup language whose tags are used to provide information about the content itself.

external risks Threats to a network or data originating from outside an organization.

extranet Two or more intranets connected via the Internet.

failover Redundant servers and other network components that can automatically take over operations when the primary servers or components fail.

Federal Communications Commission (FCC) The U.S. government agency that regulates use of the radio spectrum.

fiber-optic cable Glass fibers surrounded by a layer of glass cladding and a protective outer jacket. Used to carry voice and data over very long distances.

file services The network services that permit the centralized storage of data files that can be accessed by authorized users around the network.

File Transfer Protocol (FTP) A protocol that permits the uploading and downloading of files between computers on the Internet using a TCP connection.

filter A process or device that screens incoming information and allows only information that meets certain criteria to pass through to the next area.

firewall Specialized hardware or software (or a combination of both) placed between a private network and a public network to filter all incoming and outgoing transmissions and to block those that do not meet specific security criteria.

fixed wireless Wireless communications from a fixed location such as home or office.

fixed wireless broadband (FWB) High-speed fixed wireless communications.

Flash Animation technology developed by Macromedia, Inc. that allows animated Web page content to be more efficiently downloaded over a slow dial-up connection.

Flash Player A Web browser plug-in developed by Macromedia, Inc. and used to play Flash animations.

form An area on a Web page with blank spaces for entering data such as name and address; used to collect information from Web page viewers.

free space optics An optical wireless data transmission system that is based on fiber-optic technology but that uses air instead of cable as its transmission medium.

Freedom of Multimedia Access (FOMA) The 3G version of the NTT DoCoMo i-Mode digital phone service, based on 3-G CDMA technologies.

frequency The number of complete waves or cycles per second of electro-magnetic radiation.

Frequency Division Multiple Access (FDMA) An analog cellular standard that assigns frequencies to one user at a time.

Frequency hopping spread spectrum (FHSS) Spread-spectrum technologies that require a radio signal to hop or jump quickly from frequency to frequency based on a complex mathematical formula known only to the sender and receiver.

front-end operations The hardware and software with which customers interact directly and the processes (such as Web site ordering or customer support) over which consumers exert some control.

FrontPage An easy-to-use Web development package published by Microsoft Corporation.

general consumer portal A portal that provides a wide range of information suitable for a generalized audience with varied interests.

General Packet Radio Service (GPRS) A digital wireless standard (based on GSM) that separates voice and data into separate channels and provides IP data transmissions from 56 to 144 Kbps.

Geostationary Orbit (GEO) Satellites positioned 22,300 miles above the equator and whose orbiting speed matches the Earth's rotation, keeping the satellites positioned in a specific location in relation to Earth.

Global Positioning System (GPS) A network of 24 small satellites orbiting approximately 11,000 miles above the Earth in such a way that four to six satellites are always visible on the horizon.

Global System for Mobile communication (GSM) An international digital cellular standard based on a hybrid of FDMA and TDMA technologies that allow communications across country borders.

GoLive An easy-to-use Web development package published by Adobe Systems Incorporated.

hacker A slang term for anyone who deliberately gains unauthorized access to individual computers or computer networks.

Hertz A measure of electromagnetic radiation frequency where one Hertz is equal to one complete wave (or one peak and one valley) each second.

HomeSite An inexpensive Web development package published by Macromedia, Inc. that requires some knowledge of HTML.

horizontal portal A consumer portal that allows viewers to customize content in order to satisfy their own particular interests.

host Any device on an IP network that runs an application.

hubs An inexpensive device used to connect a group of computers (generally fewer than 64) on a LAN.

hybrid topology A LAN topology that contains elements of two or more topologies.

hypertext A system in which text and other objects are linked to each other.

Hypertext Markup Language (HTML) The markup language used to create Web pages.

Hypertext Transfer Protocol (HTTP) A protocol that governs the way Web servers transmit Web pages to a Web browser.

IEEE 802.11 Wireless Fidelity Standard (Wi-Fi) The 802.11b wireless LAN standard promoted by the WECA.

IEEE 802.11a A wireless LAN standard that supports data transmission speeds up to 54 Mbps and operates in the 5.4 GHz RF range. 802.11a products are not backwards compatible with 802.11b products.

IEEE 802.11b The first commercially successful wireless LAN standard that supports data transmissions up to 11 Mbps and operates in the 2.4 GHz RF range up to 300 feet.

IEEE 802.11g A wireless LAN standard that is backward-compatible with older 802.11b products and allows a 54 Mbps data transmission rate.

IEEE 802.15 A wireless LAN standard for mobile and portable devices such as cell phones and PDAs.

i-Mode An IP-based digital cellular phone service developed by the Japanese firm NTT DoCoMo in 1999.

industry portal A subtype of the vertical portal that attracts viewers looking for information about a specific industry.

infrared (IR) transmissions Wireless transmissions that rely on electromagnetic waves with a frequency range above that of microwave but below the visible spectrum.

Infrared Data Association (IrDA) An association created in 1993 to establish standards for the hardware and software used in IR communications; IR technologies are also referred to as IrDA technologies.

Institute of Electrical and Electronics Engineers, Inc. (IEEE) An international nonprofit association of technical professionals and the leading international authority in technical fields such as biomedical technology, consumer electronics, and computer engineering.

intelligent agent A computer program that can act independently by using simple logic to carry out scheduled tasks.

intelligent device A device that can analyze information passing through it and make decisions about which information to transmit and where to send it.

internal risks Threats to an organization's network or data originating from within the organization itself.

International Electrotechnical Commission (IEC) An international organization whose mission is to promote international standards in electronics, magnetics, and related fields.

International Mobile Telecommunication-2000 (IMT-2000) An initiative supported by the ITU that provides a framework for the development of 3G digital cellular standards.

International Organization for Standardization (ISO) A global alliance of national standards bodies drawn from more than 140 countries.

International Telecommunication Union (ITU) A specialized agency of the United Nations that provides an international forum for government agencies and members of the telecommunications industry.

Internet A vast public network of multiple individual private networks.

Internet backbone That part of the public network made up of high-speed lines spanning long distances to which local or regional networks can connect.

Internet Control Message Protocol (ICMP) A protocol that sends error messages to routers and host computers when problems occur with data transmissions.

Internet Corporation for Assigned Names and Numbers (ICANN) A nonprofit corporation working under the supervision of the U.S. Department of Commerce that assigns groups of IP addresses to businesses and organizations and manages the 13 root name servers.

Internet Protocol (IP) A protocol that breaks data into packets and routes the packets over an intranet or the Internet, and then reassembles the packets at their destination.

Internet service providers (ISPs) Companies who buy Internet access wholesale and then resell it to businesses and consumers.

Internet services The network services that provide external Internet access, internal intranet services, and management of Internet-related technologies such as Web servers, Web browsers, and Internet-based e-mail.

Internet Society (ISOC) An international organization that supports the development of Internet standards and protocols through member organizations.

Internet2 A high-speed network used by the scientific and academic world.

internetworking The processes and devices needed to allow users to communicate between two or more networks.

intranet A network that uses Internet technologies to allow employees to view and use internal Web sites that are not accessible to the outside world.

IP address A complex numerical address that identifies each device such as computer or printer connected to the Internet.

IP datagram A data packet created in the Network layer of the OSI Model by the IP protocol.

Java A programming language developed by Sun Microsystems, Inc. that is compatible with different operating systems.

Java 2 Enterprise Edition (J2EE) Flexible low-level Internet technologies developed by Sun Microsystems, Inc. that allow Java-based programs to run on any operating system.

Java Virtual Machines (JVMs) Protected virtual sandboxes used to run applets written in the Java programming language.

Joint Technical Committee on Information Technology (JTC1) The IEC technical committee that works closely with ISO to develop standards for the IT industry.

key The pattern used to unscramble encrypted data.

knowledge base Everything an organization collectively knows, including information found in paper documents, electronic files, and employees heads.

knowledge management The process of organizing, analyzing, and sharing documents, resources, and employee skills.

knowledge management system A system that includes the employees, processes, procedures, policies, and technologies that enable employees to transform their knowledge and expertise into electronic documents.

knowledge worker Employees whose intellectual capacities and experience make them an indispensable asset to a business.

latency The amount of time it takes for a data packet to travel from server to client or vice versa.

Liberty Alliance Project A group dedicated to developing standards for a decentralized open-platform authentication service.

live splitting caching Caching and delivering streaming media as it is being created.

local area network (LAN) A network that is limited to a relatively small geographical area such as an office or a single building.

Location-based Services (LBS) E-business offerings, such as discount coupons or special pricing, to a customer based on the customer's physical location.

logical topology The way in which data is transmitted between computers on a LAN.

Low-Earth Orbit (LEO) Satellites positioned 400-1,600 miles above the Earth and whose orbiting speed is fast enough to avoid the Earth's gravitational pull; one satellite in a LEO network is always visible from Earth.

MAC address A device's unique physical address which is permanently set in the device's NIC by the card's manufacturer.

macro A short program, written in the Visual Basic programming language, which is generally used to automate keystrokes when creating Microsoft Word documents or Excel worksheets.

macro virus A virus that infects macros.

mail services The network services that enable the sending, receiving, routing, and storage of e-mail messages.

management services The network service that allow network administrators to perform tasks such as determining how much data transmission and processing is occurring on the network or detecting and solving hardware or software problems on the network.

marketspace An electronic arena for buying and selling products and services.

markup languages Programming languages based on the SGML standard. Examples of markup languages include HTML and XML.

materials resource planning (MRP) A system used to allocate resources for a manufacturing operation.

Medium-Earth Orbit (MEO) Satellites positioned 1,500-6,500 miles above the Earth. MEO satellites provide a compromise between GEO and LEO networks by requiring fewer satellites than LEO and generating less transmission latency than GEO.

meta tags Small segments of HTML code that are read by search engines.

Metropolitan Area Ethernet Exchange (MAE) A short, high-speed Ethernet NAP connection within a metropolitan area.

metropolitan area network (MAN) A high-speed network connecting two or more LANs in a single metropolitan area such as a large city and its suburbs.

middleware Software that helps two different applications communicate by translating and transmitting messages between the applications.

mobile commerce (m-commerce) E-business activities conducted over a wireless connection.

Mobile Data Networks (MDNs) Wireless networks designed to transmit data from portable terminals to LANs and mainframes using hand-held devices similar to PDAs or via laptop computers.

modem bank   A box that accommodates several incoming phone lines and includes an individual modem card for each phone line.

modem card   A device that converts an incoming analog phone signal to a digital signal and then sends the digital signal on to a terminal server via a serial cable.

modem pool   A group of modems to which the incoming connections to an ISP are randomly allocated.

multilateral peering   A peering agreement between more than two entities.

name servers   Servers that contain databases of domain names and their equivalent IP addresses.

nanoscale computing   Computing with devices or components smaller than a nanometer.

network   Two or more computers and other devices (such as printers or faxes) connected by some form of data transmission media such as cable.

network access point (NAP)   An Internet connection point that joins the networks of multiple NSPs.

Network Address Translation (NAT)   A firewall technology that permits internal IP addresses to be converted to different IP addresses for external communications.

network interface card (NIC)   A circuit board or expansion card which is added to a computer or other device to enable the device to connect to a network.

network operating system (NOS)   A special kind of operating system used to connect computers and other devices into networks. Examples of network operating systems include Windows XP, Windows 2000, Linux, and NetWare.

network service providers (NSPs)   Telecommunication companies that provide part of the Internet backbone.

network topology   The way the parts of a network are connected.

node   A communication connection on a network; also an individual device on a LAN that can process a data transmission.

NSFNET   A high-speed system of interconnections sponsored by the National Science Foundation.

Object Naming Service (ONS)   A naming system (similar to the Domain Name System) that uses ePC tag addresses to locate data on tagged items.

octet   An 8-bit number.

on-demand caching   Streaming media caching that stores audio or video clips and then delivers them upon request.

Open Systems Interconnection (OSI) Model   A generic model that divides networking design into seven layers: Physical, Data Link, Network, Transport, Session, Presentation, and Application.

operational CRM   That portion of a CRM system concerned with direct customer interactions.

orbit   The elliptical or circular path followed around the Earth (or any planet) by a man-made or natural satellite.

Packet Internet Groper (Ping)   A utility that sends a test message from one computer to another; usually used to determine if a network connection is functioning. The test message itself is commonly called a "ping". DDoS attacks may use a never-ending stream of pings to disable a network.

packet-filtering firewalls   Firewalls that operate at the Network layer of the OSI Model and compare information in a packet header with predetermined filtering rules to decide which packets to accept and which to block.

pager A small battery-operated device that is used to receive RF transmissions.

parsing The process of interpreting the HTML codes that structure a Web page so that it can be displayed in a Web browser.

passive caching The process by which a cache server chooses to store content based on what is passing through the cache.

password A group of characters used to identify a specific computer user and grant that user access to a computer or network.

peering An agreement between two or more NSPs or ISPs to exchange Internet traffic destined for each other's network.

peer-to-peer computing (P2P) The uploading and downloading of files (stored on individual computer hard drives) using an IP network.

peer-to-peer network A LAN that usually consists of six or fewer general-purpose personal computers, each of which contains a NIC and is sometimes attached to a peripheral device such as a printer.

penetration testing Hacking attacks by security audit personnel with the goal of identifying network vulnerabilities.

Personal Communication Services (PCS) (digital cellular) Digital wireless phone systems that use multiple antennas in a calling area or cell.

Personal Home Page (PHP) An open source server-side technology that allows a Web author to create templates and embed non-HTML programming commands into them.

personal portal A consumer portal that allows viewers to customize content in order to satisfy their own particular interests.

personalization The use of CRM to ensure that each customer's Web experience is tailored to his or her specific needs.

Photoshop A high-end graphic-editing software package developed by Adobe Systems Incorporated.

Physical Markup Language (PML) An XML-based markup language used to describe physical objects.

physical risks Physical damage to network components and data from natural or man-made disasters or deliberate destruction of equipment and data by employees or outside intruders.

physical topology A network's physical layout or pattern in which its devices and cabling are organized.

plaintext Ciphertext returned to its plain, unencrypted form.

plug-in Software that adds special features to a Web browser such as the ability to play sound and video.

port address The address that identifies the logical connection between a server and a client application.

Portable Document Format (PDF) A universal document exchange format developed by Adobe Systems Incorporated.

portal A Web site that serves as a starting point for finding user information.

ports Physical plugs or sockets used to make a connection between computers and other devices; also, a logical (virtual) connection between server and client applications such as a Web browser (the client) and a Web server.

Post Office Protocol 3 (POP3) A protocol that provides centralized storage of e-mail messages on a mail server and the forwarding of messages between a mail server and a user's mailbox.

Practical Extraction and Reporting Language (Perl) A programming language used to extract information from text files.

print services The network services that enable employees to share printers across a network.

private IP address   An administrator-assigned IP address for use internally on a private network.

private network   An internal network such as a business LAN.

private peering   Dedicated connections between NSPs or ISPs used to exchange Internet traffic.

protocol   An agreed upon format for transmitting data between computers.

proxy server   A server (hardware or software or both) that sits between a user and the Internet and forwards HTTP requests.

public IP address   An IP address that can be accessed by devices via the Internet.

public key infrastructure (PKI)   The combination of e-businesses with assigned public and private keys, public key directories, and certificate authorities that issue and verify security credentials.

public network   An external network such as the Internet.

public peering   The exchange of Internet traffic at a pubic switch such as a NAP or MAE.

publishing portal   A portal that provides a wide range of information suitable for a generalized audience with varied interests.

quantum computing   Computing with individual atoms used to store data.

query   A search for specific records in a database table.

Quicktime   A streaming media plug-in developed by Apple Computer, Inc.

Radio Frequency Identification (RFID)   Radio frequency technologies that absorb energy from an incoming radio signal and use the absorbed energy to send a response to a special reading device.

radiofrequency (RF) transmission   Wireless transmissions that rely on signals sent over specific frequencies, similar to radio broadcasts.

RealOne   A streaming media plug-in developed by RealNetworks, Inc.

Request for Comment (RFC)   A tool used by Internet scientists to help publicize or improve an idea for a new system or function.

Resource Description Framework (RDF)   An XML-based technology used to enable computers to require less human intervention in order to find and manipulate data via the Semantic Web.

restore   Returning electronic files to their most recently backed-up status.

Reverse ARP (RARP)   A utility that converts a host's physical MAC address to its IP address.

ring topology   A LAN topology in which each node is connected to the next node via a single circle of twisted-pair or fiber-optic cable.

ROI   An acronym for "return on investment." The measurement of a business's profitability or an e-business's Web site effectiveness.

root servers   Thirteen Domain Name System servers (managed by ICANN) that contain databases that keep track of TLD and ccTLD registered domain names.

routers   Intelligent devices similar to but much more powerful than switches that are designed to manage data transmissions over large LANs and WANs.

sandbox   An enclosed environment in which applets are allowed to run.

satellite   A natural or man-made object that revolves around the Earth (or any planet) in an elliptical or circular path.

satellite networks   Networks that consist of strategically positioned earthbound antennae, ground control facilities, and orbiting satellites.

scripts   Small programs embedded in ASP pages that actually perform functions such as modifying Web page layout.

search engine   A Web site that maintains a searchable index of keywords found in Web pages; the index is automatically updated via software called spiders that browse the Web.

Secure Electronic Transactions (SET)   A security protocol that uses digital certificates, digital signatures, public and private key encryption and SSL to present credit card transactions on the Internet and that is supported by Visa, MasterCard, Microsoft Corporation, and others.

Secure Sockets Layer (SSL)   A security protocol (developed by Netscape Communications) that uses public and private key encryption and digital certificates.

security audit   A comprehensive review and assessment of an e-business's security vulnerabilities.

segments   A piece of a network that consists of computers that share a common function. For example, all the computers in a company's accounting department might make up one segment.

Semantic Web   The possible future of the Internet as seen by Tim Berners-Lee and others at the W3C in which intelligent agents radically improve a viewer's ability to find and manipulate data.

server-side technologies   Technologies that operate on the server side of a client/server relationship. One example of such a relationship is the one between a Web browser (the client) and a Web server (the server).

session keys   Temporary keys that are used in a highly secure initial conversation between the sender and the recipient and then discarded after the current session is finished. Session keys are shorter than public and private keys.

shared connection   A business LAN that uses a router and a telecommunications connection to access the Internet.

Shared Registration System (SRS)   The ICANN managed system that allows private companies to participate in the registration of domain names.

Short Message Service (SMS)   A point-to-point method of transmitting short text messages between wireless devices such as cell phones.

Simple Mail Transfer Protocol (SMTP)   A protocol that sends e-mail messages between mail servers on an IP network.

Simple Object Access Protocol (SOAP)   The protocol used to exchange XML files between applications on different operating systems using HTTP and an IP network.

smart card   A small plastic card similar to a credit card that contains an embedded memory chip.

speculative bubbles   Situations where overly exuberant optimism and often pure greed on the part of investors drive a market far beyond its sustainable performance.

spread spectrum technologies   The technologies that spread radio signals over a much larger portion of bandwidth than the original signal uses.

standalone tags   HTML tags that denote an individual Web page element.

standard   A rule, description, or design approved by an established organization or accepted by an industry through common usage.

Standard Generalized Markup Language (SGML)   An ISO standard published in 1986 that specifies a standard format for embedding information called "descriptive markup" within a document.

star topology   A LAN topology in which each node is connected to a central hub by a separate twisted-pair or fiber-optic cable.

static IP address   A permanent IP address assigned to a specific host when it originally connected to a network.

streaming cache server   A server that caches streaming media thereby providing a smoother and more predictable delivery to viewers.

streaming media   Sound and video files that are transmitted continuously over the Web.

supernodes   Computers with fast connections that act as hubs in a peer-to-peer network.

supply chain execution software (SCE)   Software used to automate different steps in the supply chain such as sending purchase orders to vendors.

supply chain management (SCM)   A system that manages the material, money, information, and other resources that go into a business's products for resale.

supply chain planning software (SCP)   Software that uses mathematical models to predict inventory levels based on the efficient flow of resources into the supply chain.

switch   A central processing location in a communication system. Also, intelligent devices that are similar to hubs in that they transmit a signal from one computer or device to another.

Synchronous Optical Network (SONET)   An ANSI standard for connecting fiber-optic networks.

systems integration   The process of integrating business practices and software applications into an ERP system.

systems integrators   Consultants who supervise the systems integration process, provide all or part of the systems integration team, and often provide employee training on the new ERP system.

tags   Codes, placed within a document, that mark the beginning and end of each document element.

TCP segments   A data packet created in the Transport layer of the OSI Model by the TCP protocol.

technology bubble   Term used to refer to investors' unbridled infatuation with the commercial possibilities of new Internet technologies and the resulting meteoric rise (and astounding fall) of many e-businesses in the late 1990s and early 2000.

throughput   The amount of data that can be transmitted during any specified period of time.

Time Division Multiple Access (TDMA)   A digital cellular standard that allows up to six synchronized conversation fragments over a shared channel and supports data, voice, fax, multimedia, videoconferencing, and short text messaging.

Time Division Synchronous Code Division Multiple Access (TD-SCDMA)   A 3G digital cellular standard based on CDMA.

Token Ring   A logical topology popularized by IBM in the mid-1980s that combines a star-wired physical topology with a special kind of access method known as token-passing.

top-level domains (TLDs)   Major domain names, organized by computer function, as part of a hierarchical domain naming scheme.

Traceroute   An operating system utility that sends a packet of information to a destination and then reports a list of all the intermediary routers through which the packet flowed.

Transmission Control Protocol (TCP)   The format for transmitting data on the ARPANET developed by Vinton Cerf and Robert Kahn; TCP establishes the connection between two computers, transmits data in packets, verifies data integrity, and assures that data is received undamaged.

Transmission Control Protocol/Internet Protocol (TCP/IP stack or suite) A group of subprotocols that operate within specific layers of the OSI Model.

transmission media The means of carrying data from one network node to another; examples of transmission media include cable or radio wave transmissions.

transparent commerce E-business transactions that take place without a consumer's explicit participation.

transponders Devices in communication satellites that receive and transmit signals.

Transport Layer Security (TLS) A security protocol suite used to assure that no third party can access and alter Internet communications.

Trojan horse A special kind of program that pretends to be something useful or fun but that actually does something malicious (such as destroying files or creating an entry point that a hacker can use later to infiltrate a network).

tunneling The process by which one protocol is encapsulated within another protocol.

twisted-pair cable Insulated copper wires twisted around each other in pairs and enclosed in a plastic covering; originally used for telephone transmissions but now also used as a LAN transmission media.

UltraDev A high-end, professional Web development package published by Macromedia, Inc.

Uniform Resource Identifier (URI) The term preferred by the W3C to define addresses for the broad set of Web resources including Web pages.

Uniform Resource Locator (URL) A short text address, entered into a Web browser, that identifies the location of a Web page and its related files.

Universal Description, Discovery, and Integration (UDDI) An XML-based directory in which e-businesses list themselves and the Web services they provide.

Universal Mobile Telecommunications System (UMTS) A 3G digital cellular standard based on GSM.

unregulated radio spectrum That part of the radio spectrum that can be used without a license.

User Datagram Protocol (UDP) A protocol that sends data in packets without error checking or receipt verification and is often used to broadcast live video or audio over the Internet.

vertical market A specific industry or industry sector in which similar products or services are developed and sold.

vertical portal A portal that attracts a narrow group of viewers with common interests.

virtual private network (VPN) A private network that uses a large public network such as the Internet to transmit its data.

virus A small, usually destructive program that inserts itself into other files that then become "infected" in the same way a human virus embeds itself in a body.

Visual InterDev A high-end, professional Web development package developed by Microsoft Corporation.

war driving The process of driving around in a car or parking near office buildings and using an 802.11b-enabled laptop, an inexpensive antennae, and WLAN access point detection software to locate WLAN access points.

Web browser The software application used to download and view Web pages.

Web content management The management of content that viewers access via a Web browser.

Web content management system A system that includes the people, policies, procedures, processes, and technologies used to manage Web site content.

Web hosting company An e-business that allows other e-businesses to warehouse their own servers or that leases space on the hosting company's own Web servers.

Web metrics Measurement tools such as pages viewed, number of Web site visitors, or the ratio of actual orders to Web site visitors which are used to measure Web site ROI.

Web mining The process of using data mining techniques to identify unknown patterns or trends in data gathered via the Web including Web server logs.

Web page A specially formatted document that resides on a Web server.

Web server A computer that stores and then delivers (or serves up) Web pages upon request by a Web browser; also the software that holds Web pages on a Web server and that allows Web browsers to download the pages.

Web services The technologies involved in exchanging data between different applications and systems over an IP network.

Web Services Description Language (WSDL) An XML-based markup language used to create descriptions in a UDDI directory.

Web site A collection of related Web pages owned and managed by a single individual, organization, or commercial enterprise.

Web site defacement Vandalism that occurs when a hacker deliberately changes Web page content.

white hat hacker Hackers who supposedly use their skills to find and make known weaknesses in computer systems without regard for personal gain.

wide area network (WAN) A high-speed network connecting two or more LANs

over a large geographical area such as across the nation or across the world.

Wide Bank Code Division Multiple Access (W-CDMA) A 3G digital cellular standard based on CDMA.

Windows Media Player A streaming media plug-in developed by Microsoft Corporation.

Wireless Application Protocol (WAP) The wireless protocol suite or stack that makes it possible to access Internet resources via a small-display wireless device such as a cell phone or PDA.

Wireless Equivalent Privacy (WEP) The security protocol used with the IEEE 802.11b Wi-Fi wireless standard to provide encryption and authentication of wireless transmissions to and from a WLAN.

Wireless Ethernet Compatibility Alliance (WECA) The wireless industry group that promotes the IEEE 802.11b wireless standard as a global standard and certifies 802.11b products.

Wireless LAN (WLAN or W-LAN) Wireless local area network that generally consists of a wired LAN and portable devices such as laptop computers that connect to the LAN via access points (radio base stations).

Wireless Markup Language (WML) A markup language, based on XML, that is used to design content for small-screen devices such as cell phones and PDAs.

Wireless Personal Area Networks (WPANS) Wireless networks set up to allow nearby mobile and portable devices to communicate without need of cable connections within a range up to 10 meters (approximately 30 feet).

Wireless Transport Layer Security (WTLS) The internal security standard for WAP that uses encryption and digital certificates to establish a secure wireless session between a WAP server and a cell phone.

wireless virus   A virus that infects wireless devices such as PDAs.

WMLScript   A scripting language, similar to JavaScript, that is used to manipulate content on small screens and to perform math functions.

World Intellectual Property Organization (WIPO)   An international organization associated with the United Nations that globally enforces copyrights and trademarks.

World Wide Web (Web or WWW)   A subset of the Internet that consists of Web pages stored on Web servers that are linked together via hyperlinks.

World Wide Web Consortium (W3C)   An organization founded by Tim Berners-Lee (in association with MIT, DARPA, CERN, and the European commission) to promote Internet standards and interoperability.

worm   A special kind of virus that doesn't alter program files directly but instead resides in memory where it replicates itself.

WYSIWYG   An acronym for "What You See Is What You Get." Often used to refer to documents containing formatting or special codes. Such documents look the same on screen as when printed.

X Internet   A term coined by futurists who predict that the Web will evolve into an environment where consumers and e-businesses download and use disposable executable programs (the executable Internet) and where nearly every electrical device is Internet-enabled (the extended Internet).

Index

Photo Credits

Figure Number	Credit Line
Figure 1-1	MIT Museum
Figure 1-2	Courtesy of National Academy of Engineering
Figure 1-3	Courtesy of Caspian Networks, Inc.
Figure 1-4a	Courtesy of National Academy of Engineering
Figure 1-4b	UK Crown copyright 1974. Reproduced by permission of the Controller of HMSO. Courtesy of the National Physical Laboratory
Figure 1-5	Computer History Museum
Figure 1-7	AP/Wide World Photos
Figure 1-8a	MIT Museum
Figure 1-8b	Courtesy of Ted Nelson/Project Xanadu
Figure 1-8c	Courtesy of the Bootstrap Alliance
Figure 1-9	AP/Wide World Photos
Figure 1-19	AP/Wide World Photos
Figure 2-22	Courtesy of Dan Bricklin with permission from Robert Metcalfe
Figure 3-7	Courtesy of BBN Technologies, A Verizon Company
Figure 5-3	©Hulton-Deutsch Collection/CORBIS
Figure 5-6	Courtesy of Ericsson Microelectronics
Figure 5-9a	Courtesy of Linksys
Figure 5-9c	Courtesy of D-Link Systems, Inc.
Figure 5-13a	©Bettmann/CORBIS
Figure 5-13b	©Bettmann/CORBIS
Figure 5-19b	Courtesy of Nokia
Figure 5-19c	Courtesy of Handspring, Inc.
Figure 6-1	Courtesy of AT&T
Figure 6-2	Courtesy of US Sprint
Figure 6-3	Courtesy of WorldCom, Inc.
Figure 6-4	Courtesy of Level 3 Communications, Inc.